Addison-Wesley Secondary Math

An Integrated Approach

Foundations of Algebra and Geometry

Cathy L. Seeley
Barbara Alcala

Penelope P. Booth • Virginia Gray • J. Irene Murphy • Andy Reeves

PROGRAM CONCEPTUALIZERS

Barbara Alcala

Randall I. Charles

John A. Dossey

Betty M. Foxx

Alan R. Hoffer

Roberta Koss

Sid Rachlin

Freddie L. Renfro

Cathy L. Seeley

Charles B. Vonder Embse

Addison-Wesley Publishing Company

Menlo Park, California • Reading, Massachusetts • New York • Don Mills, Ontario
Wokingham, England • Amsterdam • Bonn • Paris • Milan • Madrid • Sydney
Singapore • Tokyo • Seoul • Taipei • Mexico City • San Juan

Cover Images

Front

Photo of financial district, Toronto, Ontario/ Klee, Paul. Castle and Sun. 1928. Private Collection, London, Great Britain.

Back

Top left: Photo of financial district, Toronto, Ontario/ Klee, Paul. Castle and Sun. 1928 Private Collection, London, Great Britain. *Top right:* Kabotie, Michael (Hopi). Kachina Song Poetry. 1985. Acrylic on canvas/ Photo of circuit board. *Bottom left:* Armillary (predecessor to the astrolable) from the Vatican/ Black, Mary (Navajo/Paiute). Wedding Basket. 1989. Museum of Northern Arizona. *Bottom right.* Italian ceramic tile/ Fractal from the Mandelbrot Set.

ISBN 0-201-86700-1

5 6 7 8 9 10-VH-99 98 97

PROGRAM CONCEPTUALIZERS

Barbara Alcala
Whittier High School
Whittier, California

Randall I. Charles
San Jose State University
San Jose, California

John A. Dossey
Illinois State University
Normal, Illinois

Betty M. Foxx
Collins High School
Chicago, Illinois

Alan R. Hoffer
University of California
Irvine, California

Roberta Koss
Redwood High School
Larkspur, California

Sid Rachlin
East Carolina University
Greenville, North Carolina

Freddie L. Renfro
Goose Creek Independent
School District
Baytown, Texas

Cathy L. Seeley
(Formerly) Texas
Education Agency
Austin, Texas

Charles B. Vonder Embse
Central Michigan University
Mt. Pleasant, Michigan

FOUNDATIONS OF ALGEBRA AND GEOMETRY AUTHORS

Cathy L. Seeley
Lead author
(Formerly) Texas
Education Agency
Austin, Texas

Barbara Alcala
Associate lead author
Whittier High School
Whittier, California

Penelope P. Booth
Baltimore County Public Schools
Towson, Maryland

Virginia Gray
South Medford High School
Medford, Oregon

J. Irene Murphy
North Slope Borough
School District
Barrow, Alaska

Andy Reeves
Florida Department of Education
Tallahassee, Florida

OTHER SERIES AUTHORS

Jerry D. Beckmann
East High School
Lincoln, Nebraska

Randall I. Charles
San Jose State University
San Jose, California

James R. Choike
Oklahoma State University
Stillwater, Oklahoma

David S. Daniels
Longmeadow High School
Longmeadow, Massachusetts

John A. Dossey
Illinois State University
Normal, Illinois

Phillip E. Duren
California State University
Hayward, California

Trudi Hammel Garland
The Head-Royce School
Oakland, California

Pamela Patton Giles
Jordan School District
Sandy, Utah

Julia L. Hernandez
Rosemead High School
Rosemead, California

Alan R. Hoffer
University of California
Irvine, California

Howard C. Johnson
Syracuse University
Syracuse, New York

Roberta Koss
Redwood High School
Larkspur, California

Stephen E. Moresh
City College of New York
(Formerly) Seward Park
High School
New York, New York

Kathy A. Ross
(Formerly) Jefferson Parish
Public School System
Harvey, Louisiana

Beth M. Schlesinger
San Diego High School
San Diego, California

Alba González Thompson
San Diego State University
San Diego, California

Charles B. Vonder Embse
Central Michigan University
Mt. Pleasant, Michigan

Catherine Wiehe
San Jose High Academy
San Jose, California

Sheryl M. Yamada
Beverly Hills High School
Beverly Hills, California

CONSULTANTS AND REVIEWERS

CONTENT REVIEWERS

Cheryl L. Arévalo
Des Moines Independent
Community School District
Des Moines, Iowa

Mary F. Babb
Liberty High School
Liberty, South Carolina

Cathy Brown
Oregon Department of
Education
Salem, Oregon

Fred Dunn-Ruiz
Berkeley High School
Berkeley, California

Gerry Greer
Broward County Schools
Fort Lauderdale, Florida

Elgin Schilhab
Austin Independent School
District
Austin, Texas

Albert P. Shulte
Oakland Schools
Waterford, Michigan

Janie Zimmer-Long
Howard County Public Schools
Ellicott City, Maryland

MULTICULTURAL REVIEWERS

LaVerne Bitsie
Oklahoma State University
Stillwater, Oklahoma

Claudette Bradley
University of Alaska
Fairbanks, Alaska

Yolanda De La Cruz
Arizona State University West
Phoenix, Arizona

Genevieve Lau
Skyline College
San Bruno, California

William Tate
University of Wisconsin
Madison, Wisconsin

INDUSTRY CONSULTANTS

Joseph M. Cahalen
Xerox Corporation
Stamford, Connecticut

Clare DeYonker
AMATECH
Bingham Farms, Michigan

Harry Garland
Canon Research Center America,
Inc.
Palo Alto, California

Carol E. Holcomb
AMCORE Bank NA
Rockford, Illinois

Diane Sotos
Maxim Integrated Products
Sunnyvale, California

Earl R. Westerlund
Kodak Corporation
Rochester, New York

Charles Young
General Electric Research and
Development Center
Schenectady, New York

John Zils
Skidmore, Owings & Merrill
Chicago, Illinois

Table of Contents

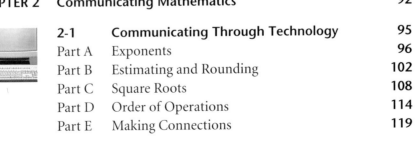

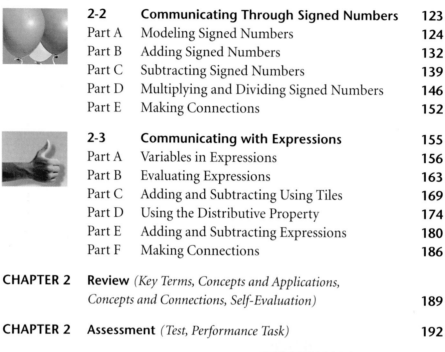
America Hurrah Antiques, NYC

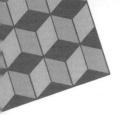

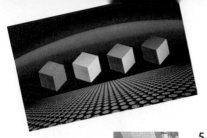

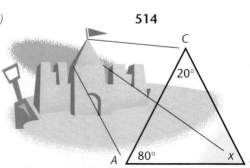

REFERENCE CENTER

What Do YOU Think

In the twenty-first century, computers will do a lot of the work that people used to do. Even in today's workplace, there is little need for someone to add up daily invoices or compute sales tax. Engineers and scientists already use computer programs to do calculations and solve equations. By the twenty-first century, a whole new set of skills will be needed by almost everyone in the workforce.

Some important skills for the next century will be
- the ability to think creatively about mathematics,
- to reason logically,
- to work as a team member, and
- to be able to explain your thinking.

Although it will still be necessary to be able to do computations, it will become increasingly necessary to analyze problems and determine the most appropriate way to solve them. After all, what good is it to solve an equation if it is the wrong equation?

This course will help you develop many of the skills you will need for the future. On the way, you will see the value of creative thinking. The students shown here will be sharing their thinking throughout this book. But the key question will always be "What do YOU think?"

1. **Why do you need to take this math class?**
2. **In your last math class, what was the most interesting or useful thing you learned?**
3. **Why is it important to be able to analyze and solve problems, even if a computer is available to help you do calculations?**

← C O N N E C T →
There are many times when working together can be more productive and motivating than working alone. If you've had experience working in groups, you are aware that it takes skill and planning to work together effectively. We will look at some of the ways to make working together more effective.

Working effectively in a team is an important skill in today's workplace, just as important as teamwork is in sports.

To work together effectively, you must be able to communicate clearly with others. Communicating your ideas in a convincing way can help you to clarify your own thoughts.

CONSIDER

1. **What was the best team you were a part of? Why?**

Here are some suggestions to consider when you are working in a group.

- Let everyone have a chance to participate.
- Everyone has a responsibility to participate.
- Support each other. Each group member must be willing to help any other member of the group.
- Be open minded and show respect for one another. Criticize ideas rather than people.
- Talk only to members of your own group.
- Ask your teacher for help *only* after every member of your group has had a chance to resolve the issue.

1. Form a group of two.
2. Determine who will be player 1 and who will be player 2.

To play the game, each of you will "play" a color. The object is to get as many points as you can. You are not playing against each other. Don't play yet!

3. By yourself, find the result on the board that will get you the most points. Secretly write down the color you will choose to get this amount.
4. Play the game using the color you chose. See where your colors meet to find the result of the game. What happened?
5. Play the game again, but this time talk to each other. Is there a way you can work together to get a better result?

Working cooperatively in groups can be an exciting and effective way to learn math. You will have many opportunities to team up in this course.

REFLECT

1. Describe a situation, other than learning mathematics, in which teamwork plays an important role.
2. Are there situations when working individually is preferable to working in a group? Explain.
3. Do teams exist in the animal world? How do you know?

Exercises

1. What strengths do you bring to a team?

2. What is the best number of people to do a jigsaw puzzle? to do a crossword puzzle? to carry a bookcase? How do you know if a team is too big?

Multiply or divide.

3. 0×5

4. $0 \div 7$

5. $16,236 \times 1$

6. $0.0237 \div 1$

7. $\frac{1}{5} \times 5$

8. $\frac{5}{8} \times \frac{8}{5}$

PART B Solving Problems

← C O N N E C T → *You have solved many problems before taking this class, and you have probably used some type of problem-solving guidelines and strategies. All of these strategies and techniques can be used in this class.*

Give *me a fish, I can eat for a day.*
Teach *me to fish, I can eat for the rest of my life.*

To *problem solve* does not mean just finding the answer to a problem in a math book! Throughout our lives, we are presented with new and challenging situations. It means solving all types of problems, including everyday problems with and without mathematics.

CONSIDER

?

1. **What are some strategies you have used to solve problems?**

Without a strategy or plan, a problem situation becomes a real problem! But a toolkit of techniques can help you toward a solution. Whenever the solution to a problem is not immediately apparent, it may be helpful to follow some guidelines and questions such as those listed below.

PROBLEM-SOLVING GUIDELINES	
Understand the Problem What is the situation all about? What are you trying to find out? What are the key data/conditions? What are the assumptions?	**Develop a Plan** Have you ever worked a similar problem before? Will you estimate or calculate? What strategies can you use?
Implement the Plan What is the solution? Did you interpret correctly? Did you calculate correctly? Did you answer the question?	**Look Back** Could you work the problem another way? Is there another solution? Is the answer reasonable?

EXPLORE: FOLLOW YOUR GUIDE

An EnergyGuide is included with any large appliance. This one accompanied a washing machine.

1. How many loads of clothes per week is considered to be average? (Hint: Use the Estimated yearly energy cost and the National average rate.)

2. How did you decide?

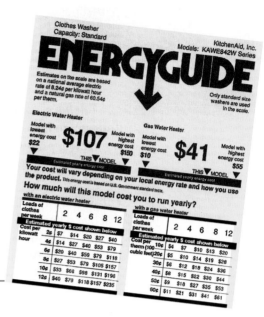

REFLECT

- **1.** Describe any strategies or guidelines that helped you in the Explore.
- **2.** Describe a helpful question or strategy you would add to the list of Problem-Solving Guidelines.

Exercises

1. I am a two-digit odd number. My tens' digit is different from my ones' digit. I am divisible by both digits. What number am I?

2. Folding a piece of paper as shown results in layers. How many layers will result from the next two folds?

2 layers high   4 layers high   8 layers high

3. The following sign is posted on a bridge. What should the weight limit be for a six-axle big rig?

WEIGHT LIMIT	
AXLES	TONS
2	7
3	9
4	11

← C O N N E C T →
You have worked in groups and used problem-solving guidelines and strategies to help you solve problems. There is often more than one approach to solving a problem. The features in this book can help you develop your mathematical skills and choose problem-solving methods wisely.

You will have many opportunities to work in groups (Explore) and to practice what you have learned (Try It) throughout this book. You will also see a feature called "What Do YOU Think?" in which you can share and compare the thinking of other students as they solve problems.

WHAT DO **YOU** THINK?

A company is purchasing an automatic chain assembly machine. It is estimated that this will reduce the cost of chain assembly by 12%. The cost of assembling chain the old way is currently 25 cents per foot. The company assembles about 40,000 feet of chain monthly. How much will the company save in a year by using the new machine?

Rachel thinks ...

I will calculate how much it currently costs in a year and then calculate the savings. It costs $0.25 a foot, and they make 40,000 feet per month.

$0.25(40,000) = $10,000 a month

In 12 months, that's 12(10,000) = $120,000

They will save 12% of $120,000: 0.12(120,000) = $14,400

Eugene thinks ...

I will calculate the savings per foot, then find the monthly and yearly savings.

It costs $0.25 a foot, but they will save 12% of this.

12%(0.25) = 0.03   They save 3¢ a foot.

0.03(40,000) = $1200   They save $1200 a month.

12(1200) = $14,400   This is the yearly savings.

> **1.** Do you think problem-solving strategies are only useful for mathematics problems? Explain.
>
> **2.** Why do you think it is important to understand the connections between mathematics and other disciplines?

Exercises

1. In 1992, Aquatic Systems sold between 20,000 and 25,000 pounds of bass per week. Each bass weighed between 1.5 and 2 pounds. How many bass did Aquatic Systems sell each week?

2. Gil dialed a phone number without looking, thinking the phone had the numbers in the same locations as his calculator. Luckily, he got the correct phone number anyway. How could this have happened?

Calculator

Telephone

3. Two sentries stand by a fork in the road. One way leads to great riches, one to certain death. One sentry always tells the truth, the other always lies. Only one question may be asked. A clever traveler arrives and asks:

"Sentry 1, if I ask Sentry 2 if his road leads to great riches, will he say yes?"

After the sentry answers, the traveler runs down one road shouting "I'm rich!" How was the traveler so sure?

> **Problem-Solving Tip**
>
> Draw a diagram showing the possibilities.

 LOOK AHEAD

4. Which of the following does not represent multiplication?
  (a) 44×7 (b) $\frac{1}{3}(9)$ (c) $2 \cdot 3$ (d) Not here

Diameters of drill bits are given below. Choose the larger size.

5. $\frac{1}{4}$ in. or $\frac{7}{32}$ in.   **6.** $\frac{9}{64}$ or $\frac{1}{8}$ in.   **7.** $\frac{15}{32}$ in. or $\frac{1}{2}$ in.

8. Increase 100 by 50%. Then decrease the result by 50%. What is the answer?

Chapter 1 Working with Data

Project A
Ready for Take Off
How do pilots keep
their planes on course?
How do planes stay
a safe distance apart?

Project B
Ten-Speed Workout
How can cyclists and
hikers judge a trail's
hill-climbing challenge
using a flat map?

Project C
Rain or Shine
How does a meteorologist
create a weather map
and what does it reveal?

2

I liked math in high school. I thought it would be good for science.

I'm proud of what I can do as an air traffic controller. One of the most important things is to keep the planes the required distances apart. We keep track of a plane's altitude, location, and speed. On radar, the plane itself just looks like a blob. We take the use of mathematics for granted. To use sophisticated machines, you need math.

Margarita Arroyo
Air Traffic Controller
   Specialist
*Federal Aviation
   Administration
Luis Muñoz Marin
   International Airport*
Carolina, Puerto Rico

Chapter 1

Working with Data

1-1 Grids and Spreadsheets

Coordinates on number lines, circular grids, and coordinate grids are used to identify locations and to plot points. You will understand how to locate points and read and interpret maps and spreadsheets.

1-2 Graphing Data

Graphs are used in newspapers, magazines, and business reports to help us understand numbers in the world around us. You will use a variety of information displays including bar graphs, circle graphs, line graphs, and pictographs to present and compare data.

1-3 Analyzing Data

Stem-and-leaf diagrams and scatter plots represent data. You will use these along with mean, median, and mode to summarize and analyze data. You will also be able to make predictions based on your analyses. These skills can be used in business communication and in decision making.

Air Traffic Control

GOOD EYESIGHT — CLEAR SPEECH — QUICK THINKING

These are qualities that make an air-traffic controller successful.

Air-traffic controllers direct the movements of aircraft in the air and on the ground near the airport. They use radar, radio, signal lights, and other equipment to control as many as 190 landings and take-offs an hour during the busiest traffic periods.

Fog, snow, and other bad weather conditions can make their job even more difficult. When visibility is poor, controllers need to rely completely on radar to locate and guide aircraft safely.

Controllers must remain calm during critical events, and they need to be able to handle a lot of stress.

Pilots also play an important role in air traffic control. They use many modern navigation aids to help them land their planes safely. One device, the Instrument Landing System (ILS), sends four radio signals to receivers on the plane. Another, the Microwave Landing System (MLS), allows pilots to select the best approach path for their aircraft.

Controllers, pilots, and the engineers who invent and refine these modern tools all cooperate to make flying an even safer way to travel.

1. What school subjects do you think are important in training air-traffic controllers?
2. How do you think the development of computers has been important to air traffic control?
3. What are some ways in which you could describe the position of an aircraft in relation to a control tower?
4. What do you think air-traffic controllers see on their screens in the control tower?

← **C O N N E C T** → *Air traffic controllers must keep track of many planes. You will learn to use a pair of numbers and a circular grid to pinpoint locations of planes. You will also learn how to use a simple number line for locating points and finding distances.*

The grid used by air traffic controllers to track planes is made up of concentric circles. The control tower is at the center of the grid. Lines from the center make an angle from 0° to 360° measuring clockwise from due north. These angles are called *bearings*.

Concentric circles have the same center.

This is a 60° bearing.

N

Bearing is the angle measured from due north.

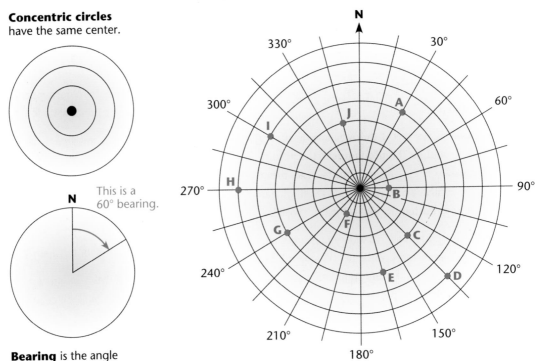

The circular grid appears on the radar screen. The location of each plane appears as a bright dot. The air traffic controller can then tell the distance and the bearing of each plane from the control tower.

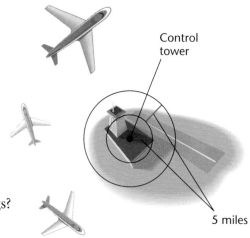

Control tower

Ten planes show as bright dots (A–J) on the radar screen on page 6. The distance from one concentric circle to the next is 5 miles.

1. Find two planes that are the same distance from the control tower. How can you tell?

2. Why does the number pair (25, 30°) describe the position of plane A?

3. Which planes are closest to the control tower? How far away are they? What are their bearings? What number pairs describe the positions of these planes?

4. Copy and complete the table. (You will need to add rows for planes D through J.)

5 miles

Plane	Distance from Control Tower (mi)	Bearing	Position (number pair)
A	25	30°	(25, 30°)
B			
C			

5. How can two planes be positioned at the same number pair and still not be in the same spot in the sky? What other information about a plane do you think air traffic controllers need to know? Explain.

The two values in a number pair are **coordinates.** For the circular grid, the first coordinate is the plane's distance from the control tower, and the second coordinate is the plane's bearing.

A **number line** is also a useful tool for representing quantity and position.

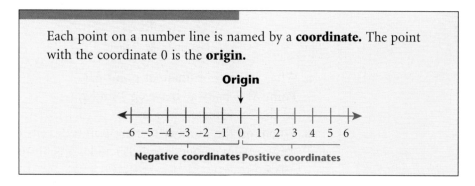

Each point on a number line is named by a **coordinate.** The point with the coordinate 0 is the **origin.**

Origin

−6 −5 −4 −3 −2 −1 0 1 2 3 4 5 6

Negative coordinates **Positive coordinates**

CONSIDER
?

1. Where on the number line is the point with coordinate 3.5? with coordinate −2.7?
2. How many points are there on the number line between 1 and 2?

A ruler is like a number line.

EXAMPLES

1. Samantha wants to measure the distance between point *A* and point *B* with her centimeter ruler. What is the distance?

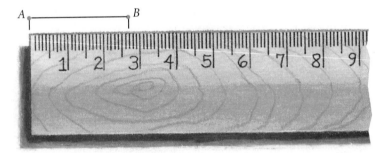

Samantha can think of the tick marks on the ruler as coordinates. There are 10 of them between centimeter marks. That means that each tick mark shows 0.1 cm.
Line up point *A* with the left edge, or 0 coordinate, of the ruler. Then read the coordinate of point *B*.
The ruler coordinate of *B* is 2.7.
So the distance between *A* and *B* is 2.7 cm.

2. Emilio **plots,** or marks, point *M* on the number line.

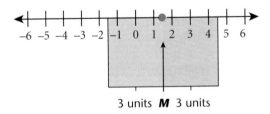

3 units **M** 3 units

a. What is the coordinate of point *M*?
Point *M* is halfway between 1 and 2.
So the coordinate of *M* is 1.5.
b. Where on the number line are points 3 units or less from *M*?
Any coordinate between −1.5 and 4.5 is 3 units or less from *M*.

Draw and label a number line.

a. Mark all points that are exactly 4.5 units from the origin and give their coordinates.

b. What are the coordinates of all points 2 units or less from the origin?

c. Plot the point *P* whose coordinate is 3. Where on the number line will you find points 4 units or less from this point?

Numbers used as coordinates locate positions on number lines and grids.

1. How can you use number pairs to give the position of a point on a circular grid?

2. How can you tell when two planes are at the same distance from the control tower on the grid?

3. How can you tell from the grid when two planes are at the same bearing from the control tower?

4. Now Samantha decides to use the ruler to measure the distance between point *A* and point *B* (see Example 1) by lining up point *A* with the 0.5 coordinate. What does she read as the coordinate of point *B*? How can she use these two coordinates to find the distance between the points?

Exercises

CORE

1. **Getting Started** On a circular grid, the number pair (27, 233°) gives the position of a plane.
   a. The values 27 and 233° are called ____.
   b. What information about the plane's position does the first value tell?
   c. What information about the plane's position does the second value tell?

2. Write the word or phrase that correctly completes the statement. Two circles that have the same center are ____.

3. Name two planes that have the same bearing.

Industry
4. Which planes, if any, are due east of the control tower?

Industry
5. Plane R (not shown on the grid) is 15 miles directly southeast of the control tower. What number pair gives its position?

Industry
6. Give the position of a plane that is 18 miles from the control tower.

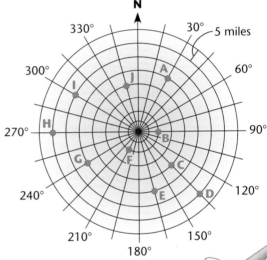

Some of the planes shown on the radar screen have changed their positions.
Use a number pair to give each new position.

Industry
7. Plane A is the same distance from the control tower on a bearing of 15°.

8. Plane I has landed.

9. Plane C flew 10 miles farther from the tower along the same bearing.

10. Plane E flew halfway around the tower but stayed the same distance away.

11. Plane F moved 32 miles from the tower along the same bearing.

12. Plane J flew counterclockwise through an angle of 90° but stayed the same distance away.

13. What is the coordinate of the origin on a number line?

Draw a number line to show points

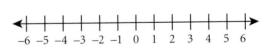

14. exactly 1 unit from the origin.

15. exactly 2 units from the point whose coordinate is −2.

16. 5 units or less from the origin.

17. Where are coordinates greater than 3? greater than −3?

18. Where are coordinates less than 2.5? less than −2.5?

19. Where are coordinates less than 2 *and* greater than −2?

20. Where are coordinates greater than 2 *and* less than −2?

21. An ant starts at the origin and travels along a number line. It goes 1 unit right, then 1 unit left, then 2 units right, then 2 units left, then 3 units right, then 3 units left. Where is the ant now? How far has it traveled?

22. An inch ruler is shown. Each tick mark is $\frac{1}{8}$ in. What is the distance between *A* and *B*?

23. A centimeter ruler is shown. Each tick mark is 0.1 cm. What is the distance between *C* and *D*?

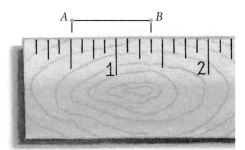

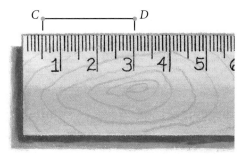

**24. California Dreaming** The highest point in California is the top of Mt. Whitney at 14,494 ft above sea level. The lowest point is in Death Valley at 282 ft below sea level. Show these points on a number line. Which number is larger? By how much?

Death Valley

Mt. Whitney

**25.** On the same day in January, the temperature was 22°F below zero at Point Barrow in Alaska and 85°F above zero at Key West in Florida. Show this on a number line. How much warmer was it in Key West?

👀 *LOOK AHEAD*

26. Draw a vertical line that you can use as a number line. Mark an origin.

27. Where would you mark the positive coordinates? Make tick marks and label five positive coordinates on your vertical number line.

28. Where would you mark the negative coordinates? Make tick marks and label five negative coordinates on your vertical number line.

MORE PRACTICE

29. On a circular grid showing a plane's position, what would each number pair mean?

a. (5, 180°) **b.** (14, 0°) **c.** (0, 270°) **d.** (0, 0°)

Copy the circular grid. Plot the position of each plane.

The distance from one concentric circle to the next is 5 miles.

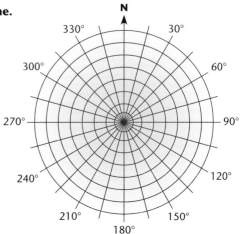

30. Plane K is 30 miles from the control tower at a bearing of 210°.

31. Plane L is at (15, 30°).

32. Plane M is at the same bearing as plane L but twice as far from the control tower.

33. Plane N is at (30, 15°).

34. Plane P is the same distance from the control tower as plane N, but P's bearing is due west.

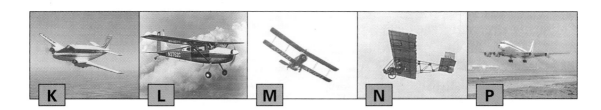

K   L   M   N   P

Where on the number line are points

35. exactly 3 units from the origin?

36. 3 units or less from the origin?

-6 -5 -4 -3 -2 -1 0 1 2 3 4 5 6

37. exactly 4 units from the point whose coordinate is −2?

38. with coordinates greater than −3?

39. with coordinates less than −1?

40. with coordinates less than 4 *and* greater than −2?

41. with coordinates greater than 2 *and* less than −4?

42. Draw a number line. Plot each point.
  a. Point *A* is 4 units to the left of the origin.
  b. Point *B* is halfway between −3 and 3.
  c. Point *C* has a negative coordinate and is 2 units from the origin.
  d. Point *D* is halfway between 4 and 1.
  e. Point *E* is 3 units to the left of the point with coordinate 2.

43. An inch ruler is shown. What is the distance between *A* and *B*?

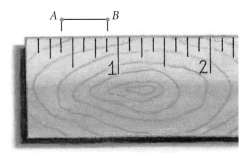

44. A centimeter ruler is shown. What is the distance between *C* and *D*?

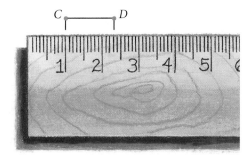

MORE MATH REASONING

45. The table shows the 1980 and 1990 census figures for five U.S. cities.

City	1980 Census	1990 Census	% Change
New York	7,071,639	7,322,564	
Detroit	1,203,339	1,027,974	
Chicago	3,005,072	2,783,726	
Seattle	493,846	516,259	
Phoenix	789,704	983,403	

a. Copy the table and complete the last column.

b. Plot the percentage changes on a number line. List the five cities in order from smallest to largest growth rate.

> **Problem-Solving Tip**
>
> Use signed numbers to give the amount of increase or decrease.

46. Shooting the Rapids You are part of a movie-making crew. You plan to film a 4-hour raft trip beginning at 10:00 a.m. at Reeves Rock. Rafts travel about 5 miles per hour, and a film crew will be at each point marked along the river.

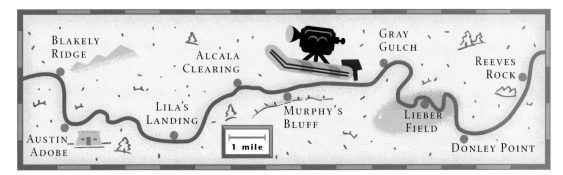

a. Use string and a ruler to draw a number line that will straighten out the river.

b. Make a schedule showing what time the raft will pass each point.

Coordinate Grids

← C O N N E C T → *You've located objects and points on circular grids and number lines. By using positive and negative numbers and a coordinate system, you also can locate points on a rectangular grid.*

Most road maps and street maps are marked with rectangular grids. You can use the grid to locate points of interest.

EXPLORE: GETTING AROUND

The grid is a street map of Shilo's home-town. Shilo is standing in the town center at point *O*.

To get to the basketball court (*B*), Shilo can walk west 3 blocks and north 2 blocks. He writes the location of point *B* as (W3, N2).

1. Use Shilo's method to give the location of each point from the town center.

2. Can Shilo write the location of the basketball court as (N2, W3)? Does the order of the coordinates matter? Explain.

LEGEND
The Bijou Theater (*T*)
Happy Hamburgers (*H*)
Linda's Laundromat (*L*)
Ye Old Swimming Hole (*S*)
Disco Records (*R*)

Shilo decides to improve his notation by letting "+" on the first coordinate mean east and "−" mean west. On the second coordinate, "+" means north and "−" means south. He writes the basketball court location as (−3, +2).

3. In this new notation, will Shilo be describing the same location if he says that the basketball court is at (+2, −3)? Explain.

In an **ordered pair** of numbers the order of the coordinates is important.

4. Write coordinates for the points *T, H, L, S,* and *R* using Shilo's improved notation. Are these ordered pairs? Why?

In mathematics we use a similar grid, called a **coordinate grid,** to locate points. The **x-axis** is like Shilo's east-west axis. The **y-axis** is like Shilo's north-south axis. The **origin** is where the **x-axis** meets the **y-axis.**

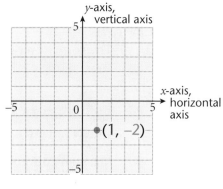

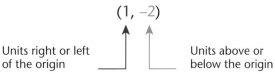

Plot **(1, –2)** by moving from the origin **1** unit right and **2** units down.

TRY IT

Give the coordinates of each point.

a. A
b. B
c. C
d. D
e. E

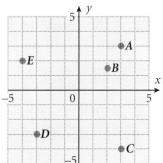

Give the directions from the origin to plot each point.

f. $(-2, 1)$ **g.** $(3.5, 4)$ **h.** $(-5, -2)$ **i.** $(2, 0)$
j. $(-4, 0)$ **k.** $(0, -4.5)$ **l.** $(0, 0)$ **m.** $(-3, -2)$

We can use coordinate grids to draw familiar geometric figures.

A •————————————• B

Line segment AB has **endpoints** A and B, and it can be written as $\overline{AB}$. It consists of point A and point B and all points between A and B, and it has measurable length.

A line segment is named by its endpoints.

EXAMPLE

The corner points of a triangle are $A(0, 3)$, $B(3, -2)$, and $C(-4, -1)$. Draw triangle ABC on a coordinate grid.

Draw the *x*-axis.

Draw the *y*-axis.

Mark off convenient units on each axis to help count.

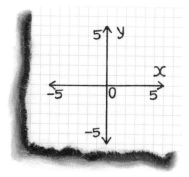

Plot each point starting at the origin.

Plot *A:* right 0, up 3

Plot *B:* right 3, down 2

Plot *C:* left 4, down 1

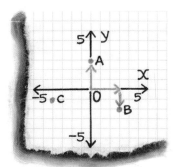

Draw segment *AB*, segment *BC*, and segment *AC*.

The corner points of the triangle are the three **vertices** of triangle *ABC*.

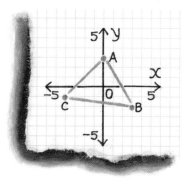

REFLECT

1. How do ordered pairs locate points on a coordinate grid?
2. $(4, -3)$ locates a point on a coordinate grid. Why is $(4, -3)$ called an *ordered* pair?
3. How are the number pairs for circular grids in 1-1 Part A similar to the ordered pairs for coordinate grids in this part? How are they different?
4. What is the ordered pair for the origin? Where are all points whose first coordinate is 0? whose second coordinate is 0?

Exercises

CORE

1. **Getting Started** Consider plotting point $P(2, -6)$.
   a. In what direction and how many units should you move along the x-axis?
   b. In what direction and how many units should you move along the y-axis?

Give directions, starting from the origin, for plotting each point on a coordinate grid. Then plot the points on graph paper.

2. $A(-5, 3)$ 3. $B(0, -2)$ 4. $C(4, 4)$

5. $D(-2, 2.5)$ 6. $E(0, 0)$ 7. $F(5, -2)$

Directions from the origin to a point are given. What are the point's coordinates?

8. left 3, down 2   9. down 1, right 4.5   10. right 3

11. down 5   12. left 1, up 2   13. left 2, right 1, up 3

14. Which ordered pair does *not* locate a point on a coordinate grid?
   (a) $(-1, 0)$ (b) $\left(2.7, -3\frac{1}{2}\right)$ (c) $(0, 0)$ (d) $(-1, -1)$ (e) not here

15. The vertices of triangle ABC are $A(3, 2)$, $B(-3, 2)$, and $C(0, 7)$. Draw the triangle on a coordinate grid.

16. The origin on a coordinate grid is
   (a) the x-axis   (b) the y-axis   (c) a point   (d) a segment

17. **Dot to Dot** Make a simple drawing of an animal or another object on graph paper. Write a set of coordinates so that a friend can plot the points and connect the dots to get an identical picture.

Science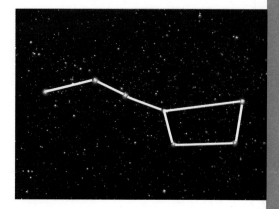

18. Give the coordinates of four points that will form a rectangle on a coordinate grid so that the perimeter, or the sum of the lengths of its sides, is 14.

19. Points M, N, O, and P are the vertices of a rectangle with length 3 and width 2. Give a set of possible coordinates for the four points.

20. Which point is 3 units right and 2 units below the point $(-2, 3)$?
   (a) $(-5, 1)$ (b) $(1, 1)$ (c) $(1, 5)$ (d) not here

21. What is the place value of the digit 4 in 2431? [Previous course]

22. What is the place value of the digit 4 in 138.45? [Previous course]

23. Write in standard form: 5 ten-thousands + 4 thousands + 1 hundred + 2 tens + 6 ones. [Previous course]

24. If the decimal point in 23.742 is moved one place to the right, what is the new number? How does the value of the new number compare with the value of the original? [Previous course]

25. If the decimal point in 234.56 is moved 2 places to the left, what is the new number? How does the value of the new number compare with the value of the original? [Previous course]

MORE PRACTICE

Give the coordinates of each point.

26. A

27. B

28. C

29. D

30. E

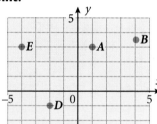

Give directions, starting from the orgin, for plotting each point.
Then plot the points on graph paper.

31. $A(-2, 1)$ **32.** $B(4, -2)$ **33.** $C(3.5, 0)$

34. $K(0, -5)$ **35.** $Y(10, -1)$ **36.** $Z\left(2\frac{3}{4}, 5\right)$

37. $D(-2, -2)$ **38.** $E(-3, 0)$ **39.** $F(-3, -2)$

Directions from the origin to a point are given. What are the point's coordinates?

40. left 1, down 3.5   **41.** down 2, right 7   **42.** right 4

43. up 3, up 4   **44.** down 7   **45.** left 2, right 4, up 1

46. down 2   **47.** up 6   **48.** up 2, left 2

49. Draw triangle ABC with vertices $A(0, 3)$, $B(-1, 2)$, and $C(6, 0)$.

MORE MATH REASONING

50. Begin by plotting the given ordered pairs. Use graph paper and a ruler to build each shape. Then list the coordinates of the points you added.

　a. Square; $(-3, 2)$, $(1, 2)$

　b. Triangle with two equal sides; $(-2, 0)$, $(0, -4)$

　c. Parallelogram; $(3, 6)$, $(-3, 3)$, $(-4, 0)$

　d. Kite; $(2, 5)$, $(0, 2)$, $(2, -4)$

51. You can use a coordinate grid to make three-dimensional figures.

　a. Copy the square onto graph paper. Add three units to the coordinates of each vertex. Connect the new points to form a square. Use a ruler to make diagonal lines so that the figure looks like a cube.

　b. Write a set of directions for how to add lines to a triangle to make it look like a wedge of cheese.

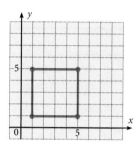 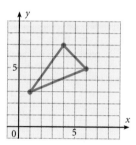

1-1
PART C — Spreadsheets and Maps

← CONNECT → *Number pairs describe locations on a circular grid. Ordered pairs give a shorthand for locating points on a coordinate grid. You will see how to use a similar system to pinpoint information on spreadsheets and maps.*

The keys on a calculator are in columns and rows.

A **spreadsheet** organizes information in columns and rows, too.

Cell C2 is where column C and row 2 meet. The number 75 is stored in cell C2.

	A	B	C	D
1	80	12	14	32
2	101	65	75	10

Computer spreadsheets help business managers keep track of finances. Some people with home computers use spreadsheets for their finances.

EXPLORE: WELCOME TO FLORIDA

Glenn is going on vacation to Florida with his family. After shopping for some items, he decides to keep track of his expenses for the trip

	A	B	C	D
1	Item	Price ($)	Sales Tax	Total Cost
2	Swimsuit	15.75		
3	Sunglasses	7.50		
4	T-shirts	19.00		
5	Sunscreen	4.25		
6	Total			

The sales tax in Glenn's city is 6.5%.

1. Copy and complete Glenn's spreadsheet.

2. What information will Glenn find in column A? in row 1?

3. Which cell shows the sales tax on his T-shirts?

4. What was the total cost of his new swimsuit?

5. Which cell shows the total cost? Which cells would you add together to find Glenn's total cost for all four items?

Column and row labels on spreadsheets are like number pairs on a grid. They describe the position of information on the spreadsheet.

The coordinates on a road map work like columns and rows on a spreadsheet. They help us locate cities and points of interest.

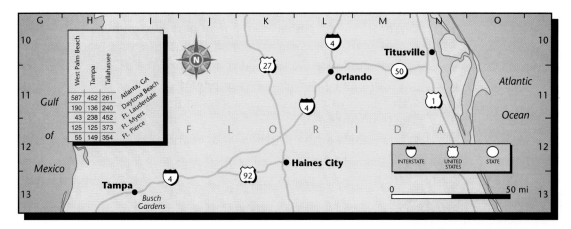

Most road maps include a map index and a legend. The map index gives the row and column coordinates for each city. The legend identifies the highway symbols. The numbers between markers along the roads show mileage. Mileage charts give you the distance between major cities in rows and columns.

EXAMPLES

1. The map index says that Titusville is located at N10. How can you find Titusville on the map?
   Look in the rectangle where column N meets row 10.
2. The *Sights to See* listing says that many attractions, including Disney World, are near the city of Orlando. Give the map coordinates for Orlando.
   Orlando is located in the rectangle where column L intersects row 11. So the map coordinates for Orlando are L11.

TRY IT

a. The map index says that Haines City is located at K12. How can you find Haines City on the map?
b. *Sights to See* lists Busch Gardens at I13. What large city is located near Busch Gardens?
c. Use the mileage chart shown above. How far is it from Tampa to Fort Lauderdale?

You can use number and letter coordinates as keys for finding information from spreadsheets and maps.

1. Describe how you use letters and numbers as coordinates to locate information on a spreadsheet.
2. What do a spreadsheet and a map have in common?
3. How is the column/row method for locating information on a spreadsheet similar to the method of using ordered pairs to locate points on a coordinate grid? How is it different?
4. Explain how you would go about finding your hometown on a road map of your state.
5. What kinds of mathematical information can you find on a road map?

Exercises

CORE

1. **Getting Started** Kevin is trying to find a piece of information on a large spreadsheet. His friend tells him that the information is in cell D15. Where should Kevin look to find the information on the spreadsheet?

2. A Texas road map shows the coordinates of Amarillo as A2. Carmen says this is an ordered pair. Is she right? Explain.

For Exercises 3–9, use these facts about the Great Lakes.

	A	B	C	D	E	F	G
1		Superior	Michigan	Huron	Erie	Ontario	Total
2	Length (mi)	350	307	205	241	193	1,296
3	Width (mi)	160	118	183	57	53	571
4	Depth (ft)	1,330	923	750	210	802	4,015
5	Amount of water (mi³)	2,900	1,180	850	116	393	5,439
6	Area of water surface (mi²)	28,000	22,300	23,000	9,190	7,550	90,040

In which cell would you find

3. the width of Lake Erie?

4. the deepest point for the shortest lake?

5. the amount of water in the longest lake?

6. the total length of the Great Lakes if you placed them end to end?

7. the area of the water surface for all the lakes?

8. What value do you get for the sum B5 + C5 + D5 + E5 + F5? What geographical fact does this give?

9. Which cell shows the least amount of water? Which lake has the least amount of water?

The map shows a section of Arizona.

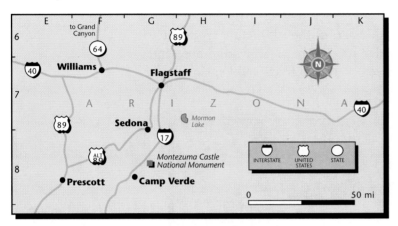

10. *Sights to See* says that Route 64, the access road for Grand Canyon National Park, starts near Williams. What are the coordinates for Williams?

11. What map coordinates would the Arizona map index show for Flagstaff?

Find each place on the map and give its coordinates.

12. Prescott   **13.** Mormon Lake   **14.** Sedona

The mileage chart is from a Texas road map.
Find each distance.

15. San Angelo to Del Rio

16. Big Spring to Lubbock

17. Del Rio to Odessa

18. Lubbock to Dallas

19. Odessa to Albuquerque, NM

20. Carlsbad, NM, to San Angelo

San Angelo	Odessa	Lubbock	
92	178	167	Abilene
510	399	319	Albuquerque NM
301	257	120	Amarillo
86	60	107	Big Spring
261	132	179	Carlsbad NM
258	348	318	Dallas
155	246	332	Del Rio

21. Gil finds the expenses for January in cell B4 of a spreadsheet. He tells Davida to look two cells to the right and three cells down to find the profits for March. Which cell shows March profits?

	A	B	C
1			
2			

 **LOOK BACK**

Find each value. [Previous course]

22. 50% of 397   **23.** 15% of $24.57   **24.** 4% of $5.98

25. You can model fractions with pictures.
[Previous course]

    a. What fraction does the shaded part of the left picture represent?
    b. What fraction does the shaded part of the right picture represent?
    c. Is there a relationship between these two fractions? Explain

MORE PRACTICE

Social Science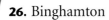

Find each place on the New York State map and give its coordinates.

26. Binghamton

27. Syracuse

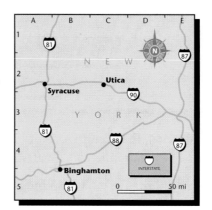

Social Science

Use the mileage chart to find each distance.

28. New York City to Buffalo

29. Lake Placid to Albany   **30.** Binghamton to New York City

Social Science

Homeless in U.S. Cities

	A	B	C	D
1		Total	In Shelters	On Streets
2	New York City	33,830	23,383	10,447
3	Los Angeles	7,706	4,597	**a.**
4	Chicago	6,764	**b.**	1,584
5	San Francisco	**c.**	4,003	1,506
6	Washington, DC	**d.**	4,682	131

31. What information is in column A?   **32.** Fill in the missing numbers **a–d.**

33. How many people were in shelters in Washington, DC?

34. What is the relationship among columns B, C, and D?

35. Find B2 + B3 + B4 + B5 + B6. What does this sum mean?

Lorena, a political science student, is studying the workload of the U.S. Supreme Court. She prepares a spreadsheet to organize her data.

	A	B	C	D	E	F
1	**U.S. Supreme Court Cases (1970–1990)**					
2		**1970**	**1975**	**1980**	**1985**	**1990**
3	Total cases on docket	4212	4761	5144	5158	6316
4	Cases argued	151	179	154	171	131
5	Number of signed opinions	109	138	123	146	112

36. What information is in column A? column B? column F?

37. What information is in row 2? row 4? What is the purpose of row 1?

38. What cell should you look in to find the number of signed opinions argued in 1975? in 1985?

39. What does *Total cases on docket* mean? How many more total cases were there on the docket in 1990 than in 1985?

40. The number of cases on the docket increases for each year shown from 1970 to 1990. What happens to the number of cases argued? Is this reasonable? Explain.

MORE MATH REASONING

41. Crazy for Cars The bar graph shows motor vehicle production 1988–1991.
   a. Make a spreadsheet that shows this data.
   b. What patterns do you see in the data?

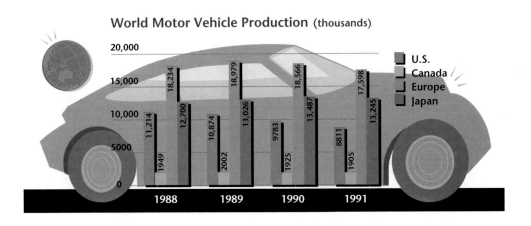

World Motor Vehicle Production (thousands)

42. This map of southeast Asia is marked with lines of latitude and longitude.

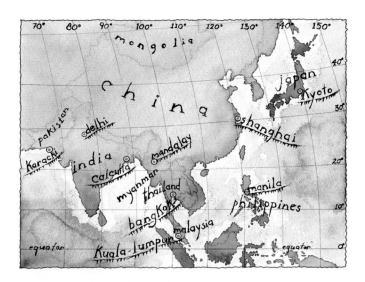

a. Which lines are latitude? Which are longitude?

b. Explain how a map with lines of latitude and longitude is like a coordinate grid.

c. Pick five cities. Give their approximate latitude and longitude.

← C O N N E C T → *You have seen how numbers, used as coordinates, are a convenient way to pinpoint positions. Number lines, grids, and spreadsheets have real-life applications, such as thermometers, aircraft radar grids, maps, and financial reports.*

Air traffic controllers, like other professionals and scientists, can use the power of and together to get a more complete picture of their data.

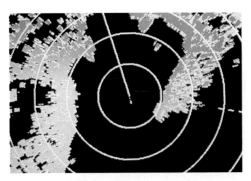

Here's a chance to put yourself in the shoes of a group of oceanographers who are studying ocean conditions.

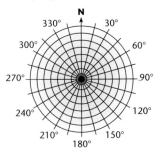

MATERIALS

Graph paper, Ruler

To measure depth, oceanographers use an echo sounder. Ultrasonic beams are directed at the ocean floor. The sound bounces off the ocean floor and its echo returns to the echo sounder.

Sound travels about 4800 ft/sec in ocean water.

If you put the total travel time, in seconds, of the sound signal into this formula, it gives you the ocean depth, in feet.

$$\text{ocean depth} = 4800 \cdot \frac{\text{sound travel time}}{2}$$

1. Draw a sketch to show the path of the signal. Why do you think you need to divide the seconds by 2?

From their shipboard lab, the oceanographers go out and take soundings at six sites. They decide to organize their information in a spreadsheet.

2. Copy the spreadsheet and complete column D.

	A	B	C	D
1	Site Number	Horizontal Distance from Ship (ft)	Sound Travel Time (sec)	Depth (ft)
2	1	0	3.1	
3	2	20	4.3	
4	3	40	2.4	
5	4	60	3.7	
6	5	80	5.1	
7	6	100	4.9	

Horizontal distance from ship (ft)

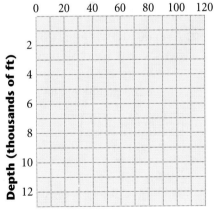

3. Make a copy of the grid on graph paper. Plot the distance and depth as ordered pairs (distance, depth).
4. Connect the points that you've plotted. What does your graph show?
5. How does this grid differ from a standard coordinate grid? Why is this grid a more effective display than a standard coordinate grid?

REFLECT

1. Does a number line always show negative as well as positive numbers? Explain your thinking.
2. Give three real-life situations that use number lines.
3. Why do you think air traffic radar screens use circular grids rather than rectangular grids to track airplanes?
4. On a rectangular grid, how do you use the signs of the coordinates in an ordered pair like $(-2, 3)$?
5. Suppose that a Colorado map index lists Denver at C5. How can you consider this as a number pair? What are the two coordinates? Is this an ordered pair?
6. How are maps and spreadsheets similar? How are they different?

Colorado Map Index	
Alamosa	F4
Aspen	D3
Boulder	C4
Canon City	D4
Colorado Springs	D5
Cripple Creek	D4
Denver	C5
Durango	F2
Estes Park	B4

Self-Assessment

1. What are the coordinates of a point on a coordinate grid that is 3 units to the left of the origin and 5 units above it?

2. Alicia is studying the effects of gravity in her science class. Alicia has read that her favorite baseball player can throw a ball at 80 mi/hr directly up into the air. She uses some formulas from science class to come up with a table that shows the height of the ball every half second.

Time (sec)	0	0.5	1	1.5	2	2.5	3	3.5	4	4.5	5
Height (ft)	0	36	64	84	96	100	96	84	64	36	0

a. On graph paper set up a coordinate grid similar to the one at the right.
b. Write ordered pairs (time, height) from Alicia's data.
c. Plot the ordered pairs on your coordinate grid.
d. Connect the points with a smooth curve.
e. Describe the motion of the baseball. What can Alicia learn about gravity from this display?

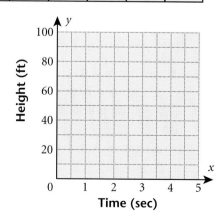

3. A ranger uses a circular grid in an observatory post to plot the location of forest fires. Starting from the center, the distance from one concentric circle to the next is 1.5 miles. Use a number pair to describe each of the five locations on the grid.

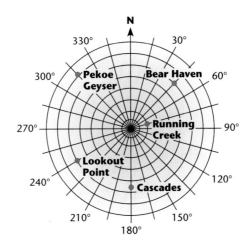

Spills from oil tankers pollute ocean water and destroy life in the sea and on land. This spreadsheet summarizes the major accidents from 1967 through 1989.

	A	B	C
1	Year	Location	Size of Spill (millions of gallons)
2	1967	England	34
3	1969	California	3
4	1976	Massachusetts	7
5	1978	France	69
6	1979	Mexico	140
7	1979	Tobago	49
8	1979	Barbados	42
9	1980	Greece	37
10	1983	Persian Gulf	80
11	1985	Persian Gulf	21
12	1989	Alaska	11

4. Which cell shows the size of the largest oil spill?

5. Which cells show oil spills of more than 50 million gallons?

6. Which cells would you add to get the total number of gallons spilled off U.S. shorelines?

7. What suggestions do you have for reducing the number of spill accidents?

8. Time to Time This map shows time zones of the United States.

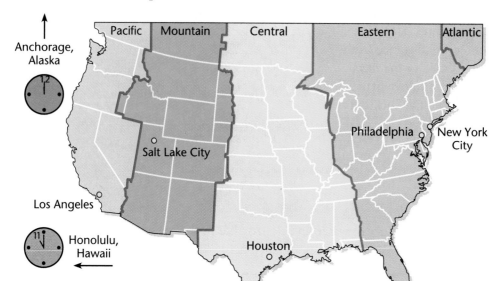

a. Draw a number line to represent the time zones. Let 0 correspond to the Pacific Time Zone.

b. If it is 12:00 noon in Los Angeles, what time is it in Salt Lake City? How can you use your number line to answer this question?

c. If it is 3:00 p.m. in Philadelphia, what time is it in Houston? in Anchorage? in New York? in Salt Lake City?

d. If it is 2:00 a.m. on Tuesday in New York, what time is it in Honolulu? What day is it? Explain your thinking.

e. Draw another number line to represent the time zones. Let 0 correspond to the Eastern Time Zone. Compare your two number lines. Discuss how it is possible to have two different number lines that represent the same U.S. time zones.

9. Which point is 5 units left and 2 units above the point $(2, -4)$?
(a) $(7, -6)$ (b) $(-3, -2)$ (c) $(-3, -6)$ (d) not here

10. Choose the term that doesn't belong to the group and tell why: point, ordered pair, axis, coordinates.

11. Write in standard form: 4 ten-thousands + 3 hundreds + 5 tens + 2 ones. [Previous course]

12. Kentucky has a state sales tax of 6%. If Leroy buys a CD priced at $12.98, how much will he have to pay including tax? [Previous course]

13. Give three examples of real-life situations where you see or use grids.

1-2 Graphing Data

The Athlete of the Century 2000

As the 20th century ends, sports historians and fans will examine the records of sports heroes to name **The Athlete of the Century.**

Many athletes who will be considered for this award have earned their place in history through the Olympics. In 1972, Mark Spitz won seven gold medals in swimming. Four years later, Nadia Comaneci earned seven perfect 10s in gymnastics. Eric Heiden won every men's speed-skating event at the 1980 Winter Games. After the 1994 Winter Games, speed-skater Bonnie Blair was the first American woman to win five gold medals.

One of the greatest sports achievements of the 20th century was the world record set in the long jump by American Robert Beamon at the 1968 Olympic Games.

Described as "The Perfect Jump," Beamon's leap measured 29 ft 2.5 in. and shattered the old 1964 record. Future Olympians did not even jump 28 feet until the 1980 Games. Beamon's amazing feat wasn't topped until American Mike Powell jumped 29 ft 4.5 in. in 1991.

We use graphs and charts to display and compare great achievements.

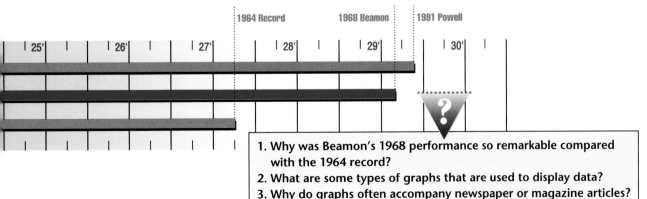

1964 Record   **1968 Beamon**   **1991 Powell**

| 25' | | 26' | | 27' | | 28' | | 29' | | 30' | |

1. **Why was Beamon's 1968 performance so remarkable compared with the 1964 record?**
2. **What are some types of graphs that are used to display data?**
3. **Why do graphs often accompany newspaper or magazine articles?**

← CONNECT → *Bar graphs and circle graphs display information in forms that make it easy to see relationships. You will learn how to decide which of these two types is best to use. You will compare and interpret data that is shown in bar and circle graphs.*

Bar graphs and circle graphs are two ways to display data.

Bar graphs compare information from several situations. The lengths of vertical or horizontal bars model the data.

Circle graphs compare information from a single situation that is broken down into parts. The sizes of wedge-shaped pieces model the sizes of the parts.

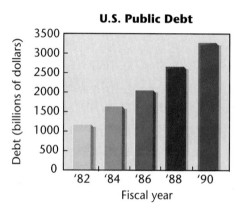

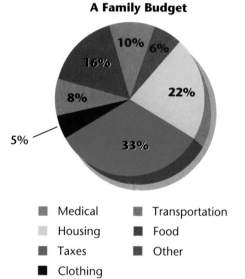

The vertical and horizontal axes show **scales** of values. The **interval** on the vertical scale is 500 billion because each tick mark on the vertical axis represents 500 billion dollars.

Each wedge-shaped **sector** shows, as a percentage, the portion of a family's budget used for each expense. The total of the expenses is 100%.

The nature of the information determines whether a bar graph or a circle graph is better.

CONSIDER
?

Which type of graph, bar or circle, would you choose to display
1. the number of nations participating in each of the Summer Olympics from 1972 to 1992?
2. the distribution of the federal budget?
3. the distribution of religions in the United States?
4. the amount of money spent on health care during the period 1970–1990?

We collect data and display it in graphs to answer questions, raise issues, or make a point.

EXPLORE: HAIL TO THE CHIEF

A weekly newsmagazine asked 1000 people to judge the President's performance in office as poor, fair, good, or excellent. An article showed the results in a circle graph.

1. What information about the poll can you get by looking at the graph?
2. What are some questions or issues that the newsmagazine editors might have been thinking about when they decided to collect the data and prepare the graph?
3. What is the total of the percentages? Why?
4. How many people in the poll rated the President's performance as poor? fair? good? excellent? Explain how you figured this out.
5. The magazine editor had a choice of showing the poll data in a circle graph or a bar graph. Do you think she made the better choice? Why?

Many computer programs prepare graphs electronically from spreadsheets. Circle graphs are often called **pie charts,** particularly when they are used in business and industry.

Most Home Runs 1985 – 1992

a. What information is shown on the vertical axis of the Home Run Leaders graph?

b. What information is shown on the horizontal axis?

c. What is the lowest number on the *Home runs* axis? the highest number? the interval?

d. Which year shows the fewest home runs?

e. Which year shows the most home runs?

f. How does the number of home runs hit in 1991 compare with the number hit in 1992?

From this graph it is difficult to tell the exact number of home runs in each year. However, the bar graph provides a way to compare information about home run records.

A circle graph often works best when you want to compare parts of the data with the whole set of data.

1. When is it best to use a bar graph to display data? a circle graph?

2. Tell at least three ways that you can use a graph.

3. What information might not be seen easily from a graph? Explain.

4. Is it better to display information in a table or in a graph? Why?

CORE

1. Getting Started This bar graph shows information about an important environmental issue.
   a. What information is shown on the horizontal scale?
   b. What is the interval on the vertical scale?
   c. Which country produces the least annual waste per person?
   d. About how many pounds of trash per person comes from the United States?

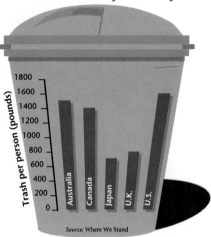

About what percentage of each circle is shaded?

2.   **3.**   **4.**   **5.**   **6.**

7. This circle graph shows five different activities in a runner's workout.
   a. On which activity does the runner spend the most time? the least time?
   b. Which two activities together make up half the workout?
   c. What is the total of the percentages? Why?

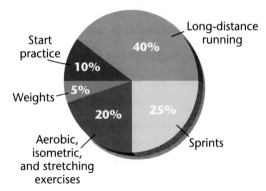

8. Write the word or phrase that correctly completes the statement. On a circle graph, each slice is called a ___.

9. In the bar graph in Exercise 1, suppose the vertical scale started at 600 instead of 0.
   a. How would it change the information that the graph shows?
   b. How could it change the impression the information gives?

The graph shows which sports people 7 years of age and older played in 1990.

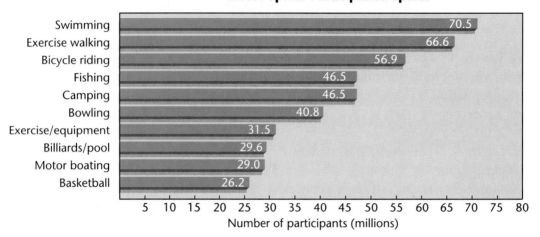

Most Popular Participation Sports

Sport	Number of participants (millions)
Swimming	70.5
Exercise walking	66.6
Bicycle riding	56.9
Fishing	46.5
Camping	46.5
Bowling	40.8
Exercise/equipment	31.5
Billiards/pool	29.6
Motor boating	29.0
Basketball	26.2

Number of participants (millions)

10. On the *Number of participants* axis, what is the lowest number? the highest number? the interval?

11. How many people participated in basketball?

12. Compare the number of participants for fishing and camping.

 Social Science
13. How many more people exercised by walking than by working out with equipment? Why do you think this is true?

14. Which sport has about one-half the number of participants as bicycle riding?

15. Which combination of sports has about the same popularity as swimming?

16. Why is a bar graph a better way to display this information than a circle graph?

Industry
17. Write the word or phrase that correctly completes the statement.
Circle graphs, especially those showing business-related information, are sometimes called ___.

For Exercises 18–22, use the circle graph, which shows the sources of immigration to the United States during 1981–1991. The number of immigrants from all countries during 1981–1991 was 7,338,000.

History
18. Almost half of the immigrants came from which continent?

19. What percentage of the immigrants came from Asia?

20. What percentage of the immigrants came from places other than Europe?

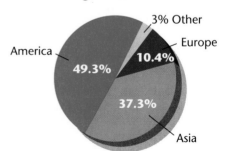

Immigration 1981–1991

3% Other
Europe
America
49.3%
10.4%
37.3%
Asia

21. About how many immigrants came from the Americas? Name five countries from which these immigrants might have come.

22. Can you tell from the graph what percentage of immigrants came from Africa? Explain.

23. **Mowing Money** Suppose your weekly earnings from yard work are $20. You spend $5 on transportation, $5 on snack foods, and $10 at the movies. What percentage of your budget do you use on each item? Draw a circle graph by estimating the size of each sector.

 LOOK AHEAD

24. Make a table that shows the same information as in the bar graph.

25. Describe how you would make a bar graph if you started with the table.

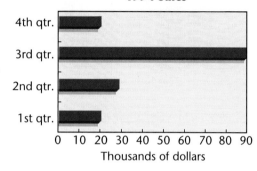

Universal Widgets 1994 Sales

MORE PRACTICE

About what percentage of each circle is shaded?

26.   **27.**   **28.**   **29.**   **30.**

 31. What fraction of the day does a dancer spend in rehearsals? in dance classes? in exercising?

 32. What activities take about twice as much time as meals and relaxation?

 33. How many hours does a dancer spend on exercises and weight training? sleeping?

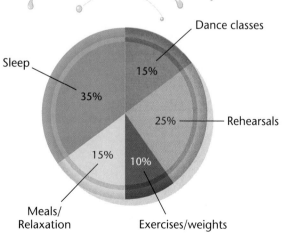

Training for the Ballet

Dance classes 15%

Sleep 35%

Rehearsals 25%

Meals/Relaxation 15%

Exercises/weights 10%

In 1988, new Olympic weightlifting records were set in all but one weight class. In the snatch weight portion of this two-part event, the contestant lifts the bar from the floor in one movement and holds it overhead for 2 seconds.

Gold Medal Weightlifting Results–1988 Summer Olympic Games

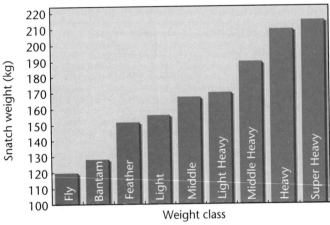

34. On the *Snatch weight* axis, what is the lowest number? the highest number? the interval?

35. How many kilograms did the super heavyweight lift?

36. Flyweights weigh 52 kg or less. How many kilograms more than this weight did the gold medal winner in this class lift?

37. The gold medalist in the featherweight class was less than 5 ft tall and weighed 132 lb.
  a. How many kilograms did the winner of this class lift?
  b. 1 kg is about 2.2 lb. How many pounds did the winner lift?
  c. What percentage of his weight did the winner lift?

History

38. What trend do you see that relates the lifter's weight and the amount lifted?

MORE MATH REASONING

39. These two bar graphs show the same data. What impression do you get about the performance of the four high schools from the first graph? Describe how the second graph changes that impression.

SAT Verbal Scores by High School

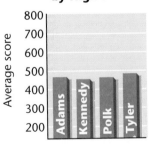

SAT Verbal Scores by High School

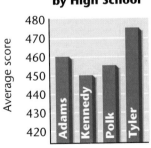

40. A Puzzling Circle A circular spinner contains eight sectors. Each sector is labeled 1, 2, 3, or 4. Use these clues to draw and label the spinner.
- There are twice as many chances to spin a 3 than a 2.
- The greatest number of sectors are labeled 4.
- The smallest number of sectors are labeled 2.
- Two numbers appear the same number of times.

1-2
PART B
Making Bar Graphs

← CONNECT → *You've seen how to read and compare data on a bar graph. People who make reports and presentations for businesses often want to take information and display it in a bar graph. In this part, you will learn how to prepare a bar graph from a table of data.*

To construct a bar graph from a table of data, you need to plan and make decisions.

Ice Cream	Gallons Sold
Chocolate	700
Strawberry	475
Vanilla	500
Chocolate Bits	425
Almond Alley	365

Q What is this comparing?
A Sales according to flavor.

Q What are the components of the bar graph?
A Axes and scales bars.

Q How do I pick what scale goes on what axis?
A If flavors go on the bottom, then sales go on the side.

Q How thick do I make the bars?
A How much space do I have on my paper?

Q How does the bar graph display the information better?
A _____?_____.

EXPLORE: THE BAR FACTS

Countries have very different customs about the average number of vacation days per year their workers are given.

MATERIALS

*Graph paper
Ruler*

Country	Vacation Days
Australia	22.4
Canada	14.7
France	27.0
Japan	24.0
Spain	32.0
United States	10.8

Suppose you are the leader of an employee group who wants to convince management to give more vacation days. You could use a bar graph to make your case in a visual way.

1. Decide which data to graph on each axis.

2. How many bars will you need to draw? Explain.

3. Decide on a scale for the axis that will contain the numbers of vacation days. Consider the following:
   a. What is the largest number you need to graph?
   b. Decide whether to use 0 or some other number as the smallest number on the axis.
   c. What is a convenient interval? What will each tick mark represent?

4. Label each axis with appropriate units.

5. Draw, shade, and label each bar.

6. Give your graph a title.

7. Compare your bar graph with the bar graphs done by other students. Did you make different decisions? What differences do you see in the graphs?

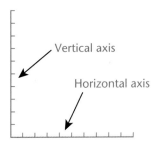

A bar graph has two axes, a **horizontal** axis and a **vertical** axis.

STEPS FOR DRAWING A BAR GRAPH

1. Choose which information to put on each axis.

2. Choose an interval and mark off a convenient scale on the axes that show numbers.

3. Draw, shade, and label the bars.

4. Give your bar graph a title.

When choosing which information to put on each axis, you must decide whether to use vertical or horizontal bars to display your information.

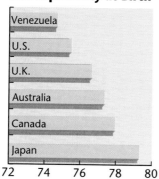

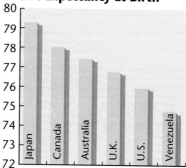

Your decision may be based on style or on what you're trying to see from the graph.

**CONSIDER ?**

1. In the Life Expectancy graphs, what information is shown on the axis with the numbers?
2. Why does the axis that shows the numbers start at 72?
3. If the axis started at 0, how would it change the way the information is displayed?

TRY IT

a. Give a convenient interval to use for graphing this set of data: 110, 170, 340, 260, 200, 285.

1. Why might you want to make a bar graph from a table of data?
2. How does your choice of which information to put on each axis affect how your bar graph will look?
3. On the axis that contains the numbers, you may decide to start with 0 or some other number as the smallest number to graph. How does your choice affect your bar graph?
4. Why is the title you choose for your bar graph important?

Exercises

CORE

1. **Getting Started** Ms. Solano is sales manager for Acme Books. She decided to make a bar graph that shows book sales in each of the company's sales regions.
   a. What information did she decide to put on the horizontal axis?
   b. What range did she decide to use on the vertical axis?
   c. What does each line on the vertical axis represent?

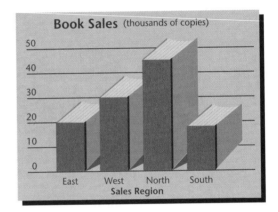

2. Ms. Solano used a *vertical* bar graph to display her information. What would she need to do to change it into a *horizontal* bar graph?

What is a convenient interval to use for graphing each set of data?

3. 10,000; 25,000; 30,000; 55,000   4. 1.2; 1.9; 1.35; 2.1; 3

5. What title would you use for a bar graph of Data Table A?

6. Make a bar graph from Data Table A. On the *Poverty level* axis, use 0 as the lowest number and 40 as the highest number.

7. Make another bar graph from Data Table A. On the *Poverty level* axis, use 25 as the lowest number and 40 as the highest number.

Data Table A	
Year	**Number Below Poverty Level (millions)**
1960	39.9
1970	25.4
1980	29.3
1990	33.6

8. Compare your two graphs from Exercises 6 and 7. Which graph is more powerful? Explain your thinking.

9. What title would you use for a bar graph of Data Table B?

10. For Data Table B, what number will you use as the largest on the *Life expectancy* axis? What number will you use as the smallest? Explain your thinking.

11. Make a bar graph from Data Table B.

12. Is life expectancy for people in Japan more or less than for people in the United States? By how much? Give at least four possible reasons for the difference.

Data Table B	
Country	**Life Expectancy (years from birth)**
Japan	79.2
Sweden	78.1
United Kingdom	76.5
United States	75.8
France	78.0
Germany	76.1

LOOK BACK

13. Where on the number line will you find points whose coordinates are greater than −4 *and* less than 0? [1-1]

14. What is the perimeter of the rectangle? What is the area? [Previous course]

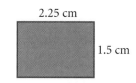

2.25 cm

1.5 cm

MORE PRACTICE

15. Mr. Menendez heads a tourist organization in Miami, Florida. He decided to prepare a bar graph to encourage people to "c'mon down" during the winter months.
   a. What information did Mr. Menendez decide to put on the vertical axis?
   b. What interval did Mr. Menendez use for the temperature axis?
   c. Did Mr. Menendez need to start the temperature axis at 0? Explain.

What is a convenient interval to use for graphing each set of data?

16. 10; 25; 35; 60   **17.** 5; 7; 8.5; 10; 11.5; 14   **18.** $75; $225; $350; $700

Data Table C	
Military Service	**1990 Strength**
Army	746,220
Navy	74,429
Air Force	535,200
Coast Guard	37,308
Marine Corps	196,652

Data Table D	
Country	**Energy Use (quadrillion BTUs)**
France	8.69
United Kingdom	9.13
Canada	10.79
Japan	18.18
United States	81.17

Data Table E	
Year	**U.S. Auto Production (in thousands)**
1985	11,653
1986	11,335
1987	10,925
1988	11,214
1989	10,874
1990	9,783

Data Table F	
Continent	**Highest Mountain (ft)**
Asia	29,028
Europe	15,771
North America	20,320
South America	22,834
Africa	19,340
Antarctica	16,864
Australia	7,310

19. What title would you use for a bar graph of Data Table C? Data Table D? Data Table E? Data Table F?

20. Anchors Aweigh! Make a bar graph from Data Table C.

21. Power to the People Make a bar graph from Data Table D.

22. Start Your Engines Make a bar graph from Data Table E.

23. Calling All Mountain Climbers Make a bar graph from Data Table F.

Describe the planning and decisions that went into making each bar graph. Note any interesting comparisons or information that you see in the bar graph.

24. Write about the bar graph from Table C.   **25.** Write about the bar graph from Table D.

26. Write about the bar graph from Table E.   **27.** Write about the bar graph from Table F.

MORE MATH REASONING

28. Melting Pot The table shows the 1990 United States population breakdown by ethnic group.

Ethnic Group	Population
European American	188,128,296
African American	29,216,293
American Indian	1,959,234
Asian American	7,273,662
Hispanic American	12,327,451
Other	9,804,937
Total	248,709,873

a. Why would a circle graph make a better display of the data than a bar graph?

b. Create a circle graph of the data. Your circle graph will need to show six sectors, one for each group in the table. Make your circle graph by following these steps:

Step 1: Calculate the percentage of total population for each ethnic group.

Step 2: Figure out the central angle measure for each sector. Use the percentages for each ethnic group and the fact that a full circle contains 360°.

Step 3: Draw the circle with a compass. Measure off the angle for each sector with a protractor.

Step 4: Label each wedge-shaped sector and title the graph.

29. The table shows marriage and divorce rates for 1970–1990. Each rate gives the percentage of people who were married or divorced in that year.

Make a single bar graph that shows all the information in the table. What conclusions can you draw from your bar graph?

Year	Marriage Rate	Divorce Rate
1970	10.6	3.5
1975	10.0	4.8
1980	10.6	5.2
1985	10.2	5.0
1990	9.8	4.7

← CONNECT → *You have seen line graphs in newspapers, magazines, and textbooks. You will see how you can make predictions based on trends displayed in line graphs.*

This line graph shows a change in the way people shop.

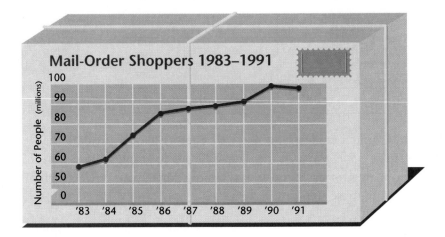

On the vertical axis the interval is 10 million. The jagged line means that the numbers between 0 and 50 million have been omitted. The horizontal axis shows time. The dots are the data points for each year.

In a **line graph,** line segments connect the data points. The overall direction of the graph describes a **trend.**

CONSIDER

?

1. How many mail-order shoppers were there in 1983? in 1987? in 1991?
2. What trend does the graph show?
3. In the 1980s large numbers of American women started working away from home. How does the graph show this?

MATERIALS

*Graph paper
Ruler*

In 1964, the men's Olympic high jump event ended in a tie when Soviet Valery Brumel and American John Thomas each broke the existing record.

Men's Olympic High Jump Results	
Year	**Height (meters)**
1964	2.18
1968	2.24
1972	2.23
1976	2.25
1980	2.36
1984	2.35
1988	2.38
1992	2.34

Step 1: Plan a line graph to display the data.
   A. What information will go on the horizontal axis? the vertical axis?
   B. What is the lowest height? What is the highest height? What interval will show the height differences most clearly?
   C. Use a jagged line like the one used on the Mail-Order Shoppers graph to start the height scale. What numbers will you cut out?

Step 2: Mark and label the axes with the intervals and scales you have chosen.

Step 3: Plot points for each data value. Draw line segments to connect the points.

Step 4: Give your line graph a title.

The mechanics of a high jump.

Use your line graph to answer the following questions.

1. What general trend do you observe? What reasons can you give for the trend?

2. In what years does the trend not hold? How can you explain this?

3. Can a true trend have exceptions? Explain your thinking.

Suppose the following pairs of points are on a line graph. Decide if the line segment connecting the two points goes up or down.

a. (1987, $157); (1989, $175)
b. (6:00 a.m., 25°F); (6:00 p.m., 18°F)
c. (January, 45.7 sec); (March, 45.07 sec)

A double line graph shows two related sets of data. This makes it easy to compare trends.

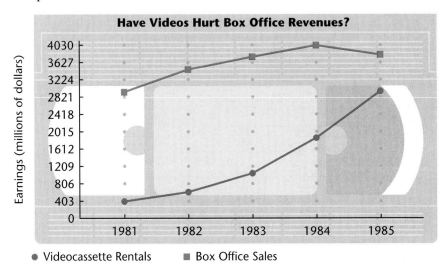

Have Videos Hurt Box Office Revenues?

Earnings (millions of dollars)

● Videocassette Rentals   ■ Box Office Sales

CONSIDER

4. What two trends are displayed in the graph above? What relationships do you see?

Connecting the points in a line graph with segments makes it easier to examine how the data is changing.

REFLECT

1. How do line graphs show trends?
2. Which axis is usually used to show time?
3. What does a jagged line mean when you see it on the scale of a graph?
4. What kind of data does a line graph display?
5. What is a double line graph? Why is it useful?

Exercises

CORE

1. Getting Started Bob used a line graph to chart book sales in his store.

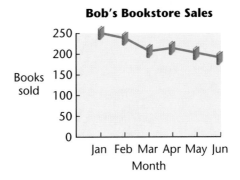

Bob's Bookstore Sales

  a. Did sales increase or decrease from January to February?

  b. Did sales increase or decrease from March to April?

  c. Would you describe the trend for book sales during the first half of the year as increasing or decreasing? Why?

2. Which type of graph is best to show trends?

(a) circle   (b) bar   (c) line   (d) not here

The 400-meter individual medley is one of the most difficult Olympic events because the swimmer must be able to do four different strokes in world-class time.

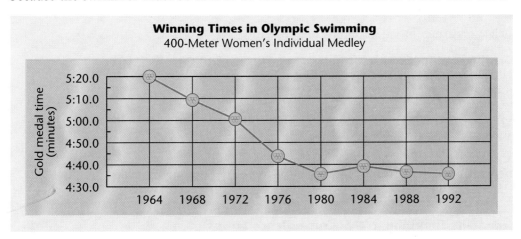

Winning Times in Olympic Swimming
400-Meter Women's Individual Medley

3. How many years are shown on the horizontal axis?

4. What is the shortest time on the vertical axis? the longest time?

5. What is the interval on the vertical axis?

6. In 1964 Donna DeVarona won the first gold medal in the 400-meter women's individual medley. Estimate her winning time.

7. How can you tell from the graph that each gold medalist in the next four Olympics broke the previous record? Estimate the winning time in 1980.

8. Describe the trend that the graph shows.

9. American Charles Hickcox won the men's 400-m medley in 1964 with a time of 4 min 48.4 sec. In which year did a woman first beat his Olympic record?

Use this double line graph comparing video rentals with box office sales.

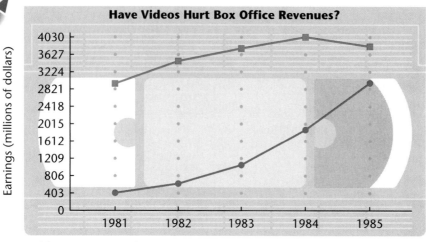

Have Videos Hurt Box Office Revenues?

● Videocassette Rentals   ■ Box Office Sales

10. How many millions of dollars does each interval represent? The graph was produced by computer. Why do you think the computer chose this value for the interval?

11. How much was earned in video rentals in 1984? in 1985?

12. What were the earnings from box office sales in 1984? in 1985?

13. Why is a double line graph a good way to compare earnings?

14. What do you predict will happen on the graph if information for years after 1985 is included?

15. **Shopping for Convenience** Small convenience stores are popping up everywhere.

Average Daily Shopping in U.S. Convenience Stores											
Year	1975	1976	1977	1978	1979	1980	1981	1982	1983	1984	1985
Customers (thousands)	510	550	640	630	630	590	600	630	640	680	710

a. What is the range of values included in the chart?
b. Draw a line graph.
c. Do you see a trend? If so, describe it.

LOOK AHEAD

This symbol 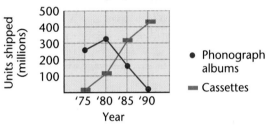 stands for 1000 telephone calls.

How many symbols would you use to show each?

16. 2000 telephone calls   **17.** 6000 telephone calls

18. 4500 telephone calls   **19.** 500 telephone calls

MORE PRACTICE

20. What is the interval on each axis?

21. Use the line graph to estimate the greatest number of phonograph albums shipped in one year.

22. Estimate the fewest number of cassettes shipped.

23. In what year did the number of cassettes first exceed the number of albums shipped?

24. In what year was the number of phonograph albums shipped the same as the number of cassettes shipped in 1985?

25. In 1985, the manufacturer valued phonograph albums at $7.67 each and cassettes at $7.12 each. About how much was the combined value of shipments of these two items?

26. What trends do you see? What new products may affect these sales?

Shipments of Cassettes and Phonograph Albums

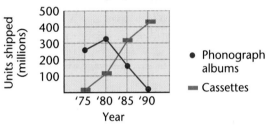

27. The Lone Star State In Texas, as in most states, land has many uses.
  a. What percentage of the land is used for crops?
  b. Which combinations of uses make up about 40% of the land?
  c. What percentage of the land is used for farming or ranching?
  d. Assume you are writing a travel guide about Texas. Write a paragraph to describe the state.

Texas Land Use

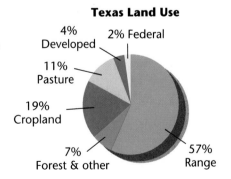

28. By 1990 almost one-third of the graduates earning medical or dental degrees were women.

History

Medical Degrees Earned by Women (1960–1990)										
Year	1960	1970	1975	1980	1984	1985	1986	1987	1988	1989	1990
Degrees	387	699	1629	3486	4454	4874	4916	5054	5080	5150	5138

a. What is the range of values included in the chart?

b. Draw a line graph.

c. Do you see a trend? If so, describe it.

MORE MATH REASONING

29. Listen Up A survey asked 1500 people how they used their walkaround radios most often. Would you use a bar graph, a circle graph, or a line graph to display the information? Explain your thinking. Draw a graph.

Use	Home	Work	Walking	Airplane	Studying	Sports	Commuting
Number	431	185	294	95	154	220	121

30. Starting Your Engine A mechanic charges a flat rate of $60 for the first hour and $50 for each additional hour to fix a car. After the first hour, if the mechanic works for part of an hour, the $50 hourly rate is multiplied by the fraction of the hour. Use the graph to find the repair cost for the following amounts of time.

a. 45 min

b. 90 min

c. 2 hr 15 min

d. 3 hr 36 min

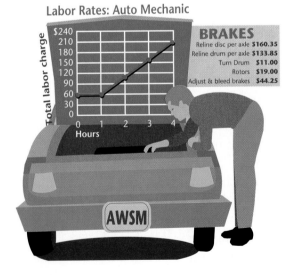

Labor Rates: Auto Mechanic

BRAKES
Reline disc per axle **$160.35**
Reline drum per axle **$133.85**
Turn Drum **$11.00**
Rotors **$19.00**
Adjust & bleed brakes **$44.25**

← CONNECT → *You can get information from bar, circle, and line graphs to help you answer questions. Pictures and symbols can also be used on graphs to give information in a very clear way that is easy to read.*

Symbols are used worldwide as a way of communicating.

Dallas/Fort Worth Airport

European Road Signs

Expo 70 Osaka, Japan

 CONSIDER ?

1. What does each symbol mean?
2. Would you understand each symbol if you didn't speak the language? Explain.

A **pictograph** uses symbols to compare data. The **key** tells how many items one symbol represents.

Average Monthly Use of Water per Household

Source: The 1992 Information Please Environmental Almanac

1. On average, how many gallons of water does a household of four in Chicago use each month?
   The pictograph uses 7.25 droplets to show the water use of a Chicago household. Each droplet stands for 1000 gallons. So a Chicago household uses about 7250 gallons of water per month.
2. Compare water usage by household in Miami and New York.
   Miami: about 8750 gallons per month (8.75 droplets)
   New York: about 7500 gallons per month (7.5 droplets)
   A Miami household uses about 1250 gallons per month more than a New York household.

WHAT DO YOU THINK?

In Tucson, 1000 gallons of water costs $1.37. Estimate the cost per month for an average household.

Lydia thinks ...

The graph shows Tucson's water use with 8.75 droplets. Each droplet is 1000 gallons. So each droplet costs $1.37. The total cost is 8.75 • 1.37 = 11.9875, or about $12.

Pei thinks ...

If 1000 gallons cost $1.37, then 1 gallon costs 1.37 ÷ 1000, or $0.00137. Tucson uses 8.75 droplets or 8750 gallons. So the cost is 8750 • 0.00137 = 11.9875, or about $12.

EXPLORE: PICK A PICTOGRAPH

MATERIALS

Almanac
Ruler
Crayons

1. Choose some interesting data from an almanac that could be displayed nicely in a pictograph. You might consider magazine circulation, TV or movie statistics, or census information. Make a table that shows the data you want to display.

2. Choose a symbol and write a key.

3. Design a pictograph that shows your data in a clear and interesting display.

4. Do you think that a pictograph is a good way to display this data? Why?

In addition to pictographs, other kinds of graphs use pictures to give information. A **glyph** is a visual display that doesn't depend on words. Once you understand the key, you can interpret it quickly.

People who live near large cities are concerned about how long it takes to get to work. This transportation glyph uses a clock to show four pieces of information.

Camden Yards

The shading in the snooze button shows the transportation as light rail.

The travel time is 15 minutes.

The train leaves at 7 o'clock.

Camden Yards

The destination (Camden Yards) is showing under the clock.

TRY IT

Describe the information you can read from these transportation glyphs.

a. Rail

Columbia

b. Trolley

Aquarium

c. Bus

Dutch Mall

Pictures help us communicate information and compare data easily.

1. Why are symbols and picture graphs useful?

2. Give examples of three symbols whose meaning you can understand without using words.

3. Why does a pictograph need a key? How do you use the key?

Exercises

CORE

1. Getting Started A market research company did a survey to find out the average number of clocks per household. What does this show?

2. One loaf of bread represents $10 worth of groceries. Draw symbols to show $25 worth of groceries.

3. A tennis racket represents winning four Grand Slam Tournaments. Draw symbols to show ten Grand Slam wins.

4. A suitcase represents 40 pounds of cargo. Draw symbols to show 50 pounds of cargo.

5. Write the word or phrase that correctly completes the statement. The ____ gives you the information you need to understand the symbols on a pictograph.

6. To attract new businesses, communities might advertise the quality of the environment, recreation facilities, public safety, and health services with glyphs. The length of the arrow on each glyph tells whether the rating is excellent, good, or poor. A longer arrow means a better rating.
  a. Describe the qualities of city A.
  b. Describe the qualities of city B.
  c. Which of these cities is a place you would like to live? Explain.
  d. Make a glyph describing the qualities of your city.

Recreation   Environment (air and water)

Health Services   Public Safety

City A   City B

Use a compass and a ruler to draw transportation glyphs.

7. A professor leaves at 9:00 a.m. for a 15-minute bus ride to University Center.

8. Ben travels from 6:00–6:45 p.m. on light rail to a concert at Pacific Arena.

 Air pollution is a big concern. Because of the large number of cars and trucks on the road, dangerous amounts of carbon monoxide are sometimes emitted.

National Carbon Monoxide Emissions 1940 to 1991

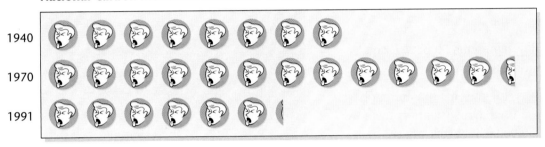

= 10 million metric tons   Information is to the nearest metric ton.

9. How much carbon monoxide was released into the air in 1940? in 1970?

10. What was the difference between the emissions in 1940 and 1991?

11. Why do you usually get estimates rather than exact numbers from pictographs?

12. How Sweet It Is On average, a typical American eats 11,113 M&M's® in a lifetime. An average bag of M&M's® contains colors in the proportions shown in the circle graph.
  a. Estimate what percentage of the M&M's® in one bag are green or tan.
  b. Estimate what percentage are brown.
  c. Compare the number of yellow with the number of orange.
  d. How many red M&M's® would you expect in a batch of 10,000?

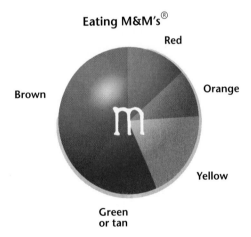

Eating M&M's®

LOOK BACK

13. Where on the number line are points whose coordinates are greater than −5? [1-1]

14. Give the coordinates of a point that is 2 units left and 5 units above (−2, 3). [1-1]

Calculate. [Previous course]

15. $0.45 + 1.08 + 0.97$ **16.** $10 - 8.54$ **17.** $32 \times 75\%$

MORE PRACTICE

18. A baseball bat represents 2000 people at the stadium for a Chicago Cubs game. Draw symbols to show 23,000 fans at the stadium.

19. A dog represents 50 pets. Draw symbols to show 300 pets.

20. A barrel represents one billion barrels of oil used. Draw symbols to show 6,250,000,000 barrels of oil.

Social Science

In a random survey, the subjects were asked about their favorite TV shows.

21. How many people claimed that they liked news shows best?

22. How many people were included in the survey?

23. What type of TV show is the most popular among the people surveyed?

Favorite TV Shows

Soap Operas
Comedy
Quiz Shows
Detective
News

 = 10 votes

A high school coach asked students about their favorite sports.

24. What percentage of the students chose soccer as their favorite sport?

25. Compare the number of students who chose baseball with those who chose tennis.

26. Make a pictograph that shows the results of the survey.

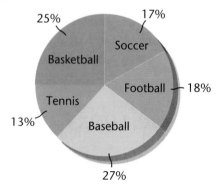

MORE MATH REASONING

Venn diagrams use intersecting circles to picture relationships.

One hundred people were surveyed about the types of electronic equipment they own. This Venn diagram shows the results. For example, 25 people have only a personal computer. Four people have a personal computer and a fax, but no car telephone.

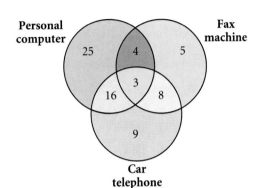

27. How many people have only a car telephone? only a fax machine? only a personal computer?

28. How many people have all three types of electronic equipment? only one type?

29. How many people have personal computers? fax machines? car phones?

30. How many people have a personal computer and a car telephone but no fax machine?

31. How many people have a fax machine and a car telephone but no personal computer?

32. How many people have none of this equipment?

1-2
PART E — Making Connections

← C O N N E C T → *You have learned about using bar, circle, and line graphs as well as some types of graphs that use pictures. You can analyze and compare information on graphs to help you plan and make decisions.*

Graphs in books, newspapers, and magazines summarize large amounts of data in an easy-to-read form. Graphs help you analyze trends and make comparisons and decisions.

MATERIALS

*Compass
Ruler*

The city of Liberty needs a new zip code area and post office to take care of the increasing amount of mail in the 12345 and 12346 zip code areas. They need to divide one of these areas into two.

The postal service needs to decide where to put the new post office. To help with the decision, city planners have supplied graphs.

Suppose you are a city council member.

Liberty Zip Code Areas

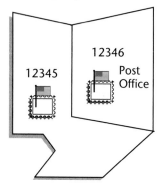

Population of Liberty by Zip Code 1996

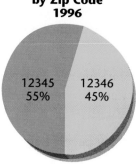

Mail Traffic by Zip Code October 1996

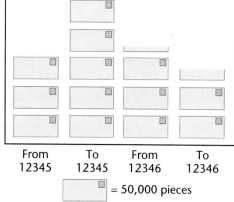

Growth in the Number of Households 1992–1996

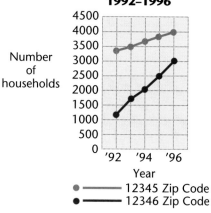

1. Study the graphs. Write as many statements as you can about the number of people and the trends in zip codes 12345 and 12346.
2. Design a glyph to show your findings.
3. Which zip code should be split into two zip code areas? Prepare a statement for the postal service that supports your position.

REFLECT

1. Why do people use graphs to display information?
2. Why do graphs usually provide only estimates of the actual numbers? Can they show actual numbers? If so, how? If not, explain.
3. What does it mean when we say, "Graphs show the big picture"?
4. When the time comes to choose the Athlete of the Century, how might graphs help?
5. Which types of graphs are used to compare data? to show parts of the whole? to show trends?

Self-Assessment

Which type of graph would you use

1. to show the number of sports injuries at five different high schools?

2. to demonstrate how the government divides your tax dollars?

3. to show the number of miles flown by spacecraft each year since 1990?

4. to show the decline in the acres of wetlands between 1975 and 1995?

5. to show the sale of Elvis Presley's various gold records?

6. What is the perimeter of the rectangle? What is the area? [Previous course]

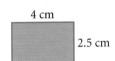

7. List three things about yourself that you could keep track of on a line graph.

8. Think of four friends. List two things about your friends that could be shown on a bar graph.

9. Is a circle graph a good way to describe a collection of tapes or compact discs? Explain.

10. What is a pictograph?

11. Which type of graph uses sectors to display information?
    (a) bar
    (b) pie chart
    (c) line
    (d) glyph
    (e) not here

12. Find a pictograph in a newspaper or magazine. Cut it out. Draw a different type of graph that shows the same information.

13. Give the coordinates of a point that is 3 units right of $(-2, 3)$ and 3 units below it. [1-1]

14. Marc is writing an article about the time employees are out due to sickness. He has collected the data shown in the chart.

Days of Work Missed Annually Due to the Common Cold

Age Group	18–24	25–44	45–64	combined
Days Missed per 100 Employees	30.3	15.5	15.8	17.6

a. Why is a bar graph a good choice to display this data?
b. Make a bar graph.

Productivity **measures how much workers produce. This line graph compares the productivity of Canadian and Japanese workers with that of U.S. workers.**

Industry

15. Estimate the percentage of U.S. productivity for Canada during the 1970s. How does this compare with Japan's productivity during the same decade?

History

16. Which country, Japan or Canada, showed the greatest increase between the 1970s and 1980s?

Social Science

17. Describe the trends you see in the graph.

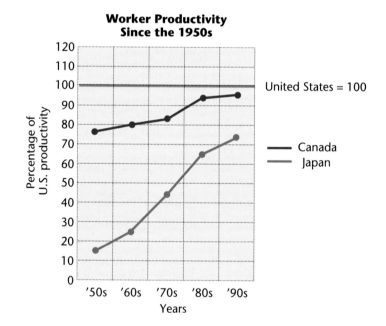

Worker Productivity Since the 1950s

United States = 100

Canada
Japan

Percentage of U.S. productivity

Years

1-3 Analyzing Data

MEASURING HEALTH AND FITNESS

"Physical fitness is the ability of your whole body, including the muscles, skeleton, heart, and all other body parts, to work together efficiently, which means [to be] able to do the most work with the least amount of effort."– *Fitness for Life*

Are you physically fit? ➤ Are you healthy? ➤ Statistics show that many Americans of all ages do not take good care of their health. ➤ You don't have to be an athlete to be healthy. Fitness experts recommend a balanced diet, plenty of sleep, and regular physical activity to look and feel good. ➤ Fitness does not need to take a lot of extra effort or be expensive. Walking or bicycling to school, work, or errands, rather than driving, can help save money and keep you in shape.

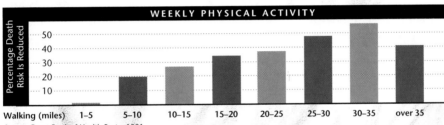

WEEKLY PHYSICAL ACTIVITY

Percentage Death Risk Is Reduced

Walking (miles) 1–5 5–10 10–15 15–20 20–25 25–30 30–35 over 35

Source: Grant Book of Health Facts, *1991*

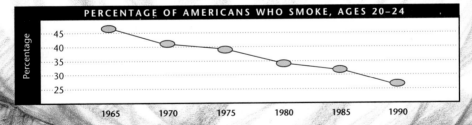

PERCENTAGE OF AMERICANS WHO SMOKE, AGES 20–24

Percentage

1965 1970 1975 1980 1985 1990

1. What problems and trends do the graphs show? What are some steps to think about taking to become more fit?
2. What do the ranges on the bar graph show?
3. What other data would you want to see to get a better picture of fitness and health?

← C O N N E C T →   *Graphs and displays give a lot of information, but sometimes we just need a snapshot. You will learn how to use special measures, each of which summarizes a set of data in a different way.*

By looking for patterns, you can summarize the information given by data that is shown in a display.

EXPLORE: HITTING THE CHARTS

Rolling Stone® magazine reports information about how well singers' albums are selling. This number line with symbols is called a **line plot.** It shows how many weeks male and female solo artists stayed on the Top 40 list. Each face represents one singer.

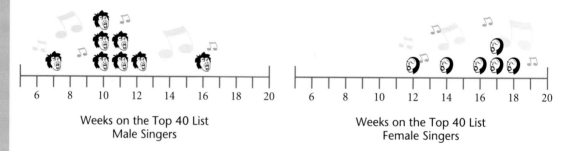

Weeks on the Top 40 List
Male Singers

Weeks on the Top 40 List
Female Singers

1. How many male singers are displayed? How many female singers?
2. Look at the pattern for male singers. Make as many statements as you can to summarize what you see. What can you say about the typical number of weeks that a male singer stays on the Top 40 list?
3. What can you say about the typical number of weeks that a female singer stays on the Top 40 list?
4. Combine the two displays into a single-line plot that shows males and females together. You can use x's and o's to represent males and females. Does looking at your combined line plot change the way that you would summarize the information? If so, how?

In the Explore, you may have used the **range,** the **mean,** the **median,** or the **mode** to describe a typical number of weeks a singer was on the Top 40 list.

The **range** of a list of values is the difference between the highest and lowest value.

The **mean** is the average of a list of numbers.

The **median** is the middle number in a list arranged in order.

The **mode** is the value that occurs most often.

For the values 84, 90, 65, 52, and 90:

The range is 90 − 52, or 38.

MEAN (Average)

To find the mean, add the values and divide by the number of values.

$$\frac{84 + 90 + 65 + 52 + 90}{5}$$

The mean is 76.2.

MEDIAN

To find the median, order the numbers smallest to largest. For an odd number of values, find the middle value. For an even number of values, find the average of the two middle values.

52, 65, 84, 90, 90   52, 60, 75, 82

The median is 84.   The median is 67.5.

MODE

To find the mode, use the number in the list that occurs most often. There may be more than one mode or no mode.

90 appears twice, while the other numbers appear just once.

The mode is 90.

Mean, median, and mode are called **measures of central tendency.** Each measure describes the data in a different way.

EXAMPLE

1. Number of copies of *Black Beauty* sold per week at Allen's Bookstore during the past 8 weeks: 14, 21, 12, 18, 15, 17, 15, 16
Find the range, the mean, the median, and the mode.
List the numbers from smallest to largest: 12, 14, 15, 15, 16, 17, 18, 21.

Range: $21 - 12 = 9$
The largest value is 21. The smallest is 12.

Median: $\dfrac{15 + 16}{2} = 15.5$ copies
The two middle values are 15 and 16.

Mean: $\dfrac{12 + 14 + 15 + 15 + 16 + 17 + 18 + 21}{8}$
There are 8 values. Add them and divide by 8.

$= \dfrac{128}{8}$, or 16 copies

Mode: 15 copies
All values appear just once except 15, which appears twice.

TRY IT

a. Five brands of sneakers are sold in Foot Emporium. They are priced at $65.97, $52.00, $25.72, $39.98, and $49.75. Find the mean price.

b. Anita Kaplan was high scorer on the 1993–1994 Stanford University women's basketball team. In the last 10 games of the season, she scored 34, 20, 13, 16, 15, 18, 23, 12, 29, and 12 points. What number of points did she score most often? Which measure of central tendency are you using?

c. Six houses were sold in Peoria today for $93,500, $87,250, $135,000, $109,200, $79,240, and $151,100. Find the median price.

Usually, the mean is the central value used. But when there is one very high or very low value, the median will summarize the data better than the mean. We might use the mode as the typical value in a small set of data if several values are the same.

EXAMPLE

2. The six employees in the mayor's office earn $18,000, $18,000, $21,000, $23,000, $30,000, and $65,000 per year. What should they report as an "average" salary?
The $65,000 salary is very high compared with the others. So the median will represent the data better than the mean.

The salaries are in order from smallest to largest:

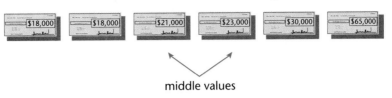

middle values

The median salary is $\frac{21,000 + 23,000}{2}$ or $22,000 per year.
The average employee has a salary of $22,000 per year.

REFLECT

1. If you know the complete set of data, why would you be interested in the mean, median, or mode?
2. The school nurse measured the heights of five teenagers.
   163 cm, 168 cm, 168 cm, 168 cm, 172 cm
   Which measure of central tendency would you use? Why?
3. Give a situation where you might use a mode. Why do you think the mode is the right measure to use in this situation?
4. Give a situation where you might use a mean. Why do you think the mean is the right measure to use in this situation?
5. Give a situation where you might use a median. Why do you think the median is the right measure to use in this situation?

Exercises

CORE

History

1. **Getting Started** At the 1986 world championship, Debi Thomas became the first African-American woman skater to win a women's figure skating competition. In 1988, she won an Olympic bronze.

Debi Thomas
Compulsory Figures XV Olympic Winter Games

| 11.0 | 12.2 | 11.3 | 11.4 | 10.8 | 11.0 | 11.5 | 11.4 | 11.6 |

   a. Arrange the scores in order. What is the range?
   b. What is the median score? the mean score? the mode?

2. In Exercise 1, does the mean, median, or mode best represent Debi's typical score?

3. Dwayne went shopping for a used car and saw six that he liked. The asking prices were $675, $495, $375, $625, $395, and $750. What was the average asking price?

4. Samantha measured the heights of five classmates. She got 60 in., 64 in., 58 in., 67 in., and 65 in. What is the range of these heights?

(a) 5 in.   (b) 64 in.   (c) 7 in.   (d) 57 in.   (e) not here

Health

5. An "arm and shoulder reach" test checks flexibility by measuring the number of inches a person can lift a broomstick overhead while lying face down with the chin on the floor.

Lift in Inches	Tally	Frequency
8	///	3
9	++++	5
10	++++ //	7
11	////	4
12	/	1

Arm and Shoulder Reaches (20 people)

a. Find the mean, mode, and median.

b. Which measure of central tendency would you use to describe the data? Why?

Social Science

6. Getting a Jump on College Between 1978 and 1992 the number of high school students who took exams for college credit quadrupled. In 1992, the number of exams taken per 1000 eleventh- and twelfth-grade students in the western United States appears on the map.

a. Which measure of central tendency would you use to summarize the data?

b. What is its value?

**College Credit Exams
(per thousand students)**

57
44
65
47
42
80
211 128
147
85
80

Careers

7. Salespeople for large manufacturing companies often work for commission and drive their cars to call on customers in person. A manager compared the mileage and the monthly commissions for six salespeople.

a. What is the range for the miles driven? for commissions?

b. Find the mean, mode, and median for each set of data.

c. If you were writing a job advertisement to hire a new salesperson, which numbers would you use for mileage and commissions? Why?

	Mileage	Commission
Kelley	521	$764
Radcliffe	633	$850
Garvin	485	$832
Habib	590	$778
Vesely	421	$692
Parks	388	$764

8. Puppy Pounds A veterinarian weighs a litter of five cocker spaniel puppies. She finds their weights to be 0.9 kg, 1.2 kg, 0.8 kg, 1 kg, and 1.4 kg. What should she say is the typical weight for a puppy in the litter?

9. The Amityville Water Board looked up records at random for 20 houses in the community to be able to make a report to the city council about community water use.

Annual Household Water Use (gallons)				
100,500	102,000	107,200	102,300	98,600
105,400	95,100	103,250	96,250	103,000
101,400	88,000	102,050	94,600	95,000
100,600	140,500	99,000	110,000	125,500

a. Do you think it was a good idea for the water board to choose records at random? Why?

b. Do you think any of the measures of central tendency are not suitable to represent this data? If so, why?

c. Use the measure of central tendency that you think is best to describe the typical water use of these 20 houses.

 ## *LOOK BACK*

What is a convenient interval to use for graphing each set of data? [1-2]

10. 1000; 2500; 575; 100

11. 12; 19; 135; 21; 30

12. Carl is trying to find a piece of information in a large spreadsheet. His friend Georgette tells him that the information is in cell B4. Where should Carl look to find the information on the spreadsheet? [1-1]

Write the name of the place value for the underlined digit in each number.
[Previous course]

13. 3<u>5</u>04

14. <u>8</u>9,441

15. 7.0<u>6</u>2

16. 0.00<u>9</u>4

MORE PRACTICE

Industry

Seats at a summer concert sold for $25, $22.75, $19.50, and $18.25, depending on their location.

17. What is the range?

18. What is the mean cost?

Industry

The average daily circulation, in thousands, for the five largest newspapers are 857, 1347, 1196, 1108, and 1098.

19. Find the median.

20. What is the mode?

21. The number of minutes of commercials for eight 2-hour television movies were 35, 38, 32, 31, 28, 30, 29, and 32. What is the mode for this set of data?

Industry

22. The chart shows the estimated incomes of the highest-paid entertainers in 1989 and 1990 according to *The Top Ten Almanac.*

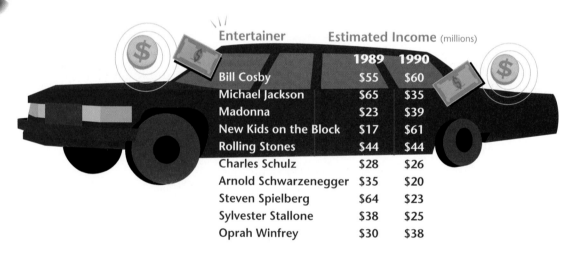

Entertainer	Estimated Income (millions)	
	1989	1990
Bill Cosby	$55	$60
Michael Jackson	$65	$35
Madonna	$23	$39
New Kids on the Block	$17	$61
Rolling Stones	$44	$44
Charles Schulz	$28	$26
Arnold Schwarzenegger	$35	$20
Steven Spielberg	$64	$23
Sylvester Stallone	$38	$25
Oprah Winfrey	$30	$38

a. What is the range of estimated incomes for 1989? for 1990?
b. Find the mean and median for each year.
c. Find the mode for 1989 and 1990 combined.
d. Calculate the 2-year total for each entertainer.
e. Which measure of central tendency would you use to summarize these 2-year totals? Why?

MORE MATH REASONING

23. Averaging an A What score would you need on Test 5 to have an A average in your school? Explain how you got your answer.

Test 1	Test 2	Test 3	Test 4	Test 5
88	92	97	78	

24. Numbers that Buzz The population of bees in a typical hive increases dramatically in the spring. The population then decreases after the bees swarm. The population also decreases during the winter when the bees on the edge of the hive freeze and die.

   a. In which month is the number of bees the smallest? the largest?

   b. What is the range of bees in the population?

   c. Explain how you would estimate a number to summarize the usual population of bees in a hive.

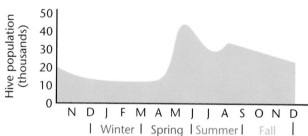

1-3
PART B
Stem-and-Leaf Diagrams

← **CONNECT** → *You have seen how you can use the mean, mode, and median to summarize a set of data. Now you are going to use a stem-and-leaf diagram to describe the shape of the data.*

A dynamometer is a device used to measure hand strength. Squeezing the grip moves the needle to show in kilograms the strength of a hand. Researchers collect data from hundreds of people to set norms for different age groups.

A **stem-and-leaf diagram** is a display that organizes data to show its shape and distribution.

EXAMPLE

Ninth graders at Waynesboro High School take a dynamometer test to measure their right-hand strengths.

Make a stem-and-leaf diagram of the data.

Step 1: Put the numbers in order from smallest to largest.

28, 34, 36, 38, 38, 38, 40, 41, 42, 42, 43, 44, 44, 45, 47, 48, 50, 51, 51, 54, 54, 58, 60, 62

Waynesboro Ninth Graders Right-Hand Strengths

34, 43, 60, 28,
41, 38, 42, 51,
44, 36, 42, 47,
38, 54, 51, 38,
44, 50, 48, 40,
54, 45, 62, 58

Step 2: Separate each number into a stem and a leaf.

Because each number is two digits, use the tens digit as the stem and the ones digit as the leaf. The number 45 becomes

Stem	Leaf
4	5

Step 3: Group numbers with the same stem.

List the stems from largest to smallest. Line up the leaves next to their stem.

The stem-and-leaf diagram shows you the shape and distribution of the data. The data clusters around the row with a stem of 4.

Right-Hand Strength

Stem	Leaf
6	0 2
5	0 1 1 4 4 8
4	0 1 2 2 3 4 4 5 7 8
3	4 6 8 8 8
2	8

CONSIDER

?

1. How would you use a stem and leaf to show a one-digit number like 9?
2. How can you use a stem-and-leaf diagram to find the median? the range?

To compare the data from two sets, you can use a **back-to-back stem-and-leaf diagram.**

30 and 31 from Set A →

Set A		Set B
Leaves	Stem	Leaves
1 0	3	4 5

← 34 and 35 from Set B

Left-hand strength data is now shown for the same group of Waynesboro students.

Waynesboro Ninth Graders Left-Hand Strengths

54, 41, 56, 50, 36, 43, 26, 41, 35, 41, 50, 29, 42, 37, 29, 39, 50, 28, 36, 26, 47, 28, 33, 37

1. Make a back-to-back stem-and-leaf diagram of the strength scores for both hands.
2. Compare the two sets of data. What impressions do you get from the diagram? Explain the differences that you discover.
3. Which set of scores has the greater range?
4. What could you say about the left-hand strength of a ninth grader? Explain your thinking.

When the numbers in the data set contain three or more digits, you can choose the stem in several different ways.

Average Speeds (mi/hr) by Indy 500 Winners Each Year										
1971–1980	158	163	159	159	149	149	161	161	159	143
1981–1990	139	162	162	164	153	171	162	145	168	186
1991–1994	176	134	157	161						

Because the first digit is 1 for each value, it makes sense to use the first *two* digits for the stem.

The stem-and-leaf diagram shows a large group of scores for the stems 14, 15, and 16 in the middle of the data.

Stem-and-leaf diagrams help picture data when there are at least 20 values that are all close together.

Stem	Leaf
18	6
17	1 6
16	1 1 1 2 2 2 3 4 8
15	3 7 8 9 9 9
14	3 5 9 9
13	4 9

REFLECT

1. Compare the information you get from a stem-and-leaf diagram with the information you get from measures of central tendency.
2. When would you use a back-to-back stem-and-leaf diagram?
3. Describe or show a set of data for which a stem-and-leaf diagram is not a helpful display.

Exercises

CORE

1. **Getting Started** An interviewer asked the ages of the first 20 people to walk into the First National Bank on a Saturday morning: 17, 25, 52, 45, 22, 35, 27, 33, 41, 66, 18, 56, 41, 43, 35, 32, 27, 48, 50, 30. Show the responses in a stem-and-leaf diagram.
   a. Put the numbers in order.
   b. How many digits will you use for the stems? Separate each number into a stem and a leaf.
   c. List the stems from largest to smallest.
   d. Line up the leaves next to their stems.

2. The secretary of the Striders Club made a stem-and-leaf diagram of the number of miles walked by group members.
   a. What does 2 | 4 8 mean?
   b. How many people belong to the Striders?
   c. During the week of March 1, what is the least number of miles walked by a member? the greatest number of miles?
   d. How many Striders walked between 30 and 40 miles?
   e. If you were writing this article, how would you describe the number of miles most of the Striders walked?

Miles Walked Week of March 1

Stem	Leaf
4	0 1 1 2 2 3 4 4 5
3	2 3 5 6 6 7 7 8 9
2	4 8
1	6 9

3. Think about how teenagers spend their time. Each stem-and-leaf diagram shows the results of a survey on the number of hours per month one group of teens participated in different activities. Which diagram do you think shows the hours spent watching television? doing chores at home? talking on the telephone? Tell how you decided.

Striders Walk for Fitness

What are you doing at 6:30 am every day? While you are rolling over and hitting the snooze button on your alarm, a group of health-conscious citizens has already hit the mall. Merchants at the Towsontown Center open the four floors of the mall to the Striders, a group of people who have had heart transplants. Members walk between 2 and 10 miles daily for fitness and then chat over a breakfast of fresh fruit and yogurt before going off to area hospitals to counsel patients awaiting new hearts.

(a)

Stem	Leaf
4	0 2 4 5
3	1 1 3 4 6 6 7 8 9
2	0 2 5 6 7
1	2 3

(b)

Stem	Leaf
4	0
3	2 4 7
2	0 1 3 3 4 6 7
1	0 0 1 1 2 2 2 6

(c)

Stem	Leaf
4	0 0 1 2 3 4 6 8 9
3	4 5 7 8 8 8 9 9
2	6 8
1	5

4. The student council at Owings Mills High School is planning to sell back-packs to raise money. A large pack holds 40 lb. A small pack holds 30 lb. The 21 homeroom representatives weighed their school books to determine which size backpack to order.

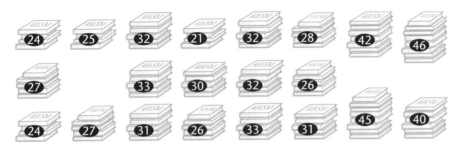

a. What is the smallest data value? the largest? the range?
b. Make a stem-and-leaf diagram of the data.
c. Describe the shape of the data.
d. Which backpack do you think the student council should order? Why?

5. How is a back-to-back stem-and-leaf diagram different from a stem-and-leaf diagram?

6. This back-to-back stem-and-leaf diagram shows the average yearly amount of general sales tax, in thousands of dollars, collected by states to get money for education, highway construction, and other services.

States West of the Mississippi River		States East of the Mississippi River
	11	
61	10	
18	9	
	8	
	7	43
67	6	33
51 23	5	
57 48 27 10	4	05 07 14 15 23 25 26 60 80
80 71 61 58 57 57 52 39 21	3	25 28 30 33 42 55 56 96
99 68 50	2	18 41 57 67 95
	1	
0 0 0	0	0 0

Source: The Universal Alamanac

a. What does 67 | 6 | 33 represent? 4 | 05 07 14?
b. In which region does the amount of tax vary more?
c. What would be a good way to describe a typical amount of tax in states east of the Mississippi River? in states west of the Mississippi River?
d. Are there any numbers in the data set that seem unusual? Explain.

You have been hired by a company planning to build an amusement park in Baltimore, Maryland, or Seattle, Washington. Your job is to analyze temperature and precipitation data to help the owners decide where the park will be more successful.

Social Science

7. What facts does the notebook show?

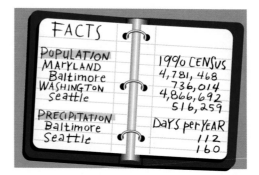

FACTS

POPULATION   1990 CENSUS
MARYLAND   4,781,468
 Baltimore   736,014
WASHINGTON   4,866,692
 Seattle   516,259

PRECIPITATION   Days per YEAR
Baltimore   112
Seattle   160

Social Science

8. The chart shows the average monthly temperatures for the two cities.

Average Monthly Temperatures (°F)												
	J	F	M	A	M	J	J	A	S	O	N	D
Baltimore	41	44	53	65	74	83	87	86	79	68	56	45
Seattle	45	50	53	58	65	69	75	74	69	60	51	47

a. Make a back-to-back stem-and-leaf diagram to compare the temperatures.
b. Which city has the smallest range of average temperatures each year?
c. Which city has the greatest number of months with an average temperature above 60°F? below 50°F?

Social Science

9. The chart shows the average monthly amount of rain or snow for the two cities.

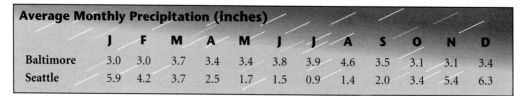

Average Monthly Precipitation (inches)												
	J	F	M	A	M	J	J	A	S	O	N	D
Baltimore	3.0	3.0	3.7	3.4	3.4	3.8	3.9	4.6	3.5	3.1	3.1	3.4
Seattle	5.9	4.2	3.7	2.5	1.7	1.5	0.9	1.4	2.0	3.4	5.4	6.3

a. Make a display to compare the precipitation amounts.
b. Which city has the greatest range in precipitation?
c. How would you compare the precipitation for the two cities?

Careers

10. Use all the information available to make a recommendation about the park to your company. What would you say in your report? What other factors would you want to consider?

LOOK AHEAD

11. Set up axes on a coordinate grid.

   a. Plot the points (4, 3) and (1, 4) on graph paper and connect them with a line labeled ℓ.

   b. Use the same set of axes to plot the points (6, 4) and (3, 5) and connect them with a line m.

   c. Do you see a relationship between line ℓ and line m? If so, describe it.

MORE PRACTICE

Make a stem-and-leaf diagram for each set of numbers.

12. Fines for speeding violations: $95, $75, $110, $80, $75, $75, $110, $80, $75, $60, $125, $90, $120, $110, $90, $85

13. Number of prisoners in state and federal prisons (in thousands), from 1980 through 1991: 330, 370, 414, 437, 462, 503, 545, 585, 632, 713, 775, 823

14. A high school lecture hall contains 100 seats. As part of a safety study, a teacher counted the number of students in the room every half hour. She did this 21 times, and she got these counts: 30, 88, 88, 0, 85, 85, 84, 84, 0, 82, 82, 0, 0, 0, 0, 83, 83, 0, 88, 88, 0.

   a. Make a stem-and-leaf diagram of the data.

   b. Describe the shape of the data.

   c. Write three statements to describe the data.

15. Fast Food Hamburgers are popular throughout the world.

The Cost of a Burger

Australia	$1.74	Belgium	$2.80	Canada		$1.89
Denmark	$3.99	France	$3.14	Germany		$2.56
Ireland	$2.06	Italy	$3.17	Japan		$2.33
Netherlands	$2.79	Russia	$6.25	United Kingdom	$2.30

   a. Make a stem-and-leaf diagram of the data showing the cost of a burger. Use the dollar amount as the stem and the cents as the leaf.

   b. If you were traveling, what would you expect to pay for a burger?

   c. Find the mean, mode, and median price.

16. In the first 10 games of their premiere 1993 season, the Florida Marlins scored the following number of runs: 10, 2, 5, 7, 2, 6, 14, 11, 4, 9.

  a. What is the range?

  b. Find the median and the mean. Which best represents the data?

17. A poultry ranch kept a yearly record of the eggs laid by each chicken.

  a. How many chickens did they raise?

  b. What was the median production?

  c. If they want to ship 15,000 eggs a year, how many chickens should they raise?

Stem	Leaf
24	1 1 3 5 5 7 8 9
23	0 1 2 2 2 2 4 7 8 8
22	1 3 4 4 5 5 5 8 9 9
21	0 0 0 0 3 3 5 6 7
19	5 7 7 8 8 9

MORE MATH REASONING

18. Copy the data on right-hand strength of Waynesboro ninth graders given earlier.

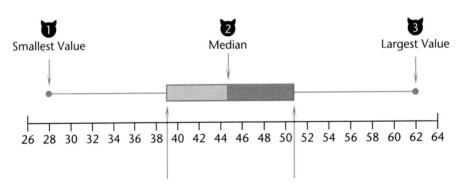

  a. Find the median of the data.

  b. The **lower quartile** is the middle value of the data *below* the median. What is the lower quartile point?

  c. The **upper quartile** is the middle value of the data *above* the median. What is the upper quartile point?

  d. What fraction of the scores is represented by the whisker to the left of the box? to the right of the box?

  e. A stem-and-leaf diagram shows the shape and distribution of data. What does a box-and-whisker diagram show about the data?

19. This chart shows the percentage of murder cases solved by police in different countries.

Percentage of Murder Cases Solved by Police

Australia	91.6	Austria	93.5	Belgium	77.2	Canada	86.0
Denmark	89.4	Finland	93.9	France	83.1	Germany	94.4
Ireland	91.2	Italy	39.0	Japan	97.1	Norway	83.0
Spain	86.0	Sweden	59.0	United Kingdom	95.0	United States	70.0

a. Arrange the numbers in order from smallest to largest. What is the range?

b. What is the median value? the lower quartile? the upper quartile?

c. Draw a number line containing the smallest and largest values. Make a box showing the lower quartile, the median, and the upper quartile values. Draw whiskers to the smallest and largest values in the data set.

d. What conclusions can you draw from the box-and-whisker diagram?

1-3 PART C · Scatter Plots and Trend Lines

← CONNECT → *A back-to-back stem-and-leaf diagram is one way to compare data in two sets. A scatter plot is another tool that shows relationships between two sets of data.*

You have taken corresponding numbers from two sets of data and plotted them as ordered pairs. You then connected the points with line segments to make a line graph. This helped you analyze trends.

Sometimes, you want to check how closely the two sets of data are related. You can take the corresponding numbers in two sets of data and plot them as ordered pairs on a coordinate grid. The graph is called a **scatter plot.**

The pattern of points suggests how closely the data is related. Drawing a trend line gives a model of the data that you can use to make predictions.

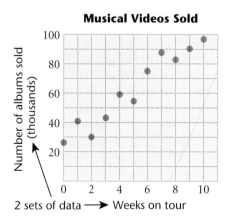

Musical Videos Sold

1. What two sets of related data are plotted as ordered pairs in the scatter plot above?
2. How would you describe the pattern of the points?
3. What information would you use the trend line to predict?

EXPLORE: LEONARDO'S SCATTER PLOT

MATERIALS

Graph paper, Ruler

The Renaissance painter Leonardo da Vinci carefully studied human anatomy and calculated the proportions of physically fit bodies. He kept huge notebooks with sketches.

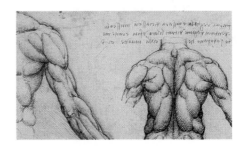

You can use a scatter plot to explore a relationship between total height and height from the waist down (waist height).

1. Copy and complete the table for 15 students in your class.

Height							
Waist Height							

2. Use graph paper and a ruler to make a grid like the one shown. What did you think about in deciding how to mark off the scales on each axis?

3. Plot each pair on your table: (height, waist height). You should end up with 15 points on your scatter plot.

4. Place the edge of your ruler along the line of the points. Try to place the ruler so there is an equal number of points above and below the line. Use the ruler to draw and extend the line to the edges of the grid. This is a trend line.

5. Use your trend line. Predict the waist height for a 72-inch-tall person and an 84-inch-tall person. Is either prediction reliable? Is one of the predictions more reliable? Why?

6. Could you have drawn your trend line in a different position? Explain.

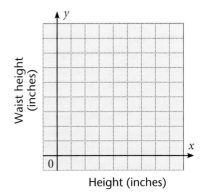

There are mathematical methods for getting the best trend line, called a **line of best fit.** However, if you eyeball carefully, you often can get a good fitting trend line.

You can use the pattern of points on your scatter plot to analyze how closely the data is related.

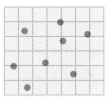
No relationship

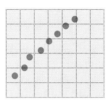
Moderate relationship

Strong relationship

REFLECT

1. Can you use just one set of data to make a scatter plot? Explain.
2. How do you decide where to draw a trend line on a scatter plot?
3. Describe a scatter plot where a trend line helps you make predictions.
4. Identify a set of data whose scatter plot would show a strong relation-ship. What will the pattern of points look like?

Exercises

CORE

1. **Getting Started** Kyle and Hannah each draw a trend line for a scatter plot showing the average monthly cost to rent an apartment in a Virginia suburb.

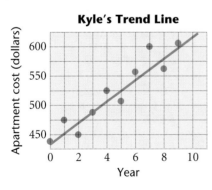

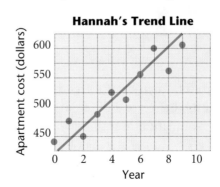

a. What year is shown by the label 0 on the horizontal axis? by the label 4?
b. Is Kyle's trend line the same as Hannah's? How can you tell?
c. What do you think Kyle would predict as the cost to rent an apartment in 1990? Hannah's prediction? Who do you agree with? Explain.

2. Jon and Sally were learning about scatter plots. Jon claimed that a trend line is always useful for making predictions. Do you agree or disagree? Explain.

This scatter plot compares the crime rate and the high school graduation rate for 17 states.

3. What is plotted on the horizontal axis? the vertical axis?

4. What was the actual graduation rate(s) when the crime rate was 300 units?

5. What was the actual crime rate when the graduation rate was 60%?

6. Through which data points does the trend line pass?

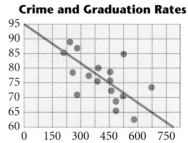

Crime and Graduation Rates

High school graduation rate (percentage)

Crime rate (units per 100,000 population)

7. What can you say about the relationship between the crime rate and the graduation rate? Why?

8. Use the trend line.
 a. Predict the graduation rate when the crime rate is 900.
 b. Predict the crime rate when the graduation rate is 90%.
 c. Do you think these predictions are dependable? Explain.

Social Science

9. Counting the Votes In a presidential election, a state's electoral votes go to the candidate who gets the most votes. The candidate who gets the greatest electoral vote total becomes President. The number of electoral votes for each state, which is adjusted at each census, depends on its population.

Electoral Vote Data—10-State Sample										
State	AL	AR	CO	ID	IA	KS	MN	MO	NV	OK
Population (millions)	4	2	3	1	3	3	4	5	1	3
Electoral Votes	9	6	8	4	7	6	10	11	4	8

 a. Make a scatter plot. Then draw a trend line.
 b. Why do you think there are a different number of electoral votes for states with the same population in millions?
 c. South Dakota is one of the states not listed in the table. Its population is about 700,000 people. Use the trend line to predict how many electoral votes South Dakota has.
 d. The U.S. territory of Puerto Rico doesn't have any electoral votes because it isn't a state. So its 3,552,000 people don't get to help elect the President. About how many electoral votes would Puerto Rico have if it were a state?
 e. About how many million people live in a state with 12 electoral votes?

 **LOOK BACK**

10. A check mark represents 5000 votes. Draw symbols to show 40,000 votes. [1-2]

11. Which ordered pair gives a point that is *not* on the *x*-axis? [1-1]
  (a) $(0, 3)$ (b) $(0, 0)$ (c) $(3, 0)$ (d) $(23, 0)$ (e) not here

Perform the indicated operation. [Previous course]

12. $7\frac{1}{5} - 1\frac{4}{5}$ **13.** $3\frac{3}{4} - \frac{1}{2}$ **14.** $\frac{2}{3} \cdot \frac{30}{4}$ **15.** $10 \div \frac{5}{2}$

MORE PRACTICE

Health care costs are constantly rising. This scatter plot shows the daily cost to stay in a hospital in large metropolitan areas.

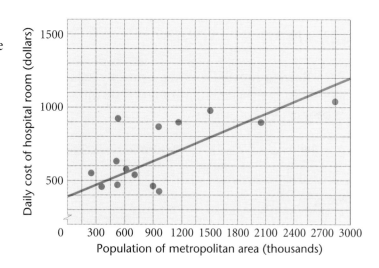

16. Columbus, Georgia, has a population of 247,000. Use a point on the scatter plot to give the average daily cost to stay in a Columbus hospital.

17. What values are plotted along the horizontal axis? the vertical axis? What does the broken line along the vertical axis mean?

18. Hospital costs in Boston are about $1048 per day. Use a point on the scatter plot to estimate the number of people who live in the Boston area.

19. Use the trend line to give the hospital cost for a metropolitan area of about 1,200,000 people.

20. Does the pattern of points suggest a moderate or strong relationship? How would this affect your confidence in using the trend line to make predictions?

21. Hit the Brakes Students at a driving school did a study of the stopping distance of a car. They used a simulator to get some data.

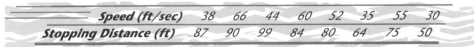

Speed (ft/sec)	38	66	44	60	52	35	55	30
Stopping Distance (ft)	87	90	99	84	80	64	75	50

a. Make a scatter plot of the data.

b. Draw a trend line.

c. Does the pattern of the points suggest a strong relationship between speed and stopping distance? Explain.

d. Use your trend line to predict the stopping distance when a car is traveling 100 feet per second (68 miles per hour).

MORE MATH REASONING

22. Barn Raising A manufacturing company made a scatter plot showing the amount of time it took different groups of people to construct a two-story barn.

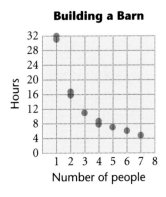

Building a Barn

Hours vs. Number of people

Workers	Hours
1	32
1	31
2	17
2	16
3	11
4	9
4	8
5	7
6	6
7	5

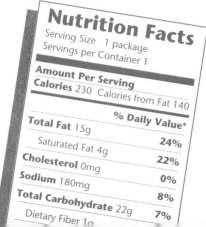

A line is not always the best pattern to fit a scatter plot.

a. Do you think there is a strong relationship? Explain. What pattern do the points suggest as a best fit?

b. As the number of people building the barn increases, what happens to the time required? Multiply the number of workers by the number of hours for each ordered pair. What appears to be true?

c. How many hours do you think it would take eight people to build the same barn?

23. Find at least 10 boxes or packages of food that list the calories per serving and grams of fat per serving. Make a scatter plot. Discuss and support any observations and conclusions that you make.

Nutrition Facts

Serving Size 1 package
Servings per Container 1

Amount Per Serving
Calories 230 Calories from Fat 140

% **Daily Value***

Total Fat 15g   24%

Saturated Fat 4g   22%

Cholesterol 0mg   0%

Sodium 180mg   8%

Total Carbohydrate 22g   7%

Dietary Fiber 1g

Making Connections

← CONNECT → *You have looked at measures of central tendency to summarize data. You've seen that stem-and-leaf diagrams as well as scatter plots can be used to organize data, analyze the distribution of data, and even make predictions.*

You can get a more complete picture about a set of data by using a combination of ways to summarize and analyze the information.

EXPLORE: A CLASS PROFILE

As a class, collect data on sleep and television watching. Complete a chart that shows the number of hours that each person sleeps and watches TV in one week. Keep track of males and females separately.

Use the measures of central tendency, stem-and-leaf diagrams, and scatter plots to develop a profile of your class. Write a description of your findings.

Hours per Week		
Males	**Sleeping**	**Watching TV**
Jose	56	21

Hours per Week		
Females	**Sleeping**	**Watching TV**
Tanya	42	18

1. Most doctors agree that teen-agers should average between seven and eight hours of sleep each night. How does your data compare with this recommendation?
2. What conclusions can you draw about the TV-watching habits of your classmates?
3. Did you discover any differences between the data for males and females?

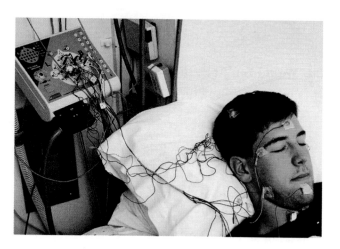

REFLECT

1. Why are mean, median, and mode called "measures of central tendency"?
2. What kind of data do you need to know to make a stem-and-leaf diagram? a scatter plot?
3. Why is order important in arranging data on a stem-and-leaf diagram? Why is order important in graphing points on a scatter plot?
4. How would you decide whether to use a stem-and-leaf diagram or a scatter plot?
5. How can you use a scatter plot to make predictions?
6. Is it possible to have more than one trend line? Explain.

Self-Assessment

1. As of July 5, 1992, these were the five longest running original plays on Broadway and the number of performances for each. Find the range, the mean, and the median.

Chorus Line	Cats	42nd Street	Grease	Fiddler on the Roof
6137	4069	3486	3388	3242

2. **Would You Keep the Money?** A world survey asked people whether they think they should keep money they find on the street or in public places

Percentage of People Who Think They Should Keep the Money			
Australia 47%	Belgium 48%	Canada 51%	Denmark 36%
Finland 36%	France 38%	Germany 39%	Ireland 42%
Italy 35%	Japan 27%	Netherlands 46%	Norway 23%
Spain 57%	Sweden 28%	United Kingdom 31%	United States 57%

a. Find the range, mean, median, and mode for the data.
b. Which measure of central tendency would you use to describe the data?
c. Make a stem-and-leaf diagram of the data.
d. What conclusions can you draw from the shape of the diagram?

Perform the indicated operation. [Previous course]

3. $5\frac{4}{5} - 2\frac{1}{5}$ **4.** $4\frac{1}{6} - 1\frac{5}{6}$ **5.** $\frac{4}{9} \cdot \frac{36}{4}$ **6.** $5 \div \frac{10}{3}$

Twelve teenagers took part in a hospital study of the effect of exercise on pulse rate.

Before Exercise	96	72	96	80	92	76	85	68	96	80	68	76
After Excersise	120	109	125	108	122	117	113	115	129	120	105	108

7. Find the range, mean, median, and mode for each set of data. Which measure of central tendency best summarizes the data? Why?

8. Make a back-to-back stem-and-leaf diagram of the before and after pulse rates. Compare the shape of the data on each side of the diagram.

9. Make a scatter plot of the data. What relationship, if any, do you see from the pattern of points?

10. Draw a trend line.

Health

    a. If a teenager had a pulse rate of 70 before exercise, predict the pulse rate after exercise.

    b. Do you think your prediction is dependable? Explain.

Decide whether the statement is true or false.

11. The median of a set of numbers is always one of the numbers.

12. A stem-and-leaf diagram shows the shape of a set of data.

13. Which ordered pair gives a point that is on the y-axis? [1-1]

    (a) $(0, -5)$ (b) $(1, 1)$ (c) $(3, 0)$ (d) $(-3, 0)$ (e) not here

14. Kitchen Mathematics Grab a plate, a bowl, a cup, a glass, some jar lids, a piece of string, and a centimeter ruler. Measure the diameter of each object. Then measure the circumference of each circle by wrapping the string around the edge and measuring its length.

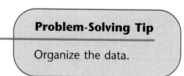
Problem-Solving Tip

Organize the data.

    a. Make a scatter plot of the results. Draw a trend line.

    b. Is $(0, 0)$ a point on your trend line? Does this make sense? Explain.

    c. Use the trend line to predict the circumference for a circle with a diameter of 25 cm.

    d. If you could find a huge piece of paper, would you be able to predict the circumference of a circle with a diameter of 1000 m? Explain your thinking.

    e. The circumference of a human-made pond is 126 m. Explain how you could find the diameter of the pond.

Chapter 1 Review

In this chapter, you practiced reading data from graphs, glyphs, and spreadsheets and made your own displays of data. After becoming familiar with measures of central tendency, you made stem-and-leaf diagrams and scatter plots. You used these ideas to compare data, analyze patterns of data, spot trends, and make predictions.

KEY TERMS

bar graphs [1-2]

circle graphs [1-2]

coordinate grid [1-1]

coordinates [1-1]

glyph [1-2]

line graph [1-2]

mean [1-3]

median [1-3]

mode [1-3]

ordered pair [1-1]

origin [1-1]

pictograph [1-2]

range [1-3]

scatter plot [1-3]

segment [1-1]

spreadsheet [1-1]

stem-and-leaf diagram [1-3]

trend line [1-3]

vertices [1-1]

x-axis [1-1]

y-axis [1-1]

Write the word or phrase that correctly completes each statement.

1. In the ordered pair $(-3, 25)$, -3 and 25 are called ___.

2. A(n) ___ organizes information using columns and rows.

3. Another name for the average of a list of numbers is the ___.

CONCEPTS AND APPLICATIONS

4. Draw a number line. Where are the points 5 units or less from the origin? [1-1]

5. Points A, B, and C are the vertices of $\triangle ABC$. [1-1]
   a. Give the ordered pairs of the vertices.
   b. Identify a line segment.

6. a. What ordered pair locates the point where the *x*-axis crosses the *y*-axis? [1-1]
   b. What is the name of this point? [1-1]

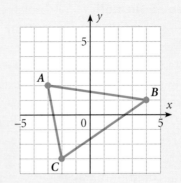

7. Which ordered pair locates a point 3 units above and 2 units right of the origin? [1-1]

(a) (3, −2)   (b) (−2, −3)   (c) (−2, 3)   (d) (2, 3)   (e) not here

8. Ashareen looked at the spreadsheet and said, "The cost of apple pie is shown in C17." What did she mean? [1-1]

9. After researching the cost of a year's tuition at local colleges, Tom made an ordered list: $900, $1800, $2250, $2250, $3600, and $12,000. [1-3]

a. Find the range, mean, mode, and median.

b. Which measure of central tendency best describes the data? Explain.

10. The double-line graph displays the population, in thousands, for Wyoming and Alaska from 1950 to 1990. [1-2]

a. What is the interval on the Population axis?

b. What was the population of Alaska in 1975?

c. Which state has grown the most, in population, in the past 40 years? How can you tell from the graph?

d. Compare the growth pattern of the two states.

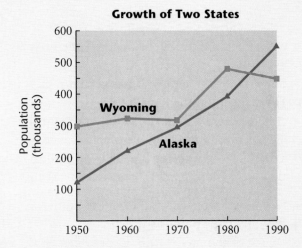

Growth of Two States

11. What is a reasonable stem to use for a stem-and-leaf diagram containing values between 300 and 400? between 10,000 and 10,100? [1-3]

12. If you make a scatter plot, what can the pattern of the points tell you? [1-3]

CONCEPTS AND CONNECTIONS

13. Literature As part of a presentation to the city council, the library staff counted the fiction books checked out during one week and made a pie chart.

a. Find the number of books of each type that were checked out.

b. Use the data to make a bar graph.

c. Which graph best displays the data?

800 Fiction Books

Historical
Other
Science fiction
12% 7%
18%
36%
27%
Romance
Mystery

SELF-EVALUATION

Make a list of the ways data can be organized or displayed. Describe when you might use each method. What vocabulary words are needed for each display? Be sure to review anything you found difficult.

Chapter 1 Assessment

TEST

1. It was 42°F the morning of the big Green Bay football game and 14°F at 4:00 p.m.
   a. Show these two temperatures on a number line.
   b. How much did the temperature drop during the day?
   c. If between 4:00 p.m. and 12:00 midnight the temperature dropped an average of 2°F per hour, how cold was it at midnight?
   d. Where on the number line will you find the coordinates for temperatures that are colder than 75°F and warmer than −7°F?

2. a. Plot on graph paper and label the points $A(-1, -2)$, $B(0, 4)$, and $C(4, 0)$.
   b. Plot and label point D, which is 3 units left and 5 units up from point A.
   c. Which of the points A, B, C, or D lies on the vertical axis?
   d. What is the point $(0, 0)$ called?

3. The table shows Ahmed's scores in a five-game bowling tournament.

	A	B	C	D	E	F	G
1	**Game**	1	2	3	4	5	Mean
2	**Score**	130	121	162	120	65	

   a. What is a name for this kind of table?
   b. Which cell shows Ahmed's score in Game 3?
   c. Which cells would you use to find his total score for the tournament?
   d. Find the value for cell G2.

4. For 9 years, Christina played goalie on a soccer team. Find the range, mode, and median of her saves per year: 23, 39, 68, 17, 39, 39, 25, 17, 45.

5. Use the circle graph to answer the questions.
   a. Which two activities together take up as much time as school work?
   b. How many hours of the day does Gabriela spend sleeping and eating?
   c. What is another name for this kind of graph?

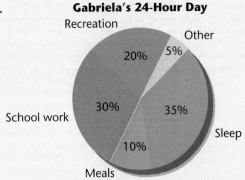

Gabriela's 24-Hour Day

Recreation 20%
Other 5%
School work 30%
Sleep 35%
Meals 10%

6. David made a pictograph to display how many rabbits the members of the Hare Raisers 4-H club plan to raise and show at the county fair.
   a. How many rabbits will the Hare Raisers club raise?
   b. It costs the club $34 to feed 8 rabbits for 3 weeks. How much will it cost to feed all the rabbits for 3 weeks?

Each symbol = 8 rabbits.

7. A group of freshmen answered a survey after taking a test. This grid shows the results of the survey.
   a. Does the pattern of the points suggest no relationship, a moderate relationship, or a strong relationship for the data? Explain.
   b. A student studies 6 hours for a similar test. Estimate the student's grade on the test.
   c. What is this type of display called?

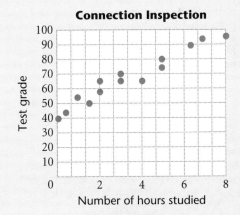

Connection Inspection

Test grade (y-axis): 10 to 100
Number of hours studied (x-axis): 0 to 8

PERFORMANCE TASK

History

In the 1992 presidential election, Bill Clinton received about 43.7 million popular votes, George Bush, 38.1 million, and H. Ross Perot, 19.2 million. Name the types of data displays you could use to show this information. Make at least two of these displays and describe how each helps you understand the data.

Chapter 2

Project A
Across the Isthmus
Where are the world's
most famous canals?
Why do they need locks?

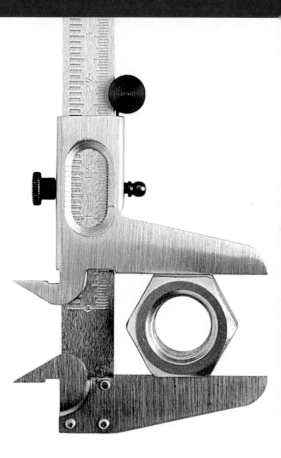

Project B
Give and Take
What is tolerance? How exact
are manufacturing standards
for nuts and bolts?

Project C
Ebb and Flow
What causes high and
low tides? Whose lives
are ruled by the tides?

KENNETH ORCUTT

I always wanted to become a sea captain. To navigate my "course" I needed math.

A canal pilot must guide every yacht and ship passing through the Panama Canal. Ships have to pass through three sets of locks to raise them 85 feet and then through three more locks to lower them back to sea level. Transit across the isthmus takes 8 hours. When computers came out, I wrote programs to simplify navigation. As a pilot, I had the canal in my head.

Kenneth R. Orcutt
Panama Canal Pilot,
Retired
Whittier, California

Chapter 2

Communicating Mathematics

2-1 Communicating Through Technology
Calculators and computers have made mathematical calculations much easier and faster. You will work with scientific calculators to perform computations and to estimate answers. In today's society, calculators are used at home and on the job.

2-2 Communicating Through Signed Numbers
Algebra tiles, balloons and scales, and number lines are used to help calculate expressions that have both positive and negative numbers. Time, temperature, sporting events, and money are only a few examples of where you will use signed numbers.

2-3 Communicating with Expressions
Algebraic expressions are used to model real-world problems and to find their solutions. You will write expressions using signed numbers as constants and variables. You will add, subtract, multiply, and divide algebraic expressions using mathematical properties.

GREEN COMPUTERS

A few years ago, the Environmental Protection Agency (EPA) decided that the approximately 10 million personal computers in use in this country weren't very friendly to the environment. The average personal computer used about 120 watts of power.

So the EPA encouraged manufacturers to redesign their machines and make "green" computers that would use 30 watts of power or less.

The EPA certifies these computers as "Energy Star" computers.

The total electricity used by an appliance is measured in kilowatt-hours.

$$\text{kilowatt-hours} = \frac{\text{power in watts} \times \text{number of hours power is on}}{1000}$$

Not only do green computers save energy, they save money as well. The cost of electricity varies around the country; on average, 1 kilowatt-hour of electricity costs about 10 cents.

In 1993, President Clinton signed an executive order requiring federal agencies to buy only Energy Star personal computers. Because the federal government is the world's largest purchaser of electronic equipment, manufacturers were quick to produce Energy Star computers.

1. Why are Energy Star computers called "green" computers?
2. What percentage of the power used by an average older computer does an Energy Star computer use?
3. If an average computer is on 4000 hours per year, how many kilowatt-hours per year would be saved by using an Energy Star computer instead of an older computer?

← C O N N E C T → *Technological advances such as calculators and computers have taken much of the tedious work out of mathematics. In this part, you will learn about some special keys that will help you use your scientific calculator effectively. You will also learn to use exponents to show repeated multiplication.*

Calculators have been in use for many years. But it wasn't until the 1980s that calculators could be made inexpensive enough so that many people could own them.

Since that time, calculators have changed the way people work. Many calculators today are actually small computers.

EXPLORE: KEYING IN

MATERIALS

Scientific calculator

1. Calculate $2 \times 4 + 3$ by entering 2 $\boxed{\times}$ 4 $\boxed{+}$ 3 $\boxed{=}$.

Calculate $3 + 2 \times 4$ by entering 3 $\boxed{+}$ 2 $\boxed{\times}$ 4 $\boxed{=}$.

Did you get the same answer for both calculations? If you did, your calculator uses an algebraic operating system. Most scientific calculators use an algebraic operating system.

2. You've seen that negative numbers are used for coordinates on a number line. Find the $\boxed{+/-}$ key. Enter a number and then press $\boxed{+/-}$. What effect does the key have on the number you entered?

To calculate $-8 + (-5)$, enter 8 $\boxed{+/-}$ $\boxed{+}$ 5 $\boxed{+/-}$ $\boxed{=}$. What is the answer?

You will see how to do arithmetic with negative numbers later in this chapter.

3. Find the key $\boxed{x^2}$.

Enter any number and then press the $\boxed{x^2}$ key.

Enter a two-digit or three-digit number and press the $\boxed{x^2}$ key.

What does the $\boxed{x^2}$ key do to each number that you entered?

4. Find the $\boxed{\sqrt{x}}$ key.

Enter any number and press the $\boxed{\sqrt{x}}$ key. Then press the $\boxed{x^2}$ key.

Enter any number and press the $\boxed{x^2}$ key. Then press the $\boxed{\sqrt{x}}$ key.

What is the relationship between these two keys?

5. Most calculators have a $\boxed{\pi}$ key. If yours does, press it and write down the number you see on the screen.

Calculate $22 \div 7$. Write that number down under your number for π. Compare these two numbers. How are they alike? How are they different?

6. Find the $\boxed{y^x}$ key. Enter these four calculations and determine what the $\boxed{y^x}$ key seems to do.

$$3 \boxed{y^x} 2 \boxed{=} \qquad 2 \boxed{y^x} 3 \boxed{=} \qquad 5 \boxed{y^x} 2 \boxed{=} \qquad 2 \boxed{y^x} 5 \boxed{=}$$

Multiplication indicates repeated addition. For example, 3×8 means $8 + 8 + 8$.

There are three common symbols that all show multiplication.

$$3 \times 8 \qquad\qquad 3 \cdot 8 \qquad\qquad 3(8)$$

The **factors,** or the numbers being multiplied, are 3 and 8. The **product** is 24.

An **exponent** indicates repeated multiplication.

Notation	Expanded Form	Read	Value
3^4	$3 \cdot 3 \cdot 3 \cdot 3$	**Three** to the **fourth** power.	**81**

(with labels: "exponent" pointing to the 4, "base" pointing to the 3)

The $\boxed{y^x}$ key, called a power key, lets you work with exponents on your calculator.

EXAMPLES

1. Find 2.05^3.

Enter 2.05 $\boxed{y^x}$ 3 $\boxed{=}$.
The screen shows 8.615125.

> 8.615125

2. Find $\left(\frac{2}{5}\right)^5$.

Enter 2 $\boxed{\div}$ 5 $\boxed{=}$ to change $\frac{2}{5}$ to its decimal
form. The screen shows 0.4.

> 0.01024

With 0.4 still on the screen, enter $\boxed{y^x}$ 5 $\boxed{=}$.
The screen shows 0.01024.

The $\boxed{x^2}$ key is a special key you can use when
the exponent is 2.

For 5^2, press either 5 $\boxed{x^2}$ or 5 $\boxed{y^x}$ 2 $\boxed{=}$ and the
screen will show 25.

TRY IT

Find each of the following.

a. 3^2 **b.** 6^3 **c.** $(1.5)^2$ **d.** $\left(\frac{1}{2}\right)^3$ **e.** $(0.2)^4$ **f.** 25^1

There are many ways that exponents are used in applications. You have
probably used exponents to find the areas and volumes of geometric
shapes.

The area of a square is measured in **square units**.

The volume of a cube is measured in **cubic units**.

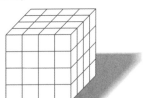

A short way to count the square units is to multiply

4×4 or $4^2 = $ **16**.

The area is **16 square units**.

A short way to count the cubic units is to multiply

$4 \times 4 \times 4$ or $4^3 = $ **64**.

The volume is **64 cubic units**.

CONSIDER

?

1. Why do you think *four to the second power*, 4^2, is often read as "four squared"? What is another way that *four to the third power*, 4^3, might be read?

EXAMPLES

3. Find the area of a square with sides measuring 5.8 inches.

The area is $5.8^2 = 33.64$ square inches.

5.8 in.

5.8 in.

4. Find the volume of a cube with edges measuring 2.5 centimeters.

The volume is $2.5^3 = 15.625$ cubic centimeters.

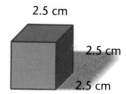
2.5 cm

2.5 cm

2.5 cm

REFLECT

1. On your calculator, when would you use the $\boxed{=}$ key? the $\boxed{y^x}$ key?
2. In doing a calculation like $6.95 + 0.06 \times 6.95$, which operation will the calculator do first if it uses an algebraic operating system?
3. How is 2×5 different from 2^5?
4. Is 2^3 the same as 3^2? Explain.

Exercises

CORE

Getting Started   Give the answer that your calculator screen shows for each calculation.

1. $2.7 + 0.5$: Enter $2.7 \boxed{+} 0.5 \boxed{=}$

2. $-5 + 2$: Enter $5 \boxed{+/-} \boxed{+} 2 \boxed{=}$

3. 8% of 48: Enter $0.08 \boxed{\times} 48 \boxed{=}$

4. 4.16^2: Enter $4.16 \boxed{x^2}$

5. 17^3: Enter $17 \boxed{y^x} 3 \boxed{=}$

6. $2 \div 3$: Enter $2 \boxed{\div} 3 \boxed{=}$

7. Darryl is decorating a floor with small square tiles that measure 7.25 cm on each side. What is the area covered by one tile?

Find each power.

8. 7^2

9. 31^2

10. 6^4

11. 9^3

12. 0.625^2

13. $\left(\frac{2}{3}\right)^2$

14. 10^1

15. 1.5^3

1.7 in.

16. Esther's little brother is playing with a set of colored blocks. Each block has edges measuring 1.7 inches. What is the volume of one of the blocks?

1.7 in.

1.7 in.

What exponent goes in each box?

17. $5 \cdot 5 \cdot 5 \cdot 5 = 5^{\square}$

18. $(3 \cdot 3 \cdot 3)(3 \cdot 3 \cdot 3) = 3^{\square}$

19. Giselle and her five friends are having lunch at a diner. They want to leave a 15% tip. The bill comes to $15.25. How much should they leave as a tip?

20. Determine whether the statement is true or false. If the statement is false, change the underlined word or phrase to make it true.
The square of a number is <u>always</u> greater than the number.

21. Boxed In The six squares are all the same size. If you trace the diagram and cut it out, you can fold the figure to form a box.
a. What is the area of each square?
b. What is the total area?
c. What is the volume of the box?

4 in.

4 in. 4 in.

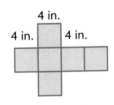

 **LOOK BACK**

22. Find the perimeter of the rectangle. [Previous course]

23. Give directions to plot the point $(-4, 3)$ on graph paper. [1-1]

3 in.

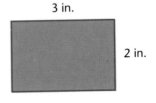

2 in.

24. About what percentage of the circle is shaded? [1-2]

    (a) 25%   (b) 40%   (c) 60%

    (d) 120%   (e) not here

MORE PRACTICE

Give the answer that your calculator screen shows for each calculation.

25. 57.4×2.3 **26.** 16% of 75   **27.** $\pi(3.75)$

28. $18.95 \div 0.05$ **29.** $(-3)(4)$ **30.** 4.7^3

31. $2 + 3 \times 7$ **32.** $(95 + 90 + 85) \div 3$ **33.** $\pi \cdot 5^2$

34. Each side of this cracker measures 1.2 inches. Find the area of the cracker.

Find each power.

35. 8^3 **36.** 20^4 **37.** 4.5^2 **38.** $\left(\frac{5}{12}\right)^2$

39. 0.05^2 **40.** $(-7)^2$ **41.** $\left(\frac{3}{4}\right)^3$ **42.** 5^0

43. Mrs. Rodriguez gets a weekly paycheck of $423. The family budget sets aside 25% for food. How much money should Mrs. Rodriguez put aside for food?

MORE MATH REASONING

44. What is the last digit in 7^{25}?

> **Problem-Solving Tip**
>
> Look for patterns by exploring the first few powers of 7.

45. Contractors are tiling the bathroom floor in a new house. The floor measures 72 inches by 48 inches. They are using square tiles with sides measuring 6 inches. How many tiles will they need?

Industry

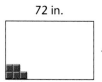

72 in.

48 in.

Estimating and Rounding

← **C O N N E C T** → *When you use a calculator, it is a good idea to have an estimate of the answer to check a calculated answer. In this part, you will learn methods to help you estimate. You will also learn how to adjust numbers by rounding them.*

When you use a calculator, you may have seen that it's easy to press the wrong key or to enter numbers and operations in the wrong order. It is important to decide if your answer makes sense.

EXPLORE: IS IT REASONABLE?

1. Determine whether each answer is reasonable or not. Explain how you decided.
  a. Mindy has collected checks for 34 sweatshirts. The sweatshirts range in price from $15 to $25. She lists the check amounts on her deposit slip and adds them up with her calculator. She gets a total of $1050.
  b. Mark has taken a test that has four sections. He adds up the scores for each section so he can get his total grade on the test. The scores are 22, 18, 20, and 17. He gets a sum of 77.
  c. The waiter has just computed the total bill for 20 students attending an awards dinner. The food bill came to $215, but the restaurant automatically includes a 15% tip. The waiter hands you a bill for $268.75 including the tip.
2. You are taking a test in your science class. One of the questions is the multiple-choice question shown below. Explain how you can tell, without doing any calculations, that two of the possible answers are not reasonable.

One horsepower is the same as 0.75 kw (kilowatts).

An engine rated at 133 horse-power is a

(a) 100-kw engine
(b) 30-kw engine
(c) 150-kw engine

3. Make a list of different ways to determine whether an answer is reasonable.

You used number sense to make your decisions in the Explore. You have developed number sense over the years from all of the experiences you've had. You may have used one or more of these methods for estimating. The symbol ≈ means *is approximately equal to.*

Clustering

$47 + 52 + 53 + 45$

Estimate sums by using multiplication. Find a number that is close to the addends.
Estimate:

The four numbers cluster around 50.

$4 \cdot 50 = 200$

So, $47 + 52 + 53 + 45 \approx 200$.

Compatible Numbers

$617 \div 37$

Replace the original numbers with compatible numbers that make the calculation simpler.
Estimate:

Replacing 617 with 600 and 37 with 40 gives compatible numbers.

$600 \div 40 = 15$

So, $617 \div 37 \approx 15$.

WHAT DO YOU THINK?

Jorge and Dawn are buying some school supplies. They have $12 to spend. They pick up a loose-leaf notebook that costs $4.25, a package of paper that costs $1.98, and a pen marked $2.75. Will they have enough money?

Jorge thinks ...

The notebook and the pen are about $4 plus $2 plus another dollar for the cents. That's $7. The paper is a little less than $2. So that's a total of just under $9. Even after the cashier adds in sales tax, $12 will be more than enough.

Dawn thinks ...

To make sure we have enough, I'll round all three items up to the nearest dollar. I'll figure $5 for the notebook, $2 for the paper, and $3 for the pen. That's $10. We've got $12, so that should easily cover the sales tax as well.

Jorge and Dawn used different methods. They came up with different estimates, but both estimates are good ones.

Rounding is an important skill for estimating and for adjusting your answer to fit the situation.

EXAMPLE

1. A customer's purchases came to $34.32. The cashier used a calculator to figure out the 6% sales tax. How much tax should the cashier add?

6% is 0.06. Enter the calculation 0.06×34.32. The calculator screen shows 2.0592. The cashier needs to round up to the next penny. 2.0592 is between 2.05 and 2.06. It is closer to 2.06. So the cashier adds $2.06.

Sometimes you have a choice of where to round. In these cases, you round to make the answer as precise as you want.

EXAMPLES

2. Ms. Appleton adds up her expenses on a calculator. The total is $755. She wants to report this to the nearest 10 dollars. What number should she report?

755 is halfway between 750 and 760. When rounding numbers, mathematicians have agreed to round up when it is exactly halfway. So Mrs. Appleton reports $760.

3. Philip is doing a calculation for his science experiment. He needs to give his answer to the nearest hundredth. What answer should he give?

4.823571427 is between 4.82 and 4.83.
It is closer to 4.82.
Philip should give 4.82 as his answer.

4.823571427

4.820   4.825   4.830

4.823571427

Sometimes the situation determines how you should round.

Suppose you have $5.00 to buy goldfish that cost $1.39 each.

$5 \div 1.39 = 3.597122302$

You can't buy a part of a goldfish, and you don't have enough money to buy four goldfish. So you round down to the nearest whole number. You only have money for three goldfish.

Calculate as indicated. If it makes sense to round, then round your answer to fit the situation.

a. The restaurant bill for Mary and Joe totals $15.32. They want to leave a 15% tip. How much should they leave as a tip?

b. Johann compared weights of five boxes he had to mail. They weighed 1.95 lb, 2.25 lb, 2.15 lb, 1.98 lb, and 2.12 lb. What was the average weight?

c. The library collection has 123 science-fiction books. The new budget allows for an increase of 15%. How many new science-fiction books can the library buy?

Suppose your calculator screen shows each number. Round to the indicated place.

d. 4254; nearest hundred

e. 9.601; nearest unit (one)

f. $3.24; nearest dime

g. 89.403; nearest tenth

h. 64,254; nearest thousand

i. $3.24; nearest dollar

Phrases such as *nearest tenth* or *nearest hundred* describe the **accuracy** of your answer. When you round a number, you want to decide how accurate you need to be for the situation you are in.

1. If you are using a calculator, is it necessary to check whether the answer is reasonable? Why or why not?

2. Describe a situation in which you would want to use an estimate.

3. Describe a situation in which you would need an exact answer.

4. Each year, wage earners fill out income tax forms. If you are using your calculator to do the computations, what accuracy should you use when you write down the results?

5. Describe a situation in which you would always round up and one in which you would always round down.

Exercises

CORE

1. **Getting Started** Amelia uses her calculator for a difficult calculation. She needs the answer to the nearest hundredth. The answer on her calculator screen, 2.236067978, is between 2.23 and 2.24. Which is closer?

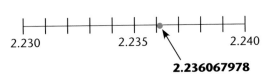

2.230   2.235   2.240

2.236067978

Suppose your calculator screen shows each number. Round to the indicated place.

2. 13,500; nearest thousand

3. 0.29952; nearest thousandth

4. $29.54; nearest dollar

5. $9.63; nearest dime

6. **Eggstra! Eggstra!** People who decorate eggs with wax and dye are practicing the Ukrainian craft called *Pysanky.* Dmitri wants to buy 5 eggs priced at $44.98, $45.25, $45.75, $44.90, and $45.02. How can Dmitri quickly find the exact total cost? What is the total cost?

7. Kwan bought a new ski jacket for $59.95. The sales tax was 4%. Is the answer shown on the calculator screen reasonable to show the total cost? If not, tell why.

$$83.93$$

Estimate.

8. 27×132

9. $279 + 312 + 293 + 331$

10. $971 \div 89$

11. $287 - 31$

12. A store advertises a special 10% discount off marked prices. Marty took an item marked $25.98 to a sales clerk. How much should Marty expect the sales clerk to subtract from the marked price?

Problem-Solving Tip

Make sure your answer makes sense.

13. Check It Out Dave checked out groceries for five customers at his register. The totals came to $19.54, $12.78, $20.33, $18.40, and $21.89. What was the average amount per customer?

14. Which is the best estimate of 27% of 31?
(a) 4   (b) 8   (c) 11   (d) 5

15. Lonnie lives in a state that has an 8% sales tax. His purchases come to $23.98. He uses his calculator to figure the sales tax and comes up with $19.18. Is the answer reasonable? Explain.

 LOOK AHEAD

Find the missing number.

16. $\_\_\_^2 = 4$ **17.** $\_\_\_^2 = 25$ **18.** $\_\_\_^2 = 49$ **19.** $\_\_\_^2 = 100$

MORE PRACTICE

Suppose your calculator screen shows each number. Round to the indicated place.

20. 32,642; nearest thousand   **21.** 432,413; nearest hundred

22. $136.50; nearest dollar   **23.** $10.73; nearest dime

24. 44.0548; nearest hundredth   **25.** 927.499; nearest unit

26. Kachina wants to take some friends to the movies. She has $20. Tickets for the matinee show cost $3.50. How many tickets can she buy?

Estimate.

27. 304×48 **28.** $587 + 673 + 621 + 598$ **29.** $382 \div 22$

30. $881 - 222$ **31.** $149 \div 7$ **32.** $3839 + 4837$

33. $19.99 + 14.99$ **34.** 73×73

35. The Hong Kong Bakery sells 2 moon cakes for 39 cents. If Chang has $2, how many cakes can she buy?

Social Science

MORE MATH REASONING

36. Save or Spend Alonzo has a summer job working as a waiter. Each night, he rounds his tips *down* to the nearest 10 dollars for deposit to his college fund and uses the rest for extra spending money. For the week of August 1, how much did he deposit to his college savings? How much did he use for spending money?

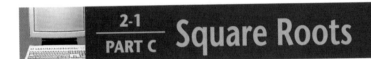

Tips for Week of August 1

Tuesday	Wednesday	Thursday	Friday	Saturday
$34.80	$28.35	$24.65	$41.20	$49.50

37. Counting the Seconds Estimate the number of seconds that have gone by so far this year. Explain how you got your estimate.

2-1 PART C Square Roots

← CONNECT → *You've seen how to use exponents to show repeated multiplication. Squaring a number means raising it to the second power. Sometimes you will need to do the reverse. That is, sometimes you start with a value and you need to find the original number that was squared. You will see a process for undoing the squaring operation.*

The Great Pyramid of Khufu has a square base that covers about 53,000 square meters of the Sahara Desert.

Remember how the area of a square is related to the length of its side.

To find the dimensions of the base, you need to learn a little more about working with squared numbers.

Square is 4 units on a side. Area is 4^2, or 16 square units.

1. List the squares of each of the whole numbers between 1 and 10.

2. The number 49 should be on your list. What is the number whose square is 49?

This number is called the **square root** of 49.

3. What is the square root of 81? of 25?

4. Is 27 one of the numbers on your list? If not, what are the two square numbers on your list closest to 27? What are the square roots of these two numbers? Use your answer to estimate the square root of 27 between two consecutive whole numbers.

> *Remember—*
> Numbers such as 5 and 6 are **consecutive whole numbers.** Their difference is 1.

5. Estimate the square root of each number between two consecutive whole numbers.
  a. 5
  b. 20
  c. 75

In the Explore, you estimated square roots of several numbers.

The square root operation undoes the squaring operation.

For example, the square root of 9 is 3.

$$\sqrt{9} = 3$$

$\sqrt{9} = 3$ because $3^2 = 9$

To see that the square root operation undoes, or is the opposite of, the squaring operation, enter a number on your calculator, press the $\boxed{x^2}$ key, and then press the $\boxed{\sqrt{x}}$ key. Your result is the original number that you entered.

You can use your calculator to get values for square roots.

The plan for a new house calls for a square patio with an area of 15 square meters. What is the length of a side to the nearest tenth of a meter?

We are looking for $(?)^2 = 15$.

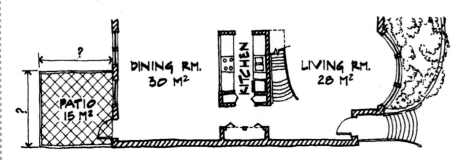

Estimate:

Look for two consecutive whole numbers.

2^2	3^2	$?^2$	4^2
4	9	**15**	16
Too small	Too small		Too large

$\sqrt{15}$ is between 3 and 4 and very close to 4.

Here's the goal.

To get an accurate answer:

Enter 15 $\boxed{\sqrt{x}}$ on your calculator.

> 3.872983346

Now you can round the answer to the nearest tenth.

$\sqrt{15} \approx 3.9$. The patio should measure 3.9 meters on each side.

TRY IT

Between which two consecutive whole numbers is each square root? Use your calculator to find the square root to the nearest tenth.

a. $\sqrt{8}$ **b.** $\sqrt{21}$ **c.** $\sqrt{75}$ **d.** $\sqrt{121}$

Sometimes a square root turns out to be an exact whole number.

Enter 9 $\boxed{\sqrt{x}}$.

> 3.0

The calculator screen shows that 9 is a **perfect square.** A perfect square is a number whose square root is an exact whole number.

1. Name all the perfect squares less than 50.
2. How many perfect squares are there less than 100?
3. If you multiply a perfect square by another perfect square, is the product a perfect square?

Surveyors, architects, and scientists use square roots when they work with the areas of squares and circles.

REFLECT

1. Why does looking at a picture of a square help us understand raising a number to the second power?
2. Jaime guesses that $\sqrt{150}$ is 13. She can't find her calculator. How can she tell whether her guess is exactly right or too large or too small?
3. Why do we call the squaring operation and the square root operation reverse, or inverse, operations?
4. Use your calculator to find $\sqrt{5}$. Is 5 a perfect square? How can you tell?

Exercises

CORE

1. **Getting Started** Is $\sqrt{26}$ more than 5 or less than 5?

2. Fill in the blank with the word or phrase that best completes the statement. Because $25 = 5 \cdot 5$, we say that 5 is the ____ of 25.

3. **Square Living** An architect planning a new home wants to design a square living room with about 500 ft² of floor space. What dimensions should the architect show on the blueprint?

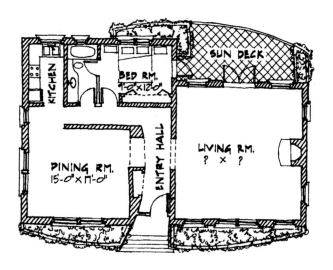

Between which two consecutive whole numbers is each square root?

4. $\sqrt{50}$ **5.** $\sqrt{22}$ **6.** $\sqrt{65}$ **7.** $\sqrt{10}$

Find each square root to the nearest tenth.

8. $\sqrt{20}$ **9.** $\sqrt{81}$ **10.** $\sqrt{0}$ **11.** $\sqrt{0.09}$

12. Tick-Tock You can find the number of seconds that it takes a pendulum to swing back and forth. First, find the square root of the pendulum's length in meters, then double it. How long will it take a pendulum that is 1.2 meters long to swing back and forth?

> **Problem-Solving Tip**
>
> Write a calculation for the time.

13. Which number is a perfect square?
(a) 5   (b) 144   (c) 50   (d) 200   (e) not here

Find at least one number that fits each description. If no number fits the description, write *impossible*.

14. Its square is the same as its square root.

15. Its square is less than its square root.

16. Its square is double its square root.

17. You can see a photo of the Great Pyramid of Khufu on page 108. Its square base covers an area of about 53,000 square meters. What are the dimensions of the square base?

18. Into the Fire A smoke jumper figures out how many seconds it will take to fall while parachuting. To do this, he finds the square root of the distance in feet and divides by 4. How long will it take the smoke jumper to free fall a distance of 2000 feet?

19. Calculate $5\sqrt{3} + 2$ to the nearest tenth. (Hint: $5\sqrt{3}$ means $5 \cdot \sqrt{3}$.)

20. Mr. and Mrs. Glickstein paid \$595 for a square rug that measured 12.5 feet on a side. How much did they pay per square foot?

21. If you give a waiter a tip of 20% of the bill in a restaurant, what fraction of the bill are you giving? [Previous course]

22. On a pictograph, a suitcase represents 5000 tourists. Draw symbols to show 17,500 tourists. [1-2]

23. What are the coordinates of a point that is three units below the origin on the *y*-axis? [1-1]

MORE PRACTICE

Between which two consecutive whole numbers is each square root?

24. $\sqrt{98}$ **25.** $\sqrt{12}$ **26.** $\sqrt{57}$ **27.** $\sqrt{105}$

28. $\sqrt{30}$ **29.** $\sqrt{21}$ **30.** $\sqrt{61}$ **31.** $\sqrt{14}$

Find each square root to the nearest tenth.

32. $\sqrt{169}$ **33.** $\sqrt{0.0016}$ **34.** $\sqrt{10,000}$ **35.** $\sqrt{18}$

36. $\sqrt{225}$ **37.** $\sqrt{12.3}$ **38.** $\sqrt{81}$ **39.** $\sqrt{0.25}$

40. A square cover for a small wading pool uses 150 square feet of fabric. What is the length of a side?

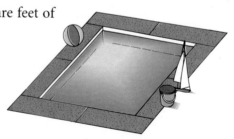

41. A house sits on a square lot. The lot covers about 100,000 square feet. What are the dimensions of the lot?

Calculate each value to the nearest tenth.

42. $2\sqrt{3}$ **43.** $\sqrt{12} \div 4$ **44.** $100 - \sqrt{6}$ **45.** $\sqrt{5} + \sqrt{10}$

MORE MATH REASONING

careers

46. A furniture maker is building a round kitchen table. The plan calls for the table top to have an area of about 7200 square inches. What radius should the furniture maker use?

> **Problem-Solving Tip**
>
> Draw a sketch and use the area.

47. A surveyor marks off three points of a right triangle to find the length of a pond. In a mathematics course, he learned a method using the Pythagorean Theorem to find the missing length. He needs to add the squares of the measured sides and then take the square root of the sum. How long is the pond?

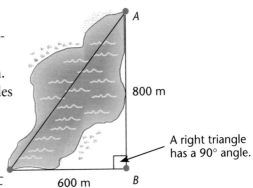

800 m

A right triangle has a 90° angle.

C   600 m   B

Careers

2-1
PART D   Order of Operations

← C O N N E C T →   *You've used your calculator to add, subtract, multiply, and divide. You've also simplified expressions with exponents and with square roots. A single calculation will often contain two or more of these operations. Now you will learn some rules to follow when a calculation calls for more than one operation.*

Andre and Lydia each simplified the expression 6 + 3 × 5. Andre said that the answer was 45. Lydia got an answer of 21.

CONSIDER

1. Show how Andre got 45. Show how Lydia got 21.
2. Can a calculation like 6 + 3 × 5 have more than one correct answer?
3. Would the answer be different if the calculation were written 3 × 5 + 6?

In 2-1 Part A, you explored the keys on your calculator. Now you will explore the order in which your calculator performs operations when expressions have more than one operation.

MATERIALS

Scientific calculator with algebraic operating system

1. Enter 6 [+] 3 [×] 5 [=]. What answer does your calculator screen show? Which of the operations, the addition or the multiplication, does the calculator perform first?

2. Enter each calculation. What answer does the calculator screen show? Explain the order in which the calculator does the operations.

   $16 - 3 \times 5$
   $5 + 7 \div 2$
   $2 \times 6 + 4 \times 2$
   $27 + 12 \div 4 + 3$
   $3 \times 5 \div 3 - 4$
   $5 + 9^2 \div 3 \times 7$

3. Make up three similar calculations. Use paper and pencil to predict what answer your calculator will show. Then enter the calculation and check your prediction.

4. Write a summary to describe the order that your calculator uses for expressions with more than one operation.

To make sure that everyone comes up with the same answer for a calculation, mathematicians have developed a set of rules for the order of operations.

ORDER OF OPERATIONS	$18 \div (8 - 2) + 2^2 \cdot 7 - 11$
1 Do the operations inside parentheses.	$18 \div \mathbf{6} + 2^2 \cdot 7 - 11$
2 Do all powers and roots.	$18 \div 6 + \mathbf{4} \cdot 7 - 11$
3 Do all multiplication and division from left to right.	$\mathbf{3} + \mathbf{28} - 11$
4 Do all addition and subtraction from left to right.	$\mathbf{20}$

Scientific calculators are made so that they follow these rules. If your calculator has parentheses keys, you can enter the parentheses as they appear in the expression. If your calculator doesn't have parentheses keys, you will have to calculate the parts of the expression in parentheses first.

TRY IT

Calculate.

a. $15 - 21 \div 7$

b. $36 \div (19 - 13) + \sqrt{16}$

c. $81 \div 3^2 + (2^3 + 1)$

d. $4 \cdot (3 + 2)$

An expression like $4 \cdot (3 + 2)$ is often written as $4(3 + 2)$. The multiplication symbol "$\cdot$" can be left out when parentheses are used in this way.

Some expressions contain a division bar. The bar acts like a set of parentheses grouping the numerator and the denominator. For example, $\frac{6 + 4}{5 \cdot 1}$ is the same as $(6 + 4) \div (5 \cdot 1)$.

WHAT DO **YOU** THINK?

Calculate $\frac{21 + 9}{3 \cdot 2 - 1}$.

Yeaphana thinks ...

I'll use the order of operations to work out the numerator and the denominator separately.

Numerator: $21 + 9 = 30$

Denominator: $3 \cdot 2 - 1$ Multiply first.

$$= 6 - 1 = 5$$

So I get $\frac{30}{5}$, or 6.

Desrie thinks ...

I'll rewrite with parentheses by changing the fraction into a division.

$(21 + 9) \div (3 \cdot 2 - 1)$

My calculator has parentheses keys.

(21 + 9) ÷ (3 × 2 − 1) =

My calculator screen shows the answer is 6.

1. Why do we need to have an order of operations?
2. Describe the order to follow when you calculate an expression that has several operations.
3. A student who had difficulty remembering the order of operations invented a word, PEMDAS, to help. What do you think this word means to the student?
4. Explain the difference, if any, between $2 \cdot (3 + 5)$ and $2 \cdot 3 + 5$.
5. What is the value of $5 \cdot 12 \div 3 + 1$? Using parentheses, rewrite $5 \cdot 12 \div 3 + 1$ so that it has a value of 15.

Exercises

CORE

1. **Getting Started** What should you do first in calculating $56 \div (3 + 4) + 9$?

2. Use the steps shown at the right to calculate $56 \div (3 + 4) + 9$. What are the values for **a, b,** and **c**?

$$56 \div (3 + 4) + 9$$
$$= 56 \div [\, \mathbf{a} \,] + 9$$
$$= [\, \mathbf{b} \,] + 9$$
$$= [\, \mathbf{c} \,]$$

3. Use your calculator to calculate $56 \div (3 + 4) + 9$. Explain how you calculate this on a calculator with parentheses. Explain how you calculate on a calculator without parentheses.

Calculate.

4. $29 - 4 \cdot 5$

5. $8(9 - 5) + 1$

6. $64 \div 8 + 77 \div 11$

7. $3 + 4^2$

8. $2(3 + 1) \div 8$

9. $60 \div (15 - 3)$

10. $\dfrac{96 - 54}{7 \cdot 3}$

11. $(19 + \sqrt{36}) \div 10$

12. $23 - 4^2 \div (2 + 3 \cdot 2)$

Write a mathematical expression for each. Then calculate.

13. the amount of juice in three 10-ounce cans and one 6-ounce can all divided among four people

14. the cost of two loaves of bread at $1.09 each and three jars of peanut butter at $1.89 each

15. Angel's calculator doesn't follow the order of operations. Describe how he can use it to calculate $13 - 3^2 \div (8 - 3 \cdot 2)$. What answer should he get?

16. Your Serve Four women played in a tennis tournament. The players earned five points for each game they won. Two points were taken away for each game they lost. A trophy was given to the player with the greatest number of points. Which player won the trophy?

Tennis Tournament Results

Sue Cox	6 6	Sue Cox	2 1	Sue Cox	6 3
Dena Gill	4 3	Brenda Fry	6 6	Tanya Pum	1 6

Brenda Fry	6 4	Brenda Fry	6 2	Dena Gill	6 4
Tanya Pum	0 6	Dena Gill	4 6	Tanya Pum	1 6

Copy each statement and place one of these signs in each box to make the sentence true: +, −, •, or ÷.

17. $15 \ \Box \ 0.2 + 8 = 11$

18. $4 \cdot 3.5 \ \Box \ 7 = 2$

19. $6.5 \ \Box \ 15.75 \ \Box \ 3 = 1.25$

20. $9.2 \ \Box \ 4 \ \Box \ 1.5 = 3.8$

21. Cost of Government In 1994, President Clinton received a salary of $200,000, and Vice President Gore received $166,200. Each of the 14 cabinet members got a salary of $143,800. What is the total amount of these salaries?

22. Coming Up Daisies A gardener figures out the number of flowers to plant along a fence by dividing the length in inches by 9 and adding one flower for the end. How many flowers will the gardener plant for a 6-ft length of fence?

LOOK AHEAD

Calculate each pair.

23. $2(3 + 5)$ and $2 \cdot 3 + 2 \cdot 5$

24. $5(1 + 7)$ and $5 \cdot 1 + 5 \cdot 7$

25. $4(3 + 5 + 7)$ and $4 \cdot 3 + 4 \cdot 5 + 4 \cdot 7$

26. $2(2 + 1 + 2)$ and $2 \cdot 2 + 2 \cdot 1 + 2 \cdot 2$

MORE PRACTICE

Calculate.

27. $4(8 - 2.3)$

28. $2(19 - 11) - 16$

29. $84 \div 12(9 - 4)$

30. $4^3 - 8^2 + 5(8 + 3)$

31. $14 \cdot 8 \div 7 + 3$

32. $49 - 6^2 - 9$

Write a mathematical expression for each. Calculate the expression.

33. the total number of miles in two trips of 52 miles each and three trips of 13 miles each

34. the cost of two roast beef dinners at $8.99 each and a meatloaf dinner at $6.98 divided equally among three diners at a restaurant

Calculate.

35. $\frac{45}{5} + 3^4$

36. $36 \div \sqrt{81} \div 5$

37. $\frac{11 \cdot 6 - 50}{13 - 9}$

38. $\sqrt{900} \div 2 \cdot (15 \div 5)$

39. $121 - \sqrt{121} \cdot 5$

40. $\sqrt{225} - 81 \div 27$

41. A tour charges $75 per person for a day trip and deducts $25 for every fourth person in a group of four or more. What is the cost for a group of four? a group of nine?

MORE MATH REASONING

42. The dots along each side are 0.9 cm apart.
    a. What is the area of rectangle *PQRS*?
    b. What is the area of triangle *PQR*?

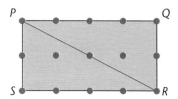

43. At Western Wear, $18 shirts were on sale at 25% off. Boots that usually cost $85 were marked down 30%. What is the cost of three shirts and two pairs of boots?

2-1
PART E **Making Connections**

← C O N N E C T → *You have worked with your calculator using operations on numbers including exponents and square roots. It is important to have estimating skills and a knowledge of order of operations to help you use your calculator effectively. You also saw how to do some calculations mentally by using a technique based on the distributive property.*

On page 95, you read about "green" computers. The Energy Star computers that federal agencies now must buy save the government money. These computers also conserve natural resources such as oil and gas by reducing by 25% the amount of electrical power being used.

The total amount of electricity used by an appliance is measured in kilowatt-hours (kwh). To calculate this, you multiply the power used in watts by the number of hours that the appliance is on, and then divide by 1000.

$$\textbf{kilowatt-hours} = \frac{\textbf{power} \text{ in watts} \times \text{number of } \textbf{hours} \text{ power is } \textbf{on}}{1000}$$

Although the cost of electricity varies around the country, one kilowatt-hour of electricity costs about 10 cents.

This spreadsheet shows average power used by some electrical appliances and how many hours per year these appliances are typically used.

	A	B	C	D	E
1	Appliance	Power (watts)	Hours per Year	Kilowatt-hours per Year	Cost per Year (10¢ per kwh)
2	Broiler	1200	75.0		
3	Toaster oven	1500	25.0		
4	Coffee maker	1100	95.0		
5	Hair dryer	1000	33.3		
6	Iron	1100	104.0		

Source: Association of Home Appliance Manufacturers

1. Copy the spreadsheet. Fill in the missing numbers in columns D and E. Use your calculator and what you have learned about number properties to get exact values. Check by making estimates.

2. Suppose manufacturers could improve the appliances listed above to use 25% less power. How much electricity in kilowatt-hours would the typical household save per year on these appliances? How much money would it save per year?

1. When is it convenient to use exponents? Do you need to use them?
2. How are square roots and exponents related?
3. How can you write a calculation expression so that someone who has never heard of the order of operations would still come out with the answer you expect?
4. Give three examples of when it would be helpful to use estimates.

Self-Assessment

Give the answer that your calculator screen shows for each calculation.

1. $4^2 - 3 \cdot 5$
2. $45 \div 9 + \sqrt{81}$
3. $12 + 56 \div 7 - 5$
4. $3{,}000{,}000 \cdot 48$
5. $4 \cdot 9 \div 10^6$
6. $72 \div 5\%$

7. **Circling the Bases** The distance between bases on a baseball diamond is 90 feet. Hank Aaron hit 755 home runs in his career as a professional baseball player.
   a. Estimate how far he ran.
   b. Explain how you calculated your estimate.

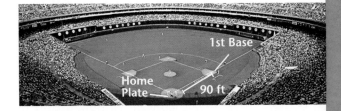

8. Use the numbers 1, 2, 3, and 4 to write expressions with 3 different answers.

9. Between which two consecutive whole numbers is $\sqrt{72}$? Use your calculator to give the value to the nearest hundredth.

10. On a pictograph, a wheel represents 200 cars. Draw symbols to show 1400 cars. [1-2]

11. Mr. Himes calculates grades by multiplying the test average by 5, the quiz average by 3, and the homework average by 2. One point is taken away from the sum for each missing homework assignment. The result is divided by 10.

Student	Test Avg.	Quiz Avg.	Homework Avg.	Missing Assignments
Mia	80	90	92	3
Ted	85	80	85	0

   a. Write a mathematical expression for Mia's grade.
   b. Write a mathematical expression for Ted's grade.
   c. Which student got the better grade?

12. Pierre used a calculator to figure out the total number of days in the first eight months of the year. His calculator screen showed an answer of 273. Is this reasonable? Explain.

13. Find the perimeter of the rectangle. [Previous course]

5.3 cm

2.1 cm

Calculate using mental math. Be prepared to explain your method.

14. $391 - 295$

15. 7×39

16. $77 + 12 + 3$

17. On weekends, Pedro installs car alarms. It takes him 1 hour and 45 minutes to complete an installation. About how many alarms can he put in during an 8-hour work day?

Round to the indicated place.

18. 4235; nearest hundred

19. 85.498; nearest unit

20. $18.68; nearest dime

21. The Washington Monument in Washington, DC, was dedicated in 1885. Its square base covers an area of about 3040 square feet. Approximate the dimensions of the base to the nearest tenth of a foot.

22. A coffee maker uses 1100 watts of power per hour. A deep fryer uses 1500 watts of power. How many kilowatt-hours of electricity are used by a small restaurant when it keeps 3 coffee makers and 3 deep fryers going for 8 hours?

Maryland

Virginia   **Washington, DC**

23. Three designers have submitted blueprints to compete for a prize. Experts rank the designs. Five points are awarded for each first-place vote, four points for each second-place vote, and three points for each third-place vote. Who has the most total points, designer A, B, or C?

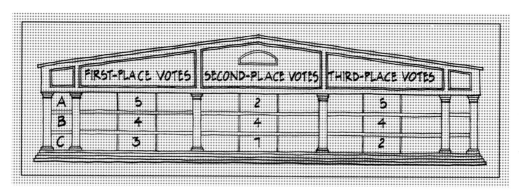

	FIRST-PLACE VOTES	SECOND-PLACE VOTES	THIRD-PLACE VOTES
A	5	2	5
B	4	4	4
C	3	7	2

Up, Up, and Away

According to *Up, Up, and Away* by   Mary E. Santilli and Marjorie Carss:

On June 5, 1783, the first public demonstration of hot-air ballooning took place in Annonay, France. A balloon with a circumference of 110 feet that held 22,000 cubic feet of air took eight men to hold down until the signal to let go was given. The huge balloon rose about 6000 ft. and landed a mile and a half away after a ten minute flight.

For more than 200 years people have been flying in balloons that are lighter than air. At first, hot air was the only thing used to lift the balloons because hot air is lighter than the surrounding air in the sky. Hot air is still used today for sporting and recreational ballooning.

For scientific and business uses, however, gases such as hydrogen and helium are used to lift balloons. Because these gases weigh less than air, they are able to lift the balloons. You've seen helium balloons at birthday parties, festivals, and celebrations. The Goodyear blimp that you sometimes see in the sky is a giant helium balloon.

1. The hot-air balloon mentioned in the reading "held 22,000 cubic feet of air." You use feet to measure length. You use square feet to measure area. What does "22,000 cubic feet" mean?
2. Why do you think that people prefer to use balloons filled with hot air instead of hydrogen or helium for sports and recreation?
3. A vendor was selling helium-filled balloons. Each balloon she sold contained just enough helium to lift a 1-pound weight slightly off the ground. What would happen to you if you bought the same number of these balloons as you weigh in pounds?

Modeling·Signed Numbers

← C O N N E C T → *You've used positive and negative numbers to show positions on a number line and on a coordinate grid. You've seen how positive and negative numbers can describe time, temperature, and money. You will now explore models for calculations with signed numbers.*

On number lines and coordinate grids, positive and negative numbers are used as coordinates to show the locations of points.

We use positive and negative numbers in other ways, too. We might say that a football team gained 4 yards by writing "+4" or that the team lost 4 yards by writing "−4."

You can think of −4 and +4 as opposites.

Night and day are opposites.

Up and down are opposites.

Back and front are opposites.

Right and left are opposites.

1. Give other pairs of opposites. What are opposites?

When our number system is expanded to include negative numbers, every number then has an opposite number on the number line. A number line is one model for this expanded set of numbers.

Every positive number has an opposite negative number, and every negative number has an opposite positive number.

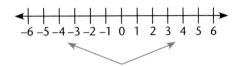

–4 and +4 are a pair of opposites.

A number and its opposite add to 0.

TRY IT

Give the opposite of each number.

a. 7 **b.** −5 **c.** 5.3 **d.** −12

CONSIDER

2. What is the opposite of 0?

A positive number like 7 is sometimes written as +7. Positive and negative numbers are called **signed numbers.**

Algebra tiles have little squares to represent +1 and −1.

You can use algebra tiles to help you think about signed numbers.

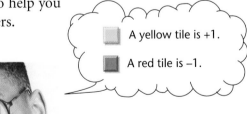

A yellow tile is +1.

A red tile is –1.

EXPLORE: PILES OF TILES

MATERIALS

Algebra tiles

A yellow tile is +1.
A red tile is −1.
A yellow tile and a red tile are opposites.
Opposites add to 0.

= 0

Experiment with your tiles.

1. Start with a collection of yellow tiles.
  a. What signed number does your collection represent?
  b. Take one yellow tile and one red tile. Add the pair to your collection. What signed number does this new collection represent? Why?
  c. Add another pair of yellow and red tiles to your collection. What signed number does your collection represent now?

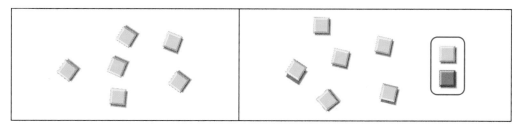

2. Start with a collection of red tiles.
  a. What signed number does this collection show?
  b. Add in five pairs of yellow and red tiles. What signed number does this collection show?
  c. Remove two of the pairs of red and yellow tiles. What signed number does the collection show now?

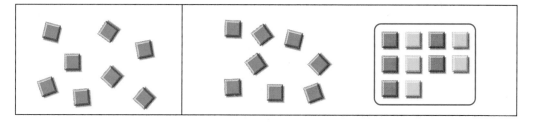

3. Show three different ways to have a collection of tiles that represents zero. Draw a sketch.
4. Show three different ways to have a collection of tiles that represents +4. Draw a sketch.
5. Show three different ways to have a collection of tiles that represents −3. Draw a sketch.

Another way to think of signed numbers uses a scale. Remember that positive and negative numbers are opposites.

A weight, caused by gravity, pushes down a scale. We use the positive numbers to show this.

gravity pulls down

(a)

Balloons do the opposite. They pull up and lessen the weight. We use negative numbers to show this.

balloon pulls up

(b)

The kitten weighs 7. The balloon has a pull of −7. So the reading on the scale is 0.

gravity pulls down

balloon pulls up

(c)

Our special scales show both positive and negative numbers. An empty scale reads 0.

CONSIDER

3. Why does the scale with both the kitten and the balloon read 0?
4. What will that scale read if the balloon's upward pull is −6? −8?
5. What effect does attaching a hot air balloon to a scale have on the total weight?
6. What effect does removing a hot air balloon from a scale have on the total weight?
7. How can you represent the kitten and the balloon together using the scale? using algebra tiles?

You can use the model that you like best to think about signed numbers.

Mr. Contreras had $5 in his bank account. The bank charged him a fee. The new bank balance was $2.

What is the missing number? $5 + \underline{} = 2$

Rachel thinks ...

I can use algebra tiles.

I'll start with 5 yellow tiles.

I want to end up with 2 yellow tiles.

Ah! I'll need to use 3 red tiles.

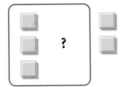

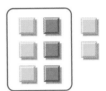

This will need to be zero.

This is zero.

So, $5 + \boxed{-3} = 2.$

Ben thinks ...

I can think of the numbers as weights and balloons on a scale.

The balloon must lift the dog with a pull of -3 to make the weight go from 5 to 2.

So, $5 + \boxed{-3} = 2.$

Yeaphana thinks ...

I can use a number line.

If I start at 5, how should I move to get to 2?

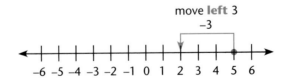

move **left** 3
-3

Oh, I need to move left 3.

So, $5 + \boxed{-3} = 2.$

What is the missing number? Draw tiles, balloons, or a number line to decide.

e. $1 + \underline{} = 0$ **f.** $6 + \underline{} = 2$

g. $5 + \underline{} = 1$ **h.** $-3 + \underline{} = -1$

No matter which model you use to think about signed numbers, remember that positive numbers and negative numbers have opposite effects.

REFLECT

1. What number would you attach to a helium balloon that could just barely lift your desk off the ground? Explain and draw a picture.
2. How many yellow tiles would it take to approximate your math book's weight in pounds? What tiles would you need to represent the opposite of this?
3. Explain with tiles why a number and its opposite add to 0.
4. Explain with weights and balloons on a scale why a number and its opposite add to 0.
5. Explain with a number line why a number and its opposite add to 0.

Exercises

CORE

Getting Started Give the opposite of each number.

1. -5 **2.** 3 **3.** -10

What is the missing number? Draw tiles, balloons, or a number line to decide.

4. $-5 + \underline{} = 0$ **5.** $3 + \underline{} = 0$ **6.** $-10 + \underline{} = 0$

Tell what each negative number could represent. Give the opposite. What could this opposite number represent?

7. $-\$4.5$ trillion **8.** $-18.7°C$ **9.** -1.6 yards

10. Three of the points are labeled incorrectly. Tell which three points are labeled incorrectly. Explain.

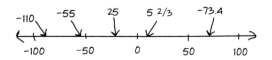

11. Ten seconds before the launch of a rocket from the Kennedy Space Center, the announcer said, "minus 10 and counting."
   a. What did she mean?
   b. What might the announcer say 15 seconds later?
   c. How is the announcer using signed numbers?

12. Photography Is Art Darkness and light are opposites. Ansel Adams is famous for his photographs of Yosemite National Park. Why do you think that Ansel Adams almost always used black-and-white instead of color film?

Fine Arts

13. Sheng is using yellow and red algebra tiles to find the missing number: $-2 +$ ___ $= 3$.

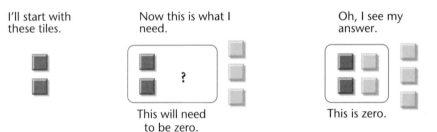

I'll start with these tiles.

Now this is what I need.

This will need to be zero.

Oh, I see my answer.

This is zero.

Explain what her thinking might be and her conclusion.

What is the missing number? Draw tiles, balloons, or a number line to decide.

14. $4 +$ ___ $= 1$ **15.** $5 +$ ___ $= 2$ **16.** $-4 +$ ___ $= 1$

17. Robert is using balloons to finish this number sentence.
   $23 +$ ___ $= 18$

Explain what his thinking might be and his conclusion.

18. Midnight in Moscow One night in Moscow, Russia, the temperature dropped from −5°F to −17°F. Show on a number line the change in temperature.

19. Look in a newspaper or a magazine. Find at least two examples that show negative numbers. Cut them out and tape them to your homework paper.

20. In the Red How might a business, when preparing its budget, use both positive and negative numbers?

LOOK AHEAD

Manuella is working with algebra tiles.

Figure 1   Figure 2   Figure 3   Figure 4

21. What number is shown in Figure 1?   **22.** What number is shown in Figure 2?

23. What number is shown in Figure 3?   **24.** What number is shown in Figure 4?

MORE PRACTICE

Give the opposite of each signed number.

25. −15   **26.** 3.2   **27.** −2   **28.** $-2\frac{1}{2}$

What is the missing number? Draw tiles, balloons, or a number line to decide.

29. $-15 + \underline{\quad} = 0$ **30.** $3.2 + \underline{\quad} = 0$

31. $-2 + \underline{\quad} = 0$ **32.** $-2\frac{1}{2} + \underline{\quad} = 0$

33. Paying Up Mrs. Donaldson has a checking account. The bank says that the account is overdrawn by $25. What signed number represents the balance in her account?

What is the missing number? Draw tiles, balloons, or a number line to decide.

34. $4 + \underline{\quad} = -2$ **35.** $-1 + \underline{\quad} = 5$ **36.** $10 + \underline{\quad} = 5$

37. $3 + \underline{\quad} = 5$ **38.** $-7 + \underline{\quad} = 2$ **39.** $12 + \underline{\quad} = -2$

Copy this number line. Place these numbers about where they belong.

40. $\frac{1}{4}$

41. -3.25

42. 5.4

43. -3.5

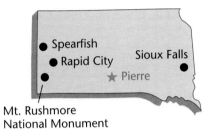

MORE MATH REASONING

Social Science

44. According to the *Guinness Book of World Records*, the temperature in Spearfish, South Dakota, went from $-4°F$ to $45°F$ in only 2 minutes on January 22, 1943.
  a. What was the total change in temperature?
  b. How many degrees per minute was this world-record temperature change?
  c. What is the approximate outside temperature for your city right now? If the same change happened in your city, what would the temperature be in 2 minutes?

Science

45. A New Scale The coldest temperature possible is $-459.7°F$. It is called absolute zero. This is the point at which the motion of molecules stops. Suppose we used this as the zero point of our temperature scale. What number would represent the freezing point of water? What would be the boiling point of water?

2-2
PART B
Adding Signed Numbers

← **CONNECT** → *Earlier, you saw that you can use algebra tiles, balloons, or a number line to help you think about signed numbers. Now you will use these models to help you add signed numbers.*

The word "add" is defined by *Merriam-Webster's Collegiate® Tenth Edition Dictionary.*

add \\'ad\ *vb* [ME, fr. L *addere*, fr. *ad-* + *-dere* to put — more at DO] *vt* (14c) **1 :** to join or unite so as to bring about an increase or improvement 〈~s 60 acres to his land〉 〈wine ~s a creative touch to cooking〉 **2 :** to say further : APPEND **3 :** to combine (numbers) into an equivalent simple quantity or number **4 :** to include as a member of a group 〈don't forget to ~ me in〉 ~*vi* **1 a :** to perform addition **b :** to come together or unite by addition **2 a :** to serve as an addition 〈the movie will ~ to his fame〉 **b :** to make an addition 〈~ed to her savings〉 — **add•able** *or* **add•ible** \\'ad-ə-bəl\ *adj*

You may have learned to add positive numbers using objects.

The numbers being added are called **terms.**

$3 + 2 = 5$

terms   sum

The result is the **sum.**

Likewise, you can add negative numbers.

$-3 + (-2) = -5$

You can use what you learned about opposites to add positive and negative numbers.

$5 + (-2) = 3$

This is zero.

EXPLORE: TILING IT ON

1. Add $2 + 1$. What sign is the sum of two positive numbers?

2. Add $-2 + (-1)$. What sign is the sum of two negative numbers?

3. Use tiles to show that $4 + (-3) = 1$. Draw a picture to illustrate.

4. Use tiles to find each sum. Draw pictures to illustrate.
   a. $2 + (-1)$ **b.** $-2 + 1$
   c. $3 + (-5)$ **d.** $-3 + 5$

5. Show at least two more examples of adding a positive and a negative number. Use your tiles to find the sum. Is the sum of a positive and a negative number always a positive number? Is it always a negative number? Write a conclusion about the sign when you add a positive number and a negative number.

6. Explain how to add two signed numbers.

MATERIALS

Algebra tiles

$= 0$

An algorithm is a process. You can use your work in the Explore to write your own algorithm for adding two signed numbers.

As you've seen already, a positive number is often written without its sign.

For example, $-7 + (+3)$ is the same as $-7 + 3$.

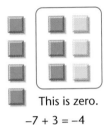

This is zero.

$-7 + 3 = -4$

Add $-6 + 2$.

Eugene thinks ...

I can use algebra tiles. I need to start with six red tiles for -6 and two yellow tiles for $+2$.

So, $-6 + 2 = -4$.

4 red tiles is -4.

This is zero.

Lydia thinks ...

I have a weight of 2 on the scale. The balloon pulls up on the weight with a force of -6.

So, $-6 + 2 = -4$.

The balloon pulls up with a force that is 4 more than the weight's downward pull.

Jorge thinks ...

I can think of adding as moving along a number line. I start at 0 on the number line.

-6 means I move *left* 6. Then, $+2$ means I move *right* 2.

I end up at -4.

So, $-6 + 2 = -4$.

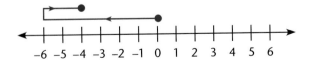

Add.

a. $8 + (-5)$ **b.** $-8 + 5$ **c.** $+13 + 12$ **d.** $-13 + (-12)$
e. $+14 + (-80)$ **f.** $-75 + (-50)$ **g.** $-2.3 + (-3)$ **h.** $4.5 + (-10)$

When there are more than two terms, we add them two at a time.

EXAMPLE

Add $30.3 + (-10) + 45.3 + (-25) + 100$.

One way is to add the positive numbers and the negative numbers separately.

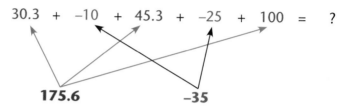

So, $30.3 + (-10) + 45.3 + (-25) + 100 = 175.6 + (-35)$.

$$= 140.6$$

When you add signed numbers, you can rearrange the terms to make the work more convenient.

REFLECT

1. Can the sum of two negative numbers ever be positive? Explain.
2. When will the sum of a positive and a negative number be positive? When will it be negative?
3. What is an advantage of rearranging the terms when you are adding more than two signed numbers with different signs?
4. How can you use this number line to add $3 + (-5)$?

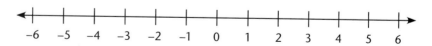

5. Which model do you like best to help you think about adding signed numbers: tiles, balloons, or the number line? Why?

Exercises

CORE

1. **Getting Started** Cheung is calculating $5 + (-8)$ using tiles.

   What is the sum?

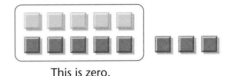

This is zero.

2. Write the word or phrase that correctly completes the statement. In $30.3 + (-10) + 45.3$, the numbers 30.3, −10, and 45.3 are called ___.

Illustrate each calculation with a picture of tiles, balloons, or a number line.

3. $5 + (-3) = 2$

4. $-5 + (-4) = -9$

5. $-7 + 2 = -5$

Add.

6. $-7 + (-4)$

7. $5 + (-2)$

8. $5 + (-7)$

9. $-7 + 4$

10. $-27 + 4$

11. $25 + (-35)$

12. $18 + 2.5$

13. $-18 + (-2.5)$

Copy the temperature scale.

14. Mark an approximate location for 70°.

15. Mark an approximate location for 80° more than 70°.

16. Mark an approximate location for 90° less than 70°.

17. What do the arrows at the ends mean?

100°

0°

−100°

Add.

18. $-32.6 + (-50)$

19. $-1.5 + (-40.1) + 17$

20. $67.4 + (-30.1) + 35.6 + (-15) + 2.4$

21. $-16\frac{2}{3} + \left(-4\frac{2}{3}\right)$

22. **Money Talks** Lucretia's old bank balance was $102. She wrote her brother a check for $16, her company deposited her $25 holiday bonus electronically, and she paid $18.50 for a concert ticket.

   a. Write an expression that models Lucretia's new balance.

   b. Use the expression to find Lucretia's new balance.

23. Amy says that the glasses must weigh +5. Do you agree? Why or why not?

24. Samson needed to calculate $-5.4 + (-4.3) + 2.1$. He started at 0 on a number line and moved 5.4 left, then 4.3 left, then 2.1 right. Did he use an appropriate process? What is the sum?

25. Stock Exchange A share of stock for Universal Widgets sold for $30 on Monday. On Tuesday, the stock price dropped $0.50 per share. On Wednesday, it dropped another $1.25, on Thursday it gained $1.13, and on Friday it gained $0.38. What was the selling price per share at the end of the week?

> **Problem-Solving Tip**
>
> Write an expression to show the changes.

26. Going Up The Sears Tower in Chicago, Illinois, is considered an engineering marvel because of its height. It has 110 stories with several basements below ground level. Marcus and Jane took a ride on the elevator. Starting on the 10th floor, they went up 2 floors, down 15 floors, and finally, up 25 floors. On what floor did they end up?

 LOOK BACK

27. On a calculator, the screen shows a result of 641.568123. How would you report the answer rounded to the nearest unit? [2-1]

28. In 1990, there were 10,800,000 people 18 to 20 years old. Only 45% of them reported that they voted. How many 18 to 20 year olds did not vote in 1990? [Previous course]

Use a ruler. Draw a line segment with the given length. [1-1]

29. 2.5 cm

30. $3\frac{1}{4}$ in.

31. $\frac{1}{3}$ ft

MORE PRACTICE

Add.

32. $-5 + (-3)$ **33.** $7 + (-8)$ **34.** $-5 + (-17)$ **35.** $-6 + 14$

36. $-2 + 24$ **37.** $35 + (-35)$ **38.** $18 + 12.7$ **39.** $-20 + (-3.7)$

40. Minimum Payment Mr. Nicolov's credit card statement showed that he owed $235. He paid $10. Then he charged another $75. What was his new balance?

Add.

41. $170.4 + (-20) + (-65)$

42. $-450 + (-100) + (-25)$

43. $5003 + (-1000) + 1000 + (-3)$

44. $130 + (-20) + (-5) + 45$

45. $-1500 + (-75) + 25$

46. $50\frac{3}{10} + 20\frac{4}{10} + (-10.2)$

47. $-919 + 10 + (-3.2)$

48. $13.2 + (-2) + (-5) + 4.5$

49. Serena's bank account was overdrawn. Her balance was $-\$4.32$. She didn't realize it, and she wrote another check for $25.00. The bank charged her $20.00. What was her bank balance then?

MORE MATH REASONING

50. On the Greens A high-school golf team had a score of -5 (that is, 5 under par) halfway through a tournament. They finished with a final score of $+2$. How many points over or under par did they score in the last half of the tournament?

51. Take My Heart Away In one version of the card game Hearts, the player with the fewest number of points left in his or her hand at the end of the game wins. Each of the 13 hearts is 1 point, the queen of spades is 13 points, the jack of diamonds is -10 points, and all other cards count 0. Andy, Rosemarie, Louise, and Dillon played 3 rounds of Hearts. Their total scores were $+44$, -6, $+25$, and -9, respectively.
a. Who was winning?
b. They played one more round and finished with scores of $+51$, -4, $+18$, and $+5$, respectively. Who got the jack? Who got the queen of spades?

← C O N N E C T →

You have explored how to add signed numbers. Now you will work with tiles to see how to subtract them.

We use subtraction to find the difference of two numbers.

ITEM NO. OR TRANS. CODE	DATE	TRANSACTION DESCRIPTION	SUBTRACTIONS AMOUNT OF PAYMENT OR WITHDRAWAL (−)	✓ T	(−) FEE IF ANY	ADDITIONS AMOUNT OF DEPOSIT OR INTEREST (+)	BALANCE	
							625	30
368	12/3	Jackson's Grocery	17 93				17	93
							607	37
369	12/5	Andware's Cleaners	6 75				6	75
							600	62
	12/6	Refund- Jody's Toys				16 50	16	50
							617	12
370	12/8	Classic Copy Center for resumes	30 34	✓			30	34
							586	78

PLEASE BE SURE TO **DEDUCT** CHARGES THAT AFFECT YOUR ACCOUNT

If you are using tiles, you can think of subtracting as taking away.

Using algebra tiles, $5 - 2$ means:

Start with 5 yellow tiles.

Take away 2 yellow tiles.

So, $5 - 2 = 3$

Start with 5 yellow tiles.

Take 2 away.

EXPLORE: YOURS FOR THE TAKING

MATERIALS

Algebra tiles

1. Sabrina is using algebra tiles to help her calculate $5 - (-2)$.
She needs to start with 5 yellow tiles. She must take away 2 red tiles.

Use the three pictures above to explain how Sabrina did the calculation with her tiles.
Complete the statement: $5 - (-2) =$ ___.

2. Use your tiles to work out each of these subtractions. Or you might prefer to make up your own subtraction calculations.

$$-5 - (-2) \qquad -4 - 6 \qquad 6 - (-1) \qquad -6 - 4$$

3. Do you see a pattern? How can you subtract signed numbers?

CONSIDER

1. If you subtract a positive number will the original value increase or decrease?
2. If you subtract a negative number will the original value increase or decrease?

Subtracting signed numbers has connections to our balloon model.

Balloonists can toss off a weight called a ballast to make the balloon weigh less and rise. Think about subtracting positive numbers as removing ballast.

Balloonists can release some hydrogen to make the balloon weigh more and descend. Think about subtracting negative numbers as releasing hydrogen.

Subtracting a signed number is the same as adding its opposite.

$$-3 - (-4)$$

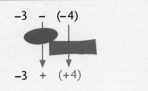

$$-3 + (+4)$$

You can verify this using the balloon model.

Removing the -10 balloon on the left increases the scale reading by 10.

$$25 - (-10) = 35$$

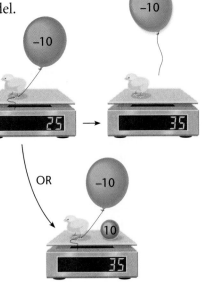

OR

Adding a weight of 10 on the right also increases the scale reading by 10.

$$25 + (+10) = 35$$

So *subtracting* -10 is the same as *adding* $+10$.

1. Subtract $-85 - (-45)$.

$$-85 - (-45) = -85 + 45$$ Subtracting -45 is the same as adding 45.

$$= -40$$ Add the two signed numbers.

2. Subtract $-17 - 8$.

$$-17 - 8 = -17 + (-8)$$ Subtracting 8 is the same as adding -8.

$$= -25$$ Add the two signed numbers.

Subtract.

a. $-3 - (-4)$ **b.** $5 - (-2)$ **c.** $-7 - (+5)$

d. $-3 - 4$ **e.** $30 - 46$ **f.** $-27 - (-40)$

g. $-50.6 - 30$ **h.** $3\frac{1}{2} - \left(-4\frac{1}{2}\right)$ **i.** $17.3 - (-3.1)$

Adding and subtracting are inverse, or opposite, operations.

1. What effect does removing a weight from a scale have on the scale reading? What effect does removing a balloon from a scale have on the scale reading? How does this relate to subtracting positive and negative numbers?

2. Explain what happened to get from the first scale reading to the second one. Include a number sentence.

First this.   Then this.

3. To calculate $4 - (-6)$ using tiles, you need to start with 4 yellow tiles and then remove 6 red ones. How can you do this?

4. One day in Fairbanks, Alaska, the temperature was 5°F at 7:00 p.m. and −6°F an hour later. How can you use subtraction to find the temperature change?

Exercises

CORE

1. Getting Started Amanda is trying to calculate $1 - (-3)$ using tiles.

She starts with 1 yellow tile.

She needs to remove 3 red tiles. So she uses 3 pairs of red and yellow tiles.

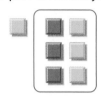

This is zero.

Now she can remove 3 red tiles.

Remove 3 red tiles.

What answer does Amanda get for $1 - (-3)$?

2. Jorge needs to calculate $-14 - (-12)$.
  a. Write the calculation as an addition of signed numbers.
  b. What answer should Jorge give?

Rewrite each as an addition calculation.

  3. $-14 - (-12)$ **4.** $-4 - 8$ **5.** $-14 - (-12) - (-3)$

Calculate.

  6. $-4 - (-9)$ **7.** $-3 - 7$ **8.** $-5 - (-2) - (-3)$

9. Friday Night Football Jeremy was told he had nearly broken the school record of 142 yards total for a single game by running for 140 yards. On reviewing the films, the coaches found Jeremy had mistakenly been credited with a -4-yard run made by another player, but then he was not credited with a -2-yard run that he did make. Did Jeremy break the record after all?

> **Problem-Solving Tip**
>
> Be sure you have answered the question.

10. What number sentence do these tiles illustrate?

This is zero.

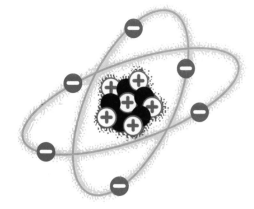

Remove
3 yellow tiles.

Calculate.

11. $-10 - (-20)$

12. $-100 - 99$

13. $-58.2 - (-75)$

14. $-49 - 25 - (-3)$

15. $-47 + 3 - (-4) + 55$

16. $2.7 - (-3.1) - 0.8$

17. Atoms are made up of three types of particles.

protons

positive
charge

neutrons

no
charge

electrons

negative
charge

A natural carbon atom has six protons and six electrons.

a. Is the charge of a natural carbon atom positive, negative, or zero? Explain.

b. When an electron jumps off the atom it creates electricity. Is the charge of the atom then positive, negative, or zero? Explain.

18. Avram is using his calculator to calculate $(-30) - 5$.

30 [+/-] [−] 5 [=]

a. What does the [+/-] key do?

b. What answer should Avram expect to get? Check using your calculator.

c. Show the buttons to press for calculating $5 - (-7)$. What is the answer?

19. War Between the States In 1863, during the Civil War, President Abraham Lincoln delivered the Gettysburg Address to dedicate the Gettysburg National Cemetery. He began with this often-quoted statement:

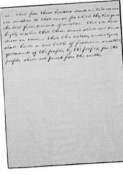

Four score and seven years ago, our fathers brought forth on this continent a new nation, conceived in liberty and dedicated to the proposition that all men are created equal.

A score is 20. What year is he referring to in this opening line? What happened in that year?

20. The highest point in the world is Mt. Everest, in Asia, at 29,028 feet above sea level. The lowest point is in the Mideast. It is the Dead Sea, and it is 1312 feet below sea level. What is the range of altitudes across the Mideast and Asia?

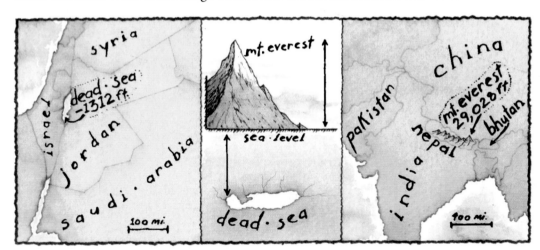

 LOOK AHEAD

21. Calculate 5 × 4. Calculate 4 + 4 + 4 + 4 + 4. Are the answers the same?

22. Write an addition calculation that has the same answer as 3 × 2.4.

Divide.

23. 150 ÷ 3   **24.** $\frac{64}{4}$ **25.** 17 ÷ 2   **26.** $\frac{127}{5}$

MORE PRACTICE

Rewrite each as an addition calculation.

27. $-24 - (-12)$

28. $-6 - 3$

29. $-1 - (-14) - (-32)$

Subtract.

30. $-52 - (-35)$

31. $-10 - 9$

32. $-29 - 25$

33. In a set of data, the highest number is 292 and the lowest is -31. What is the range?

Calculate.

34. $70.3 - 34.5$

35. $-73.6 - 28$

36. $2 - (-1) + (-1.7)$

37. $2.8 - (-4.1) - 1.8$

38. $-41 + 3 - (-3) + 5$

39. $-3.5 - (-42.1) + 7$

40. $271.4 + (-20.3) - (-35)$

41. $-81.2 - (-31) - (-2.3)$

42. $-45.3 - (-300) + (-2.5)$

43. $6004 + (-2000) - 2000 - (-3)$

44. $-16\frac{3}{4} - 4\frac{1}{2}$

45. $167.4 + (-36.1) + 35.6 - (-1.5) + 2.4$

MORE MATH REASONING

46. Down Under A submarine is at -400 ft, or 400 ft below sea level. It is ordered to descend 550 ft, then to ascend 250 ft, then to descend 220 ft, then to ascend 150 ft, and then to descend to the ocean floor at 1000 ft below sea level.

a. Draw a diagram of the trip.

b. What was the amount of the final descent?

c. Write a number sentence to show the trip.

d. If the first move were transmitted incorrectly to the ship as "descend 650 ft," what would happen?

e. This whole exercise was monitored on radar from a plane 1 mile overhead. How many feet above the ocean floor was the plane?

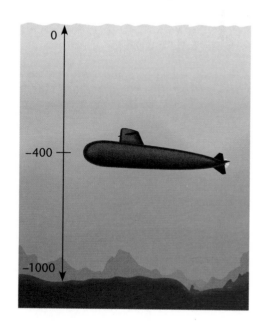

47. Each of the four boys on the mile relay team could run his lap in about 1 minute. Jesse's best time was 1.5 seconds less than 1 minute, which could be written as "−1.5." Mario's time was 0.8 seconds more than a minute, Patwin's was 0.3 seconds more, and Salim's was 1.9 seconds less.

a. Write an expression with signed numbers to show how much slower or faster than 4 minutes the whole team could run the relay, if each ran his best.

b. Salim got hurt before the state meet and was replaced by Malcolm who could run −0.9 seconds as a signed number relative to 1 minute. If they all ran their best, what was their total time in the state meet?

48. Checks and Balances Elizabeth's checking account had a balance of $87.32. She deposited a $32.50 paycheck and $25.00 from a birthday gift. That month she wrote checks for $82.00, $17.50, $6.35, $14.00, and $33.00. Her bank charges her $0.20 for each check and $15 for each check that is written when the account is overdrawn. How much must she deposit to pay the overdrawn fee and bring her balance back up to $100.00?

2-2
PART D Multiplying and Dividing Signed Numbers

· ·

← CONNECT → *The four basic arithmetic operations are adding, subtracting, multiplying, and dividing. You've seen how to do adding and subtracting with signed numbers. In this part, you will look at how to multiply and divide.*

You may already know that multiplying positive numbers is a shortcut for repeated addition.

3×7	5×2	2×1
means	means	means
$7 + 7 + 7$	$2 + 2 + 2 + 2 + 2$	$1 + 1$

You can use this to help you multiply signed numbers.

EXPLORE: PRODUCING PRODUCTS

1. Each stapler weighs 20 grams. What will the scale read after the staplers are placed on it?

   Adding 20 three times is the same as multiplying 20 by 3. Finish this sentence: $3 \times 20 =$ ____.

2. What will the scale read after the 4 balloons are attached?

   Adding -30 four times is the same as multiplying -30 by 4. Finish this sentence: $4 \times (-30) =$ ____.

3. If each marble weighs 10 grams, what will the scale read after 2 marbles are removed? What will be the change in the scale reading?

   Removing 10 two times is the same as multiplying 10 by -2. Finish this sentence: $-2 \times 10 =$ ____.

4. What will the scale read after Maurice removes 3 balloons? What will be the change in the scale reading?

   Removing -11 three times is the same as multiplying -11 by -3. Finish this sentence: $-3 \times (-11) =$ ____.

5. If you multiply two signed numbers, how can you tell the sign of the product from the signs of the factors? Explain how to multiply signed numbers.

The answer when you multiply is called the **product.**

These guidelines give a way to tell the sign of a product of two signed numbers.

> The product of two numbers with the *same* signs is *positive.*
>
> $$(+)(+) = (+)$$
> $$(-)(-) = (+)$$
>
> The product of two numbers with *different* signs is *negative.*
>
> $$(+)(-) = (-)$$
> $$(-)(+) = (-)$$

1. What sign is the product of three negative numbers: (−)(−)(−)? Explain.

TRY IT

⋮ Tell whether the product will be positive or negative. Then give the product.

⋮ **a.** $20 \times (-8)$ **b.** $(-11)(-4)$ **c.** $(-25)(10)$ **d.** $-4 \times (-5) \times (-2)$

⋮ Find the missing value.

⋮ **e.** $-10 \times$ ___ $= -150$ **f.** $-20 \times$ ___ $= -400$

Congratulations—you've made it through the hard part! Dividing signed numbers should be easy.

Remember that dividing and multiplying are inverse operations.

$24 \div 6 = 4$	because	$4 \times 6 =$	24
$150 \div 5 = 30$	because	$30 \times 5 =$	150
$-150 \div (-5) = 30$	because	$-5 \times 30 =$	-150
$150 \div (-5) = -30$	because	$-5 \times (-30) =$	150

The answer you get when you divide is called the **quotient.**

These division calculations suggest that the guidelines to determine the sign of a quotient are similar to the guidelines to tell the sign of a product.

The quotient of two numbers that have the *same* signs is *positive.*

$$(+) \div (+) = (+)$$
$$(-) \div (-) = (+)$$

The quotient of two numbers that have *different* signs is *negative.*

$$(+) \div (-) = (-)$$
$$(-) \div (+) = (-)$$

Divide $400 \div (-50)$.

Tyler thinks ...

First, I'll ignore the signs. $400 \div 50$ is 8.

400 and -50 have different signs so the quotient is negative.

So, $400 \div (-50) = -8$.

Desrie thinks ...

For $400 \div (-50)$, I'm looking for $? \times (-50) = 400$.

First, I'll ignore the signs. $8 \cdot 50 = 400$.

The sign is negative because $(-)(-) = (+)$.

So, $400 \div (-50) = -8$.

TRY IT

Divide.

g. $126 \div (-6)$ **h.** $-44 \div 2$ **i.** $35 \div 5$ **j.** $\dfrac{-500}{-50}$ **k.** $\dfrac{-12}{-3}$

REFLECT

1. How can you predict the sign of the product when you multiply two signed numbers?

2. Explain how to do a division calculation with signed numbers.

3. What happens when you multiply a signed number by zero? Explain.

Exercises

CORE

1. Getting Started Which is the correct product for $-5 \times (-3)$, 15 or -15?

The sign of each number is shown. Give the sign of the answer.

2. $+\blacktriangledown \times -\blacksquare$ **3.** $-\blacktriangledown \times -\blacksquare$ **4.** $+\blacktriangledown \div -\blacksquare$

5. $-\blacktriangledown \div -\blacksquare$ **6.** $+\blacksquare \div +\bullet$ **7.** $(-\blacktriangledown \times -\blacksquare) \times +\bullet$

Calculate.

8. $4 \times (-7)$

9. $(-3)(-10)$

10. $7 \cdot (-25)$

11. $75 \div (-25)$

12. $-100 \div 10$

13. $\frac{25}{-2}$

14. Carlito needs to find the quotient $(-4.2) \div (-2)$.
    a. Write a related multiplication sentence to help figure this out.
    b. What does he get if he ignores the signs?
    c. What is the sign of the quotient?
    d. What answer should Carlito give?

15. Chilly Chile Weather forecasters took early morning temperature readings for five consecutive days during mid-winter in southern Chile: 4°C, −2°C, −5°C, 1°C, and 0°C. What was the mean temperature?

16. Which doesn't show a calculation for a quotient?

    (a) $2 \div (-4)$
    (b) $\frac{3}{-2}$
    (c) $(-3)(+1.7)$
    (d) $7\overline{)-3}$
    (e) not here

17. Money Drain Alison writes a check for $25.75 every month to pay for her cable television service. Write a number that shows the effect this payment has on her checking account balance during a 1-year period.

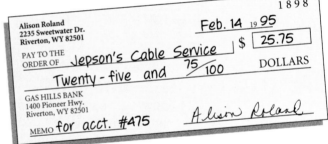

Calculate.

18. $-40 \times (-70)$

19. $(33)(-101)$

20. $750 \div (-25)$

21. $-2.1 \times (-3)$

22. $-30 + 45 - (-20.4)$

23. $\frac{-800}{-50}$

24. Watch that Watch Mario set his watch to the correct time on Sunday. The following Sunday he noticed that the watch was 5 minutes behind. How long would it take for the watch to be 1 hour off?

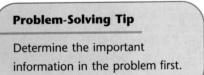

Problem-Solving Tip

Determine the important information in the problem first.

25. Brrr! The higher you go, the colder it gets. For each kilometer that you increase your altitude, the temperature decreases by 7°C. A plane is flying at an altitude of 5 km directly over an airport where the ground temperature is 0°C. What is the temperature outside the airplane?

 ***LOOK BACK***

 26. Smith & Co. puts 6% of an employee's salary into a stock fund. If an
employee earns $23,000, how much money is contributed to the stock fund?
[Previous course]

27. What is a glyph? [1-2]

28. Which choice best describes the value of $18.25 − $8.97? [2-1]
(a) less than $10   (b) more than $10

MORE PRACTICE

**The numbers below are covered by a geometric shape, but the signs are shown.
Give the sign of the answer.**

29. $+\blacktriangledown \div -\blacksquare$

30. $-\blacktriangledown \div -\blacksquare$

31. $(-\blacktriangledown \times -\blacksquare) \div +\bullet$

32. $-\bullet \times -\blacksquare$

33. $-\blacksquare \times +\blacktriangledown$

34. $+\bullet \div (-\blacktriangledown \times +\blacksquare)$

Calculate.

35. $\dfrac{1818}{-18}$

36. -100×14

37. $-12.1 \times (-6)$

38. $12.5 - 7.0 - 2.5 + 17$

39. $12.5 + 7.0 + 2.5 - 17$

40. $\dfrac{-375}{75}$

41. $-30 \times (-72)$

42. $75 \div (-5)$

43. $\dfrac{-2700}{9}$

44. $-20 + 42 - (-20)$

45. $122.3 - 6.0 - 4.5 + 34$

46. $58 - (-21) + (-5)$

47. $-4 \times (-5 + (-2))$

48. $518 - (-20) + (-7)$

49. $15\frac{3}{4} + \left(-2\frac{1}{2}\right)$

MORE MATH REASONING

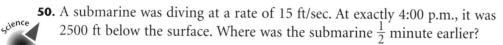 **50.** A submarine was diving at a rate of 15 ft/sec. At exactly 4:00 p.m., it was
2500 ft below the surface. Where was the submarine $\frac{1}{2}$ minute earlier?

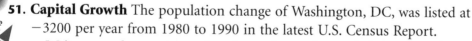 **51. Capital Growth** The population change of Washington, DC, was listed at
−3200 per year from 1980 to 1990 in the latest U.S. Census Report.
a. Write a number sentence that shows the total population gain or loss
during that 10-year period.
b. If the population in the 1990 census was 606,900, what was the population
in the 1980 census?

Making Connections

← C O N N E C T → *You've seen that you need both positive and negative numbers to handle applications from social studies, science, business, and many other fields. You've used several different models including algebra tiles, balloons, and a number line to help you understand signed number relationships.*

EXPLORE: A PERFECT MODEL?

1. For each of the four arithmetic operations—adding, subtracting, multiplying, and dividing—make up a display poster. Illustrate how to do sample calculations. Use your favorite models—tiles, balloons, or a number line. Be sure to show illustrations for different combinations of signs.

2. Did you use the same model for all four of your posters? Why or why not?

MATERIALS

*Poster paper
Colored pencils or crayons*

REFLECT

1. How do you add numbers if both are negative? if one is positive and one is negative?
2. How is subtracting signed numbers related to adding signed numbers? Illustrate with an example.
3. How can you tell the sign of the answer when you multiply two signed numbers?
4. What will be the sign of the quotient for $-15 \div (-3)$? Explain your thinking.
5. Which model—tiles, balloons, or a number line—do you like best for thinking about signed numbers? Why?

Self-Assessment

Calculate.

1. $-17 - (-23)$

2. $47 + (-31) - 10$

3. $-2.3 \times 4 \times (-5)$

4. $(-5 + (-3) - 2) \div 3$

5. $-2.3 \times 4 - (-1)$

6. $4 - (-1) \times (-2.3)$

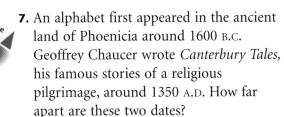

 7. An alphabet first appeared in the ancient land of Phoenicia around 1600 B.C. Geoffrey Chaucer wrote *Canterbury Tales,* his famous stories of a religious pilgrimage, around 1350 A.D. How far apart are these two dates?

What is the missing number?

8. $-17.4 + (-10.1) = \underline{\quad}$

9. $\underline{\quad} - (-100) = 138.3$

10. $-11.1 \times \underline{\quad} = 88.8$

11. $\underline{\quad} \div -6 = -126$

Find the numbers described. If no number fits the description, write _Impossible_.

12. Find a number that, when added to itself, gives -25.

13. Find a number that, when multiplied by itself, gives -16.

14. Find two numbers such that when one is divided by the other, the answer is -18.

15. Find two negative numbers such that when one is subtracted from the other, the answer is positive.

16. On a calculator, the screen shows a result of 45.87659. What is this result rounded to the nearest hundredth? [2-1]

17. In 1991, of the 102,786,000 people in the work force, about 18% were represented by a labor union. [Previous course]
   a. What percentage were not represented by a labor union?
   b. How many workers were not represented by a labor union?

18. Spreading the Debt In 1992, the U.S. national debt was about $4.3 trillion, and there were about 250 million Americans. What number sentence tells how much each of us would owe if the national debt were divided evenly among every man, woman, and child? Use this example to explain why a negative number divided by a positive number gives a negative number.

19. **Spell Check** Some teachers mark −2 for each
    misspelled word in an essay and −3 for each
    grammar error. The score for a perfect paper is 100.
    a. If the teacher returns a paper that is perfect in
       every other way, but has 3 misspelled words and
       4 grammar mistakes, what is the score?
    b. What is the fewest number of mistakes you could
       make of these types and still score 85?
    c. What is the greatest number of mistakes you
       could make of these types and still pass with a 70?

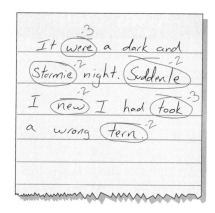

20. What is the answer called when numbers are multiplied?
    (a) sum   (b) quotient   (c) term   (d) product   (e) not here

21. **Par for the Course** Although golf is popular all over the world, it is a
    national passion in Scotland. In golf, the lowest score wins. Par is the
    expected number of strokes to complete the course. A player whose
    score is −10 (read as 10 under par) has completed the course using 10
    fewer strokes than the expected number. If golfer A gets a score of
    −12 and golfer B gets a score of −15, who wins? By how much?

22. The highest peak in Africa is Mount Kilimanjaro in Tanzania. It is
    19,340 feet above sea level. The lowest point is Lake Assal in Djibouti.
    It is 512 feet below sea level. What is the range of altitudes?

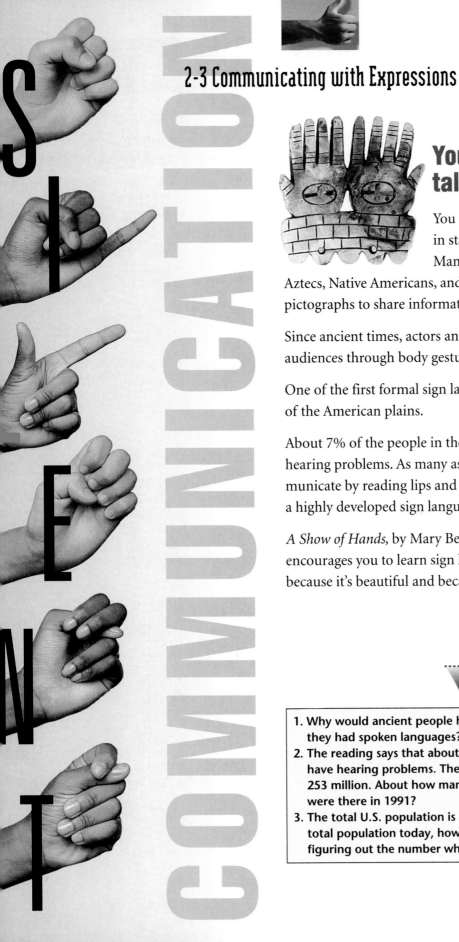

S I L E N T

2-3 Communicating with Expressions

You don't have to talk to communicate.

You don't even have to write in standard alphabets to communicate. Many early cultures, including Mayans, Aztecs, Native Americans, and Egyptians, used carvings and pictographs to share information.

Since ancient times, actors and dancers have spoken to their audiences through body gestures.

One of the first formal sign languages was used by native tribes of the American plains.

About 7% of the people in the United States are deaf or have hearing problems. As many as 14 million of them can communicate by reading lips and speaking. But many others use a highly developed sign language.

A Show of Hands, by Mary Beth Sullivan and Linda Bourke, encourages you to learn sign language "because it's expressive, because it's beautiful and because it's lots of fun."

COMMUNICATION

1. Why would ancient people have used sign language even if they had spoken languages?
2. The reading says that about 7% of people in the United States have hearing problems. The U.S. population in 1991 was about 253 million. About how many deaf or hearing-impaired people were there in 1991?
3. The total U.S. population is always changing. If *P* stands for the total population today, how would you write an expression for figuring out the number who are deaf or hearing impaired?

← C O N N E C T → *You have been looking at signed numbers and ways to do signed number arithmetic. Now, by using variables and signed numbers, you will be able to write algebraic expressions.*

In mathematics, we communicate by using the language of algebra. Ordinary expressions in words can be written as **algebraic expressions,** which use two kinds of quantities—constants and variables.

the number of sides in a square

the number of cents in a dollar

the number of feet in a mile

These quantities don't change. They are constants. A square has 4 sides; a dollar has 100 cents; a mile has 5280 feet. **Constants** are quantities with values that do not change.

your pulse rate or number of heart beats per minute

the number of people who become U.S. citizens each year

the price of a loaf of bread in the supermarket

Each quantity here is a variable. A **variable** is a quantity with a value that can change or vary.

You have seen variables in formulas such as that for the perimeter of a triangle: $P = a + b + c$.

You have seen variables in rules, such as the commutative rule: $a + b = b + a$.

TRY IT

Decide whether each quantity is a constant or a variable.

a. the number of donuts in a dozen

b. the temperature of a cup of coffee

c. the percentage rate of state sales tax in Ohio in 1990

d. the amount of state sales tax you pay in Ohio when you buy something

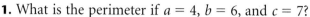

EXPLORE: MODEL EXPRESSIONS

The letters *a*, *b*, and *c* are the lengths of the sides of this triangle. The expression $a + b + c$ gives the perimeter of a triangle.

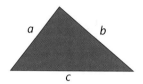

1. What is the perimeter if $a = 4$, $b = 6$, and $c = 7$?

2. Does the same expression work if $a = 16$, $b = 20$, and $c = 24$?

The rule $x + y = y + x$ tells us that we can add two numbers in any order and the sums will be the same.

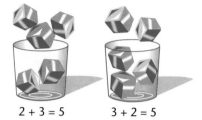

3. Which are true?

$3 + 4 = 4 + 3$

$3 - 4 = 4 - 3$

$3 \times 4 = 4 \times 3$

$3 \div 4 = 4 \div 3$

$2 + 3 = 5 \qquad 3 + 2 = 5$

Suppose your math teacher said, "I'm adding 10 points to everyone's grade, no matter what the grade is."

Your grade is **x**.
Your grade will be **x + 10**.

4. Think about these situations.

Suppose your grade is 76. What will it be?

Suppose your grade is 90. What will it be?

What if your grade is 100. What will it be?

CONSIDER

Think about the ways that variables and expressions were used in the Explore above.

1. Which tells you a relationship between different quantities?
2. Which tells you a method for doing something?
3. Which tells you a relationship that is true for all numbers?

Variables are used when we change word expressions into algebraic expressions.

EXAMPLE

1. Suppose x represents an unknown length. Write an expression for the following.

a. twice that length $2x$

b. 5 less than that length $x - 5$

c. that length decreased by 5 $x - 5$

d. half that length $\frac{1}{2}x$ or $\frac{x}{2}$

Algebraic expressions can be modeled by algebra tiles.

You've already used unit tiles to represent the constants 1 and -1.

Now you will use x-tiles to represent a variable.

1   –1

x $-x$

We put tiles next to each other to show expressions.

Word phrase:

Two more than three times a number.

3 x-tiles

and
2 unit tiles

Expression:

$3x + 2$

$3x$ means $3 \cdot x$ or $x + x + x$.

EXAMPLE

2. What expression is shown by the tiles?

Because there are two x-tiles, we write $2x$.
For the three negative unit tiles, we write -3.

The expression is $2x - 3$.

3. Write an algebraic expression that follows this rule: Cut my portion (*p*) off the 24-inch submarine sandwich. Divide what's left evenly among 4 people.

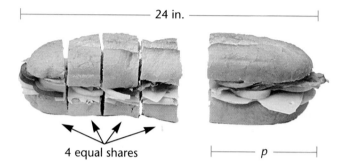

|⟵ ———— 24 in. ———— ⟶|

4 equal shares |⟵ —— *p* —— ⟶|

The expression $24 - p$ is the amount remaining after *p* is taken away. This amount must be evenly divided by 4.

So the expression is $(24 - p) \div 4$ or $\dfrac{24 - p}{4}$.

A fraction bar is commonly used to show division.

Write an algebraic expression. Then model it with algebra tiles.

e. 5 more than 2 times a number
f. twice the length of the rectangle, less 1 cm
g. 8 mi/hr more than 3 times as fast as last year's winning speed
h. 11° more than today's temperature
i. 3 miles, less twice the distance

CONSIDER

4. Identify the constants in $3x + 2$. Identify the variables.
5. What are the arithmetic operations in $3x + 2$?
6. Can there be two different pictures with tiles that both show the same expression? Explain.
7. Must *x* be used as the variable when the value is unknown?

In Example 2 we used *x* to represent the unknown, while in Example 3, we used *p*. You can use *any* letter to represent the unknown in an algebraic expression.

1. The side of a square measures *s*. The expression 4*s* gives the perimeter of, or distance around the square. Is 4 a variable or a constant? Is *s* a variable or a constant? Explain.
2. Can the same quantity be both a constant and a variable?
3. Is *x* an algebraic expression? Why or why not?
4. An expression for the area of a rectangle is ℓ*w*. What does the expression mean? Why does the expression use two different variables?

Exercises

CORE

1. **Getting Started** What expression do these algebra tiles show?

Decide whether each quantity is a constant or a variable. Explain your choice.

2. the value of an ounce of gold

3. the number of justices on the U.S. Supreme Court

4. the length of a centipede

5. the speed of light

6. how long it takes to eat breakfast

Draw algebra tiles for each expression.

7. $x + 3$ 8. $4x - 2$ 9. $2 - 3x$

10. Which expression shows "5 times a number, *n*, decreased by 7"?

  (a) $5(n - 7)$ (b) $7 - 5n$ (c) $5n - 7$ (d) $\frac{5n}{7}$ (e) not here

11. Write an algebraic expression for the number of nickels in *d* dollars. (Hint: Find a pattern.)

For Exercises 12-16, write an algebraic expression.

12. *t* degrees more than 98.7°

13. $\frac{1}{3}$ as long as *j*, decreased by 3.54 inches

> **Problem-Solving Tip**
>
> Draw a sketch if it helps.

14. 5 minutes more than twice the number of minutes Alvin jogged

15. remove 5 feet from the length, *v*, then divide the remainder into 7 equal pieces

16. the number of years equal to *t* months

Write a possible word phrase for each algebraic expression.

17. $15t - 3.2$

18. $1.25 + 3t$

19. $\frac{k}{9} - 0.3$

20. Each sketch below shows the expression $5x + 8$ in a different way. Draw three similar sketches to show the expression $6x + 9$.

  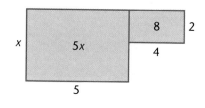

21. The area of a rectangle is the length times the width. The large rectangle has a small rectangle cut from its corner. Measurements are in inches. Write an algebraic expression for the area of the shaded part.

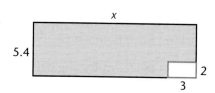

Use the pictures to write algebraic expressions.

 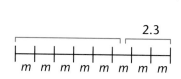 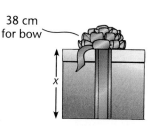

Front view   Top view

22. the total weight on the scale

23. the length of the unlabeled line

24. the length of ribbon needed to wrap the gift

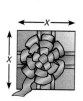 *LOOK AHEAD*

Calculate.

25. $3 \cdot 4 - 7$

26. $3(21.3) - 7$

27. $-3 \times 21.3 + 5$

28. $3 - 2(-4)$

29. $30 + 0.25 \cdot 52$

30. $1.8(-5) + 32$

MORE PRACTICE

Decide whether each quantity is a constant or a variable.

31. the radius of a circle

32. the number of days in a week

33. the speed of a car on a highway

34. the number of terms that a U.S. President serves

35. the number of meters in a kilometer

36. the amount of a monthly telephone bill

Draw algebra tiles for each expression.

37. $x - 2$

38. $2x - 3$

39. $1 - 2x$

Write an algebraic expression.

40. the number of inches in y feet, less $5\frac{1}{2}$ inches

41. the number of pennies worth the same as q quarters and 1 dime

42. the number of days in n weeks minus 2 days

43. $5.50 less than 3 times the money Gil makes working for h hours at $4.35 an hour

44. double the record for the half-mile run, t, increased by 6 seconds

45. 15% of your salary, less $48

46. 10 years more than $\frac{1}{2}$ your age

MORE MATH REASONING

47. Health Note Systolic pressure keeps blood flowing through your body. Normal systolic pressure depends on your age. Multiply your age by 0.54, then add 110 to get a close value for normal systolic pressure.

a. What quantity is variable when calculating normal systolic pressure? Write an algebraic expression for normal systolic pressure.

b. Does normal systolic pressure increase or decrease with age?

c. Use your expression to find your normal systolic pressure.

d. About how old is someone whose normal systolic pressure is 130?

e. What physical reasons might account for change in systolic pressure with age?

> **Problem-Solving Tip**
>
> Analyze your expression.

48. Temperatures are measured using the Fahrenheit scale in the United States. Most other countries use the Celsius scale. To change a Fahrenheit reading to Celsius, subtract 32, then multiply by $\frac{5}{9}$.

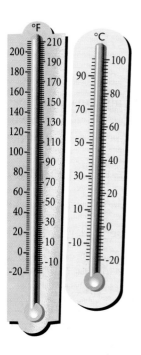

a. Write an algebraic expression for changing a Fahrenheit temperature to Celsius. Use F as the Fahrenheit temperature.

b. If a temperature is a positive number on the Fahrenheit scale, will it be more or less on the Celsius scale? Explain.

c. If a temperature is a positive number on the Fahrenheit scale, will it be a positive number on the Celsius scale? Explain.

d. Normal room temperature is 68°F. What temperature is this on the Celsius scale?

> **Problem-Solving Tip**
>
> Make sure your answer makes sense.

2-3 PART B Evaluating Expressions

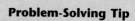

← CONNECT →   *You have seen that algebraic expressions model real-life situations. In this part, you will replace variables with numbers in an algebraic expression.*

To **evaluate an expression** you replace the variables with numbers. Then you calculate to find the value of the expression.

In the same way a substitute replaces a player in a game, a number can substitute for a variable in an expression.

Manufacturing companies use algebraic expressions to help manage warehouse space. They must have enough stock on hand to fill orders, but not so much that it gets old or out of date. Awesome Products stocks three sizes of TV monitors.

Model S (small) takes 4 square feet of storage space.

Model M (medium) takes 6 square feet of storage space.

Model L (large) takes 10 square feet of storage space.

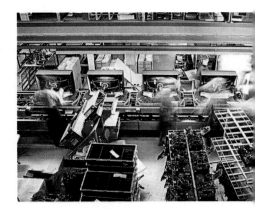

1. If s is the number of model S in stock, what does $4s$ represent?
2. If m is the number of model M in stock, what does $6m$ represent?
3. If ℓ is the number of model L in stock, what does 10ℓ represent?
   This expression shows how much storage space is used by these three models:
   $4s + 6m + 10\ell$.
4. Suppose $s = 20$, $m = 50$, and $\ell = 25$. Find the value of $4s$, $6m$, and 10ℓ. Then find the value of $4s + 6m + 10\ell$.
5. Refer to the Stock Goals at the right. How many square feet of storage space are needed at the lowest stock level? at the highest?
6. Find some values of s, m, and ℓ that are close to using the maximum storage space shown on the Stock Goals sign.
7. The warehouse manager reports that there are 25 model S, 35 model M, and 40 model L in stock. What can you learn from this report?

Stock Goals

S between 15 and 30
M between 40 and 80
L between 20 and 40

Maximum storage space
is 700 square feet.

CONSIDER

1. What are some costs that could result if a company has too much stock in its warehouse?
2. What other expressions can you think of that would be useful in a business?

An algebraic expression can have different values. It depends on the numbers being substituted for the variables.

EXAMPLE

1. If C is the Celsius temperature, the expression $1.8C + 32$ gives the temperature on the Fahrenheit scale. A radio announcer in Detroit hears that the temperature is $-5°C$ in Paris. What Fahrenheit temperature should the announcer tell his listeners? The expression $1.8C + 32$ gives the Fahrenheit temperature.

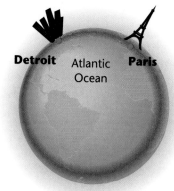

Detroit   Atlantic   **Paris**
      Ocean

$1.8C + 32$
$= 1.8(-5) + 32$ Replace C by -5.
$= -9 + 32$

The radio announcer should tell listeners that the Paris temperature of $-5°C$ is $23°F$.

In the example above, the variable C is replaced by a negative number. Replacements for variables can be positive, zero, or negative depending on the situation.

EXAMPLE

2. A pizzeria decides to price its pizzas by their areas. The small pizza has a 4-inch radius, the medium pizza has a 5-inch radius, and the large pizza has a 6-inch radius. Find the area of the large pizza. Decide if $0.10 per square inch is a reasonable price.

Evaluate the expression πr^2 for the value $r = 6$ in.

Large, $r = 6$ in.: $\pi r^2 \approx (3.14)(6^2)$
$\approx (3.14)(36)$
≈ 113.04 in.^{2}

At 10 cents per square inch, the price would be $11.30, which seems reasonable.

> **Remember—**
> π is a symbol that stands for a special constant whose value is about 3.14.

TRY IT

Evaluate each expression.

a. $y - 5.3$ for $y = -3.1$ **b.** $5t^2 - 2.3$ when $t = -3$
c. πr^2 when $r = 10$ **d.** $4x + 6y - 40$ if $x = 10$, $y = 5$
e. $a + b + c + d$ for $a = 10$, $b = 3$, $c = -5$, $d = -1$

1. Why would you use an algebraic expression to model a calculation?
2. When you evaluate an algebraic expression, will the result always be a number?
3. Give an expression whose value is always positive no matter what number you use to replace the variable.
4. Is the arithmetic expression $5\frac{1}{2} - 3$ the same as the algebraic expression $5x - 3$ when $x = \frac{1}{2}$? Explain.
5. Suppose you need to write an expression for the perimeter of a rectangle. How many variables do you need to use? Why?

Exercises

CORE

1. **Getting Started** Judith is evaluating the expression $2x + 2y$ for $x = 4$ and $y = 3$.

$$2x + 2y$$
$$= 2(4) + 2(3) \quad \text{Replace } x \text{ with 4 and } y \text{ with 3.}$$

If she completes the calculation correctly, what will she get as her answer?

2. **Green Thumb** Jeremiah knows that the expression $2\ell + 2w$ gives the perimeter of his flower garden. What does ℓ represent? w? What is the garden's perimeter?

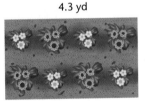

4.3 yd

2.5 yd

Calculate.

3. $17.5(18^2 - 6.4)$

4. $280 - (4.1)(-5)$

5. $\frac{24}{3} + (7)(5^2)$

Evaluate each expression.

6. $3n - 7$ when $n = 1000$

7. $n^2 + 2n + 3$ for $n = 10$

8. $15 - 2x$ for $x = 3.5$

9. $45 + 3f$ when $f = -19$

10. $4x - 3y + 5$ if $x = 3$, $y = -4$

11. $2x^2 - 3xy + y^2$ if $x = 5$, $y = -2$

12. Mr. Jones told the class, "Evaluate the expression $2x - 5$." No one raised a hand. Finally, Julia said, "I think we need more information, Mr. Jones." What did she mean?

13. How Long Can They Get? Fingernails grow about 1.5 inches per year. If the length of the cuticle is 0.5 inches when your nail starts to grow, the expression $1.5y + 0.5$ gives the total length of your fingernail.

  a. What does y represent?

  b. How long would your nail be if you didn't cut it for 10 years? for 20 years?

  c. How long would it take to grow the world's record fingernail of 37 inches?

> **Problem-Solving Tip**
>
> Guess and check.

14. Bridging the Gap Metal expands or contracts as temperature changes. When a highway bridge is built, a small gap is left between bridge sections to allow for these changes. If t represents a temperature on the Celsius scale, the expression $21 - 0.4t$ is the width of the gap in millimeters.

  a. What is the width of the gap on a hot summer day if the temperature is 25°C?

  b. What is the width of the gap on a cold winter night when the temperature is −10°C?

  c. What is the width of the gap when the temperature, 0°C, is just cold enough to freeze a small puddle of water?

15. Weather reporters on TV use the expression $1.8C + 32$ to change a temperature from Celsius to Fahrenheit. Use the expression to change the five Celsius readings to Fahrenheit. Then plot the resulting ordered pairs (C, F) on a coordinate grid like the one shown. What is the pattern in the points?

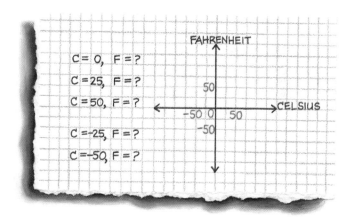

LOOK BACK

16. Calculate $(-2)^2 - 4(-3) + 7$. [2-2]

17. As a lab supervisor, you are told the new budget allows up to a 12% staff increase. If you now have 23 lab technicians, how many more can you hire? [2-1]

18. How would you locate a piece of data in a spreadsheet that is in cell B3? [1-1]

MORE PRACTICE

Evaluate the expression.

19. $4f - 17$ if $f = 21$

20. $n^2 + 2n + 3$ if $n = 10$

21. $\frac{x}{6} + 28$ if $x = 60$

22. $10(x - 4)$ if $x = 20$

23. $\frac{2}{3}h - 20$ if $h = 30$

24. $3(x + 15)$ if $x = -4$

25. $x^2 - (10 - 1)$ if $x = 10$

26. $5x - 8$ if $x = 7.1$

27. $y - (5.3 - 3.3)$ if $y = 12$

28. $n^2(11 - 5)$ if $n = 8$

29. $12x + 8y + 7$ if $x = 2, y = -3$

30. $x^2 + 2x + 4 - 3y$ if $x = 2, y = -3$

31. Mouth Watering A jumbo bucket of chicken costs $10. Adding or subtracting a piece of chicken in the bucket changes the price by $0.50 a piece. Let p represent the change in the number of pieces. The expression for the price of the bucket is $10 + 0.50p$.

a. How much will a bucket cost if Pearl wants four extra pieces?

b. How much will a bucket cost if Nick asks to take out two pieces?

c. How much will a bucket cost if Zeke wants it just the way it comes?

MORE MATH REASONING

32. Wire Code The National Electrical Code specifies that up to 40% of a conduit, a pipe for wiring, can be filled with electrical wires.

a. Complete the table below.

b. Can Steve run three types of wire through the conduit without violating the code? Explain.

c. Why is 60% of the space in a conduit unavailable for wiring?

Product	Diameter	Area of 1 End	Number Needed	Total Area
Conduit	1.25 in.		//////////	//////////
Wire A	0.27 in.		3	
Wire B	0.14 in.		12	
Wire C	0.18 in.		5	
Total area of the ends of the wires:				

33. Dialing Dollars The cost of a weekday phone call from Raleigh to Durham is $0.31 for the first minute and $0.22 for each additional minute. Write an expression for the cost of a call. How long could you talk for $2.00 or less?

Adding and Subtracting Using Tiles

← CONNECT → *You have seen how to use variables in algebraic expressions and how to evaluate them. In this part, you will see how you can use tiles to add and subtract algebraic expressions.*

Situations often call for combining two or more algebraic expressions.

Earlier you used unit tiles and x-tiles to help you work with signed numbers and variables in expressions.

Now we will also use x^2-tiles. As with other tiles, a square tile and its opposite add up to 0.

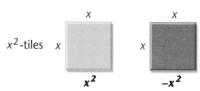

These tiles model the expression

$2x^2 - 3x - 4$.

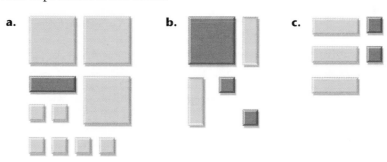

TRY IT

What expression is modeled?

a.

b.

c.

Use tiles to model these expressions.

d. $x^2 + 5$ **e.** $x^2 - 2x + 3$ **f.** $2x^2 + 3x - 2$

Now you will explore the idea of adding and subtracting expressions by using tiles.

To add two expressions, combine their tiles to get the sum.

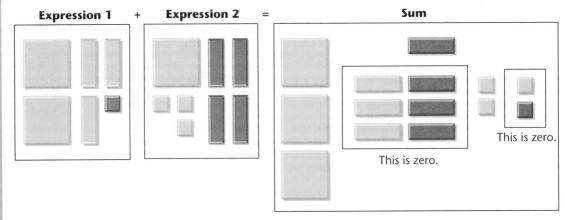

Expression 1 + **Expression 2** = **Sum**

This is zero.

This is zero.

1. What two expressions are being added? What is the sum? Explain the zero combinations.
2. Use algebra tiles or make drawings to add these expressions.
   a. $(5x + 7) + (3x - 2)$ **b.** $(4x - 3) + (-2x - 7)$
   c. $(4x^2 + 5x - 6) + (2x^2 - x + 4)$
3. How could you add algebraic expressions if you didn't have tiles and you didn't want to make drawings?
4. Test your method by using it on the three examples above. Do you get the same answer in each case as you did using tiles?

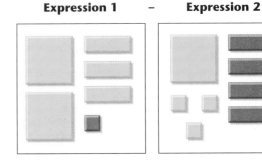

Expression 1 − **Expression 2**

In 2-2 Part C, you learned to subtract a negative number by adding its opposite. Now to subtract an expression, you can just add its opposite expression.

To make the opposite of an expression, replace each tile by its opposite.

Opposite of
Expression 2

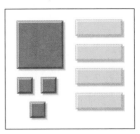

5. Compare Expression 2 and the Opposite of Expression 2. How can you tell they are opposites?
6. What are the two original expressions? What is the opposite expression? What is the answer?
7. Use tiles to show $5x + 1$, then show its opposite. Use that result to find $(7x - 4) - (5x + 1)$.

1. Use or think about algebra tiles to add
   $(x^2 + 2x - 1) + (3x^2 - 5x + 2)$.

   So the sum is $4x^2 - 3x + 1$.

Think:

2. Find the opposite of the second expression,
   $3x^2 - 5x + 2$.

   The expression is $-3x^2 + 5x - 2$.

Think:

3. Use the same expressions to subtract.
   Find $(x^2 + 2x - 1) - (3x^2 - 5x + 2)$.

   Using the opposite expression in Example 2,
   the combined result is:

   $-2x^2 + 7x - 3$.

Think:

Use or think about algebra tiles to complete this table.

	Expression 1	Expression 2	Expression 1 + Opposite of Expression 2
g.	$3x - 11$	$6x + 2$	
h.	$3x^2 + 5x + 7$	$2x^2 + 5x - 8$	
i.	$7x^2 + 4x - 10$	$3x^2 - 3$	

1. Is the expression $x + 1$ positive or negative? Is the expression $x^2 + 1$ positive or negative?
2. Sandra is adding two expressions with algebra tiles. When may she remove tiles?
3. When do two expressions have a sum of zero? Give an example.
4. How is the rule about subtracting signed numbers like the rule for subtracting expressions?

Exercises

CORE

1. Getting Started The picture shows Alice using algebra tiles to add $(2x^2 + 2x - 3) + (-4x + 1)$.

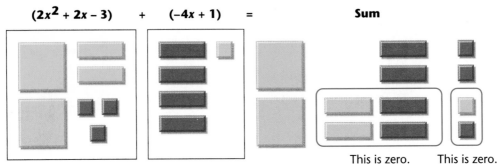

$(2x^2 + 2x - 3)$ + $(-4x + 1)$ =   **Sum**

This is zero.   This is zero.

What is the sum?

2. Draw algebra tiles to show each of the expressions $(x^2 + 2x - 3)$ and $(-5x + 7)$. Next replace $(-5x + 7)$ by its opposite. Then find the difference, $(x^2 + 2x - 3) - (-5x + 7)$.

Use or think about algebra tiles to combine these expressions.

3. $(3x + 5) - (x + 2)$ **4.** $(7x - 3) + (-4x + 7)$

5. $(2x^2 + 7x + 6) + (x^2 + 3x - 4)$ **6.** $(3x^2 + 6) - (5x - 6)$

Use or think about algebra tiles to complete this table.

	Expression 1	**Expression 2**	**Expression 1 + Opposite of Expression 2**
7.	$2x - 18$	$33x + 7$	
8.	$4x^2 + 6x + 9$	$2x^2 + 5x - 8$	
9.	$3x^2 + 2x - 10$	$3x^2 + 3$	

10. Use the variable x to write an expression for the perimeter of this rectangle.

$x - 2$

4

Find the missing term.

11. $(6x + \underline{\hspace{0.5cm}}) + (2x + 4) = 8x + 7$

12. $(x^2 + 8x + 6) - (4x^2 + \underline{\hspace{0.5cm}} + 1) = -3x^2 + 2x + 5$

13. Write an expression for the area of the shaded part.

T

3

13

5

LOOK AHEAD

14. Does $5(2 + 3) = 5 \cdot 2 + 5 \cdot 3$? How do you know?

Evaluate both expressions.

15. $5(x + 7)$ and $5x + 35$ if $x = -2$

16. $-2(y + 4)$ and $-2y - 8$ if $y = 5$

MORE PRACTICE

Use or think about algebra tiles to combine these expressions.

17. $(5x - 1) + (10x^2 + 7x)$

18. $(7x + 4) + (-7x + 4) + (2x)$

19. $(10x - 25) - (3x + 14)$

20. $(-5y^2 + y + 6) + (-3y^2 - 2y + 1)$

21. $(4x^2 + 5x + 8) + (2x^2 + 7x - 5)$

22. $(3m - 2p + 8) - (2p + 5)$

23. $(x^2 + 28x + 14) - (3x^2 + 10x - 10)$

24. $(x^2 + y^2 + 5) + (3x^2 - 2y^2 - 7)$

25. $(20x^2 + 3) + (14x^2 - 10) + (5x^2 - 8)$

26. $(-6m + 4) - (6m + 4)$

27. $(10x - 25) + (15x + 25) + (7x)$

28. $(7x + 3y + 8) + (-2x - 5y - 7)$

Use or think about algebra tiles to complete this table.

	Expression 1	Expression 2	Expression 1 + Opposite of Expression 2
29.	$5x - 10$	$21x + 7$	
30.	$3x^2 + x + 9$	$x^2 + 4x - 11$	
31.	$x^2 + 12x - 11$	$-7x^2 + 3$	

32. Write an expression for the perimeter of this triangle.

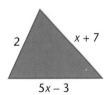

Find the missing term.

33. $(4x + \underline{\quad}) + (x + 4) = 5x - 17$

34. $(x^2 + 8x + \underline{\quad}) - (\underline{\quad} + 7x + 4) = -3x^2 + x + 11$

MORE MATH REASONING

35. Planning for Profit The expression $xy - 500$ describes the profit expected for a dance. The price of a ticket is x, the number of people who would buy tickets at that price is y, and 500 is the expense of hiring a band and renting a room.

a. Give five reasonable values for the price of a ticket, x.

b. For each of the five x values above, estimate a reasonable y value.

c. Evaluate the expression $xy - 500$ for your five pairs of x's and y's.

d. What is the price of a ticket that will produce the biggest profit for your dance?

36. The expression $ax^2 + 3x - 4$ is equal to 1 when x is 1. What is the value of a?

2-3
PART D Using the Distributive Property

. . . .

← CONNECT →   *You have added and subtracted expressions using algebra tiles. In this part, you will see that the distributive property gives you another way to think about these operations.*

EXPLORE: WRECK TANGLE

MATERIALS

Algebra tiles

1. The algebra tiles below model the expression $3(2x - 1)$. If the dotted lines were not there, how would you write the expression?

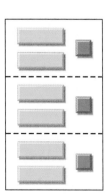

2. Write two different expressions for each group of algebra tiles. (Hint: For one of the expressions, ignore the dotted lines.)

a. 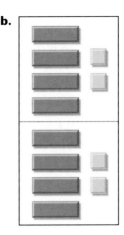 **b.** 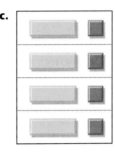 **c.**

3. Create an algebra tile model for the expression $3(x - 4)$. Create an algebra tile model for the expression $3x - 12$. What is the difference between your two models?

4. Create an algebra tile model for the expression $6x + 2$. What is another expression for the same algebra tile model?

You just explored an important property called the distributive property.

THE DISTRIBUTIVE PROPERTY
For any numbers a, b, c,
$a(b + c) = ab + ac$ and $(b + c)a = ba + ca.$

We can use this property to write $5(10 + 7)$ as $5 \cdot 10 + 5 \cdot 7$.

Note that both expressions have the same value.

$$5(10 + 7) = 5(17) \qquad \text{and} \qquad 5 \cdot 10 + 5 \cdot 7 = 50 + 35$$
$$= 85 \qquad\qquad\qquad\qquad\qquad = 85$$

CONSIDER

?

1. Which expression is easier to compute mentally, $5(10 + 7)$ or $5 \cdot 10 + 5 \cdot 7$? Why?

The distributive property is also true for subtraction: $a(b - c) = ab - ac.$

EXAMPLE

Use the distributive property to write a new expression that has the same value.

1. $3(5 + 10)$

$3(5 + 10) = 3 \cdot 5 + 3 \cdot 10$

	(5 + 10)			5			10
3	45	=	3	15	+	3	30

> **Problem-Solving Tip**
>
> Draw a diagram.

Check:

$3(5 + 10) \overset{?}{=} 3 \cdot 5 + 3 \cdot 10$

$3(15) \overset{?}{=} 15 + 30$

$45 = 45$

Both expressions have the same value.

You can use the distributive property to rewrite algebraic expressions without parentheses. When you do this, you **simplify** the expression.

EXAMPLES

Simplify each expression.

2. $4(3b - 1) = 4 \cdot 3b - 4 \cdot 1$
$\qquad = 12b - 4$

$4(3b - 1)$

3. $(3x^2 + 4x - 5)(-4)$
$\qquad = 3x^2 \cdot (-4) + 4x \cdot (-4) - 5(-4)$
$\qquad = -12x^2 - 16x + 20$

$(3x^2 + 4x - 5)(-4)$

In an algebraic expression, the parts that are added or subtracted are called **terms** of the expression.

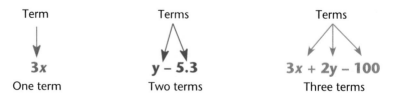

Term	Terms	Terms
$3x$	$y - 5.3$	$3x + 2y - 100$
One term	Two terms	Three terms

Simplify each expression.

a. $3(4a - 2)$ **b.** $-4(x + 3)$ **c.** $(x + 2y)5$ **d.** $-3(2y^2 + 4y - 1)$

1. How could you use the distributive property to calculate $8(15)$ mentally?

2. Why do you think that this property is called the distributive property?

3. Why do you get the same expression when you simplify $2(x + 4)$ and $(x + 4)2$?

Exercises

CORE

1. Getting Started Clarissa starts using the distributive property to rewrite $-3(4x + 7)$.

$$-3(4x + 7) = -3 \cdot 4x + (-3) \cdot (7)$$
$$= \boxed{?}$$

$$-3 \, (4x \ + 7)$$

What expression should she write down to finish her solution?

Simplify.

2. $7(6x + 4)$

3. $(x - 20)(-5)$

4. $-2(4.3x^2 - 8x - 1)$

5. $5(2x^2 + 10x + 7)$

6. $-3(10y - 3)$

7. $\left(\frac{1}{4}d^2 + d\right)100$

8. Going in Style Four siblings plan to rent a limousine for their parent's thirtieth anniversary. They will each pay $\frac{1}{4}$ of the cost. It costs \$55 an hour for the limousine and driver. The expression for the total cost is given by $55H + 40$, where H is the number of hours used, and \$40 is the tip. How much should each pay? (Hint: Write an expression using the distributive property.)

9. Find an expression in the columns on the right to match each expression in the column on the left. Some expressions will not be used.

a. $3(a + 5)$ $3a + 5$ $21b$

b. $(12b)6$ $18b$ $30x$

c. $7x - 5x$ $3a + 15$ 2

d. $9b + 12b$ $9 + 12b$ $72b$

e. $(4x - x)10$ $2x$ 30

10. Heathcliff and Cathy Karl works as a student assistant. He processed an order for the book *Wuthering Heights* for the English department. Let t represent the cost of a teacher's edition and s represent the cost of a student edition of the book.

a. Write an expression for the cost of 2 teacher's editions.

b. Write an expression for the cost of 24 student editions.

c. Write an expression for the total cost of 2 teacher's editions and 24 student editions.

d. Show another way to write the same expression.

Laurence Olivier and Merle Oberon in the 1939 film adaptation of Emily Brontë's Wuthering Heights

LOOK AHEAD

What is the opposite of each number?

11. 1 **12.** 3 **13.** -12 **14.** -1

Subtract.

15. $5 - 2$ **16.** $5 - (-2)$ **17.** $-5 - 2$ **18.** $(-3) - (-7)$

Use the distributive property to do some "hard" calculations mentally.

19. $12(21) = 12(20 + 1) = 12(20) + 12(1) = ?$

20. $3(299) = 3(300 - 1) = 3(300) - 3(1) = ?$

MORE PRACTICE

Simplify.

21. $7(3x + 11)$

22. $3(4x^2 + 2x - 6)$

23. $(x^2 + 8)5$

24. $-3(2a^2 + a)$

25. $(m - 35)(-2)$

26. $-2(b^2 + 5b + 8)$

27. $(3x + 2y + 11)7$

28. $\frac{1}{3}(30x^2 + 45x - 6)$

29. $-4(2x^2 - 5)$

30. Write a simplified expression for the area of this rectangular patio.

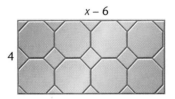

Evaluate.

31. $3(x^2 + 4x + 9)$ if $x = 3$

32. $(4y^2 + 9) + (8y^2 + 18)$ if $y = -7$

33. $(a^2 + 7) + (a^2 + a - 6)$ if $a = -2$

MORE MATH REASONING

Industry

34. Explain how you can tell that the salesperson who entered this into the sales register didn't know about the distributive property.

```
One shirt              $15.75
           Discount   $1.58
One shirt              $15.75
           Discount   $1.58
One shirt              $15.75
           Discount   $1.58
One shirt              $15.75
           Discount   $1.58
One shirt              $15.75
           Discount   $1.58
   Subtotal:           $78.75
   Less discount        $7.90
   Total            $70.85
```

35. Tax Your Brain! For a sales tax of 7%, the total price you pay for an item priced at P dollars is given by $P + 0.07P$. If the purchase price is $1.98, how can you use the distributive property to work this out on your calculator in an easy way?

Adding and Subtracting Expressions

← C O N N E C T → *Now that you've seen how to add and subtract algebraic expressions with tiles, let's see how to use the distributive property directly.*

When you add an expression with tiles to another expression, you just group similar tiles and count them. When you subtract an expression from another expression, you need to find the opposite expression first.

In the Explore, you will see how these rules for tiles relate to the distributive property.

EXPLORE: FIND THE MATCH

MATERIALS

Algebra tiles

Study this picture that shows the sum of two expressions.

  +  =

1. Write the expressions being added and their sum.
2. a. In adding expressions with tiles, do you ever add x^2-tiles and x-tiles?
   b. In written expressions, do you ever add x^2 terms and x terms?
3. a. With tiles, do you ever add x-tiles and unit tiles?
   b. In written expressions do you ever add x terms and constants?
4. a. Working with tiles, do you combine x-tiles only with other x-tiles?
   b. In written expressions, do you ever combine constants with any other kind of term?
5. State a way to find the sum or difference of expressions that each have several terms.

Terms that involve exactly the same variables and powers are called **like terms.** To use the distributive property quickly, we combine like terms.

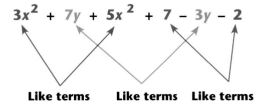

$$3x^2 + 7y + 5x^2 + 7 - 3y - 2$$

Like terms   Like terms   Like terms

When we combine like terms in an expression, we are **simplifying** it. We can extend this idea to find a way to simplify expressions quickly.

To **add** expressions, combine like terms.

To **subtract** an expression, find its opposite, and then combine like terms.

CONSIDER

1. Why can't we combine unlike terms into a single term?
2. Is there any fixed number of x-values that add up to x^2?

EXAMPLE

1. Simplify $(5x^2 + 7y^2 + 4x + 3) + (4x^2 + 2x + 5)$.
   Combine like terms:

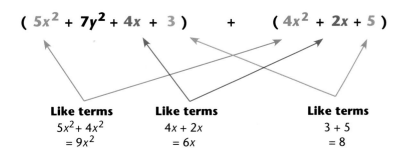

$$(5x^2 + 7y^2 + 4x + 3) \quad + \quad (4x^2 + 2x + 5)$$

Like terms	**Like terms**	**Like terms**
$5x^2 + 4x^2$	$4x + 2x$	$3 + 5$
$= 9x^2$	$= 6x$	$= 8$

There is no like term to combine with the $7y^2$ term, so it remains unchanged in the sum.

$(5x^2 + 7y^2 + 4x + 3) + (4x^2 + 2x + 5) = 9x^2 + 7y^2 + 6x + 8$

Simplify.

a. $(5y + 3) + (2y - 4)$ **b.** $(2x^2 + 2) + (x^2 + 8)$

c. $(5y^2 - 3y - 3) + (2y^2 + y - 3)$

EXAMPLE

2. Simplify $(3x^2 + 5x + 7) - (2x^2 + x - 5)$.
Instead of subtracting, add the opposite expression.
The opposite of $(2x^2 + x - 5)$ is $(-2x^2 - x + 5)$
$(3x^2 + 5x + 7) + (-2x^2 - x + 5)$

Combine like terms:

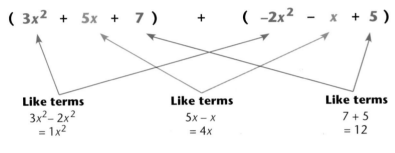

Like terms	**Like terms**	**Like terms**
$3x^2 - 2x^2$	$5x - x$	$7 + 5$
$= 1x^2$	$= 4x$	$= 12$

$(3x^2 + 5x + 7) - (2x^2 + x - 5) = x^2 + 4x + 12.$

TRY IT

Simplify.

d. $(3x + 5) - (x + 1)$ **e.** $(2x^2 + 2) - (x^2 + 8)$

f. $(5y + 3) - (2y - 4)$ **g.** $(5y^2 - 3y - 3) - (2y^2 - y - 3)$

h. Find the missing term. $(2x + 4) - (\underline{\quad} + 2) = -5x + 2$

REFLECT

1. Is $(-x^2 - 1)$ the opposite of $(x^2 - 1)$? How can you tell?
2. Describe a method for finding the opposite of an expression like $(12y^2 + 5x + y - 1)$.
3. Describe a method for subtracting algebraic expressions.
4. Can you combine the terms $-8x$ and $5x$? Why or why not? If you can, what is the result?

Exercises

CORE

1. Getting Started What is the opposite of $(3x + 7)$?

2. Rebecca needs to simplify $(x^2 + 2x - 3) - (3x + 7)$.
a. Write an expression that shows the opposite of $(3x + 7)$ added to $(x^2 + 2x - 3)$.
b. Combine like terms to get the answer.

Simplify.

3. $(3x + 5) - (x + 2)$

4. $(15y - 3) + (10y - 7)$

5. $(10x^2 + 6) - (x^2 - 4)$

6. $(x + 2) - (x - 2)$

7. A park has a rectangular sandbox. Write an expression in terms of x for the area of the sandbox. (Hint: The area is the length times the width.)

$4x^2 - 2$

10

8. Fast Talking, Fast Walking Carissa is a race walker. When she is trying to break a record, Carissa asks Nicole, who walks slower, to help. Nicole starts walking 60 meters ahead, and Carissa walks quickly to catch up.

After s seconds, Nicole is a distance of $6s + 60$ from the starting line and Carissa is a distance of $7s$.
a. How far ahead of Carissa is Nicole after s seconds? (Hint: Subtract Carissa's distance from Nicole's.)
b. Evaluate this expression for $s = 15$, $s = 30$, and $s = 45$.
c. Does Carissa ever catch up with Nicole? If so, after how many seconds?

Simplify.

9. $(3x + 5) + (x - 4)$

10. $(x^2 + 7) + (2x^2 - 5)$

11. $(5x - 1) - (10x^2 + 7x - 9)$

12. $2x^2 + (5x^2 - 30) - (-40)$

13. $(y^2 + y) + (y^2 + 7y)$

14. $(4x - 7) + (x + 5y + 1)$

Find the missing term.

15. $(8x^2 + 6) - (4x^2 + \underline{\quad} + 1) = 4x^2 - 18y^2 + 5$

16. $(x + 5y + \underline{\quad}) + (2x + y + 7) = 3x + 6y - 4$

17. The length of segment AC is $7a - 1$. Write an expression for the length of segment $\overline{BC}$. If $a = 1.2$, what is the length of $\overline{AB}$, $\overline{BC}$, and $\overline{AC}$?

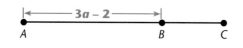

> **Problem-Solving Tip**
>
> Make sure your answer makes sense.

 LOOK BACK

Calculate. Try to get the answer mentally. [2-2]

18. $-3 \times 8 \div (-2)$ **19.** $(22)(-11)$ **20.** $2 \times (-3 + (-2))$

21. According to the 1990 census, the population of Little Rock, Arkansas, was 175,795 with a 1980–1990 growth of 10.5%. If the growth remains at 10.5%, what do you expect the population will be in the year 2000? [Previous course]

MORE PRACTICE

Simplify.

22. $(2x + 9) - (3x - 2)$ **23.** $(6m + 7) + (-3 - 2m)$

24. $(4x^2 + 8) - (2x^2 - 5)$ **25.** $(100x + 50y - 25) + (3x + 14y + 3)$

26. $(28y + 14) - (3y^2 + 10y - 10)$ **27.** $(-2x + 3y - 7) + (2x - 5y - 3)$

28. The circular park has an area of $3 - x^2$.

　a. What is the area of the square court?

　b. Write an expression for the shaded lawn area.

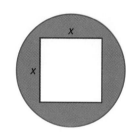

Simplify.

29. $(k^2 + 4k + 9) + (2k^2 - 6)$

30. $(4y^2 + 9) + (8y^2 + 18)$

31. $(20x^2 + 3y^2) - (14x^2 - 10) + 5x^2$

32. $(10x - 25) + (15x + 25) - (-3x + 2)$

33. $(10x^2 + 12y^2 + 6x) - (5x^2 + 12y^2 - 6)$

34. $(7x + 21y) + (7x + 21y) + (7x + 21y)$

35. $(-4x + 2y - 6m) + (-2x - 2y - 6m)$

36. $(3y + 2) - (3y + 4) + (3y + 2)$

Find the missing term.

37. $(9x^2 + 7) - (11x^2 + \underline{\ \ \ }) = -2x^2 - 18$

38. $(t^2 - 6) + (\underline{\ \ \ } - 1) = -2t^2 - 7$

39. $(x + 5y + \underline{\ \ \ }) + (2x + y + 7) = 3x + 6y$

40. $(x - \underline{\ \ \ }) + (x + 4) = 2x + 25$

MORE MATH REASONING

41. Evaluate $(x^2 + 7x - 3) + (2x^2 + 3x + 1)$ if $x = -2$. Is there more than one way to do this? Explain.

42. Dinosaur Dynasty A timeline is shown below.

　x years　　　　y years　　　　　　　　　　　0　1995 AD
　　BC　　　　　　　BC

　a. The dinosaur shows the Jurassic Period. Write an expression for the length of the Jurassic Period.

　b. Use $x = 190,000,000$ and $y = 136,000,000$ to find the duration of the Jurassic Period in years.

43. Romeo, the elephant, and his mother currently share a 20 ft by 20 ft pen. The vet suggests that Romeo needs some space of his own and uses a variable y to show a y-by-y pen.

Write a simplified expression that gives the perimeter for the whole area shown including the landscaped portions.

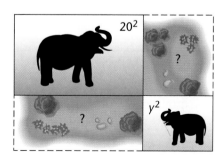

Making Connections

← **C O N N E C T** → *You have seen how to write algebraic expressions to describe real-world situations. You've also used the methods and language of algebra to simplify and evaluate algebraic expressions.*

Spoken language, the language of Braille, and sign language are all ways to communicate ideas.

The language of algebra is a way to communicate mathematical information.

The magician in the Explore knows enough about the language of algebra to entertain and amaze the audience with a neat trick.

EXPLORE: ALGEBRAIC MAGIC

The magician can tell you the number of brothers and sisters you have if you follow his five steps and show him your answer.

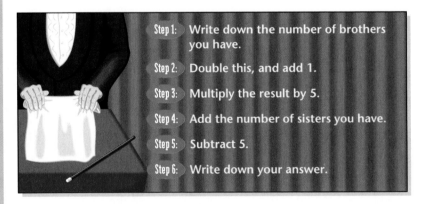

Step 1: Write down the number of brothers you have.

Step 2: Double this, and add 1.

Step 3: Multiply the result by 5.

Step 4: Add the number of sisters you have.

Step 5: Subtract 5.

Step 6: Write down your answer.

1. Pretend that you are the magician and try the trick out on classmates. How do you know the number of brothers and sisters from the answer that you get in Step 5?

2. Use variables and the algebra you have learned to show how the trick works. Tell what methods or properties you are using and how you are using them.

3. Make up your own number trick using age, last two digits of your house number, or some other fact. Make a display that shows how your number trick works. You can use any algebraic methods or properties.

REFLECT

1. Why are expressions with variables helpful to describe real-world situations?
2. Write down some things you feel are important to remember about working with algebraic expressions.
3. Why would you need to evaluate an algebraic expression?
4. Do you find that algebra tiles help you understand how to simplify an algebraic expression? Why or why not?
5. What is the opposite of an algebraic expression? How is the idea of "opposite" used in simplifying?

Self-Assessment

Write an algebraic expression for each word phrase.

1. 4 times the length (ℓ) minus 7 inches

Science

2. the population of Minnesota (p) increased by 1000

Evaluate.

3. $-3y - 57$ if $y = -6$

4. $2n^2 - 3$ if $n = 15$

Science

5. An animal rights group rents an auditorium to hold a special meeting. They will pay a rent of $125 plus $5 for each adult and $2 for each child that attends. They can figure out how much to pay by writing $5a + 2c + 125$, where a is the number of adults who attend the meeting and c is the number of children. If 35 adults and 17 children show up for the meeting, how much rent will they pay?

Simplify.

6. $14x + 9x^2 - 3x^2 + 13y - 18x - 2x^2 + 8y$

7. $(10a - 30b^2) + (15a - 24a^2)$

8. $(3x - 8y) - (4y + 2x)$

9. $-3(5b - 7)$

10. $24(2x + 6y)$

11. $2(3c + 5d) - 8(3c - 5d)$

12. Number Please! Is there a person in class you've been wanting to meet but were too shy to ask for a phone number? If this doesn't impress that special someone, nothing will!

Of course they'll get 5 if they did all the computations correctly, but in your checking, you automatically get their phone number!

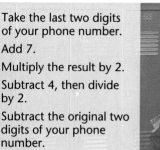

Take the last two digits of your phone number.

Add 7.

Multiply the result by 2.

Subtract 4, then divide by 2.

Subtract the original two digits of your phone number.

Do you get 5?

Let me check your phone number to see if you did it right.

Show how this number trick works by using *n* for the original number. Show that you always wind up with 5, no matter what 2-digit number *n* stands for. Use drawings or algebraic expressions to prove your point.

13. Describe the mistake, if any, in each calculation. If you find a mistake, correct it.
   a. $5(6x + 7t - 4) = 30x + 7t - 4$
   b. $4(2x - 5) = 8x - 20$
   c. $3(5x + 4) - (7x + 2) = 15x + 12 - 7x + 2 = 8x + 14$
   d. $7(5y - 4) + 2(4y - 6) = 35y - 28 + 8y - 12 = 43y - 30$

14. You have a job with a company that manufactures packing materials for sporting goods. You are asked to design boxes for all of the round balls they ship (basketballs, baseballs, soccer balls, etc.) and to determine how much packing is needed to fill the empty space inside the box.
   a. If the diameter of a ball is *d*, what would be the dimensions of the smallest box to hold the ball?
   b. The volume of a cube is the length × width × height.
   • For a cube with sides *d* in length, the volume is d^3.
   • The volume of a ball with diameter *d* is $\frac{1}{6}\pi d^3$.
   What expression gives the volume of the empty space inside the box surrounding the ball?
   c. What volume of packing foam needs to go around a basketball with a 9.47-in. diameter? a baseball with a 2.9-in. diameter? a volleyball with an 8.28-in. diameter? a soccer ball with an 8.75-in. diameter?

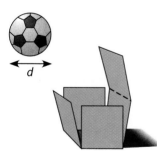

15. Greenhorns Ahead Explain how you can tell that the cowpokes who wrote this didn't know how to combine like terms.

Population 74
Elevation 437
Fine for Dirty Boots 10
521

Chapter 2 Review

In Chapter 2, you explored operations with both positive and negative numbers including exponents and square roots. You used techniques for estimating, and you worked with properties that help you do calculations mentally. Algebraic expressions, made up of numbers and variables, let you describe real situations mathematically. You saw how to simplify expressions by adding, subtracting, and using the distributive property.

KEY TERMS

algebraic expression [2-3]	factors [2-1]	signed numbers [2-2]
algorithm [2-2]	like terms [2-3]	simplify [2-3]
constants [2-3]	order of operations [2-1]	square root [2-1]
distributive property [2-3]	perfect square [2-1]	sum [2-2]
evaluate an expression [2-3]	product [2-1]	terms [2-2]
exponent [2-1]	quotient [2-2]	variable [2-3]

Determine whether each statement is true or false. If the statement is false, change the underlined word or phrase to make it true.

1. When you <u>divide</u>, the answer is called the product.

2. The square root of a perfect square is <u>always</u> a whole number.

3. In the sum $2 + 5$, 2 and 5 are <u>factors</u>.

Write the word or phrase that correctly completes the statement.

4. An exponent shows repeated ___.

5. A ___ is a quantity whose value changes.

CONCEPTS AND APPLICATIONS

Calculate. [2-1, 2-2]

6. $(1.2)^3$

7. $-5 + \sqrt{36}$

8. $\sqrt{3^2 + 4^2}$

9. $10 + (-2) + 3$

10. $2 - 9 - 7$

11. $64 - 72 + 8$

12. $3^2 - 36 \div (-6)$

13. $52 - (-3) \cdot 2$

14. $-3 \cdot 2 + 7^2$

15. Estimate how much material Anne will need to make an outfit. The skirt takes $2\frac{7}{8}$ yards of material; the vest, $1\frac{1}{2}$ yards; and the jacket, $3\frac{3}{4}$ yards. [2-1]

Suppose your calculator screen shows each number. Round to the indicated place. [2-1]

16. 7254; nearest ten   **17.** $57.3845; nearest cent   **18.** 45.236; nearest tenth

19. Keiko took five tests in Spanish class. She got grades of 78, 82, 75, 84, and 86. Keiko used her calculator to find her average. Is the answer shown on the calculator screen reasonable? If not, tell why not. [2-1]

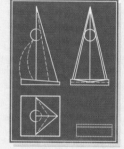

79.2

Estimate. Describe your method. [2-1]

20. 201×51 **21.** $351 + 347 + 345 + 358$ **22.** $462 \div 21$

Careers **23.** An architect is designing a small monument whose square base should cover about 125 square feet of ground. What should be the length and width of the square base? [2-1]

24. Which number is a perfect square? [2-1]
(a) 50   (b) 2   (c) 25
(d) 75   (e) not here

25. Marcus needed to calculate $7 \cdot 43$ quickly in his head. He came up with an answer of 301. Describe a method that he might have used to work out the answer. [2-1]

26. In plotting the ordered pair $(2, -4)$, which coordinate tells you how much to move right or left? [1-1]

What is the missing number? Draw tiles, balloons, or a number line, if it helps. [2-2]

27. $-5 + \underline{\quad} = 0$ **28.** $7 + \underline{\quad} = -3$ **29.** $\underline{\quad} - (-3) = 8$

Industry **30.** Mrs. Alexander's charge card account started the month with a balance due of $25.34. At the end of the month, her bill showed a balance due of $123.45. How much did she charge to her account that month? [2-2]

31. List the numbers in order from largest to smallest: 0.6, 0.5, 0.7, 0.06, 0.52, 0.621. [Previous course]

Copy this number line. Mark and label each point. [2-2]

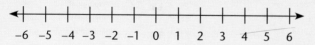

32. 3.7   **33.** -3.7 **34.** -2.25 **35.** $\frac{1}{3}$

36. The weather bureau has data that gives the daily maximum temperature in Sioux City, Iowa, for a full year. The highest recorded temperature is 97°F. The lowest is −5°F. What is the range? [2-2]

37. Because of a falling demand for its products, the Blue Sky company plans to lay off 16% of its staff. If the company employs 1032 people, how many may be laid off? [Previous course]

38. What expression is modeled by the algebra tiles shown? [2-3]

Simplify. [2-3]

39. $(5x + 7) + (4x − 2)$ **40.** $(5k + 2) − (2k + 1)$ **41.** $−5(2y − 3)$

42. $(7x^2 − 4) − (8x^2 − 6)$ **43.** $(−3x + 7)4$ **44.** $3(b − 1) + 2(b + 1)$

45. A camera store charges $6.29 to develop a roll of 24-exposure color film plus $0.17 for each print. [2-3]
  a. Use p to represent the number of prints. Write an expression for the total cost of developing the film.
  b. What will the camera store charge if it makes prints of all 24 exposures?
  c. What will the store charge if it can't make prints of 2 exposures?

46. Write an expression in terms of x for the perimeter of the rectangle. What is the perimeter if $x = 3$? if $x = 2$? [2-3]

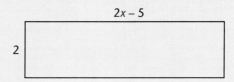

47. The area of a circle is given by the expression πr^2, where π is about 3.14 and r is the radius of the circle. A quarter has a radius of about 2.4 cm. What is the area of one of its faces? [2-3]

CONCEPTS AND CONNECTIONS

48. Astronomy Scientists use signed numbers, called absolute magnitude, to describe the brightness of a star. The brighter the star, the smaller the number that identifies its magnitude. The sun has a magnitude of −26.7. The star Polaris has a magnitude of +2. Which is brighter? What is the difference in their magnitudes? Why do you think that scientists decided to use both positive and negative numbers to express the magnitudes of stars?

SELF-EVALUATION

The title of Chapter 2 is *Communicating Mathematics.* Write a paragraph explaining how the concepts, methods, and tools that you've seen in this chapter relate to the title. Be sure to include specific examples and illustrations to show how topics in this chapter relate to communicating about real-life situations.

Chapter 2 Assessment

TEST

Determine whether each statement is true or false. If the statement is false, change the underlined word or phrase to make it true.

1. The square of a number is <u>sometimes</u> negative.

2. In the expression $2x - 3$, x is a <u>variable</u>.

Calculate.

3. 5^3

4. $\sqrt{6^2 + 8^2} - 10$

5. $(-7) + 3 + (-4)$

6. $(2 - 6)7$

7. $2(3^2 - 5)$

8. $48 \div (-8) - (-5)$

Write an algebraic expression.

9. half the height (h), decreased by 4 inches

10. 30 mi/hr more than twice the speed

11. Give an example of a calculation that you could find mentally by using the distributive property. Then describe how you would think out the answer.

Simplify.

12. $(7x^2 + 6) + (3x^2 + 5)$

13. $2(x + 5) + 10(-2x + 3)$

14. $(x^2 + 3x + 6) - (3x - 6)$

15. $(4b - 2)3$

16. Emilio claimed that $\sqrt{60}$ is between 8 and 9. Is he correct? Explain.

17. A submarine starts to dive from sea level. It drops 500 ft, then rises 50 ft, then rises another 60 ft, then drops 150 ft, and finally rises 15 ft. Draw a diagram to show the submarine's movements. What is its depth?

18. What is the length of a side of a square garden whose area is one-half the area shown at the right?

8 ft

8 ft

19. Penny is buying a $5.98 item at a hardware store. Sales tax is 6%. Describe how she can estimate how much the salesperson will add for the sales tax.

20. Elizabeth is working with algebra tiles.
   a. What expression do her tiles represent?
   b. Draw a picture of tiles to represent the opposite of this expression.
   c. What expression does your picture of the opposite represent?

21. A small sugar cube has the dimensions shown. What is its volume?

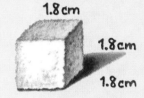

1.8 cm
1.8 cm
1.8 cm

Science

22. The expression $0.07s^2$, where s is your speed in miles per hour, gives the stopping distance of a motorcycle, in feet, on a wet tar road. How far will a motorcycle travel before stopping if its speed is 10 mi/hr when the rider hits the brakes? 30 mi/hr? 60 mi/hr?

23. Which number is larger, -5.1 or -5.2? Use a number line to defend your answer.

PERFORMANCE TASK

Work with the numbers 6, 3, and 2 in order. Use your knowledge of the order of operations and the distributive property, and insert the symbols, $+$, $-$, $\times$, $\div$, and any needed parentheses to get the answer.

Example: 6, 3, 2 **20**

   $6 \times 3 + 2$ is 20

1. 6, 3, 2   **30**   **2.** 6, 3, 2   **36**   **3.** 6, 3, 2   **1.5**

4. 6, 3, 2   **−6**   **5.** 6, 3, 2   **9**   **6.** 6, 3, 2   **4**

Can you find three more expressions and answers using 6, 3, and 2?

Now use 8, 6, 4, and 2. If you keep the numbers in order, how many different expressions can you write and find the answers to?

Why do you think mathematical symbols might be called the "road signs" of algebra?

Chapter 3

Drawings and Patterns

Project B
What's Mine's My Own
What's the most elegant way
to show ownership?

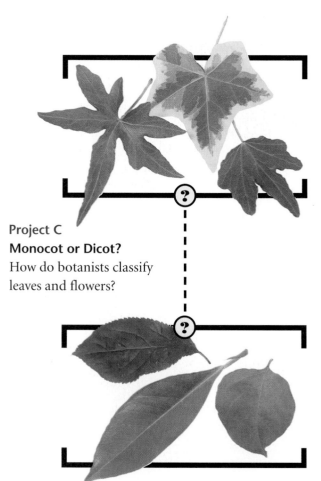

Project C
Monocot or Dicot?
How do botanists classify
leaves and flowers?

Project A
Highland Fling
How do Scottish clans
distinguish themselves?

LISA TRUJILLO

I did OK in math in high school. I thought I'd use math as a scientist or as a doctor.

Today I work in a very old weaving tradition at a Rio Grande loom, using pattern in colors, in shapes, and in overall design. I establish rules for the pattern. Then I code it on paper so I can use it to turn the pattern around, to repeat it, or to reproduce it later to make the piece symmetrical. My biggest accomplishment is a piece called *Passion in the Web*, which represents an entire year's work.

Lisa Trujillo
Weaver and Business
    Owner
Centinela Traditional Arts
Chimayo, New Mexico

Chapter 3

Drawings and Patterns

3-1 Designs

Patterns using geometric shapes can be found in art, architecture, interior design, and nature. You will investigate shapes that have the property of symmetry. You will see that some familiar geometric shapes can fit together to create a tiling pattern called a tessellation.

3-2 Transformations

Translations, reflections, and rotations are geometric transformations that can be used by anyone who creates designs. You will see real-life examples of these designs, create your own, and analyze their point locations and symmetry.

3-3 Patterns

The study of patterns has applications in mathematics and in scientific research. By considering patterns of numbers, letters, and figures, you will learn to identify and continue the pattern. You will see how to use an algebraic expression to provide a rule for finding a sequence of numbers.

The Mysterious

A G A T H A C H R I S T I E

78 mystery novels written

Her name was Agatha Christie, and she was born in Torquay, England, in 1890.

Christie introduced the Belgian detective Hercule Poirot in *The Mysterious Affair at Styles* (1920). Since then, Poirot has delighted readers of dozens of Christie's books with his neatly groomed mustache and his insistence on order, symmetry, and method in all things. Poirot never failed to solve his case by using his "little gray cells."

In many of Christie's other novels, Jane Marple is the sleuth. A lovable, slightly nosy, elderly English-

2 billion copies sold

woman, Marple has an uncanny way of getting to the bottom of a case.

After she married the archaeologist Max Mallowan in 1930, Christie spent several months each year on archaeological digs in Syria and Egypt.

Translated into 44 languages

Agatha Christie created a real-life mystery of her own when she disappeared for ten days in 1926. She left clues that made many suspect she'd been murdered, but she turned up alive after a huge, nationwide search. She never told the story behind her disappearance.

Most murder mysteries ever written

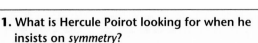

?

1. What is Hercule Poirot looking for when he insists on *symmetry*?
2. How can mathematics be helpful to a detective?
3. What objects might have been unearthed in Agatha Christie's archaeological digs? What are some ideas from geometry that could help in studying these objects?

Symmetry

← CONNECT → *Artists and professionals often try to give a feeling of balance to their work. Designers of clothing and jewelry are concerned that their work is pleasing to the eye. Car designers and architects have similar concerns. You will study an important part of design called symmetry.*

Hercule Poirot, Agatha Christie's Belgian detective, took great pride in his mustache. He waxed and brushed it many times each day to make sure that the right half looked exactly like the left half.

This is one type of symmetry.

Another type of symmetry is shown in this flower.

CONSIDER

?

1. What do you think of when you hear the word *symmetry?*

MATERIALS

Scissors
Mirror (optional)

1. Which of these shapes, designs, and letters do you think have symmetry? Which do you think are not symmetric at all? You may want to trace some of the figures and cut them out. You can try turning them or looking at them in a mirror.

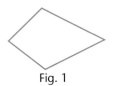

Fig. 1

Fig. 2

Fig. 3

Fig. 4

Fig. 5

Fig. 6

S

Fig. 7

Fig. 8

A

Fig. 9

2. In some symmetric figures, you can draw a line that acts like a mirror so that each part of the figure is a mirror image of the other. This is called line symmetry. Which of the figures above have line symmetry?

3. In other symmetric figures, you can draw a point that acts as a center, and the figure can spin around that point matching itself before making a complete spin. This is called rotational symmetry. Which figures above have rotational symmetry?

4. List any of the figures that have more than one line that acts as a mirror.

5. List any of the figures that have both line symmetry and rotational symmetry.

Designers and artists create symmetric objects that we see and use all the time. Dishes, windows, cars, and jewelry often have symmetric designs.

There are many types of symmetry. For now, let's concentrate on the type where we see mirror images.

Line symmetry, or just symmetry, occurs when two halves of a figure mirror each other across a line. The **line of symmetry** is the line that divides the figure into two mirror images. If you fold a figure along its line of symmetry, both halves match each other perfectly.

You saw some of these shapes in the Explore. They all have line symmetry.

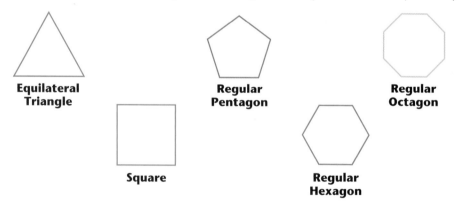

Equilateral Triangle

Square

Regular Pentagon

Regular Hexagon

Regular Octagon

These shapes are regular polygons. A **polygon** is a geometric shape made up of line segments. A **regular polygon** is one in which all sides have the same length and all angles have the same measure.

Tell whether each figure has line symmetry. If it does, copy the figure and draw a line of symmetry.

a.   **b.**   **c.**   **d.**

By now you may realize that a figure can have more than one line of symmetry.

EXAMPLE

Find all lines of symmetry for each letter.

1. E   **2.** N   **3.** H

one line of symmetry   no lines of symmetry   two lines of symmetry

Many objects in nature have symmetry. People also create designs to have symmetry. Symmetry gives designs balance and makes them pleasing to the eye.

REFLECT

1. How is a mirror image related to line symmetry?
2. What is a line of symmetry?
3. What is rotational symmetry?
4. Describe a figure that has two lines of symmetry.
5. Describe a figure that has more than two lines of symmetry.

Exercises

CORE

1. **Getting Started** Copy the figure and fold it along the line. Is the line a line of symmetry for the figure? Explain.

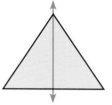

For each figure, is the red line a line of symmetry? Explain.

2.   3.   4.

5. Which letter has no lines of symmetry?

    (a) **A**   (b) **B**   (c) **C**   (d) **D**   (e) not here

6. Write the word or phrase that correctly completes the statement. If two halves of a figure mirror each other across a line, the figure has ___.

7. Describe at least five things outside of school that have line symmetry or rotational symmetry.

Copy each figure. Then draw the other half of the figure so that the red line is a line of symmetry.

8.    9.    10.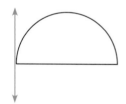

11. Brenda Spencer, a Navajo rug weaver, used the traditional *burntwater* design in her rug shown at the right. How has she used symmetry?

12. Copy the design at the right. Shade additional squares so that the figure has line symmetry.

13. Does the photograph at the right show symmetry? Explain your thinking.

Fine Arts

14. Crown Jewels Suppose you are designing a pair of earrings. Draw a sketch for a design that has line symmetry. Draw another sketch that does not have line symmetry.

15. Determine whether the statement is true or false. If the statement is false, change the underlined word or phrase to make it true.

A polygon with six sides is called an <u>octagon</u>.

Copy each letter and draw any and all lines of symmetry.

16. A   **17.** F   **18.** M   **19.** X   **20.** Z

21. Digging Up Agatha Christie went on many archaeological expeditions with her husband Max Mallowan.

Careers

  a. What do archaeologists do on an expedition?
  b. What could symmetry have to do with archaeology?

 *LOOK AHEAD*

Plot the point P(2, 3) on graph paper.

22. If you move the point right 3 units and down 4 units, what will the new coordinates be?

23. Think of the *y*-axis as a mirror. Find a point that is the mirror image of *P*. What are its coordinates?

MORE PRACTICE

For each figure, is the red line a line of symmetry? Explain.

24.
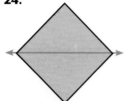

25.
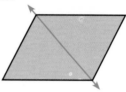

26.
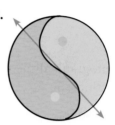

Copy each figure. Then draw the other half of the figure so that the red line is a line of symmetry.

27.
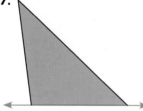

28.

29.

30.

31.

32.

Copy each letter and draw any and all lines of symmetry.

33. **D**   34. **G**   35. **Y**   36. **S**   37. **P**

MORE MATH REASONING

38. The word **TOOT** has a vertical line of symmetry. Find at least three other words that have a vertical line of symmetry.

39. a. Copy and complete the table to show how many lines of symmetry you see in each of these regular polygons.

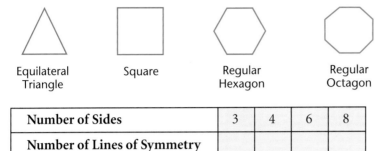

Equilateral Triangle · Square · Regular Hexagon · Regular Octagon

Number of Sides	3	4	6	8
Number of Lines of Symmetry				

b. Look for a pattern. How many lines of symmetry would you expect to find for a regular pentagon—a figure with five sides?

3-1
PART B Tessellations

← C O N N E C T → *You've seen designs that have line symmetry. Artists use many methods to create spectacular designs. In this part, you will learn about some shapes that you can use to create a tiling pattern.*

The Dutch artist M. C. Escher is noted for his work in the early 1900s. He created works using **tessellations.**

A **tessellation** is an arrangement of figures that fills a flat surface but does not overlap or leave gaps.

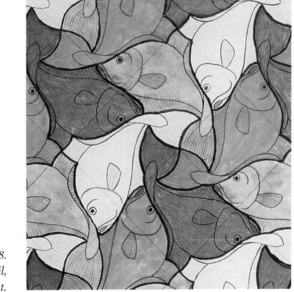

*Fish, 1938.
Drawn in India Ink, pencil, watercolor, and gold paint.*

In the Explore, you will be using triangles and quadrilaterals. A **quadrilateral** has four sides. Some quadrilaterals have special names.

Square   Rectangle   Trapezoid   Parallelogram

EXPLORE: TESSEL EARLY, TESSEL LATE

You've probably seen square tiles used to tessellate a floor.

Your task is to find some other shapes that also tessellate.

1. Stack two sheets of paper together and fold them twice to make eight layers. Draw a triangle on the paper and cut it out so that you get eight identical triangles.

2. Try to arrange the pieces so they cover a flat surface without overlapping and without leaving gaps. Can you make a tessellation with your triangles?

3. Now make eight copies of a quadrilateral in a similar way. (Don't draw a rectangle or a square.) Can you make a tessellation with your quadrilateral?

4. Trace this regular octagon. Make eight copies using the same method. Try to make a tessellation with your octagons.

5. What conclusions can you draw?

MATERIALS

Scissors
Tracing paper

Not all shapes will fit together in a way that makes a tessellation possible. But you can make a tessellation using any triangle or quadrilateral.

Tessellations can be made with many different geometric figures. M. C. Escher made designs like the one shown at the beginning of this part by using irregular shapes. In a later part, you will explore how to make irregular shapes that tessellate.

Name the figures used in each tessellation.

a.    **b.**    **c.**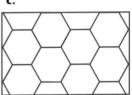

These tessellations are made by repeating a single figure. When the same figure is used throughout, the tessellation is called a **pure tessellation.**

You see tessellations on floor covering, wallpaper, fabric, and other decorated objects.

REFLECT

1. What is a tessellation?
2. Are tessellations art or mathematics?
3. How are jigsaw puzzles like tessellations? How are they different?
4. Describe a tessellation that you have seen somewhere outside of school.
5. Can a circle be used to make a tessellation? Explain.

America Hurrah
Antiques, NYC

Exercises

CORE

1. Getting Started What is the name for an arrangement of figures that fill a flat surface but do not overlap or leave gaps?

Identify the tessellated shapes.

2. 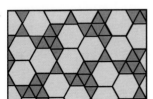   **3.**

4. **Spanish Mystery** The Alhambra is a famous palace in southern Spain.
   a. Look up the Alhambra in an encyclopedia or other source. Who built it? When was it built? Write a brief description.
   b. If you visit the Alhambra, where might you see tessellations?

5. Is coordinate grid paper an example of a pure tessellation? Why or why not?

6. Copy the figure at the right. Is the figure symmetric? If so, draw its line(s) of symmetry. Can the figure be used to make a tessellation? If so, draw it. If not, explain why not.

7. Name three regular polygons that you can use to make a tessellation.

8. Sketch a tessellation that uses equilateral triangles.

9. Jane Marple, Agatha Christie's sharp-minded detective, is on a budget. She wants to get her kitchen floor tiled using small square tiles of one color. Sketch three different patterns that she could use to lay out the tiles.

10. The Republic of Chad, in Africa, is known for having some unusual stamps. Why are most postage stamps shaped like rectangles?

Determine whether each statement is true or false.

11. Only polygons can be used to make a tessellation.

12. A polygon that is not a regular polygon can be used to make a tessellation.

13. Is a honeycomb a tessellation? If so, what shape is used?

14. Which quadrilateral is a regular polygon?
    (a) rectangle   (b) trapezoid   (c) square
    (d) parallelogram (e) not here

15. Which polygon cannot be used to make a tessellation?
    (a) triangle   (b) trapezoid   (c) square
    (d) hexagon   (e) not here

LOOK BACK

16. Calculate $21 + \sqrt{9} - 6^2$. [2-1]

17. Finish the sentence: $-2 + \underline{\quad} = -7$. [2-2]

18. Find the median of these prices for an Elvis Presley compact disc: $12.98, $9.49, $14.25, $9.95, $11.99, and $5.95. [1-3]

MORE PRACTICE

Identify the tessellated shapes.

19. 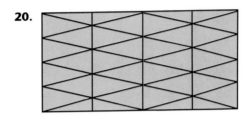   **20.**

21. Sketch three patterns bricklayers can use to arrange bricks to build a wall.

22. Write a letter to a friend explaining tessellations. Include diagrams.

23. In which professions might people make use of tessellations?

24. Write the word or phrase that correctly completes the statement. A tessellation that uses just one shape is called a _____ tessellation.

25. Sketch five different shapes that you can use to make a tessellation.

MORE MATH REASONING

26. Copy the shape at the right. Use it to design a tessellation pattern.

27. Copy this tessellation of equilateral triangles. Color it so that it shows a tessellation of regular hexagons and trapezoids.

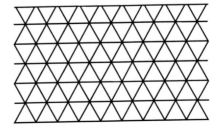

← C O N N E C T → *You've seen how to recognize line symmetry and how to complete a design so that it has line symmetry. Tessellating, or covering a surface with identical figures, is another way to create designs. You've discovered some figures that you can use to make tessellations.*

A detective, who is as talented as Agatha Christie's fictional characters, discovered an interesting relationship for tessellations. By starting with a basic shape that tessellates and changing it into a shape with the same area, you will get another shape that tessellates.

EXPLORE: TASTY TESSELLATIONS

1. Start with a square.

MATERIALS

Scissors, Tape, Colored pencils or crayons

2. Cut a curved area from one side of the square. Tape the cutout to the other side.

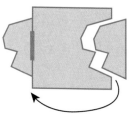

3. Use your new basic shape to make a tessellation pattern. Color and design your tessellations.

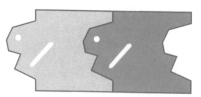

4. Does your design have line symmetry?

1. How can you tell whether a figure has line symmetry?
2. What is a tessellation? How are tessellations used?
3. What will you see if you fold a symmetric drawing along its line of symmetry?
4. If you cut a square along its diagonal, what new figure do you get? Can you make a tessellation with this figure?
5. How many lines of symmetry does a square have?

Self-Assessment

1. Is the figure at the right a polygon? Explain.

2. Sketch a shape that has a line of symmetry.

3. Sketch a shape that you can use to make a tessellation.

4. The four cities in Georgia that had the greatest population in the 1990 census are Atlanta (394,017), Columbus (178,681), Macon (106,612), and Savannah (137,560). What is the median population of these four cities? [1-3]

5. Calculate $\dfrac{(-5)^2 \cdot (-2)}{\sqrt{100}}$. [2-2]

6. A stop sign is in the shape of a(n)
(a) triangle
(b) hexagon
(c) square
(d) octagon
(e) not here

State whether the red line is a line of symmetry.

7.
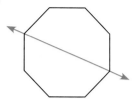

8.
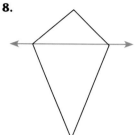

9.
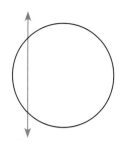

What shape is used to make each tessellation? Where might you see each tessellation?

10.

11.

Copy each letter and draw any and all lines of symmetry.

12. **B**   13. **W**   14. **F**   15. **T**   16. **K**

17. What shapes are used to make the design shown? Is this a tessellation? Is it a pure tessellation? Explain.

3-2 Transformations

The Navajo, the largest tribe of Native Americans in the United States, live mainly in Arizona, New Mexico, and Utah. Their woven rugs and textiles are recognized all over the world.

The earliest Navajo weavers made blankets, mostly with geometric patterns. Colors included gray, cream, black, and brown—the natural colors of sheep's wool; and shades of red from vegetable dyes. Today Navajo weavers primarily make rugs.

Although some men do weaving, it is the Navajo women who are mostly responsible for weaving the wonderfully artistic patterns.

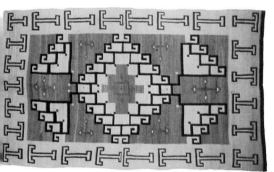

Navajo weavers often repeat shapes and lines in geometric rug patterns by sliding, flipping, shrinking, and enlarging them. The overall patterns and the smaller sections within a main pattern can include many examples of line symmetry.

NAVAJO ART

?

1. Where would you be able to fold the large rug so that the two parts of the design will match?
2. To continue the pattern of the small rug down the left-hand side, starting at the top left corner, would you slide, flip, or turn the $\mathbb{T}$ (or make a combination of these moves)?
3. To make the pattern of the small rug across the bottom from left to right would you slide, flip, or turn the $\mathbb{T}$ (or make a combination of these moves)?

← CONNECT → *The patterns that you find in the folk art of many cultures are often made by repeating a basic design. In this part, you will get an introduction to three ways to move a basic design as you repeat it.*

Figures that have exactly the same shape and size are **congruent figures**.

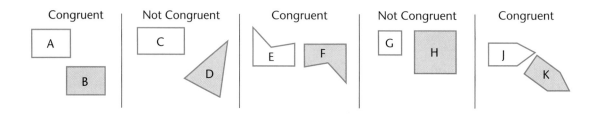

| Congruent | Not Congruent | Congruent | Not Congruent | Congruent |

 **CONSIDER**

1. How can you use tracing paper to tell if two figures are congruent?
2. Why are Figure C and Figure D not congruent? Why are Figure G and Figure H not congruent?

Congruent shapes appear in many designs. The same basic shape is used over and over, but it is transformed by using slides, flips, and turns.

| Slide | Flip | Turn |

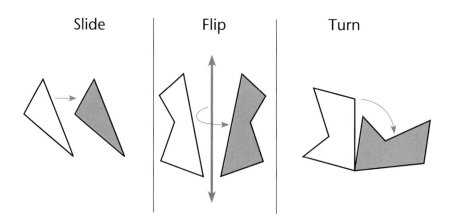

MATERIALS

Cardboard
Scissors
Tracing paper

Now create your own design.

Step A

Draw a shape on the cardboard and cut it out.

Step B

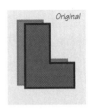

Trace a copy of the shape on a piece of paper. Label this tracing ORIGINAL.

Step C

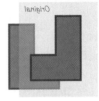

Create a design by making tracings of your shape in different positions. The tracings are called images.

Step D

Compare the images in your design with the original shape. Label which images are slides, which are flips, and which are turns.

You can use tracing paper to help you decide whether an image is a slide, a flip, or a turn.

EXAMPLE

Decide whether to slide, slide and flip, or slide and turn Figure A to fit on Figure B.

1.

Trace Figure A on tracing paper.

2.

Start by sliding the traced image over to Figure B without turning it.

3.

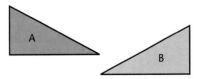

Since it doesn't match up, try turning the tracing paper or flipping it.

You can slide and then flip Figure A to fit on Figure B.

Decide whether to slide, slide and flip, or slide and turn Figure A to fit on Figure B.

a.

b.

Slides, flips, and turns are **transformations.** A transformation is a movement of points that transforms, or changes, a figure. Slides, flips, and turns transform figures into congruent figures.

REFLECT

1. How can you tell if two figures are congruent?
2. If two triangles are congruent, can they have different perimeters?
3. If two circles have the same radius, are they congruent?
4. If Figure B is a flip image of Figure A, can it also be a turn image?
5. What is a transformation?

Exercises

CORE

1. Getting Started Trace Figure A on cardboard and cut it out. Draw images and label them by

a. sliding the cutout.
b. flipping the cutout.
c. turning the cutout.

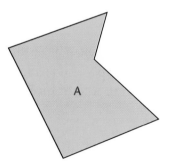

2. Write the word or phrase that correctly completes the statement.
When two figures have exactly the same shape and size, we say the figures are ____.

Decide whether to slide, slide and flip, or slide and turn Figure A to make it fit on Figure B.

3.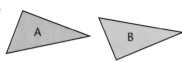

4.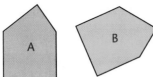

5.
Fig. A
Fig. B

6.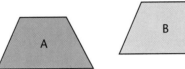

7. Which two letters of the alphabet are flip images of each other?

Tell whether each statement is always true, sometimes true, or never true.

8. Two squares are congruent.

9. Two hexagons have the same shape.

10. If two figures are not congruent, you cannot slide, flip, or turn one onto the other.

11. Name a sport for which an official playing field in one location is congruent to one in another location. Name sports for which playing fields don't have to be congruent.

Is Figure A congruent to Figure B? Explain.

12.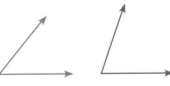
Fig. A   Fig. B

13.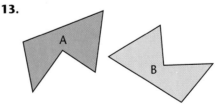

 LOOK AHEAD

Set up axes on a coordinate grid.

14. Plot the point $A(-3, -1)$.

15. Point A is moved 2 units left and 1 unit up to a new point B. What are the coordinates of B? Plot point B.

MORE PRACTICE

Decide whether to slide, slide and flip, or slide and turn Figure A to make it fit on Figure B.

16.

17.

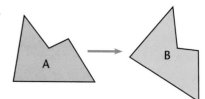

18.

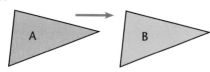

Fig. A   Fig. B

19.

Fig. A   Fig. B

20.

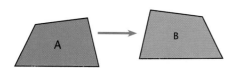

21.

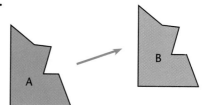

Is Figure A congruent to Figure B? Explain.

22.

23.

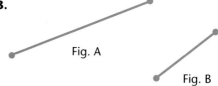

Fig. A

Fig. B

24.

Fig. A   Fig. B

25.

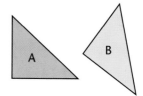

MORE MATH REASONING

26. Which letter of the alphabet looks the same whether you slide it, flip it, or turn it?

27. Give two ways that Figure A can be made to fit onto Figure B.

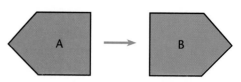

← C O N N E C T → *You've seen that slides, flips, and turns are three ways to transform points. Now you will use coordinates to learn more about the slides.*

You have seen that you can move a figure by sliding it. Another name for a slide is a **translation.**

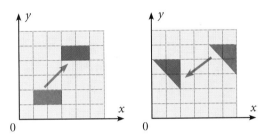

Translating a figure means sliding all points in the figure the same distance in the same direction.

You can find many everyday examples of translation patterns in clothing and in architecture.

The **image** of a translation is the new figure that results from the slide. In the pictures above, original figures are in red and the translation images are in blue.

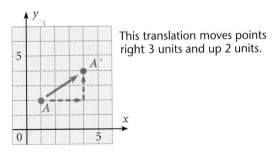

This translation moves points right 3 units and up 2 units.

Translations move points. *Prime notation* is used to relate an image point, A', to its original, A. The symbol A' is read "A prime."

EXPLORE: MOVE IT, BUDDY!

$\triangle ABC$ has vertices $A(-1, -2)$, $B(2, -2)$, and $C(0, 3)$.

MATERIALS

Graph paper
Ruler

1. Set up axes on a coordinate grid. Plot and label A, B, and C. Then draw $\triangle ABC$.

2. Slide point A 2 units right and 3 units up. Label the point A'.

3. Use the same slide to move point B to B' and point C to C'.

4. Draw $\triangle A'B'C'$. This triangle is the translation image of $\triangle ABC$.

5. How is a point on $\triangle ABC$ related to its corresponding image point on $\triangle A'B'C'$?

6. Write as many statements as you can that compare the original $\triangle ABC$ with its translation image $\triangle A'B'C'$.

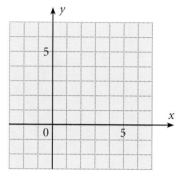

A translation moves each point a fixed distance in a given direction. The original and its image have the same shape and size, and they face in the same direction.

We use a shorthand notation to describe a translation of points. For example, we can write the translation that moves points 2 units right and 3 units up as **<2, 3>**.

CONSIDER

1. What is the translation <0, 0>?

2. What is the notation for a translation that moves points 5 units straight down?

We can find the coordinates of the translation of a figure. The new figure is called the translation image.

The vertices of a rectangle are $P(-1, 2)$, $Q(-1, 5)$, $R(3, 5)$, and $S(3, 2)$. Find the coordinates of the vertices of the image after the translation $<-1, 2>$.

Find the image of any point by subtracting 1 from the x-value and adding 2 to the y-value: $(x, y) \rightarrow (x - 1, y + 2)$.

$P(-1, 2) \rightarrow P'(-2, 4)$

$Q(-1, 5) \rightarrow Q'(-2, 7)$

$R(3, 5) \rightarrow R'(2, 7)$

$S(3, 2) \rightarrow S'(2, 4)$

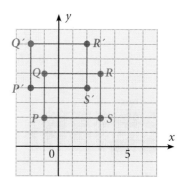

Each point on the original rectangle is moved 1 unit left and 2 units up.

a. Tell how the translation $<-6, -4>$ moves a point.

Find the image of each point after the given translation.

b. $A(2, -5)$; $<1, 0>$ **c.** $M(-1, 0)$; $<-2, 3>$
d. $K(2, 0)$; $<0, -2>$ **e.** $O(0, 0)$; $<1, -1>$

Translating the same figure in the same way again and again makes a design that has a type of symmetry different from the line symmetry and the point symmetry that you've already seen. Artists and creators of handicrafts use **translational symmetry** to create interesting designs.

1. Why do you think mathematicians use the word *translation* to describe the transformation that slides figures?
2. Can a translation image of a line segment be longer than the original segment? Explain.
3. Describe how you can tell if one figure is a translation image of another figure.
4. How is translational symmetry different from line symmetry?

Exercises

CORE

1. **Getting Started** The translation <2, −3> moves a point right 2 units and down 3 units. What is the image of $A(1, 4)$ after a translation of <2, −3>?

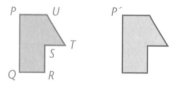

2. Tell how the translation <6, −2> moves a point.

3. Copy the figures. Finish labeling the vertices on the translation image.

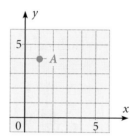

4. Write the letter of the second pair that best matches the first pair.
   Translation: transformation as (a) dog: collie, (b) square: quadrilateral, (c) axis: graph, (d) male: female

Find the image of each point after the given translation.

5. $B(−3, −5)$; <−1, −1>   6. $E(2.3, −1.7)$; <4, −2>   7. $F(0, −3)$; <2, 0>

8. The coordinates of the vertices of $\triangle PQR$ are $P(2, 5)$, $Q(6, 1)$, and $R(4, −3)$. Find the coordinates of the vertices of the image after a translation of <−2, −3>. Plot both the original and its image on graph paper.

9. Make a template of the figure on cardboard. Create a design by using the template to draw four translations.

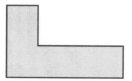

10. Draw a picture showing an original figure and its congruent image that is not a translation.

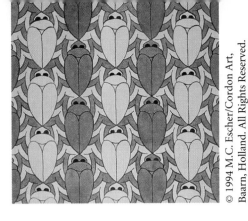

11. How did M. C. Escher use the idea of translation in this picture?

Beetle, *1953, Drawn in India ink and watercolor.*

12. Making Music Beethoven changed two measures of his Fifth Symphony by translating them. Describe how he did it.

13. Assembly Line What does this assembly line have to do with translations?

 LOOK BACK

14. Copy the figure and draw all lines of symmetry. [3-1]

15. Simplify $(3x^2 - 2x + 8) - (3 - 4x)$. [2-3]

16. Write the word or phrase that best completes the statement. A wedge-shaped section of a circle graph is called a ___. [1-2]

MORE PRACTICE

Tell how each translation moves a point.

17. $<2, 6>$

18. $<-2, 6>$

19. $<2, -6>$

20. $<-2, -6>$

21. $<-2, 0>$

22. $<0, -2>$

Find the image of each point after the given translation.

23. $B(-1, 2); <-1, -6>$

24. $E(2.2, -3.7); <-4, 5>$

25. $S(-1, -3); <2, 1>$

26. $D(4, 0); <-2, 5>$

27. $M(3.1, -1.8); <-0.1, 2>$

28. $V(2, -5); <-2, -1>$

29. $F(1, 3); <-2, -4>$

30. $S(0, -1); <-4, -5>$

31. $K(-1.3, -2.5); <-2, 0>$

32. The coordinates of the vertices of $\triangle KLM$ are $K(2, 0)$, $L(0, 2)$, and $M(2, -3)$. Find the coordinates of the vertices of the image after a translation of $<-2, 3>$. Plot both the original and its image on graph paper.

MORE MATH REASONING

33. What single translation accomplishes the same as the translation $<5, 3>$ followed by the translation $<2, -1>$ followed by the translation $<-3, -4>$?

34. Write a description and show the notation for a translation that moves rectangle $ABCD$ into rectangle $A'B'C'D'$.

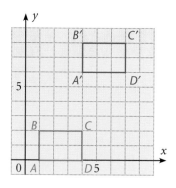

Reflections

← CONNECT → *You have seen that a translation slides a figure into its image. Now you will look at another kind of transformation, a reflection. A reflection flips a figure into its image.*

Earlier you saw how to create a congruent figure in a different position by flipping it.

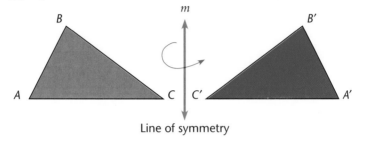

Line of symmetry

If a figure is flipped over a line, the image is a **reflection** of the original. You get a design that has line symmetry.

△*A'B'C'* is a reflection of △*ABC*.

CONSIDER

?

1. **Why do you think line *m* above is called a line of symmetry?**

Recall some special angle and line relationships that can help you explore reflections.

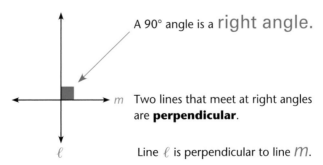

A 90° angle is a right angle.

m Two lines that meet at right angles are **perpendicular**.

Line *ℓ* is perpendicular to line *m*.

Now it's your turn to make a design with line symmetry.

MATERIALS

Key
Tape
Ruler

Step A

Fold a piece of paper. Lightly tape a key or other small, flat object inside the folded paper.

Step B

Firmly press the paper around both sides of the key. Open the paper and remove the key. You will see an impression of the key and a reflection.

Step C

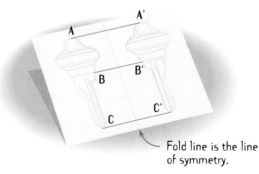

Draw three lines connecting corresponding points as shown.

Fold line is the line of symmetry.

1. At what angle do the three lines you drew meet the line of symmetry? Where is the halfway point for each of the three lines?

2. Compare the original figure and its reflected image. What similarities do you see? What differences do you see?

A reflection transforms points into mirror images. An object and its reflection have the same shape and size, but the figures face in opposite directions.

Line symmetry is also called **reflectional symmetry.**

We can use properties of the line of symmetry to find reflections on a coordinate grid.

EXAMPLES

1. Point $A(-3, 4)$ is reflected over the y-axis. Give the coordinates of its reflection image.

Draw a line from A perpendicular to the y-axis. Continue the line the same distance so that $(3, 4)$ is the reflection image over the y-axis.

2. Point $A(-3, 4)$ is reflected over the x-axis. Give the coordinates of its reflection image.

Draw a line from A perpendicular to the x-axis. Continue the line the same distance so that $(-3, -4)$ is the reflection image over the x-axis.

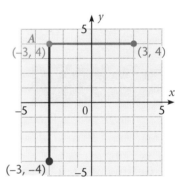

TRY IT

Name the coordinates of the image point if the given point is reflected over the y-axis.

  a. $A(-2, 3)$ **b.** $B(1, 2)$ **c.** $C(4, -2)$

Name the coordinates of the image point if the given point is reflected over the x-axis.

  d. $A(-2, 3)$ **e.** $B(1, 2)$ **f.** $C(4, -2)$

You can get a good feeling about how a reflection transforms a figure by standing in front of a mirror. Is that freckle on the left side of your face or on the right side?

REFLECT

1. How can you tell if a figure is a reflection image of another figure?
2. How could you use a mirror when making a reflection transformation?
3. If the point (a, b) is reflected over the y-axis, what are the coordinates of the image?
4. If the point (a, b) is reflected over the x-axis, what are the coordinates of the image?
5. Describe the relationship between line symmetry and reflection.

Exercises

CORE

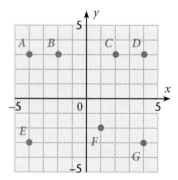

1. **Getting Started** Point A is shown on the coordinate grid.
   a. Which point is the reflection of A over the y-axis?
   b. Which point is the reflection of A over the x-axis?

Name the coordinates of the image point if the given point is reflected over the y-axis.

2. $A(2, -3)$
3. $C(-1, 2)$
4. $X(-3, -5)$
5. $L(4, 0)$

Name the coordinates of the image point if the given point is reflected over the x-axis.

6. $A(1, -3)$
7. $C(4, 3)$
8. $X(-2, -1)$
9. $L(0, -2)$

10. Make a design by filling all five boxes. Use reflections.

11. $\triangle PQR$ has vertices $P(-1, 4)$, $Q(3, 2)$, and $R(-1, 1)$. The triangle is reflected over the x-axis. Find the coordinates of the vertices of the image $\triangle P'Q'R'$. Draw $\triangle PQR$ and $\triangle P'Q'R'$ on graph paper.

12. Why are reflection and symmetry important to architects? What other professionals might use ideas about reflection and symmetry in their work?

Monticello, Virginia

 LOOK AHEAD

Which angle has a measure of

13. 90°?

14. 45°?

15. 135°?

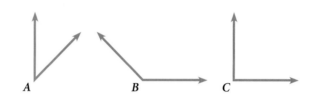

MORE PRACTICE

16. Is point D a reflection image of point C over the y-axis? How can you tell?

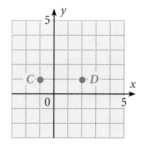

Give the coordinates of the image point if the given point is reflected over the y-axis.

17. $A(-3, 1)$ **18.** $C(3, 4)$ **19.** $X(-1, -2)$ **20.** $L(-2, 0)$

21. $A(-3, 2)$ **22.** $C(2, -1)$ **23.** $X(-5, -3)$ **24.** $L(0, 4)$

Give the coordinates of the image point if the given point is reflected over the x-axis.

25. $A(-3, 2)$ **26.** $C(2, -1)$ **27.** $X(-5, -3)$ **28.** $L(0, 4)$

29. $A(-3, 1)$ **30.** $C(3, 4)$ **31.** $X(-1, -2)$ **32.** $L(-2, 0)$

33. $\triangle ABC$ has vertices $A(1, -4)$, $B(3, -2)$, and $C(-3, 3)$. The triangle is reflected over the y-axis. Find the coordinates of the image $\triangle A'B'C'$. Draw $\triangle ABC$ and $\triangle A'B'C'$ on graph paper.

MORE MATH REASONING

34. The L-shaped polygon is reflected over the *y*-axis. The image is then reflected over the *x*-axis. Find the coordinates of the vertices of the final image. Is there another way of manipulating the figure that will have the same effect as these two reflections?

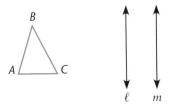

35. Line *ℓ* is parallel to line *m*. △*ABC* is reflected over line *ℓ*. The image, △*A'B'C'*, is then reflected over line *m* to get a new image, △*A"B"C"*. Copy and complete the sketch. How does △*ABC* compare with △*A"B"C"*?

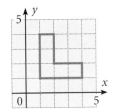

3-2
PART D Rotations

← C O N N E C T → *Translations and reflections are the two types of transformations that you saw earlier. You learned that they result from slides and flips. You will now learn about rotation. Rotation is the type of transformation that results when you turn a figure about a pivot point.*

These designs use a basic pattern that rotates.

Hmong tapestry

Hopi pottery

1. What type of symmetry, if any, do you see in the two rotation designs on page 230? Explain.

You can make your own rotation design.

EXPLORE: PUTTING A SPIN ON IT

MATERIALS

Compass
Key with round hole at top

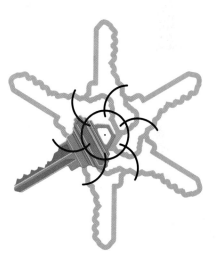

1. Make a circle. It should have a radius between 5 cm and 8 cm.

2. Keep your compass at the same radius you used to make the circle. Place the compass at any point on the circle. Make an arc on the circumference. Repeat until you have six arcs as shown.

3. Place the hole of the key on the center of the circle and turn the key so that its flat edge intersects an arc. Trace the key. This tracing is your original figure.

4. Repeat the process by rotating the key to each arc. Each new trace is an image of the original that is formed by turning about the center of the circle.

5. Label the original trace *O*. Number each succeeding turn image 1 through 5. Remember that a circle, or a complete turn, contains 360°. Measure the angle of turning from the original trace to each of its five images. Complete the table with the degree measures of each angle of turning.

Image	1	2	3	4	5
Angle of Turning					

6. Compare the shape and size of the original with the shape and size of the turn images.

A **rotation** is a transformation that turns a figure about a fixed point called the **center of rotation.** The angle of turning is called the **angle of rotation.**

CONSIDER

2. What is the degree measure of the angle of rotation for a one-half turn?

3. What is the degree measure of the angle of rotation for a one-quarter turn?

EXAMPLES

Square *ABCD* is rotated about its center *O*.

1. What is the image of *B* if it is rotated 90° counterclockwise?

Counterclockwise 90° is a one-quarter turn that takes *B* to *C*.

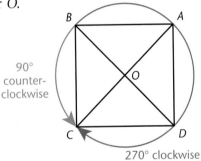

2. What is the image of *B* if it is rotated 270° clockwise?

Clockwise 270° is a three-quarter turn that takes B to C.

A rotation of 90° counterclockwise moves a point to the same position as a rotation of 270° clockwise.

Two rotations are the same if they are in opposite directions and the measures of the angles of rotation add up to 360°.

TRY IT

Give a rotation that is the same as the given rotation.

a. 60° clockwise   **b.** 30° counterclockwise
c. 90° clockwise   **d.** 25° counterclockwise
e. 45° clockwise   **f.** 180° counterclockwise

You have learned that this ceiling fan
has rotational symmetry. Rotational
symmetry also is called point symmetry.

*This figure can be rotated less than
a full turn so that it matches itself.*

REFLECT

1. If you rotate a figure, what will happen to its area?
2. Does a square have rotational symmetry? If so, where is the center of
   rotation?
3. What is the effect of rotating a figure 360°?
4. What should be the measure of the angle of rotation to fit a design
   exactly four times around a point?
5. Can two rotations of a figure result in the same image? Explain.

Exercises

CORE

1. **Getting Started** What is the angle
   of rotation that moves Figure A to
   Figure B?

   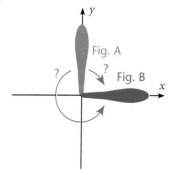

2. **Aerodynamics** Make a sketch of what
   this propeller design will look like if it
   is rotated 90° about the origin.

   Industry

   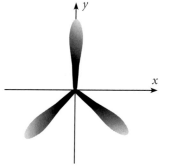

3. From the group of terms, choose the term that does not belong and explain why.
   Rotation, Congruent, Translation, Reflection

4. Make a template of the L-shaped figure on cardboard. Mark a point *O* on your paper. Create a design by rotating the template about point *O* and making tracings using four different angles of rotation.

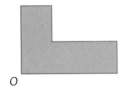

Regular hexagon *ABCDEF* is rotated about its center *O*.

5. What is the image of *B* if it is rotated 120° counterclockwise?

6. What is the image of *F* if it is rotated 240° clockwise?

7. What is the image of *C* if it is rotated 180° clockwise?

8. What is the image of $\overline{CD}$ if it is rotated 60° counterclockwise?

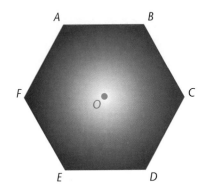

Give a rotation that is the same as the given rotation.

9. 20° clockwise

10. 150° counterclockwise

11. Zelda starts turning the octagonal nut clockwise from the position shown. Through what angle of rotation must she turn it so that *H* moves to *E*?

12. Does a stop sign have rotational symmetry? Explain.

13. In a Turkish Market In the Middle Ages and early Renaissance, nomads carried **kilims,** small loomed spreads, for praying, eating, and sleeping.

    a. How is rotation used in this more recent kilim from Western Turkey?

    b. What other transformations or symmetry do you see?

14. Copy the figure. Draw the figure you would get if you held point D fixed and turned the figure one-quarter turn (90°) in a clockwise direction.

15. How many degrees must you turn the figure to give it a complete turn? How will the figure look after a complete turn?

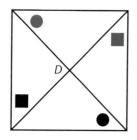

 ## *LOOK BACK*

16. A house sits on a square lot that covers about 22,500 square feet. What is the length of a side? [2-1]

17. Simplify $-3(2x - 4)$. [2-3]

MORE PRACTICE

A boat steering wheel is like a regular hexagon *ABCDEF* that rotates about its center O.

18. What is the image of B if it is rotated 240° counterclockwise?

19. What is the image of F if it is rotated 60° clockwise?

20. What is the image of $\overline{AF}$ if it is rotated 300° counterclockwise?

21. What is the image of C if it is rotated 180° counterclockwise?

22. What is the image of $\overline{AB}$ if it is rotated 120° clockwise?

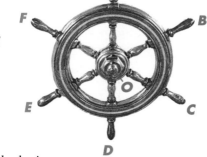

Give a rotation that is the same as the given rotation.

23. 35° clockwise

24. 110° counterclockwise

25. 70° clockwise

26. 100° clockwise

MORE MATH REASONING

27. Design a pattern that has both rotational symmetry and reflectional symmetry. Draw the lines of symmetry on your pattern.

28. Draw rectangle *PQRS* with vertices $P(-3, 4)$, $Q(3, 4)$, $R(3, -3)$, and $S(-3, -3)$ on graph paper. *PQRS* is rotated 90° clockwise about the origin. Draw the image and give the coordinates of its vertices.

29. Describe how the final design was generated starting with the original pattern.

Original

Final Design

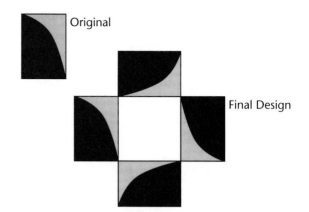
← **CONNECT** → *Mathematicians use transformations to help them understand nature. Artists use transformations to help them create works of art. You've explored translations, reflections, and rotations to transform basic figures. Transformations can produce designs that have translational, reflectional, or rotational symmetry.*

Navajo weavers, African basket makers, and pioneer American quilt makers all have used geometric patterns in their creations. Geometric patterns also have been found in Egyptian, Greek, Roman, Arabian, and Japanese art.

Using the same original pattern, you can make different designs by using a variety of transformations.

Pottery jars from Acoma Pueblo , New Mexico

EXPLORE: ORDER OUT OF CHAOS

MATERIALS

Graph paper, Ruler, Coin, Colored pencils or crayons

1. Make a copy of the divided square as shown.

2. For each of the eight sections, flip a coin to decide whether to shade it. Do each shading in a different color.

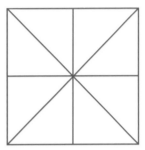

3. Create a 16-block design by using translations, reflections, and rotations of the original basic pattern.

4. Look for smaller, new patterns within the 16-block design. Explain how the new design relates to the original design. Identify any symmetries.

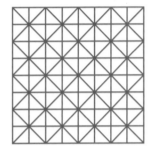

REFLECT

1. How are translations, reflections, and rotations similar? How are they different?

2. Why do you think that many people find designs based on translations, reflections, and rotations to be visually pleasing?

3. How can you find the translation image of a point on a coordinate grid? the reflection image of a point?

4. What is the difference between reflectional symmetry and rotational symmetry?

Self-Assessment

1. Which transformation can you use to make a picture of a daisy starting with a picture of a petal?

2. Which transformation can you use to make a picture of a butterfly starting with a picture of a wing?

Give a rotation that is the same as the given rotation.

3. 25° clockwise

4. 180° counterclockwise

5. 330° clockwise

6. Sketch a design that has translational symmetry and reflectional symmetry at the same time.

7. Simplify $4(x^2 - 4x)$. [2-3]

Determine whether each statement is true or false.

8. The image of a figure after a reflection faces in the same direction as the original figure.

9. No point remains in the same place after a translation.

10. Which of the following is not a type of transformation?
   (a) translation   (b) rotation   (c) symmetry
   (d) reflection   (e) not here

11. The vertices of $\triangle ABC$ are $A(2, 2)$, $B(5, 2)$, and $C(5, 7)$.
   a. Find the vertices of the image $\triangle A'B'C'$ under the translation $<-3, 2>$.
   b. How does the translation move the points of the triangle?
   c. Verify your answer by drawing $\triangle ABC$ and $\triangle A'B'C'$ on graph paper.

12. Copy the figure and draw all lines of symmetry. [3-1]

13. $\triangle KLM$ has vertices $K(-5, 6)$, $L(-2, 6)$, and $M(-4, 1)$. The triangle is reflected over the y-axis. Find the coordinates of the vertices of the image $\triangle K'L'M'$. Draw the original figure and its reflection image on graph paper.

14. **Off the Wall** How did the designer of this wallpaper pattern make use of transformations?

Careers

Cooper-Hewitt, National Design Museum, Smithsonian Inst./Art Resource, NY

3-3 Patterns

T R A C I N G
Ancestry

Alex Haley, Author

In the book *Roots,* author Alex Haley traced his own family's history in Africa, the American colonies, and the United States. People from all ethnic groups are interested in their heritage. The study of ancestry is called "genealogy."

Archaeologists on digs in India, Egypt, and other countries in Asia and the Middle East have turned up stone tablets inscribed with records of family ancestry.

Two types of diagrams are often used in tracing lines of ancestry. The top diagram shows a person's ancestors. The bottom diagram shows a person's descendants.

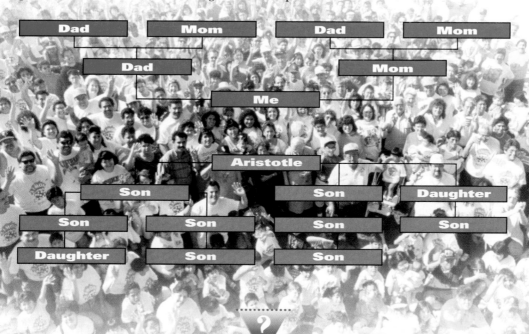

1. Why might it be more difficult for people in the United States to trace their ancestry than for people in many other countries?
2. What are other books or movies that have a theme of ethnic or family pride?
3. Which of the two types of drawings above is usually used in making a "family tree"?
4. Can you see a pattern for the generations in either diagram?

← CONNECT → *You have seen that patterns using translations, reflections, and rotations can be found in nature as well as in handicrafts. Now you will learn to recognize and extend patterns.*

Pattern of Numbers:

2   4   8   16

Pattern of Letters:

S   M   T   W   T

Pattern of Figures:

A set that has elements that seem to be in a certain order has a **pattern.** You can use the pattern to predict the next element. The set may contain numbers, letters, or figures.

CONSIDER

?

1. What pattern do you see for 2, 4, 8, 16? What is the next number?
2. Can you recognize the pattern in the letters SMTWT? What will be the next two letters?
3. How many dots will be in the fourth figure for the pattern of dots above? the fifth figure?

EXPLORE: A MALE BEE'S FAMILY TREE

Bees have an interesting reproductive system. A male bee comes from an unfertilized egg. A female bee comes from a fertilized egg. The male bee has only one parent, the female. The female has both a male and a female parent.

Use this male bee family tree.

1. What is the pattern for the numbers: 1, 1, 2, 3, 5, and 8 in the total column? Predict the next number.
2. Test your prediction by copying the diagram and completing the family tree for the sixth generation back. How many bees are in that generation?
3. How many bees should be in the seventh generation back? the eighth generation back? Check by drawing the family tree back two more generations.
4. Make up a pattern using numbers, letters, or figures. Give the first four elements. Describe the pattern.

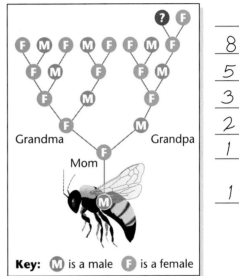

Total Number:

___
8
5
3
2
1

1

Key: Ⓜ is a male Ⓕ is a female

The pattern of numbers given by the total in each generation of bees (1, 1, 2, 3, 5, 8, ...) comes up in science, art, music, and nature. It is called the Fibonacci sequence. The Italian merchant Leonardo of Pisa, called Fibonacci, found this pattern in a problem he studied around the year 1200.

If you count the number of hexagons on the spiral of a pineapple, you will get a Fibonacci number.

Give the next two elements in each pattern.

a. 1, 4, 9, 16

b. AB, DE, GH, JK

c.

d. 2, 5, 8, 11

Recognizing a pattern can help you solve a problem.

EXAMPLE

A building-supply house is gathering blocks for building steps of various heights. How many blocks are needed for a staircase that is six steps high?

> **Problem-Solving Tip**
>
> Look for a pattern.

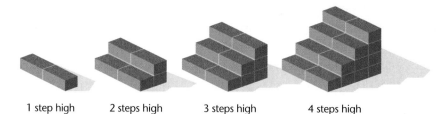

| 1 step high | 2 steps high | 3 steps high | 4 steps high |

a 1-step-high staircase uses 2 blocks → 2

a 2-step-high staircase uses 6 blocks → 2 + 4

a 3-step-high staircase uses 12 blocks → 2 + 4 + 6

a 4-step-high staircase uses 20 blocks → 2 + 4 + 6 + 8

In each case, the next addend is 2 more than the previous addend.

So a six-step-high staircase needs 2 + 4 + 6 + 8 + 10 + 12, or 42 blocks.

REFLECT

1. Does a set always show a pattern?

2. Give an example of a number pattern that uses multiplication.

3. Is it possible for two people looking at the same pattern to come up with different ways to continue the pattern? If you think so, give an example.

Exercises

CORE

1. Getting Started Consider the set of three figures.

Fig. 1   Fig. 2   Fig. 3

a. How many sides are in Figure 1? Figure 2? Figure 3?
b. Describe the pattern.
c. Draw the next figure in the pattern.

Find the next three elements in the pattern.

2. 3, 4, 7, 11, 18

3. 1, −3, 9, −27

4. I, II, III, IV

5. $\frac{1}{2}, \frac{2}{3}, \frac{3}{4}, \frac{4}{5}$

6. 81, 27, 9, 3

7. YZ, XY, WX, VW

8. Explain how you agree or disagree with the following statement.
Every set of elements shows a pattern.

9. How many blocks are in the 4th building?
the 5th building? the 10th building?

> **Problem-Solving Tip**
>
> Look for a pattern.

Bldg. 1   Bldg. 2   Bldg. 3

Give the missing elements in the pattern.

10. ____, ____, ____, ____, 32, 64, 128, 256

11. J, F, M, A, M, ____, ____, ____

12. 2, 6, 12, 20, 30, 42, ____, 72, 90, ____, 132

13. Make a pattern of dots that shows the same
pattern as 1, 4, 9, 16.

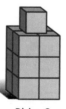

●

Fig. 1

14. Half and Hole Punch a hole in a sheet of paper and you'll have one hole. Fold the paper and punch another hole and you'll have a total of three holes in the paper. Fold again and punch a third time and you'll have seven holes.

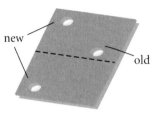
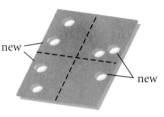

1st fold   2nd fold

The number of holes is given by the pattern 1, 3, 7, 15. Find the next five numbers in the pattern.

15. A Fine Thing At Youngstown Library, the fee for overdue books is 2 cents for the first day and 5 cents for the second day. For each day after that, the fine is twice the sum of the fines for the two preceding days. How much must Emanual pay when he returns his book if it is 5 days overdue?

 LOOK AHEAD

Evaluate each expression for $n = 1, 2, 3, 4, 5.$

16. $2n$　　　　**17.** $3n - 2$　　　　**18.** n^2　　　　**19.** $2n^2 + 1$

MORE PRACTICE

Find the next three elements in each pattern.

20. 23, 20, 17, 14, 11, 8, 5

21. $\frac{1}{2}$, 2, 5, 11, 23, 47

22. 0, 2, 6, 12

23. I, III, V, VII

24. 0.1, 0.51, 0.511, 0.5511

25. 12, −22, 32, −42

26. $\frac{1}{1}, \frac{1}{4}, \frac{1}{9}, \frac{1}{16}$

27. 64, 32, 16, 8

28. −42, −17, 8, 33, 58, 83

29. 0, 3, 8, 15

Give the missing elements in the pattern.

30. 2, 5, 7, 12, 19, ____, ____, ____

31. O, T, ____, F, F, ____, S, ____, N

32. 2, 5, 10, 17, 26, 37, 50, ____, 82, 101, ____, 145

33. −1, −5, −9, −13, −17, ____, −25, −29, ____, −37

34. Digging Deep An archaeologist digging in some ancient Roman ruins found a strange group of symbols:

Write a paragraph explaining the pattern. Where might the symbols have come from?

35. Consider this pattern of blocks.

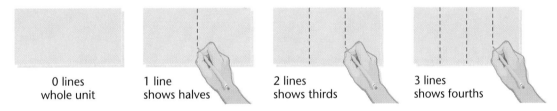

Bldg. 1   Bldg. 2   Bldg. 3   Bldg. 4   Bldg. 5

How many blocks would be in Building 6? Building 7? Building 10?

36. Draw the next five figures in the pattern.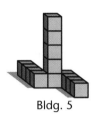

MORE MATH REASONING

37. Dividing It Up To help a friend understand fractions, you might make a rectangle and divide it into halves, thirds, and fourths showing fractions with denominators 2, 3, and 4.

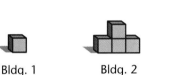

0 lines   1 line   2 lines   3 lines
whole unit   shows halves   shows thirds   shows fourths

a. How many lines would you draw to show fifths (fractions with denominator 5)? sixths? sevenths?

b. How many lines would you draw to show fractions with denominator x?

c. Write an explanation that would help another student see the pattern.

38. The figure at the right shows three line segments: $\overline{AB}$, $\overline{BC}$, and $\overline{AC}$.

A   B   C

How many segments are shown in each of these figures?

Fig. 1   Fig. 2   Fig. 3   Fig. 4

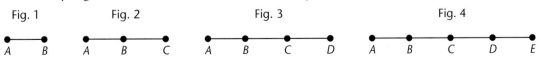

How many line segments will be in Figure 5?

← **CONNECT** → *You've seen patterns formed with numbers, letters, and figures. When patterns are formed with numbers, algebraic expressions can be used to model the pattern. You now will see how to use variables to write expressions that model number patterns.*

A number pattern like 2, 4, 8, 16, ... is an ordered list of numbers. We can associate the value of each number on the list with its position. To help see this, let's look at how this number pattern models a process in biology, the study of life.

The paramecium, a single-celled animal, reproduces by splitting apart. A new generation is born every 5 hours. Each generation has twice as many organisms as the previous one.

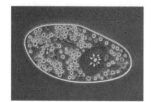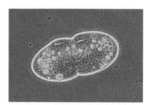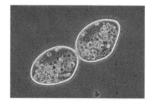

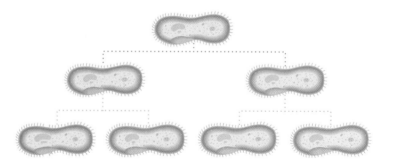

We can use a pattern to find out how many of these organisms will be in any generation.

The number pattern, 2, 4, 8, 16, ..., models the paramecium generations.

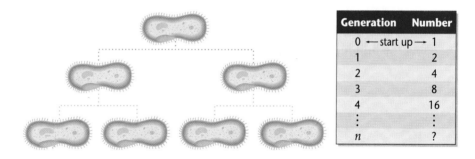

Generation	Number
0 ← start up →	1
1	2
2	4
3	8
4	16
⋮	⋮
n	?

We can relate the numbers in the pattern to their position in the list.

1st generation → 2^1 or 2 animals

2nd generation → 2^2 or 4 animals

3rd generation → 2^3 or 8 animals

We can use a variable (n) to represent the nth generation. Now we can write an expression for the number of animals:

nth generation → 2^n animals

So 2^n is an expression for the number pattern 2, 4, 8, 16, ...

CONSIDER ?

1. **What do the three dots mean in the number pattern?**
2. **How can you use the expression 2^n to find out how many animals are in the 8th generation? the 10th generation?**

An ordered list of numbers like 1, 2, 4, 8, 16, ... is called a **sequence.**

Each number in the sequence is called a **term.**

Sequences often have patterns that can be described by expressions.

MATERIALS

Blocks or sugar cubes

Using sugar cubes or blocks, make the five buildings shown. Label the buildings.

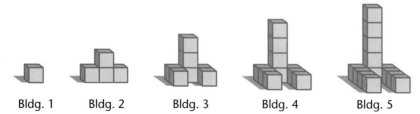

Bldg. 1   Bldg. 2   Bldg. 3   Bldg. 4   Bldg. 5   ...

You are going to look for a relationship between the building number and the number of blocks it takes to make the building.

Problem-Solving Tip

Organize the data.

1. Make a table with a similar layout and complete it for all five buildings.

Building Number	Blocks in Each Wing	Blocks in Tower	Total Blocks
1			
2			

2. Look for patterns in the numbers in each column. Let *n* stand for the building number. What is an expression for the number of blocks in each wing? in the tower? What is an expression for the total number of blocks in the building?

3. Describe Building 6. How many blocks in each wing? in the tower? How many blocks in all? Describe Building 8.

In the Explore, you found three expressions using the variable *n* to describe the number patterns for the wings, towers, and total blocks in the sequence of buildings.

When you are able to describe a pattern with an expression, you can tell what happens down the line in the sequence. Just replace the variable by the term's position number.

Describe the pattern for the sequence 4, 7, 10, 13, ... What is the 10th term?

Elena thinks ...

That's easy!

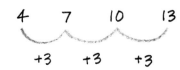

Each term is 3 more than the one before it.

So I can list 10 terms: 4, 7, 10, 13, 16, 19, 22, 25, 28, 31.

The 10th term is 31.

Pei thinks ...

I'll try to relate each term's value to its position in the list.

Since the term values are separated by 3, I'll try tripling the position numbers to start.

3(1)	3(2)	3(3)	3(4)
3	6	9	12

Those are almost the right values. I just need to add 1.

If I triple the position numbers and add 1, I get the right values.

That was tough to see. Using n to give the position number, I can write an expression to describe the sequence:

$$3n + 1.$$

Pos. 1	**Pos. 2**	**Pos. 3**	**Pos. 4**
3(**1**)+1	3(**2**)+1	3(**3**)+1	3(**4**)+1
4	7	10	13

Now I can get the 10th term without listing the first 9 terms.

10th term → 3(10) + 1

The 10th term is 31.

CONSIDER

?

3. How do you start to find a pattern for a sequence?
4. What clues do you use to decide if multiplying, dividing, adding, subtracting, or even squaring is involved?

Describing a pattern is like solving a puzzle.

Write an expression to describe the pattern. What is the 20th term?

a. 2, 4, 6, 8, ...   **b.** 3, 5, 7, 9, ...
c. 1, 4, 9, 16, ...   **d.** 2, 5, 8, 11, ...

Suppose that an expression like $4n + 2$ describes a sequence. The next Example shows how to replace n by position numbers to get terms of the sequence.

EXAMPLE

Write the first five terms of the sequence described by $4n + 2$.

Replace n with 1 to get the first term, with 2 to get the second term, and so on.

Term **1**   Term **2**   Term **3**   Term **4**   Term **5**

$4(1) + 2$ $4(2) + 2$ $4(3) + 2$ $4(4) + 2$ $4(5) + 2$

So the first five terms are 6, 10, 14, 18, and 22.

An expression with a variable is a powerful way to describe a pattern for a sequence.

REFLECT

1. Why do we say that a number pattern like 3, 6, 9, 12, ... is an ordered list?
2. Why is an algebraic expression a useful way to describe a number pattern?
3. Do you think you can describe every number pattern with an expression? Illustrate with examples.
4. If the expression $n^2 + 2$ describes a sequence, how would you find the value of the third term?

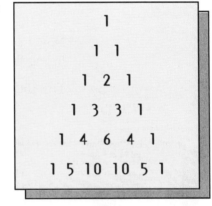

Pascal's Triangle is a famous arithmetic triangle that contains number patterns occurring in algebra, geometry, and nature.

Exercises

CORE

1. **Getting Started** What are the first five terms of the sequence given by the expression $2n - 3$? Find out by evaluating the expression for $n = 1, 2, 3, 4,$ and 5.

2. Write the letter of the second pair that best matches the first pair.
   Term: sequence as (a) age: height, (b) letter: word, (c) dog: cat, (d) vertex: triangle

Write the first five terms of the sequence given by each expression. To organize your work, copy and complete the chart.

	Expression	$n = 1$	$n = 2$	$n = 3$	$n = 4$	$n = 5$
3.	$n + 5$					
4.	$3n + 1$					
5.	$2n - 1$					
6.	$(n + 1)(n - 1)$					
7.	$n^2 - 1$					

8. Compare your answers in Exercises 6 and 7. What do you observe? What relationship does this suggest for the expressions $(n + 1)(n - 1)$ and $n^2 - 1$?

Write an expression to describe the pattern. Then find the indicated term.

9. 5, 10, 15, 20, ... (9th term)

10. $-1, -2, -3, -4, ...$ (12th term)

11. $1, \frac{1}{2}, \frac{1}{3}, \frac{1}{4}, ...$ (25th term)

12. 0, 2, 6, 12, ... (100th term)

13. **Good and Bad Growth** The chart shows the estimated number of four types of containers in the United States in 1995 and the projected growth rate per year. Use your calculator to find the number of containers of each type in the year 2000.

Type of Material	Billions of Containers Used in U.S. (1995)	Estimated Annual Growth Rate
Aluminum	87	3%
Glass	33	−2%
Steel	11	−10%
Plastic	62	10%

87×1.03

89.61×1.03

89.61

14. **Digging for Roots** Start a family tree using yourself or someone you admire as the starting point. Get as much information as you can, including names and dates.

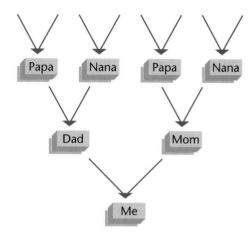

   a. Is there a pattern in the number of relatives going back by generation? If so, describe the pattern.

   b. Is the pattern similar to the paramecium pattern? If so, how?

   c. How many years back can you trace the ancestry? Write a brief family history.

 LOOK BACK

15. Which of the following transformations does this figure show? [3-2]

   (a) translation   (b) reflection   (c) rotation
   (d) expansion   (e) not here

16. Decide whether the quantity is a constant or a variable: the distance between lines of longitude on a globe. [2-3]

17. Simplify $18 \div (8 - 2) + 2^2 \cdot 7 - 11$. [2-1]

MORE PRACTICE

Write the first five terms of the sequence whose pattern is given by each expression. To organize your work, copy and complete the chart.

	Expression	$n = 1$	$n = 2$	$n = 3$	$n = 4$	$n = 5$
18.	$n(n + 1)$					
19.	$2n + 5$					
20.	$n^2 + 5$					
21.	$(n + 1)(n + 2)$					

Write an expression to describe the pattern. Then find the indicated term.

22. 4, 6, 8, 10, ... (15th term)

23. 1, 3, 9, 27, ... (8th term)

24. 2, 8, 18, 32, ... (25th term)

25. 0, 3, 8, 15, ... (10th term)

26. 5, 9, 13, 17, ... (8th term)

27. $-5, -1, 3, 7, ...$ (12th term)

MORE MATH REASONING

28. Gearing Up for Patterns Think of how the five gears shown would turn each other—clockwise or counterclockwise. The first gear turns counterclockwise.

5th   3rd   1st

4th   2nd

...

a. What do the three dots mean?

b. In what direction would the 2nd gear turn? the 3rd? the 4th? the 5th? the 6th? the 100th?

c. How would the nth gear in the row turn if n is an odd number?

d. How would the nth gear in the row turn if n is an even number?

e. If the first gear rotated clockwise instead of counterclockwise, how would the answers for **28b, 28c,** and **28d** change?

29. According to the *Guinness Book of World Records* (1988), the world record for setting up dominoes and toppling them over with one push is 281,581. The person shown at right has made a triangular pattern of dominoes that will all fall when the front one is pushed.

Copy the table. Use the pattern to fill in the "?"s in the chart for rows 6–25.

Row #	1	2	3	4	5	6	7	.	.	.	25
Total Dominoes Used	1	3	6	10	15	?	?	.	.	.	?

30. What is the next number in the sequence 1, 2, 6, 24, 120, ... ?

Making Connections

← C O N N E C T → *You've looked at patterns that are made with numbers, letters, and figures. Number patterns are sequences of terms. You've seen that sometimes the pattern for a sequence can be described using an algebraic expression. When you can write an expression, it makes it easy to calculate the value of any term.*

Recall that the family tree of a male bee, a pattern of figures, suggested a pattern of numbers called the Fibonacci sequence.

Other patterns of figures
can also suggest sequences
of numbers.

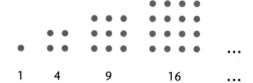

1   4   9   16   ...

EXPLORE: FIGURING IT OUT

For each pattern of figures,

a. draw the next two figures.
b. write a number sequence related to the pattern.
c. write an algebraic expression to describe the pattern of the number sequence.

1.

2.

3.

4.

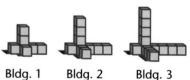

Bldg. 1   Bldg. 2   Bldg. 3

1. Where are some places that you might see patterns?

2. Why would you want to write an algebraic expression for a number sequence?

3. Give an illustration of a pattern using letters. Describe the pattern.

4. Why is the position of an element in a pattern important?

Detail from Georges Seurat's
Le Cirque.
Musee d'Orsay, Paris.

Self-Assessment

Find the next three elements in each pattern.

1. 10, 1, 9, 2, 8, 3, ...

2. 3, 4, 7, 8, 11, 12, ...

3. X, XI, XII, XIII, ...

4. AZ, YB, CX, WD, ...

5. What figure comes next if the pattern below continues as it has started? Explain.

Write the word or phrase that correctly completes the statement.

6. A sequence is a ____ of numbers.

7. Each element in a sequence is called a ____.

8. Simplify $36 \div (20 - 16) + \sqrt{25}$. [2-1]

9. An Ancient Rhyme People are not the only things with family histories. This Mother Goose nursery rhyme can be traced all the way back to its roots in ancient Egypt (1500 BC).

a. Draw a diagram to explain how to solve this problem.

b. Describe a pattern to solve the problem.

c. Use a calculator to find how many were going to St. Ives.

d. Some people claim that the answer to the riddle is 1. How can this be correct?

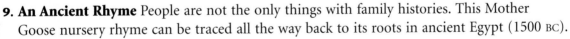

As I was going to St. Ives,
I met a Man with seven Wives.
Every wife had seven Sacks,
Every sack had seven Cats.
Every cat had seven Kits,
Kits, Cats, Sacks, and Wives,
How many were going to St. Ives?

10. Jorge has a plan for building geometric figures from toothpicks.

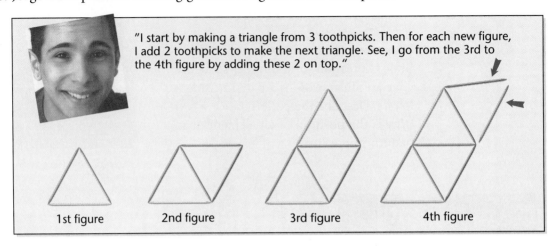

"I start by making a triangle from 3 toothpicks. Then for each new figure, I add 2 toothpicks to make the next triangle. See, I go from the 3rd to the 4th figure by adding these 2 on top."

1st figure   2nd figure   3rd figure   4th figure

If Jorge bought a box with 100 toothpicks in it, how many triangles would be in the largest shape he could make?

11. Use a calculator, a ruler, and the pages of a book to help you compute the thickness of a single sheet of paper. Use the measure that you get to answer the questions below.

a. If you fold a sheet of paper one time, how thick is the stack?

b. If you fold a sheet of paper two times, how thick is the stack?

c. If you fold a sheet of paper three times, how thick is the stack?

d. If you fold a sheet of paper four times, how thick is the stack?

e. If you fold a sheet of paper n times, how thick is the stack?

f. Someone said that if you could fold a sheet 50 times, the stack would reach the moon. Is this true?

Find the first five terms of each sequence.

12. Start with -1 as the first term. Each term is three more than the square of the preceding term.

13. The sequence is described by the expression $4n - 3$.

14. Start with -1 as the first term and 1 as the second term. Each term is the sum of the preceding two terms.

Chapter 3 Review

In Chapter 3, after investigating three types of transformations and their symmetry, you identified and worked with figures that tessellate. Using sets of numbers, letters, and geometric figures, you learned to find and extend patterns. Then you used mathematical expressions to represent number patterns. You found that many of the ideas in this chapter can be seen in nature and are used by designers and artists.

KEY TERMS

angle of rotation [3-2]

center of rotation [3-2]

congruent figures [3-2]

equilateral triangle [3-1]

Fibonacci sequence [3-3]

hexagon [3-1]

image [3-2]

line of symmetry [3-1]

line symmetry [3-1]

octagon [3-1]

pattern [3-3]

pentagon [3-1]

perpendicular [3-2]

polygon [3-1]

quadrilateral [3-1]

reflection [3-2]

reflectional symmetry [3-2]

regular polygon [3-1]

right angle [3-2]

rotation [3-2]

rotational symmetry [3-2]

sequence [3-3]

square [3-1]

term [3-3]

tessellation [3-1]

transformation [3-2]

translation [3-2]

translational symmetry [3-2]

Determine whether each statement is true or false. If the statement is false, change the underlined word or phrase to make it true.

1. A tessellation is an arrangement of figures that fill a flat surface but do not overlap or leave gaps.

2. The measure of an acute angle is 90°.

3. Every polygon is a quadrilateral.

Write the word or phrase that correctly completes the statement.

4. A ____ has five sides.

5. A sequence is an ____.

CONCEPTS AND APPLICATIONS

6. How many lines of symmetry does an equilateral triangle have? [3-1]

7. Which figure cannot be used to make a tessellation? [3-1]
    (a) square   (b) circle   (c) trapezoid   (d) rectangle   (e) not here

Is Figure A congruent to Figure B? Explain. [3-2]

8.

Fig. A   Fig. B

9.

Fig. A   Fig. B

10.

Fig. A   Fig. B

11. Decide whether you must slide, slide and flip, or slide and turn Figure A to make it fit on Figure B. [3-2]

a.

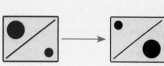

Fig. A   Fig. B

b.

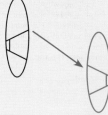

Fig. A   Fig. B

c.

Fig. A   Fig. B

12. What is the mathematical name for a slide? a flip? a turn? [3-2]

13. a. Tell how the translation $<-5, 2>$ moves a point. [3-2]
    b. $\triangle ABC$ has vertices $A(1, -2)$, $B(2, 5)$, and $C(4, 2)$. Find the coordinates of the vertices of the image after a translation of $<-5, 2>$. Plot and label both the original and its image on graph paper.

Name the coordinates of the image point if the point is reflected over the given axis. [3-2]

14. $M(3, 0)$; y-axis   **15.** $T(7, -2)$; y-axis   **16.** $P(-4, -8)$; x-axis

17. Copy the figure. Then draw the other half of the figure so that the red line is a line of symmetry. [3-1]

18. Which of the following transforms a figure into its mirror image? [3-2]
(a) reflection   (b) separation   (c) rotation   (d) translation   (e) not here

19. Which of the following transformations describes a figure that has been moved 73° clockwise about a point? [3-2]
(a) reflection   (b) separation   (c) rotation   (d) translation   (e) not here

20. Calculate $20 \div (68 - 3) + 3^2 \cdot 7 - 10$. [2-1]

21. Simplify $(4x^2 - 5x + 1) + (2x^2 + 3x - 5)$. [2-3]

22. Simplify $-3(2x - 4)$. [2-3]

Find the missing elements in each of the following patterns. [3-3]

23. 3, 6, 11, 18, 27, 38, ___, ___, ___

24. J, D, F, N, M, O, A, S, M, ___, ___, ___

25. What figure comes next if the pattern below continues? Explain. [3-3]

26. Write an expression to describe the pattern. Then find the indicated term. [3-3]

5, 8, 11, 14, ... (16th term)

CONCEPTS AND CONNECTIONS

27. History This pendant models a circular window in the Iolani "Royal Hawk" Palace in Honolulu. The only royal palace in the United States, it was the home of King Kalakaua, the last Hawaiian monarch, and his sister, Liliuokalani.
  a. What is the image of *A* if it is rotated 135° clockwise?
  b. Give a rotation that is the same as 135° clockwise.
  c. Where is the center of rotation?
  d. Does this pendant show reflectional symmetry? rotational symmetry?

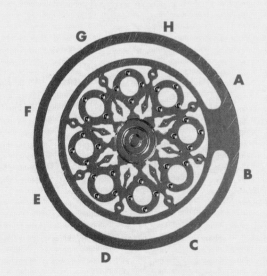

SELF-EVALUATION

Use the ideas you learned in Chapter 3 to sketch and label examples of transformations and a tessellation. Then make up several figures and number patterns of your own. Try to find expressions to represent your number patterns. You will want to review the definitions and examples of the chapter.

Chapter 3 Assessment

TEST

Determine whether each statement is true or false. If the statement is false, change the underlined word or phrase to make it true.

1. If you fold a figure over its <u>line of symmetry</u>, both halves match exactly.

2. A regular <u>hexagon</u> has eight sides of the same length.

3. <u>Polygon</u> figures have exactly the same size and shape.

4. Which figure has no lines of symmetry?
   (a) circle   (b) square   (c) regular octagon   (d) rectangle   (e) not here

5. a. Explain why this design is a tessellation.
  b. Name two kinds of figures that were used.
  c. Name another figure that tessellates.

6. Tell how the translation <−2, 4> moves a point.

Find the image of each point after the given translation.

7. $M(7, -2)$; <4, 5>   **8.** $E(0, 4)$; <−2, 1>   **9.** $T(-7, -5)$; <3, −2>

10. a. Explain why Figure A is congruent to Figure B.
   b. What kind of transformation does this design show?
   c. What is the relationship between M and M'?

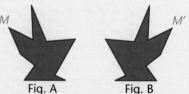

Fig. A   Fig. B

Name the coordinates of the image if the original point is reflected over the *y*-axis.

11. $M(6, -3)$ **12.** $T(-5, 0)$ **13.** $X(4, 1)$

14. $\triangle ABC$ has vertices $A(3, 1)$, $B(-2, 5)$, and $C(-1, 2)$. The triangle is reflected over the x-axis. Find the coordinates of the image $\triangle A'B'C'$. Draw $\triangle ABC$ and $\triangle A'B'C'$ on graph paper.

15. a. What is the angle of rotation that moves the hour hand from 3:00 p.m. to 12:00 p.m. in a clockwise direction?
   b. Give a second rotation that is the same.
   c. Where is the center of rotation?

16. Calculate $18 \div (8 - 2) + 2^2 \cdot 7 - 11$. [2-1]

17. Simplify $(5x^2 + 4x + 2) + (2x^2 + 3x - 7)$.

18. Simplify $7(x^2 + 5)$.

Find the missing elements in each of the following patterns.

19. 22, 16, 10, 4, -2, ____, ____, ____

20. AC, BD, EG, FH, ____, ____, ____

21. What figure comes next if the pattern continues as it has started? Explain.

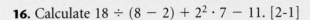

Write the word or phrase that correctly completes each statement.

22. A ____ is an ordered list of numbers like 2, 5, 8, 11, ...

23. In the list above, each number is called a ____.

Write the first five terms of the sequence whose pattern is given by each expression. To organize your work, copy and complete the chart.

	Expression	$n = 1$	$n = 2$	$n = 3$	$n = 4$	$n = 5$
24.	$4(n + 3)$					
25.	$n^2 + 5$					

26. Why do you think mathematicians find the Fibonacci sequence fascinating?

PERFORMANCE TASK

Now it's your turn to be creative. Rearrange the 50 stars and 13 stripes of the U.S. flag into a new design that could be used as a poster, quilt top, or Olympic Games insignia patch for a team jacket. You may use the stars and stripes in a variety of sizes. Explain which ideas you used from Chapter 3 and how you used them.

Chapter 4 Equations

40% Off

½ Price Sale

GIANT CLEARANCE!

Project A
Two for One
How do retail managers decide on a sales strategy? How much do you really save on special offers?

SPARKLE
Detergent
AWESOME
CLEANING
POWER!

SPARKLE
Detergent
AWESOME
CLEANING
POWER!

Project C
Break the Code
What is cryptography? How are patterns and messages coded and decoded?

Project B
Economy Size
What is unit pricing and how does it help you get the most for your money?

DEBBY McCLOSKEY

I didn't think I would ever use the math I learned in high school. It was difficult for me and very structured.

Today I use math to make a design become real. First I "image" the ornament in my mind, then the drawing has to be brought into the scale of the wood I'm using. The ornaments are three-dimensional. It's like solving a puzzle. Math is extremely important. You just don't realize how much you use it everyday."

Debby McCloskey
Ornament Designer
and Producer
*Snowy Mountain
Ornament* Co.
Cincinnati, Ohio

Chapter 4

Overview | Equations

4-1 Using Variables
Equations are used in business and science to show the relationship between quantities. Expressions with variables are used in these equations. You will solve equations using number sense and algebra tiles.

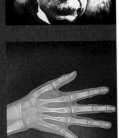

4-2 Solving Equations
Some real-world problems expressed as equations are not easily solved using number sense. You will learn to apply the properties of equality to solve equations that require more than mental calculations.

A Universal Language

What's in the universe?

First, nothing.

Second, nothing.

Third, nothing.

Fourth, a little radiation

...h, a little dirty hydrogen.

Stars in the universe and "dust bunnies" under your bed actually have something in common. The dust bunny starts as a small speck of dirt. More and more dust collects around it as time goes by. It grows and grows.

A star is made when "dirty hydrogen atoms" begin to collect in the sky. As time passes, more and more hydrogen is attracted and starts swirling around the center. This goes on and on until the swirling mass gets hot enough to burn. A "nuclear reactor in the sky"—a star—is formed, changing hydrogen into helium. Energy is given off in this process, according to a law that the physicist Albert Einstein discovered in 1905: $E = mc^2$.

Einstein's famous formula tells the amount of energy produced when matter is completely changed to energy. In this formula, E stands for **energy** produced, m stands for mass of **matter** converted, and c is the **speed of light,** or about 300,000 kilometers per second. This natural law relates to stars in the sky as well as to nuclear reactions here on earth.

1. How is $E = mc^2$ an example of using variables to express a special relationship?
2. Are all three letters used in the formula $E = mc^2$ variables? Explain.
3. Is there a difference between the formulas $E = mc^2$ and $mc^2 = E$? Explain.

265

4-1
PART A
Using Formulas

← C O N N E C T → *You have worked with many different expressions. You have found ways to simplify them, and you have learned to evaluate them. Sometimes an expression is used to create a formula.*

A formula shows how to use numbers, variables, and operations to find a value for a quantity that is used frequently.

For the science fair, Rachel decides to plant 12 daisy seeds and report on how they grow. She plans to keep careful records about how much water and sunlight she gives the plants. She expects to use the following formula.

Sum of all the heights

Average height of plants ⟶ $A = \dfrac{S}{N}$ The fraction bar stands for division.

Number of plants

Rachel will add the individual heights of her plants to find the sum (S). She will then divide that sum by the number of plants (N) to find the average height.

CONSIDER

?

1. **What number would Rachel use for N? Suppose two of her plants did not grow at all. Do you think she should use a different value for N?**

MATERIALS

Three circular objects of different sizes
Ruler, String

Use three circular objects of different sizes. You might use the top of a flower pot, a lamp shade, and a coin.

1. Make a table like this one and list your objects by name.

Circular Object	Measured Diameter	Measured Circumference	Calculated Circumference

2. Use a ruler to measure across the widest part of each circle. This measure is called the **diameter.** Enter each measured diameter in the table.

3. Measure the distance around each circle, called the **circumference.** Do this by wrapping a piece of string around the object. Then measure the amount of string it took to circle the object. Enter each measured circumference in the table.

4. For each object, divide the circumference by the measured diameter. Is there a relationship between the circumference and the diameter? Explain.

5. Use the formula $C = \pi d$ to find the circumference of each circle. For π, use 3.14 or the π key on your calculator. Enter each calculated circumference in the table.

6. Compare the last two columns of the table. What relationship do you see? Describe your findings.

7. Consider the formula $C = \pi d$.
  a. Is d a variable? Is π a variable? Explain.
  b. Are there any operation symbols on the right side of the formula? Explain.

8. Recall that half the diameter is called the **radius** or r. That means $2r$ is the same length as d. Write a different formula for C using the variable r.

You found that you didn't need to measure around a circle to find its circumference. Instead, if you know the diameter or radius of a circle, you can take a shortcut and just use a formula.

The formula $C = \pi d$ means to multiply the number 3.14 by the length of the diameter to find the circumference. Formulas also help us remember the steps of calculations.

EXAMPLE

When you exercise, your heart beats faster. In fact, your heart rate is a good indicator of whether exercise is helping, hurting, or not really doing anything for you.

For exercise to be worthwhile, your heart rate, in beats per minute, should not be less than the value of L in the formula:

$$L = 0.72(220 - A), \text{ where } A \text{ is age.}$$

What is the lowest worthwhile heart rate if you are 14 years old?

$$
\begin{aligned}
L &= 0.72(220 - A) \\
&= 0.72(220 - 14) \qquad \text{Substitute 14 for } A. \\
&= 0.72(206) \\
&= 148.32
\end{aligned}
$$

For exercise to be worthwhile, your heart rate should not be less than about 148 beats per minute.

CONSIDER

2. Why does it make sense to round 148.32 in the Example?

TRY IT

a. A bicycle wheel has a radius of 14 inches. Use the circumference formula to find the distance around the wheel.

b. For exercise to be safe as well as worthwhile, your heart rate should not be more than the value of H in the formula $H = 0.87(220 - A)$, where A is age. While exercising, what is the highest safe heart rate for someone 30 years old?

What is the perimeter of this rectangle?

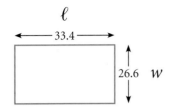

Yeaphana and Eric agree that they could find the perimeter just by adding the four numbers.

$$P = 33.4 + 26.6 + 33.4 + 26.6$$

But they want to find a formula they could use for *any* rectangle.

Yeaphana thinks ...

Instead of adding each number twice, I'll find $2 \times \ell$ and $2 \times w$. Then I'll add those two answers together.

My formula is $P = 2\ell + 2w$.

$$P = 2(33.4) + 2(26.6)$$

My answer is $P = 66.8 + 53.2$, or 120.

Eric thinks ...

If I add ℓ and w, that will equal half the perimeter. So I can just double that amount to get the whole perimeter.

My formula is $P = 2(\ell + w)$.

$$P = 2(33.4 + 26.6)$$

My answer is $P = 2(60)$, or 120.

Both Yeaphana and Eric thought about the formula correctly.

REFLECT

1. When is it easier to use the formula $C = \pi d$ than to measure a circumference directly?
2. Write any formula that you recall. Identify the variables in the formula. Identify any symbols that are not variables. Describe in words the relationship that the formula shows.
3. Is it faster to write a formula or to write the steps in words? Explain.
4. Formulas are most useful in situations where you must do the same kind of calculation over and over. Name some situations in daily life that call for a formula.

Exercises

CORE

1. **Getting Started** The formula for the area of a rectangle is $A = bh$. Find the area of a rectangle whose base (b) is 6 ft and height (h) is 4 ft.

2. Marsha kept track of how long it took her to drive to her computer programming class the first week: 45, 75, 40, 55, and 90 minutes. What was the average time?

Use $A = \frac{1}{2}bh$ to find the area of each triangle.

3.

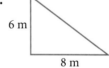

6 m

8 m

4.

5 in.

9 in.

5.

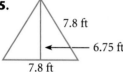

7.8 ft

6.75 ft

7.8 ft

Use the formulas and compute each value.

6. $A = \ell w$; $\ell = 6$ ft, $w = 7$ ft

7. $d = rt$; $r = 55$ mi/hr, $t = 3$ hr

8. A ____ is a line segment across the widest part of a circle.

Careers

9. **Press "1"** An architect is planning the number of phone outlets needed in a new office building. There will be 8 on each floor, an extra 6 in the lobby, and 2 in each conference room. The architect writes this formula: $P = 8F + 6 + 2C$.
   a. What do the variables F, C, and P stand for?
   b. If there will be 12 floors and 10 conference rooms, what is the value of $8F$? of $2C$?
   c. How many phone outlets will the architect specify for the new building?

Industry

10. **Spare Change?** People paying back simple interest loans use $I = prt$.

$I = $ the interest due	$p = $ the amount borrowed
$r = $ interest rate	$t = $ the time it takes to pay the money back

   a. Compute the interest due if $p = \$500$, $r = 0.07$, and $t = 3$ years.
   b. Compute the interest that would have to be paid at an 8% interest rate. (Hint: 8% = 0.08.)
   c. Compute the interest due if $500 was borrowed at a rate of 9% for 3 years.

11. What! No Push-ups? A popular formula for a person's arm strength (S) is:

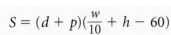

$$S = (d + p)(\tfrac{w}{10} + h - 60)$$
  d = dips on a parallel bar
  p = pull-ups
  w = weight in pounds
  h = height in inches

Compute S for these students.
  a. Herta: 5 dips, 7 pull-ups, 140 lb, 66 in.
  b. Manny: 6 dips, 4 pull-ups, 130 lb, 70 in.
  c. Ricardo: 2 dips, 3 pull-ups, 120 lb, 64 in.
  d. List the students from strongest to weakest.

12. The Burning Sun Sunscreen products are rated by an SPF, or sun protection factor. SPF #15 means $T = 15n$.

T = amount of time the sunscreen will protect you from burning
n = amount of time you could go without sunscreen and not burn

a. Find T for SPF #15 if you could stay out 20 minutes without sunscreen and not burn.
b. Find T for SPF #15 if you could stay out 30 minutes without sunscreen and not burn.
c. Write a formula for a sunscreen product rated SPF #10 and explain what it means.

13. Use Albert Einstein's formula, $E = mc^2$. Compute E, the energy produced, if $m = 5$ kg and $c = 300{,}000$ meters per second.

14. Country Salt Shaker Find the surface area of the salt lick by following these steps.
  a. Use $S = \ell \times h$ to find the area of side S
  b. Use $E = w \times h$ to find the area of side E.
  c. Now use $A = 4S + 2E$ to find the total surface area.

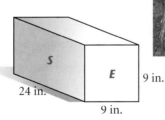

24 in.
9 in.
9 in.
S
E

LOOK AHEAD

15. There are 5 identical helium balloons on the scale.
  a. What would the scale read without the balloons?
  b. What is the total weight of all the balloons together? (Hint: Remember, balloon weights are negative numbers.)
  c. Use trial and error to find the weight (b) of each balloon.

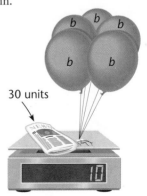

30 units

MORE PRACTICE

Explain what the variables mean in each formula. Then draw a picture or describe a situation for each formula.

16. For a rectangle: $A = \ell w$

17. For travel: $d = rt$

18. For a square: $P = 4s$

19. For a circle: $A = \pi r^2$

20. Use $P = 2(\ell + w)$ and find the perimeter of a parking lot that is 160 ft long and 85 ft wide.

21. Use $C = \pi d$ and find the circumference of a round mirror with a 63.5-cm diameter.

22. Sam timed his brother's model airplane flights at 85 seconds, 82 seconds, 80 seconds, 82 seconds, and 78 seconds. What was the airplane's average flight time?

Use the formulas and compute each value.

23. $A = \ell w$; $\ell = 6$ ft, $w = 7$ ft

24. $d = rt$; $r = 25$ mi/hr, $t = 3$ hr

25. $V = \ell wh$; $\ell = 13.2$ cm, $w = 5$ cm, $h = 7.1$ cm

26. $A = \pi r^2$; $r = 10$ yd

27. Erendira designed a plastic tray.
  a. Use $B = \ell w$ to find the area of B.
  b. Use $R = \ell h$ to find the area of R.
  c. Use $E = \frac{1}{2}wh$ to find the area of a side, E.
  d. Find A, if $A = B + R + 2E$. What does A tell her about her tray?

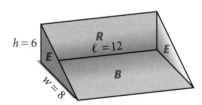

28. For 2 years, Brenton had $350 in an account that paid 5% simple interest. $A = p + prt$ shows the total amount in savings after the interest has been added to the principal. What was the total amount he had in savings at the end of the 2 years? (Hint: Remember the order of operations.)

29. This Won't Taste Bad To determine how much adult medicine to give a child, doctors sometimes use:

$$M = \frac{C}{C + 12} \times A.$$

The formula says to divide the child's age by the child's age plus 12 years.

Then multiply that answer by the adult dose.
  a. Tell what each variable stands for.
  b. Find the dose for a 4-year-old child when the adult dose is 2 tablespoons.

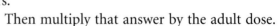

30. Heart Throbs Copy and fill in the table using the two formulas.

$$L = 0.72(220 - A) \qquad H = 0.87(220 - A) \qquad A \text{ is your age}$$

	Your Age	Middle-Aged (45)	Senior Citizen (80)
Lowest worthwhile exercise heart rate			
Highest safe exercise heart rate			

MORE MATH REASONING

31. Apply Those Brakes How far does a car go after you hit the brakes? The stopping distance depends on the speed.

$$D = 0.05s^2 + s, \text{ where } D \text{ is the distance in ft and } s \text{ is the speed in mi/hr.}$$

a. What is the stopping distance for a car going 15 mi/hr?
b. What is the stopping distance for a car going twice as fast, or 30 mi/hr?
c. When the car's speed doubles, does the stopping distance double? Explain what happens and why.

32. What Did You Say? Have you ever stood near a passing train or near the speakers at a concert? If so, you know that the intensity of the sound decreases very quickly as you move away.

$I = \dfrac{100}{d^2}$, where I is the intensity of sound and d is the distance away.

a. What is the intensity level at 1 foot away? at 4 feet? at 10 feet?
b. How much more intense is the sound at 1 foot than at 10 feet?

Using Number Sense

← CONNECT → *You have seen that formulas use mathematical expressions to help calculate some special value. Now you will study equations. Equations are mathematical sentences that also use expressions with variables.*

An **equation** says that two expressions represent the same quantity. Some equations are true and some are false.

$12 + 6 = 3 \times 6$	True
$5 = 2 + 1 - 4$	False
$3x + 10 = 19$	Neither

Most equations that you will study contain one or more variables. We cannot tell if an equation is true or false until we know the value of the variables.

In the equation $2x + 13 = 4x + 7$, the variable x appears twice. We can pick some values for x and see if one of them makes the equation true. Let's try 0 and 3. We will need to substitute the same value for x into the equation each time.

$$2x + 13 = 4x + 7$$

First, let's try 0.	$2(0) + 13 \stackrel{?}{=} 4(0) + 7$	Use 0 for x.
	$0 + 13 \stackrel{?}{=} 0 + 7$	Multiply.
	$13 = 7$	False!
Now let's try 3.	$2(3) + 13 \stackrel{?}{=} 4(3) + 7$	Use 3 for x.
	$6 + 13 \stackrel{?}{=} 12 + 7$	Multiply.
	$19 = 19$	True!
How about 5?	$2(5) + 13 \stackrel{?}{=} 4(5) + 7$	Use 5 for x.
	$10 + 13 \stackrel{?}{=} 20 + 7$	Multiply.
	$23 = 27$	False!

Because 3 is the only value of x that makes the equation true, we call 3 a **solution** of the equation. We **solve** an equation when we find a solution of the equation.

TRY IT

a. Pick some values for x. See if one of them makes the equation $x + 10 = 5x - 6$ true.

You can also find solutions to some equations simply by using your *number sense*.

EXPLORE: GETTING NUMBER SENSITIVE

Use number sense and the hints, if needed, to solve these equations.

Equation	Number Sense Hint
1. $\frac{x}{8} = 5$	**Calculation skill:** How do you know that x must be a multiple of 8?
2. $5x + 20 = 555$	**Estimation skill:** Do you think x is greater or less than 100?
3. $5x = -17$	**Negative-number skill:** How do you know that x must be a negative number?
4. $\frac{1}{2}x = 100$	**Cover-up:** Half of what number is 100?
5. $6x = 37.8$	**Trial and error:** How do you know the number must be between 6 and 7?
6. $x + 10 = x$	**Test values:** What pattern do you see?
7. $x + 2 + x = 2x + 2$	**Make a table:** When does the left side equal the right side?

8. Did you find an equation with no solution?

9. Did you find an equation with more than one solution?

10. What are some other common-sense techniques you can use?

1. Solve $5x + 25 = 35$.

$$5x + 25 = 35$$

 $+ 25 = 35$ Cover $5x$ with your hand.

Think: What number added to 25 is 35?

$$5x = 10$$

Think: What number times 5 is 10?

$$5 \cdot \text{✋} = 10$$

$$x = 2$$ $2 \cdot 5 = 10$, so x must be 2.

Let's check:

$$5x + 25 = 35$$

$$5(2) + 25 \stackrel{?}{=} 35$$ Substitute 2 for x.

$$10 + 25 \stackrel{?}{=} 35$$ Multiply.

$$35 = 35$$ It checks.

2 makes the equation true.

So 2 is the solution.

2. Solve $\frac{1}{4}x - 1 = 99$.

$$\frac{1}{4}x - 1 = 99$$

$$\text{✋} - 1 = 99$$ Cover $\frac{1}{4}x$ with your hand.

Think: What number minus 1 is 99?

$$\frac{1}{4}x = 100$$ $100 - 1 = 99$, so $\frac{1}{4}x$ must equal 100.

$$\frac{1}{4}\text{✋} = 100$$ Think: $\frac{1}{4}$ of what number is 100?

$$x = 400$$

The cover-up method can help you take the guesswork out of solving equations. And you can check your solution. Just replace the variable with the value you found and do the calculation. Then see if both sides of the equation are the same value.

b. Check to see if 400 is the solution to $\frac{1}{4}x - 1 = 99$.

Solve each equation. Use any number-sense technique.

c. $25t = 125$ **d.** $\frac{1}{5}x = 300$ **e.** $3y - 10 = 290$

CONSIDER

?

1. What do you do if your solution does not make the equation true?

Equations are often used to model everyday situations.

EXAMPLE

3. Emperor penguins are disappearing from Antarctica due to a reduction in their food supply. Scientists use several estimation techniques to count penguins. Use number sense to estimate the number of penguins in this photo.

We can divide the photo into boxes of equal area. There are 12 boxes. Count the number of penguins in a box that has an average number of penguins. There are 6 in the box with the thick red border.
Let p represent the approximate number of penguins in the photo.

$$\frac{1}{12}p = 6$$

$$p = 12 \times 6 \qquad \text{If } \frac{1}{12} \text{ of the number is 6, then I need to multiply 12 by 6.}$$

$$p = 72$$

The number of penguins in the photo is about 72.

f. Jim built a basketball court at the side of his garage. The court was 20 feet wide because of trees and a hill. He used 70 feet of fencing to keep the ball from rolling down the hill. Find the length (x) of the court.

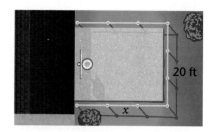

20 ft

x

REFLECT

1. Look at the two equations on the pad. It looks like one could be solved with simple number sense, but the other might take some serious calculating. Why?

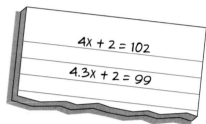

$4x + 2 = 102$

$4.3x + 2 = 99$

2. How do you know when you have solved an equation?

3. Write an equation that is easy enough to solve mentally using number sense. Describe how you would solve it.

4. How do estimation skills help you find solutions to equations?

5. Suppose you have a problem described in words. What are some steps you might take to find an equation to model it?

Exercises

CORE

1. Getting Started If $x = 4$, is the equation $2x - 1 = 7$ true?

2. Use the cover-up method to solve $3x + 1 = 7$.

3. A statement in which two expressions represent the same quantity is called
   (a) an equation   (b) a solution   (c) a formula   (d) not here

Use number sense to answer each question. Then solve the equation.

4. $14v = 154$. How do you know v must be larger than 10?

5. $4x - 3 = 401$. How do you know x must be near 100?

6. $15 - \frac{1}{3}t = 9$. Cover $\frac{1}{3}t$ with your hand. What can you subtract from 15 to get 9? What new equation does that give you?

7. $4x = -20$. Why must x be a negative number?

Solve each equation using number sense. Then check your solution.

8. $500 = 2w$ **9.** $15.7 = x + 2.7$ **10.** $3y - 10 = 65$ **11.** $75 + 2n = 150$

Write an equation to model each situation. Then solve the equation.

12.
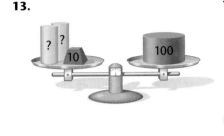
27
x
137

13.

? ?
10
100

14.

DALTON
550 MILES
SPEED LIMIT
55 MPH

distance = rate x time

15. What a Leaf The hand covering the end of the palm leaf is 6 inches long. Use number sense to estimate the length of the leaf.

16. T.I.P. To Insure Promptness Missy works at a diner. She makes $5 per hour plus tips. Last week she made $42 in tips. Her total wages and tips were $97. Follow these steps to find how many hours she worked.

Careers

a. Choose a variable. What does it represent?
b. Write an expression for how much Missy earned.
c. What does this expression equal?
d. Write and solve an equation for this situation. Check your solution.

Write an equation for each situation. Then solve and check the equation.

17. Need a Lift Carrie can lift 80 lb. Her goal is to lift 120 lb two months from now. On average, how much *more* weight should she lift each month to reach her goal?

18. Paging Joaquin Joaquin has five days to finish reading a 200-page library book. He's already read 50 pages. How many pages per day must he average to finish on time?

19. Grading Yourself! What grade do you have to earn on the final test to get an average of 90 for all five tests?

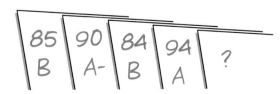
85 B   90 A-   84 B   94 A   ?

 ## *LOOK AHEAD*

A mother and child balance a father on a seesaw. The mother weighs 127 lb and the father weighs 169 lb. Let the weight of the child be *x*.

20. Write an equation for the picture.

21. What does the balanced seesaw tell you about expressions on the two sides of your equation?

MORE PRACTICE

Use number sense to answer each question. Then solve the equation.

22. $11x = 99$. Can x be a negative number? Can x be as large as 10?

23. $3t - 10 = 290$. Cover up $3t$ with your hand. What must $3t$ be equal to?

24. $175 - n = 160$. Why can you be sure that n is a whole number?

25. $13.9 = x + 2.5$. Which is a value closer to x: 10 or 16?

26. $\frac{2}{3}x = 12$. Why is x obviously greater than 12?

27. $6x = 10.2$. Why is the solution between 1 and 2?

Solve each equation using number sense. Then check your solution.

28. $2x + 1 = 17$ **29.** $12 = 12y$ **30.** $z - 10 = 16$ **31.** $6s = -60$

32. $\frac{1}{3}t + 5 = 15$ **33.** $8t - 12 = 86$ **34.** $2r - 14 = 656$ **35.** $4q + 1 = 0.2$

Write an equation to model each situation.

36.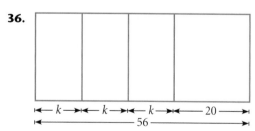

37.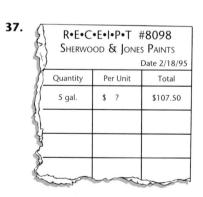

38. Number Sense at Lunch Deron's lunch in the cafeteria costs $3.29. He gave the clerk a five-dollar bill and four pennies.

  a. Why did he give the clerk the four pennies?

  b. How much change should he get?

MORE MATH REASONING

39. Suppose an equation shows that $A - B = 0$. What do you know about A and B if the equation is true? if the equation is false?

40. Strawberries, crayons, and pencils are on the scales. Find the weight of a pencil. Tell how you thought about the problem.

41. Fast Stuff Write and solve a problem using this data and a calculator. Write an equation if it helps.

  • Light travels 186,000 miles per second.
  • The sun is approximately 93,000,000 miles from the earth.

42. True Boole Computers evaluate equations. Using a system called *Boolean algebra,* a computer evaluates a true equation as a 1 and a false equation as a 0. Because $(2 + 2 = 5)$ is false, it is evaluated as 0 in this system. Use this system to evaluate the following.

  a. $(3 + 1 = 5 - 1)$

  b. $(2 = 2) + (3 = 3)$

  c. $(4 = 3 + 1) \cdot (3 = 9 - 6)$

  d. How would a computer evaluate $(2x + 1 = 7)$ if it had a value of 2 for x? if it had a value of 3 for x?

Data entered into a computer are changed into on-off electrical signals that pass through circuit boards.

4-1
PART C   Solving Equations Using Algebra Tiles

← CONNECT →   *Earlier you used algebra tiles to model expressions and to simplify them. In this part, algebra tiles will be used again—this time to model equations.*

As you experiment with the algebra tiles and find solutions to simple equations, you will develop even greater number sense.

The basic algebra tiles that you will use are shown below.

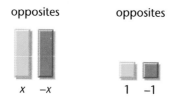

To multiply an expression by 2, just double the number of tiles.

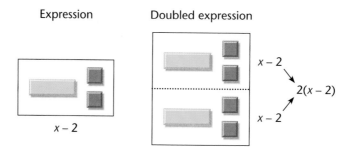

If you can divide the tiles into two equal groups, then one group is half the tiles.

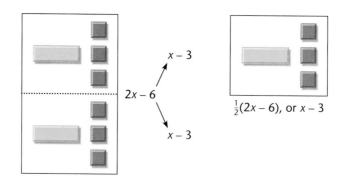

An equation box models both sides of an equation.

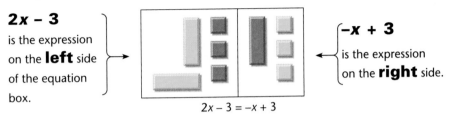

2x − 3
is the expression
on the **left** side
of the equation
box.

−x + 3
is the expression
on the **right** side.

$2x - 3 = -x + 3$

Write the equation represented by each equation box.

a.

b.

To solve an equation, use some simple rules to get a single *x*-tile on one side of the equation box.

Rules

1. You can add or remove tiles, but you must do the same thing to both sides.

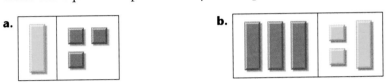

$2x - 1 = 3$

Add 1
to both sides.

2. Any pair of opposite tiles on the same side of an equation box equals 0. Pairs of opposite tiles can be removed.

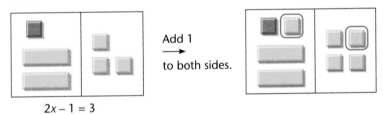

Remove 0
from left side.

3. If you can divide the equation box into two or more equal parts, you can solve the equation using only one of these new boxes.

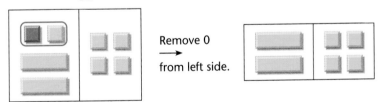

Take half of the
equation box.

$x = 2$

MATERIALS

Algebra tiles

Use the algebra-tile rules to add or remove tiles. Try to get a single *x*-tile on one side and only unit tiles on the other side. Write the original and final equations.

1.

2.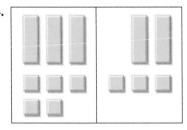

3.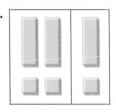

4.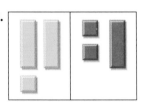

5. Make up your own equation. Model the equation with algebra tiles and solve it.
6. Describe any special technique you may have learned while working with algebra tiles.

REFLECT

1. Describe how an equation box looks when the equation is solved.
2. Decide if Maurie solved the following equation correctly. Explain how you decided.

Maurie's equation   Maurie's solution

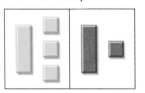

3. What would the tiles look like if you were able to take one-third of the equation box?

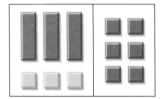

Exercises

CORE

1. Getting Started What algebra tiles would you have to add to each expression to get 0?

a.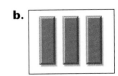

b.

c.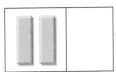

2. Write the word or phrase that correctly completes each statement.
   a. A number and its ___ add up to 0.
   b. An equation shows that two ___ are equal.

Write the equation modeled by each equation box. Then solve the equation.

3.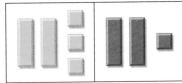

4.

5.

6. Larry added one negative unit tile to both sides of this equation box. When Nola tried the problem, she removed one positive unit tile from both sides of the box. Who was correct? Explain.

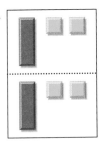

Write two expressions shown by each set of tiles.

7.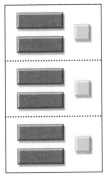

8.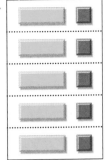

9.

10. There is more than one way to begin solving this equation. How many can you find?

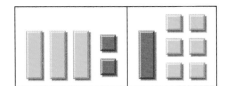

Write the equation modeled by each equation box. Then solve the equation using any method you like.

11.

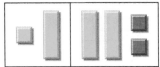

12.

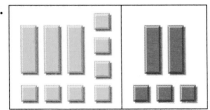

 ## LOOK BACK

13. Which is the best estimate of 72% of 63? [2-1]
   (a) 45   (b) 89   (c) 36
   (d) 115   (e) not here

14. Give a rotation that is the same as each of the following. [3-2]
   a. 30° clockwise
   b. 72° counterclockwise

15. Find the next three elements in the pattern. [3-3]

   1, 3, 6, 10, 15

MORE PRACTICE

What must you add to each of these diagrams to get 0?

16.

17.

18.

Write the equation modeled by each equation box. Then solve the equation using any method you like.

19.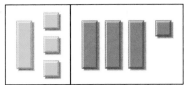

20.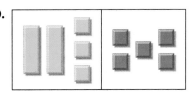

Write two expressions shown by each set of tiles.

21.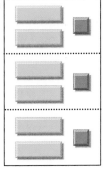

22.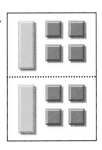

23.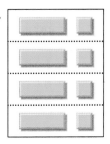

MORE MATH REASONING

24. What would you need to be able to do to solve this with tiles?

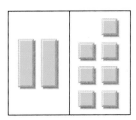

25. What do you think the large tiles below represent? Why?

← C O N N E C T → *You have seen different ways that formulas and equations are used in mathematics. Now you will choose your own variables to write a formula for readability.*

In the 1920s, formulas were developed to measure how difficult material was to read. Unfortunately, the formulas were difficult to use. In 1944, the Fog Index^SM scale was developed to measure the reading level of a book quickly and reliably.

To find the Fog Index^SM score of a paragraph:

■ Compute the average number of words per sentence.

> There are 127 words and 8 sentences.
>
> 127 ÷ 8 is 15.875. About 15.9 words per sentence

■ Compute the percentage of words with three or more syllables.

■ Add this percentage as a whole number to the first number.

■ Multiply this sum by 0.4.

> 15.9 + 11.0 = 26.9
> 26.9 x 0.4 = 10.76
>
> **Fog Index^SM**

> There are 14 *long* words out of those 127 words.
>
> 14 ÷ 127 is 0.110 That's about 11%

The Fog Index^SM score indicates the approximate years in school needed to understand the paragraph. The 10.6 result above means that an average 10th or 11th grader will understand the paragraph.

The Fog Index^SM points out when people use confusing language.

4-1 opened with this essay.

A star is made when "dirty hydrogen atoms" begin to collect in the sky. As time passes, more and more hydrogen is attracted and it starts swirling around the center. This goes on for centuries, until the swirling mass gets hot enough to burn. A "nuclear reactor in the sky"—a star—is formed, changing hydrogen into helium. Energy is given off in the process, according to a law that the physicist Albert Einstein discovered in 1905: $E = mc^2$.

1. Write a mathematical formula for the Fog Index[SM] score. Explain what your variables mean.
2. Use your Fog Index[SM] score formula on the above paragraph. Treat equations and numbers just like the words they represent.
3. Should your class be able to understand this paragraph? Discuss why or why not.
4. What makes a book harder or easier to read? Explain.
5. Suppose a paragraph has an average sentence length of nine words. Could its Fog Index[SM] score be 7? Why or why not?
6. A paragraph has a Fog Index[SM] score of 8, with 10% long words. Estimate or compute the average sentence length. Explain how you got your answer.

You have used expressions in formulas and as part of equations. You looked at several common-sense ways to solve equations. Next you will learn about other ways to solve equations.

REFLECT

1. Explain why your Fog Index[SM] score is a formula.
2. Describe ways in which a formula is like an equation. How is a formula different from an equation? Explain your thinking.
3. When is it helpful to use a variable?
4. Describe some methods for solving an equation. Show an example of each method.

Self-Assessment

1. The first 25 pages in a science book describe how the universe began. The graph shows the Fog Index^sm score for each page.

a. What happens in the book when the graph goes up?

b. What happens when the graph goes down?

c. If this book were rewritten for elementary grades, what might the graph look like?

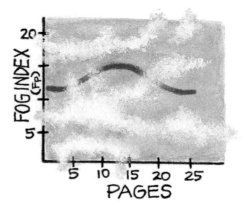

Use the formulas in the chart to write the first five terms of each sequence of numbers.

	Formula for nth Term	Term Number (value of n)				
		1	2	3	4	5
2.	$4n$	4	8	12	?	?
3.	$n + \frac{2}{3}$	$1\frac{2}{3}$	$2\frac{2}{3}$	?	?	?
4.	$-n$	-1	?	?	?	?
5	$-n^2$	?	?	?	?	?

Write an equation for each scale. Then find the value of x.

6.

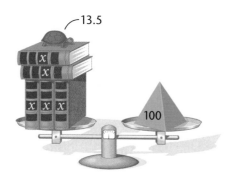

7.

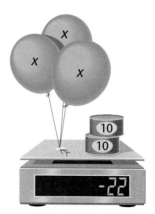

8. To make a 30-ft fence with poles 10 ft apart, you
need 4 poles.

   a. Write a formula that shows how many poles
   you need for a fence *n* ft long.
   b. Use the formula to find the number of poles
   needed for a fence that is 120 ft long.

9. The percentage of gold in an object is given by the formula $P = \frac{25k}{6}$,
where *k* is the number of karats and *P* is the percentage of gold.

   a. Gold jewelry comes in 10, 12, 14, or 18 karats. Find the percentage
   of gold in each type.
   b. A gold bar stored in Fort Knox is 100% gold.
   How many karats is that?

10. Write the equation modeled by the equation box.
Then solve the equation using algebra-tile rules
and write your final equation.

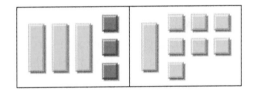

11. **How Big Is a Star?** The volume of a sphere is
given by the formula $V = \frac{4}{3}\pi r^3$. The sun's radius
is about 108 times as large as the earth's. Assume
the earth's radius is 1 unit.

   a. What is the volume of the earth?
   b. What is the volume of the sun?
   c. How many earths would it take to fill up a
   sphere as big as the sun?

12. **Skate Rate** Mark worked at the skating rink. He made a wall chart to show
costs. There is a fixed cost for skate rental and an hourly rate for skating.
   a. What would 5 hours cost? 6 hours? 7 hours?
   b. What would it cost to skate all night (8:00 p.m.
   to 8:00 a.m.)?
   c. What is the fixed cost of renting skates?
   d. What is the hourly rate?
   e. Write a formula like the one Mark used to make
   up this chart.
   f. Many people have their own skates. Create a new
   chart entitled "Without Skate Rental."

Hours	Cost* per Person
1	$3.50
2	$5.00
3	$6.50
4	$8.00
⋮	⋮

*Cost includes skate rental

13. Suppose 1 pound of matter could be changed entirely into energy. According to $E = mc^2$, this matter would produce more than 11 billion kilowatt-hours of electricity. Austin, Texas, uses about 5 billion kilowatt-hours per year.
  a. How long could 1 pound of matter keep Austin supplied with electricity?
  b. What are some advantages and disadvantages of using nuclear energy?

14. Find all lines of symmetry for each figure. [3-1]

a.   **b.**    **c.**   **d.**    **e.**

15. A box manufacturer uses the formula $A = 8s^2$ to find the amount of cardboard needed to manufacture boxes like the one shown. The formula includes the extra cardboard needed for tabs that overlap to keep the box together. The formula also accounts for waste.
  a. What do the variables A and s represent?
  b. How much cardboard is needed to make a box 10 inches on each side?
  c. What would the formula be if there were no tabs or waste?

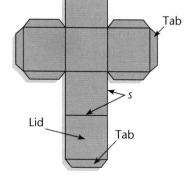

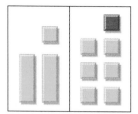

16. Which of the following is *not* a possible next step for the equation box shown at the right?

(a) 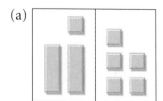   (b) 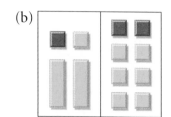   (c)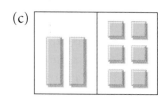

4-2 Solving Equations

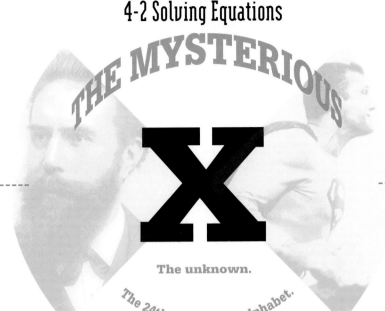

THE MYSTERIOUS

X

helm
ntgen ←- - - - - - - - - -

- - - - - - - - - -→ **Superman**

The unknown.

The 24th letter of the alphabet.

X-rays may make you think of Superman. He could turn
on his X-ray vision and see through anything except lead. But
the real "super man" behind X-rays was the scientist who discovered
them, quite by accident, in 1895. ✳ At that time, physicist Wilhelm Roentgen
was experimenting with cathode rays in his laboratory. Isaac Asimov, in his book *X
Stands for Unknown,* describes what Roentgen went through. ✳ **It seemed to Roentgen
that the cathode-ray tube was producing a penetrating radiation that no one had reported
before. ✳ Roentgen spent seven weeks exploring the penetrative power of this radiation: what it
could penetrate; what thickness of what material would finally stop it, and so on. He must have been
te a trial to his wife during that period. He came to dinner late and in a savage mood, didn't talk, and raced
ck to the laboratory. ✳ On December 28, 1895, he finally published his first report on the subject. He knew
hat radiation did, but he didn't know what it was. Mindful of the fact that in mathematics, x is usually
used to signify an unknown quantity, he called the radiation "X-rays". ✳** Asimov closes the introduction to
his book with a tribute to the researchers and scientists whose daily lives are dedicated to discovering the
unknown. He adds, "May *x* always be with us to afford us pleasure."

1. What did Asimov mean when he
   said, "May *x* always be with us to afford
   us pleasure"?
2. What are other ways to use the letter
   X? Does it always mean "unknown"?
   If not, what else does it mean?
3. We often use *x* for "unknown" in

mathematics, but we also use other
letters for this purpose. What are some
other letters we use to show an unknown
quantity? When might it be helpful to
choose a specific letter?
4. What great "unknown" would you like
   to find if you were a scientist?

293

← CONNECT →   *You have used common-sense methods and algebra tiles to solve equations. Now you will see the ways in which equations are balanced.*

To solve an equation that contains a variable, you must find values of the variable that make the equation true. This can be difficult using number sense alone. You need to find other methods.

A balanced scale is a good model of an equation because each side must have equal weight.

This scale is *not* balanced.
The left side is heavier than the right side.

This scale *is* balanced.
The left side has the same weight as the right side.

This scale is *not* balanced.
The left side is lighter than the right side.

You can make a balance scale using a ruler and some milk cartons or small aluminum dishes.

EXPLORE: KEEP YOUR BALANCE

Start by placing three identical objects on the left side. Then place pennies on the right side until the scale balances.

MATERIALS

*Balance scale
Several identical objects to weigh, such as pens, chalk, and spoons
A large amount of pennies to use as weights*

1. Place some identical objects on each side. What happens if the same thing is added to both sides of a balanced scale?

2. Remove an object from one side and the identical object from the other. What happens when you remove the same thing from both sides of a balanced scale?

3. Start again with three objects on the left side and enough pennies to balance them.

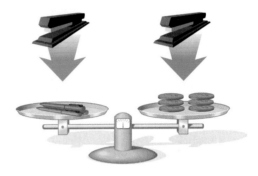

4. Now double the objects on the left side. What can you do to the side with the pennies to balance the scale?

5. Start again with three objects in balance, but triple the objects on the left side. If you double, triple, or even quadruple the objects on one side, what must you do to the other side to keep the scale balanced?

6. Group the objects on the left side into three identical bunches. Group the pennies into three equal stacks.

7. Remove one bunch of objects. Now there are $\frac{2}{3}$ as many objects as before. What must you do to the pennies to balance the scale?

8. How can you balance a scale if you take a fraction of what is on one side?

9. How do your conclusions compare with the rules you learned for algebra tile equations? Explain.

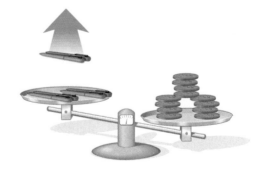

In the next few parts, you will learn to use these ideas about equality to **solve** equations.

TRY IT

If two objects look alike, assume they have the same weight.

I'm balanced!

The scale at the right is balanced. Use it to answer the following.

Is the scale balanced? Explain.

a.   b.   c.

Balanced?   Balanced?   Balanced?

You can use balance-scale ideas when you need to find unknown quantities.

EXAMPLES

1. Write an equation to model this situation.

If **s** stands for the weight of one stapler, then an equation is

$$2s + 7 = 19$$

2 staplers   ↑   19 blocks
plus 7 blocks

weigh the
same as

2. Find the weight of one stapler in Example 1.

Begin by removing two 1-blocks and a 5-block from each side.

Two staplers weigh 12. One stapler must weigh 6.

CONSIDER

1. How does the weight of the stapler relate to the equation in the Example?

Understanding the balance scale will help you understand the mathematics of solving equations.

REFLECT

1. How is a balance scale like an equation?

2. Tell how the four operations of addition, subtraction, multiplication, and division are related to the activities with the balance scale.

3. Write a statement telling what you learned from the Explore.

4. Why should the variable always be identified carefully when you write an equation?

Exercises

CORE

1. Getting Started The scale is balanced. Tell how to keep it balanced in each case.

a. if 10 lb is added to the right

b. if the weight on the right is tripled

c. if $\frac{2}{5}$ of the weight on the left is removed

d. if 17.5 oz is removed from the right

2. Trace the scales on your paper. Then draw a picture to show each equation.

a.

$3x = 15$

b.

$31 = 2x + 5$

c.

$x + {}^-7 = 10$

Write an equation to model each of these balanced scales.

3.

Let *c* stand for cake's weight.

4.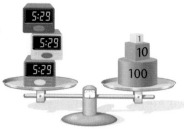

Let *c* stand for clock's weight

5.

Let *c* stand for coin's weight

Use the scales shown in Exercises 3–5. Describe the steps needed to find each weight. Remember to keep each scale balanced.

6. a piece of cake's weight

7. one clock's weight

8. one coin's weight

9. They're Still Hungry? Harry thought he fed his three puppies 2.5 pounds of puppy food. But he made the mistake of including the weight of the bowl! If the bowl weighs 0.7 pound, how much did each puppy eat?

10. Use number sense to find the weight of one muffin.

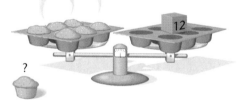

11. If *m* stands for the weight of one muffin, write an equation that models the situation above. Explain how you might use the properties of equality to solve your equation and get the same solution as you did using number sense.

LOOK AHEAD

12. The equation $\frac{7}{8}p + 12 = 40$ models the weight of the remaining fritatta and the 12-ounce plate. How much did the *whole* fritatta weigh, not including the plate? Use your number sense.

MORE PRACTICE

The scale is balanced. Tell how to keep it balanced in each case.

13. if a clock is added on the left side

14. if the coins on the right side are tripled

15. if $\frac{2}{3}$ of the clocks are removed

16. if $\frac{1}{3}$ of the coins are removed

Write an equation to model each of these balanced scales.

17.

18.

19.

Let *c* stand for calculator's weight   Let *p* stand for pencil's weight   Let *d* stand for dispenser's weight

Use the pictures above. Describe the steps needed to find each weight.

20. the calculator's weight   **21.** the pencil's weight   **22.** the tape dispenser's weight

Use your number sense to solve the equation. Check your solution.

23. $4x = 4000$ **24.** $n + 9 = 99$ **25.** $\frac{3}{4}y = 75$ **26.** $x - 50 = 850$

MORE MATH REASONING

27. This scale is unbalanced.
- **a.** If you add the same weight to both sides, will it stay unbalanced? Explain.
- **b.** If you remove the same weight from both sides, will it stay unbalanced? Explain.
- **c.** If you double or triple what is on each side, will it stay unbalanced? Explain.

28. This scale is balanced.   What can you add to the right side to balance this one?

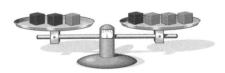

Isolating the Variable

You have solved equations using number sense and algebra tiles. Now you will see how to solve equations using inverse operations.

Many equations that model real situations are too difficult to solve in your head, and when fractions, decimals, or large numbers are involved, tiles and balance scales may be awkward to use.

The equation at the right is like that. If *x* were by itself on the left side, then the calculation on the right would tell us the value of *x*.

$x + 19.7$ 98.13 x $98.13 - 19.7$

We call this *isolating the variable.*

EXPLORE: WHAT IS THE QUESTION?

Imagine that you and your classmate are on a TV quiz show. You are given an answer, and you must find the matching question on the list. If you pick the correct question, you also get to solve the equation. Otherwise, your classmate chooses the question.

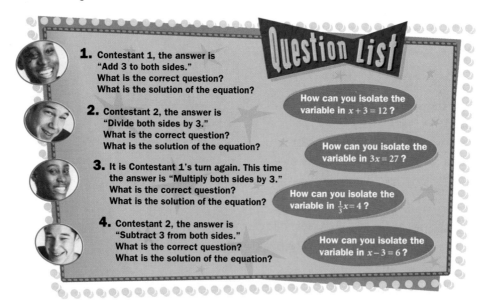

1. Contestant 1, the answer is "Add 3 to both sides."
What is the correct question?
What is the solution of the equation?

2. Contestant 2, the answer is "Divide both sides by 3."
What is the correct question?
What is the solution of the equation?

3. It is Contestant 1's turn again. This time the answer is "Multiply both sides by 3."
What is the correct question?
What is the solution of the equation?

4. Contestant 2, the answer is "Subtract 3 from both sides."
What is the correct question?
What is the solution of the equation?

Question List

How can you isolate the variable in $x + 3 = 12$?

How can you isolate the variable in $3x = 27$?

How can you isolate the variable in $\frac{1}{3}x = 4$?

How can you isolate the variable in $x - 3 = 6$?

Subtraction is the opposite of addition. These are called **inverse** operations. Multiplication and division are inverse operations. In the following Examples, inverse operations will help us isolate the variables.

EXAMPLES

1. Point T is on the x-axis. Then it is translated 53 units to the right and the image point T' is at 75. What was the location of point T?

   Let x be the location of point T.

   We need to solve $x + 53 = 75$.   The location of point T + the translation is the location of the image point T'.

   Notice that 53 is *added* to x. We use *subtraction* to isolate the variable.

   $x + 53 - 53 = 75 - 53$ Subtract 53 from both sides.
   $x = 75 - 53$ x is isolated.
   $x = 22$ $75 - 53$ is 22.

   Point T was located at 22.

2. The school secretary has 546 student folders to file. She wants to put the same number of folders in each file drawer. If there are 13 file drawers available, how many folders can go in each drawer?

   n

   ← 13 file drawers with 546 folders →

   n is the number of folders in each drawer.

   We need to solve $13n = 546$.   The number of drawers × the number in each drawer is the total number of files.

   Notice that n is *multiplied* by 13. We can isolate the variable and keep the equation balanced by dividing both sides by 13.

   $13n = 546$
   $\frac{13}{13}n = \frac{546}{13}$ Divide both sides by 13.
   $n = \frac{546}{13}$ n is isolated.
   $n = 42$ $\frac{546}{13}$ is 42.

   The secretary can put 42 files in each drawer.

As before, you can check your solution by replacing the variable with its value. The two sides of the equation should match after you do the calculations. If it is helpful, use your calculator for the computations.

CONSIDER

1. Can you isolate the variable in $x + 31.2 = 47.5$ by adding 31.2 to both sides? Explain.
2. Can you isolate the variable in $\frac{1}{2}x = 22.7$ by subtracting $\frac{1}{2}$ from both sides? Explain.
3. Can you isolate the variable in $3x = 4.7$ by dividing both sides by 3? Explain.
4. Can you isolate the variable in $5.6 = x - 2.3$ by adding 2.3 to both sides? Explain.

TRY IT

a. What operation and what number do you need to use on both sides of the equation to isolate the variable?

   1. $x + 17.9 = -63.2$ **2.** $14\frac{2}{3} = 6.34 + v$ **3.** $3.2y = 15.6$

b. Solve each equation. Always try number sense first. Check your solution.

   1. $32.5 + z = 170$ **2.** $28\frac{1}{2} = x - 17.5$ **3.** $v + 47 = -3$

c. Juanita ran 5090 feet during her morning jog. Her goal was 1 mile, which is 5280 feet. By how many feet did she miss her goal?

> **Problem-Solving Tip**
>
> Write and solve an equation.

Although you have been solving equations in different ways, each method is based on the **properties of equality.** The properties of equality are very powerful tools because they allow us to solve any linear equation.

The **Addition Property of Equality** states that adding or subtracting the same quantity to both sides of a true equation will not change the solution of the equation.

The **Multiplication Property of Equality** states that multiplying or dividing both sides of a true equation by the same non-zero amount will not change its solution.

REFLECT

1. Explain how an inverse operation undoes an operation.
2. Using a calculator, enter any number. Multiply by 3, then divide by 3. How does the result show that multiplication and division are inverse operations?
3. Why would you want to isolate the variable when solving an equation?

Exercises

CORE

1. Getting Started Copy these steps to solve $y - 73 = 313$. Fill in **a–c** with a description or explanation of each step.

$$y - 73 = 313$$
$$y - 73 + 73 = 313 + 73 \qquad \textbf{a.}$$
$$y = 313 + 73 \qquad \textbf{b.}$$
$$y = 386 \qquad \textbf{c.}$$

2. Copy the scale.
   a. Draw a picture to show the equation $x + 18 = 45$.
   b. Tell how to get your unknown object by itself on the balance scale.

3. Choose the word that best completes the sentence.
The inverse operation for division is
   (a) subtraction   (b) multiplication   (c) division   (d) addition   (e) not here

Solve each equation using number sense. Check your solution.

4. $10y = 430$ **5.** $2x = 12.8$ **6.** $w + 78 = 101$ **7.** $44 = -4x$

8. $\frac{1}{8}x = 6$ **9.** $25 = h - 25$ **10.** $\frac{v}{3} = 100$ **11.** $-3.2 = 3.2k$

Solve each equation. Use a calculator whenever it helps.

12. $w + 76.93 = 853.1$ **13.** $230 = y + 9\frac{1}{2}$ **14.** $x - 4.5 = 15\frac{1}{2}$

15. $150 = t + 90$ **16.** $-53 = x - 1.12$ **17.** $s + 4 = -7.3$

18. How are the two pictures below related to the following problem?

The New York Limited Express was traveling the 114.1 miles from New York to Philadelphia. It stopped at a station 38.7 miles from New York. How much farther did it need to go to complete the trip?

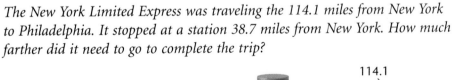

19. Solve the problem given in Exercise 18.

**Write an interesting problem and draw a picture for each world record below.
Write an equation if it helps.**

20. The record for limbo dancing under a flaming bar is $6\frac{1}{8}$ inches off the floor. The record for roller skating under a bar is $5\frac{1}{4}$ inches.

21. The longest continuous voluntary crawl on record, with one or the other knee always in contact with the ground, is 27 miles. A marathon, a running event in track, is exactly 26.21875 miles long.

22. The world's heaviest man, Jon Minnoch, weighed an estimated 1400 lb. The lightest, full-grown, normal-height man weighed 48 lb.

23. The only person to have been both a dwarf and a giant grew from 3 ft 10.45 in. at age 21 to 7 ft 1.75 in. at age 32.

LOOK AHEAD

24. You would not completely solve $5t + 49 = 78$ by subtracting 49 from both sides. Explain why not.

25. Find the unknown length (t). Describe your method.

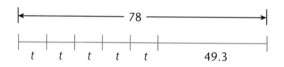

MORE PRACTICE

Solve each equation using number sense. Check your solution.

26. $3y = 60$

27. $5x = 1.5$

28. $m + 12 = 23$

29. $14 = 2x$

30. $\frac{1}{4}x = 6$

31. $7 = t - 7$

32. $\frac{n}{7} = 10$

33. $1 = 0.5y$

34. $x + 15 = 45$

35. $100 - y = 91$

36. $t + 60.3 = 60.3$

37. $1011 = x - 2$

38. Copy the scale.
    a. Draw a picture to show the equation $32 = y + 7$.
    b. Tell how to get your unknown object by itself on the balance scale.

Solve each equation. Use a calculator whenever it helps.

39. $14t = 1400$ **40.** $5.23 + x = 17.9$ **41.** $28k = 868$

42. $4.92 = w - 3.18$ **43.** $\frac{n}{4} = 25$ **44.** $m + 125 = 125$

45. $\frac{1}{9}x = 200$ **46.** $7.00 + t = 10.00$ **47.** $x - 75.3 = 14.3$

48. $y + 5.8 = 25.4$ **49.** $132 = v - 48.3$ **50.** $x - 1479 = 3000$

MORE MATH REASONING

51. Choose a positive number.
    a. Multiply it by a number so that you still get your number. What number did you multiply it by?
    b. Subtract a number from it so that you still get your number. What number did you subtract?
    c. Add a number to it so that you still get your number. What number did you add?
    d. Divide it by a number so that you still get your number. What number did you divide it by?
    e. Which answers in 51a–51d were the same?

52. Write four equations. You should be able to solve one with *number sense,* one by *adding or subtracting,* and one by *multiplying or dividing.* Write the last one so that it can't be solved by any of these strategies. Discuss why each equation fits its category.

53. How are these two pictures alike?

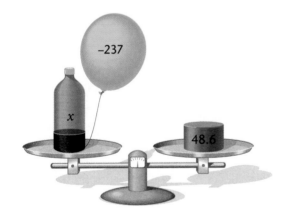
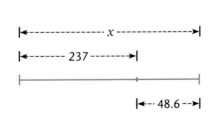

A Look at Some Math Concepts

← CONNECT → *You've solved equations using number sense and inverse operations. You've also seen that isolating the variable is a very powerful method. Now you are ready to look into some of the mathematics behind these methods.*

Notice that each variable in the following equations has a multiplier. That multiplier is called a **coefficient.**

$$-3x + 2 = 8$$

$$\frac{1}{4}y = 2$$

-3 is the coefficient of **x.**

$\frac{1}{4}$ is the coefficient of **y.**

Usually, you can read the coefficient right from the equation, as in the equations above. But sometimes the coefficient is hidden.

$$x - 7 = 5$$

$$\frac{z}{6} + 2 = 7$$

Since x is the same as $1x$, 1 is the coefficient of x.

Since $\frac{z}{6}$ is the same as $\frac{1}{6}z$, $\frac{1}{6}$ is the coefficient of z.

Because x is the same as $1x$, whenever you isolated the variable by multiplying or dividing, you were making the coefficient of the variable equal to 1. When you multiply a number by its **reciprocal,** the product is 1.

EXAMPLE

1. What is the reciprocal of each number?

a. 2 $\frac{1}{2}$ is the reciprocal of 2 because $\frac{1}{2} \times 2 = 1$.

b. $\frac{2}{5}$ $\frac{5}{2}$ is the reciprocal of $\frac{2}{5}$ because $\frac{5}{2} \times \frac{2}{5} = 1$.

c. -4 $-\frac{1}{4}$ is the reciprocal of -4 because $-\frac{1}{4} \times (-4) = 1$.

TRY IT

What is the reciprocal of each number?

a. 3   **b.** 1   **c.** $\frac{1}{4}$ **d.** $\frac{4}{7}$

CONSIDER

?

1. Dividing a number by $\frac{2}{5}$ is the same as multiplying it by

   ____.
2. Why is the reciprocal of a negative number always negative?
3. Can you find the reciprocal of 0?

You will use these ideas in the Explore. Variables with fractions as coefficients may look hard at first, but the same ideas are used to isolate them.

EXPLORE: A FRACTION OF THE WHOLE

A six-pack of sparkling water will not fit on the scale. So four cans, or $\frac{2}{3}$ of the six-pack, were weighed. We want to use this weight to find the weight of all six cans.

y is the weight of the whole six-pack.

1. Why does the equation $\frac{2}{3}y = 100$ model the problem?
2. Should y be more or less than 100? Use your number sense to find y.
3. What is the coefficient of y in the equation?
4. What can you multiply this coefficient by so that it becomes 1?
   If you do this multiplication, what must you do to balance the equation?
5. What does this tell you about solving $\frac{2}{3}y = 100$? Explain.

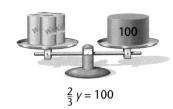

$\frac{2}{3}y = 100$

Polly says, "Why would a person put four cans on the scale when they could just weigh one can?"

6. What fraction of the six-pack is one can?
7. How does the equation $\frac{y}{6} = 25$ model this situation? Is this the same as $\frac{1}{6}y = 25$?
8. What can you multiply both sides by to solve the equation? Explain.
9. What does this tell you about solving $\frac{y}{6} = 25$? Explain.
10. Describe how you can get a coefficient of one for the variable in order to isolate it.

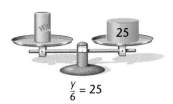

$\frac{y}{6} = 25$

Reciprocals can help us isolate the variable and solve equations.

EXAMPLE

2. A symphony orchestra contains four sections: woodwinds, brass, percussion, and strings. The string section usually makes up about three-fifths of an orchestra.

If the string section has 54 musicians, about how many musicians are in the orchestra?

Let x be the number of musicians in the orchestra.

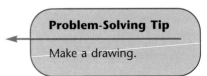

Problem-Solving Tip

Make a drawing.

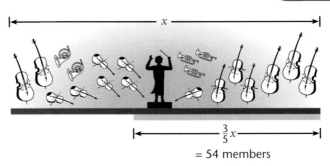

Then $\frac{3}{5}x = 54$ is the equation we must solve.

$$\frac{3}{5}x = 54$$

$$\frac{5}{3} \cdot \frac{3}{5}x = \frac{5}{3}(54) \qquad \text{Multiply both sides by the reciprocal of } \frac{3}{5}.$$

$$1x = 90 \qquad \frac{5}{3} \cdot \frac{3}{5} \text{ is 1.}$$

$$x = 90 \qquad x \text{ is the same thing as } 1x.$$

There are about 90 musicians in the orchestra.

TRY IT

What can you multiply or divide by to isolate the variable? Solve each equation. Use a calculator if it helps.

e. $\frac{2}{5}n = \frac{4}{5}$

f. $-\frac{2}{5}n = \frac{4}{5}$

g. $\frac{x}{9} = 231$

h. $135 = 0.3n$

There are many ways to solve an equation.

At the copy center, Mr. Arden prints fliers about the family's lost cat. Each of the five family members takes an equal number of fliers. Norma puts all 24 of hers on trees and fences near her house. Can you tell how many fliers Mr. Arden originally printed?

Pei thinks ...

I'll let x stand for the total number of fliers. Then $\frac{1}{5}x$ stands for the number Norma took, which is 24. The equation is

$$\frac{1}{5}x = 24.$$

$$5 \cdot \frac{1}{5}x = 5 \cdot 24 \qquad \text{Multiply both sides by the reciprocal of } \frac{1}{5}.$$

$$x = 120$$

Mr. Arden printed 120 fliers.

Eugene thinks ...

To show $\frac{1}{5}$ of the whole amount, I'll divide x by 5:

$$\frac{x}{5} = 24.$$

$$5 \cdot \frac{x}{5} = 5 \cdot 24 \qquad \text{To undo division by 5, I can multiply by 5.}$$

$$x = 120$$

Mr. Arden printed 120 fliers.

Dawn thinks ...

I like to work with decimals and the calculator.

$$1 \boxdot 5 \boxdot \boxed{\quad 0.2 \quad}$$

The equation is

$$0.2x = 24.$$

I'll divide each side by 0.2.

$$x = \frac{24}{0.2} \qquad \text{I know } \frac{0.2}{0.2}x \text{ is } 1x, \text{ so the left side is just } x.$$

$$24 \boxdot 0.2 \boxdot \boxed{\quad 120 \quad}$$

Mr. Arden printed 120 fliers.

Use the method that seems easiest for you, but check your solution to make sure that it is correct.

1. What does isolating the variable do?
2. How many different ways can you think of to solve $\frac{3}{5}x = 300$?
3. What method do you prefer for solving equations? Justify your answer with an example.
4. Can you always find the reciprocal of a number n by dividing 1 by n? Show some examples.

Exercises

CORE

1. Getting Started What can you multiply or divide by to isolate the variable?

a. $4s = 28.3$ **b.** $\frac{3}{5}x = 74$ **c.** $-\frac{3}{5}x = 74$ **d.** $\frac{x}{9} = 34.2$ **e.** $1v = 12.4$

2. In the equation $2x = 15$, 2 is the
(a) reciprocal of x
(b) coefficient of 15
(c) coefficient of x
(d) reciprocal of 15

Give the coefficient of the variable, name its reciprocal, and write the equation that results from multiplying both sides by that reciprocal.

3. $5y = 430$ **4.** $\frac{1}{2}x = 12.5$ **5.** $w + 15 = 91$ **6.** $44 = -4x$

7. $\frac{3}{8}x = 15$ **8.** $25.4 = h - 23.5$ **9.** $\frac{v}{3} = 100$ **10.** $-14.1 = 3.2k$

Solve.

11. $\frac{2}{7}x = 104$ **12.** $8p = 100$ **13.** $\frac{r}{4} = 16.4$

14. Write a real-world problem for each figure. Write an equation to solve your problem.

a.

Area = 18 cm²   5 cm

x

b.

15. We Can! In 1992, a class of New York students decided to collect aluminum cans to raise money. They received $0.05 for each can returned. How many cans (c) did they need to collect to make their goal of $100? Write and solve an equation to find out.

16. Solve this problem.

> 3.4 lb of meat cost $8.29.
> How much for 1 lb?
>
> $3.4x = 8.29$
>
> $x =$

Problem-Solving Tip

Make a drawing.

17. The "Chunnel" is the new tunnel connecting England and France beneath the English Channel. It runs underwater farther than any tunnel in the world. However, the Seikan Tunnel in Japan, which also has an underwater section, is the longest tunnel in the world. Solve the equations $0.433s = 14.5$ and $0.758c = 23.5$ to find the length of each tunnel.

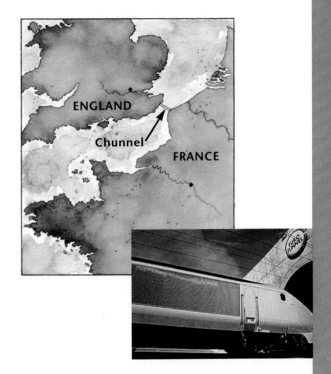

14.5 miles under water

Seikan Tunnel = s miles long

23.5 miles under water

Chunnel = c miles long

LOOK AHEAD

18. Kym bought nine pencils at the school store. She paid with $2 and got 11¢ back in change. How much did each pencil cost?
  a. Without using an equation, solve this problem. Use number sense.
  b. Use p for the cost of one pencil. Write an equation that models the problem.
  c. Tell how to solve the equation.

MORE PRACTICE

What can you multiply or divide by to isolate the variable?

19. $14t = 1400$ **20.** $5x = 17.9$ **21.** $28k = 868$ **22.** $4.92 = 0.18w$

23. $\frac{n}{4} = 25$ **24.** $125m = 125$ **25.** $\frac{5}{9}x = 200$ **26.** $7.00t = 10.00$

Give the coefficient of the variable, name its reciprocal, and write the equation that results from multiplying both sides by that reciprocal.

27. $\frac{1}{3}x = 20$ **28.** $\frac{2}{5}x = 18$ **29.** $-\frac{1}{5}y = 7$ **30.** $-\frac{3}{4}t = -9$

31. $200t = 4$ **32.** $-\frac{4}{5}m = 44$ **33.** $-\frac{1}{6}x = 1$ **34.** $-\frac{1}{6}x = -1$

35. $3y = 2$ **36.** $19g = 76$ **37.** $w + 78.3 = 101$ **38.** $10 = -2x$

Solve.

39. $\frac{2}{9}x = 4$ **40.** $0.4 = k - 0.25$ **41.** $\frac{t}{5} = 0$ **42.** $-0.1 = 10w$

43. $\frac{3}{5}x = 12$ **44.** $15x = 75$ **45.** $-7x = 154$ **46.** $\frac{x}{7} = -28$

47. The school council gets to keep $0.07 for each carton of milk sold in the lunchroom. How many cartons of milk must be sold before the council has $250?

MORE MATH REASONING

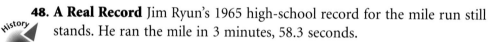

48. A Real Record Jim Ryun's 1965 high-school record for the mile run still stands. He ran the mile in 3 minutes, 58.3 seconds.

Find out his average speed or rate in miles per hour.

Remember—
$d = rt$

49. Ground Transportation Write and solve a problem using some or all of these world records. Use an equation if it helps.

The longest distance traveled by a go-cart in a 24-hour race is 1018 miles.

The longest distance traveled by a truck riding on two side wheels is 2864 miles.

The highest speed attained by a solar-powered vehicle is 24.74 mi/hr.

The fastest long-distance drive backwards in a car went 501 miles in 17.6 hours.

50. a. Write an equation that shows multiplication or division by 3 and also addition or subtraction with 3. Solve your equation.
   b. Write an equation that uses the two unused operations with 3. Solve your equation.

4-2
PART D
Solving Two-Step Equations

← **C O N N E C T** → *You have solved equations that needed only one step to isolate the variable. Now you will learn how to solve equations that need two steps to isolate the variable by combining the methods from the past two parts.*

EXPLORE: A WEIGHTY SITUATION

When Chris tried to weigh herself, her new piglets, and her dog, the scale showed a total of 280 pounds. She knows the dog weighs about 26 pounds and she weighs about 123 pounds. If the piglets all weigh about the same, how much does each piglet weigh? How can she tell?

1. The total weight is 280 pounds. What would it be without the dog?
2. What would the weight be without the dog and Chris?
3. How much do the three piglets weigh together? How do you know?
4. What is the weight of one piglet? How did you decide?
5. What equation models Chris' problem? Explain.
6. See if you can solve this equation by isolating the variable. Use what you have learned about combining like terms first.

In equations like these, the variable has a coefficient, but there is also something added or subtracted.

If number sense doesn't work to solve such equations, you will need to take two steps to isolate the variable.

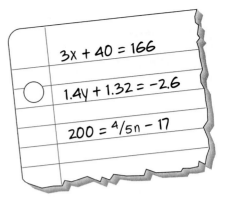

$$3x + 40 = 166$$

$$1.4y + 1.32 = -2.6$$

$$200 = \tfrac{4}{5}n - 17$$

Undo addition or subtraction first. Then undo multiplication or division. Remember, by doing these steps you are using properties of equality and keeping the scale balanced.

EXAMPLES

1. Solve $14y + 62 = -29$.

Most people would agree that this equation is too hard to solve by number sense alone. So we will isolate the variable.

$$14y + 62 = -29$$
$$14y + 62 - \mathbf{62} = -29 - \mathbf{62} \qquad \text{Subtract 62 to isolate the term } 14y.$$
$$14y = -91 \qquad \text{Simplify each side.}$$

This looks easier to solve.

$$\frac{14y}{\mathbf{14}} = \frac{-91}{\mathbf{14}} \qquad \text{Isolate } y \text{ by dividing by 14. Now 1}$$
$$\text{is the coefficient of } y.$$

$$y = -6.5 \qquad y \text{ means } 1y. \text{ Find } -6.5 \text{ using your calculator.}$$

To check your solution, replace y with -6.5 in $14y + 62 = -29$. After doing the calculation, both sides of the equation should equal -29.

2. Solve $\tfrac{4}{5}n - 17 = 200$.

$$\tfrac{4}{5}n - 17 = 200$$

$$\tfrac{4}{5}n - 17 + \mathbf{17} = 200 + \mathbf{17} \qquad \text{Add 17 to isolate the term } \tfrac{4}{5}n.$$

$$\tfrac{4}{5}n = 217 \qquad \text{Simplify each side.}$$

Now we can just use the reciprocal.

$$\tfrac{5}{4} \times \tfrac{4}{5}n = \tfrac{5}{4} \times 217 \qquad \text{Multiply by } \tfrac{5}{4} \text{ to get 1 as the coefficient of } n.$$

$$n = 271.25 \qquad n \text{ means } 1n. \text{ Use your calculator to get the solution.}$$

TRY IT

Solve each equation. Use your calculator if it helps.

a. $5m + 7 = 67$ **b.** $\frac{1}{2}x - 11 = 19$ **c.** $63t - 13 = 50$

d. $-3x + 9 = -10.5$ **e.** $\frac{3}{4}k + \frac{1}{2} = 9\frac{1}{4}$ **f.** $3a - 0.5 = 4.1$

CONSIDER

?

1. **How does undoing an equation seem to relate to the usual order of operations?**

An equation may also contain like terms. Combine like terms before you begin to solve the equation.

EXAMPLE

3. Find the length of this rectangle that has a perimeter of 50 units.

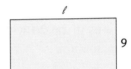

ℓ

9

Perimeter is 50.

$$9 + \ell + 9 + \ell = 50 \quad \text{Perimeter means the distance around.}$$
$$2\ell + 18 = 50 \quad \text{Combine like terms.}$$
$$2\ell = 32 \quad \text{Subtract 18 from both sides.}$$
$$\ell = 16 \quad \text{Divide both sides by 2.}$$

The length of the rectangle is 16 units.

TRY IT

g. Clay says that he will be eligible to run for the U.S. Senate when he is 4 years older than twice his current age. If senators must be at least 30 years old, how old is Clay now?

1. How do you know whether you will need two steps to isolate a variable?

2. When solving an equation like $12x + 50 = 140$, why do you undo addition first?

3. How could you use your calculator to solve the equation $12x + 50 = 140$?

Exercises

CORE

1. Getting Started What would you do first to solve $5x - 7.5 = 12$?

2. An equation that models this situation is $12x + 5.5 = 125.5$, where x is the weight of one egg. Copy these steps in the equation's solution. Replace the questions in **2a–2d** with a description or explanation.

$$12x + 5.5 = 125.5$$

$$12x + 5.5 - 5.5 = 125.5 - 5.5$$ **a.** Why subtract 5.5?

$$12x = 120$$ **b.** How do you get 120 on the right side?

$$\frac{12x}{12} = \frac{120}{12}$$ **c.** Why divide both sides by 12?

$$x = 10$$ **d.** What is the coefficient of x?

Solve each equation.

3. $5x - 17 = 108$ **4.** $\frac{2}{3}m + 84 = 144$ **5.** $10h = 230$

6. $3k - 2 = 1198$ **7.** $0.25s - 2.24 = 1.76$ **8.** $4x - 5 = 95$

9. $-4 + 2x = -14$ **10.** $13 + \frac{4}{5}x = 53$ **11.** $-\frac{1}{4}x = 25.5$

For Exercises 12–14, write an equation for each problem. Solve by using number sense or by isolating the variable.

12. Four letterman jackets cost $140.40, including tax of $10.40. How much does each jacket cost without tax?

13. Maria put 5 puppies in a cage to send them on an airplane. The total weight was 88 pounds. The cage by itself was 22.5 pounds. On average, how much did each puppy weigh?

14. Garth gets to watch 12 hours of TV each week. If he chooses three 1-hour shows, how many half-hour shows can he watch?

Solve each equation. Simplify the left side of each equation before isolating the variable. Check your solution.

15. $3x + 2 + 4x = 44$

16. $(x + 15) + (2x - 10) = 11$

17. $m + m + m + 25 - 20 = 38$

18. $2y + 4 + (6y - 9) + 1 = 21$

19. A Fine Problem In Morton City, the fine, in dollars, for a speeding ticket is $F = 30 + 4x$, where x stands for the miles per hour *over the speed limit.*

   a. What is the fine for going 32 miles per hour in a 20 mi/hr school zone?

   b. Donna got a fine of $122 for speeding in this school zone. How fast was she traveling?

   c. For what speeds do you think the formula makes sense? Why?

20. Leon said the chance of winning the state lottery was the same as the solution of the equation

$$1325x + 2786 = (150 \times 20) - 214$$

What did Leon mean? Why?

21. Solve for the variable.

a.

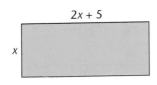

2x + 5

x

Perimeter = 70

b.

12

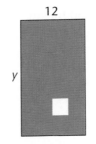

y

An area of 5 was removed.

Shaded area = 175

22. Dental Details According to the *Unofficial U.S. Census* (Heymann 1991), just over half of the adults in the United States use dental floss regularly. Each adult uses an average of about 33 feet per month.

   a. If an adult flosses every night, about how many feet is this per night?

   b. About how many feet will an adult use in a year? How many miles of floss?

Simplify. [2-3]

23. $2x - 3x$

24. $3(y - 2)$

25. $\dfrac{3y - 6}{3}$

26. Describe the symmetry of this figure. [3-1]

27. Describe the shape of the window shown. [3-1]

MORE PRACTICE

Solve each equation.

28. $25x = 250$

29. $70 + 3t = 100$

30. $1.4y + 9 = 11.8$

31. $-5x = 35$

32. $27y - 8 = 46$

33. $\frac{2}{3}x = 18$

34. $150 = 30n$

35. $0.6t = -3.12$

36. $5.6 = 6x - 6.4$

Solve each equation. Simplify the left side of each equation before isolating the variable. Check your solution.

37. $2x + x + x - 7 = 13$

38. $27x - 14x + 3 - 10 = 19$

39. $4m - 10m + 17 = 5$

40. $\frac{7}{8}x + 7 - \frac{5}{8}x = 11$

41. $y + 8 + 7y = 64$

42. $-4x + 2 - (6x - 2) = -28$

43. Renting a videotape costs $2.50 for one day. There is a late charge of $2.00 a day. Hank's bill was $30.50 when he returned the tape he rented. How many days did Hank have the tape? Write an equation that models the situation.

MORE MATH REASONING

44. How much will one drink cost, after getting a nickel back for recycling the can?

ON SALE
6–pack for
$1.98

Recycle your cans

We pay 5¢

The perimeter is the distance around a figure. Write and solve an equation for each problem.

45. How long is each side of this pentagon if the perimeter is 36 cm? (Hint: Write an equation showing the sum of the 5 sides.)

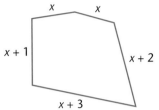

46. Maurice has to draw a triangle with all three sides equal in length. The perimeter must be 15 cm. How much longer than 4 cm must each side be?

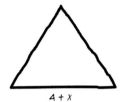

47. Solve an equation to find what x should be to build a 100-foot low wall around this scenic viewpoint.

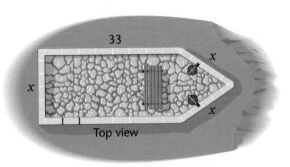

Top view

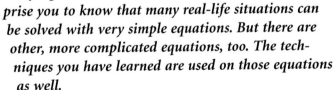

4-2
PART E
Making Connections

← C O N N E C T →
You've solved many equations that have one unknown. It may surprise you to know that many real-life situations can be solved with very simple equations. But there are other, more complicated equations, too. The techniques you have learned are used on those equations as well.

You've seen that X the *unknown* can become X the *known* by using different types of equation-solving skills. The Explore gives you a chance to combine your number sense and your new skills.

EXPLORE: UNMASKING THE UNKNOWN

1. *Search for the unknown* in each of these equations. Apply your number sense and the methods you studied in this chapter.

Hints:

a. $x^2 + 2 = 11$ Isolate the variable.

b. $5b - 3 = 2b + 6$ You solved equations like this with tiles.

c. $2(y + 3) = 14$ Think about taking $\frac{1}{2}$ of each side.

d. $(x - 3)(x - 2) = 0$ When you multiply by 0, what is the result?

e. $3x + 2y = 22$ When there are two variables, there can be more than one right answer. What if $y = 5$?

f. $5x + 6y + 8z = 0$ Sometimes all variables can have the same value.

2. After solving an equation by number sense, try to write a mathematical solution.
3. Did you find more than one solution for any of the equations? Explain.
4. Write a problem that matches any one of the equations.
5. Tell why the equation is a model for the problem. Explain your steps to solve the equation. Relate your search for the unknown in the equation to the solution of your problem.

REFLECT

1. Why should number sense be the first strategy you try when searching for the unknown?
2. Describe in your own words the idea behind the strategy of isolating the variable.
3. How do you know when you've solved an equation? How can you check that your solution is correct?
4. How are equations and their solutions related to real-life problem solving?
5. Compare the equations $\frac{2}{3}x = 18$ and $x + \frac{2}{3} = 18$. Tell the differences in the ways you would solve them.

Self-Assessment

Evaluate the expression for the given value of the variable.

1. $2.3x$ if $x = 1.2$

2. $2(y - 6)$ if $y = 6$

3. $\frac{b + 2}{3}$ if $b = 7$

4. $\frac{b}{3} + 2$ if $b = 7$

5. Use the equation $5x - 10 = 20$ to answer the following questions.
   a. What does it mean to solve the equation?
   b. If number sense won't work, how would you begin to isolate the variable?
   c. Give the resulting equation.
   d. What must you do to both sides to complete the isolation of x?
   e. What is the solution of $5x - 10 = 20$?

6. Two basic ways to solve equations are:

Use number sense alone. **or** *Isolate the variable in steps.*

Which do you prefer if both work for solving an equation? Why? Give an example to show what you mean.

Solve each equation in a way that makes sense to you.

7. $12x - 17 = 163$

8. $\frac{w}{3} + 21 = 46$

9. $0.4t = 40$

10. $230 = 10x$

11. $-2r = 70$

12. $\frac{3}{5}d = 100$

13. $3q - 2 = 15 + 9$

14. $0x = 9$

15. Jacqueline runs a small souvenir shop and often uses the formula $P = s - e$, where P stands for profits, s stands for the dollar amount she sold, and e stands for her expenses.

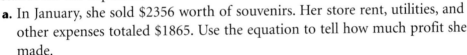

   a. In January, she sold $2356 worth of souvenirs. Her store rent, utilities, and other expenses totaled $1865. Use the equation to tell how much profit she made.
   b. She knew her February expenses would remain the same as January's. She wanted to make $4000 profit. Write an equation to show how many dollars worth of souvenirs she had to sell.
   c. Solve the equation. How much did she need to sell to make her goal?
   d. In March, she sold twice as many souvenirs as she had sold in January. Her expenses were the same as in January. Did her profits double? Explain what happened and give an equation for her profits in March.

16. In 4-1 Part D, you used the Fog Index^{SM} score to measure the reading level of a paragraph. The formula is $F = 0.4A + 0.4P$. F is the reading level in years. A is the average number of words in a sentence. P is the percentage of words with three or more syllables.

> *We, the people of the United States, in order to form a more perfect Union, establish justice, insure domestic tranquility, provide for the common defense, promote the general welfare, and secure the blessing of liberty to ourselves and our posterity, do ordain and establish this Constitution for the United States of America.*

a. Find the value of A in the paragraph.
b. What is the value of P in the paragraph?
c. Find the fog index or reading level of this paragraph.
d. Suppose the Preamble was rewritten into two sentences. Would the reading level be higher or lower? How does the addition property of equality help you explain what happens?

Write a problem to match these equations.

17. $105 = 5x + 25$

18. $\frac{2}{3}t - 10 = 8$

19. What is alike about the mathematics in these two pictures?

20. Explain the distributive property in your own words. [2-3]

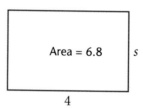

Area = 6.8

21. Purr-reduced Jamal has a coupon for $0.75 off 12 cans of Purr Cat Food. Without the coupon, he would pay $4.44 for the cans. How much will he actually pay for each can?

22. "Performance Assessment—An International Experiment" includes this problem that has been given to students all over the world. Try it yourself.

Suppose you have a scale, some clay, a 20-g weight, and a 50-g weight. Produce a lump of clay that weighs exactly 15 g.

Write an explanation of how to create the 15-g lump of clay.

Chapter 4 Review

In Chapter 4, you learned how formulas and equations are related. After investigating the idea of equality using balance scales and algebra tiles, you saw how to solve equations by using number sense or by isolating the variable. You've learned what an equation is and how it is used to model a mathematical situation.

KEY TERMS

circumference [4-1]

coefficient [4-2]

diameter [4-1]

equation [4-1]

formula [4-1]

inverse operations [4-2]

isolating the variable [4-2]

properties of equality [4-2]

radius [4-1]

reciprocal [4-2]

solution [4-1]

solve [4-1]

Write the letter of the word or phrase that best completes the sentence.

1. The distance around a circle is called the
 (a) circumference   (b) perimeter   (c) diameter   (d) radius   (e) not here

2. A mathematical statement that says two expressions are equal is called
 (a) an operation   (b) a comparison (c) a variable   (d) a negation   (e) not here

CONCEPTS AND APPLICATIONS

Use the formulas and compute each value. [4-1]

3. $P = 2\ell + 2w$; $\ell = 17$, $w = 5$

4. $C = \pi d$; for π use 3.14, $d = 21$

Use number sense to answer the question. [4-1]

5. $4.1x = 100$. How do you know that x is close to 25?

6. $\frac{1}{3}t = 10.5$. How do you know that t is greater than 30?

Solve each equation using number sense. Then check your solution. [4-1]

7. $250 = 5t$

8. $2.36 = d + 2.01$

9. $y - 7 = 4$

10. Choose the letter of the equation that the situation models. [4-1]

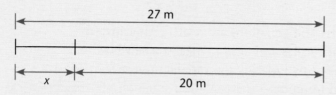

(a) $x - 27 = 20$ (b) $x - 20 = 27$ (c) $x + 27 = 20$ (d) $x + 20 = 27$ (e) not here

11. What algebra tiles would you have to add to this expression to get 0? [4-1]

Write the equation modeled by each equation box. Solve each equation. [4-1]

12.

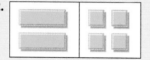

13.

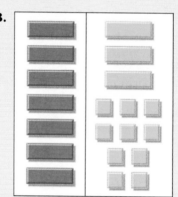

14.

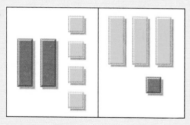

15.

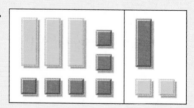

Write an equation to model each balanced scale. Describe the steps needed to find the weight of each item. Remember to keep each scale balanced. [4-2]

16.

Let *e* represent the
weight of 1 egg.

17.

Let *p* represent the
weight of 1 pencil.

18.

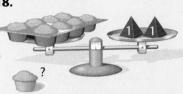

Let *m* represent the
weight of 1 muffin.

19. Sketch a scale. Then draw a picture to show the equation. [4-2]
$$x + 7 = 15$$

What is the reciprocal of each number? [4-2]

20. 6

21. $\frac{4}{7}$

22. -3

23. $-\frac{1}{4}$

Solve each equation. Check your solution. [4-2]

24. $\frac{3}{5}s = 20$

25. $d + 17 = 157$

26. $d - 17 = 65$

27. Use the equation $-3x + 17 = 65$ to answer the following questions. [4-2]
   a. Name the variable.
   b. Name the coefficient of *x*.

Solve each equation. [4-2]

28. $2x + 4 = 8$

29. $\frac{2}{3}s = -12$

30. $-\frac{2}{5}t = 10$

31. Write a problem to match the equation $3q - 2 = 17$. [4-2]

32. a. Write an expression that shows the
   perimeter of the pentagon shown. [4-2]
   b. If the perimeter of the figure is 45 cm,
   write an equation using the expression
   you wrote and 45.
   c. Solve your equation.
   d. How would the perimeter change if
   you doubled the value of *s*?
   e. How would the perimeter change
   if you cut the value of *s* in half?

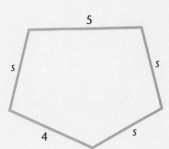

CONCEPTS AND CONNECTIONS

Industry Lou's Market is offering a new line of soda. The introductory price is $2.04 for two 6-packs. There is a 3¢ refund for each can returned. [4-2]

33. How would you find the cost for one 6-pack before refund?

34. If all 12 cans were returned, what would the total refund be?

35. How would you find the cost of 1 can after the refund on the 12 cans?

36. Write an equation to find the cost of 1 can after the refund on the 12 cans.

SPECIAL   Try the NEW
Sippin' Good Soda
Two 6-packs only **$2.04**
3¢ refund per can

SELF-EVALUATION

Explain what an equation is. Describe three different ways to solve equations. Then use examples of equations to show how each way works. Decide which method of solving equations you like best and explain why. Explain how to check your solution. Use as many of the vocabulary words from the beginning of this review as you can.

Chapter 4 Assessment

TEST

Use the formulas and compute each value.

1. $A = \frac{1}{2}bh$; $b = 15.25$, $h = 4$

2. $I = prt$; $p = 500$, $r = .05$, $t = 1$

3. For the equation $w - 75 = 16$, how does number sense tell you that w is a positive number?

Solve each equation. Check your solution.

4. $x + 1 = 2$

5. $-0.2c = 9.2$

6. $28 = 5 + 3x$

7. What algebra tiles would you have to add to this expression to get 0?

8. Write the equation modeled by the equation box. Solve the equation.

9. Write an equation to model this balanced scale. Describe the steps needed to find the weight of each item. Remember to keep each scale balanced.

Let p represent the weight of one bag of popcorn.

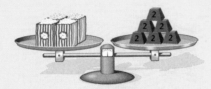

10. Sketch a scale. Then draw a picture to show the equation.

$2x + 4 = 15$

11. Use the equation $\frac{2}{7}x + 17 = 65$ to answer the following questions.

a. Name the variable.

b. Name the coefficient of x.

c. Name the reciprocal of the coefficient of x.

Solve each equation. Check your solution.

12. $d - 20 = 39$ **13.** $d + 3.4 = 157.8$ **14.** $\frac{5}{9}s = 72$

15. Write an expression that shows the perimeter of the hexagon shown.

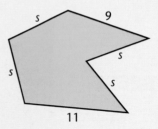

a. If the perimeter of the figure is 84 cm, write an equation using the expression you wrote and 84.

b. Solve your equation.

c. How would the perimeter change if you doubled the value of s?

d. How would the perimeter change if you cut the value of s in half?

PERFORMANCE TASK

Choose one equation listed below and write a problem for it. Choose a different equation to illustrate how to use algebra tiles or a balance scale. Explain in detail how you would use number sense to solve the third equation. In each case, explain why you chose that equation for the task.

a. $3x + 1 = 10$ **b.** $3x - 1 = 10$ **c.** $\frac{1}{3}x - 1 = 10$

Chapter 5

Spatial Relations

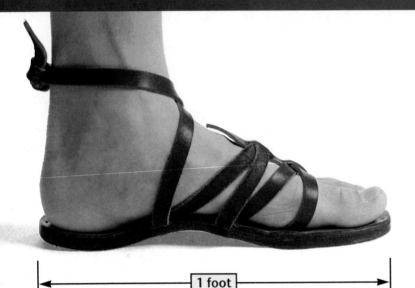

← 1 foot →

Project A
Great and Small
What are SI units? How did we arrive at our system of weights and measures?

Project B
One Person, One Vote
Who is Elbridge Gerry and what effect did he have on how congressional district lines are drawn?

S.S.S. 7.
BALLOT
BOX.
1882

Project C
What a Relief!
How do the features of a flat map look in relief?

JEFFREY RAINE

I enjoyed math in high school. I knew I would use it. Sometimes it seems that every decision I need to make comes down to numbers.

I started work at entry-level. Now I supervise a whole warehouse the size of a city block. When I receive a product in multiple truck loads, I have to know how many pallets are on each truck, how many layers are on each pallet, and how many cases are on a layer. The computer keeps track, but I have to know in my head where everything is.

Jeffrey Raine
Warehouse Supervisor
Addison-Wesley
Distribution Center
Indianapolis, Indiana

Jeffrey Raine

Chapter 5

Overview

Spatial Relations

5-1 Size

Architects, designers, and other professionals need to be able to represent objects on paper. You will learn some techniques for drawing three dimensional figures. You will be able to find sizes of geometric objects in terms of perimeter, area, and volume.

5-2 Polygons and Circles

Formulas for areas of polygons and circles are equations that make calculations easier for everyone from seamstress to landscaper. You will explore some commonly used formulas. You will use orthographic projections to "break apart" solids into polygons and circles.

5-3 Nets, Surface Area, and Volume

Manufacturers need precise measurements of objects they make. You will draw nets to find surface areas of solids. You will find volumes and surface areas of prisms, pyramids, cylinders, and cones.

A Cube, a Solid, and Good Luck!

According to writer Clovis Heimsath, Texas pioneers had a simple method for building houses. She calls the method "a geometry lesson:"

> 1. Take a cube and a solid.   2. Put them together.   3. Punch in a door for good luck!

Although many pioneer homes in Texas were more elaborate than the so-called "Texas basic," all were based on the simple geometry of a cube topped by a triangular solid. The simplicity of the design reflected the simplicity of the setting, a landscape as pure and undisturbed as any in America.

Like all well-designed buildings, early Texas houses consisted of solids and spaces arranged to make the buildings as functional as possible. The solid walls, floors, and ceilings were made of stone, timber, and other materials from the surrounding country-

side. Some of the spaces, such as windows and doorways, were *two-dimensional*. Others, such as room spaces and open porches, were *three-dimensional*. The size and placement of each part of a home were chosen carefully by the builder to make the structure as comfortable and convenient as possible for those who lived in it. Taken in its entirety, the "Texas basic" was a clear confirmation of the saying that "architecture is geometry."

?

1. The article says that early Texas houses were built to be "as functional as possible." Explain this phrase.
2. What do we usually mean by the three dimensions?
3. Explain how a space can be two-dimensional.
4. Describe your school building in terms of the spaces and geometric solids of which it is composed.

← CONNECT → *You know how to draw two-dimensional figures, such as squares and rectangles. Now you will learn several methods for showing three-dimensional objects on paper.*

The world in which we live is three dimensional, and the most common geometric shapes are three-dimensional **solids,** or "space" figures. These two-dimensional drawings represent three-dimensional solids.

Cube   **Rectangular Prism**   **Tetrahedron**

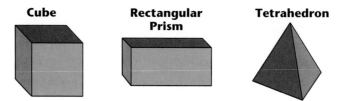

CONSIDER

?

1. What do the solids above have in common?

Drawing a three-dimensional object on a two-dimensional piece of paper is not an easy task.

To give a three-dimensional quality to a drawing, an architect may create an **isometric projection.** An isometric projection, such as this one, shows an object as it would appear if you viewed it from an angle.

This isometric projection depicts a $1 \times 1 \times 1$ cube. Each corner is a **vertex.** Each segment connecting two vertices is an **edge.** Each surface is a **face.**

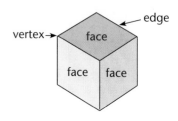

2. What are the geometric shapes that form each face of a cube?

3. How many faces are visible in the drawing? How many faces are hidden?

4. How many vertices does a cube have? How many edges does a cube have?

EXPLORE: CUBES AND PRISMS TO A "T"

1. Draw a cube on isometric dot paper.

2. Draw a second cube that is twice as long in each direction.

3. How can you compare the size of the second cube with that of the original cube?

The drawing shows a **rectangular prism,** which measures 2 units by 3 units by 1 unit, and a block-letter T.

4. Draw an isometric view of the prism as it would appear if you viewed it from the bottom rather than from the top. (Hint: Draw the bottom first or rotate this page 180°.)

5. Study how the block-letter T was constructed. Then draw your initials in block letters.

MATERIALS

Isometric dot paper
Ruler

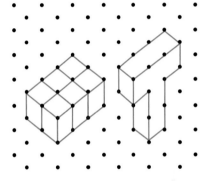

Isometric projections do not show the shrinking that seems to happen to the parts of an object that are farther from a viewer's eye.

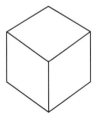

All edges of the cube appear equal.

During the Renaissance, artists discovered how to use this shrinking effect, known as **perspective,** to make their drawings and paintings appear more lifelike.

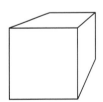

All edges of the cube do not appear equal.

Draw a rectangular prism in **one-point perspective,** which is the simplest type of perspective drawing.

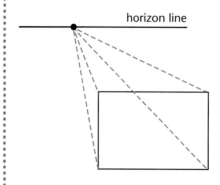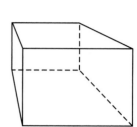

First connect each vertex of the front face of a rectangle to a vanishing point on the horizon.

Then sketch the back face of the prism, draw the edges, and erase the perspective lines.

a. Copy the triangle, the horizon line, and the vanishing point. Then complete a one-point perspective drawing of a prism.

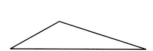

1. In a perspective drawing, why is the point on the horizon called a vanishing point?

2. Why do railroad tracks seem to meet at a point off in the distance, when you know they are really parallel?

3. What techniques, in addition to perspective, could you use to make a drawing of a cube appear more lifelike?

Painting by Amsterdam artist Maynert Hobbema, Avenue at Middelharnis *(1698). The National Gallery, London.*

Exercises

CORE

1. Getting Started How many faces does a rectangular prism have?

Identify the view of the rectangular prism as isometric projection or one-point perspective.

2.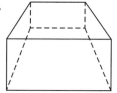

3.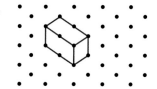

4.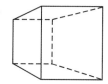

5. Match each item from Column 1 with an item from Column 2 and one from Column 3.

Column 1	Column 2	Column 3
a. edge		**A.** a 3-dimensional figure
b. face		**B.** a surface of an object
c. isometric projection		**C.** an object viewed from an angle
d. perspective drawing		**D.** uses a vanishing point
e. solid		**E.** a segment connecting two vertices

i.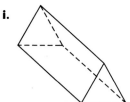

ii.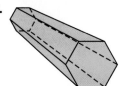

iii.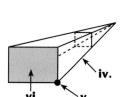

6. a. Draw an isometric view of a row of three cubes.
   b. Draw a different isometric view of the same row of three cubes.

7. Copy the trapezoid, the horizon line, and the vanishing point. Then complete a one-point perspective drawing of a prism.

Give the number of vertices, edges, and faces for each solid.

8.

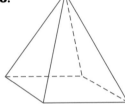

9.

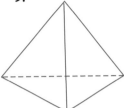

10.

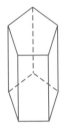

Study the two scenes and tell whether the artists used isometric projection or one-point perspective. If perspective was used, try to locate the horizon line and vanishing point.

11.

Fine Arts

12.

Industry

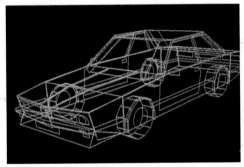

 LOOK BACK

13. The formula $E = \frac{9R}{I}$ is used to calculate the earned run average (E) of a pitcher who has given up R earned runs in I innings. Find the number of earned runs given up in 54 innings by a pitcher who has an earned run average of 3.5. [4-1]

14. Evaluate the expression $3yz - z^2$ if $y = 2$ and $z = -1$. [2-3]

Solve for x. [4-2]

15. $2x + 7 = 43$

16. $\frac{x}{2} = 9$

17. $\frac{2}{5}x = -4$

MORE PRACTICE

18. a. Draw an isometric view of your textbook.
   b. Draw an isometric view of a three-story building.

19. Copy the trapezoid, the horizon line, and the vanishing point. Then complete a one-point perspective drawing of a prism.

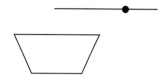
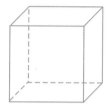

20. Why do many engineering blueprints contain isometric projections?

Give the number of vertices, edges, and faces for each solid.

21. 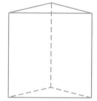   **22.** 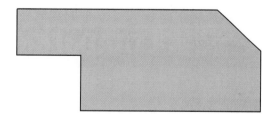   **23.**

24. Use this shape as the front face of a solid. Draw the solid in one-point perspective.

25. Can you locate the vanishing point in this one-point perspective photo? Make a sketch of one object from the photo, its horizon line, and its vanishing point.

MORE MATH REASONING

26. Complete the first three lines of the chart using data from Exercises 8–10. Complete the next three lines using data from Exercises 21–23. Use your results to make a statement about the relationship among the numbers of faces, vertices, and edges in a solid figure.

Figure	Number of Faces (F)	Number of Vertices (V)	Number of Edges (E)	$F + V - E$

5-1 PART B Comparing Sizes

← **CONNECT** → *You have measured lengths with rulers. Comparison is the basis of all measurement. Now you will learn to measure or tell the size of an object by comparing it with the measurement of other objects.*

We can start our study of measurement by comparing the sizes of the two houses below.

CONSIDER

?

1. What are five ways you could compare the sizes of the two houses?
2. Which way might be used when a realtor compares the size of one house with another? an air-conditioning salesman? a painter? Explain.

EXPLORE: DESKTOP COMPUTERS

You have been asked to calculate the size of your desktop. The data will be used to estimate the cost of applying a plastic coating to the desktop and its edge to extend its life.

MATERIALS

Pen or pencil
Index cards, envelopes, or comparable paper rectangles

1. Use an index card, an envelope, or some other small paper rectangle. Find the size of the surface of your desktop in number of rectangles.
2. Use a pen or pencil. Find the distance around the edge of your desktop in number of pens or pencils.
3. Which measurement, the size of the surface or the distance around your desktop, would be more useful to the maintenance staff? Why?
4. Are your measurements exact or approximate? Explain.
5. If you measured the surface of your desktop again, this time using a smaller rectangle, would you count the same number of rectangles, more rectangles, or fewer rectangles?
6. If you measured the distance around the edge again, this time with a longer pen or pencil, how would the number of pen or pencil lengths change?
7. What difficulties would the maintenance staff face if students reported desktop sizes in numbers of rectangles and pencils?

Is a house large or small?

The distance around the outside of a house would probably be several thousand ant lengths. Compared with an ant, a house is huge.

However, the distance around the outside of a house would be a very small part of the circumference of the earth. Compared with the earth, the house is tiny.

When you take a measurement or find a size, you are comparing the object being measured with a unit of measurement. You used *rectangles* or *pens* or *pencils* as your units of measurement when you found the size of your desk.

You may recall that **perimeter** is the length around the edge of a figure. It is measured in **linear units.**

Area is the number of squares it takes to cover the region within a figure. It is measured in **square units.**

EXAMPLES

Find the perimeter and the area of each region.

1.

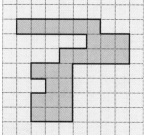

2.

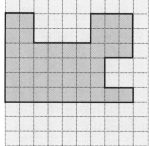

Perimeter: The distance around the edge of the region is 40 units.
Area: The size of the region within the figure is 25 square units.

Perimeter: The length around the edge of the figure is 38 units.
Area: It takes exactly 42 squares to cover the figure. The size is 42 square units.

Find the perimeter and the area of each region.

a.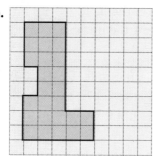

b.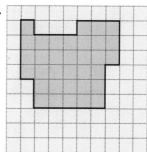

WHAT DO **YOU** THINK?

Find the area of the rectangle.

12 inches

3 inches

Tyler thinks ...

I will count the square units. There are 36 square units. Each unit is a square inch, so the area is 36 square inches.

Elena thinks ...

I will use the formula $A = \ell w$

$$= 12 \times 3$$
$$= 36$$

So the area must be 36 square inches.

CONSIDER

?

3. What unit of measurement did Tyler and Elena use?
4. How is counting the squares similar to using the formula $A = \ell w$ for finding the area of a rectangle?
5. Why is area measured in square units?

Areas of irregular shapes can be estimated by counting squares on a grid.

3. Estimate the area of the lake.

Most maps have grids on them. To find the lake's area, count the number of squares it covers.

The lake covers 23 full squares. It also covers pieces of squares that appear to add to about 10 more squares.

23 + 10 = 33 square units

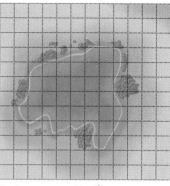

Each square = 1 mi²

Because each square unit is 1 square mile, the area of the lake is about 33 square miles.

Notice that we can write "square miles" as "mi²" to save space.

TRY IT

Find each area.

c.

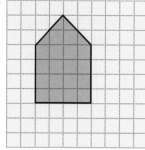

Each square = 1 cm²

d.

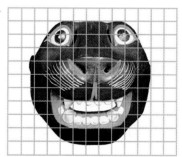

Each square = 1 cm²

REFLECT

1. Explain the difference between the part of your desk you measured with a pen or pencil in the Explore and the part of your desk you measured with a rectangle.

2. Suppose you measured the size of an object twice, using different-sized units of measurements each time. Describe how the measurements would compare.

3. Suppose you measured two different objects, using the same unit for each measurement. Which would be greater, the measurement of the larger object or the measurement of the smaller object?

4. Explain why we call the measurement of distance along the edge of a figure "one-dimensional." Explain why we call the measurement of the region inside the edge of a figure "two-dimensional."

Exercises

CORE

1. Getting Started
   a. How long is each of the four sides in units?
   b. What is the perimeter of the rectangle?
   c. How many squares are in the rectangle?
   d. What is the area of the rectangle?

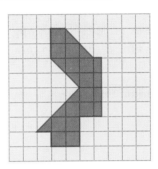

2. Find the perimeter and area.

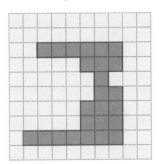

3. Estimate the area.

4. Determine whether the statement is true or false. If the statement is false, change the underlined word or phrase to make it true.

The perimeter of a figure is measured in <u>square</u> units.

Find the perimeter and area of each rectangle. Be sure to use the correct units.

5.   2 m

3 m

6.   6 mm

2 mm

7. Three different figures each have an area of 12 square units. Use unit squares and draw three possible figures.

8. a. Draw three different rectangles, each with a perimeter of 12 units.
   b. Find the area of each rectangle.

9. How many square feet are in 1 square yard?

> **Problem-Solving Tip**
>
> Draw a diagram of 1 square yard.
> Mark the dimensions in square feet.

10. One wall of a living room measures 12 ft by 8 ft. If you want to put masking tape around the 4 edges of the wall before you paint, how much tape do you need? How much paint do you need if a gallon covers 400 ft², and you want to apply 3 coats of paint?

11. Find the perimeter and area of the figure. All measurements are in feet. (Hint: Find the missing lengths first.)

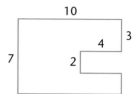

12. A rectangular lawn measures 80 feet by 60 feet. Meredith's lawn mower cuts a 1.5-foot path as it mows. If Meredith mows parallel to the long side of the lawn, how many paths must she cut to mow the entire lawn?

Problem-Solving Tip

Draw a diagram.

13. **Keeping Pace** Tony paced off the distance of the Class Day foot race and measured it as 256 paces. Then Annette, whose pace is slightly smaller than Tony's, stepped off the distance. Which of the following describes Annette's measurement of the distance?
   (a) fewer than 256 paces   (b) 256 paces   (c) greater than 256 paces

14. **State of the Union**

   a. Estimate the perimeter of each state.
   b. Estimate the area of each state.
   c. Compare the areas of the two states.

Georgia

□ = 40 mi   ■ = 1600 mi²

Ohio

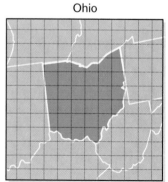

Estimate each area.

15.
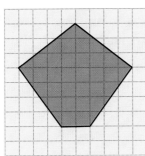
Each square = 1 m²

16.

Each square = 1 km²

17. Juan ordered a carpet that is 4 yd × 5 yd at $12.95 a square yard. Find the cost of the carpet.

 LOOK BACK

Simplify. [2-1]

18. $5 + 4 \cdot 3 - 2$

19. $(5 + 4) \cdot (3 - 2)$

20. $5 + (4 \cdot 3 + 2)$

21. Find the next three elements in the pattern. 97, 72, 47, 22, ___, ___, ___ [3-3]

Solve each equation. [4-2]

22. $a + 2a = 18$

23. $3 = 4n - 9$

24. $1.2b - 18 = -3$

MORE PRACTICE

Find the perimeter and area of each figure.

25.
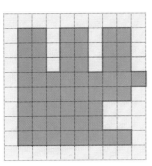

26.
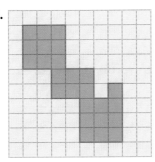

27.
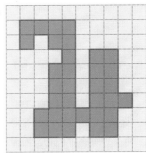

28. Write the word or phrase that best completes the sentence.
The length around a circle is called its ____ .

Find the perimeter and area of each figure. Be sure to use the correct units.

29.

4 in.

4 in.

30.

6 yd

1 yd

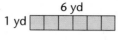

31.

4 km

1.5 km

32. A building rents for $1.24 per square foot per month. If Maxine rents three 12 ft by 15 ft rooms for her office, calculate her monthly rent.

Estimate the areas.

33.

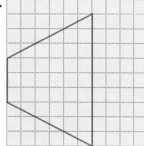

Each square = 1 m^2

34.

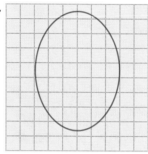

Each square = 1 m^2

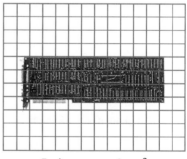

35. Computer Circuitry Electrical circuits cover boards located inside a computer. Data entered into a computer are changed into on-off electrical signals.
a. Find the perimeter of the circuit board.
b. Find the area of the circuit board.

Each square = 1 cm^2

Give the perimeter and area of each rectangle. Be sure to use the correct units.

36.

7 in.

4 in.

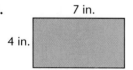

37.

15.3 yd

3 yd

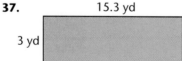

38.

20.3 km

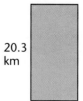

8.6 km

39. Carcassonne, France, contains one of the finest remaining examples of a walled city of the Middle Ages. It is about a mile in perimeter, and enclosed by 2 walls with 54 towers. Estimate the area within the outer wall of the city.

MORE MATH REASONING

40. Crater from Mars NASA's *Mariner 7* sent photos of the surface of Mars to Earth. These photos revealed many craters on Mars's surface. Describe how you could use graph paper to estimate the area of this crater in square units. What else would you need to know to estimate the area of the crater?

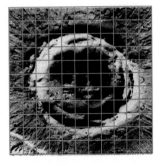

41. Jessie found a way to tessellate a large region using exactly 40 congruent figures. Give the size of the region in terms of one congruent figure's size.

42. A rectangle measures *m* units by *n* units. Give the size of the rectangle in terms of 1 × 1 squares.

43. The circle graph shows the results of a "Favorite Spectator Sport" poll. The circumference of the circle is 7.25 in. Find the radius.

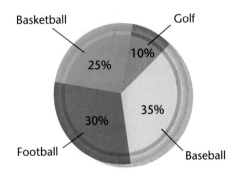

Sizes in Three Dimensions

← C O N N E C T → *You have measured lines using one dimension and figures using one and two dimensions. Now you will examine solids, which have measures in one, two, and three dimensions.*

We have seen that we measure lengths with units, and surfaces with square units. We will now look at the measure of space.

EXPLORE: BOX BUILDING

MATERIALS

Cubes

You will use small cubic blocks to build some three-dimensional, box-shaped solids. For the activity, assume that the length, width, and height of each of your blocks are 1 unit. So each block fills 1 cubic unit of space.

1. Lay out a layer of blocks as shown.
   a. What is the length, width, and height of the solid?
   b. Count the blocks or cubic units that make up your box. This is its volume.

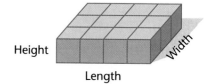

Height · Length · Width

2. Expand your box so it is two layers high instead of one.
   a. What is the length, width, and height of the solid now?
   b. What is the volume of the solid now? Describe how it compares with the original volume.

3. Expand your box so it is six rows wide instead of three.
   a. What is the length, width, and height of the solid now?
   b. What is the volume of the solid now? Describe how it compares with the original volume.

4. How could you use what you have learned to find the volume of this box?

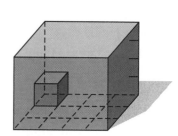

The size of the region inside a solid is its **volume.** It is the number of cubes that exactly *fills* a solid. Volume is measured in **cubic units.**

Length	Area	Volume

Length is measured in linear units.

For example: in., ft, km, cm.

Area is measured in square units.

For example: in.^{2}, ft^2, cm^2.

Volume is measured in cubic units.

For example: in.^{3}, ft^3, km^3, cm^3.

TRY IT

Determine whether each measurement is length, area, or volume and if it requires linear, square, or cubic units.

a. the grass on a soccer field
b. the span of a bridge
c. the amount of juice in a jar
d. the available ad space on a cereal box

EXAMPLES

1. How many cubic units are contained in this box?
Each layer contains 4 rows of 3 cubes, or 12 cubic units.
There are 3 layers, so the box contains 3 × 12, or 36 cubic units.

2. Find the volume of the hay bale in cubic feet, or ft^3.

If each cube was 1 cubic foot, it would take 16 × 1, or 16 cubes to fill the bale.
The volume of the hay bale is 16 cubic feet, or 16 ft^3.

e. Find the volume of this rectangular prism.

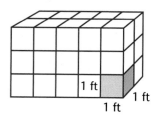

1 ft

1 ft

1 ft

REFLECT

1. In your own words, explain the difference between perimeter and area; between area and volume.

2. When you are calculating perimeter, area, or volume, why is it important that you specify the units?

3. Describe how you would find the volume of a box.

4. Describe what happens to volume if you double the length, width, and height of a box?

Exercises

CORE

1. Getting Started What measurement are you finding when you count the total number of cubic units?

2. How many cubic units are contained in this box?

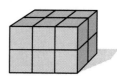

Find the volume of each box.

3.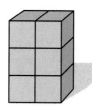

4.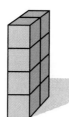

5.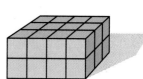

6. Which is an appropriate unit of measurement for the size of a painting?
(a) in.   (b) cm³   (c) ft²   (d) not here

7. Find the volume of the box if
   a. its length is increased by 1 unit.
   b. its width is increased by 1 unit.
   c. its height is decreased by 1 unit.
   d. its width is doubled.

Height

Width

Length

Determine whether each measurement is length, area, or volume and if it requires linear, square, or cubic units.

8. amount of wall space for exhibits in an art museum

9. storage room for food in a freezer

10. maximum safe diving depth without oxygen tanks

11. drinking water in a water tower

12. diameter of a tree

13. the amount of wood you can get from a tree

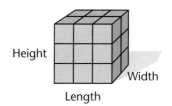

14. Find the volume of the compost container.

Science

15. Re-box Elaine says a box that is 2 ft × 2 ft × 2 ft is *much* smaller than a box that is 3 ft × 3 ft × 3 ft. Do you think this is true? Explain.

16. Draw a box that has a volume of 32 cubic units. Draw or describe a different box that has the same volume.

17. Truth in Advertising Many labels on products contain the note, "Contents are sold by weight and not by volume." Explain what this means. Why is this note on the products?

Industry

18. Predict the volume of the 10th figure in this series. What rules did you use to find it?

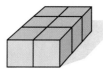

19. A candy maker dipped all sides of a piece of candy in icing. The recipe said to make the candies with edges of 3 cm before icing them. He made them much smaller. Explain why he ran out of icing.

LOOK AHEAD

20. Find the total area. (Hint: Find the areas of the three rectangles first.)

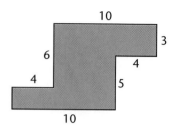

21. What is the total area of the box before it is assembled?

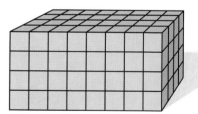

22. A manufacturer packs children's blocks, each measuring $1\frac{1}{2}$ in. on a side, in boxes measuring 6 in. × 6 in. × 12 in. How many blocks can be packed in each box?

MORE PRACTICE

23. How many cubic units are contained in this box?

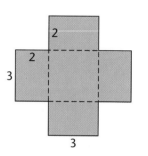

Determine whether the measurement requires linear, square, or cubic units.

24. the distance across a circular rink

25. the amount of oxygen in a cave

26. the size of a poster frame

27. the floor space in a tent

28. the capacity of an oil drum

29. the size of a wall that can be painted with 1 gallon of paint

Find the volume of each box.

30.

31.
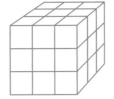

32.

33.
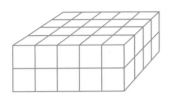

34.
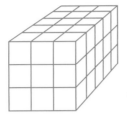

35.
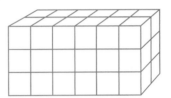

36. Draw a square to represent 1 square foot.
  a. Label the dimensions in inches.
  b. How many square inches are in 1 square foot?

MORE MATH REASONING

37. Postal Puzzle A package that weighs more than 15 pounds per cubic foot must be mailed in an extra strong box. Max will pack up a machine that is 18 inches wide, 2 feet long, and 1 foot high and that weighs about 55 pounds. He will protect it with 6 inches of foam pellets on each side that weigh about 2 pounds total.
  a. Sketch a box that will hold the machine and the foam material. Label its length, width, and height.
  b. Will he need to use an extra strong box? Explain.

38. Each edge of cube A measures 4 inches. Each edge of cube B measures 1 inch. Give the size of cube A in terms of the size of cube B.

39. These are three views of a box. What is the volume of the box?

Top view

Side view

Front view

Making Connections

You have seen that the dimensions of an object can be expressed in units of measurement and that its size can be expressed in terms of length, area, or volume. Now you will apply what you have learned to the room where you study mathematics.

EXPLORE: ROOM WITH A VIEW

MATERIALS

Yardstick or meter stick
Drawing materials

You can find the size of your math classroom and create a drawing of the room.

1. Decide how to express the size of your classroom. You may wish to express the size in terms of perimeter, area, or volume.
2. Find the dimensions of the room. If you estimate any measurements, explain how you made the estimates.
3. Calculate the size of the room and explain why you used the method that you did.
4. Make an isometric or perspective drawing of the room and indicate your room's dimensions on your drawing.

REFLECT

1. Suppose that an architect is preparing drawings of a new house for you. What type(s) of drawing(s) would you find most useful?
2. Describe some similarities and differences between two-dimensional figures and three-dimensional solids. Use some of the terms you learned in 5-1.
3. When are the measurements of length, area, and volume useful?

Self-Assessment

1. On the cube, $\overline{CG}$ is
   (a) a vertex   (b) a face
   (c) an edge   (d) a prism

2. Is this view of the prism an isometric projection or one-point perspective?

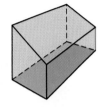

3. Write the next three terms of the pattern.
   2, 5, 10, 17, ____, ____, ____ [3-3]

Write the letter of the word or phrase that correctly completes the statement.

4. Volume is to cube as area is to ____.
   (a) perimeter   (b) line   (c) square   (d) length   (e) not here

5. Find the area and perimeter of the quadrilateral.

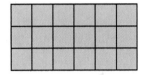

6. a. What is the length of $\overline{AB}$ in centimeters? [1-1]
   b. What is the length of $\overline{AB}$ in inches?

A ———————————————————— B

7. A letter L is formed from a row of three cubes plus a fourth cube placed beside one of the end cubes in the row. Use isometric dot paper to draw an isometric view of the L.

8. Find the mean of these highway speeds (mi/hr): 61, 59, 60, 72, 61, 65. [1-3]

Give the perimeter and area of each figure. Be sure to use the correct units.

9.
1 in.
1 in.

10.

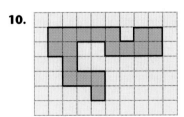

11.
12 ft
18 ft

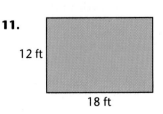

12. Monica is planning to install an automatic sprinkler system in her yard. The yard is 18 feet wide and 34 feet long. Each sprinkler head will water a square area six feet on each side. She needs to know how many sprinkler heads will be needed to water the whole yard.

    a. Draw and label a sketch of her situation on graph paper.

    b. Using your sketch, how many sprinkler heads should she buy?

    c. Write an equation that models the situation.

    d. Solve your equation and check your solution.

    e. Is there a difference between your answer using the sketch and your answer using an equation? Explain.

Estimate the areas.

13.

Each square = 1 yd²

Social Science

14.

Each square = 1 m²

15. Evaluate each expression if $b = 3$, $b_1 = 2$, $b_2 = 4$, and $h = 5$. [2-3]

    a. $A = bh$

    b. $A = \frac{1}{2}(b_1 + b_2)h$

    c. $A = \left(\frac{1}{2}b_1 + \frac{1}{2}b_2\right)h$

    d. $A = \frac{1}{2}h(b_1 + b_2)$

16. Copy the figure, the horizon line, and the vanishing point. Then complete a one-point perspective drawing of a prism.

17. Complete the following statements.

    a. Perimeter and circumference are measured in ____ units.

    b. Volume is measured in ____ units.

    c. Area is measured in ____ units.

Find the volume of each box.

18.

19.

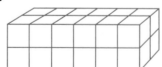

20.

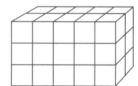

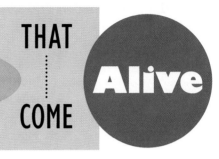

Shapes THAT COME Alive

.. bare, awkward silhouettes of running or stumbling animals ...

Unexpectedly, they brought the figure back into an art world that had learned to reject it.

In Susan Rothenberg's **Cabin Fever** (1976), the horse image is handsome and forceful. Critics first paid attention to Rothenberg's art in the mid-1970s, when she did a series of paintings that showed horses. ● Her first horse, done in 1973, was "a watery sketch." But it was one of those art pieces that led the way to a new interest in figures as subjects for paintings. The rise of abstract art in the early twentieth century had caused many well-known artists to lose interest in depicting recognizable shapes. The rediscovery of such shapes by Rothenberg and other artists in recent decades has led to the decline of abstract art and a renewed interest in representational art, with its recognizable figures and scenes. ● How do you make a three-dimensional object look lifelike on a flat piece of canvas? Many artists put together basic shapes—circles, ovals, segments, triangles, rectangles—to bring to life representations of three-dimensional objects on canvas. Their work demonstrates the mathematical structure that is an essential ingredient in every work of art.

1. What does the phrase "a watery sketch" in the second paragraph mean?
2. What are some techniques that artists use to make images lifelike?
3. Using only simple geometric shapes, draw a sketch of a horse or another figure of your choice.
4. What connections between mathematics and art can you think of?

357

Triangles, Parallelograms, & Trapezoids

← CONNECT → *You have learned how to find the area of a figure by counting the number of square units that are needed to cover the figure. Now you will look at polygons and find their areas by using dimensions.*

Figures that have straight sides are called **polygons.** You are already familiar with triangles, rectangles, and squares. Here are some other common polygons.

Right triangle–Has a right angle.

Parallelogram–Opposite sides are parallel.

Trapezoid–Two opposite sides are parallel.

EXPLORE: GETTING IN SHAPE

MATERIALS

Tangrams or tracing paper

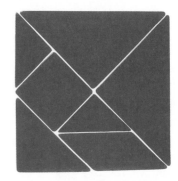

1. Use tangrams, or trace and cut out the polygons at the right.
2. Classify each of these seven polygons as a triangle, rectangle, square, parallelogram, or trapezoid. Can a shape be classified in more than one way?
3. Combine several tangram shapes to create more polygons. Then classify these figures.
4. Find the area of each figure. Compare the area of the first tangram figure with that of the second tangram figure. Explain how you found the area of the second figure.

a.

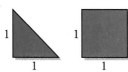

b.

c.

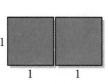

You can calculate the area of a triangle or a parallelogram if you know just two measurements—the length of one side and the height of the figure.

The length of one of the sides is called a **base.** The **height,** or **altitude,** is the perpendicular distance from a vertex to a line containing *that* base.

There is more than one way to label the base and height of a triangle.

For △*ABC,*

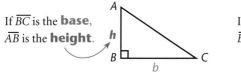

If $\overline{BC}$ is the **base**, $\overline{AB}$ is the **height**.

If $\overline{AB}$ is the **base**, $\overline{BC}$ is the **height**.

We can also label the base and height of a parallelogram in more than one way.

For parallelogram *ABCD,*

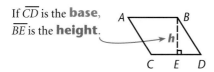

If $\overline{CD}$ is the **base**, $\overline{BE}$ is the **height**.

or extend the **base** $\overline{CD}$ and then $\overline{AE}$ is the **height**.

EXAMPLES

1. Find the height of △*DEF.*
   a. Measure the height from vertex *E* to base $\overline{DF}$.

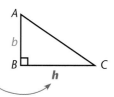

3 in.

   b. Or, measure the height from vertex *D* to base $\overline{EF}$.

3.2 in.

2. Find the height of △*ABC.*
   a. Measure the height from vertex *B* to base $\overline{AC}$.

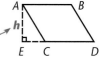

0.5 cm

   b. Or, measure the height from vertex *A* to the extended base line of $\overline{BC}$.

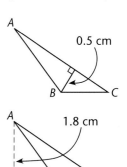

1.8 cm

It is important to identify a base with an altitude or height related to it.

TRY IT

Copy the polygons. Use the named line segment as the base. Draw, if necessary, and label a height from a vertex to the base.

a. $\overline{AC}$ **b.** $\overline{AD}$ **c.** $\overline{BC}$

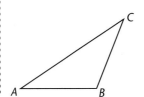
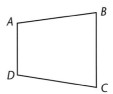
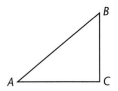

You can use the following formulas to find areas of triangles, parallelograms, and trapezoids. The base is represented by the variable b. The height is represented by h.

Parallelogram	Triangle	Trapezoid
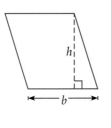	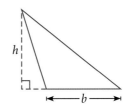	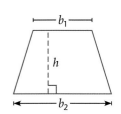
$A = bh$	$A = \frac{1}{2}bh$	$A = \frac{1}{2}(b_1 + b_2)h$

TRY IT

Find each area. Measurements shown are in inches.

d. Triangle ABC **e.** Parallelogram $PQRS$ **f.** Trapezoid $DEFG$

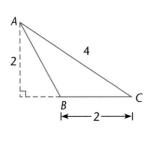
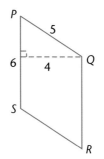
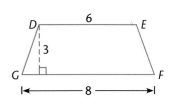

CONSIDER
?

1. Which formula can you use to find the area of a rectangle? Explain why it works.
2. What part of the formula for the area of a trapezoid represents the average of the bases?

WHAT DO **YOU** THINK?

Find the area of the triangle.

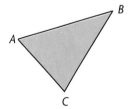

Lydia thinks ...

I will measure the base, $\overline{AB}$.

$\overline{AB} \approx 11$ inches

Then I'll measure the related height, $\overline{CD}$.

$\overline{CD} \approx 7$ inches

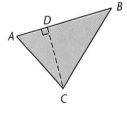

Using the formula $A = \frac{1}{2}bh$,

$$A \approx \frac{1}{2} \cdot 11 \cdot 7,$$
$$A \approx \frac{1}{2}(77), \text{ or } 38.5.$$

The area of $\triangle ABC$ is about 38.5 square inches.

Dawn thinks ...

I will use the base, $\overline{BC}$.

$\overline{BC} \approx 10$ inches

Then $\overline{AE}$ is the height.

$\overline{AE} \approx 7.7$ inches

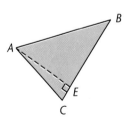

Using the formula $A = \frac{1}{2}bh$,

$$A \approx \frac{1}{2} \cdot 10 \cdot 7.7,$$
$$A \approx \frac{1}{2}(77), \text{ or } 38.5.$$

The area of $\triangle ABC$ is about 38.5 square inches.

1. Does it matter which side is the base of a polygon? How can you find the height for each base?
2. How are parallelograms and trapezoids similar? How are they different? Explain.
3. How does the area of a triangle with base b and height h compare with the area of a parallelogram with the same base and height?
4. The formula for the area of a rectangle is $A = \ell w$; for the area of a square, $A = s^2$; for the area of a parallelogram, $A = bh$. How are these formulas alike? Explain.

Exercises

CORE

1. **Getting Started** Copy the following columns. Match the items in each column by drawing connecting lines.

Column 1	**Column 2**	**Column 3**
$A = \frac{1}{2}(b_1 + b_2)h$		triangle
$A = bh$		parallelogram
$A = \frac{1}{2}bh$		trapezoid

Find each area. Measurements are in inches.

2. Triangle ABC

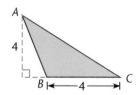

3. Parallelogram $PQRS$

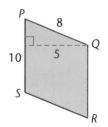

4. Trapezoid $DEFG$

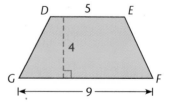

5. Melissa is designing earrings. The drop piece is a thin gold-plated triangle. Find the perimeter and area of the drop piece.

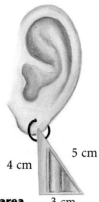

> **Problem-Solving Tip**
>
> Look for perpendicular sides.

5 cm

4 cm

3 cm

Measure the dimensions of each polygon in centimeters and find its area.

6.

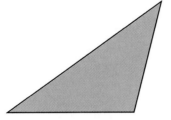

7.

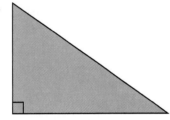

8.

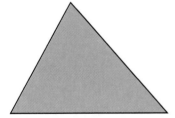

9.

10. Trapped in the City You are a land developer who would like to own all the land between the four cities shown on the map. Use the scale 1 inch = 40 miles to find the area of land within the trapezoid.

Careers

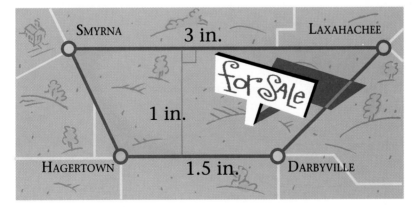

SMYRNA   3 in.   LAXAHACHEE

for SALE

1 in.

HAGERTOWN   1.5 in.   DARBYVILLE

Measure the dimensions of each trapezoid and find its area.

11.

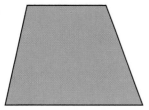

12.

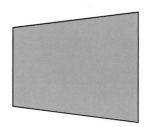

13. The painting with frame measures 4 feet by 3 feet. The width of the frame is 3 inches.

a. Find the area of the painting (not including the frame).

b. Find the perimeter of the painting (not including the frame). Why would this information be useful?

c. Find the area of the painting including the frame.

Fine Arts

14. The Size of It Use the map and key to estimate the area of Oklahoma.

Social Science

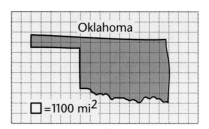

Oklahoma

$\square = 1100 \text{ mi}^2$

15. The base of a parallelogram is 4.5 cm and its area is 18 cm². What is the height?

LOOK BACK

Give the perimeter and area of each rectangle. [5-1]

16.

1 m

2 m

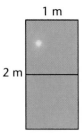

17.

10 in.

4 in.

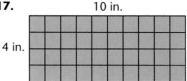

Solve each equation. [4-2]

18. $x + x = 3$ **19.** $3x - 2 = 8$ **20.** $4 - x = 10$

21. Give the coordinates of the image point if $P(2, -5)$ is reflected over the x-axis. [3-2]

History

22. The formula for the area of a triangle, $\frac{1}{2}bh$, appears in the *Ahmes Papyrus*, which was written about 3550 years ago. In approximately what year was the Papyrus written? [2-2]

MORE PRACTICE

Name each figure.

23. 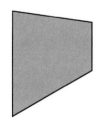   **24.**    **25.**

Find each area. Measurements shown are in centimeters.

26. Triangle ABC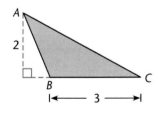

27. Parallelogram $PQRS$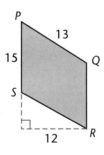

28. Trapezoid $DEFG$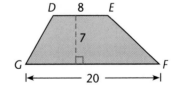

29. Find the area of a triangle with base 5.2 cm and height 3.7 cm.

30. A parallelogram has a base of $2\frac{1}{4}$ ft and a height of $1\frac{1}{2}$ ft. Find its area.

Measure the dimensions of each polygon in centimeters and find its area.

31.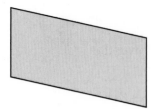

32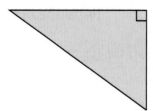

33.

34.

35. The school band is selling pennants. Each pennant is cut in the shape of a triangle. A pennant is 4 feet long and 1 foot high. How many square feet of fabric are needed to make 200 pennants (assuming no waste)?

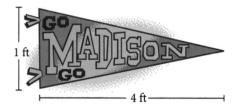

1 ft

4 ft

Measure the dimensions of each trapezoid in centimeters and find its area.

36.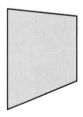

37.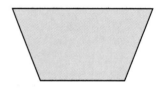

38. Water Over the Drain Alexis is making plans for a water drainage gutter that has an opening in the shape of a trapezoid. What is the area of the opening in Alexis's design?

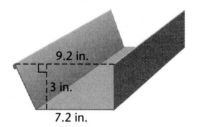

9.2 in.

3 in.

7.2 in.

39. South Carolina is nearly triangular shaped. Approximate its area.

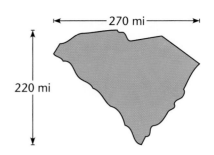

270 mi

220 mi

MORE MATH REASONING

40. The diagonals of a **rhombus,** a parallelogram with congruent sides, are perpendicular and they cut each other in half. Find the area of rhombus *ABCD* if the diagonals $\overline{AC}$ and $\overline{BD}$ measure 4 inches and 5 inches.

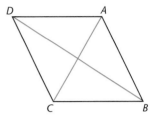

D   A

C   B

41. Estimate the area of this regular pentagon. (Hint: Use lines from the center to break the area into congruent triangles.)

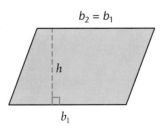

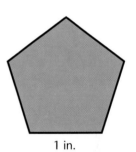

1 in.

42. Is It a Trap? Carolina says she can use the trapezoid area formula $A = \frac{1}{2}(b_1 + b_2)h$ for the area of a rectangle, parallelogram, and triangle. She shows you these drawings.

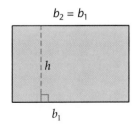

$b_2 = b_1$

h

b_1

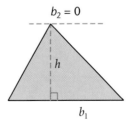

$b_2 = b_1$

h

b_1

$b_2 = 0$

h

b_1

Is she correct? Show why or why not by substituting numbers for b_1 and h in each case.

← **C O N N E C T** → *You have used isometric projection and perspective to draw three-dimensional objects. Now you will look at another way to represent objects, surfaces, and circular regions in two dimensions.*

An architect creates an orthographic projection to show the shape and dimensions of a building. An orthographic projection is a drawing that shows front, top, and side views of a building as they would appear if you looked directly at each. Compare the three views of the orthographic projection with the isometric projection you saw in 5-1.

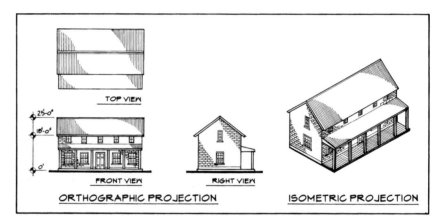

EXPLORE: THAT'S ONE VIEWPOINT

1. Make a structure of 20 cubes so that the cubes connect at their faces or edges.
2. Make an isometric drawing of the cube structure.
3. Now make an orthographic projection. First draw the cube structure as it appears from the front.
4. Then, draw the cube structure as it appears from the top.
5. Finally, draw the cube structure as it appears from the right side.
6. Which type of drawing was easier to make? Why would you want to make each type of drawing?

MATERIALS

Cubes

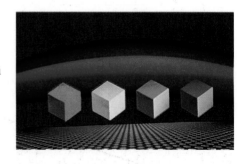

1. What does one of the towers of the World Trade Center look like from directly overhead?

EXAMPLE

1. Draw the front, top, and right view of the figure.

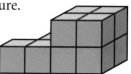

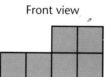
Front view

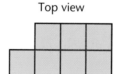
Top view

Side view

Designers, scientists, engineers, machinists, and draftsmen use orthographic drawings to describe objects. Orthographic drawings can be thought of as a universal language, understood all over the world.

EXAMPLE

2. Draw the orthographic views of the figure.

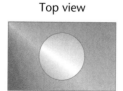
Top view

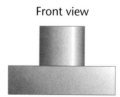
Front view

Right-side view

Draw the front, top, and right orthographic views of each figure.

a.

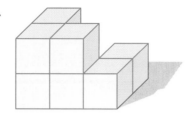

b.

Recall the formulas for circles:
Area $(A) = \pi r^2$ and
circumference $(C) = \pi d$.

Use $\pi \approx 3.14$, or the π key on your calculator.

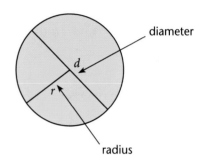

diameter

radius

EXAMPLES

3. Find the circumference of the circular region marked A.

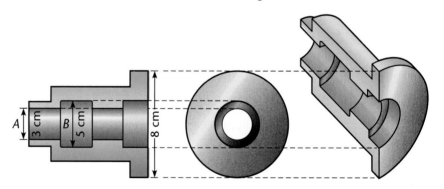

You can see from the top view that each piece of the valve is circular. From the side view, we see that the diameter of the circular region marked A is 3 cm.

$$C = \pi d$$
$$\approx 3.14(3)$$
$$\approx 9.42$$

The circumference of the smallest circle is approximately 9.42 cm.

4. Find the area of the tan part of the front of the birdhouse.

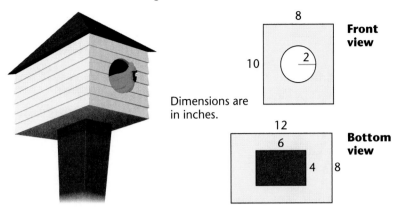

Dimensions are in inches.

Front view — 8, 10, 2

Bottom view — 12, 6, 4, 8

The area of the tan portion is the area of the rectangle minus the area of the circle.

$$A = \ell w - \pi r^2$$ Use the two area formulas.

$$\approx (8 \cdot 10) - (3.14 \cdot 2^2)$$ Substitute values for ℓ, w, and r. Use 3.14 for π.

$$\approx 80 - (3.14 \cdot 4)$$ Use order of operations.

$$\approx 80 - 12.56$$

$$\approx 67.44$$

The area of the tan part of the front of the birdhouse is approximately 67.44 square inches.

TRY IT

c. Find the circumference of the circular portion, marked B, of the valve shown in Example 3.

d. Find the area of the yellow portion of the valve in Example 3.

e. In Example 4, what is the area of the tan part of the bottom of the birdhouse?

REFLECT

1. Compare orthographic drawing with isometric projection.

2. Is the front view of a can of soup a rectangle? Explain.

3. Describe an object for which all the views are the same.

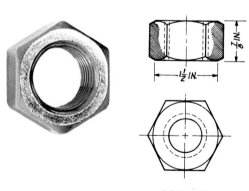

HEX. NUT

Exercises

CORE

1. **Getting Started** Study the figure made from cubes.
   a. How many cubes are in this figure?
   b. Draw the front view.
   c. Draw the top view.
   d. Draw the right view.
   e. Draw the left view.

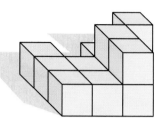

2. Use the circle shown.
   a. What is its radius?
   b. What is its diameter?
   c. Give its circumference using the correct units.
   d. Give its area using the correct units.

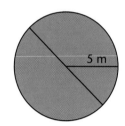

5 m

Draw the front, top, and right orthographic views of each solid.

3.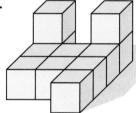

4.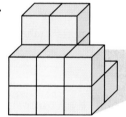

5. A quarter has a diameter of 2.5 cm. Find the circumference and area of a face of a quarter.

6. A circular well has an opening with a 12.25-in. radius. How much material is needed for a canvas top that will cover just the opening?

Draw the front, top, and right orthographic views of each solid.

7.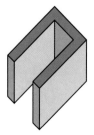

8.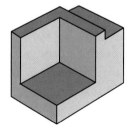

9. The earth's circumference at the equator is about 25,000 miles. Find the approximate equatorial diameter of the earth.

10. Perimeter is to length as circumference is to ___.
(a) area   (b) length   (c) volume   (d) not here

Draw the isometric projection of the solid that has the following orthographic views.

11.

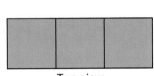

Top view

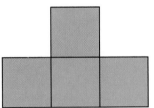

Front view

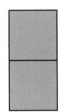

Side view

12. Making It Pan Out Aisha is making brownies. The recipe calls for a 9 in. square pan. She has a round pan with a 9-in. diameter and a 9-in. × 10-in. rectangular pan. Which pan should she use? Why?

13. A square plaza, 18 feet on each side, has a circular statue at its center. The rest of the plaza is brick. The radius of the base of the statue is 3 feet.
   a. What is the area of the plaza?
   b. What is the area of the brick part of the plaza?

14. On the Road Again A bicycle tire has a diameter of 26 inches.
   a. How far will the bicycle travel in 1 rotation of the tire?
   b. How far will the bicycle travel in 20 rotations of the tire?
   c. How many rotations will the wheel make in 1 mile of travel?

15. Could these be three views of a box? Why or why not?

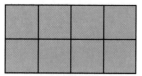

Top view   Side view   Front view

Social Science

16. Sherman's Memorial General Sherman in Sequoia National Park in California is one of the largest trees on Earth. In 1991, its circumference at 4.5 feet above ground was 83 feet.
a. What was its diameter at that height?
b. If the tree were cut, what would be the area of the top of the 4.5-foot-high stump?

17. a. Find the area of the circle by estimating.
b. Find the area by formula.
c. Compare your answers.

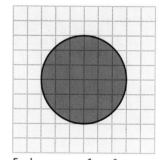

Each square = 1 cm²

Social Science

18. Skin Deep The drum head of this tabla drum from India has a diameter of 14 inches. The skin is stretched around the ring, approximately 1.5 inches below the top of the drum. Estimate or calculate the area of the skin used on the drum.

14 in.

19. The Name's Norman An architect is planning to install a Norman window in a house she is designing. The window glass will have a square bottom with a **semicircle,** or half circle, on top. The width of the window glass is 1.3 feet. What is the area of the glass that the architect needs?

 LOOK AHEAD

20. How many of the small cubic blocks will fit in the large one?

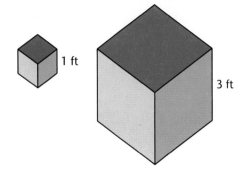

1 ft

3 ft

21. The volume of the second figure is 3 cubic inches. What is the volume of the cube?

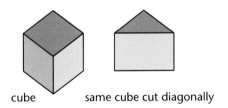

cube   same cube cut diagonally

MORE PRACTICE

22. Use the circle shown.
   a. What is its radius?
   b. What is its diameter?
   c. What is the formula for the circumference of a circle?
   d. Give the circumference of the circle using the correct units.
   e. What is the formula for the area of a circle?
   f. Give the area of the circle using the correct units.

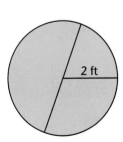

2 ft

Draw front, top, and right orthographic views of each solid.

23.

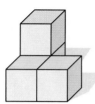

24.

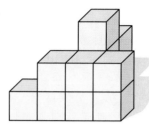

25.

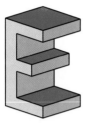

26.

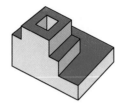

27. Circling the Scene Detectives investigating a crime want to check every gas station within a 3-mile radius of the scene of the crime. How big is the area that they will need to search?

Careers

28. What is the area of the shaded region?

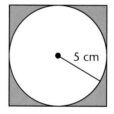

5 cm

29. The mammoth stones at the celebrated archaeological site of Stonehenge, England, are arranged in a circle approximately 30 meters in diameter. Find the circumference of the circle.

History

MORE MATH REASONING

30. **Go, Team, Go** Susan is making a cheerleader's skirt. The circumference of her waist is 24.5 inches, and she wants her circular skirt to be 21 inches long. How much braid will she have to buy to trim around the bottom of her skirt? (Hint: Use the formula for the circumference of a circle to find the radius of her waist.)

31. **Ring, Ring** Saturn's rings are made up of chunks of ice, some as large as a car. Three of the rings are visible from Earth. The brightest is the B Ring, which is about 17,000 miles in width.

    Use the diagram and find the approximate area of the B Ring.

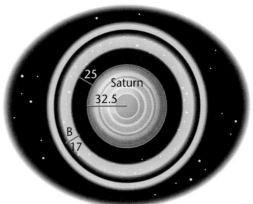

32. **Spy on Pi** Does your calculator hide some digits of pi? No calculator can hold all the digits of π because there is an infinite number. Some calculators use more numbers than they display. How many digits does your calculator hold?

    a. Press $\boxed{\pi}$. Write down the number. Now enter $\boxed{-}$ 3 $\boxed{=}$ and $\boxed{\times}$ 10 $\boxed{=}$. Compare the digits shown with the ones you wrote down. Do they end the same way?
    Replace the last digit of your original number for pi with the last two digits of your new number.

    b. Now enter $\boxed{-}$ 1 $\boxed{=}$ and $\boxed{\times}$ 10 $\boxed{=}$ and revise your number again. Keep subtracting the integer part, multiplying by 10, and rewriting your number until the end numbers stay the same.

    c. What value does your calculator use for π?

π = 3.14159265358979323846264338327950 2

← **C O N N E C T** → *You have learned to find the perimeters and areas of many types of two-dimensional figures. Now you will look at each of those figures in turn to determine which one produces the greatest area for a given perimeter.*

In nature and in everyday life, the effort to find the greatest area possible under limiting conditions is never-ending.

- A lily pad tries to achieve a shape that will collect the most sunlight with the least effort.
- A wolf marks a territory that has the greatest possible area that the animal can cover during an all-night hunt.
- A rancher attempts to enclose the largest possible corral with a length of fence he found stashed in a loft of a barn.

EXPLORE: THE BIG PICTURE

MATERIALS

String
Customary ruler
Tape measure or yardstick

An artist has a strip of flexible framing material measuring 36 inches in length. With the material, the artist can construct a straight-sided or curved frame with a perimeter of 36 inches. The artist wants to enclose the largest possible area with the frame. What shape should the artist choose?

1. Make a loop of string with a perimeter of 36 inches. Cut a length slightly longer than 36 inches so you will have extra string for tying a knot.
2. Experiment with various frame shapes. Which one appears to have the greatest area? Why?
3. Copy and complete the table. For each row, choose dimensions for the given figure. Sketch the figure and show its dimensions. Then calculate its area. Row 1 has been done to get you started.

Remember that each figure must have a perimeter of 36 inches. Strive for a variety of shapes and sizes. You may add rows if you wish to investigate additional figures.

Figure	Sketch	Perimeter (in.)	Area (in.²)
Rectangle 1	12 / 6 ▭	36	72
Rectangle 2		36	
Rectangle 3		36	
Square		36	
Trapezoid		36	
Triangle 1		36	
Triangle 2		36	
Triangle 3		36	

4. What shape should the artist choose? Give reasons for your answer.

5. Would you choose a different shape if the strip of framing material were more or less than 36 inches long?

REFLECT

1. Describe situations in 5-2 where you used formulas that use π.

2. Describe situations where you used formulas that do not use π.

3. Write a paragraph about how some of the situations in 1 and 2 are similar.

4. Write a paragraph about how some of the situations in 1 and 2 are different.

Self-Assessment

Find each area. Measurements are in inches.

1. Triangle *ABC*

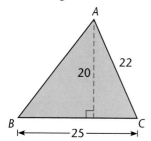

2. Parallelogram *PQRS*

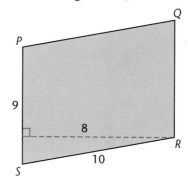

3. Trapezoid *DEFG*

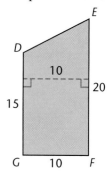

4. a. What segment represents the altitude to the base $\overline{CB}$ in $\triangle ABC$?

    (a) $\overline{CB}$ (b) $\overline{AB}$

    (c) $\overline{DB}$ (d) $\overline{AC}$

b. What segment represents the altitude to the base $\overline{AC}$?

    (a) $\overline{CB}$ (b) $\overline{AB}$

    (c) $\overline{DB}$ (d) $\overline{AC}$

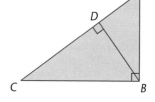

5. Which of the following describes $\overline{AB}$?

    (a) a radius   (b) a diameter

    (c) the circumference   (d) the perimeter

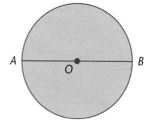

6. The radius of a circle is 5 cm. What is its diameter?

    (a) 25 cm^2 (b) 5π cm   (c) 10 cm   (d) 10π cm

7. A square has an area of 100 cm^2. What is its perimeter?

    (a) 10 cm   (b) 400 cm   (c) 40 cm   (d) 20 cm

8. Draw a rectangle that is 2 units longer than it is wide.

    a. Label each side with an expression for length using *x*.

    b. Write an equation for the area of the rectangle using your expressions.

    c. Write an equation for the perimeter of the rectangle.

Find the perimeter, or circumference, and area of each figure. Use 3.14 for π, or the π key on your calculator.

9.

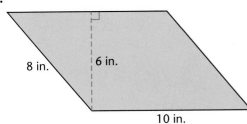

10.

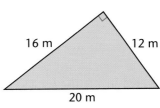

11.

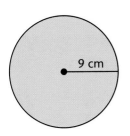

12.

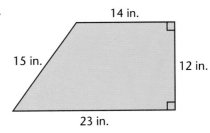

Solve. [4-2]

13. $2x + x = 18$

14. $3 - x = 20$

15. $\frac{3}{5}x + 2 = 11$

16. $4y + 7 = 10$

17. $5b - 7 = 15$

18. $10m + 3 = 5m - 1$

19. Pan Cake Matter Scott is making a cake but doesn't have the right pan. The recipe calls for a 10-in. diameter pan. He has an 8-in. square pan, a 9-in. square pan, and a 10-in. square pan. Which pan comes closest in area to the one that the recipe suggests? Which pan should Scott use? Why?

20. Draw the front, top, and right orthographic views of the solid.

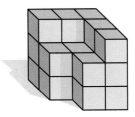

21. A Top Coat A paving company will coat a parking lot with a blacktop sealer. The lot is in the shape of a trapezoid. Its two base lengths are 60 ft and 92 ft. The side lengths are each about 50 ft. The height is 38.4 ft.
a. What is the area of the lot?
b. If a $21 can of sealer covers 200 ft^2, how much will the sealant cost?

22. A 20-ft × 15-ft swimming pool is surrounded by a 2-ft-wide sidewalk. A fence encloses the whole area.

   a. Find the length of the area enclosed by the fence.

   b. Find the width of the area enclosed by the fence.

   c. What is the area inside the fence?

   d. What is the area of the sidewalk?

   e. How much fencing is used?

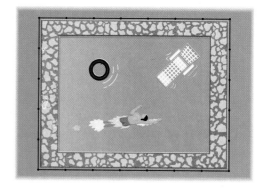

23. The Equality State Wyoming's state seal represents the fact that it was the first state in the nation to give women the right to vote.

   a. If a flag is 5 feet long and 3 feet high and the center seal has a diameter of 1 foot, what is the area of the rest of the flag?

   b. Copy the flag, make a grid with 1 foot by 1 foot squares and approximate the area of the buffalo.

24. Radio Active A radio station claims it can be heard over an area of "A million square miles!" Its signal reaches 500 miles in all directions. Evaluate the station's claim.

25. Some art uses illusions to make a point.

   a. Is the small rounded figure a circle? How can you tell?

   b. Which gray circle is larger? How can you tell?

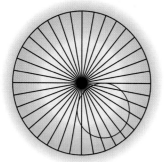

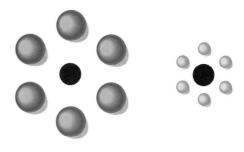

5-3 Nets, Surface Area, and Volume

Since ancient times, people have been inspired to design and construct grand buildings. About 5000 years ago, Egyptians constructed the Great Pyramid in the sands of the Sahara Desert. About 1000 years ago, Native Americans put up massive pyramids, Tibetans erected the 1000-room Potala, and Europeans built elaborate cathedrals. All of these masterfully designed and constructed structures are still visited and enjoyed today.

Will the great buildings of our own time still stand and be admired in 1000 years? Architects like I. M. Pei are doing what they can to ensure that the answer is yes. Pei has pioneered the uses of new materials and new methods of construction. Born in Guangzhou, China, in 1917, Pei came to the United States in 1935 to study architecture. He soon became a U.S. citizen.

In 1989, Pei completed a structure at the entrance to the Louvre art museum in Paris. Similar to many buildings of ancient times, Pei's creation was a pyramid. Unlike them, it was built of glass! Pei is confident that, barring earthquakes and batted baseballs, his pyramid will stand for 1000 years.

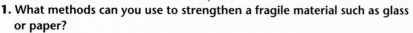

1. What methods can you use to strengthen a fragile material such as glass or paper?
2. Why might Pei have chosen to build a pyramid at the Louvre?
3. How might an architect use mathematics?

← C O N N E C T → *Area is a measure of the size of a two-dimensional figure. One way to measure the size of a three-dimensional object is to "unfold" it into a two-dimensional figure, then find the area of the new figure.*

An architect must be able to visualize in three dimensions, to imagine how solids and spaces in a building design interrelate, to see how a three-dimensional structure can be represented in two dimensions.

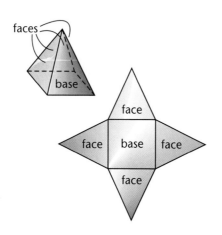

The top illustration shows a pyramid like one I. M. Pei might have imagined for the entrance to the Louvre. Below it the pyramid has been unfolded into two dimensions.

A flat pattern, like the bottom figure, that can be folded without gaps or without overlapping into a three-dimensional object is called a **net.**

C O N S I D E R

1. Explain how a pyramid could be constructed from the net.
2. How could you find the total surface area of the pyramid?
3. How would the net look if the pyramid had a pentagonal rather than a square base? How would it look with a rectangular base twice as long as it is wide?
4. What other nets can you design for a pyramid that has a square base?

MATERIALS

*Graph paper or
orthographic dot paper
(1 inch or greater)
Scissors*

You have been asked to design a glass cube for the entrance
to New York's Museum of Modern Art. Figure **a** shows one
way the cube could be unwrapped into a net.

1. Fold a cube using the net in figure **a.**

a.

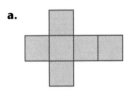

2. Use graph paper to design and cut out cube nets that have shapes
different from those in the net in figure **a.** Notice that the shape
in figure **b** is not really different from that in figure **a.**

b.

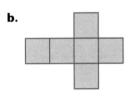

3. Is figure **c** a net? Why or why not?

c.

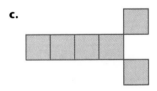

4. Fold each of your patterns to confirm that it is a cube net.

5. If you knew the length of one edge of your cube, how could
you find the surface area of the cube?

6. Choose one of your nets. Show how it would change if the
height of the cube were greatly decreased; if the length of the
cube were greatly increased.

Nets help us measure the surface area of three-dimensional
objects. The surface area of a solid is the total of the areas
of each of its faces.

1. Find the surface area of the solid.
Dimensions are in inches.

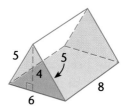

Sketch a net of the solid. One possible net is shown.
Find the area of each face of the solid.
Find the sum of the areas of the five faces.

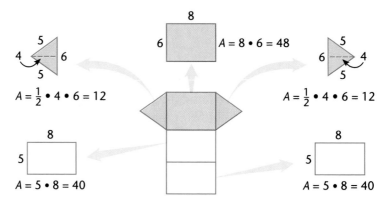

$A = \frac{1}{2} \cdot 4 \cdot 6 = 12$ $A = 8 \cdot 6 = 48$ $A = \frac{1}{2} \cdot 4 \cdot 6 = 12$

$A = 5 \cdot 8 = 40$ $A = 5 \cdot 8 = 40$

$48 + 40 + 40 + 12 + 12 = 152$ The sum of the areas of the five faces
The surface area is 152 square inches.

TRY IT

a. Sketch a net of the solid. Then find
its surface area. Dimensions are in
centimeters.

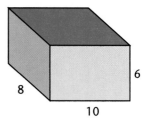

 **CONSIDER**

5. A soup can has a 4-inch wide
label. What do you know about
the can top?

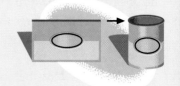

2. An oatmeal box is in the shape of a cylinder. The bases have a radius of 3 in. The height of the box is 6 in. What is its surface area?

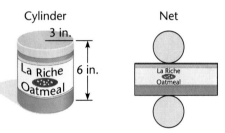

A net for the surface area is made up of 3 two-dimensional figures. (Note: A circle in a net may touch a straight edge at a single point.)

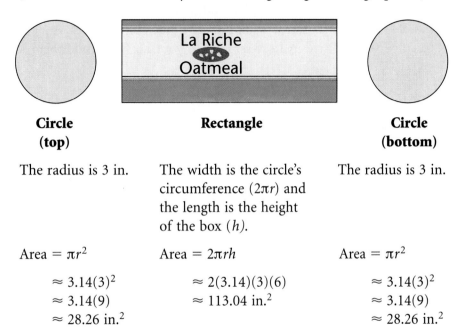

Circle (top)	**Rectangle**	**Circle (bottom)**
The radius is 3 in.	The width is the circle's circumference ($2\pi r$) and the length is the height of the box (h).	The radius is 3 in.

Area $= \pi r^2$	Area $= 2\pi rh$	Area $= \pi r^2$
$\approx 3.14(3)^2$	$\approx 2(3.14)(3)(6)$	$\approx 3.14(3)^2$
$\approx 3.14(9)$	≈ 113.04 in.^{2}	$\approx 3.14(9)$
≈ 28.26 in.^{2}		≈ 28.26 in.^{2}

The surface area is approximately $28.26 + 113.04 + 28.26$, or 169.56 square inches.

REFLECT

1. In everyday life, when might it be useful to draw a net of a solid object?

2. In what jobs might people find it useful to draw nets of solid objects?

3. Describe a three-dimensional object that would be difficult, or impossible, to unwrap into a net.

4. Make a list of all the types of two-dimensional figures for which you know area formulas. How would you find the surface area of a refrigerator? of a barrel? of a slice of pie? of an ice-cream cone?

Exercises

CORE

1. **Getting Started** Sketch a net for this rectangular prism. Use the following steps as a guide.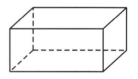
   a. Which two-dimensional figures make up the faces of the box? How many of each type are there?
   b. Choose one of your figures to be the base of the net and sketch it.
   c. Decide which other shapes touch the base. Add them to your net by sketching them adjacent to the sides of the base.
   d. Sometimes the base of a solid doesn't touch all the sides. Are any of the figures you listed in **1a** missing from your net? If so, add them.

2. Write the letter of the second pair that best matches the first pair. Net: solid as
   (a) envelope: letter   (b) pattern: dress
   (c) curtain: window   (d) washed clothes: folded clothes

3. Which is a correct net for this figure?

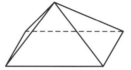

(a) 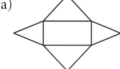   (b)    (c)

4. Sketch a net for this hexagonal prism.

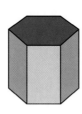

Sketch a net of the solid. Then find its surface area.

5.
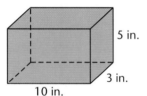

5 in.
3 in.
10 in.

6.
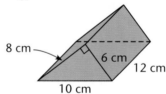

8 cm
6 cm
12 cm
10 cm

7.
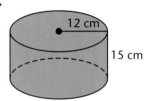

12 cm
15 cm

The dimensions of this net are given in centimeters. Rectangles with the same shading are identical.

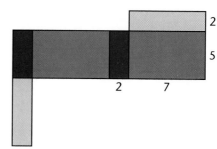

8. Describe the solid that has been unfolded to make the net.

9. What is the surface area of the solid?

10. Crunch a Bunch The net at the right will fold into a solid. Sketch a different net that will fold into the same solid.

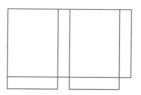

11. Sketch three different nets of the solid. Include dimensions in centimeters on the nets.

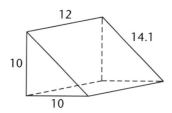

12. Is this pattern a net for a solid? Explain.

 LOOK BACK

13. The bases of a trapezoid measure 14 in. and 20 in. If the trapezoid has a height of 15 in., what is its area? [5-2]

14. Solve $3x + 5 = 29 - x$. [4-2]

15. Evaluate $-4 - 28 \div (-4)$. [2-2]

MORE PRACTICE

16. A tetrahedron is a pyramid with four triangular faces. Sketch a net for a tetrahedron.

17. Describe the solid that has been unfolded to make the net.

18. Find the surface area of the solid from Exercise 17.

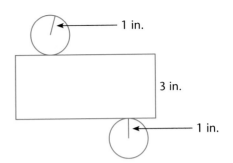

Sketch a net of the solid. Then find its surface area.

19.

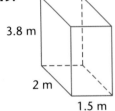

20.

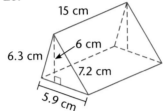

21.

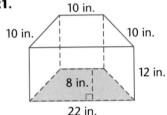

22. a. Sketch a net for the five surfaces of the swimming pool.
   b. Find the cost of resurfacing the pool at $2.25/ft².

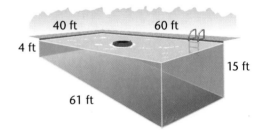

MORE MATH REASONING

23. A die is a cube. Each of its six faces is numbered from 1 to 6. The number of dots on opposite faces of the die add up to 7. Draw at least three nets for a die that is a one-inch cube.

24. A soccer ball has a pattern of pentagons and hexagons as shown. Draw a net for a soccer ball.

25. Inter-Net Look at a world globe. How many pieces make up the surface? Is there a net that can form a ball or sphere? Explain.

> **Problem-Solving Tip**
>
> Try to draw the net.

5-3 PART B Prisms and Volume

← C O N N E C T →

In the last part, you measured the size of a solid by unfolding it and calculating the area of its outside surface. Now you will look at how you can measure the size of its inside, beginning with the important class of solids called prisms.

A right prism is a solid with

1) rectangular sides,
2) parallel bases, and
3) congruent polygons as bases.

We will refer to right prisms simply as **prisms.**

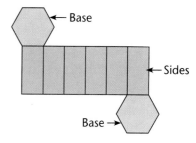

Prisms are classified by their base shapes. An unsharpened pencil is a **hexagonal prism.**

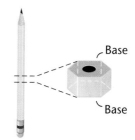

You have already seen prisms like this. It is a **rectangular prism** because its bases are rectangles.

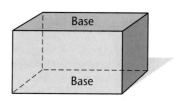

1. Describe a triangular prism.
2. Give examples of rectangular prisms you see everyday.
3. If you laid a hexagonal pencil on one of its rectangular sides, would it still be a prism?
4. How could you determine the surface area of a prism?

Surface area measures the outside of a solid. Recall that *volume* measures the region inside a solid. The volume of the cube is 8 in.³ because eight cubes, each measuring 1 in. by 1 in. by 1 in., could be packed inside the cube.

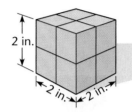

Now you will explore how the volume of a prism is affected when its shape is changed but its base and height are not.

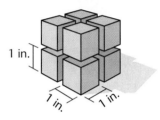

EXPLORE: STACK 'EM UP

MATERIALS

Stack of index cards, playing cards, sheets of paper, or other congruent rectangles

1. This stack has a height of eight cards. Suppose that you knew the area of the base card. How could you find the volume of the entire stack?
2. Straighten up your stack of cards to form a rectangular prism. Let B represent the area of your base card. Write an expression for the volume of the stack.
3. Reshape the stack several times into forms that are not rectangular prisms. For each new shape, answer the following questions.
   a. Has the height of the stack changed?
   b. Has the area of the base card changed?
   c. Has the volume of the entire stack changed?
   d. If B represents the area of the base card, what is the volume of the stack?

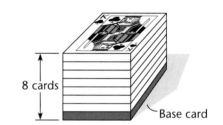

8 cards

Base card

The Explore suggests that if the cross-section of a solid is the same size at every height, the volume can be found by multiplying the area of the base by the height of the solid.

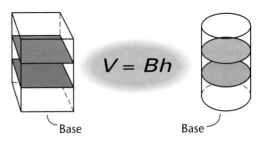

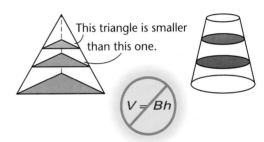

$V = Bh$

Base   Base

If the cross-sectional shape of a solid is *not* the same at every height, the formula cannot be used.

This triangle is smaller than this one.

$V \neq Bh$

EXAMPLES

Find the volume of each solid, if possible.

1.

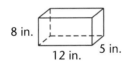

8 in.

12 in.   5 in.

2.

7 cm

Area = 30 cm²

3.

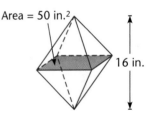

Area = 50 in.²

16 in.

Area of base = 12 × 5 = 60

Height = 8

$V = Bh$

$= 60 \times 8$

$= 480$

The volume is 480 in.³.

Area of base = 30

Height = 7

$V = Bh$

$= 30 \times 7$

$= 210$

The volume is 210 cm³.

The shape of the solid is not the same at each height, so the formula for volume cannot be used.

Look at Example 1 again. The area of the base (*B*) is the product of the prism's length and its width. This means that the volume of a rectangular prism equals the product of its length (ℓ), its width (*w*), and its height (*h*): $V = \ell w h$.

Find the volume of each solid.

a.

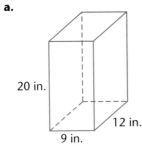

20 in.

12 in.

9 in.

b.

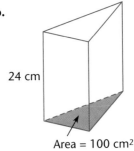

24 cm

Area = 100 cm²

REFLECT

Temple in Tikal, Guatemala

1. Is a pyramid a prism? What about a cube? Explain your answers.

2. Describe how you could find the volume of a triangular prism.

3. What is the difference between the volume and surface area of a prism?

4. If you knew the volume and height of a hexagonal prism, how could you find the area of the prism's base?

5. A pyramid has a height of 4 in. and a base with an area of 10 in.². Would the volume of the pyramid be greater than, less than, or equal to 40 in.³?

Exercises

CORE

1. Getting Started A rectangular prism measures 10 inches by 8 inches by 2 inches.

a. Sketch the prism and show its dimensions.

b. Find the volume of the prism.

Find the volume of each prism.

2.

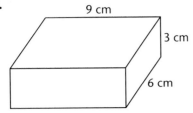

9 cm

3 cm

6 cm

3.

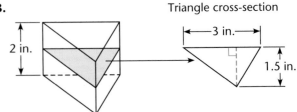

Triangle cross-section

2 in.

3 in.

1.5 in.

4.

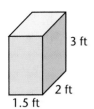

3 ft

2 ft

1.5 ft

5.

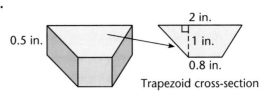

0.5 in.

2 in.

1 in.

0.8 in.

Trapezoid cross-section

6.

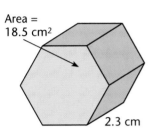

Area = 18.5 cm²

2.3 cm

7.

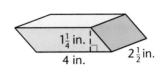

$1\frac{1}{4}$ in.

4 in.

$2\frac{1}{2}$ in.

Find the surface area of the prism. Draw a net, if it is helpful.

8. Exercise 1   **9.** Exercise 2   **10.** Exercise 4

11. Keeping It Clean The basin of a kitchen sink measures 18 in. by 12 in. It is 5 in. deep.
   a. Find the maximum volume of water that the basin will hold.
   b. If 1 gallon is 231 in.³, how many gallons of water can the basin hold?

12. How much cement, in cubic feet, is needed to make these steps?

1.5 ft

2 ft

3.5 ft

1 ft

3 ft

13. How many cubic inches are in 1 cubic foot?

Problem-Solving Tip

Draw two diagrams and label them with different units.

14. A refrigerator carton has a volume of 36 ft³. The carton is 6 ft tall and 3 ft wide.

   a. Draw the carton and label the dimensions, using x for the missing length.

   b. Write the formula for volume, using x. Solve for x to find the length of the carton.

   c. What is the surface area of the carton?

15. Cement is measured by the cubic yard. How much would it cost to pour a 3.5-yard by 2.5-yard by 3.6-inch slab for a patio if cement sells for $75 per cubic yard?

LOOK AHEAD

A car is traveling steadily at 55 mi/hr.

16. Copy and complete this table to show the distance traveled after the given number of hours.

Time in Hours (*t*)	0	1	2	3	4	5
Distance in Miles (*d*)						

17. Use the variables d and t to write an equation that shows the relationship between distance and time.

MORE PRACTICE

Find the volume of each prism.

18.

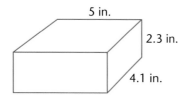

5 in.
2.3 in.
4.1 in.

19.

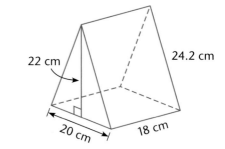

22 cm
24.2 cm
20 cm
18 cm

20.

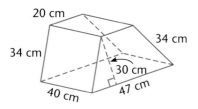

20 cm
34 cm
34 cm
30 cm
40 cm
47 cm

21.

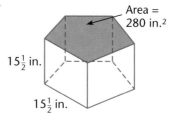

Area = 280 in.²
$15\frac{1}{2}$ in.
$15\frac{1}{2}$ in.

Find the surface area of the prism. Draw a net, if it is helpful.

22. Exercise 18   **23.** Exercise 19

24. Exercise 20   **25.** Exercise 21

26. The base of a recycling bin is a 3-ft by 2-ft rectangle. Its height is 1.4 ft. What is the volume of the recycling bin?

Science

MORE MATH REASONING

27. Something Fishy A 50-cm-tall fish tank has a uniform cross-section. The overhead view is a regular hexagon. In the metric system, liquid volume is measured in liters, where 1 liter is 1000 cm³. How much water can the tank hold?

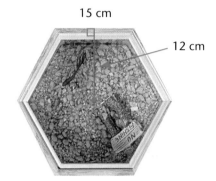

15 cm

12 cm

28. Find the volume of an 18-cm cube that has a hole with a 36-cm² opening cut through from one side to the opposite side.

29. A hot springs swimming pool is 50 feet wide.
  a. What is the volume of the pool?
  b. A gallon of water is 231 cubic inches. How many gallons of water will the pool hold?

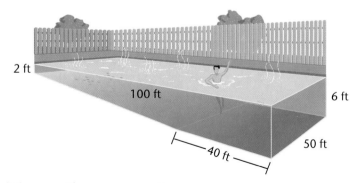

2 ft

100 ft

6 ft

40 ft

50 ft

30. Sketch at least two solids that don't have uniform cross-sections.

5-3
PART C
Cylinders, Pyramids, and Cones

← CONNECT → *The method you used earlier to find the volume of a prism also can be used to find the volume of a cylinder, cone, or pyramid. Now you will explore volumes and surface areas of all of these solids.*

Recall that a **prism** is a solid with parallel bases that are congruent polygons and sides that are rectangles. In this Part, we will investigate three more important classes of solids, the **cylinder,** the **pyramid,** and the **cone.**

Rectangular Prism
(a box)

Cylinder
(a can)

Square-Base Pyramid

Cone

CONSIDER

?

1. What are some everyday examples of cylinders, pyramids, and cones?
2. Sketch a net of a cylinder and of a pyramid.
3. How could you find the surface area of a cylinder? of a pyramid?

Earlier, you learned that if the cross-sectional shape of a solid is the same at every level, the volume of the solid is the product of the area of its base and its height: $V = Bh$. We can use the fact that a cylinder has this property to find its volume.

Find the volume of this cylinder.

Find the area of the base first.

$$B = \pi r^2$$

$$= \pi(8)^2 \qquad \text{Substitute 8 for } r.$$

$$= 64\pi$$

Now find the volume of the cylinder.

$$V = Bh$$

$$= 64\pi(12) \qquad \text{Substitute } 64\pi \text{ for } B \text{ and 12 for } h.$$

$$= 768\pi$$

The volume of the cylinder is 768π cm³.

Because $V = Bh$ and $B = \pi r^2$, you can use the formula $V = \pi r^2 h$ to find a cylinder's volume.

TRY IT

a. A cylinder has a height of 4.5 in. and a base with a radius of 1.5 in. Find the volume of the cylinder. Use 3.14 for π.

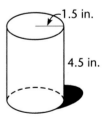

In the following Explore, you will discover that the volume of a cone is closely related to that of a cylinder.

MATERIALS

*Paper, Compass, Scissors
Tape, Ruler, Popcorn*

1.

Use your compass to draw as large a circle as possible on a sheet of paper. Then cut it out.

2.

Slit the circle along one radius. Pull in and tape the areas adjacent to the slit to produce a cone.

3.

With another sheet of paper, make a cylinder with the same height and radius as the cone. Cut out a circle from a separate sheet of paper and tape it to close one end of the cylinder.

4.

How do you think the volumes of the cone and the cylinder compare? Explain your reasoning.

5. Fill the cylinder with popcorn.

6. How many times will the popcorn from the cylinder fill the cone? Make a statement.

7. Use the popcorn from the cylinder to fill the cone. Repeat until all the popcorn in the cylinder is used. How many times did you fill the cone from the cylinder?

8. What conclusion can you make about a cone's volume?

Now we can look at some volume formulas.

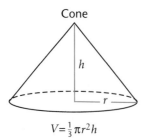

Cone

$$V = \tfrac{1}{3}\pi r^2 h$$

Pyramid

$$V = \tfrac{1}{3} B h$$

Find the volume of the cone.

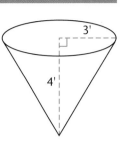

Jorge thinks ...

The volume of a cone is *one-third* the volume of a cylinder with the same base radius and height. First, I'll find the volume of a *cylinder* with the same base radius and height as the cone.

$$B = \pi r^2 \qquad \text{Area of the base of the cylinder}$$
$$\approx 3.14 \cdot 9$$
$$\approx 28.26$$

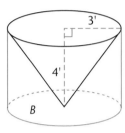

The base of the cylinder is approximately 28.26 ft².

$$V = Bh \qquad \text{Volume of a cylinder}$$
$$= 28.26 \cdot 4$$
$$= 113.04$$

Then one-third the volume of the cylinder is $\frac{1}{3} \cdot 113.04$, or 37.68 ft³.

Desrie thinks ...

I'll use a formula to find the volume.

$$V = \frac{1}{3}\pi r^2 h \qquad \text{Use formula for volume of a cone.}$$
$$\approx \frac{1}{3} \cdot 3.14(3)^2(4) \quad \text{Use 3.14 for } \pi.$$
$$\approx \frac{1}{3} \cdot 3.14 \cdot 9 \cdot 4$$
$$\approx 37.68 \text{ ft}^3$$

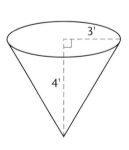

The volume of the cone is approximately 37.68 ft³.

To find the surface area of a cone, you must know the cone's **slant height** (ℓ). Slant height is the distance from the **vertex,** or point, of the cone to the base, measured along the cone's surface.

Surface area $= \pi r \ell + \pi r^2$

This table summarizes methods for finding surface areas and volumes of solids.

Solid		Surface Area	Volume
Prism		Sketch a net. Then find the area of the net.	$V = Bh$
Cylinder		Sketch a net. Then find the area of the net.	$V = Bh$ $= \pi r^2 h$
Pyramid		Sketch a net. Then find the area of the net.	$V = \frac{1}{3}Bh$
Cone		$\pi r \ell + \pi r^2$	$V = \frac{1}{3}Bh$ $= \frac{1}{3}\pi r^2 h$

REFLECT

1. How can a net help you find the surface area of a solid?
2. How can knowing the volume of a cone help you find the volume of a cylinder?
3. Suppose you know the dimensions of a pyramid but have forgotten the formula for the volume of a pyramid. How could you find the volume?

Exercises

CORE

1. **Getting Started** Copy the columns below. Draw lines connecting items in each column.

Column 1	Column 2	Column 3
Cone	Bh	Surface area
Cylinder	$\frac{1}{3}\, Bh$	Volume
Prism	$\pi r \ell + \pi r^2$	
Pyramid		

Find the surface area and volume of each solid.

2.

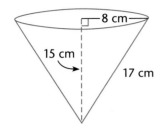

3.

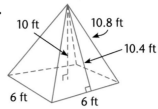

4.

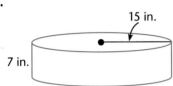

5.

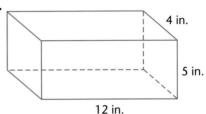

6. A can of tomato sauce has a circular cross-section with a 2-in. radius. The height of the can is 3.75 in.
   a. What is the area of the top of the can?
   b. What is the volume of the can?

7. Drink Up The diameter and height of a can of juice are 2.4 inches and 4.75 inches. The label says the can holds 12 fluid ounces.
   a. What is the volume of the can in cubic inches?
   b. One cubic inch equals 0.554 fluid ounces. Use your answer above to figure out how many fluid ounces should be in the can.
   c. Is the label correct? Explain.

8. A small monument is in the shape of a pyramid with a 2-ft square base. Find the volume of the pyramid if its height is 1.2 ft.

9. A water cup is in the shape of a cone. The opening has a diameter of 5 inches and the cup is 3.5 inches deep.
   a. How much water does the cup hold?
   b. If one gallon is 231 in.³, does the cup hold more or less than a pint of water? (Hint: There are 8 pints in a gallon.)

10. The volume of a cylinder is 30 cm³. A cone has the same base and height as the cylinder. What is the volume of the cone?

11. Great Wonder of the World The Great Pyramid of Egypt has a square base that measures 225 m on each side. The pyramid is about 137 m tall. What is its volume?

12. Describe how you would find the approximate volume of this funnel.

13. The altitude from the tip of the roof to the floor is 14 meters. Find the volume of the chicken coop.

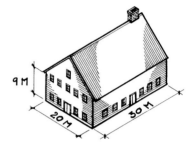

14. This net will build a solid with a volume of 70 cm³. Find the missing dimension.

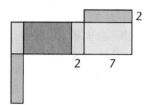

15. a. Name the solid that this net will build.
b. Find the surface area and volume of the solid.

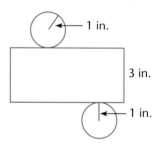

 LOOK BACK

16. Find the volume of a shoe box 14 in. long, 8 in. wide, and 5 in. high. [5-3]

17. Find the area of a triangle with $b = 4$ cm and $h = 5$ cm. [5-1]

Simplify. [2-3]

18. $4(x + 2) - (2x + 4)$ **19.** $3.7^2 + 4(2^3 - 1)$ **20.** $16x - (4x + 2)5$

MORE PRACTICE

Find the volume of each solid.

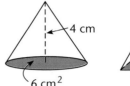

21. a prism with 6-cm^2 base area and 4-cm height

22. a pyramid with 6-cm^2 base area and 4-cm height

23. a cone with 6-cm^2 base area and 4-cm height

24. a cylinder with 6-cm^2 base area and 4-cm height

25. a cone with 10-in. radius and 9-in. height

26. a cylinder with 10-in. radius and 9-in. height

27. How much ice cream will fit into a 4-inch-tall cone if the opening has a 1.8-inch radius?

28. A paperweight in the shape of a pyramid has a triangular base with an area of 12.3 in.^{2}. The paperweight has a volume of 9.43 in.^{3}. How high is it?

29. Find the surface area and volume of a cylindrical oatmeal box that has a radius of 3 inches and a height of 6 inches.

30. A pipe that has a 1-in. diameter and that is 50 ft long is to be given a special rust-proofing treatment on its outer surface. Find the area of the surface that will be covered.

31. Find the volume of a 10-in.-high pyramid that has a base in the shape of a right triangle. The legs of the right triangle measure 7.3 in. and 5.7 in.

32. The altitude from the tip of the roof to the floor is 8 feet. Find the volume of the tool shed.

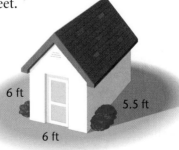

6 ft

5.5 ft

6 ft

33. The two crystals shown each have a base area of
20 cm² and a height of 3 cm. How do their
volumes compare? Explain.

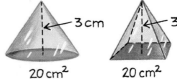
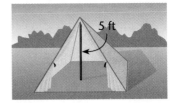

MORE MATH REASONING

34. A tent with a square base has a volume of 90 ft³ and
a height of 5 ft. What is the length of each side of
the base?

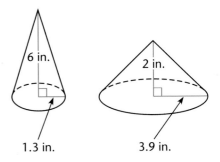

35. Find and compare the volumes of the cones.

6 in.

1.3 in.

2 in.

3.9 in.

36. This rocket has a diameter of 16 feet. Fuel will fill
35% of it, not including the nose cone. What
volume of fuel will be needed?

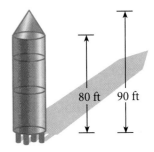

80 ft   90 ft

37. Sketch two solids that have the same volumes but different surface areas.

38. Use this drawing to explain why slant height is used rather than height to find
surface area.

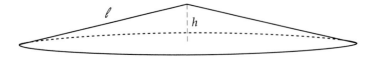

ℓ   h

39. Have a Ball! A can holds three tennis balls, each with a 3.25-cm radius. What is the volume of the can not taken up with tennis balls?

The volume of a ball, or sphere, is $\frac{4}{3}\pi r^3$.

5-3 PART D Making Connections

← CONNECT → *You have learned to draw nets of unfolded three-dimensional solids. You have also used the nets to help you find the surface areas of solids. Using formulas, you have found the volumes of prisms, pyramids, cylinders, and cones. Now you will make some discoveries about the relationship between a solid's volume and its surface area.*

When deciding on the dimensions of a package for a new product, a package designer may consider the artistic design, company traditions, and methods of manufacturing and storage.

Because the most important factor may be cost, a designer is always looking for ways to decrease the surface area of a package.

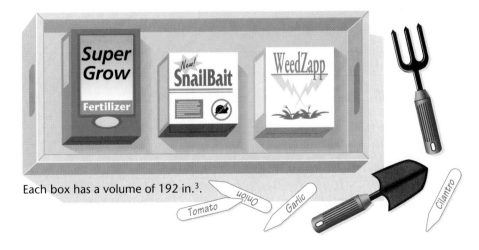

Each box has a volume of 192 in.³.

Many other businesses need to cut down on the surface area of a project to control costs.

An architect has been asked by a nursery owner to design a rectangular prism-shaped solar greenhouse with a volume of 6000 ft³.

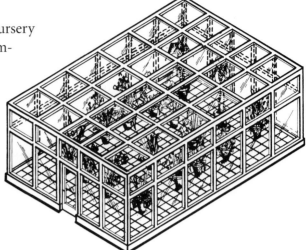

Because the greenhouse will be constructed on bare ground, the structure will consist of four walls and a roof. The building material is quite expensive, so the nursery owner has asked the architect to use as little glass as possible.

1. Sketch a net of a greenhouse that has four walls and one roof.
2. Describe a method to find a length, width, and height of a greenhouse so that its volume is 6000 ft³.
3. Use your method to find an appropriate set of dimensions.
4. Find the surface area of a greenhouse with the dimensions you chose.
5. Repeat steps 3–4 using different sets of dimensions. Your goal is to find the dimensions that will produce the smallest possible surface area for the green-house. Record your data in a table like this one:

Trial	Length (ft)	Width (ft)	Height (ft)	Volume (ft³)	Surface Area (ft²)
1				6000	
2				6000	
3				6000	
4				6000	

6. What patterns did you observe in your results?
7. Describe your results. Do you think you found the smallest possible surface area? Explain.

1. Describe everyday situations in which people might want to find the smallest possible areas or volumes that satisfy certain conditions.
2. Why does a manufacturer save money by cutting down on the surface area of a package?
3. Write a paragraph comparing what you have learned about pyramids, prisms, cones, and cylinders.

Self-Assessment

1. Draw a net for this closed box.

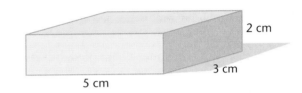

2. Use the closed box in Exercise 1.
   a. Find its volume.
   b. Find its surface area.

3. What is the volume of this square-base pyramid?
   (a) 36 m²   (b) 36 m³
   (c) 12π m³   (d) 12 m³

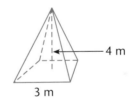

Find the surface area and volume of each solid.

4.

5.

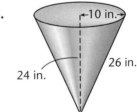

6. The design for a truck's gas tank has this shape. If a gallon is 231 in.³, how much gasoline will the tank hold?

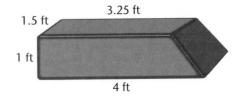

7. St. Paul's Cathedral in London has a volume of 190,000 m³. A large living room in a home might have dimensions 5 m × 7 m with a 3-m-high ceiling. Compare the size of the living room with the size of St. Paul's Cathedral.

8. To measure each, which unit should you use: meters, square meters, cubic meters?
  a. the amount of water used daily in Phoenix, Arizona
  b. the amount of glass enclosing a fish tank
  c. the distance a soccer player runs

9. An appliance manufacturer is designing a refrigerator.
  a. Decide on suitable dimensions. Draw a sketch with the dimensions marked.
  b. How much enamel is needed to paint the refrigerator? Explain.

10. The height of a cylinder is doubled, but its radius remains the same.
  a. What happens to its volume?
  b. What happens to its surface area?

Problem-Solving Tip

Draw and label a sketch of each cylinder.

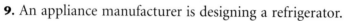

11. The owner of Abram's Market has decided to double the market's floor space. The current floor measures 100 ft by 100 ft. The ceiling is 10 ft high.
  a. Like the current floor, the new one will be square. What are the new floor dimensions?
  b. By how much will the volume of the store increase?
  c. How much more will it cost to wax the new floor than it costs to wax the current one? A bottle of wax that covers 400 ft² costs $4.95.

12. Chad's Chips packs its potato chips in cylindrical cans that are 8 in. high and that have a 3-in. diameter. Twelve cans are packed in a carton. What percentage of the carton's volume is empty?

CHAD'S CHIPS

13. A rectangular park measures 500 m by 700 m. A sidewalk 1 m wide is built inside the outside edge. What is the area of the sidewalk?

500 m.

700 m.

14. Zeke needs to solve the equation $3.2x - 5.1 = 10.3$. [4-2]

    a. Write a plan to help him.

    b. Solve the equation.

15. Find the coordinates of four points in the coordinate plane that are each 3 units from the origin. [1-1]

16. Footprints In many suburban areas, zoning codes regulate the size of buildings on lots. In Jake's city, the *footprint* of a single-story structure in lots smaller than 5000 square feet can be no larger than 45% of the lot size.

    a. What is the area of the lot?

    b. What is the area of the footprint?

    c. Can Jake expand the house as shown?

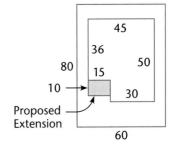

All dimensions are in feet.

17. The dimensions of a rectangular prism are doubled. The volume of the new prism is how many times the volume of the original prism?

    (a) 2   (b) 4

    (c) 6   (d) 8

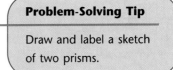

Problem-Solving Tip

Draw and label a sketch of two prisms.

18. John uses his calculator on five homework questions. He gets answers of 29.47826087, 8447.786, 0.2513, 4.66666666, and 100.00025. The directions say that he should report the answers rounded to the nearest hundredth. What answers should he report? [Previous course]

19. Draw as many types of different figures as you can that have a volume of 64 cm³.

20. The area of the crop art is 24 acres. Estimate its dimensions in yards and in feet.

> "Artists, especially muralists, have long utilized a basic grid to project a smaller sketch to larger dimensions. On my large image, the scale I usually use is one inch on the sketch representing one hundred feet on the field. To lay out the giant grid accurately, two assistants set flags at coordinates found through the lens of a surveyors transit."
>
>   *Stan Herd*

The Harvest, *crop art near Lincoln, Nebraska, planted with wheat, corn, and field grains.*

Chapter 5 Review

In Chapter 5, you explored ways to find and express the size of an object. After working with isometric projection and one-point perspective, you used length and area to determine the size of polygons and circles. You drew orthographic projections and found the length, area, and volume of three-dimensional objects. The use of nets helped you compute the surface area of solids.

KEY TERMS

altitude [5-2]

area [5-1]

base [5-2]

circle [5-2]

cone [5-3]

cubic units [5-1]

cylinder [5-3]

diameter [5-2]

edge [5-1]

face [5-1]

height [5-2]

isometric projection [5-1]

linear unit [5-1]

net [5-3]

one-point perspective [5-1]

orthographic projection [5-2]

parallelogram [5-2]

perimeter [5-1]

polygon [5-2]

prism [5-3]

pyramid [5-3]

radius [5-2]

rectangular prism [5-1]

right triangle [5-2]

slant height [5-3]

solid [5-1]

square unit [5-1]

surface area [5-3]

trapezoid [5-2]

vertex [5-1]

volume [5-1]

Write the word or phrase that best completes the sentence.

1. Another name for the altitude of a triangle is the ____.

2. A(n) ____ depicts the apparent shrinking in size that occurs when an object moves farther and farther from the eye.

3. A(n) ____ is a segment that connects two vertices of a prism.

4. Circumference is measured in ____ units.

CONCEPTS AND APPLICATIONS

5. A picture frame measures 9 in. × 12 in.
   a. Find the perimeter of the frame.
   b. What is the area of the picture?

A solid figure consists of a row of two cubes. Draw the row from the following views.

6. isometric projection

7. one-point perspective

8. orthographic projection

9. Find the area of the triangle.

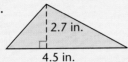

10. A piece of tile with an area of 5.4 in.² is in the shape of a parallelogram. The length of one side of the tile is 3 in. Find the length of the altitude to that side.

11. Give the median of these temperatures: 88°, 85°, 93°, 91°, 95°, 88°. [1-3]

12. A trapezoidal piece of stained glass has the dimensions shown. Find the perimeter and the area of the glass.

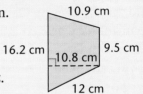

13. The diameter of a wheelbarrow wheel is 14 in. Use 3.14 for π.
  a. Give the radius of the wheel.
  b. How far will the wheel roll in one revolution?

14. Simplify. [2-3]
  a. $2(a^2 + 3a - 2) - (a^2 + 5a - 1)$
  b. $2(a^2 + 3a - 2) + (a^2 + 3a - 2)$

15. Find the area of the front face of the machine nut.

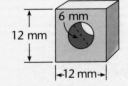

16. A rectangular prism measures 3 in. × 4 in. × 5 in.
  a. Sketch its net.
  b. Find its surface area.
  c. Find its volume.

17. For the prism shown, give the number of each.
  a. faces   **b.** edges   **c.** vertices
  d. Sketch a net of the prism.

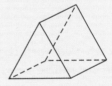

Write the next three numbers in each pattern. [3-2]

18. 19, −23, 27, −31, 35, ____, ____, ____

19. 196, 169, 144, 121, 100, ____, ____, ____

20. A pyramid has a rectangular base measuring 5 in. × 6 in. and a height of 4 in. Find the volume of the pyramid.

21. An unsharpened cylindrical pencil is 19 cm long and 0.8 cm in diameter. Use 3.14 for π.
  a. Give the surface area of the pencil.   **b.** Give the volume of the pencil.

CONCEPTS AND CONNECTIONS

22. Earth Science The greater the surface area of the particles in soil, the more water the soil can hold.
   a. Find the difference in the surface areas of **A** and **B**. (Cube **A** is formed by breaking cube **B** into eight congruent cubes.)
   b. Which absorbs water more efficiently, small-grained soils or large-grained soils? Explain.

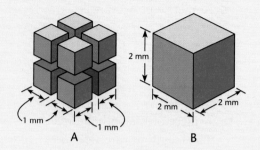

SELF-EVALUATION

Max said that he lives in a large house. Use the ideas in this chapter to explain how he might have arrived at this conclusion and how he might back up his conclusion with facts and sketches. Make a list of the ideas or vocabulary that still trouble you, and plan to review them.

Chapter 5 Assessment

TEST

1. a. Use the dots to sketch a cube.
   b. Identify the view you have drawn as isometric or orthographic projection or one-point perspective.

Determine whether each statement is true or false. If the statement is false, change the underlined word or phrase to make it true.

2. A cone has one-third the volume of a cylinder.

3. The value of π is approximately 3.14.

4. Square units are used to measure volume.

5. A line segment that connects two points on the circle and passes through the center is called a circumference.

6. Evaluate the expression $4(x + y)^2$ if $x = 2$ and $y = 3$.

Find the perimeter and area of each figure.

7.

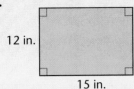

12 in.

15 in.

8.

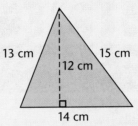

13 cm   15 cm

12 cm

14 cm

9.

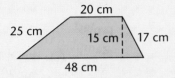

20 cm

25 cm

15 cm   17 cm

48 cm

10. a. Sketch a net of the prism.
b. Find the surface area of the prism.
c. Find the volume of the prism.
d. Give the number of edges on the prism.

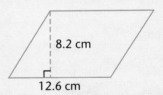

6 in.   5 in.

3 in.

4 in.

11. A vitamin bottle in the shape of a cylinder is 5 cm in diameter and 9 cm tall.
a. A rectangular label pasted on the bottle reaches halfway around the bottle's circumference. Give the width of the label.
b. Find the volume of the bottle.

12. The contents of a cereal box measuring 3 in. × 10 in. × 12 in. were poured into a box measuring 2 in. × 8 in. × 10 in. Give the volume of cereal remaining in the larger box.

13. The parallelogram shown is the base of a pyramid that has a height of 16 cm.
a. How many faces does the pyramid have?
b. How many vertices?
c. Find the area of the parallelogram.
d. Find the volume of the pyramid.

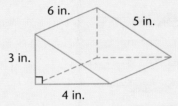

8.2 cm

12.6 cm

14. Explain how grids help us estimate
a. lengths on a map.   **b.** size of an area on a photograph.

PERFORMANCE TASK

If you cut out the two nets, you would find that you could fold the second one into a cube but not the first one. There are ten more cube nets in addition to the one shown. Find as many of them as you can. Be sure that each is truly different from the others.

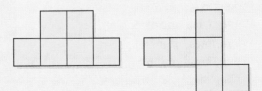

Chapter 6

Ratio and Proportion

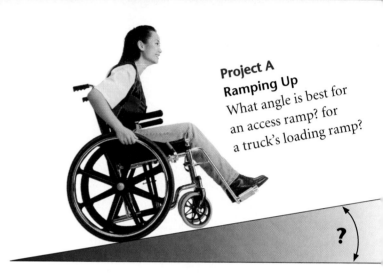

Project A
Ramping Up
What angle is best for an access ramp? for a truck's loading ramp?

Project B
Perfect Harmony
What notes belong to a major chord in the key of C?

Project C
Get the Scoop
Why are newspapers and newsletters printed in columns?

Examples of Ramp D...	
Slope	Maximum Rise (incl...
1:12	

60" min.

Intermediate level platform

Fig. 5.7 Straight ramp run

Bottom level platform

As required

DISABLED ACCESS REGULATIONS

60"

As required

NICHOLAS ZIRPOLO

When I was in high school, I thought math was cool stuff. For instance, you could understand how speed, time, and distance were related.

I designed an access ramp for the student union at Stanford University. I had to know what is needed as well as what the rules require. I'm proud of helping make Stanford proactive in the arena of access for people with disabilities. There is a lot of math in the planning. Math helps us know what's real about the present and what the future will be like.

Nicholas Zirpolo, Ph.D.
Architectural Accessibility
  Consultant
*Access Planning and
  Design*
Palo Alto, California

Nicholas Zirpolo

Chapter 6

Overview

Ratio and Proportion

6-1 Using Ratios to Compare
Ratios and proportions are tools for making accurate representations, such as maps or blueprints. You will use ratios in fraction, decimal, and percentage form to compare quantities. You will find missing quantities by solving proportions.

6-2 Similarity and Scaling
Scaling is used to maintain proportions as size is increased or decreased. Scaling is important in sculpture, model building, and medicine. You will find quantities using indirect measurement, and you will make scale models and scale drawings using concepts of proportionality in similar figures.

6-3 Trigonometry
Surveyors and engineers use ratios to find measurements of sides or angles in a triangle. You will use trigonometric ratios to calculate measures in right triangles.

Rodgers, Hammerstein, and Pythagoras

Doe, a deer, a female deer, Ray, a drop of golden sun,

Me, a name I call myself ...

Do-Re-Mi by Richard Rodgers & Oscar Hammerstein

Richard Rodgers and Oscar Hammerstein built their song *Do-Re-Mi* around the ascending musical scale that is the basis of all Western music:

do re mi fa sol la ti do

About 2500 years before Rodgers and Hammerstein wrote their song, the Greek mathematician Pythagoras discovered the mathematical principles behind the scale. Pythagoras knew that musical sounds were produced by vibrations. For example, a guitar string makes a sound when it is plucked, and a trumpet player must vibrate his lips to make music. The **frequency** of the vibration—the number of vibrations per second—determines how high or low the sound will be. Pythagoras discovered that simple mathematical relationships can be used to find the frequencies of the sounds that produce the notes of the scale.

Note	Frequency
do (1 octave up)	$\frac{2}{1}n$
ti	$\frac{15}{8}n$
la	$\frac{5}{3}n$
sol	$\frac{3}{2}n$
fa	$\frac{4}{3}n$
mi	$\frac{5}{4}n$
re	$\frac{9}{8}n$
do (middle C)	n

1. A guitar string vibrates 264 times per second to produce the note *do* (middle C). Find the frequencies of the other notes of the scale.
2. Describe some other connections between music and mathematics.
3. What does it mean to say that the *do-re-mi* scale is the basis of all "Western" music? What other types of music exist? How do they differ from Western music?

← C O N N E C T → *You have used math to measure, calculate, and solve equations. But math also is used to compare quantities. Now you will investigate some comparisons that are related to fraction and percentage concepts you studied in the past.*

Each statement below compares two quantities.

The population of Iowa is $\frac{1}{4}$ the population of Illinois.

I'll take only half as much spinach as you gave Uncle Phil.

In 1986, 29% of the population was under twenty years old.

CONSIDER

?

1. **What are the quantities being compared in each statement above?**

EXPLORE: TRAFFIC PATROL

Roosevelt Market is located on a busy corner that does not have any traffic signals. The math class broke up into groups to take a traffic survey.

Jan's group reported that 7 cars out of 25 were exceeding the speed limit.

Roberto's group reported that out of 15 cars making left turns, 10 held up traffic.

Sami's group reported that of the 20 pedestrians, 12 crossed the street.

1. The class assumes the traffic pattern will continue in the same way during the rest of the day. Copy and complete each table.

Number of Cars Speeding 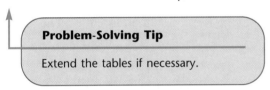	7				
Total Number of Cars	25	50	75	100	1000

Number of Cars Holding Up Traffic	10				
Total Number of Cars Turning Left	15	30	45	60	120

Number of Pedestrians Crossing	12				
Total Number of Pedestrians	20	40	50	60	100

2. According to the first table, how many speeders are there out of 100? What percentage is this?
3. Out of 60 cars turning left, how many held up traffic?
4. Out of 50 pedestrians, how many crossed the street?
5. Based on this traffic survey, find each of these quantities.

> **Problem-Solving Tip**
>
> Extend the tables if necessary.

   a. the number of speeders out of 300 cars
   b. the number of cars that held up traffic out of 75 cars turning left
   c. the number of pedestrians who crossed the street out of 75 pedestrians
6. In a survey they made the next day, Sami's group found that 10 out of 16 pedestrians crossed the street. How does this compare with the day before?

A ratio is a comparison of two quantities. A ratio such as 3 cars out of 15 cars can be written in several ways.

    3 out of 15   3:15 $\frac{3}{15}$

Two ratios that show the same comparison, such as 3:15 and 6:30, are called **equivalent ratios.**

Because a ratio can be written as a fraction, it can be written in any form that is equivalent to that fraction. So the ratio 3:15 also can be written as

    1 out of 5   1:5 $\frac{1}{5}$ 20%   0.20

CONSIDER

2. What are the ratios in the three sentences at the beginning of this part?

3. Does the ratio of cars holding up traffic to cars turning left, written as 10:15, tell how many cars actually turned left?

EXAMPLE

1. Miriam earns $60 each month at her library job after school. She puts $24 of this amount into her savings account for a trip to Washington, DC. Write this ratio in different forms and in words.

$24 out of $60 is 24:60 or $\frac{24}{60}$ or $\frac{2}{5}$ or 40%.

You can say, "Miriam saves 40% of her pay each month."

When you work with ratios you may use fractions, decimals, and percentages. You already may know some of the methods for finding equivalent ratios.

Let's look at methods for changing the ratio 24:60 to equivalent ratios. Note that the ratio $24:60 = \frac{24}{60}$.

There are several ways to find an *equivalent fraction* for the ratio 24:60.

Divide or multiply both numerator and denominator by the same number.

$$\frac{24}{60} = \frac{24 \div 12}{60 \div 12} = \frac{2}{5} \qquad \text{or} \qquad \frac{24}{60} = \frac{24 \cdot 2}{60 \cdot 2} = \frac{48}{120}$$

Division can be used to find an *equivalent decimal* for the ratio 24:60.

Use division.   To find $\frac{24}{60}$ by using your calculator,

$\frac{24}{60} = 24 \div 60 = 0.4$ enter 24 ÷ 60.

Display: [0.4].

To find an *equivalent percentage* for the ratio 24:60:

Find the equivalent decimal first.

$\frac{24}{60} = 24 \div 60 = 0.4$

Write the decimal as hundredths, then write as a percentage:

$0.4 = 0.40 = 40\%.$

Using your calculator,

enter 24 $\boxed{\div}$ 60 $\boxed{\%}$.

Display: $\boxed{\qquad 40}$ = 40%.

EXAMPLE

2. Find the ratio of skull bones to total bones in the human skeleton. What is the ratio of bones in the arms and legs to the total number of bones in the body? Express these ratios as percentages.

Human Skeletal System
Skull bones: 29
Main body bones: 51
Arm and leg bones: 130
Total bones: 210

Ratio of skull bones to total bones:

$29{:}210 = \frac{29}{210} \approx 0.138 = 13.8\%,$
or about 14%

Ratio of bones in arms and legs to total bones:

$130{:}210 = \frac{130}{210} \approx 0.619 = 61.9\%,$
or about 62%

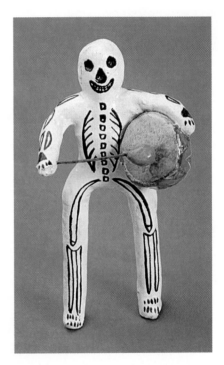

TRY IT

a. The Louisiana Super Dome, the largest indoor arena in history, can hold 90,000 people. If 36,000 fans came to a football game there, what percentage of the Super Dome's capacity would be used?

REFLECT

"Gift Box," 1981, by Wayne Thiebaud

1. Why would someone use a ratio instead of actual measurements?
2. What arithmetic operation is associated with ratio? Explain.
3. What are two common forms used to express ratios? Give advantages and disadvantages of each form.
4. If a newspaper reports that 65% of the voters voted "Yes" on the school bonds, can you figure out how many people voted?
5. What does it mean to share the cost of a gift 50–50?

Exercises

CORE

Getting Started   Determine the ratio for each situation.

1. Yesterday, 3 out of 30 students were absent from class.

2. Out of every $10 spent on food and drinks, Americans pay $1 for packaging.

3. In 1990, there were approximately 6.5 million Asian Americans out of 250 million people in the United States.

4. In 1987, 53% of all crimes were reported to the police.

5. Assume that the patterns continue. Copy and complete the table.

Number of Cars Turning on Elm St.	2				
Total Number of Cars Approaching the Intersection	15	30	60	90	150

6. Choose the letter of the word or phrase that best completes the sentence.
   A ratio is
   (a) an equation   (b) a comparison   (c) a variable   (d) not here

7. Bart kept track of the weather for 30 days. Write ratios for the following comparisons.
   a. sunny days to the total number of days
   b. cloudy days to the total number of days
   c. cloudy days to sunny days
   d. sunny days to cloudy days

Weather Record

SUNNY 𝗛𝗛 𝗛𝗛 𝗛𝗛 𝗛𝗛 20
CLOUDY 𝗛𝗛 𝗛𝗛 10

Write the equivalent fraction in lowest terms for these ratios.

8. 4:6   **9.** 8:20   **10.** 10:100

11. Good Vibrations The frequency of a musical note is the number of vibrations of the sound wave per second. Frequency is measured in Hertz. A major
scale has seven tones (do, re, mi, fa, sol, la, ti). The ratio of the frequencies of
one note to the same note seven notes lower is 2:1. If the first "la" has a
frequency of 440 Hertz, what is the frequency of the "la" that is an octave, or
seven notes, lower?

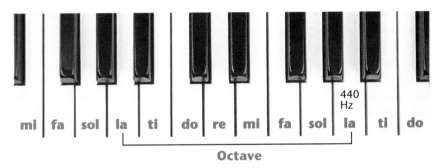

Write the decimal equivalent to each ratio. Round your answer to two places.

12. 1:2   **13.** 2:5   **14.** 3:4

Write the percentage that is equivalent to each ratio.

15. 4:5   **16.** 14:200   **17.** 1:3

Write an equivalent ratio for each expression. Write the new ratio in words.

18. Six out of eight people had the right change.

19. Two out of ten visitors to the White House have been there before.

20. Out of the first 41 presidents of the United States, 9 were living in New York
when they were elected.

21. Strrrrike! Baseball player Ted Williams was hitting so well in 1941 that if
he had been at bat 1000 times, he would have had 406 hits. Write a ratio, in
decimal form, to describe this record. This ratio is his *batting average*. Can
you determine how many times he was at bat or his number of hits from his
batting average? Explain.

22. In each picture, what is the ratio
of the shaded area to the entire
area? to the unshaded area?

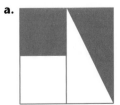

a.   **b.**

LOOK BACK

Solve each equation. [4-2]

23. $2x + 3x = 35$ **24.** $-8x - 1 = 19$ **25.** $15 - x = 32$

Evaluate each expression for $a = -5$ and $b = 6$. [2-3]

26. $3(a + b)$ **27.** $3a + 3b$ **28.** $3a + b$

29. Find the area of the trapezoid. [5-2]

MORE PRACTICE

30. Groups of light bulbs were tested, and the defective bulbs were counted. Copy and complete this table, assuming the numbers continue in the same way.

Defective Light Bulbs	3						
Number Tested	50	100	150	200	250	300	1000

31. Copy and complete this table. It shows the number of correct problems needed to score 80% on any test.

Number Correct	4			16			80
Total Number of Problems	5	10	15		25	30	

Write a ratio for each expression.

32. Out of 50 flips of a coin, Tanner got 27 heads.

33. For each $5 admission, $1 will be sent to a charity organization.

34. Mrs. Crandon got 2 out of every 3 votes that were cast for mayor.

Write an equivalent fraction in lowest terms for each ratio.

35. 3:6   **36.** 5:20   **37.** 14:14   **38.** 10:50

For each picture, what is the ratio of the shaded area to the entire area? to the unshaded area?

39.

40.

41.

Write the equivalent decimal for each ratio. Round your answers to two places.

42. 1:8   **43.** 2:10   **44.** 7:8   **45.** 3:5

Write the equivalent percentage for each ratio.

46. 2:3   **47.** 5:100   **48.** 16:320   **49.** 1:5

50. Which of the following ratios is equivalent to the ratio 3:4?
(a) 75%   (b) 4:3   (c) 4:5   (d) not here

Write each ratio as an equivalent fraction, decimal, and percentage.

51. Each month Bill spends $10 of his $25 allowance on bus fare.

52. An inch on each side of the $8\frac{1}{2}$-inch paper is used for margins.

53. We spend 8 hours out of 24 sleeping.

54. All 24 of the photographs were blurred.

MORE MATH REASONING

55. Ad Lib Liz finds that during the late news, $3\frac{1}{2}$ minutes out of 10 of broadcast time are devoted to commercials. She says that this ratio is the same as 35%. What do you think?

Industry

56. Musical Pitch The pitch of a musical note's sound is related to its frequency. Musicians usually use the note A at a frequency of 440 Hertz to tune their instruments. Two notes that have the frequency ratio of 2:1 are an *octave* apart on the musical scale. The ratio of the frequency of two notes is 3:2 for every fifth note of the scale. This distance is called a *fifth*. Decide whether notes with these ratios are octaves, fifths, or neither.

Fine Arts

a. 880:440   **b.** 440:220
c. 660:440   **d.** 165:110
e. 990:660   **f.** 220:110

6-1 PART B Understanding Ratios

← CONNECT → *You have seen that ratios compare two quantities by using fractions and percentages. Now you will see that one ratio can be compared with another ratio. You also will see that ratio concepts can apply to quantities expressed in different units.*

Using ratios to compare the results from one year with the results from another year is very common in business, education, and government. Comparisons—and ratios—are necessary for us to analyze the way things change.

EXPLORE: SIDE OUT

The girls' volleyball team at Union High School has won the championship for the past three years. Here are the results of the games they played each season.

1. Which year did the volleyball team have the best record? Explain why you think so.

2. For each of the three years above, write a ratio of the form: $\frac{\text{number of games won}}{\text{number of games played}}$. How can you compare these ratios?

3. Use your calculator to write each ratio as a decimal or percentage.

4. Three years ago, the team played only six games. They won five games and lost one game. How does this record compare with the other years?

5. Tell how percentages make it easy to compare ratios.

In most sports, a team's standing is computed using this ratio:

$$\frac{\text{number of games won}}{\text{number of games played}} \cdot$$

It is often written as a decimal correct to three decimal places or as a percentage.

CONSIDER

1. Why is it easier to compare ratios written as decimals or percentages, rather than as fractions?
2. What is meant when someone says, "We're behind you 100%"?

EXAMPLE

1. Bonnie's Bargain Basement started selling video games in 1992. That year video games were $\frac{1}{15}$ of the store's profit. The next year video games were $\frac{1}{20}$ of the profit, and the following year video games were $\frac{1}{10}$ of the profit. In which year did video games make up the largest share of the profit? the smallest?

1992: $\frac{1}{15} \approx 0.067$, or about 7%   Use a calculator.

1993: $\frac{1}{20} = 0.05$, or about 5%

1994: $\frac{1}{10} = 0.10$, or about 10%

The largest share was in 1994, and the smallest share was in 1993.

Most of the ratios you have seen so far compare part of something with the total amount. Ratios can also compare different kinds of quantities.

EXAMPLE

2. At Edgewater High School, there are 1720 students and 85 teachers. The principal says the student-to-teacher ratio is about 20 to 1. Is this correct?

The ratio of students to teachers is 1720:85.

$$1720{:}85 = \frac{1720}{85} = \frac{1720 \div 85}{85 \div 85} \approx \frac{20.2}{1}$$

Because 20.2 to 1 is approximately 20 to 1, the principal's statement is correct.

Decide which ratio is greater. Explain how you decided.

a. 15 problems correct out of 50 problems or 20 problems correct out of 60 problems

b. 25 games won out of 30 played or 20 games won out of 25 played

c. What is the ratio of teachers to students in Example 2?

d. The Statue of Liberty without its pedestal is 151 ft high. When Cindy holds a torch, or flashlight, above her own head, the top of the torch is 6.5 ft high. Write the ratio of Cindy's height, including the torch, to the statue's height, and the ratio of the statue's height to Cindy's height, including the torch. Then write a sentence that would help someone understand the enormous size of the Statue of Liberty.

REFLECT

1. The ratio of the number of students who walk to school compared with the number who use public transportation is $\frac{2}{3}$. Does this mean that only two people walk to school?

2. In 1992, the population of Sweden was about $\frac{9}{7}$ the population of Switzerland. Which country had the larger population? Explain.

3. When you write a ratio in fraction form, how do you decide which number to use as the numerator?

Exercises

CORE

1. **Getting Started** Which ratio shows the best record?
   (a) 8 wins out of 10 games (b) 4 wins out of 5 games
   (c) 18 wins out of 20 games

Fill in the blank to make equivalent ratios.

2. 100 dollars:1 week = 1000 dollars:___ weeks

3. 3 pounds:2 dogs = ___ pounds:6 dogs

Which ratio is greater? Explain how you decided.

4. 14 games won out of 20 played or 12 games won out of 18 played

5. $300 for 4 weeks or $1000 for 15 weeks

6. 45 miles in half an hour or 50 miles in 42 minutes

7. 2 bins out of 24 bins or 5 bins out of 55 bins

8. Oranges are selling at 3 pounds for 66 cents.
   a. Copy and complete this table using ratios. Then use the table to answer the questions that follow.

Pounds of Oranges	3	6		12		x
Cost	$0.66		$1.98		$3.30	

   b. What is the cost of oranges per pound?
   c. How many pounds can you buy for $1?

9. Write a ratio for each comparison.
   a. morning orders to afternoon orders
   b. afternoon orders to morning orders
   c. evening orders to total orders
   d. morning orders to total orders

Larry's Delivery Service
Total Orders Today: 16
Morning Orders: 2
Afternoon Orders: 8
Evening Orders: 6

10. What is the ratio of seconds to minutes in one day? of minutes to hours?

11. **The Reign in Spain** Queen Isabella of Spain reigned for 30 years. Queen Elizabeth I of England reigned for 45 years. Use ratios to compare the lengths of their reigns in two ways.

12. Researchers placed 25 female and 10 male fleas on Thomas the cat each day and counted the egg production.

a. In 27 days, Thomas's fleas produced 14,921 eggs. Use your calculator to find the rate of eggs produced in one day for Thomas's fleas.

b. Researchers placed a different type of flea on Creole, a cat in the same laboratory. In 25 days, Creole's fleas produced 11,719 eggs. Find the rate of eggs produced in one day for Creole's fleas.

c. Which cat had fleas that produced the most eggs in one day? How can you tell?

13. The radius of the small circle is 5 m. The radius of the large circle is 10 m.

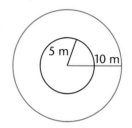

a. Find the area of the small circle.

b. Find the area of the large circle.

c. What is the ratio of the area of the large circle to the area of the small circle?

14. Write a ratio comparing the heights of each pair of famous landmarks.

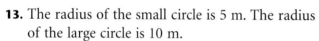

Landmark	Height (nearest ft)
Empire State Building	1250
Statue of Liberty	305
Washington Monument	555
San Jacinto Column	570
Sears Tower	1454
Gateway Arch	630

a. Empire State Building and San Jacinto Column

b. Statue of Liberty and Sears Tower

c. Gateway Arch and Washington Monument

d. San Jacinto Column and Gateway Arch

15. Suppose you are asked to display the data in the Landmark table as a graph. Which would make a better display, a bar graph or a circle graph? Explain.

 *LOOK AHEAD*

Write the number that correctly completes each statement.

16. 1 mi = ___ ft   **17.** 1 year = ___ days   **18.** 1 gallon = ___ quarts

19. 1 yd = ___ in.   **20.** 1 pound = ___ ounces   **21.** 1 yd^2 = ___ ft^2

22. George flips a coin 10 times. Here are his results:

What was his percentage of heads after 2 flips? after 5 flips? after 7 flips? after 10 flips?

MORE PRACTICE

Fill in the blank to make equivalent ratios.

23. 10,000 books:1000 students = ___ books:1 student

24. 5 dollars:1 day = 100 dollars:___ days

25. 55 miles:1 hour = ___ miles:2.5 hours

Which ratio is greater? Explain how you decided.

26. 16 red marbles out of 75 marbles or 4 red marbles out of 21 marbles

27. 17 freshman band members out of 57 band members or 67 freshman chorus members out of 183 chorus members

28. 5 infertile eggs out 91 eggs or 1 dozen infertile eggs out of 10 dozen eggs

29. $1.69 tax paid on $25.95 or $4.03 tax paid on $64.50

30. Apples sell for 2 pounds for 64 cents.
   a. Copy and complete the table. Then use the table to answer each question.

Pounds of Apples	2	4		10	12	100	x
Cost	$0.64		$1.92				

   b. What is the cost of these apples per pound?
   c. How many pounds can you buy for $1?

31. Lincoln High School has 1638 students and 78 teachers.
   a. What is the teacher-to-student ratio?
   b. What is the student-to-teacher ratio?

32. Sunrise Serial The local supermarket sells cereal at $2.26 for a 12-oz box or $3.29 for an 18-oz box. Which is less expensive? Explain.

33. Color Me Yellow Some students performed an experiment to see whether insects are attracted to different colors. They placed colored sticky boards around a field for 6 days. The yellow board collected 283 beetles. The white board collected 94. The green and blue boards collected 189 and 89 beetles, respectively. For each color, find the rate at which beetles were collected each day.

34. A small cube is 4 cm on each edge. A large cube is 5 cm on each edge.
  a. Find the volume of the small cube.
  b. Find the volume of the large cube.
  c. What is the ratio of the volume of the small cube to the volume of the large cube?

35. Write a ratio comparing the size of Texas with the size of California. Write another ratio comparing the size of California with the size of Texas. Write statements that compare their areas.

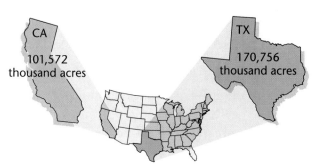

MORE MATH REASONING

36. Water, Water, Everywhere The estimated volume of the earth's salt water is about 1,285,600,000 cubic kilometers. The fresh water on the earth is about 35,000,000 cubic kilometers. Express the ratio of fresh water to salt water in decimal form. What percentage of the earth's water is fresh? What percentage is salt water?

37. Round About Because of the earth's rotation, a person standing at the equator is traveling 1040 miles per hour. How could you find the circumference of the earth with this information? (Hint: How long would it take the person to make a complete rotation?)

38. The area of Alaska is 591,004 square miles. The area of the continental United States including Alaska is 3,612,299 square miles. If the area of Alaska is subtracted from that of the continental United States, what fraction of the continental United States would be left?

Rates

← CONNECT → *Ratios are used to compare quantities that have the same units as well as quantities that have different units. Now you will see a special kind of ratio known as a rate.*

A ratio compares two quantities.

The quantities may have the same units.

This room has a length of 30 feet and a width of 20 feet. The ratio of the length to the width is 3:2.

The quantities may have different units.

To beautify the streets, the city will plant 500 trees evenly throughout an area of 100 blocks. The ratio is 500 trees:100 blocks, or 5 trees per block.

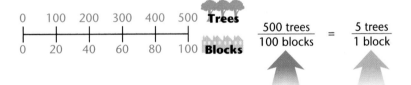

$$\frac{500 \text{ trees}}{100 \text{ blocks}} = \frac{5 \text{ trees}}{1 \text{ block}}$$

Rate   Unit Rate

When a ratio compares quantities that have different units, it is called a **rate.** We call it a **unit rate** when the comparison is made to one unit. We often use the word **per** to mean **for each.** Miles per hour, hits per time at bat, dollars per day, and points per test are all examples of unit rates.

Rate	Ratio	Unit Rate
6 books for 2 students	6:2	3 books per student
5 pencils for 2 students	5:2	2.5 pencils per student
3 computers for 8 students	3:8	0.375 computers per student

1. **Suppose you have a ratio, such as 40 miles in 4 hours, that you want to write as a unit rate. How can you change it to a unit rate?**

EXAMPLE

1. An airplane makes the 2800 mile trip from Portland, Oregon, to Miami, Florida, in 5.5 hours.

What is the ratio of miles to hours? Find the unit rate.

The ratio is $\dfrac{2800 \text{ mi}}{5.5 \text{ hr}} = \dfrac{2800 \text{ mi} \div 5.5}{5.5 \text{ hr} \div 5.5} = \dfrac{509.09 \text{ mi}}{1 \text{ hr}}$.

Divide the ratio's numerator and denominator by 5.5.
The unit rate is 509.09 miles per hour.

TRY IT

a. Morris has a coupon for 50 cents off a 12-ounce package of his favorite breakfast cereal. About how much will this coupon save him per ounce?

EXPLORE: THE RIGHT RATE

Compare the rates in each situation.

1. In 1939, an ad for a train boasted that passengers would travel a mile a minute from Chicago to New York. How can you compare this with miles per hour?

2. Suppose a train travels one mile per minute. What information do you need to find the number of feet it travels per second?

> **Problem-Solving Tip**
>
> Draw a diagram.

3. During the Midwest floods of 1993, the rising rivers were sometimes measured each hour. State which measurement shows that the river is rising faster: $\dfrac{5 \text{ inches}}{1 \text{ hour}}$ or $\dfrac{3 \text{ feet}}{1 \text{ day}}$.

4. Describe any techniques you found for comparing rates.

One way to convert rates is to multiply by a fraction in which the numerator equals the denominator. Because these kinds of fractions equal 1, the value of the original rate is not changed. Such fractions are called **conversion factors.** Here are a few examples.

$$\frac{1\ hour}{60\ minutes} \qquad \frac{7\ days}{1\ week} \qquad \frac{12\ inches}{1\ foot} \qquad \frac{24\ hours}{1\ day}$$

CONSIDER ?

2. Determine some other conversion factors. What is always true about the numerator and denominator of conversion factors?

EXAMPLES

2. Convert the rate of 5 miles per minute to miles per hour.

$$\frac{5\ miles}{1\ \cancel{minute}} \times \frac{60\ \cancel{minutes}}{1\ hour} = \frac{300\ miles}{1\ hour}$$

5 miles per minute = 300 miles per hour

Multiply the ratio by a useful conversion factor and cross out the minutes.

3. Convert 5 inches per day to feet per week.

$$\frac{5\ \cancel{inches}}{1\ \cancel{day}} \times \frac{7\ \cancel{days}}{1\ week} \times \frac{1\ foot}{12\ \cancel{inches}} = \frac{5 \times 7\ feet}{12\ weeks} \approx \frac{2.9\ feet}{1\ week}$$

5 inches per day ≈ 2.9 feet per week

Multiply the ratio by two useful conversion factors and cross out the inches and days.

TRY IT

b. Convert 4 centimeters per hour to units involving minutes instead of hours.

It is often easier to solve problems with a unit rate.

4. Myra earned $360 in the first 3 weeks of her summer job. How much will she earn at this rate during the 10 weeks she works during the summer?

$$\frac{360 \text{ dollars} \div 3}{3 \text{ weeks} \div 3} = \frac{120 \text{ dollars}}{1 \text{ week}}$$ Find the unit rate.

$$\frac{120 \text{ dollars}}{1 \text{ week}} \times \frac{10}{10} = \frac{1200 \text{ dollars}}{10 \text{ weeks}}$$ Find the rate for 10 weeks.

Myra will earn $1200 for 10 weeks at this rate.

REFLECT

1. What is the value of any fraction in which the numerator equals the denominator?

2. How does a fraction's value change when it is multiplied by 1?

3. Many rates used in this Part equal 1. What other rates can you think of that equal 1?

Exercises

CORE

1. Getting Started
   a. Write the rate 20 miles in 5 hours as a fraction.
   b. Write this fraction as an equivalent fraction with a denominator of 1.
   c. Write the unit rate for 20 miles in 5 hours.

2. Which of the following is a unit rate for $\frac{10 \text{ gallons}}{20 \text{ plants}}$?

   (a) $\frac{1 \text{ gallon}}{2 \text{ plants}}$ (b) $\frac{0.5 \text{ gallon}}{1 \text{ plant}}$ (c) $\frac{2 \text{ gallons}}{1 \text{ plant}}$

Write each as a unit rate.

3. 6 quarts of water per 4 tablespoons of dry plant food

4. 135 books per 6 shelves

5. 5 calculators for every 3 students

6. 4 ounces for 2 dollars

Complete the following conversion factors. (Hint: Make each ratio equal 1.)

7. $\dfrac{16\ \text{ounces}}{\boxed{}\ \text{pound}}$

8. $\dfrac{1\ \text{gallon}}{\boxed{}\ \text{quarts}}$

9. $\dfrac{100\ \text{pennies}}{\boxed{}\ \text{dimes}}$

10. $\dfrac{9\ \text{square feet}}{1\ \text{square}\ \boxed{}}$

Replace each variable with the number that correctly completes each statement.

11. $\dfrac{15\ \text{words}}{7\ \text{minutes}} \times \dfrac{60\ \text{minutes}}{1\ \text{hour}} = \dfrac{x\ \text{words}}{1\ \text{hour}}$

12. $\dfrac{1030\ \text{gallons}}{25\ \text{hours}} \times \dfrac{x\ \text{hour}}{y\ \text{minutes}} = \dfrac{z\ \text{gallons}}{1\ \text{minute}}$

13. Copy and complete to find the number of cups in a gallon.

$\dfrac{4\ \text{quarts}}{1\ \text{gallon}} \cdot \dfrac{x\ \text{pints}}{1\ \text{quart}} \cdot \dfrac{y\ \text{cups}}{1\ \text{pint}} = \dfrac{z\ \text{cups}}{1\ \text{gallon}}$

14. Convert 12 heartbeats per 10 seconds to heartbeats per minute.

15. Toe to Toe Assume that each person at the beach has five toes on each of two feet.

   a. What is the ratio of toes per foot? of toes per person? of persons per foot? of persons per toe?

   b. Eli watches from the lifeguard platform. He counts 85 people. How many feet? How many toes?

16. a. Find the area of the figure shown.

   b. Find the area of the red circle.

   c. Find the area of the blue portion of the figure.

   d. What is the ratio of the area of the red circle to the area of the blue portion of the figure?

   e. What is the ratio of the area of the red circle to the area of the whole figure?

4 m

8 m

17. The maker of a new foreign car advertises that the car gets 22 kilometers per liter. Find the number of miles per gallon of gasoline.

1 kilometer ≈ 0.62 miles $\dfrac{22\ \text{km}}{1\ \text{L}} \cdot \dfrac{x\ \text{mi}}{1\ \text{km}} \cdot \dfrac{y\ \text{L}}{1\ \text{gal}}$

1 gallon ≈ 3.785 liters

18. Koki is driving from Des Moines to Kansas City, a distance of 197 miles.

   a. About how long will it take if he averages 55 miles per hour?

   b. About how far will he travel in 80 minutes?

Social Science

19. The fastest stilt walker on record is Roy Luiking, who took only 13.14 seconds to travel 328 feet.
   a. What is the rate in seconds per foot?
   b. What is the rate in feet per second?

20. About 49.7 billion gallons of water per day are used in California.
   a. How many gallons per second is that?
   b. Describe an experiment to figure out the weight of water per gallon. How would you use the results of this experiment to find the weight of the water used in California per year?

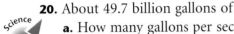 ## LOOK BACK

The figure is a square pyramid. Each base edge measures 2.5 meters. The height of each triangular face is 3 meters.

21. Draw a net for this square pyramid. [5-3]

22. Find the surface area of this pyramid. [5-3]

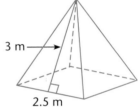
3 m
2.5 m

23. Find the area of the front cover of your math book. [5-1]

24. Find the volume of your math book. [5-3]

25. Write an expression to describe the sequence. What is the 20th term? [3-3]

   3, 6, 9, 12, …

MORE PRACTICE

Tell whether each ratio is equal to the ratio 48 drops:16 ounces.

26. 48 drops:1 pound   **27.** 3 drops:2 ounces   **28.** 4 drops:1 ounce

Replace each variable with the number that correctly completes each statement.

29. $\dfrac{25 \text{ words}}{3 \text{ minutes}} \times \dfrac{60 \text{ minutes}}{1 \text{ hour}} = \dfrac{x \text{ words}}{1 \text{ hour}}$

30. $\dfrac{10 \text{ gallons}}{3 \text{ hours}} \times \dfrac{24 \text{ hours}}{1 \text{ day}} = \dfrac{x \text{ gallons}}{1 \text{ day}}$

31. $\dfrac{100 \text{ gallons}}{35 \text{ hours}} \times \dfrac{x \text{ hour}}{y \text{ minutes}} = \dfrac{z \text{ gallons}}{1 \text{ minute}}$

32. Copy and complete to find the number of inches in a mile.

$$\frac{1760 \text{ yd}}{1 \text{ mi}} \cdot \frac{x \text{ ft}}{1 \text{ yd}} \cdot \frac{x \text{ in.}}{1 \text{ ft}} = \frac{z \text{ in.}}{1 \text{ mi}}$$

33. A hogshead is a unit of measure representing 63 gallons. How many pints are in a hogshead? Use the rates $\frac{4 \text{ quarts}}{1 \text{ gallon}}$ and $\frac{2 \text{ pints}}{1 \text{ quart}}$.

34. Luis's driving manual tells him to keep a six-car-length distance from the car ahead of him when he is traveling at a speed of 88 feet per second. Use these rates to find how fast this is in miles per hour.

> 1 mile is 5280 feet.
> 60 seconds is 1 minute.
> 60 minutes is 1 hour.

35. Move Over, Please The total surface area of the earth is about 196,940,000 square miles. The total population of the earth is about 5,292,200,000.

  a. A square mile is 27,878,400 square feet. If the population of the earth were distributed evenly, how many square feet would each person be allowed?

  b. How useful is your answer? What changes could you make in the given information to make the answer more useful? Explain.

MORE MATH REASONING

36. Time Is Money Help Congress understand the annual federal budget.

  a. How many years are 1 million seconds?

  b. How many years are 1 billion seconds?

  c. How many years are 1 trillion seconds?

  d. The annual federal budget is more than 1 trillion dollars. If you paid $1 per second, how many years would it take you to pay 1 trillion dollars?

37. In 1990, the U.S. government had a budget of $1,393,121,000,000, and the population was 248,709,873.

  a. What is the ratio of dollars per person that the government spent?

  b. What is the ratio of dollars per day that the government spent?

38. In 1988, a team of 32 divers pedaled a tricycle underwater for a distance of 166.7 miles. It took them 75.3 hours.

  a. Express the ratio of miles to hours as a fraction. Use your calculator to express the ratio of miles to hours as a decimal. Which form of the ratio is easier to use? Why?

  b. Express the ratio of hours to miles in both fraction and decimal form.

  c. What is the rate expressed in miles per hour?

← **C O N N E C T** → *A proportion is a special type of equation that uses ratios. You will see how to find missing values in ratios by solving proportions.*

A recipe that serves 8 people calls for 3 eggs. A cook at a diner must serve 16 people. To do this, he must find an equivalent ratio.

8 servings:3 eggs = 16 servings:6 eggs

We can also write this ratio as: $\dfrac{8 \text{ servings}}{3 \text{ eggs}} = \dfrac{16 \text{ servings}}{6 \text{ eggs}}$.

This equation is a proportion. A **proportion** is an equation showing that two ratios are equal.

EXPLORE: KEEPING THINGS IN PROPORTION

All of these ratios are equivalent.

6:9   12:18   4:6   8:12   20:30   5:7.5

1. How can you check to be sure that they are all equivalent?

2. A proportion is an equation that says two ratios are equal. Using the ratios above we can write true proportions like these:

$\dfrac{6}{9} = \dfrac{4}{6}, \dfrac{8}{12} = \dfrac{6}{9}, \dfrac{4}{6} = \dfrac{8}{12}, \dfrac{20}{30} = \dfrac{5}{7.5}$.

Write as many true proportions as you can using the ratios listed above.

These proportional nesting dolls are a traditional folk art form of Russia.

3. How can you check to be sure that these are true proportions? What happens if
  a. you use a calculator to change both ratios in each proportion to decimals to compare them?
  b. you reduce all fractions to see if they are the same?
  c. you change both ratios to fractions with a common denominator?
  d. you multiply the first numerator times the second denominator and compare this with the first denominator times the second numerator?

4. Determine three true proportions. Test your proportions using **3d**. Are the two products always the same?

5. Test these proportions to see if they are true.
$$\frac{3}{5} = \frac{6}{10}, \frac{5}{3} = \frac{4}{12}, \frac{5}{8} = \frac{8}{12}$$

6. Write in your own words some ways to test a proportion to see if it is true.

7. Describe whether the methods you've explored work for every proportion.

To find equivalent ratios, we *solve a proportion.* Because the proportion is an equation, you can solve it using the properties of equality or number sense.

When you set up a proportion, be sure to put corresponding quantities in the same position in each ratio.

Both ratios have the form dollars:weeks.

dollars $\frac{5}{3} = \frac{x}{1}$ *dollars*
weeks   *weeks*

EXAMPLE

1. The ratio of the flying speed of a spine-tailed swift to the running speed of an experienced runner is 13:1, assuming that the runner goes 8 miles per hour. How fast can the spine-tailed swift fly?

Let b represent the speed of the spine-tailed swift.

Set up a proportion using two ratios in the form: $\dfrac{\text{speed of swift}}{\text{speed of runner}}$.

$\dfrac{b}{8} = \dfrac{13}{1}$ $\dfrac{\text{Speed of swift}}{\text{Speed of runner}} = \dfrac{\text{Speed of swift}}{\text{Speed of runner}}$

$\dfrac{b}{8} \cdot 8 = \dfrac{13}{1} \cdot 8$ Multiply both sides of the equation by 8.

$b \cdot 1 = 13 \times 8$ Simplify.

$b = 104$ Simplify.

The spine-tailed swift can fly 104 miles per hour.

Solve $\frac{20}{11} = \frac{x}{3}$.

Rachel thinks ...

I can multiply both sides by 3 to isolate the variable.

$$3 \cdot \frac{20}{11} = \frac{x}{3} \cdot 3 \qquad \text{Multiply by 3.}$$

$$\frac{60}{11} = x \cdot 1 \qquad\qquad 3 \cdot \frac{20}{11} = \frac{3}{1} \cdot \frac{20}{11} = \frac{60}{11}$$

$$5\frac{5}{11} = x$$

So $x = 5\frac{5}{11}$, or about 5.45.

Eric thinks ...

In a proportion, the first numerator times the second denominator equals the first denominator times the second numerator.

$$\frac{20}{11} \underset{\nearrow}{\overset{\searrow}{=}} \frac{x}{3}$$

$$20 \cdot 3 = 11x$$

$$60 = 11x$$

$$\frac{60}{11} = x$$

$$5.45 \approx x \qquad\qquad \text{Use a calculator.}$$

So x is about 5.45.

Eric's technique is called cross multiplication.

In the true proportion

$$\frac{a}{b} = \frac{c}{d},$$

a, b, c, and d are numbers or variables that represent numbers, and

$$\frac{a}{b} \underset{\nearrow}{\overset{\searrow}{=}} \frac{c}{d}$$

$ad = bc$.

Cross multiplication may often be the easiest method to use when there are fractional values or when the variable appears in a denominator. However, you can use cross multiplication to solve any proportion. Your *number sense* skills can also be helpful when solving proportions.

2. The Eiffel Tower in Paris, France, is 986 feet tall, and the Space Needle in Seattle, Washington, is 606 feet tall. Suppose a model of the Eiffel Tower is 15 inches high. How high should you build a model of the Space Needle, if you want the two models to be in proportion?
Let x represent the height of the model of the Space Needle.

$$986:15 = 606:x$$ Write each ratio in the form: Actual monument in feet:model in inches.

$$\frac{986}{15} = \frac{606}{x}$$

$$986(x) = 15(606)$$ Cross multiply.

$$\frac{986}{986}x = \frac{9090}{986}$$

$$x = 9.2$$

The Space Needle model should be 9.2 inches high. This seems reasonable because 9.2 is a little more than half of 15, and the Space Needle is a little more than half as tall as the Eiffel Tower.

CONSIDER

1. In the Example, both ratios used the units feet:inches. Would your answer be correct if one ratio used the form feet:feet?

TRY IT

Write each statement as a proportion and tell whether the proportion is true or false.

a. $16 per 10 hours = $6 per hour
b. 40 hot dogs for 25 people = 8 hot dogs for 5 people.

Solve these proportions.

c. $\frac{y}{12} = \frac{4}{3}$ d. $\frac{0.4}{0.6} = \frac{8}{k}$ e. $\frac{28}{x} = \frac{4}{5}$

f. Certain bacteria that are 6 millionths of a meter long can swim 600 millionths of a meter in 1 second. If a 5-foot 6-inch person (5.5 feet tall) could run as fast as this bacteria in proportion to her height, how many feet could she run in 1 second?

1. What is the difference between a ratio and a proportion?
2. Give three illustrations of a proportion.
3. Write a problem that can be solved using proportions.
4. Can you use the cross-multiplication method to calculate $\frac{1}{9} + \frac{2}{3}$? Explain. When can you use the cross-multiplication method?

Exercises

CORE

Getting Started Write each statement as a proportion and tell whether the proportion is true or false.

1. 4 successes out of 10 tries = 40 successes out of 100 tries

2. 10 dollars per day = 1 dollar per 10 days

3. $\dfrac{60 \text{ miles}}{1 \text{ hour}} = \dfrac{15 \text{ miles}}{15 \text{ minutes}}$

Solve each proportion.

4. $\dfrac{a}{25} = \dfrac{2}{5}$

5. $\dfrac{x}{2} = \dfrac{3}{4}$

6. $\dfrac{14}{8} = \dfrac{c}{10}$

7. $\dfrac{100}{7} = \dfrac{b}{14}$

8. Mort and Mert earned $50 washing 30 windows. Mort says the ratio 10:6 describes the relationship. Mert says the ratio is 5:3. Who is right? Explain.

Solve each proportion.

9. $\dfrac{7}{3.5} = \dfrac{12}{x}$

10. $\dfrac{45}{x} = \dfrac{9}{10}$

11. $\dfrac{4}{24} = \dfrac{1}{x}$

12. $\dfrac{10}{15} = \dfrac{2}{b}$

13. **Turning Green** When mixing green paint, Cornelius uses a ratio of 4 quarts of yellow to 2 quarts of blue.
    a. How much yellow paint will he need if he uses 10 quarts of blue?
    b. How much blue paint will he need if he uses 10 quarts of yellow?
    c. How much blue paint will he need if he uses 5 quarts of yellow?
    d. How much total paint will he need if he uses 5 quarts of blue?

14. An advertisement for a new car says that the car gets 51 miles per gallon.
    a. Explain what the ratio 51 miles per gallon tells us.
    b. Use a proportion to find how much gas it takes to travel 120 miles.
    c. If you use 120 gallons of gas, how far will you travel?

Industry

15. An ant can carry 50 times its total weight. If a person could carry the same proportional weight, how much could you carry? Explain.

16. In his first-period class, Mr. Hatcher compared the number of students who ride the school bus with those who do not. The ratio is 3:2. There are 12 students who ride the bus. How many don't ride the bus?
  a. Use a variable for the number of non-riders, and fill in the values.

$$\frac{\text{Number of riders}}{\text{Number of non-riders}} = \frac{3}{2}$$

  b. Solve the proportion.

17. At a jogging rate of 6 miles per hour, how long would it take a jogger to run around the earth? (The earth has a circumference of about 25,000 miles.)

18. The frequency of a note is measured in Hertz (Hz), or vibrations per second. The ratio of the frequency of a note to that of the note just below it on a keyboard is approximately 1.059:1. Note A, shown on the keyboard to the left of middle C, has a frequency of 220 Hz. Find the frequency of A sharp, the next higher note.

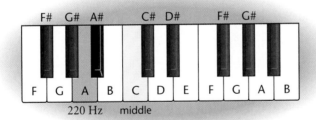

19. Traffic over the George Washington Bridge in New York City averages 249,300 cars per day.
  a. How many cars pass over the bridge in 15 days?
  b. How many days will it take for 1,000,000 cars to cross the bridge?

20. Winging It A wandering albatross has a wing span of about 200% of the arm span of an average man who is 5 feet 10 inches tall. What does this mean? How can you use this information to find the wing span of a wandering albatross?

LOOK AHEAD

In Raoul's marble collection, there are yellow, red, and blue marbles.

21. What fraction of the marbles are yellow?

22. What fraction of the marbles are red?

23. What fraction of the marbles are blue?

Find the area of the following squares.

24. 3 in. × 3 in.

25. 4 in. × 4 in.

26. 5 in. × 5 in.

MORE PRACTICE

27. Tell whether each proportion is true or false.
   a. $4000 per 5-acre lot = $800 per acre
   b. $4000 per 5-acre lot = 1 acre per $400
   c. $4000 per 5-acre lot = $5000 per 6-acre lot

Solve each proportion.

28. $\frac{x}{10} = \frac{2}{6}$

29. $\frac{x}{2} = \frac{3}{8}$

30. $\frac{45}{x} = \frac{9}{10}$

31. $\frac{5}{0.25} = \frac{x}{10}$

32. $\frac{0.5}{8} = \frac{x}{24}$

33. $\frac{4}{24} = \frac{1}{x}$

34. A person who weighs 150 pounds has about 60 pounds of muscle. Use a proportion to determine the amount of muscle on a 200-pound person.

35. A person who weighs 150 pounds would weigh only about 24 pounds on the moon. Use a proportion to find your moon weight.

36. The ratio of singers to dancers in the spring play is 3 to 4.
   a. If there are 12 dancers, how many singers are there?
   b. If there are 30 singers, how many dancers are there?

37. Hair grows about 6 inches in 12 months.
   a. Use a proportion to determine how much hair grows in 9 months.
   b. Use a proportion to determine how long it will take your hair to grow 8 inches.

Science

38. Athlete's Dream In 1988, Leonid Tranenko of the USSR lifted 586.25 pounds. On the moon, where gravity is less, he could have lifted 3664 pounds. What is the ratio of the gravity of the earth to that of the moon?

MORE MATH REASONING

39. Tooth Moves One method that an orthodontist

uses to move teeth is to attach wire to brackets that are bonded to the teeth. The wire used comes in various widths, with diameters ranging from 0.010 inches to 0.020 inches. The strength (s) of the wire is proportional to the cube of the diameter (d) of the wire.

a. Determine how much stronger a wire with a 0.020-inch diameter is than a wire with a 0.010-inch diameter. (Hint: Solve the proportion $\left(\frac{s}{0.020}\right)^3 = \left(\frac{1}{0.010}\right)^3$.)

b. Determine how much stronger a wire with a 0.012-inch diameter is than a wire with a 0.010-inch diameter.

40. Making Lots of Dough Rene, the baker, can make dough for 500 chocolate chip cookies in 1 hour.

a. How much dough could Rene make in 2 hours? Explain.

b. How long would it take four bakers working together to make dough for 500 chocolate chip cookies? Explain.

c. How long would it take 3600 bakers working together to make dough for 500 chocolate chip cookies? Explain.

d. If a pianist can play the Minute Waltz in 1 minute, how long will it take a four-person orchestra to play it? Explain.

41. Butte-Silver Bow, Montana, the least crowded U.S. city, has 47 people per square mile.

a. How is this statistic calculated?

b. How many square miles are there per person?

c. How could you compare the crowding in Butte-Silver Bow, Montana, with the crowding in Los Angeles, California?

Making Connections

← C O N N E C T → *You have used ratios to compare and interpret information in real-world situations. As you will see in this lesson, these uses of ratios have important applications to everyday life.*

Taking surveys and using the results to form ratios can provide fascinating information to sociologists about groups of people.

EXPLORE: TRIVIA HUNT

Sociologists study people in society. Doing this activity as a class may provide some unexpected information about the society of you and your classmates.

1. On the chalkboard or an easel, make a chart similar to the one below. Agree on other items of interest and add them to the chart. Take a survey to complete the information.

Characteristics	Yes	No	Total
Are naturally left handed			
Naturally fold arms with right hand on top			
Naturally clap with right hand on top			
Would try skydiving if given the chance (and instruction)			
Would sing in front of the class			
Like to listen to classical music			
Like peanut butter and jelly sandwiches			
Have seen the White House			

2. Individually decide what information you would like to highlight from the class survey. Write ratios to make clear comparisons. Express the ratios as decimals or percentages. Using your ratios, write a short report that gives a profile of your classmates.

1. How does a ratio describe a rate?
2. What is the difference between a ratio and a proportion?
3. What do we mean when we say something is "out of proportion"?
4. How can ratios be used to convert measurements?
5. If *per* means "for each," what does *percent* mean?
6. How does the fraction $\frac{1}{3}$ relate to the ratio $\frac{1}{3}$?

Self-Assessment

Write each of the following as a unit ratio.

1. 3 hours of television viewing for every 30 minutes of homework

2. 3 computers for every 7 students

3. $3.5 million for every 5 miles of roadway

4. Convert the ratio 13 gallons:4 hours to gallons per day.

5. Evaluate the expression $4(c + d)$ for $c = -3$ and $d = 7$. [2-3]

6. These airfares were the lowest fares available in August 1993.

City	Round-Trip Airfare from San Francisco	One-Way Distance from San Francisco (mi)	Cost per Mile of Air Travel
Phoenix, AZ	$74	647	
Chicago, IL	$318	1859	
Anchorage, AK	$412	1998	
Los Angeles, CA	$98	347	

a. Find the average cost per mile for each of the plane trips above.
b. To whom might this information be important? How might it be used?
c. Compare the cost per mile of air travel from San Francisco to Phoenix and from San Francisco to Los Angeles. What conclusions can you draw?

7. The label on a 12-oz box of raisins claims that there are enough raisins to make five dozen cookies. How can you figure out the number of raisins per cookie without counting all of the raisins?

8. Benjamin Harrison, who was President from 1889 to 1893, delivered 140 different speeches in 30 days. How many speeches is this per day?

9. Note Passing President Woodrow Wilson and his wife, Ellen, wrote 1000 love notes to each other in 29 years of marriage. What is the average number of love notes per day? Is this a rate? Explain.

10. Mr. Hospers drove on a 6-hour trip. He traveled 50 miles the first hour, and 60, 50, 30, 55, and 60 miles in each of the last five hours. Find his average rate.

11. Solve the equation $2.5x - 0.5x = 15$. [4-2]

12. In a recent survey, 25% of adults said "Yes" when asked if their standard of living was improving. The ratio was the same for both men and women. The survey reported that 132 women said "Yes," but it didn't say how many people were included in the survey. Was enough information given to find out? Explain.

13. Joanie took a poll of her class, asking, "Would you prefer to own a dog or a cat?" She noted that 14 classmates said "Dog," and 16 said "Cat." Joanie reported that $\frac{7}{8}$, or $87\frac{1}{2}$%, preferred dogs. What numbers did Joanie use to make her ratio? What mistake did she make?

14. Changing Money Each day the exchange rates for money vary. In the past, 1 British pound has had an exchange rate of $1.48.

    a. Show how to use the rate $\frac{1 \text{ pound}}{1.48 \text{ dollars}}$ to find how many pounds you would get for 100 dollars.

    b. Show how to use the rate $\frac{1.48 \text{ dollars}}{1 \text{ pound}}$ to find how many dollars you would get for 100 British pounds.

15. The rectangular prism is 2 cm high, 8 cm wide, and 5 cm deep. [5-3]
    a. Draw a net of the prism. Label all the dimensions.
    b. Find the surface area of the top face of the prism.
    c. Find the volume of the prism.
    d. What is the ratio of the area of the top face of the prism to the volume of the prism?

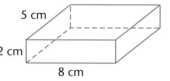

16. Heavy Subjects An elephant weighs 14,000 pounds.
    a. The ratio of the weight of a tractor to the weight of an elephant is 6:5. What does a tractor weigh?
    b. A tour bus weighs 26,600 pounds. What is the ratio, in decimal form, for the weight of an elephant to the weight of a tour bus?
    c. An excavation machine weighs 33,600 pounds. How many elephants is that?
    d. An army tank weighs as much as 8.3 elephants. Write a ratio, as a percentage, comparing the weight of an elephant with the weight of an army tank.
    e. How much does an army tank weigh?

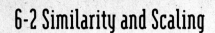

GONE WITH THE WAVES

"Sand Castles. They are the stuff afternoons at the beach are made of. In between riding the waves, searching for seashells and burying each other in the sand, there's that peaceful, creative time when you're drawn toward a point halfway between your blanket and the high-water mark — buckets and shovels in hand."

"Sand Visions" by Kathleen M. Caccavale, Vista USA, Summer, 1989.

Almost every coastal state seems to have a competition for sand-castle architects at some time during the summer. The few hours of low tide find sand engineers working at a feverish pace. And the subjects of their sculptures stretch the imagination. Miniature cities; dragons from mythology; enormous hands, feet, and faces; humorous and distorted objects from everyday life—all erupt into short-lived reality on the wet sand.

Then as the tide turns, the waves begin to take their toll, gradually restoring the beaches to smooth, wet sand. Like lost cities of Atlantis, the amazing structures modeled only hours before vanish without a trace.

1. Why would someone build a sand sculpture, knowing it will be completely washed away by the tide?
2. What are some of the difficulties in building a sand sculpture?
3. How do creators try to make their sculptures lifelike?
4. How can mathematics be involved in making sand sculptures?

Angles and Angle Relationships

← CONNECT → *Angle sizes determine the shape and size of physical objects. You will measure angles and explore angle relationships to prepare for work with similar figures.*

To find ratios in geometric figures, you need to measure the lengths of their sides and the sizes of their angles.

You have used a ruler to measure distances along a line. Units for measuring distances include inches, centimeters, feet, miles, and kilometers. A **protractor** is a tool for measuring angles. Angles are measured in degrees.

The protractor shows that the measure of ∠ABC is 50°.

We write this in a special way:

$m\angle ABC = 50°$.

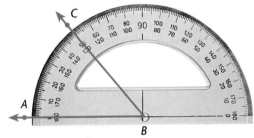

CONSIDER

?

1. How would you describe an angle with the measure of 180°?

2. How do you know that the measure of ∠ABC above is 50° and not 130°? How can you tell whether to use the top markings or the bottom markings on the protractor for the measure of an angle?

3. Suppose each side of the 50° angle above, $\overline{BA}$ and $\overline{BC}$, is increased from $1\frac{1}{2}$ inches to 3 inches long. How does this change the measure of the angle?

TRY IT

Use a protractor to measure each angle.

a.   b.  c.

Notice the 90-degree marks on the protractor. An angle that measures 90° makes a "square corner" and is called a **right angle**.

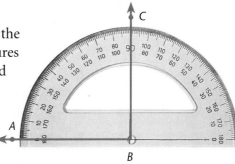

In drawings, right angles are usually marked with a small square.

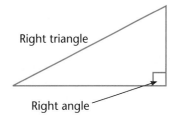

Right triangle

Right angle

A triangle that has a right angle is called a **right triangle.**

EXPLORE: SUM IT UP

MATERIALS

Ruler, Protractor

Use a ruler to draw three different triangles on your paper. Your triangles should be similar in shape to these three triangles.

Make each one large enough so that you can measure the angles with a protractor easily. For each triangle, measure and record the sizes of the three angles.

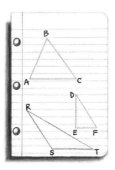

1. What is the sum of the measures of the angles in △ABC? in △DEF? in △RST?
2. What conclusion can you draw about the sum of the measures of the angles of a triangle?

Repeat the process using three different quadrilaterals, shaped similar to these.

3. What is the sum of the measures of the four angles in *ABCD*? in *GHJK*? in *WXYZ*?
4. What conclusion can you draw about the sum of the measures of the angles of a quadrilateral?
5. What relationship can you find that would relate a quadrilateral to two triangles?

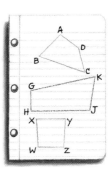

Your measurements in the Explore may have confirmed the following:

> The sum of the measures of the angles of a triangle is 180°.
>
> The sum of the measures of the angles of a quadrilateral is 360°.

EXAMPLE

A sand castle has a tower with a triangular roof shaped like $\triangle ABC$. Find the measure of $\angle B$.

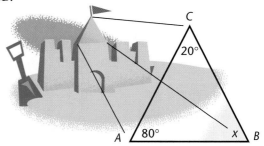

Using the angle-sum relationship above, we can write an equation.

$$m\angle A + m\angle B + m\angle C = 180$$

$$80 + x + 20 = 180 \qquad \text{Substitute values.}$$

$$x + 100 = 180 \qquad \text{Simplify.}$$

$$x = 80 \qquad \text{Subtract 100 from each side.}$$

The measure of $\angle B$ is 80°.

In the Example, notice that both $\angle A$ and $\angle B$ measure 80°. Recall that angles with the same measure are **congruent angles.** In symbols, we write $\angle A \cong \angle B$.

TRY IT

d. Find the measure of $\angle C$.

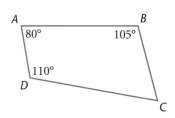

1. How do you position a protractor to measure an angle? How do you read the angle measure?
2. Suppose the three angles of a triangle are congruent. What is the measure of each angle?
3. One angle of a quadrilateral measures 90°. Do the other three angles also each measure 90°? Explain.
4. What could the term *congruent* mean for sides of a triangle? for the whole triangle?

Exercises

CORE

1. Getting Started Find the measure of each angle.

a.

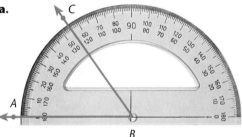

b.

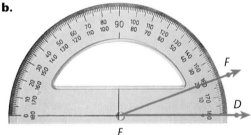

2. The sum of the measures of two angles of a triangle is 165°. What is the measure of the third angle?

Use a protractor to find the measure of each angle.

3.

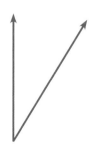

4.

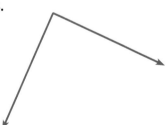

5. One angle of a triangle measures 90°. What is the sum of the measures of the other two angles?

    (a) 90°   (b) 180°   (c) 270°   (d) not here

Find the value of *x* in each figure.

6.

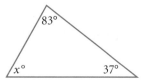

83°
x°
37°

7.

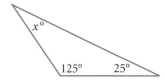

x°
125°   25°

8.

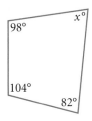

98°
x°
104°
82°

9.

95°   135°
85°   *x*°

10. What is the measure of the angle shown? How do you know?

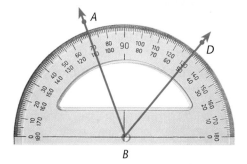

11. Steering in Circles Draw two circles, each with a different radius. Divide each circle into three sectors of different sizes. Then measure the size of each angle in the circles.
   a. What is the sum of the angle measures in your first circle?
   b. What is the sum of the angle measures in your second circle?
   c. What conclusion can you make about the sum of the angles in a circle?

12. A water-ski tow handle makes two angles that are congruent. The third angle is 50°. What are the measures of the congruent angles?

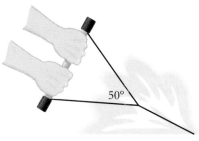

50°

13. What is the angle of rotation clockwise from *C* to *C*′? counterclockwise from *C*′ to *C*?

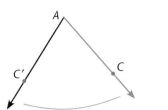

A
C′
C

 *LOOK AHEAD*

14. Find *x*, *y*, and *z*.

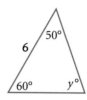

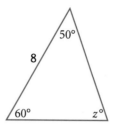

MORE PRACTICE

Find the measure of each angle.

15.

16.

17.

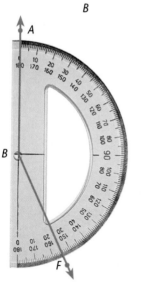

18.

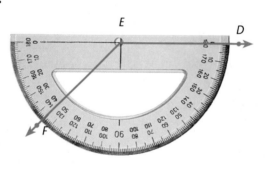

19. The sum of the measures of two angles of a triangle is 65°. What is the measure of the third angle? (Hint: Write and solve an equation that models the situation.)

20. The sum of the measures of three angles of a quadrilateral is 300°. What is the measure of the fourth angle?

Use a protractor to find the measure of each angle.

21.

22.

23.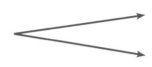

Find the missing angle measures.

24.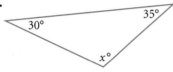

30°

35°

x°

25.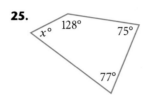

x° 128° 75°

77°

26.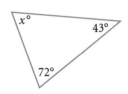

x° 43°

72°

MORE MATH REASONING

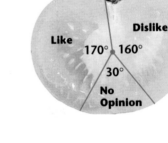

Like 170° Dislike 160°

30°

No Opinion

27. I Say Tomato Harold works as a pollster. In a recent poll, he asked 180 people whether they liked genetically engineered tomatoes. The circle graph shows the results. How many people gave each response? (Hint: Find the sum of the three angles. Then use a proportion.)

Careers

28. The base of a sand castle is a rhombus. All four sides have the same length. Two of the angles measure 100°. What are the measures of the other two angles?

29. In the diagram, $m\angle a = 130°$. Find the measures of the angles marked b, c, and d. A pair of angles positioned across from each other, such as $\angle a$ and $\angle c$ or $\angle d$ and $\angle b$, are called **vertical angles.** What do you think is true about a pair of vertical angles? Explain.

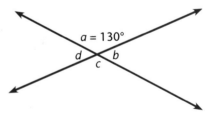

a = 130°

d b

c

30. In a **parallelogram,** any pair of **consecutive angles,** such as $\angle A$ and $\angle B$ or $\angle B$ and $\angle C$, add up to 180°.
   a. In parallelogram $ABCD$, $m\angle A = 70°$. Find the measures of the other three angles.
   b. Describe as many other relationships as you can about the angles of a parallelogram.

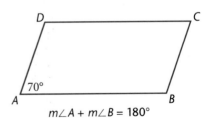

D C

70°

A B

$m\angle A + m\angle B = 180°$

Similar Figures

← CONNECT → *You have seen that the sum of the measures of the angles in a triangle is 180°, and in a quadrilateral it is 360°. You will use angle measures and proportional sides to develop the idea of similar figures.*

Blueprints, maps, and computer chips are all examples of the use of similar figures. The blueprint shows a reduced version of a building; a map is a reduced version of roads and streets; computer chips are photographically reduced versions of large-scale drawings.

These three photographs of the castle are **similar.** One is the original photo, one is an enlargement, and the third is a reduction.

SIMILAR

\'sim-ə-lər adj.

1: having characteristics in common; strictly comparable

2: alike in substance or essentials

CONSIDER

?

1. What features of these three photos are exactly the same?
2. What features are different?

You will need to explore relationships in similar figures so that you can understand the mathematical use of the term *similar* better.

MATERIALS

Centimeter ruler
Protractor
Copy machine

1. Make a large drawing of a triangle. Use a copy machine that has a Reduce/Enlarge control to make an enlargement and a reduction.

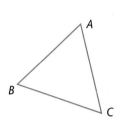

Original triangle

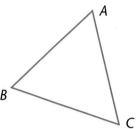

Enlarged triangle

Reduced triangle

2. Use a ruler and a protractor to measure all the sides and angles of the figures on your original drawing and the two copies. Record the angle measurements on the figures. Record the lengths of the sides in the table below.

Triangle Sides	Original Triangle	Enlarged Triangle	Reduced Triangle
$\overline{AB}$			
$\overline{BC}$			
$\overline{CA}$			

3. The three angles at *A* are called **corresponding angles.** The three angles at *B* and the three at *C* are also corresponding angles. Compare all the measures of corresponding angles. What do you find?

4. Find these ratios of **corresponding sides.**

$$\frac{\text{Original length } AB}{\text{Reduced length } AB} \qquad \frac{\text{Original length } BC}{\text{Reduced length } BC} \qquad \frac{\text{Original length } CA}{\text{Reduced length } CA}$$

Find these ratios of corresponding sides using the enlarged lengths.

$$\frac{\text{Original length } AB}{\text{Enlarged length } AB} \qquad \frac{\text{Original length } BC}{\text{Enlarged length } BC} \qquad \frac{\text{Original length } CA}{\text{Enlarged length } CA}$$

5. Write a statement about the ratios of **corresponding sides** of your triangles.

If two polygons can be matched up so that corresponding angles are congruent and corresponding sides have the same ratio, we call them **similar polygons.**

1. Show that the two triangles are similar.

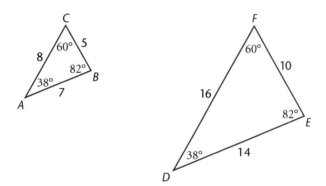

Begin by checking the corresponding angles.

$\angle A$ and $\angle D$ both measure 38°.

$\angle B$ and $\angle E$ both measure 82°.

$\angle C$ and $\angle F$ both measure 60°.

So the corresponding angles are congruent.

Next compare the ratios of corresponding sides.

$\dfrac{AB}{DE} = \dfrac{7}{14}$, or 0.5

$\dfrac{BC}{EF} = \dfrac{5}{10}$, or 0.5

$\dfrac{AC}{DF} = \dfrac{8}{16}$, or 0.5

Corresponding sides have the same ratio. So triangle *ABC* is similar to triangle *DEF.* We write $\triangle ABC \sim \triangle DEF.$

If two triangles are similar, you can use proportions to find the lengths of unknown sides.

2. Sandy Boulevard is a diagonal street that cuts through a rectangular grid of streets. This creates a few triangular lots. How can you find the missing length by using these similar triangles?

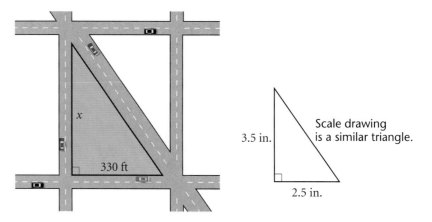

Scale drawing is a similar triangle.

3.5 in.

2.5 in.

$$\frac{2.5}{330} = \frac{3.5}{x}$$ Use corresponding sides to build a proportion.

$2.5 \cdot x = 330(3.5)$ Cross multiply.

$2.5x = 1155$

$x = 462$

The missing length is 462 feet.

You can experiment on enlargements and reductions of figures that have 4, 5, or 6 sides. You will find that all corresponding angles are congruent, and all corresponding sides have equal ratios.

EXAMPLES

3. Pentagon *JKLMN* is an enlargement of pentagon *ABCDE*. Find three ratios of corresponding sides that are equal.

$$\frac{AB}{JK} = \frac{CD}{LM}$$

$$\frac{BC}{KL} = \frac{AE}{JN}$$

$$\frac{CD}{LM} = \frac{ED}{NM}$$

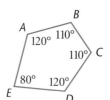
Original pentagon

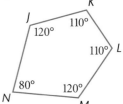
Enlarged pentagon

4. The photo on the right is a reduction of the one on the left. What is the width of the reduced photograph?

3 in.

4 in.

3.2 in.

h

The rectangular photos are similar.

$$\frac{\text{Width of original}}{\text{Width of reduction}} = \frac{\text{Height of original}}{\text{Height of reduction}}$$

$$\frac{4}{3.2} = \frac{3}{h}$$

$$4h = 9.6 \qquad \text{Cross multiply.}$$

$$h = 2.4$$

The reduced photograph is 2.4 inches high.

TRY IT

a. Show that the two triangles are similar.

b. The two figures are similar. Find the missing length.

8

16

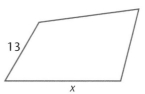

13

x

REFLECT

1. How can you tell if two triangles are similar?

2. Are all squares similar? Are all rectangles similar?

3. If $\triangle ABC$ is similar to both $\triangle DEF$ and to $\triangle PQR$, will $\triangle DEF$ and $\triangle PQR$ be similar? Explain.

Exercises

CORE

1. Getting Started △GHJ and △XYZ are similar. Complete the following statements.
a. ∠H corresponds to ∠___.
b. Side $\overline{HJ}$ corresponds to side ___.

2. These two triangles are similar.
a. What is the measure of ∠Q? How do you know?
b. What is the measure of ∠A?
c. What is the measure of ∠M?

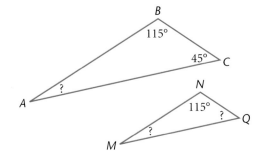

Complete each statement.

3. A ___ is used to measure angles.

4. A figure and its enlargement are ___ figures.

5. Two angles with the same ___ are congruent.

6. Corresponding ___ in similar triangles have the same measure.

7. The ratios of corresponding sides of similar triangles are ___.

8. These two triangles are similar.
a. What ratio of corresponding sides can you find?
b. Use your answer in **8a** to find the length of $\overline{AB}$.
c. What is the length of $\overline{AC}$?

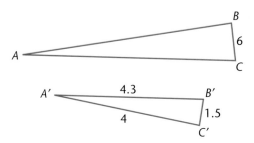

Test to see if each pair of triangles is similar.

9.

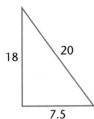 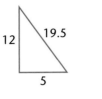

10.

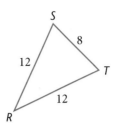 

The following pairs of figures are similar. Find the missing side lengths by using proportions.

11.

12.

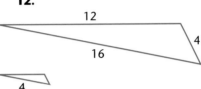

13. Draw two parallelograms with sides that have the same measure, but with different angle measures. Are they similar? Explain.

14. The trapezoids are similar. Find the missing length *b*.

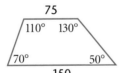 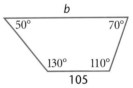

15. The triangles are similar. How do their areas compare?

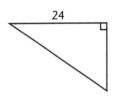

> **Problem-Solving Tip**
>
> Find a missing length first.

16. Find the figures that are similar to △*TUV*. Justify your answer.

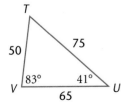 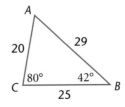 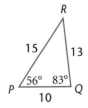

17. Crystal Clear A salt crystal cube that has been

magnified 240 times has edge lengths of 9 mm.

a. What is the length of an edge of the unmagnified
salt crystal?

b. What is its approximate volume? How did you
decide?

 LOOK BACK

Solve each equation. [4-2, 6-1]

18. $12t = 60$ **19.** $49 = 98j$ **20.** $\frac{2}{3} = \frac{8}{x}$ **21.** $\frac{m}{10} = \frac{30}{15}$

22. An air cleaner is purchased for a 20-ft by 16-ft room that is 8 ft high. [5-3]

a. What is the volume of the room?

b. What is the surface area of the room?

23. The legend on a map of New York State says that 1 inch = 100 miles. If New
York City and Albany are 1.5 inches apart on the map, what is the actual
distance between them? [6-1]

24. To make a scale drawing of this rectangle so
the sides are $\frac{1}{3}$ as long, what dimensions would
you use? [6-1]

27

9

MORE PRACTICE

25. $\triangle CDE$ and $\triangle FGH$ are similar. Complete
the following statements.

a. $\angle H$ corresponds to $\angle$____.

b. Side $\overline{FG}$ corresponds to side ____.

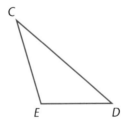

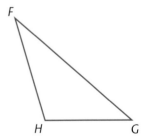

26. These two parallelograms are similar.

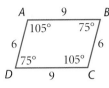
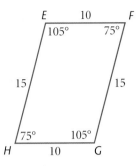

  a. Tell which pairs of angles are corresponding angles.

  b. What is the ratio of corresponding sides?

  c. Why are the parallelograms similar?

Show that the figures are similar.

27.

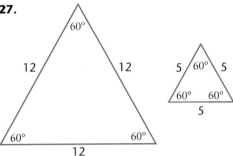

28.

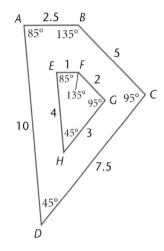

29. Draw two pictures of a hat. Draw them so that you could say they are similar according to a dictionary definition of *similar,* but so they are not similar according to the mathematical definition.

30. Draw two rectangles that are similar and two that are not similar.

31. Shedding Some Light Suzuki is 5 feet 6 inches tall. Her shadow from a street light is 10 feet long when she is 20 feet away from the street light.

  a. What do the marked symbols mean at ∠*LJK* and ∠*MNK*?

  b. Draw each of these two triangles separately, and show the measures of all sides and angles you know.

  c. Why is △*LJK* similar to △*MNK*?

  d. Find the height (*h*) of the street lamp.

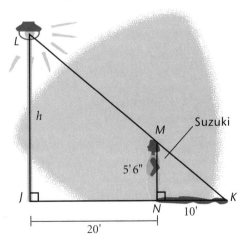

Test to see if each pair of triangles is similar.

32.

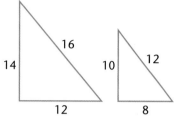

33.

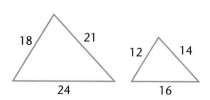

The following pairs of figures are similar. Find the missing side lengths by using proportions.

34.

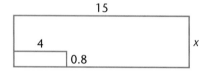

35.

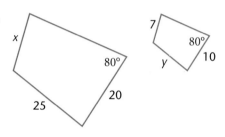

MORE MATH REASONING

36. Could these triangles be similar? Explain.

37. Could the trapezoid and parallelogram be similar? Explain your reasoning.

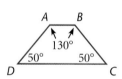 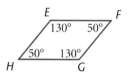

38. A 5-in. by 3-in. photograph is enlarged by 25%. Find the dimensions of the enlargement.

39. Explain how similarity is helpful to these professionals.
   a. architect   **b.** clothing designer   **c.** doctor   **d.** advertising designer

40. Circle 'Round
   a. Are these two circles similar? Describe your thinking.
   b. When will two circles be similar? Explain.
   c. What ratio would you use to compare two circles? Why?

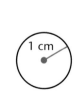 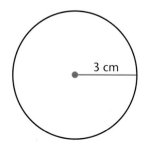

Blow It Up and Scale It Down

← CONNECT → *You've learned how to work with ratios and proportions. You also know some properties of similar polygons. Now you can combine these two ideas to make scale models and scale drawings.*

Builders of sand sculptures might make miniature castles, or they might make giant monsters. For realism, these sculptures should be similar to the original objects. The miniature castle is built on a small scale, and the monster is built on a large one.

3 in.

|← 5 in. →|
Actual critter

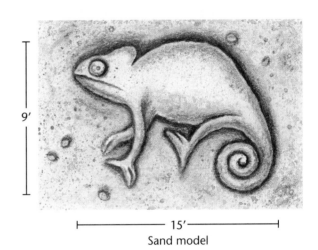

9′

|← 15′ →|
Sand model

These figures are similar. Notice how corresponding sides compare. The **scale factor,** or **scale,** is the ratio of corresponding lengths.

$$\frac{\text{Enlarged length}}{\text{Original length}} = \frac{15 \text{ ft}}{5 \text{ in.}} = \frac{180 \text{ in.}}{5 \text{ in.}} = \frac{36}{1}$$

The enlargement has a scale factor of 36 to 1, or 36:1.

If the denominator of the scale factor is 1, we may omit writing it. So if an enlargement has a scale factor of 36:1, we say that its scale is 36. That is, its linear measurements are 36 times those of the original.

Honey, I Shrunk the Kids was a popular movie that "scaled down" the problem of raising children.

Imagine yourself as one of the young stars in the movie. You need to shrink yourself.

1. What scale factor will you use? Why?
2. How can you use your scale factor, along with your own measurements, to decide the measurements of your shrunken self?
3. You need to give measurement information to the costume department. Copy the chart. Complete it by taking measurements and doing the necessary calculations.

	"Real Self" Measurements	"Shrunken Self" Measurements
Height		
Arm length		
Thumb length		
Wrist circumference		
Head circumference		
Knee-to-ankle length		

4. What scale factor would you use if you wanted to be small enough to hide in a cookie jar?
5. What scale factor would you use if you wanted to be small enough to take a shower in the kitchen sink, but big enough not to fall down the drain?
6. Discuss the effect of different scale factors on your "movie." Write some conclusions to share with your class.

CONSIDER

1. A model airplane has a scale factor of 1:50. What does this mean?
2. Can an object have more than one scale factor?

a. Rectangle *QRST* is a reduction of rectangle *ABCD*. What is the scale factor?

A ——— 125 cm ——— B

75 cm

D ——————— C

Q ——— 100 cm ——— R

60 cm

T ——————— S

b. What is the scale factor for the small rectangle below?

2.5 in.

1 in.

0.5 in.   1.25 in.

WHAT DO **YOU** THINK?

A company in South Dakota wants to design a model of Mt. Rushmore to sell as a souvenir. They know that Lincoln's head measures 66 feet tall. If the scale factor is 1:120, how tall will the model of Lincoln's head be?

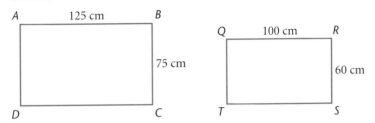

Ben thinks ...

I can multiply by the scale factor.

The measurements of the model are $\frac{1}{120}$ the measurements of the original.

$\frac{1}{120} \cdot 66 = 0.55$

The model of Lincoln's head will be 0.55 feet high.

Elena thinks ...

I can set up a proportion.

$\frac{\text{Model height (ft)}}{\text{Real height (ft)}} = \frac{1}{120}$

$\frac{m}{66} = \frac{1}{120}$

$120m = 66$ Cross multiply.

$m = \frac{66}{120}$, or 0.55   Divide both sides by 120.

The model of Lincoln's head will be 0.55 feet high.

On a map, a *legend* may describe the scale. Scale may be described with pictures, or words, or both.

Hawaii

0 ——— 100 mi
0   100 km

Snake River Idaho Falls Jackson Lake

1 inch equals about 80 miles.

Tanners Ridge

10860   10360

0   1   2 miles

Contour interval 100 feet. Elevation with respect to sea level.

Sometimes you will see scale factors given in forms such as 1 in. = 3 ft, 1 in. = 200 mi, or 3 cm = 150 km.

EXAMPLE

The scale on a map of Ohio says 1 inch equals 25 miles. The distance on the map from Toledo to Cincinnati is approximately 9 inches. About how many miles apart are these two cities?

Set up a proportion using two ratios in the form:

$$\frac{\text{Distance in inches}}{\text{Distance in miles}} : \frac{1 \text{ inch}}{25 \text{ miles}} = \frac{9 \text{ inches}}{x \text{ miles}}.$$

$1 \cdot x = 25 \cdot 9$

$x = 225$

It is about 225 miles from Toledo to Cincinnati.

Lake Erie

Toledo

★ Columbus

Cincinnati

REFLECT

1. What does it mean if a blueprint of a house is drawn on a scale of $\frac{1}{2}$ in. = 1 ft? Would this be a good scale factor for an architect to use? Explain.
2. Suppose you build a model with a scale factor of $\frac{2}{5}$. Is the model larger or smaller than the original?
3. What does a scale factor of 0.4 mean? What does a scale factor of 1 mean?
4. A map legend says 1 inch = 10 miles. How would you use this information?

Exercises

CORE

1. **Getting Started** $\triangle ABC \sim \triangle DEF$ with measurements given in centimeters.
   a. What is the ratio of AB to DE?
   b. What is the ratio of BC to EF?
   c. What is the ratio of AC to DF?
   d. What is the scale factor?
   e. What is the value of x?

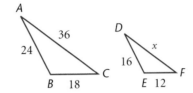

2. Rectangle $QRST$ is a reduction of rectangle $ABCD$. What is the scale factor?

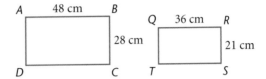

3. Solve each proportion.

   a. $\dfrac{2}{3} = \dfrac{5}{x}$ **b.** $\dfrac{6}{14} = \dfrac{3}{y}$ **c.** $\dfrac{z}{4} = \dfrac{21}{7}$ **d.** $\dfrac{p}{9} = \dfrac{2}{4.5}$

4. Choose any one of the proportions in Exercise 3. Write a related problem using the concept of scale factor.

5. A toy train is a $\dfrac{1}{50}$ scale model. How long should a model of a 50-foot coal car be?

6. A doll house is made to $\dfrac{1}{15}$ scale, and the original house is 20 feet tall. How tall is the doll house?

7. A rectangle has a width of 10 cm. Another rectangle is drawn using a scale factor of 2:5. What is the width of the second rectangle?

8. How can you tell if a scale factor will give a larger figure or a smaller figure?

9. Make a scale drawing of the figure using
   a. a scale factor of 2.
   b. a scale factor of $\dfrac{1}{4}$.

10. Draw a square. Then draw a square with a scale factor of 2:1. How do their areas compare?

11. Draw a cube. Then draw a cube with a scale factor of 2:1. How do their volumes compare?

12. The White House is 750 ft long. Suppose you want to make a model to sell as a souvenir. What scale factor would be appropriate?

(a) 1:1500   (b) 1:3   (c) 1:750   (d) 1:250   (e) 1:100

13. Suppose you had many models of the same statue. The scale factors of the models are 4, $\frac{3}{4}$, $\frac{5}{2}$, $\frac{1}{2}$, $\frac{1}{3}$, and $\frac{7}{6}$. Arrange the models in order from smallest to largest. (Hint: Write equivalent ratios with the same denominator.)

14. a. Describe a situation in which you would want to use a very large scale factor.

    b. Describe a situation in which you would want to use a very small scale factor.

Choose an appropriate scale factor. Describe your reasoning.

15. a drawing showing the elevation of Mexico City at 7340 ft; La Paz, Bolivia, at 12,001 ft; and Santiago, Chile, at 1706 ft

16. a map of your city

17. a drawing of a ladybug

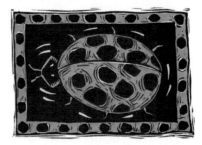

18. a drawing of the engine of a car

19. Describe the difference between a scale of 1 inch = 1 foot and a scale factor of 1.

20. Splitting Hairs Microchips are made by first
drawing them on a large scale, and then reducing
them by using photography. The chips are then
printed with a metallic ink. If you put 250
microchip lines next to each other, they would be
about as wide as one strand of hair. If a microchip
is to be 1 centimeter wide and an engineer wants to
draw it 2 meters wide, what is the scale factor?
(Hint: How many centimeters make one meter?)

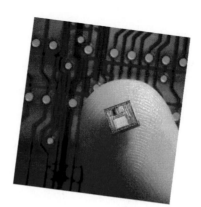

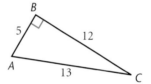

LOOK AHEAD

Use *is less than*, *is greater than*, or *is equal to* between each pair of values.

21. $1^2 + 2^2$ ____ 3^2

22. $3^2 + 4^2$ ____ 5^2

23. $6^2 + 7^2$ ____ 8^2

24. $10^2 + 10^2$ ____ 15^2

25. $12^2 + 5^2$ ____ 13^2

26. $\sqrt{12^2 + 5^2}$ ____ $\sqrt{13^2}$

27. Draw sketches of two triangles similar to $\triangle ABC$ and mark
the measurements.

MORE PRACTICE

Solve each proportion.

28. $\dfrac{1}{6} = \dfrac{5}{z}$

29. $\dfrac{P}{8} = \dfrac{3}{4}$

30. $\dfrac{2}{w} = \dfrac{16}{40}$

31. $\dfrac{k}{3} = \dfrac{28}{12}$

32. Rectangle *QRST* is a reduction of rectangle *ABCD*. What is the scale factor?

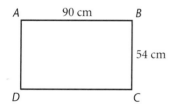

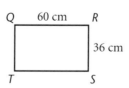

33. Triangle *ADE* is an enlargement of triangle *ABC*. What is the
scale factor?

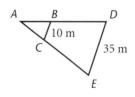

Use the given scale factor to find the missing information.

34. scale factor = 1:20, length 5 in., actual length _____

35. scale factor = 1:6, length 5 cm, actual length _____

36. scale factor = 12:1, length 12 ft, actual length _____

> **Problem Solving Tip**
>
> Draw a diagram showing relative sizes.

37. Chug, Chug, Chug A caboose on a toy train is 8 inches long. How big is a life-sized caboose if the toy is a scale model with 1 inch = 3 feet?

 38. A map has a scale of 2 cm = 10 km. The distance between Medford, Oregon, and Ashland, Oregon, is 19.2 km. How far apart are the cities on the map?

39. A model car is built on a scale of $\frac{1}{12}$.
   a. If you had the car and wanted to build the scale model, what would be the scale factor?
   b. If you started with the model and wanted to build the car, what would be the scale factor?

MORE MATH REASONING

 40. A blueprint has a scale of 1 inch = 1 foot. A room is drawn with dimensions 24 inches by 20 inches. What are the dimensions of the actual room?

41. A museum is building a scale model of the Great Pyramid of Giza, which is $481\frac{2}{3}$ feet tall and $775\frac{3}{4}$ feet along an edge of the square base.

   a. Select a scale factor so that it can fit exactly on an outdoor square plot that is 30 feet on a side.
   b. What will be the height of the pyramid model?

42. Cat Scan Data may be displayed graphically using scaled pictures.
   a. Are the cats scaled horizontally as well as vertically?
   b. Is each cat similar to the first? Explain.
   c. What data could the graph represent?

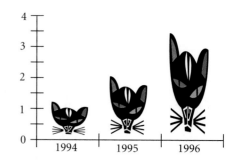

6-2
PART D
The Pythagorean Theorem

← C O N N E C T → *You have seen that similar triangles are very useful in practical ways. Now you will see that right triangles that are similar have some special properties that make them valuable in finding unmeasurable dimensions.*

Right triangles have special names for their sides.

The two sides of the right angle are called **legs.**

The long side opposite the right angle is called the **hypotenuse.**

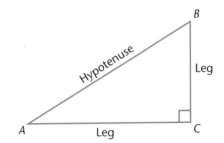

EXPLORE: FAIR AND SQUARE

1. On graph paper draw a right triangle with legs of 3 units and 4 units. Leave room to draw a square on each leg as shown.

2. Explain why it is not easy to tell the length of the hypotenuse by counting squares on the graph paper.

3. Cut a 3-by-3 square and a 4-by-4 square apart into individual squares.

4. Can you arrange these squares into a large square along the third side of the triangle? If so, what length do you find for the hypotenuse?

5. Repeat for triangles with legs of 5 and 12.

6. What relationship can you find among the squares that you have drawn for each triangle?

7. What are the values of 3^2, 4^2, and 5^2? How are they related? What are the values of 5^2, 12^2, and 13^2? How are they related?

MATERIALS

Graph paper, Scissors, Ruler
Several 3-by-3, 4-by-4, 5-by-5, and 12-by-12 graph paper squares

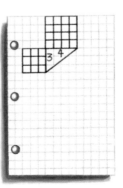

PART D • THE PYTHAGOREAN THEOREM **479**

You have been working with one of the most famous discoveries in mathematics. Ancient Egyptians used ropes with knots spaced at three, four, and five units to make square corners on their fields after the Nile flooded each spring.

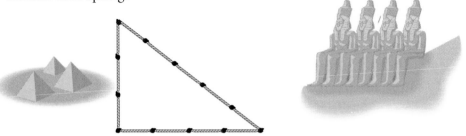

This discovery is called the Pythagorean Theorem after the Greek mathematician, Pythagoras.

THE PYTHAGOREAN THEOREM

If a and b are lengths of the legs of a right triangle, and c is the length of the hypotenuse, then

$$a^2 + b^2 = c^2.$$

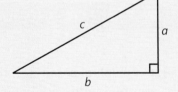

This relationship is true for all right triangles, and only for right triangles.

You can use this relationship in two ways:

• to see if a triangle is a right triangle, or
• to find the length of a side of a right triangle, if the other two lengths are known.

EXAMPLES

1. A triangle has sides of 6, 7, and 10. Is it a right triangle?

Let $a = 6$, $b = 7$, and the hypotenuse $c = 10$.
$$a^2 + b^2 \stackrel{?}{=} c^2$$
$$6^2 + 7^2 \stackrel{?}{=} 10^2$$
$$36 + 49 \stackrel{?}{=} 100$$
$$85 \neq 100$$

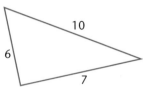

The triangle is not a right triangle.

2. The bottom of a cereal box is 2 in. by 8 in. A toy manufacturer wants to be sure that a toy will not end up stuck in the bottom of the box. How long is the diagonal of the box?

We want to find the length of the hypotenuse. Let the legs be *a* and *b*, so $a = 2$ and $b = 8$.

$$a^2 + b^2 = c^2$$
$$2^2 + 8^2 = c^2$$
$$4 + 64 = c^2$$
$$c = \sqrt{68}$$
$$c \approx 8.25$$

The triangle is a right triangle, so use the Pythagorean Theorem.

Use the square root key on a calculator to find the square root of 68.

The diagonal of the box is about 8.25 inches long.

CONSIDER
?

1. How can the toy manufacturer use the information above?

TRY IT

a. Find the length of the hypotenuse of this triangle.

Two right triangles are used often in problem solving.

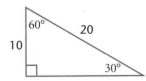

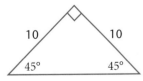

In any 30°-60°-90° triangle, the short leg is half the length of the hypotenuse.

In any 45°-45°-90° triangle, the two legs are the same length.

3. Felice is flying a kite and uses all 200 feet of string. Neil, who is watching, estimates that the string makes a 30° angle with Felice's hand holding the kite string. How high is the kite above her hand?

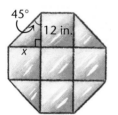

Kite

60°

200 ft of string

x ft

30°

The kite diagram makes a 30°-60°-90° triangle.

$x = \frac{1}{2}(200)$ The short side is half the hypotenuse.

$x = 100$

The kite is 100 feet above Felice's hand.

In the example above, it would be difficult to measure the height of the kite directly. Using what we know about triangles and their relationships lets us find these distances by mathematics. This is often called *indirect measurement*.

TRY IT

b. A window is made up of panes, as shown. What is the length of x?

45°

12 in.

x

REFLECT

1. How can triangle information be used to find distances that you cannot measure directly?

2. A phrase such as "directly overhead" implies that there is a right angle in a situation. What other words or situations imply right angles are present?

3. How do the side lengths of a triangle help you determine if the triangle contains a right angle?

4. In a right triangle, how can you find the length of a leg if you know the lengths of the other leg and the hypotenuse?

5. If a right triangle contains a 30° angle, what else do you know about the triangle?

6. If a right triangle contains a 45° angle, what else do you know about the triangle?

Exercises

CORE

1. Getting Started Which side is the hypotenuse of △*RST*?
 (a) $\overline{RS}$
 (b) $\overline{ST}$
 (c) $\overline{RT}$

2. State the Pythagorean Theorem for this right triangle.

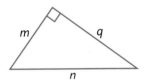

Use the Pythagorean Theorem to decide whether these triangles are right triangles.

3.

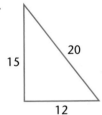

4.

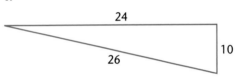

The lengths of the legs of a right triangle are *a* and *b*. The length of the hypotenuse is *c*. Find the missing length in each of the following.

5. $a = 4$, $b = 5$, $c = ?$ **6.** $a = 20$, $b = 25$, $c = ?$

7. $a = 7$, $b = ?$, $c = 25$ **8.** $a = ?$, $b = 10$, $c = 14.14$

9. Short Cut A city park has a right angle at each corner. How long is the path that cuts from corner to corner?

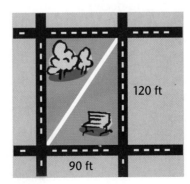

120 ft

90 ft

10. A diagonal street runs through a grid of square blocks.

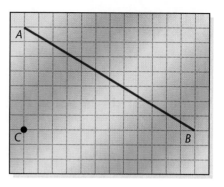

   a. Using the rectangular street system, about how many blocks is it from *A* to *B*?

   b. The diagonal street from *A* to *B* is equivalent to how many regular blocks?

   c. As a shortcut, about how many blocks are saved by taking the diagonal street?

Find the missing parts of these triangles.

11.

12.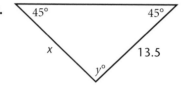

13. Raise the Roof Each hip rafter shown rises to the top of the roof at a 30° angle. How long is a hip rafter?

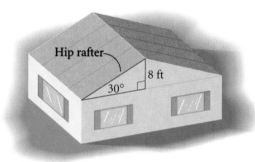

14. Kiel measured the sides of a large triangular piece of concrete and found lengths of 84 inches, 67 inches, and 107 inches. Is the triangle a right triangle? Explain.

 ## *LOOK BACK*

15. Write each ratio as a rate in decimal form. [6-1]

   a. $\dfrac{3 \text{ km}}{8 \text{ min}}$

   b. $\dfrac{1880 \text{ words}}{20 \text{ min}}$

   c. $\dfrac{22 \text{ mi}}{4 \text{ hr}}$

16. Use the circle shown. [5-2]

   a. What is the radius?
   b. What is the diameter?
   c. Find the circumference of the circle.
   d. Find the area of the circle.

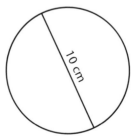

17. The formula for the area of an ellipse, in square units, is $A = \pi ab$. Find the area of an ellipse if $a = 12$ in. and $b = 6$ in. [2-3, 5-2]

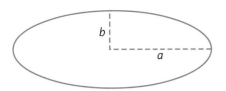

18. Add or subtract. [2-3]

  a. $-5 - 2 - 7$ **b.** $-5 - (2 - 7)$ **c.** $-5 - 2(-7)$

MORE PRACTICE

Use the Pythagorean Theorem to decide whether these triangles are right triangles.

19.

20.

21.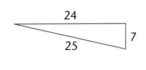

22.

The lengths of the legs of a right triangle are a and b. The length of the hypotenuse is c. Find the missing length in each of the following.

23. $a = 3, b = 5, c = ?$ **24.** $a = 30, b = 40, c = ?$ **25.** $a = 7, b = 20, c = ?$

26. $a = 7, b = ?, c = 25$ **27.** $a = ?, b = 12, c = 12.5$ **28.** $a = 10, b = ?, c = 17.32$

29. In a 30°-60°-90° triangle, the short leg is $\frac{1}{2}$ the length of

  (a) the long leg   (b) the hypotenuse
  (c) the corresponding side   (d) not here

30. Complete the following statement. In a 45°-45°-90° triangle, the length of the hypotenuse is

  (a) unknown   (b) equal to one of the legs
  (c) one-half of one of the legs   (d) not here

31. Refer to $\triangle QRS$.

  a. Find the length of $\overline{QS}$ using what you know about 30°-60°-90° triangles.
  b. Use the result in **31a** to find the length of $\overline{QR}$ by the Pythagorean Theorem.

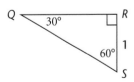

32. Refer to △*GHQ*.

    a. Find the length of $\overline{HQ}$ using what you know about 45°-45°-90° triangles.

    b. Use the result in **32a** to find the length of $\overline{GQ}$ by the Pythagorean Theorem.

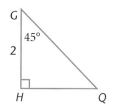

MORE MATH REASONING

33. This figure shows two 45°-45°-90° triangles placed side by side along the hypotenuse.

    a. What are the measures of the angles of quadrilateral *ABCD*?

    b. If the length of $\overline{AB}$ is 10, what are the measures of the other three sides?

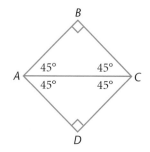

34. Water Log Christine swims 1 mile of laps at the city pool. She usually swims straight from one end to the other.

Since no one else is at the pool, she decides to swim from corner to corner to reduce her number of laps.

    a. How many feet does she travel from a corner to the opposite corner and back?

    b. How many times will she need to swim this distance in order to swim 1 mile?

    c. How many laps would it take to swim a mile going straight from one end to the other?

    d. Did she reduce her number of laps? Explain.

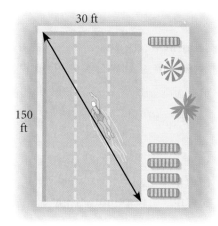

35. More Water A surveyor found the width of the Rancho River without crossing it. She made the sightings shown. How wide is the river?

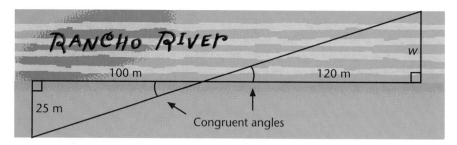

Making Connections

← CONNECT → *Using what you have learned about similarity and scale factors, you now can make models or "blow-ups" of favorite objects or pictures.*

Bob and Pat Reed's book, *Sand Creatures and Castles: How to Build Them,* suggests that to make a sculpture that looks real, you should plan and size carefully.

EXPLORE: SCALING THE BUG

Designers and cartoonists need ways to change sizes of drawings while still keeping the right proportions. For a humorous or distorted effect, making a drawing sometimes works better than using copy machines.

You may want to work with a partner to make an enlargement of this cartoon drawing.

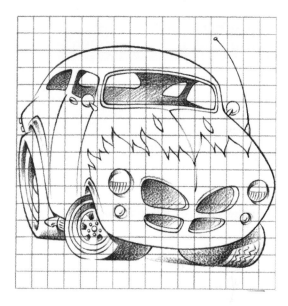

TO MAKE YOUR ENLARGEMENT:

A. Make a grid that is 16 squares by 16 squares, like the one shown, but make the squares larger.

B. In each square, draw the part of the cartoon picture that is contained in the matching square of the grid.

Using your enlargement, consider these questions and write a summary of your observations.

1. How would your enlargement be different if you used rectangles instead of squares?

2. How can you figure out the scale factor for your enlargement? Find the scale factor.

3. Measure some lengths and angles on the original cartoon and on your enlargement. Compare the results. What relationships do you see?

4. Are the two drawings really similar? Explain.

REFLECT

1. How are ratios used in architecture and in map-making?
2. Why must angle measures remain the same for similar polygons?
3. How does everyday use of the word *similar* differ from its use in mathematics?
4. If you increase the lengths of the sides of an angle, does it change the angle measure? Explain.
5. Describe how shadow measurements and similar triangles might be used to find the height of something like a tall tree or a tall monument indirectly.

Self-Assessment

1. What is the measure of the angle shown?

Find the value of *x* in each figure.

2.

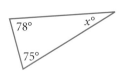

3.

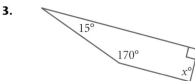

4. Briefly explain how to reproduce a drawing using a scale factor of 2.

5. A reproduction has a scale factor of $\frac{1}{3}$. How is it related to the original?

6. Choose the best comparison. Triangle: similar triangle as
   (a) mother: son   (b) enlargement: photo
   (c) twin: twin   (d) square: rectangle

7. What is the height of the flagpole?

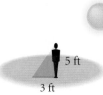

Use the Pythagorean Theorem to find the third side of each triangle.

8.

9.

10. Is a triangle with side lengths 6 cm, 10 cm, and 12 cm a right triangle? Why or why not?

11. Give the coordinates of each point. [1-1]
 a. *M*
 b. *P*
 c. *T*
 d. *Q*

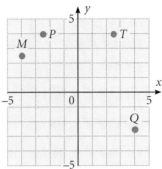

12. Scaling New Heights
 a. What scale factor is needed to make the second rectangle from the first?
 b. What scale factor is needed to make the first rectangle from the second?

13. Find the perimeter and area of the figure. All measurements are given in meters.

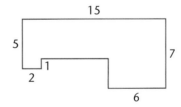

14. A yield sign is cut from a piece of metal in the shape of an **equilateral** triangle with sides measuring 27 in. (All three sides of an equilateral triangle have the same length.)
 a. What is the measure of each angle? (Hint: All three angles are congruent.)
 b. What is the height? (Hint: Use the Pythagorean Theorem.)
 c. Find the perimeter and area of the sign.

15. A 35-oz jar of nutmeg contains Mexican nutmeg and Portuguese nutmeg in the ratio 3:2. How many ounces of each type of nutmeg are in the jar? [6-1]

16. Dream House The architect claims that the floor plan is drawn to scale.

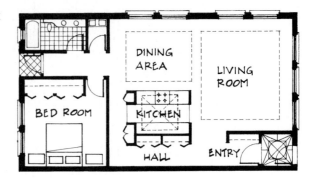

a. What scale might the architect have used? Explain your reasoning.

b. Find the actual length and width of the house using your scale factor.

17. Make a rough sketch of your home state. Choose at least five cities. Select an appropriate scale. Then place the cities on your map so that the map distances are proportional to the actual distances.

18. A telephone pole casts a 5-ft shadow at the same time that a nearby stop sign casts a 2-ft shadow. If the stop sign is 8 ft tall, how tall is the telephone pole?

> **Problem-Solving Tip**
>
> Draw a diagram.

19. How do similar polygons compare with each other?

20. You know that the sum of the measures of the angles of a triangle is 180°. How could you use this fact to find the sum of the measures of the angles of an octagon (8 sides)? What additional information would you be able to find out if the octagon is regular? Name a common object that was designed as a regular octagon.

21. Horsing Around A billboard can be made by taking a photo, dividing it into parts, and enlarging each part. What is the scale of the drawing shown? (Hint: Find the size of the billboard.)

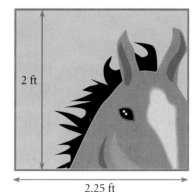

6-3 Trigonometry

MEASURING THE UNMEASURABLE

Hey Diddle Diddle,
The cat and the fiddle
The cow jumped over the moon
The little dog laughed to see such sport.

And the dish ran away with the spoon.

A nonsense rhyme—cats don't fiddle, dogs don't laugh, and dishes certainly don't run around with spoons. But that cow …

Lying in the grass, looking at the stars on a summer night, we wonder: How far away is the moon? What's it like up there? We ask the same questions that people have been asking for thousands of years. One of the first sciences was astronomy, the study of the stars.

More than 2000 years ago, Hipparchus, a Greek astronomer, drew the first accurate star map. Working without a telescope, he had only his eyes and his mathematics. Incredibly, he accurately recorded the positions of more than a thousand of the brighter stars. In developing his star map, Hipparchus devised mathematical methods of indirect measurement. The methods he came up with are the beginnings of trigonometry. Some mathematicians believe that because of Hipparchus, we use 360 degrees to divide a circle today.

1. What are some distances that are too great to measure by direct means?
2. How could similar triangles help determine "unmeasurable" distances?
3. Hipparchus used 360 degrees for a circle. Why might he have chosen 360 as a convenient number?

491

← C O N N E C T → *You have worked with similar triangles, right triangles, and the Pythagorean Theorem to solve some problems. Now you will see how some special keys on your calculator can make problem solving easier.*

On your calculator you will see some keys you may have never used.

First you will explore how to use these keys, and then you will see how to use them in solving problems.

EXPLORE: KEYS TO TRIGONOMETRY

Let's experiment with the keys labeled SIN, COS, and TAN.

1. Be sure your calculator is in degree mode. The AC button (all clear) should do this for you.

Enter a number between 0 and 90 and press one of the three keys.

For example, if you press

45 SIN,

the value 0.7071 will appear in the display. (The order for pressing the keys and the number of decimal places that appear in the display may depend on the calculator.)

Recall the 30°-60°-90° triangle. Press 30 SIN.

2. From your knowledge of 30°-60°-90° triangles, what do you think this number represents?

3. Describe how you might get this number using the sides of the triangle shown and their relationship to the 30° angle.

MATERIALS

Scientific calculator

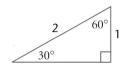

4. Press 60 [COS]. What do you think this number represents?

5. Describe how to get this number using the sides of the triangle shown above and their relationship to the 60° angle.

6. Use the Pythagorean Theorem to find the third side length in the triangle.

7. Press 30 [TAN]. Use your calculator and the numbers you see in the triangle to find how to get this number.

The three calculator keys [SIN], [COS], and [TAN] are used in **trigonometry.** Trigonometry is the study of right triangles and their application to problem solving. Early mathematicians studied the three common **trigonometric ratios:** sine, cosine, and tangent.

When you enter 30 [SIN], the display shows (**0.5000**). We say, "the sine of 30 degrees is 0.5" and we write, "sin 30° = 0.5."

TRY IT

Find these values using your calculator.

a. cos 43°   **b.** tan 79°   **c.** sin 10°

Adjacent means "next to."

In a right triangle, the length of the **leg opposite** ∠A divided by the length of the **leg adjacent** to ∠A is called the **tangent ratio** for ∠A.

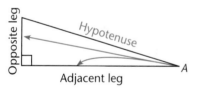

$$\tan A = \frac{\text{Opposite}}{\text{Adjacent}}$$

EXAMPLE

1. Find the ratio $\frac{\text{opposite}}{\text{adjacent}}$ and compare it with tan 76° that you find on your calculator.

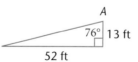

The leg opposite ∠A measures 52 ft, and the leg adjacent to ∠A measures 13 ft.

$$\frac{52}{13} = 4$$

On the calculator, tan 76° = 4.0108.
The difference is a "rounding error" and is acceptable.

d. Use the information in the figure to find tan 35°. Then find tan 35° using your calculator and compare.

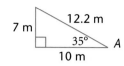

7 m
12.2 m
35° A
10 m

Using the calculator to display trigonometric ratios gives us a way to find missing lengths of sides when actual measurements are difficult or impossible.

EXAMPLES

2. Find x.

From the calculator, tan 32° = 0.6249.

In the figure, the tangent ratio for ∠B is

$$\frac{\text{opposite}}{\text{adjacent}} = \frac{x}{48}.$$

$$0.6249 = \frac{x}{48} \qquad \text{Substitute tan 32°.}$$

$$48(0.6249) = x$$

$$29.9952 = x$$

$$x \approx 30$$

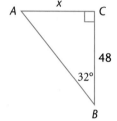

A   x   C

48

32°

B

3. On a vacation trip in California, Todd saw the world's tallest living tree. He stood 435 feet away from the tree and sighted an angle of 40° to the top of the tree. Then he made this drawing. How did he find the height of the tree?

Todd sees that he can use the proportion

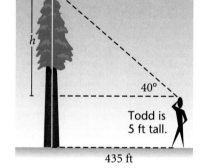

Todd is 5 ft tall.

435 ft

$$\frac{\text{opposite}}{\text{adjacent}} = \frac{h}{435}. \qquad \text{This is the tangent ratio.}$$

His calculator shows that tan 40° = 0.8391. Todd writes:

$$0.8391 = \frac{h}{435}.$$

$$435(0.8391) = h \qquad \text{Multiply both sides by 435.}$$

$$365.0085 = h$$

$$h \approx 365 \qquad \text{"Aaah, but I'm not done!"}$$

Todd adds 5 feet for his own height. He finds that the redwood tree is about 370 feet tall.

CONSIDER

1. How can you find the measure of an angle from your eye to the top of a building or a tree?

REFLECT

1. Why is the tangent a ratio? Explain.

2. What does it mean when a tangent value is greater than 1?

3. What situations can you think of where the tangent can help find a missing length?

4. In Example 3, what is the relationship between the triangle formed by Todd sighting to the top of the tree and the scale drawing he makes of the situation?

Exercises

CORE

1. Getting Started Find these values using your calculator.

   a. sin 37°   **b.** cos 37°

   c. tan 37°   **d.** sin 85°

   e. cos 85°   **f.** tan 85°

Find the tangent ratio, $\frac{\text{opposite}}{\text{adjacent}}$, for angle A.

2. 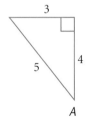   **3.**    **4.**

5. Which side of the triangle is not used in finding the tangent ratio?

   (a) adjacent leg   (b) opposite leg

   (c) hypotenuse   (d) not here

6. First see if you can guess the measure of an angle whose sine is approximately 0.5736. Then check your guess with a calculator.

7. Find the tangent ratio
  a. for $\angle D$.
  b. for $\angle E$.

8. Find the tangent ratio
  a. for $\angle S$.
  b. for $\angle T$.

9. Satellite's View The Caspian Sea, bordered by Iran, is the world's longest lake. Find its length (ℓ) using these measurements made from a satellite 53 miles directly above one end of the lake.

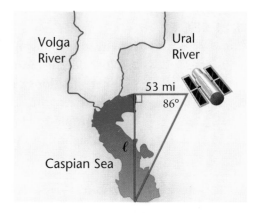

10. An engineer sights to the top of the building at an angle of 73° to find its height. What is the height of the building?

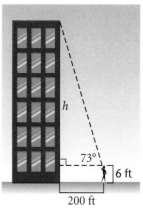

11. How deep is the well?

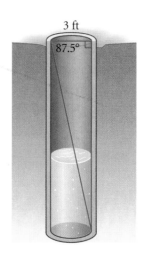

12. Mystery Measure In Sir Arthur Conan Doyle's *The Musgrave Ritual,* Reginald Musgrave said he had figured out, by using "an exercise in trigonometry," that an elm tree was 64 ft tall. Explain how he could have found the height of the tree.

13. A pilot is in a plane that is 6 miles from a point directly overhead an aircraft carrier. The pilot looks down at a 10° angle to the carrier. Find the plane's altitude (a).

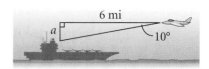

14. In flipping a coin, compare the ratio of 4 heads out of 10 tries to the ratio of 8 heads in 15 tries. [6-1]

15. What is the shape of the paper label for a soup can? How does its size relate to the circumference of the can? [5-3]

16. Find the area of a circle with a diameter of 8.5 cm. [5-2]

17. Find the circumference of a circle with diameter 8.5 cm. [5-2]

© 1994 The Andy Warhol Foundation for the Visual Arts, Inc.

MORE PRACTICE

18. Find these values using your calculator.
    a. cos 40°   **b.** tan 32°   **c.** cos 29°   **d.** sin 44°

19. The tangent ratio for $\angle M$ is
    (a) $\frac{20}{15}$ (b) $\frac{25}{15}$
    (c) $\frac{15}{20}$ (d) not here

Find the tangent ratio, $\frac{\text{opposite}}{\text{adjacent}}$, for angle A.

20.

21.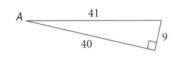

22.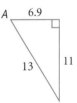

23. Find the tangent ratio
    a. for $\angle A$.
    b. for $\angle C$.

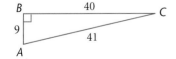

24. Find the tangent ratio
    a. for $\angle G$.
    b. for $\angle H$.

25. a. Find the length of the hypotenuse using the Pythagorean Theorem.

   b. Find tan *A* using a ratio. Find tan *B* using a ratio.

   c. Find tan 45 using your calculator.

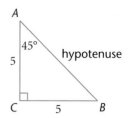

MORE MATH REASONING

26. a. Make a chart that shows the values for sin 0°, sin 90°, sin 180°, sin 270°, and sin 360°.

   b. How do you think the pattern continues? Check it with your calculator.

27. Draw two similar right triangles. Measure their angles. Use the lengths of the sides to compare the tangents of their corresponding angles.

28. For any triangle *ABC*, where *C* is the right angle, how does the tangent of angle *A* relate to the tangent of angle *B*?

29. Using a calculator, find tan 17°. Now press [INV] [TAN] or [2nd] [TAN], depending on your calculator. What is the result? What does [INV] [TAN] do?

6-3
PART B The Sine and Cosine Ratios

. . . .

← CONNECT → *By using your calculator to find ratios quickly, you have worked problems using the tangent ratio. In this part you will use the other two common ratios, sine and cosine.*

You have used the tangent ratio: $\tan A = \dfrac{\text{opposite}}{\text{adjacent}}$.

Now you will use the two ratios that involve the hypotenuse—the **sine** (sin) and the **cosine** (cos).

$$\sin A = \frac{\text{Opposite}}{\text{Hypotenuse}}$$

hypotenuse = **25** opposite = **7** $\sin A = \dfrac{7}{25}$
A adjacent = 24

$$\cos A = \frac{\text{Adjacent}}{\text{Hypotenuse}}$$

hypotenuse = **25** opposite = 7 $\cos A = \dfrac{24}{25}$
A adjacent = **24**

EXPLORE: SINE OF THE TIMES

MATERIALS

*Notebook paper or fine graph paper
Ruler, Calculator, Protractor*

On a piece of notebook paper draw a large right triangle by using a corner of the paper. The corner is the right angle and you are drawing the hypotenuse.

For triangle *ABC*,

$\angle C$ is the right angle.

$\overline{AB}$ is the hypotenuse.

Focus on $\angle A$:

The leg *adjacent* to $\angle A$ is side $\overline{AC}$.

The leg *opposite* $\angle A$ is side $\overline{BC}$.

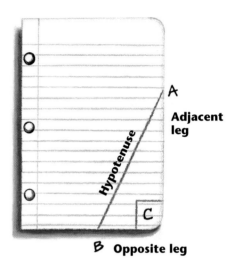

Use a centimeter ruler and a protractor to measure the three sides and $\angle A$ as accurately as possible.

Record your measurements on the drawing. Your paper will look like this but with your own measurements.

1. Fill in the first row by using the measure of $\angle A$ on your paper and the measure of the three sides. Then compute the three ratios.

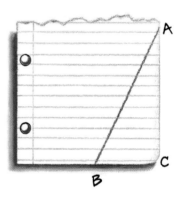

Angle Measure	Length of Opposite Leg	Length of Adjacent Leg	Length of Hypotenuse	$\dfrac{\text{Opposite}}{\text{Hypotenuse}}$	$\dfrac{\text{Adjacent}}{\text{Hypotenuse}}$	$\dfrac{\text{Opposite}}{\text{Adjacent}}$
____ °						
Now use your calculator to find these values:				sin A =	cos A =	tan A =

2. Compare the ratios you calculated with the corresponding ratios from your calculator. (The values may not be quite the same because measurements are not exact or because of rounding.)

Ratios are very useful in making indirect measurements. Just make a similar figure of an actual measurement. Then think of the ratio you need.

CONSIDER

?

1. Why are all right triangles that have one 55° angle similar? Why is the ratio of their sides the same?

EXAMPLES

1. Find *a*.

   We know the *hypotenuse* is 10, and we want to know the *adjacent* leg (*a*). These are the parts of the *cosine* ratio.

   $$\frac{\text{Adjacent}}{\text{Hypotenuse}} = \cos 50°$$

   $\dfrac{a}{10} = 0.6428$ Use a calculator to find cos 50°.

   $a = 6.428$ Multiply both sides by 10.

2. An 18-mile road through a national park is closed by a landslide. A bypass road will connect to the highway. How long is the highway portion of the detour (*x*)? We know the *hypotenuse* is 18, and we want to know the *opposite* leg (*x*). These are the parts of the *sine* ratio.

   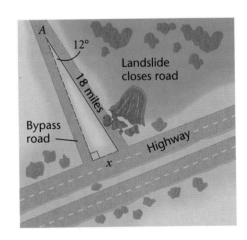

   $$\frac{\text{Opposite}}{\text{Hypotenuse}} = \sin 12°$$

   $\dfrac{x}{18} = 0.2079$ Use a calculator to find sin 12°.

   $x = 3.7422$ Multiply both sides by 18.

   The length of the highway portion of the detour is about 3.74 miles.

2. What are two ways you can find the length of the bypass road?

Be careful. Sometimes the length of a side is not the solution to the problem.

EXAMPLE

3. Whitney is holding a 250-ft wire that is attached to a flying model airplane. The wire makes a 36° angle to the horizontal line. Whitney is 5 ft tall. How high is the airplane?

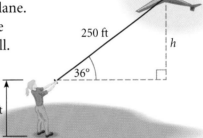

250 ft

h

36°

5 ft

Draw a right triangle with a 36° angle. We know the *hypotenuse* is 250 ft, and we want to know the *opposite* leg (*h*). These are the parts of the sine ratio.

$$\frac{\text{Opposite}}{\text{Hypotenuse}} = \sin 36°$$

$$\frac{h}{250} = 0.5878$$

$$h = 146.95 \qquad \text{Multiply both sides by 250.}$$

To find the height of the airplane, add Whitney's height (5 ft) to the value of *h*.
The model airplane is about 152 ft high.

TRY IT

a. Find *h*.

10

h

40°

b. Find *n*.

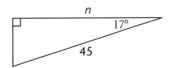

n

17°

45

1. How do the sine, cosine, and tangent ratios of an angle differ?

2. Describe a way to calculate a long distance using a right triangle.

3. Why are similar triangles important in finding measures indirectly?

4. Because the sine of an angle is a ratio, how can 0.5 be the sine of an angle?

5. What step can you take to begin solving $\frac{10}{x} = 0.5592$?

Exercises

CORE

1. Getting Started Use $\triangle ABC$. Evaluate each ratio.

a. $\sin A = \dfrac{\text{Opposite leg}}{\text{Hypotenuse}}$

b. $\cos A = \dfrac{\text{Adjacent leg}}{\text{Hypotenuse}}$

c. $\tan A = \dfrac{\text{Opposite leg}}{\text{Adjacent leg}}$

d. $\sin B = \dfrac{\text{Opposite leg}}{\text{Hypotenuse}}$

e. $\cos B = \dfrac{\text{Adjacent leg}}{\text{Hypotenuse}}$

f. $\tan B = \dfrac{\text{Opposite leg}}{\text{Adjacent leg}}$

Solve each equation.

2. $\dfrac{x}{150} = 0.4293$

3. $\dfrac{k}{5} = \dfrac{3}{5}$

4. $\dfrac{y}{9} = 0.6162$

5. $\dfrac{w}{3} = 0.1562$

6. $\dfrac{7.5}{m} = \dfrac{15}{24}$

7. $\dfrac{203}{p} = 0.4521$

Find the side given by the variable.

8.

9.

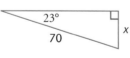

10.

11. A surveyor (S) is standing 120 ft away from the base of a tower. She sights the top of the tower (T) at an angle of 30°. Use the cosine ratio to find the distance (d) from the surveyor to the top of the tower.

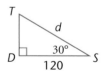

12. In right triangle *ABC*, the leg opposite ∠*A* measures 7 units, the leg adjacent to ∠*A* measures 11 units, and the hypotenuse measures 13.04. Find the sin, cos, and tan ratios for ∠*A*.

Problem-Solving Tip

Draw a diagram.

13. A support wire at an angle of 35° runs from the ground to the top of a 40.5-ft telephone pole. Find the length of the support wire.

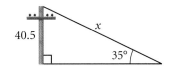

14. Cleared for Landing An airport control tower is 4285 ft east of a point directly below a plane. An air-traffic controller contacts the plane, which is at an angle of 27° from the horizontal. How far does the radio signal (*m*) travel?

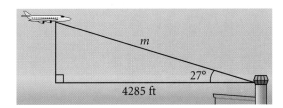

15. You are positioning a delicate sculpture at the museum. It is 22 feet high and needs three support wires, from the top of the sculpture to the floor, to keep it from toppling. If you place each support wire at an angle of 45° to the floor, how many feet of wire will you need?

16. New Jersey's 102-foot-high Sandy Hook Lighthouse is the oldest operational lighthouse in the United States. It is one of two lights that guide ships into New York Harbor.

Three students attempt to measure the height of the lighthouse. Which student will get the correct answer?

(a) Kay: $\sin 73° = \dfrac{100}{h}$

(b) Joleen: $\tan 81° = \dfrac{h}{16.2}$

(c) Royce: $\cos 65° = \dfrac{h}{150}$

(d) not here

The following pairs of figures are similar. Find the missing side lengths by using proportions. [6-2]

17.

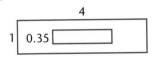

18.

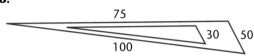

Solve each equation. [4-2]

19. $3x + 12 = 42$

20. $16 - 7m = 37$

Evaluate. [2-3]

21. $6y + 2y - 8$, if $y = -3$

22. $a^2 + b^2 + ab + 5$, if $a = 4$ and $b = -1$

23. $a^2 + b^2 + ab + 5$, if $a = -1$ and $b = 4$

MORE PRACTICE

24. Match each ratio with its trigonometric function.

a. $\dfrac{48}{64}$ **i.** $\sin A$

b. $\dfrac{48}{80}$ **ii.** $\cos A$

c. $\dfrac{64}{80}$ **iii.** $\tan A$

25. Find the ratios of sides for the triangle using $\angle B$.

a. $\dfrac{\text{Opposite leg}}{\text{Adjacent leg}}$

b. $\dfrac{\text{Adjacent leg}}{\text{Hypotenuse}}$

c. $\dfrac{\text{Opposite leg}}{\text{Hypotenuse}}$

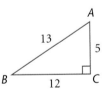

Solve each equation.

26. $\dfrac{y}{3} = 0.5$

27. $\dfrac{k}{8} = \dfrac{3}{4}$

28. $\dfrac{9}{y} = \dfrac{12}{15}$

29. $\dfrac{24}{r} = \dfrac{15}{24}$

30. $\dfrac{w}{22} = 0.1562$

31. $\dfrac{15}{p} = 0.4521$

Find the side given by the variable.

32.
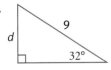
9

d

32°

33.

x

14°

25

34.
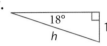
m

12 | 68°

35.

200

r

43°

36.

0.1 57°

q

37.
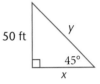
18°

1

h

38. Find the length of the base (b) of the right triangle.

20

60°

b

39. Find x and y.

50 ft

y

45°

x

MORE MATH REASONING

40. The deepest canyon in the world is El Cañon de Colca in the Andes Mountains of southern Peru.

$\sin M = 0.9956$

$\cos M = 0.0942$

$\tan M = 10.574$

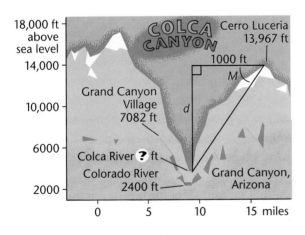

a. Find the canyon's depth.

b. How far above sea level is the river at this point?

c. Compare the depth of the Cañon de Colca with the Grand Canyon.

41. In a right triangle containing a 30° angle, name a side length you must know to find the lengths of the other two sides. Explain how you could do it. Show an equation you might use.

Problem-Solving Tip

Draw a labeled diagram.

42. In 225 B.C., the Greek astronomer Eratosthenes determined the radius of the earth. He noticed that on a certain day at noon it was possible to see the reflection of the sun in the bottom of a deep well in Aswan. At the same time, in Alexandria, 500 miles away, it was computed that the sun was at an angle of 7.2° away from being directly overhead in Alexandria.

From this information, he calculated the earth's radius.

a. In a right triangle, the ratio of the leg opposite the 7.2° angle to the leg adjacent to the 7.2° angle is 0.1263. Find the radius (r) of the earth.

b. The circumference of a circle is $2\pi r$ where r is the radius. Use $\pi = 3.1416$ and find the circumference of the earth from Eratosthenes' measurements.

c. The circumference of the earth through these cities is 24,901.55 miles. Use this to find the radius of the earth.

d. Compare Eratosthenes's calculation to the actual radius using a ratio in percentage form. Was Eratosthenes's calculation accurate? Explain your thinking.

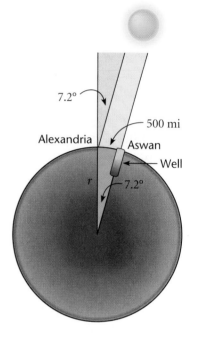

6-3
PART C
Making Connections

← CONNECT → *You have used trigonometry to find distances on the earth that might seem impossible to measure because of their size or accessibility. Trigonometry is also used to measure the vastness of our universe.*

Early astronomers noticed that certain stars moved in relation to the other stars throughout the year. These "stars" were named *planets,* from the Greek word meaning "wanderer." Venus, the brightest of the planets, always wanders within 46° of the sun, as viewed from the earth. We can use this fact to indirectly measure the distance from the sun to Venus.

When Venus is 46° from the sun, a right triangle is formed by the earth, the sun, and Venus, as shown. The mean distance from the earth to the sun is about 93,000,000 miles.

1. Use these facts to estimate the mean distance of Venus from the sun. Explain how you found the distance.
2. Mercury is closer to the sun and only gets 23° away from the sun as viewed from the earth. Draw a similar diagram to find out about how far Mercury is from the sun.
3. Venus is most often seen at dawn or dusk. Do you think Venus is ever visible at midnight? Explain.

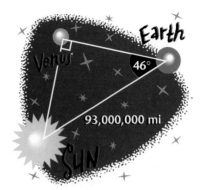

Trigonometry has been used for thousands of years by astronomers, surveyors, and cartographers.

In the seventeenth century, Tycho Brahe made the first precise measurements of angles of stars and planets in the sky. Johann Kepler later used this extensive data to derive accurate orbits for planets.

Johann Kepler, 1571–1630

Venus at Sunrise

1. What do we mean by the phrase "measuring the unmeasurable"? Describe how trigonometry is used to do this.
2. The height of the monument in Quito, Ecuador, would be difficult to find with a tape measure. Draw a diagram showing how you could measure it using trigonometry.
3. Use the parts of a triangle to describe the three trigonometric ratios.
4. How might pilots use trigonometry?
5. "Metry" at the end of a word is a suffix meaning "to measure." What do you think the word trigonometry means? What other words do you know ending in "metry"? What do they mean?

Self-Assessment

Find the length of the side given by the variable.

1.

2.

3.
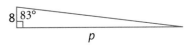

4. Fill in the blanks. The cosine of an angle is the ratio of the ____ to the ____.

5. How wide is the canyon?

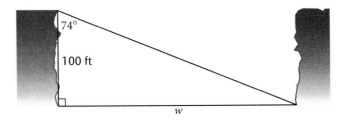

6. George has drawn this plan for a ramp to provide access for disabled people.
   a. What will be the length (L) of the ramp?
   b. Do you think this is a good design? Explain.

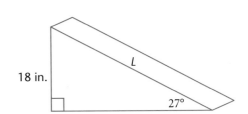

7. No Greater Crater Crater Lake in Oregon was once an active volcano. Now it is known for its blue color. Starting from a point due east across the lake from a lodge, a surveyor walked 550 ft north. Using a transit, he sighted the lodge at an angle of 89° and then calculated the length of the lake. How long is Crater Lake?

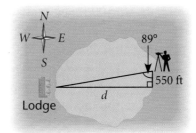

8. Carmelita can measure the angle at which she looks up to see the top of a totem pole. Explain how she can find out how tall it is.

9. Describe how you can use a scale to find the weight of 1 paper clip if you have 50 paper clips in a dish. Write an equation that models your method. [4-2]

10. A tree is growing at an angle of 30° to the ground. The tip of the tree is 40 feet off the ground. How tall would the tree be if it had grown straight up?

11. a. What is the height of the brownstone?
   b. What measurements would change if they were made from the ground?

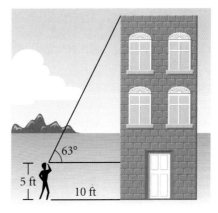

12. Ken and Brenda are 100 miles apart. Ken said that the moon was directly above his location. Brenda immediately measured her angle to the moon and found that it measured *m* degrees. Describe how Brenda and Ken could use trigonometry to find how far above Ken the moon was.

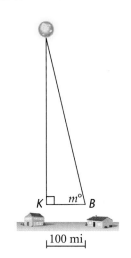

13. Karl is 600 feet northeast of Nishi, who is running straight north at a rate of 6.25 feet per second. How fast must Karl run due west to meet Nishi at the intersection point? (Hint: For each person, how far is it to the meeting point?)

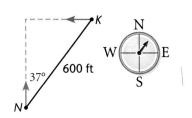

14. African Angle Viewing Africa from an altitude of 7056 miles, astronauts can see the entire continent, which is about $\frac{1}{5}$ of the land surface of the earth. Find the length $(\overline{NS})$ using the measurements shown.

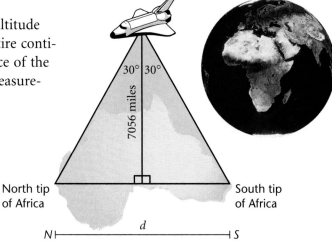

North tip of Africa

South tip of Africa

15. The Eyes Have It! If your left eye sees a lamppost at an angle of 85° and your right eye sees the same lamppost also at an angle of 85°, how far away is the lamppost? (Hint: Measure the distance between your eyes, pupil to pupil).

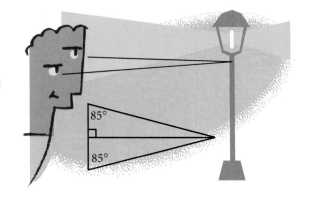

16. **Team Work**

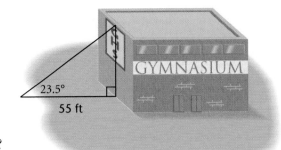

a. Nafeesa and Masanee want to make a 15-ft-wide homecoming banner that hangs halfway from the roof of the gym to the ground. How long should they make the homecoming banner?

b. How many yards of 48-in.-wide material will they need to buy to make the banner?

> **Problem-Solving Tip**
>
> Make a diagram of the banner pieces.

17. Find the perimeter and area of a right triangle with a 20-ft-long hypotenuse and with a 60° angle.

18. Swimmers were polled for a month about how the water felt. The results were compared against the actual water temperature.

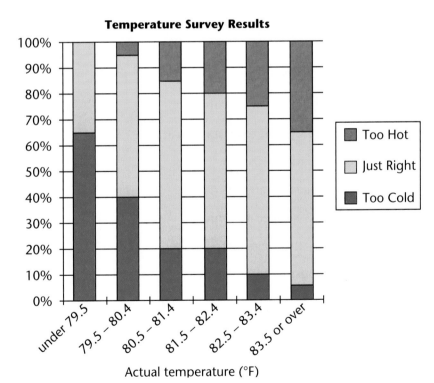

Temperature Survey Results

Actual temperature (°F)

Legend: Too Hot, Just Right, Too Cold

If you maintained the pool, what would you do? Why? [1-2]

Chapter 6 Review

In Chapter 6, you learned to recognize, write, and use ratios and proportions. With these powerful problem-solving tools, you could identify similar triangles. After working with the Pythagorean Theorem, you extended your knowledge of right triangles to include three trigonometric ratios: sine, cosine, and tangent. Now you have the mathematical tools to make comparisons, work with scaling, and find lengths you can't measure directly.

KEY TERMS

adjacent leg [6-3]	opposite leg [6-3]	right triangle [6-2]
congruent angles [6-2]	parallelogram [6-2]	scale factor [6-2]
conversion factors [6-1]	proportion [6-1]	similar polygons [6-2]
corresponding angles [6-2]	protractor [6-2]	sine [6-3]
corresponding sides [6-2]	Pythagorean Theorem [6-2]	tangent [6-3]
cosine [6-3]	rate [6-1]	trigonometric ratios [6-3]
equivalent ratios [6-1]	ratio [6-1]	trigonometry [6-3]
hypotenuse [6-2]	right angle [6-2]	unit rate [6-1]
leg [6-2]		

Write the word or phrase that correctly completes each statement.

1. An equation that states two ratios are equal is called a ___.

2. An angle that measures ___ degrees is a right angle.

3. In a right triangle, the ratio $\frac{?}{\text{hypotenuse}}$ is called the sine.

4. In similar triangles, corresponding ___ are congruent.

5. In a 30°-60° right triangle, the side opposite the 30° angle is one-half the length of the ___.

CONCEPTS AND APPLICATIONS

Write each ratio as an equivalent fraction, decimal, and percentage. [6-1]

6. John backpacked three out of the four days of his vacation.

7. For every 20 dollars collected, 5 dollars went to cover expenses.

Solve each equation. [4-2]

8. $-4x + 11x = 15.7$ **9.** $-3(x + 2) = 15$ **10.** $\frac{3}{4}x = 69$

11. Find the area of the triangle whose base is 7 cm and height is 2.5 cm. [5-1]

12. Kirie is using cross multiplication to solve the proportion $\frac{16}{x} = \frac{10}{5}$. If she starts to write, "16(5) =," how should she complete the equation? [6-1]
(a) $x(10)$ (b) 80 (c) 5(16) (d) 8

13. Solve the proportion. $1.1{:}6 = x{:}110$. [6-1]

14. A map of Wisconsin is drawn to the scale 1 inch = 64 miles. If Beloit, Wisconsin, is actually 160 miles from Green Bay, how far apart are these cities on the map? [6-2]

15. Write a short explanation of the Pythagorean Theorem. Include drawings to illustrate what you are saying. Show an example using a right triangle with legs of 5 units and 12 units. [6-2]

16. The two triangles are similar. [6-2]
  a. Can you find any of the missing angle sizes? Explain.
  b. Can you find any of the missing side lengths? Explain.
  c. How would your answers to **16a** and **16b** change if these triangles were right triangles?

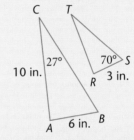

17. After a history quiz, the teacher said students' grades would be proportional to the number correct. Dizz got 22 correct and a grade of 88%. Greg's grade was 76%. How many did he get correct? [6-1]

18. Write the three trigonometric ratios for $\angle B$. [6-3]

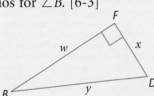

19. Calculate the three trigonometric ratios for $\angle S$. [6-3]

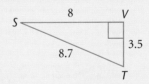

20. Explain why the rate of $\frac{3 \text{ miles}}{10 \text{ minutes}}$ is equal to the rate of 18 miles per hour. [6-1]

21. a. What is the ratio of the height of the solid to its length? its width to its length? [6-1]
  b. Which ratio is greater? How do you decide? [6-1]
  c. Find the volume and surface area of the solid. [5-3]

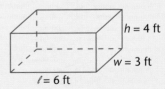

22. Jake says he can type 25 words per minute. If he spends 12 minutes typing a book report, about how many words has he typed? [6-1]

CONCEPTS AND CONNECTIONS

23. Fitness Some students were bragging about their running abilities. Nichole said she could run an 8-minute mile. Darwin said he ran at the rate of 10 miles per hour. Mike thought that in half an hour he could cover about 6 miles. Miranda said it would take her 12 minutes to run a mile. How can you compare these rates? Do all these rates seem realistic?

24. Engineering City officials want to build a bridge across a lake to connect two roads. The roads are too far apart for anyone to measure the distance between them physically. Tell how they could use trigonometry to find the length of the proposed bridge. What measurements would be needed? How could they get the needed measurements?

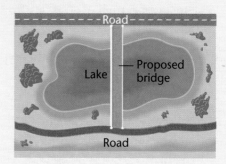

SELF-EVALUATION

Write a summary about what you know about ratio and proportions. Include examples of scale factors and trigonometric ratios. In your summary, include areas where you had trouble with the ideas and tell how you plan to review those areas.

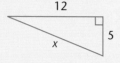
Chapter 6 Assessment

TEST

1. Which ratio does not belong?
   (a) 2:10   (b) 5:1   (c) $\frac{1}{5}$ (d) 20%   (e) 80 out of 400

2. Use the Pythagorean Theorem to find the value of x in each figure.

a.

12

5

x

b.

12

x

20

3. For each figure, find the ratio of shaded area to entire area. Then find the ratio of shaded area to unshaded area.

a.

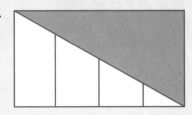

b.

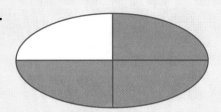

4. A sample of 1000 pens made at the Penn Factory showed 3 defective pens. After the machine was repaired, a new sample showed 4 defective pens out of 1500. Is the machine doing a better job than before it was repaired? Explain.

5. Write each ratio as a fraction, a decimal, and a percentage.
   a. $10 out of every $40 goes for taxes.
   b. Seven cans out of every ten cans could be recycled.

6. Write each rate as a comparison to 1 unit, using the word *per*.
   a. The car used 8 gallons of gas in the 200-mile trip.
   b. The car went 200 miles on 8 gallons of gas.

7. A hiker at *A* looks down at point *B* in a canyon. What trigonometric ratio would he use to find *x*?

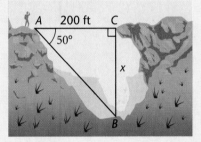

8. The depth of the canyon, distance *x*, is equal to

   (a) $200 \tan 50°$ (b) $200 \sin 50°$

   (c) $200 \cos 50°$ (d) $\dfrac{200}{\tan 50°}$

9. Use the following fractions to complete the conversions.

   $\dfrac{2 \text{ pints}}{1 \text{ quart}}$ $\dfrac{1 \text{ gallon}}{4 \text{ quarts}}$ $\dfrac{1 \text{ pint}}{2 \text{ cups}}$

   a. 6 cups per minute = ____ gallons per minute

   b. 3 gallons per minute = ____ pints per minute

10. A rectangle has a length of 12 cm. A larger rectangle is drawn using a scale factor of 2:3. What is the length of the second rectangle?

PERFORMANCE TASK

You are on a school committee that wants to paint a picture of a smiling bear on the side of the school gym. What concepts from this chapter could help you plan this project?

Chapter 7

Probability and Decision Making

Project A
Not for Profit
How do charities collect and distribute their funds?

Project B
Pooling Resources
What are the steps for setting up a public carpool system?

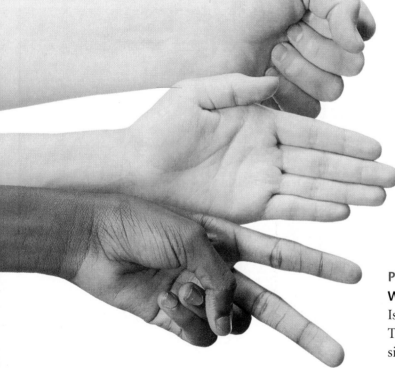

Project C
What Are the Chances?
Is winning a game like Tic-Tac-Toe or Rock-Paper-Scissors simply a matter of luck?

PATTI CADWELL

I took math in high-school because it was required. I didn't think I'd use it.

Now I plan meetings for the entire Pharmaceutical Division at Miles, including hotels, entertainment, food, and transportation for ten people to a thousand people.

I use a timetable called a Gantt chart for planning events. I use numbers constantly for reservations, deposits, cost breakdowns, and budgets.

Patti Cadwell
Associate Meeting's Coordinator
Miles Pharmaceuticals
West Haven, Connecticut

Patti Cadwell

517

Chapter 7

Overview

Probability and Decision Making

7-1 Probability

Probability is used in scientific research to express the possibilities that events will or will not happen. You will observe how probability is a factor in familiar or historical games. You will use experimental data to determine probabilities. You will work with ratios expressed as fractions, decimals, and percentages to compare probabilities and make predictions.

7-2 Counting and Probability

Techniques used in probability are helpful in determining the total number of possibilities of an event. You will investigate events involving objects where order is important and where order is not important. You will examine informal statements about the accuracy and odds of events.

Shake, Rattle, and Roll

People have been rolling dice and dealing cards for centuries in civilizations all over the world. In the ruins of ancient cities and villages, archaeologists have found dice made of peach pits, pottery, shells, and animal bones. Cards made of ivory or wood were used to tell fortunes and to play games as early as 1360. The pictures on playing cards have been used to teach young children numbers, to illustrate fables, and to honor kings and queens.

Games that have endured the longest use common objects and simple directions. Checkers, Backgammon, Parcheesi, and Go have all been played for many centuries. Thousands of years ago, Egyptians carved stone playing boards for Mancala games, which are played with small counters in a series of cups. Today, people play Mancala games in Africa, Asia, South America, and the West Indies. Such long-lasting, simple-looking games can be enjoyed by children or adults, but for players who think strategically, they become sophisticated and challenging.

1. Why do you think a simple-looking game might survive many centuries and civilizations?
2. Look at a pair of standard dice. What is the sum of the dots on opposite faces of the cube? What sum do you think you would roll most often with a pair of dice?

3. A deck of cards contains 52 cards in four suits. Why do you think the face cards have pictures of jacks, queens, and kings? Why do you think these cards are the highest numbers in a suit?
4. Think of a game that you play. What mathematics do you need to know to play it?

Games in Other Cultures

← C O N N E C T → *Games involve mathematical thinking, strategy, and luck. Now you will learn to analyze your chances of winning games played in countries around the world.*

The game of Lambs and Tigers is played in India. One player has three pieces called tigers, and the opponent has fifteen lambs. Players move pieces by sliding each one to an adjacent point on the board. The tigers try to remove lambs from the board by jumping over them. Lambs try to trap a tiger so that it cannot slide or jump.

EXPLORE: I'M GAME

Decide with a classmate which pieces each player will use. Take turns, tiger first, placing your pieces on the board. Tigers must start on the three points marked "T," but lambs can be placed anywhere else. A tiger can begin moving and capturing lambs as soon as all three tigers are in place. But lambs are not permitted to move until all fifteen have been placed on the board.

MATERIALS

Copy of the game board
3 chips for tigers
15 chips for lambs

1. What is the ratio of tigers to lambs? What is the ratio of playing pieces to positions on the board?
2. Notice the labeling of the lines A through F and the four bands 0 through 4. Can you identify all points on the board using this coordinate system?
3. Do you think the lambs or the tigers have the better chance of winning? Why? Play the game.

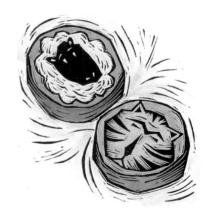

4. What is the smallest number of lambs needed to trap a tiger on the point labeled (4, E)? anywhere on line A? on the point 0? Draw pictures to show your answers.

5. What strategy should the player with the tigers use? the player with the lambs?

Suppose you are playing the tigers in the game shown.

6. Does moving from (4, C) to (4, D) improve your chances of winning? Explain.

7. How would moving the tiger on (3, D) improve your chances of winning?

8. If either the tigers or the lambs were able to win every time, would people play the game? Why or why not?

9. If you describe your chances of winning a game as a percentage, what is the highest percent chance you could have of winning? What is the lowest?

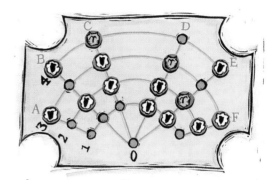

CONSIDER

1. Is winning the game of Lambs and Tigers based on luck or on strategy?

2. In your favorite games, do you *know* that you can win, *hope* that you can win, or know that you *won't* win?

3. Would you play a game if you were sure of the results ahead of time?

Dice games have always been popular. Before numbered cubes were available, children in Europe used *astragali,* or small bones from the feet of sheep, to play a game called Knucklebones.

The game of Knucklebones. Painting by French artist Jean-Baptiste-Siméon Chardin (1699–1779).

In Knucklebones, four bones are thrown at one time. Points depend on the landing positions of the bones.

Dog	Vulcan	Eagle	Prince
Flat side up	Broad, concave side up	Broad, convex side up	Sinuous side up
1 point	3 points	4 points	6 points

There are special rules for combinations of throws.

- A player wins the game immediately if all four landing positions appear in one throw.
- A player loses immediately for a throw of 4 dogs.
- A throw of two pairs earns 5 bonus points.
- A throw of three-of-a-kind earns 10 bonus points.
- A throw of 4 vulcans, eagles, or princes earns 20 bonus points plus 4 times the total value of the throw.

EXAMPLES

How many points does a player get for each of these throws?

1. a throw of 2 princes, 1 eagle, and 1 dog
$2 \cdot 6 + 4 + 1 = 17$ points

2. a throw of 1 prince and 3 vulcans
$6 + 3 \cdot 3 + 10$ bonus points $= 25$ points

TRY IT

a. How many points does a player get for a throw of 1 dog, 1 vulcan, 1 eagle, and 1 prince?

REFLECT

1. Give two differences between Lambs and Tigers and Knucklebones.
2. Which game requires skill and which involves only good luck? Which would you have a better chance of winning? Explain your answer.
3. If you play a game against someone who has played it many times, what are your chances of winning if it is a game of skill? a game of luck?

Exercises

CORE

Getting Started One variation of the game of Lambs and Tigers is played with four lambs and one tiger on a smaller board. Suppose you are the tiger. What is your best move on each board?

1.

2.

3.

4.

5. What is the ratio of playing pieces to positions on the board?

6. Why is it difficult to trap a tiger in this game?

7. Explain why the game is fair even though the number of playing pieces is different.

8. How would planning ahead improve your chances of winning a game?

Use the rules for Knucklebones to write the score for each throw.

9. 2 princes and 2 vulcans

10. 4 dogs

11. 2 eagles, 1 prince, and 1 dog

12. 3 dogs and 1 vulcan

Use the bonus points to decide which throw seems less likely to happen.

13. four of the same face or one of each face

14. three-of-a-kind or two pairs

15. Name two games you have played in which points are totaled to determine the winner.

16. Why do you think people like to play games involving chance? Name two games you have played that are based on chance.

Many games are played on a board in the shape of a star.

17. Copy the star onto your paper. Draw the lines of symmetry.

18. What rotational symmetry is present in the figure?

19. The game of Pentalpha is played in Crete on a board shaped like a star. Players must place three pebbles in a straight line on the board. In how many ways is this possible?

 ## LOOK BACK

20. At 1 mile (5280 feet) away, the top of Venezuela's Angel Falls is sighted at a 31.3° angle. What is the height of the falls? [6-3]

Find the number that correctly completes each statement. [6-1]

21. $\dfrac{300 \text{ words}}{5 \text{ minutes}} \times \dfrac{60 \text{ minutes}}{1 \text{ hour}} = \dfrac{\boxed{} \text{ words}}{1 \text{ hour}}$

22. $\dfrac{2 \text{ quarts of water}}{4 \text{ tablespoons plant food}} \times \dfrac{1 \text{ gallon}}{4 \text{ quarts}} = \dfrac{1 \text{ gallon}}{\boxed{} \text{ tablespoons plant food}}$

23. Show that the sum of the areas of △CBD and △ABD equals the area of trapezoid ABCD. [5-2]

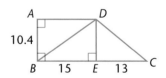

MORE PRACTICE

24. Assume the lambs move next. On which board do the lambs have the better chance of winning?

(a)  (b)

Use the rules for Knucklebones to write the score for each throw.

25. 2 eagles and 2 dogs

26. 4 vulcans

27. 1 prince, 1 vulcan, and 2 dogs

28. 3 vulcans and 1 dog

Which throws in Knucklebones would produce each score?

29. 13

30. 84

31. What is the smallest possible score on one throw? the largest possible score?

32. Why do you think people long ago played games like Lambs and Tigers and Knucklebones?

33. On which board would a tiger have a better chance of winning? Why?

(a)
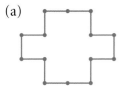

(b)

34. In one state lottery, a ticket has 1 chance in 22,957,480 of winning. At the rate of 1 per minute, how long would it take to buy this many tickets?

35. The game of Fox and Geese uses rules similar to those for Lambs and Tigers. The board begins with the playing pieces in this position.
   a. What is the ratio of foxes to geese? of playing pieces to positions on the board?
   b. How many different moves are possible by the fox on the first play? by the geese?
   c. What strategy would you use if you were playing the fox? the geese?

MORE MATH REASONING

36. Which type of game do you prefer to play—one based on luck or one based on skill? Why?

37. What would be a good method of keeping score to determine the winner in the game of Knucklebones? Explain your thinking.

38. Some games require a player to roll a specific score to win the game. What faces would you need to roll each score with the numbered cube shown?

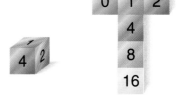

  a. 13 with 3 cubes
  b. 17 with 4 cubes
  c. 37 with 5 cubes
  d. 63 with 4 cubes

39. In the game of Tic-Tac-Toe, a player can win, lose, or draw. Players take turns placing X's or O's to try to get three in a row up, down, or diagonally. If the correct strategies are followed:

  • The player who moves first will not lose.
  • The player who moves second will not lose.

  a. What should happen if two people play 20 games of Tic-Tac-Toe?
  b. For the game shown, why is O's only game-saving move in the center?

7-1
PART B The Meaning of Probability

← **CONNECT** → *You know that many questions come up when we play games: Is skill more important than luck? Does every player have an equal chance to win? What is likely to happen on my next turn? Now you will see how to use math to figure out your chances of winning or losing.*

What will you be doing tonight at 7:00? You can't be sure, but you probably know some things that are likely and some that are unlikely.

More Likely	Less Likely
Eating	Flying in an airplane
Doing homework	Sleeping
Listening to music	Painting your room

For another person, an item on your "Less Likely" list may be very likely!

We do not know what will happen in the future. But by thinking about what is likely or unlikely, we can get an idea of what will probably happen.

MATERIALS

3 × 5 index card

Fold a 3 × 5 index card along its width, but a little off center. If you toss the card up, how will it land? Will it ever land on edge? How many times would each of the four possible outcomes pictured happen in 100 tosses? Use a table like the one below to record your guesses.

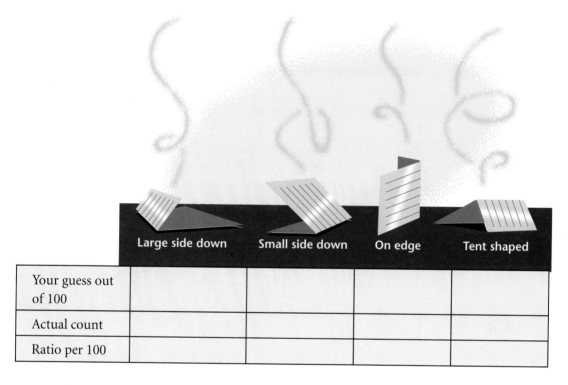

	Large side down	Small side down	On edge	Tent shaped
Your guess out of 100				
Actual count				
Ratio per 100				

1. Toss or drop the folded card 100 times. Make sure it falls at least a few feet. Keep a record of each landing. Then complete your table.
2. Which outcome occurred most often? Did you guess this result?
3. In what position will your card probably land if you toss it one more time?
4. Toss the card. Were you right? Do you think the most probable event is the one that will definitely happen?
5. How can collecting data help you predict the outcomes of future events?

We use ratios to show how likely—or unlikely—an outcome might be. Suppose your card landed tent shaped 5 times out of 100 tosses. The ratio of the number of tent-shaped landings to the number of all possible landings is $\frac{5}{100}$. This ratio is the **probability** that your card lands tent shaped.

$$\text{Probability that your card lands tent shaped} = \frac{\text{Number of times it lands tent shaped}}{\text{Total number of tosses}} = \frac{5}{100}$$

Since $\frac{5}{100} = 0.05 = 5\%$, you could say, "In 100 trials, I found the probability that my card lands tent shaped is 5%."

$$\text{Probability of an event} = \frac{\text{Number of times it can occur}}{\text{Total number of possible outcomes}}$$

The probability of an *impossible event* is 0. The probability of a *certain* event is 1. Numbers between 0 and 1 show the probability of other outcomes.

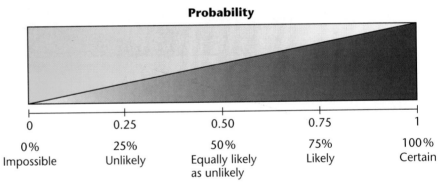

Probability

0	0.25	0.50	0.75	1
0%	25%	50%	75%	100%
Impossible	Unlikely	Equally likely as unlikely	Likely	Certain

1. Suppose your card lands large side down 34 times in 40 tosses. What is the probability of this event? Express it in words.

$$\text{Probability of landing large side down} = \frac{34 \text{ landings with large side down}}{40 \text{ total tosses}}$$

$$= \frac{17}{20}$$

$$= 0.85, \text{ or } 85\%$$

You could say, "The probability of my card's landing large side down is 0.85, or 85%."

a. The probability of a future event is 23%. Would you say it is very likely to happen?

b. A future event is described as being as likely as it is unlikely. What probability would you give this event?

For some future events, we cannot do an experiment. But we may be able to find a probability by taking a survey or by looking at past records.

EXAMPLE

2. What is the probability that the temperature will be below zero on January 1 next year where you live?

No one knows what the temperature will be that day. But if you look at past weather records, you might find that the temperature on January 1 was below zero 12 times in the past 120 years. This ratio is $\frac{12}{120}$, which equals 0.10, or 10%.

"There is a 10% probability of temperatures below zero next January 1."

CONSIDER

1. What are other words or phrases you might associate with probabilities close to 0? with probabilities close to 1? with probabilities close to 0.5?

2. Name some highly probable events that *did not* happen.

3. What are some improbable events that *did* happen?

EXAMPLES

Approximate the probability for each event. Explain your reasoning.

3. It will rain somewhere in the United States tomorrow.
This is almost definite. The probability is very close to 1—perhaps 0.999.

4. Tomorrow will have only 22 hours.
This is impossible. The probability is 0.

Approximate each probability.
Explain your reasoning.

c. A cat will live 50 years.
d. An English word contains a vowel.

1. Someone might say, "Don't hold your breath" when you are waiting for something to happen. What is that person implying about probability?

2. What are the highest and lowest probabilities? Why?

Exercises

CORE

1. Getting Started Copy the following two columns. Match items in the first column with items in the second column by drawing lines.

a. 0 probability   **i.** certain event
b. probability of 0.48   **ii.** about equally likely
c. probability of 1   **iii.** impossible event

Which event is more likely?

2. one with a probability of 35% or one with a probability of 0.3

3. one with a probability of $\frac{3}{5}$ or one with a probability of 65%

Tell whether the probability of each event is closest to 0, 1, or 0.5. Give a reason for your answer.

4. There will be school on Sunday.

5. It will snow in Louisiana on July 4.

6. You will get a grade in this class.

7. You will like your grade in this class.

8. A questionnaire was sent out to 4000 households. Only 684 were returned. What is the probability that a household returned the survey? Show the probability as a fraction, decimal, and percentage. Describe the probability in words.

9. When Jorge tossed a folded 3 × 5 card he got these results:

Large side down: 25　　Small side down: 13　　On edge: 3　　Tent shaped: 20

　a. How many times did Jorge toss the card?
　b. What is the probability that his card lands on edge?
　c. If Jorge tosses his card again, what outcome should he expect? Explain.

10. The coach asked his players to give 110% effort. Explain this request.

11. A gardener kept records of the calls he made to line up new jobs.

Season	Spring	Summer	Fall	Winter
Calls Made	196	178	244	105
Jobs	29	22	34	18

　a. In which season is the probability of getting a job from a call the greatest? Explain.
　b. How would this information help the gardener plan his time? (Hint: Where have you seen a situation like this before?)

12. **Tacky** Dawn flipped a thumbtack 200 times. She says that it landed on its head 15 times, on its side 184 times, and on its point 3 times. Can Dawn's data be correct?

 LOOK BACK

Simplify. [Previous course]

13. $1 - \frac{2}{3}$　　　　**14.** $1 - \frac{5}{8}$　　　　**15.** $1 - 0.35$　　　　**16.** $1 - 0.07$

17. Write each ratio as a percentage and as a decimal. [Previous course]
　a. $\frac{5}{8}$
　b. 11 out of 25
　c. 16 red banners out of 36
　d.

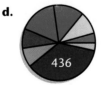

Total: 1204

436

Find the area of the shaded region. [5-2]

18.

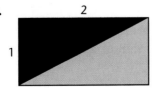

19.

20.

MORE PRACTICE

Tell which event is more likely.

21. one with probability of 0.5 or one with probability of 0.08

22. one with probability of 5% or one with probability of 50%

23. one with probability of 0.5 or one with probability of 0.9%

Tell whether the probability of each event is closest to 0, 1, or 0.5. Explain your thinking.

24. There will be fireworks tonight at 8:00.

25. You will be home from school by 4:00 p.m.

26. The moon will fall into the Atlantic Ocean next week.

27. Tuesday will follow Monday next week.

28. The first letter of someone's last name falls between N and Z.

29. "Wreck-less" Drivers Use this insurance company data.

Industry

| Ages | Number of Accidents | | Totals |
	25 miles or less from home	More than 25 miles from home	
18–25	36	14	50
26–35	24	16	40
36–45	20	12	32
46–55	18	10	28
56–65	10	12	22
Over 65	12	16	28
Totals	120	80	200

a. What is the probability that a 20-year-old customer who has an accident is 25 miles or less from home? more than 25 miles from home?

b. In which age group is the probability of having an accident the least?

c. What does this data show about the probability that an accident will be close to home as you get older?

d. For each age group, find the probability that the next accident reported will be in that age group. What is the sum of all the probabilities?

30. In a poll taken before an election, 1000 people said they would vote Yes, and 3000 people said they would vote No. What is the probability a person will vote No?

(a) $33\frac{1}{3}\%$ (b) 75%   (c) 25%   (d) $66\frac{2}{3}\%$ (e) not here

31. Rain, Rain, Go Away Meteorologist Marty Bass said there is a 60% chance of rain. Would you say this means it probably will rain? Explain your answer.

MORE MATH REASONING

32. Police conducted a study of a dangerous intersection. They found the probability that a car turns left during rush hour is 0.55.
   a. What is the probability that a car turns right or continues straight through the intersection?
   b. How does the probability explain why this was a dangerous intersection?

33. Breathe the Air The Bureau of Vital Statistics received reports of 136,000 deaths from lung cancer in 1987.
   a. What is the probability that a person selected at random from the records was male?
   b. What is the probability that a person who died of lung cancer in 1987 had been a smoker?
   c. How do you think these probabilities will change for years after 1987? Explain your thinking.

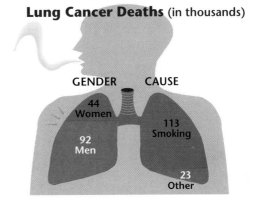

Lung Cancer Deaths (in thousands)

GENDER   CAUSE
44 Women
92 Men
113 Smoking
23 Other

34. The Big Spin A game spinner is divided into red, blue, and yellow areas.
   a. If you spin, would you be as likely to get red as blue? to get yellow as blue?
   b. Are you *certain* to get at least 1 red in 100 spins? Explain.
   c. Is it possible never to get blue in 100 spins? Explain.
   d. What would you think if you got yellow every time in 100 spins?
   e. Suppose the probability of getting yellow with the spinner is $\frac{45}{100}$ and the probability of getting red is $\frac{15}{100}$. What is the probability of getting blue?

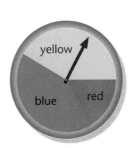

yellow

blue   red

7-1
PART C
Theoretical Probability

← CONNECT → *You have found probabilities by looking at data from past records and by making many trials of an experiment. Now you will look at some probabilities that can be found mathematically.*

Moe and Zoe go to the movies. Moe wants to sit close to the screen, but Zoe wants to sit toward the rear. They decide to flip a coin. Heads means Moe can choose the seats, and tails means Zoe can choose the seats.

Is this a fair way to decide? We can determine if it is fair by finding the probability of the coin's coming up heads or tails.

When we flip a coin we do not need to run a set of trials to find the probabilities.

The picture shows the two ways a coin can land.

We know both ways are equally likely.

The probability that a coin will land heads is

$$\frac{1 \text{ way to get heads}}{2 \text{ possible ways to land}} = \frac{1}{2}, \text{ or } 50\%.$$

The probability that a coin will land tails is the same: 50%.

Because these two probabilities are the same, Moe and Zoe feel it is a fair way to decide where to sit.

In games, and sometimes in everyday life, we flip coins, use spinners, or roll dice to make choices. We believe that by using these tools, each possibility is *equally likely* and that any result comes up *at random*. In other words, it is completely *fair*.

CONSIDER
?

1. Why couldn't you flip a coin that is identical on both sides to choose between alternatives?

1. This spinner for a jungle game has four equal regions. What is the probability of landing on tigers? We can find the probability of landing on tigers without doing any trials. The ratio of 1 tiger region to 4 total regions shows the probability:

The probability of landing on tigers =

$$\frac{1 \text{ possible region}}{\text{Total of 4 regions}} = \frac{1}{4} = 0.25.$$

There is a 25% probability of landing on tigers.

2. What is the probability of *not* landing on tigers? The probability of *not* landing on tigers means landing on a lions or an elephants region.

The probability of not landing on tigers =

$$\frac{3 \text{ possible regions}}{\text{Total of 4 regions}} = \frac{3}{4} = 0.75.$$

There is a 75% probability of not landing on tigers.

Refer to the spinner from Examples 1 and 2.

a. What is the probability of landing on lions?
b. What is the probability of *not* landing on elephants?

A single die with 6 sides has the numbers 1, 2, 3, 4, 5, and 6.

c. What is the total number of outcomes from one roll of the die?
d. What is the probability of rolling 4?
e. What is the probability of not rolling 4?

When all possible outcomes can be found without doing any trials, we can find the **theoretical probability** of an event very easily. When we must do trials or take surveys to find outcomes, we are using **experimental probability.**

In the Explore, you will compare some experimental probabilities to their theoretical probabilities.

MATERIALS

Paper clip or eraser
Sheet of paper

Make a target from a square sheet of paper divided into eight equal regions. Label them as shown.

Suppose you were to drop a paper clip or an eraser—something you can't control and something that can fall anywhere on the target at random—from a point about a foot above the center of the target.

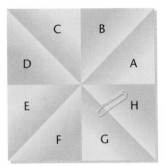

1. In a drop at random, what is the theoretical probability of landing in region A? Is the probability of landing in any of the eight regions the same?
2. Write the probability of each region as a decimal and enter it in each box in the bottom row of the table below.
3. Guess how many times the clip will land in each region in 24 random drops.

Now drop the paper clip 24 times over the center of the target. Record your landings, and enter the totals in the table. Then complete the table.

	A	B	C	D	E	F	G	H
Number of landings								
Experimental probability as a fraction								
Experimental probability as a decimal								
Theoretical probability as a decimal								

4. Do you think that the clip should land in each region the same number of times? Is it likely that you—or someone in your class—could actually hit each region the same number of times, dropping strictly at random?
5. Try 24 more drops onto this target for a total of 48 drops. Update your probabilities. Are these probabilities closer to the theoretical probabilities you calculated for 24 drops?
6. Write a statement telling how the actual outcomes of events match theoretical probability.
7. Suppose you have a robot that will make 100,000 drops for you. How do you think the experimental probabilities would compare with the theoretical probabilities?

2. Suppose you know the probability of an event, such as spinning blue on a spinner. How can you find the probability that you will *not* spin blue?

3. Why is there no theoretical probability for flipping a folded index card?

EXAMPLE

3. If you roll a fair six-sided die, what is the probability of rolling a number less than 3?

There are six equally likely ways the die can land. Two of them are numbers less than 3, namely 1 and 2.

The probability of rolling a number less than 3 =

$$\frac{2 \text{ ways}}{6 \text{ possible outcomes}} = \frac{2}{6}, \text{ or } \frac{1}{3}.$$

Another way to visualize probability ratios is by using **geometric models.** The probability ratio becomes:

$$\text{Probability of any goal} = \frac{\text{Area of goal}}{\text{Area of whole figure}}$$

EXAMPLE

4. Players throw a marker onto this game board. What is the probability of landing on the shaded boxes if the throw lands at random?

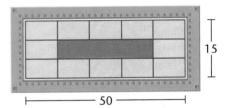

The area of the entire rectangle is $50 \times 15 = 750$ square units. The shaded area is 30×5, or 150 square units.

The ratio $\frac{150}{750}$ is the probability of landing on the shaded area. It is equal to 20%.

TRY IT

f. On the game board, what is the probability of landing on a corner box?

g. On the game board, what is the probability of landing on a yellow box?

1. Explain why experimental probabilities can be useful even when people get different values for the same experiment.
2. What would you think if the experimental probability for an event turned out to be very different from the theoretical probability?
3. Explain how a geometric model helps to show probability.

Exercises

CORE

1. **Getting Started** Think of rolling a six-sided die.
   a. What is the probability of rolling a 5?
   b. List the ways it can land to get an even number.
   c. What is the probability of rolling an even number?

2. You have two nickels and two dimes in a cup. If you shake out two coins, what is the probability that you can pay for a 15¢ purchase?

> **Problem-Solving Tip**
>
> Make a list of the possible pairs of coins.

3. Think of using a spinner with five equal regions labeled 1, 2, 3, 4, and 5. For **3a–3d,** find each probability. You may use ratio, decimal, or percentage form.
   a. landing on 2
   b. landing on an odd number
   c. landing on 3 or 4
   d. landing on a number greater than 2
   e. If you spin 20 times, how many times would you expect to get a 5?
   f. If you spin 25 times, how many times would you expect to get a 1? Explain your thinking.

Write the word or phrase that best completes each statement.

4. Seth flipped a coin 10 times and got 6 heads. He says the ___ probability of getting heads with this coin is 60%.

5. Because the spinner has three out of eight equal regions labeled *red*, the ___ probability of getting red is $\frac{3}{8}$.

6. A geometric model with 12 squares has 3 red and 9 blue squares. The probability of choosing red is ___.

7. The width of each band is the same size.

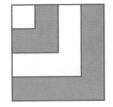

   a. How many small squares will fit in each band?

   b. Find the theoretical probability of landing on each band.

   c. How will adding the probabilities help you check your answers?

8. Suppose a fair coin is flipped eight times in a row.

   a. In any flip, what is the probability of getting heads? of getting tails?

   b. If you get tails every time, what do you think the probability of getting tails on the ninth throw will be? Explain your thinking.

   c. What do you think the probability of getting heads on the ninth flip will be? Explain your thinking.

9. This spinner has been divided into unequal regions. What is the theoretical probability that the spinner will stop in the indicated area?

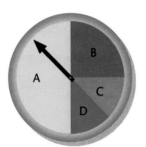

   a. A

   b. B

   c. D

   d. any shaded region

10. **Square Shooter** The smallest square in this target is 6 in. by 6 in. The lengths of the sides increase by 6 in. for each of the three larger squares. Find the probability of hitting each of the four areas if a dart is thrown at random.

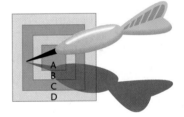

 LOOK BACK

Use this game board to answer the questions. [6-1]

11. What fraction of the dark squares is occupied by striped markers, including striped kings? light squares by dotted markers?

12. What fraction of the total squares is occupied by kings? by a marker other than a king?

13. Which ratio is greater: occupied light squares to total light squares or occupied dark squares to total dark squares?

MORE PRACTICE

14. Georgia has a list of six things she could be doing tonight at 8:15. She says that they are all equally likely.

- Shopping at Uptown Mall
- At home doing homework
- At home watching TV
- Visiting at a friend's house
- At home on the phone
- At home playing her clarinet

a. What is the probability that she will be watching TV?
b. How many things on her list are at home?
c. What is the probability she will be doing something at home?

The area of each region on the spinner is the same.

15. Make a list of all possible outcomes.

16. How many outcomes give you
    a. an odd number?
    b. a number greater than 4?
    c. a number that is not a 5?

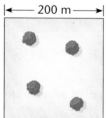

17. Write each probability.
    a. landing on a number divisible by 3
    b. landing on 2
    c. landing on a number less than 9
    d. landing on 1, 2, or 4
    e. landing on a number that is a factor of 12
    f. landing on 0

18. Safe Landings To make a safe jump, a parachutist must avoid trees in this 200-meter square. A circle with a radius of 25 meters marks each unsafe area. What is the probability of a safe jump? How do you know?

19. In a game similar to Tiddlywinks, a small cup is located in the center of four concentric circles with radii of 1, 2, 3, and 4 units, respectively. What is the ratio of the playing area of circle 3 to circle 4?

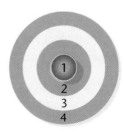

MORE MATH REASONING

20. You and a friend flip two coins to see who pays for gas. You pay if the coins match. Your friend pays if the coins are different. Does each person have the same chance of paying? Explain.

21. Two dice are tossed at the same time and the numbers are added.
  a. What are the different totals that are possible? How many totals are possible?
  b. Is each total as likely as any other?
  c. Suppose one die is red and the other die is green. List the ways these dice can land to give a total of 2 and of 12.
  d. List the ways the red and green dice can land to give a total of 7.

22. Geologists have said that the probability of a major earthquake occurring in the San Francisco Bay area in the next 30 years is about 90%. Is this experimental probability or theoretical probability? Why?

23. Three coins tossed together can land with three heads, two heads, one head, or no heads.
  a. Is each outcome equally likely? What are the theoretical probabilities?
  b. Toss three different coins 24 times and record the number of heads in each toss.
  c. How do the experimental probabilities match the theoretical probabilities you found?

7-1
PART D — Simulations

← **C O N N E C T** → *You have worked with experimental and theoretical probability. Now you will look more closely at the idea of a random event.*

Imagine …

• Ten $100 bills are handed out at random to ten students. Is it possible that someone would not get any bills?
• Two evenly matched tennis players play five games. Who would win the most games?
• 14 pens out of a box of 100 are broken. How many would be broken in another box of 100?

We can't find the theoretical probability for such events since we can't predict the ratio of the various outcomes. Experimental probability would require us to spend money, play tennis, and open boxes of pens.

Instead, we use dice or spinners to **simulate** the situation. A random-number table is another tool you can use. A **random-number table** is a list of digits chosen without any pattern. One number is as likely to appear in any position as any other number.

Random Numbers					
24430	88834	77318	07486	33950	61598
49693	99286	83447	20215	16040	41085
57159	58010	43162	98878	73337	35571
73256	02968	31129	66588	48126	52700
96312	42442	96713	43940	92516	81421
88047	68960	52991	67703	29805	42701
25545	26603	40243	55482	38341	97781
72654	24625	78393	77172	41328	95633
55102	93408	10965	69744	80766	14889
78338	77881	90139	72375	50624	91385

EXAMPLE

Ten students are lined up in order holding numbers from 1 to 10. Ten $100 bills are going to be given away at random. Use a random-number table to show what could happen.

We pick a starting point anywhere, at random, and read off 10 digits. Each digit means "give a $100 bill to the student holding that number." A zero corresponds to a student with the number 10.

5   5102   93408

The money goes to students 5, 5, 1, 10, 2, 9, 3, 4, 10, and 8. Students holding the numbers 5 and 10 each got two bills, but the students with numbers 6 and 7 have none.

TRY IT

a. Start at a different place in the random-number table and simulate giving away twenty $100 bills. Do you think any student will be overlooked this time? Will any student get as much as $500? Explain.

A group of 10 students go into the library and give their lunch bags to the librarian. When the bell rings the librarian hands each student a lunch bag at random. Will anyone get the right lunch?

1. Suppose you are one of the 10. Do you think it is likely that you will get your own lunch?

2. Do you think *anyone* will get the right lunch? Explain why you think so.

It would be very difficult to get 10 students and 10 lunches to test this situation. But you can simulate this situation by using the random-number table. Make a chart like the one below to record several trials.

3. We've chosen a random starting point. Move to the right until you find all of the numbers from 0 to 9 (ignore duplicate numbers). The first four are underlined.

24430	88834	77318	07486	33950	61598
49693	99286	83447	20215	16040	41085
57159	58010	43162	9_8_8_7_8	7_3_337	35571
73256	02968	31129	66588	48126	52700
96312	42442	96713	43940	92516	81421

The digits 9, 8, 7, and 3 were found and entered in the table below. Skip any digits that you have already listed. Complete the table by finding all 10 digits. These represent the 10 lunches. Do any lunch numbers match the student number? If so, that student got the right lunch.

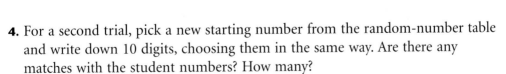

Student number ...	1	2	3	4	5	6	7	8	9	10
First trial: gets lunch number ...	9	8	7	3						
Second trial: gets lunch number ...										
Third trial: gets lunch number ...										
Fourth trial: gets lunch number ...										

4. For a second trial, pick a new starting number from the random-number table and write down 10 digits, choosing them in the same way. Are there any matches with the student numbers? How many?

5. Do the trial two more times. Enter results in your table.

6. On average, how many students seem to get their own lunches? What is the probability that some student will get the correct lunch?

1. What other situations can you think of where a group of objects must be matched with another group?
2. Look up the meaning of *simulation.* Have you ever seen an ad for a simulated diamond ring? What would such a ring be like?

WHAT DO **YOU** THINK?

The traffic light for drivers on York Road is red for 20 seconds. Then it is red for drivers on Chestnut Street for 40 seconds.

Suppose you will drive to school on Chestnut Street four times next week. What is the probability that the light will be red for you every day?

Tyler thinks ...

I can use a die. I will let 1 and 2 mean green for Chestnut Street, and 3, 4, 5, and 6 mean red for Chestnut Street.

I'll throw the die four times to simulate the days I will be driving to school. I will do this for 10 trials.

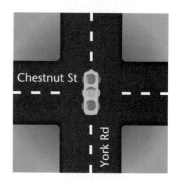

Trial 1:	1 **5 5** 1	Red every day? No
Trial 2:	**5** 2 2 2	Red every day? No
Trial 3:	**4 6 6** 2	Red every day? No
Trial 4:	**3** 2 **3 5**	Red every day? No
Trial 5:	**6 3 6 4**	Red every day? **YES**
Trial 6:	1 **4** 1 **6**	Red every day? No
Trial 7:	1 **6 3** 1	Red every day? No
Trial 8:	**4 6** 2 **3**	Red every day? No
Trial 9:	**5** 1 **4 5**	Red every day? No
Trial 10:	**5** 2 **3 4**	Red every day? No

In 1 trial out of 10, the light was red every day, so my experimental probability was $\frac{1}{10}$.

Yeaphana thinks ...

I'll put four red markers in a bag representing a red light on Chestnut Street, and two green markers representing a red light on York Road. I will pick one marker, record its color, replace it, and draw three more times. I'll do this for 10 trials.

Trial 1: **R R R R** Red every day

Trial 2: R R G R

Trial 3: G R G G

Trial 4: R R G R

Trial 5: R G R R

Trial 6: R G R G

Trial 7: R G R R

Trial 8: **R R R R** Red every day

Trial 9: G G R R

Trial 10: G R R R

In 2 trials out of 10, the light was red every day, so my experimental probability was $\frac{2}{10}$.

REFLECT

1. Why do you think it is important to select the starting digit on a random-number table without looking?

2. Will events turn out exactly as one simulation would imply? Would a more likely result be obtained by doing many simulations and averaging the results? Explain your thinking.

3. Instead of using a random-number table, would it be just as effective to draw digits from a bag, or use a spinner with 10 spaces numbered 0 to 9? Why do you think so?

4. Why do you think the probabilities found using a random-number table are estimates?

Exercises

CORE

1. **Getting Started** Pick any row in a random-number table. Count the number of times the digit 5 appears. Why should the ratio be close to 10%? What ratio do you find?

2. You draw a card at random from a bag. Do you have a better chance of drawing a vowel or a consonant?

3. Suppose this spinner is used to award a prize.

   a. Which letter would you choose?
   b. Explain why the probability of spinning either an A or a D is the same.

4. Nia has a batting average of 0.300.

   a. What is the probability that she will get a hit next time at bat?

$$\text{Batting average} = \frac{\text{Number of hits}}{\text{Number of times at bat}}$$

   b. Use a random-number table and let 0, 1, and 2 stand for hits. Let the other seven digits stand for no-hits. Find the probability that the player will get two or more hits in a row in a game if she bats five times.
   c. What is the probability of her getting no hits in her next eight times to bat?

5. Andre and Chris have agreed to play five table-tennis games.

   a. Assume the players are equally matched. What is the probability of Chris's winning every game?
   b. Use a simulation of your choice to find the probability that Andre wins exactly three games and Chris wins two.

6. A multiple-choice test has ten questions. Only one of the four possible answers beside each question is correct.

   a. What is the probability of getting the correct answer to question 1 if you guess at the answer?
   b. Make a spinner to simulate choosing answers. Use it to find your score if you guess at all ten questions.
   c. Do you ever get three questions correct in a row using this simulation?

7. A spinner containing equal-sized regions with the numbers 1, 2, 3, and 4 is used in a game. The arrow fell off the spinner. Explain how you could use a random-number table to continue the game.

8. Robert ran a simulation to see how many packs of cards he would need to buy to get all three Hot Cards. Which is the best method?

		Card 1	Card 2	Card 3
(a)	Use a random-number table	0–3	4–6	7–9
(b)	Flip a coin twice	two heads	a head and a tail	two tails
(c)	Roll a die	1 or 6	2 or 5	3 or 4
(d)	Use the hours of a clock	1, 2, 3, or 4	5, 6, 7, or 8	9, 10, 11, or 12

Science

9. Suppose the probability is $16\frac{2}{3}\%$ that a seed will sprout. Run 10 trials of a simulation to determine how many seeds should be planted to get 5 seeds to sprout. (Hint: What fraction is $16\frac{2}{3}\%$?)

What fraction of each region is shaded? [5-2]

10.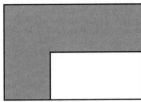

11.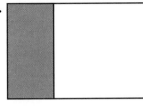

12.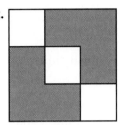

13. Find the least common denominator for the following fractions. [Previous course]

a. $\frac{2}{3}, \frac{1}{2}$ **b.** $\frac{3}{4}, \frac{5}{6}$ **c.** $\frac{7}{10}, \frac{1}{4}$

MORE PRACTICE

14. Four friends each give $5 to purchase one concert ticket. They will draw a name at random to see who gets the ticket.
  a. Would you be willing to join in a plan like this one, assuming you would like to go to the concert?
  b. Would you feel different if twenty people each gave $1 to buy one ticket? Explain your thinking.

15. Pick any column in the random-number table on page 689.
  a. Count the number of even digits.
  b. What is the probability that a digit is even in this column?

16. Pick any row in the random-number table on page 689.
  a. How many times does the digit 0 appear?
  b. What is the probability of choosing 0 from this row?

17. A basketball player makes 70% of his free throws. Suppose he attempts five free throws in one game. Use these numbers from the random-number table to simulate his free throws.

72654   24625   78393   77172   41328   95633   55102   93408   10965   69744

Let the digits from 1 to 7 stand for free throws he hits. Digits 8, 9, and 0 are misses. Read off five digits. Do this 10 times. From this simulation:
  a. What is the probability that he will make all five free throws?
  b. What is the probability that he will make at least four free throws?

18. The executive board of a company contains four men and two women. The members draw straws to determine which two will speak at the annual stockholders meeting.

   a. What is the probability that at least one of the speakers will be a woman? (Hint: Roll a six-sided die two times. Let 1 and 2 mean that a woman is chosen, and let 3, 4, 5, and 6 mean that a man is chosen.)

   b. What is the probability that neither speaker is a woman?

19. In the 1993–1994 National Basketball Association season, about one-third of the attempted three-point goals were made. What is the probability that an NBA player will make his next two three-pointers in a row? (Hint: Use simulation.)

MORE MATH REASONING

20. Left-handed people make up about $\frac{1}{7}$ of the population. The Rangers softball team contains 10 players. Tell how to use simulation to find the probability that the team has exactly two left-handed players.

21. Design a spinner with two regions, marked 1 and 2, where the probability of spinning a 1 is twice the probability of spinning a 2.

22. A company surveyed 1000 families moving to a new state to determine the results of an advertising campaign. Some data were misplaced, but one employee remembered that twice as many families were moving south as west. Complete the table.

Region of New Home	North	East	South	West
Region Ratio	0.15			0.2

7-1
PART E
Making Connections

← C O N N E C T →   *The ideal game gives all players an equally likely chance of winning. Is this true for all games and contests? In this lesson you will use what you have learned about probability to decide.*

A pretzel company includes cards with photos of teenage TV stars in the boxes. There is one card in each box and six cards in the series.

EXPLORE: COLLECTING STARS

MATERIALS

Number cube or die

Two friends want to see who can collect a complete set of cards for the least amount of money. The cost of a box is $1.25. Each box contains one picture card. How many boxes will each friend probably have to buy to get all six cards? Make your guess now!

1. Annie buys six boxes at once. Estimate the probability that she got all six cards.
2. Gregor bought 3 boxes at once. Is it probable that he got three of the same card?

Ben   Jorge   Desrie   Pei   Lydia   Elena

We assume there is an equally likely chance of getting any one of the six cards. Because a die has six faces, we can simulate buying cards by rolling a die.

3. Count how many times you roll the die until all six numbers have come up. Conduct 10 trials. Record the total number of rolls for each trial.
4. Find the average number of rolls needed to collect all six cards.
5. Compare your results with those of a classmate. Were your answers close?
6. Find the average cost to collect the series.

You could also use the random-number table to simulate collecting star cards. Start anywhere and record the digits 1, 2, 3, 4, 5, and 6 as they come up. Ignore the other digits 7, 8, 9, and 0 because they have no meaning in this situation.

1. Probability is a measure of certainty or uncertainty. Name two events that are certain and two that are impossible.
2. Why do you think people enjoy playing games involving chance?
3. What does the expression *50–50 chance* mean? Why would tossing a coin represent a 50–50 chance? Would you play a game with a 50–50 chance of winning? carry an umbrella if there were a 50–50 chance of rain? ride in a car that had a 50–50 chance of brake failure? Explain your answers.
4. How does a simulation help you understand the possible outcomes of an event?

Self-Assessment

1. A friend of yours has collected five of the six cards in the teen-star collection.
   a. What is the probability that the next card will complete the set?
   b. What is the probability that the next card will *not* complete the set?

2. Suppose the pretzel company made twice as many cards for the teenagers numbered 1, 2, and 3. How would this affect the experiment? the outcome?

3. Suppose there had been eight cards in the teen-star series.
   a. What is the probability of getting each card?
   b. What is the sum of the probabilities?
   c. What is the probability of getting a baseball card in the pretzel box?
   d. Draw a device you could use to conduct a simulation with eight possible outcomes.

4. A scientist was working on an important experiment when her chemicals spilled. Estimate the missing number.

Recovery Time	A	B	C	D
Probability	0.32	0.27	0.21	?

5. The customers at Joe's Pies spin to determine the price for a small pie.

  a. What is the probability of spinning $6.75? of spinning $5.00?

  b. What is the probability of paying more than $6.00 for a pie?

  c. If 24 customers order a small pie, how many would you expect to get the pie for free? for less than $6.50?

  d. What do you think is the actual price for a pie at Joe's? Explain your thinking.

Social Science

6. The game of Lu-Lu is played in Hawaii. Players throw stones, each marked with 1, 2, 3, or 4 dots on one side. They total the number of dots for their score. All stones landing opposite side up are thrown by the next player for bonus points.

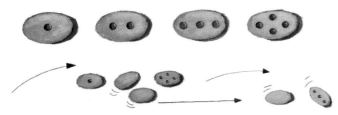

  a. What is the probability that a stone will land with the dots up?

  b. If a stone lands with the dots up, what is the probability of throwing a 1? a 2 or 3?

  c. What score might you expect on one roll if all the stones land dots up?

  d. What is the highest score you could expect if one stone thrown by the previous player landed opposite side up?

  e. Do you think winning this game is based on skill or luck? Explain your thinking.

7. Design a spinner containing the numbers 1, 2, 3, 4, and 5 such that the probability of spinning a 1 is twice the probability of spinning a 5 and the sum of the probabilities of spinning a 2, 3, or 4 is $\frac{1}{2}$.

8. A fast-food chain includes one of four toy cars in each child's meal.

  a. What is the average number of meals needed to make a complete set? Conduct a simulation of 10 trials to calculate your answer.

  b. If a child's meal costs $3.29, what is the average cost to collect all four toys?

9. An unusual dart board contains white and shaded areas.

  a. Copy the dart board and draw lines to form equal areas.

  b. What is the probability of landing on a shaded area? a white area?

  c. To win a game, would you choose to shoot darts at the shaded area or the white area? Explain your thinking.

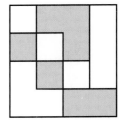

10. Based on past results, the probability of improving your score the second time you take a college entrance exam is 80%. Of five students you know who took the exam for the second time, two improved their scores. Do you think you should take the exam again? Justify your decision.

11. Which spinner is most likely to give a sum greater than seven in two spins?

(a)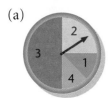
(b)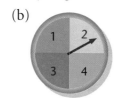
(c)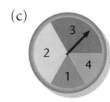
(d)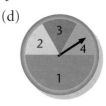

Which price is closest to the mean price of the set? [1-3]

12. (a) Finch $15   (b) Canary $55   (c) Cockatiel $38   (d) Parakeet $20

13. (a) Pup $85   (b) Hexagonal $125   (c) Hoop $160   (d) Four-person $199

Industry

14. If the probability that you will catch a cold in the next six months is 0.34, what is the probability that you will *not* catch a cold? What is the sum of these probabilities?

15. The total points scored in a basket-ball tournament by each player was recorded in a stem-and-leaf plot. What is the probability that a player scored more than 45 points in the tournament? [1-3]

Stem	Leaf
6	5 6 7 8
5	3 5 6 6 7 9
4	0 1 4 4 4 5 7 9 9
3	0 1 2 2 8
2	3 3 5 7

16. Which fountain glass holds more strawberry shake? Why? [5-3]

2 in.

6 in.

3 in.

8 in.

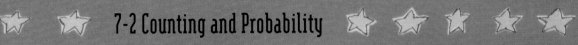

A Goat of a Chance

Marilyn vos Savant writes a question-and-answer column that appears in many newspapers. One question was about probability.

Dear Marilyn:
Suppose you're on a game show, and you're given the choice of three doors. Behind one is a car, behind the others, goats. You pick a door, say No. 1, and the host, who knows what's behind the other doors, opens another door, say No. 3, which has a goat. He then says to you, "Do you want to pick door No. 2?" Is it to your advantage to take the switch?

Ms. vos Savant's reply started a controversy that attracted national attention of mathematicians, ordinary citizens, and students from elementary school through college. Some said that the probability of picking the door with the car is 1/3 regardless of what the host shows after the choice is made. Others, including Ms. vos Savant, claimed that switching improved the probability to 2/3. Each tried to prove his or her own answer correct.

This puzzle has been named Monty's Dilemma after Monty Hall, the original host of "Let's Make a Deal," the game show that prompted the letter.

1. Look up the word *dilemma.* Is this problem a good example of a dilemma? Why or why not?
2. Suppose you were a contestant on Monty Hall's show. If he offered you $5000 instead of the chance to switch doors, would you choose the *sure thing* or take a chance on picking the right door? Give your reasons.
3. Do you agree with Ms. vos Savant that your chances of winning the prize would be better if you switched? What simulation could you use to test her answer?

← C O N N E C T →
You have seen that to find the probability of an event you need to know the total number of possibilities. Now you will see a technique that can help you find this number.

Most big decisions consist of many small decisions. Even choosing what to wear to a party can mean a long list of possibilities.

EXPLORE: WHO WAS THAT MASKED MAN?

Eugene is getting ready for a costume party. He needs to get a mustache, fake eyebrows, and a wig. The costume store has the following in stock

Handlebar moustache   Groucho moustache   Round eyebrows   Pointed eyebrows   Bald wig   Curly wig   Straight wig

1. How many mustache choices are there? eyebrow choices? wig choices?

A **tree diagram** is a way to list all possibilities.

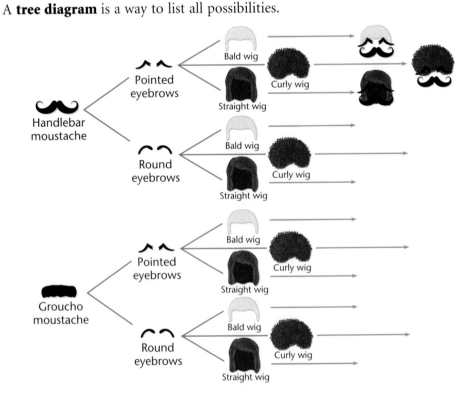

2. Copy and complete the tree diagram to show all the possibilities. How many possibilities are there?

3. Suppose Eugene makes his three choices at random. What is the probability that he chooses the Groucho mustache, round eyebrows, and the bald wig?

4. List the possibilities that include the curly wig. What is the probability of choosing a costume that includes the curly wig?

5. How many possibilities include the round eyebrows? What is the probability of choosing a costume that does *not* include round eyebrows?

6. Look at the number of choices for each part of the costume. How could you find the total number of possible costumes without making a tree diagram?

To find the probability of an event, you must know the total number of possibilities to use as the denominator of the probability ratio. A tree diagram lists all possibilities. Another way is to use an organized list.

EXAMPLE

1. Akiko has decided to improve her daily diet by meeting the recommended servings of fruit (2–4) and vegetables (3–5) given in the Food Guide Pyramid. How many different possibilities of a fruit and vegetable servings can she have for lunch if she takes carrots or broccoli with an orange, an apple, a peach, a nectarine, or strawberries?

When listing the possibilities, go through all the possibilities with one vegetable before listing the others.

There are 10 possibilities.

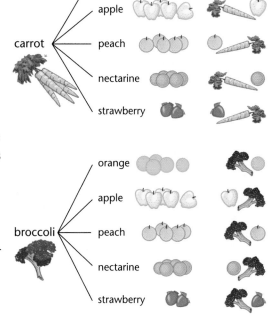

You can use the total of the possible outcomes to calculate probabilities. In the Example, it is easy to see the probability of getting a combination that has an orange is $\frac{2}{10}$, or $\frac{1}{5}$.

TRY IT

Each of the outcomes on each spinner is equally likely.

a. List the possibilities when you spin both spinners.

b. What is probability that cows will run?

CONSIDER ?

1. In the Explore, would the tree diagram look different if it started with the three wigs? Would the total number of possibilities be different?

WHAT DO **YOU** THINK?

Candy, David, and Pam all want to be president of the Ecology Club. All received the same number of votes. To break the deadlock, the president and vice president will be chosen by picking two slips of paper out of a hat that contains the names of each candidate.

Find the probability that David will be named president and Pam will be named vice president.

Eugene thinks ...

To list all possible outcomes, I will make a tree diagram.

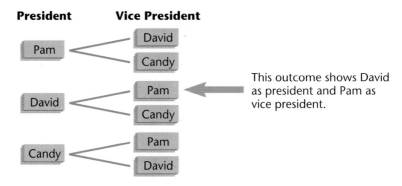

This outcome shows David as president and Pam as vice president.

There are six possibilities, one of which has David as president and Pam as vice president. The probability is $\frac{1}{6}$.

Dawn thinks ...

I will make a list of all possibilities. I'll keep them in alphabetical order, so that I don't skip any.

President, Vice President

1. Candy, David
2. Candy, Pam
3. David, Candy
4. **David, Pam**
5. Pam, Candy
6. Pam, David

Of the six possibilities, there is one with David as president of the Ecology Club and Pam as vice president. The probability is $\frac{1}{6}$.

Both students correctly found the total number of possibilities to use as the denominator of the probability ratio.

TRY IT

Use the information from the student election above.

c. Of the six possible sets of winners, what is the probability that Pam is vice president?

d. What is the probability that Pam is elected to *either* job?

In many situations we need to know only the number of possibilities that exist. We don't need a tree diagram or an organized list.

COUNTING PRINCIPLE

If a first thing can occur in *m* ways, and a second thing can occur in *n* ways, then these things can occur together in *m* × *n* ways.

The **Counting Principle** works for any number of events.

2. Miranda has a gift-wrapping business. She has 15 types of paper, 10 types of ribbon, and 12 different types of bows. How many different combinations of paper, ribbon, and bows does she have?
Using the Counting Principle, we find $15 \times 10 \times 12 = 1800$ possible combinations.

REFLECT

1. Explain why it is a mistake to say that the probability of getting two heads, one head and one tail, or two tails is each $\frac{1}{3}$ when two coins are flipped together.

2. Describe a situation in which a list might be easier to work with than a tree diagram.

3. What are some reasons why a real election might not turn out as probabilities would predict?

President Truman is holding up a newspaper that falsely claims he was defeated in the 1948 presidential election.

Exercises

CORE

1. Getting Started A deli offers a soup and sandwich special.

Soup	Bread	Filling
French onion	Whole wheat	Ham
Vegetable	Rye	Roast beef
		Chicken

a. Copy and complete this tree diagram showing all the possible lunch combinations.

b. How many different combinations does your tree diagram show?

c. How many of those combinations include chicken?

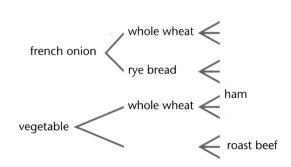

2. Make a tree diagram to show all the possible outcomes of tossing three coins.
   a. How many of the eight combinations contain exactly two heads?
   b. What is the probability of tossing exactly two heads?
   c. How many of the eight combinations contain one head and two tails?
   d. What is the probability of tossing one head and two tails?

3. Phone Home A telephone comes in a wall or desk model, four colors, and with or without an answering machine.
   a. How many different combinations are possible?
   b. What is the probability of choosing a phone with an answering machine? a wall model without an answering machine? a desk model in white with an answering machine?

4. This map shows the roads between three towns. How many different routes can a traveler choose between Columbia and Essex?

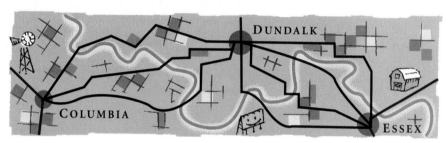

5. Paloma High School offers four different PE classes, courses in three foreign languages, and three courses in computers. How many possibilities are there for a student to take one course from each group?

6. What's Up? Consider all the possible outcomes when rolling a die and tossing a coin.
   a. How many outcomes are possible?
   b. Are the outcomes equally likely?
   c. What is the probability of getting 2 on the die and heads on the coin?
   d. What is the probability of getting any combination with a 6 on the die? a tail on the coin?

7. A raffle at a country fair will award a quilt to the person with the winning ticket. Each ticket will be red, green, or blue and printed with a letter of the alphabet and a single-digit non-zero number.

What is the maximum number of tickets that can be sold without duplicating a ticket?

8. There are 24 different ways to select an entree, a fruit, and a dessert for lunch in the school cafeteria. There are two entrees and three fruits. How many desserts are available? How do you know?

Problem-Solving Tip

Write and solve an equation.

9. A state decides to issue license plates with two letters followed by four digits. If there are no restrictions on the letters or digits, how many different license plates can the state issue?

10. Suppose your favorite letter and number are A and 7. How could you use the counting principle to find the probability of getting a ticket number A7 in a random draw? What other information would you need to know?

11. Use the counting principle to find the number of outcomes from spinning both spinners.
 a. Would the counting principle, a list, and a tree diagram all give the same result?
 b. What is the probability of spinning more than 50 tigers?

12. Plate Tectonics A license plate consists of three letters followed by three numbers.
 a. Show the first three plates and the last three plates in the complete set.
 b. Use a calculator to find the total number of possible plates.
 c. What is the probability of getting the license plate shown?
 d. What is the probability of getting a license plate with your initials on it?

FUN 123

LOOK AHEAD

Simplify each expression.

13. $5 \cdot 4 \cdot 3 \cdot 2 \cdot 1$ **14.** $9 \cdot 8 \cdot 7 \cdot 6 \cdot 5$ **15.** $12 \cdot 11 \cdot 10$

16. The letters A, B, and C can be ordered in six ways. Show these ways.

17. Sketch a graph that tells a changing story. Explain the parts of the graph.

MORE PRACTICE

18. A frozen-yogurt store offers three flavors of yogurt: vanilla, chocolate, and strawberry; two kinds of containers: cone or cup; and three toppings: raisins, granola, and peanuts.

Copy and complete this tree diagram showing all possible combinations for a frozen yogurt with one topping. How many combinations are there?

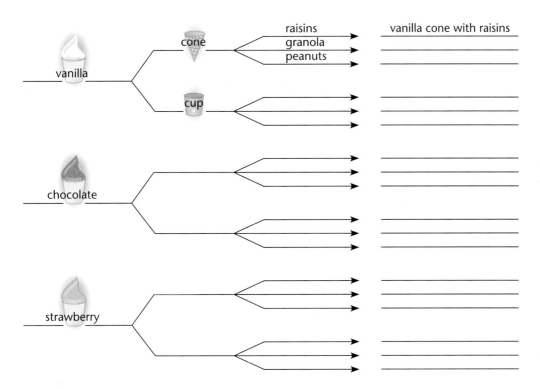

19. Burrito Rapido Salsa Taqueria offers two sizes of burritos, four different fillings, and a choice of sour cream, guacamole, or no topping. How many different combinations are there?

20. There are 36 different ways a customer can order pizza at La Pizzeria. Make a chart to show how this might be possible.

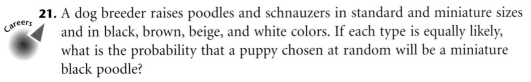

21. A dog breeder raises poodles and schnauzers in standard and miniature sizes and in black, brown, beige, and white colors. If each type is equally likely, what is the probability that a puppy chosen at random will be a miniature black poodle?

22. Imagine you need a dog, a bird, and a hamster for a commercial. Write a list showing all possible ways to select one dog from Nemo, Curly, and Kato; one parakeet from Tweety and Alfa; and one hamster from Hammie and Buzz.

23. A deli offers 3 soups, 4 salads, and 6 sandwiches. How many different lunches can be planned from this menu?

24. Map Trap There are 3 roads from Allentown to Bakersfield, 1 road from Bakersfield to Carollton, and 4 roads from Carollton to Drigsby. How many different routes are there from Allentown to Drigsby?

MORE MATH REASONING

25. Swimmers Take Your Marks ... A swim meet has eight events, two heats for each event, and six lanes for each heat. Each person swims in two events.
   a. How many swimmers can participate in the meet?
   b. What is the probability that the same swimmer will be assigned lane 1 for both events?

26. Spinners A and B are divided into four and eight equal parts, respectively. In a board game, each player spins A and then B.

   a. Make a tree diagram to show all the possible outcomes.
   b. Are the outcomes equally likely?
   c. What is the probability of spinning 1 on spinner A and 4 on spinner B?
   d. What is the probability of spinning 3 on spinner A and a number less than 5 on B?
   e. What is the probability that both numbers are divisible by 4?

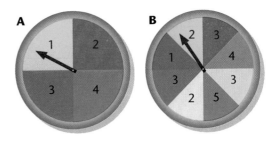

27. It's Amazing! Scientists use probability in their experiments. Suppose a mouse enters this maze. Assume that it is equally likely that the mouse will choose either A or B. It is also equally likely that it will choose C, D, or E.

   a. What is the probability the mouse will choose path A, then C? path B, then D?
   b. What is the probability that the mouse will arrive in the bottom room?
   c. What is the probability that the mouse will follow path B to the top room?

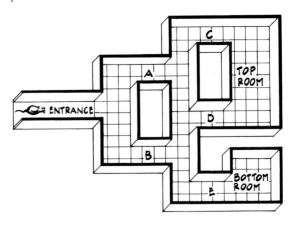

← C O N N E C T → *You have learned that to find probability, it is important to know all possibilities in a situation. Now you will get more experience in counting different arrangements of a set of objects.*

If you and three other people sit down at random at a table for four, will you probably get to sit next to your special friend?

If you and four other people sit down at random at a round table, will you probably get to sit next to your friend?

The probabilities that we use to answer these questions are based on knowing all the possible **arrangements.**

EXPLORE: SEATING THE PANEL

Jorge and his committee are in charge of setting up the stage for a panel discussion. They have invited 2 teachers (A and B), 2 guests (C and D), and 3 students (E, F, and G, the moderator). The committee wants to seat the seven panelists at a table like this:

1. Does the arrangement A E C G D F B meet the committee's requirements?
2. Does the arrangement B E G C D F A meet the requirements?
3. Find as many arrangements as possible that meet the requirements of Jorge's committee.
4. What is the probability that Student G will sit next to Ms. B?
5. What is the probability that Guest C will sit next to Student G?
6. What is the probability that Guest D will sit next to Ms. B?
7. Do you think a tree diagram or an organized list would be more useful in solving this problem? Explain.

The counting principle can be used to find how many ways you can *arrange* objects or place things in a specific *order*.

Suppose you have three objects to put in order.

We know that you can choose the first object *three* ways.

Once it's chosen, you can choose the second object only *two* ways.

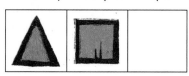

Now you can choose the last object only *one* way.

So by the counting principle, there are $3 \times 2 \times 1 = 6$ ways to put the objects in order:

1.
2.
3.
4.
5.
6.

For *n* objects, the number of **arrangements** is

$$n \times (n - 1) \times (n - 2) \times \ldots \times 2 \times 1.$$

EXAMPLE

1. Allie, Bonito, Carli, and Dawn will be putting on a Philippine folk dance demonstration. If each does one routine, how many possible ways can they dance in order?

Any one of the four could do the first routine, leaving three dancers to choose from for the next routine. After that, there are two dancers to choose from for the third routine, leaving only one choice for the last routine.

There are $4 \times 3 \times 2 \times 1 = 24$ possible ways they can dance in order.

When you need to arrange only some of the items, the number of factors in the product should match the number of items.

EXAMPLE

2. Six people have been nominated for art awards. In how many ways can 1st-, 2nd-, and 3rd-prize ribbons be awarded? What is the probability of guessing the winners in order?

There are 6 ways to award 1st prize, then 5 ways to award 2nd prize, and 4 ways to award 3rd prize.

There are $6 \times 5 \times 4 = 120$ ways to award the ribbons.

The probability of guessing the winners in order is $\frac{1}{120}$.

TRY IT

a. A machine is expected to transport boxes marked A, B, C, D, E, and F, in order, down an assembly line. What is the probability the machine could do this if it picked up the boxes in random order?

b. At a swim meet, three swimmers will compete in a pool that has five lanes. How many ways could you assign each swimmer to a lane?

1. Why do you have fewer choices once you begin arranging objects?
2. How does finding the number of arrangements compare with counting possibilities using the counting principle? How are they alike? How are they different?
3. How many factors are in the number of arrangements of 7 objects? of n objects?

Exercises

CORE

1. **Getting Started** Suppose you have four objects, labeled A, B, C, and D, to put in order.
   a. In how many ways can you select the first object?
   b. In how many ways can you select the second object, once the first is selected?
   c. In how many ways can you select the third object, once the first two are selected?
   d. In how many ways can you select the last object, once all the others are selected?
   e. What is the product of your answers? What does this number represent?

2. In how many ways can three objects be arranged in order? Give an example.

3. In how many ways can five different stones be arranged from left to right on a necklace?

4. a. In how many ways can a baseball manager make a batting order using nine players?
   b. Suppose the manager picks a lineup randomly. What is the probability that someone could guess the batting order?

5. **Line of Succession** This photograph was taken at the April 28, 1994, funeral for President Nixon. Presidents Ford, Carter, Reagan, Bush, and Clinton are lined up in chronological order of their presidencies.

   What is the probability this would occur if they had lined up randomly?

6. Make up an example where the number of ordered arrangements
  a. is greater than 1000.   **b.** is greater than 10,000.

Fine Arts

7. Ding Dong *Change ringing* is the ringing of a set of bells in all possible orders of the bells.

  a. In how many ways could a ringing order be arranged for six bells?

  b. If each bell takes one second to ring and between each order is a pause of three seconds, how long will it take to ring all possible orders?

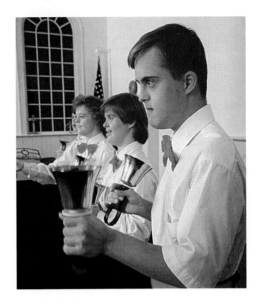

Industry

8. Fire Away An automobile engine has 4, 6, or 8 cylinders, each with a spark plug. If the spark plugs do not fire in the correct order, the car will run poorly or not at all.

  a. How many firing orders are possible for a 4-cylinder car?

  b. How many firing orders are possible for a 6-cylinder car?

  c. How many firing orders are possible for an 8-cylinder car?

  d. The wires from the distributor cap must be put on the correct plugs to get the right firing order. What are your chances of getting this right by attaching them randomly for each type of car?

9. a. Copy and complete the table below.

Number of Objects	1	2	3	4	5	6	7	8	9
Arrangements									

  b. How does adding an object (the *n*th object) change the number of arrangements?

> **Problem-Solving Tip**
>
> Look for a pattern.

LOOK BACK

Fill in the blank to make equivalent ratios. [6-1]

10. 24 hours: 1 day = ____ hours: 7 days

11. 1500 cm: 60 minutes = 600 cm: ____ minutes

Solve each equation. [4-2]

12. $2x + x = 39$

13. $4x + 13 = 5$

14. $6x + 2x = 9 - 5$

15. $3x - 8 = 2x + 3$

Reduce each fraction to lowest terms. [Previous course]

16. $\frac{12}{32}$

17. $\frac{16}{24}$

18. $\frac{9}{60}$

MORE PRACTICE

19. Find the product: $7 \times 6 \times 5 \times 4 \times 3 \times 2 \times 1$. What does this number represent?

20. In how many ways can three people line up at a ticket window?

21. In how many ways can four children be given a saxophone, trumpet, clarinet, and tuba?

22. In how many orders can five dogs jump through a flaming hoop?

23. Six taxicabs are lined up waiting for a fare.
   a. How many arrangements are possible for the line?
   b. What is the probability that the taxicabs are in line in the order of the numbers on their sides?

24. Six important people will lead a parade. The lead car seats only two people. In how many ways can two guests be chosen for the lead car?

25. Easy as 1, 2, 3? A door lock has five buttons. Three different buttons must be pressed in the correct order before the key will open the door.
   a. In how many ways can you press three different buttons?
   b. What is the probability of pressing the right buttons if you don't know the lock combination?

26. The roster of a girls' softball team contains 15 players. Find the number of batting orders possible for the first three hitters.

27. Think about arranging the last four digits of a telephone number.
   a. How many ways are possible if the numbers are all different?
   b. What is the probability that an arrangement selected at random matches the last four digits of your telephone number?

28. There are 52 cards in a deck. How many 5-card hands are possible?
   (a) $52 \times 52 \times 52 \times 52 \times 52$ (b) $52 \times 51 \times 50 \times 49 \times 48$
   (c) $5 \times 4 \times 3 \times 2 \times 1$ (d) not here

MORE MATH REASONING

29. Why is it much easier to unscramble a five-letter word jumble than a six-letter word jumble?

30. You, your best friend, and two others must seat yourselves according to a randomly placed name tag at a round table.
   a. How many different seating arrangements are possible?
   b. What is the probability that your best friend will be next to you?

31. Suppose your house number is 135. An address on an envelope has the digits in the wrong order.
   a. In how many ways can this happen?
   b. Suppose your house number is 344. How many ways can the digits be mixed?
   c. How does your answer change if your house number is 222?

32. Locate the ⟨ ! ⟩ key on your calculator. This is called the *factorial* key.

   a. Press 7 ⟨ ! ⟩. What is 7 factorial?

   b. Copy and complete the following table.

x	1	2	3	4	5	6	7	8
x!								

   c. What could this key be used for?

   d. What happens if you enter 2.5 ⟨ ! ⟩? Can you explain the result?

← CONNECT → *The counting principle and tree diagrams helped you find the number of possibilities when position and order were important. Now you will compare those situations with others in which order is not important.*

In some lotto drawings, a player chooses a **group** of numbers from a list to try to match a winning set of numbers. The order of choosing the numbers is not important. Lotto games *appear* fairly easy to win.

EXPLORE: 3 OUT OF 6 IS HALF, ISN'T IT?

Can you win your own lottery? If you don't pick the right numbers the first time, how many tries do you think it will take?

MATERIALS

*Small paper or plastic bag
Slips of paper*

1. Write the numbers from 1 to 6 on slips of paper and put them in a bag. Shake well, and pick three pieces of paper without looking. Write the numbers down. These are your personal winning lottery numbers! Return the slips to the bag.

2. Now you will try to match the three winners. Pick three more pieces of paper. Compare the numbers with the three winners. Remember that the order in which you draw the numbers is not important. Do they match?

3. If your three numbers do not match, put the slips back into the bag and try again. Keep track of how many times you must try until you match the three winners.

4. Did anyone win on the first try? Did anyone have to try more than 20 times?

5. In how many ways can the three numbers be chosen? Make an organized list.

6. Would you say that the probability of matching 3 numbers out of 6 in one try is 5%? 10%, 25%, 50%?

In the Explore, you examined ways to choose a group of numbers where the order of the choice made no difference.

Suppose the director of a play needs to select a singer and a dancer from among three candidates. The director has three choices for a singer and then two choices for a dancer. So there are $3 \times 2 = 6$ possibilities.

Singer	Dancer
A	B
A	C
B	A
B	C
C	A
C	B

But suppose the director only wants two singers. Then some of the possibilities are the same as others.

Because the order in which the singers are chosen is not important, the director has only three possible ways to choose two singers.

AB   BC   AC

Singer	Singer	
A	B	
A	C	
B	A	Same
B	C	
C	A	
C	B	

EXAMPLE

1. Show the 10 possible ways to choose 2 students from a list of 5 students called A, B, C, D, and E.
The possibilities are

AB	AC	AD	AE
	BC	BD	BE
		CD	CE
			DE

TRY IT

a. Show the 10 possible ways to choose a group of 3 students from a group of 5. Call the 5 students A, B, C, D, and E.

You can also find the probability of choosing a group.

2. Jeff is delivering newspapers to a new route. Four houses remain on the street, and he has two newspapers. If Jeff chooses two houses at random, what is the probability they will be the correct ones?

There are six ways to choose two houses from four:

Jeff's probability of choosing the correct houses is $\frac{1}{6}$.

CONSIDER

1. In Example 2, why wouldn't a mail carrier have the same probability as Jeff of matching mail to correct houses?

REFLECT

1. Describe the difference between a choice in which order is important and one in which it is not.
2. Why are there fewer possibilities when order is not important?
3. What daily life examples can you think of that are like selecting two people from a larger group for a committee?

Exercises

CORE

1. Getting Started Decide whether each phrase describes an ordered arrangement or a group.
a. the number of ways to arrange 8 trophies in a display case
b. the number of ways to choose a group of 3 trophies from 8 trophies
c. the number of ways to select 1 trophy from 8 trophies

2. In how many ways can you choose 3 objects from a group of 4 objects?

3. Ann, Bob, Carly, and Damien are players on a game show in which two players compete at one time. Make a list of all the possible pairs.

4. Suppose you pack two shirts for a trip. How many pairs of shirts are possible if you choose from six shirts in a closet?

5. In how many ways can a committee of four be selected from a group of five people? Call the people A, B, C, D, and E, and show your list.

6. A game or contest is considered fair when all participants have an equally likely chance to win. Which of the following situations would you consider fair? Explain your thinking.
   a. Winning a lottery if the numbers are chosen by a machine
   b. Using a poll to determine the winner in an election
   c. Using ballots submitted at baseball games to pick the Major League All-Stars

7. Decide whether each phrase describes an ordered arrangement or a group.
   a. the number of batting orders for a baseball team of 25 players
   b. the number of starting teams for a basketball team of 12 players
   c. the number of three-letter sets you can form from the word *games*
   d. the number of three-letter words you can form from the word *games*

8. You and a friend are playing a game. For your turn, you may choose to roll a die or spin a spinner containing the numbers 1 through 5. Give a reason for each answer.
   a. You need to get a 5 to win a game. Would you rather roll or spin?
   b. You need to match numbers to win. Would you rather roll twice or spin twice?
   c. You need an even number to win. Would you rather roll or spin?

9. In a game of musical chairs, four children are walking around three chairs. In how many ways can three children get seats to remain in the game?

LOOK AHEAD

Complete each table following the pattern shown.

10.

x	1	2	3	4	5
y	3	6	9		

11.

x	1	2	3	4	5	6
y	2	5	8			

12.

x	1	2	3	4	5	6
y	0	3	8	15		

13.

x	1	2	3	4	5	6
y	0	1	4	9		

14. This line graph shows the number of classroom teachers in the United States.

History

a. Use the graph to write three statements about the number of classroom teachers.

b. How would a community use this information?

c. What do you think caused the changes in the numbers of teachers?

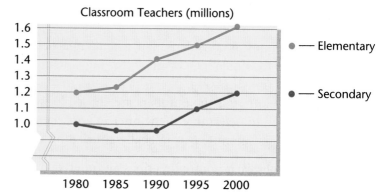

Classroom Teachers (millions)

— Elementary

— Secondary

1980 1985 1990 1995 2000

MORE PRACTICE

15. In how many ways can 4 objects be chosen from a group of 5 objects?

16. Eric says there is only one way to select 6 marbles from a bag containing 6 marbles. Explain Eric's thinking.

17. Yeaphana claims there are $6 \cdot 5 \cdot 4 \cdot 3 \cdot 2 \cdot 1$ ways to arrange 6 marbles in a line. Explain her thinking.

18. A large movie theater is showing an all-night program of horror movies. One ticket allows you to see four of the six shows. Use 1, 2, 3, 4, 5, and 6 to make a list of all the groups of movies one person can see. (Hint: Keep your list in numerical order.)

19. A basketball team has a roster of eight players. Use letters to make a list of all the possible combinations for the starting five players.

20. Players use the sum of one roll of a die and one spin of a spinner with the numbers 1, 2, 3, 4, and 5 to move in a game. Write each probability.
a. rolling a 4 and spinning a 4
b. rolling a 5 and spinning a 1
c. rolling an even number and spinning an odd number
d. moving a number of spaces greater than 9

21. To win a prize you need to draw two O's from a bag containing these six letters. You draw an O on the first draw. Is the probability of winning better if you replace the letter before drawing again? Explain your thinking.

22. The license plate on an antique car reads **NTQ 123** . Use the same letters and digits to write as many other license plates as possible.

MORE MATH REASONING

23. Six people are in a lottery for four tickets to a concert.
a. Make a list of the different groups possible.
b. If you are one of the six people, what is the probability that your name will be picked?
c. If you and three friends are in the lottery, what is the probability that the four of you will be chosen?

24. A jar contains 5 chocolate chip, 3 oatmeal, and 2 ginger cookies. Cookies are removed from the jar one at a time. Write the probability of making the following selections.
a. 2 chocolate chip cookies in a row
b. 2 oatmeal cookies in a row
c. 2 ginger cookies in a row
d. 1 chocolate chip, then 1 oatmeal, and then 1 ginger cookie

25. Ana, Barry, Cecilia, Damon, Elizabeth, Felix, Gary, and Hannah auditioned for three female roles and two male roles in the school musical.

   a. Make a list of the possible students who are chosen.

   b. If the cast members were chosen at random, what is the probability that Ana would get a part?

   c. If the cast members were chosen at random, what is the probability that Gary would get a part?

   d. What is the probability that both Ana and Gary will get a part?

   e. Does a male or a female have a better chance of getting a part? Why?

26. Hot Chance A package contains ten gum balls. Three of the pieces are red hot. What is the probability that the first three gum balls eaten are hot? Use a bag with three red chips to represent the hot gum balls. Use seven chips in a different color to represent the others.

Remove three chips from the bag, one at a time, and record whether you drew three hot gum balls. Put the three chips back in the bag and repeat the experiment until you have completed 20 trials. How would you describe your chances of getting three hot gum balls in a row?

7-2
PART D Accuracy and Odds

← C O N N E C T → *You have seen that the probability of an event is the ratio that compares the number of ways the event happens to the number of total possibilities. Now you will see a different kind of ratio that is often used in informal probability statements.*

Have you ever seen information like this?

   On an average day, the nation's trash consists of
      4,383,562 disposable pens,
      5,479,452 disposable razors, and
      43,835,616 disposable diapers.

How accurate is this data? It is obvious that no one counted all these items in the trash. Usually this kind of data comes from polls or surveys of a few people and is then expanded to the whole population.

Many colleges and universities publish information about the earnings of graduates in order to show that their graduates are successful. What questions would you ask about the data reported here?

1. People attending class reunions are probably not a random sample of graduates. How would you select a random group of graduates of Winston College?
2. Do you think the average salary of all graduates between 1985 and 1995 would be the same as those surveyed? Explain your thinking.
3. Do you think the college received responses from all 1000 people who received the survey questions? Who might not have responded?
4. Suppose five people reported salaries of $125,000, $25,000, $25,000, $25,000, and $25,000. What is the mean? Could reporting that average salary mislead the reader? How could you report the salary information fairly?

> **Winston College Grads Earn Average of $45,691**
>
> A survey mailed to 1000 Winston College students who graduated between 1960 and 1970 found that the average salary was more than $45,000 per year. Earnings were reported for occupations ranging from secretaries to company presidents. Survey participants were selected from graduates attending class reunions at the 1995 College Homecoming.

It is wise to question the accuracy of data that comes from a survey. It is important to know whether the people who responded are a random sample and whether conclusions drawn from the data are valid. It is also impossible to tell if the participants always told the truth.

One day a supermarket manager was studying sales records. The reports showed that 7 out of 10 customers paid with checks or credit cards. Only 3 out of 10 paid cash.

Of every 10 customers ...

7 paid by check or charge. 3 paid with cash.

Afterward, the manager reported that the odds were 7 to 3 *in favor* of a customer's paying by check or charge.

Odds can be expressed in several forms: 7 to 3, $\frac{7}{3}$, and 7:3.

The odds of an event (the odds *in favor* of the event) =

Number of ways the event ● Number of ways the event
can happen ● *cannot* happen

The odds against an event =

Number of ways the event ● Number of ways the event
cannot happen ● *can* happen

These statements are all ways of expressing the same idea:

The **probability** that a customer will
pay with cash is $\frac{3}{10}$.

The **odds** that a customer will pay
with cash are 3 to 7.

to

The odds **against** a customer
paying cash are 7 to 3.

to

The probability that a customer will pay by check or credit card is $\frac{7}{10}$.

The odds that a customer will pay by check or credit card are 7 to 3.

The odds *against* a customer's paying by check or credit card are 3 to 7.

CONSIDER

1. Suppose that each month 100,000 customers buy food
at the market. Do you think it is correct to say that
70,000 will pay by check or credit card? Explain.

EXAMPLE

Jawaan will win a game on his next turn if he lands on green, but he will lose if he lands on red or orange. He will neither win nor lose if he lands on purple.

What are his odds of winning on his next spin?
What are his odds of losing on his next spin?

The spinner has an equal chance of landing on each of the 4 regions.

The odds are 1 to 3 that the spinner will land here.

The odds are 2 to 2 that the spinner will land here ...

... which is the same as 1 to 1 odds.

The odds are 1 to 3 that Jawaan will win the game on his next turn.

The odds are 1 to 1, or **even,** that Jawaan will lose on his next turn.

TRY IT

a. A survey found that the probability of a commercial's being on the air when the radio is turned on is $\frac{2}{5}$. According to the survey, what are the odds in favor of hearing a commercial when you turn on the radio?

CONSIDER

2. Are odds of 9 to 6 the same as odds of 3 to 2? Explain.
3. Since radio stations usually broadcast news on the hour, how would this affect the survey results in Try It a?

REFLECT

1. Why might a claim like "2 out of every 3 doctors recommend our product" be misleading or inaccurate?
2. If you know the odds in favor of an event, how can you find the odds against it?
3. If you have a 4 to 1 chance against winning a prize, why is a claim that "Your probability of winning is 1 in 4!" incorrect?

Exercises

CORE

Industry

1. **Getting Started** From experience, a paint-store owner knows the probability that a customer will buy white paint is 75%.
   a. Write the probability as a ratio.
   b. What percentage of customers do not buy white paint?
   c. Compare the percentage who buy white paint with the percentage who do not. What are the odds that a customer will buy white paint?

2. On a radio show, 35 callers requested a song from the Top 100, and 45 callers requested an oldie. Based on this data, what are the odds in favor of a caller requesting an oldie? against a caller requesting an oldie?

Careers

3. A local weather forecaster announced a 75% chance of rain. Write the odds in favor of rain.

4. Based on his experience at dining out, Mr. Green believes that the odds in favor of receiving a correct bill are 8 to 2. Express his belief in terms of probability.

5. The odds against winning a prize pitching softballs at the Fire-fighters' Carnival are 4 to 1.
   a. If 100 people play the game, how many would you expect to win a prize?
   b. Would you be willing to try your luck if the cost to play was $1? $5? Explain.

6. A fast-food company reported that one in two Americans had a pizza delivered in the past three months.
   a. How many people do you think should be surveyed to report this information accurately? Explain your thinking.
   b. Give two reasons why this information could be inaccurate.

7. A study in Italy found that drinking coffee reduces the risk of asthma attacks.

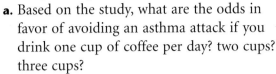

a. Based on the study, what are the odds in favor of avoiding an asthma attack if you drink one cup of coffee per day? two cups? three cups?

b. If you believe this information is true, how would it affect the amount of coffee you drink?

c. What might happen if you drank four cups of coffee each day?

d. The Italian Health Survey studied 72,284 people. How would scientists know the exact amount of coffee each person in the study drank?

e. What questions might you ask a doctor to be sure the results of a study were accurate?

8. The owner of a ski resort claims any day in January has a 75% chance of snow.

a. What does this mean?

b. Based on this claim, how many days in January would you expect snow at the ski resort?

c. Why do you think the owner of the ski resort would make this claim?

		January				
S	M	T	W	T	F	S
❄	2	❄	❄	❄	❄	7
8	❄	❄	11	❄	13	❄
❄	❄	17				

LOOK BACK

9. The triangles are similar. Find the lengths *x* and *y*. [6-2]

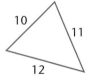

10. In 1992, there were 1223 hazardous-waste sites in the United States. What was the mean number of hazardous-waste sites per state? [1-3]

11. Jaye bought two CDs at the same price. Her torn receipt only listed $2.14 tax and the $28.10 total. What was the price of each CD? [4-2]

MORE PRACTICE

12. Statistics show the odds that an American will appear on TV sometime during his or her life are 1 to 3. What is the probability that you will appear on TV?

13. A bag contains jelly beans in three different colors.
   a. What are the odds of selecting a red jelly bean?
   b. What is the probability of selecting a red jelly bean?

14. A newspaper editorial claims the odds in favor of a candidate's winning the race for mayor are 2 to 5.
   a. What is the probability that the candidate will win?
   b. Would the odds reported in the paper influence your vote?
   c. If there are 35,000 registered voters, how many votes would you expect the candidate to receive?

15. The piece of paper containing Jared's locker combination was torn. The lock has 40 numbers. Jared remembers the third number had two digits beginning with a 3. What are the odds against his guessing the third number correctly?

16. A TV news survey asked people to call with their responses to a question.

> Should there be a 10 p.m. curfew for teenagers on school nights?
> Call 1-900-555-1414 to vote Yes.
> Call 1-900-555-2424 to vote No.
> (Each call costs $2.)

Does this survey accurately reflect the opinion of the community?

17. Conduct a survey of 20 friends to find out at what time of the day they were born.
   a. Using your data, what would you say the odds are that a baby will be born between midnight and 6 a.m.?
   b. How would this kind of information influence staffing at a hospital?

18. In one city, the fire department records show that the odds in favor of a firefighter's receiving an alarm while eating are 3 to 2. The company responds to about 65 calls per month. How many times would you expect a firefighter to be eating when a call is received?

MORE MATH REASONING

19. Draw a grid so that four nickels fit inside one square as shown. A player flicks a nickel with a finger and slides it onto the grid. Do a simulation to find the odds that the nickel will not touch on a line.

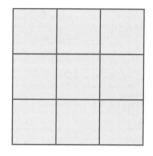

20. In a three-person political race the odds of candidate A's defeating candidate B are 2 to 1. The odds of candidate B's defeating candidate C are 3 to 2. Assume that means candidate A would therefore be favored to beat candidate C. What are the odds of candidate A's defeating candidate C?

21. Explain why odds of 5 to 2 are between the odds of 2 to 1 and 3 to 1.

7-2
PART E — Making Connections

← **CONNECT** → *You've seen that probability plays an important role in daily life. You have learned counting techniques and have applied these techniques to make smart decisions about math problems we face every day.*

Many of the situations you saw in 7-2 had surprising results. Like Monty's Dilemma, the problem about the doors on the game show, interesting questions with controversial answers can attract the attention of many people.

Another surprise to many people is the problem about the 10 students taking their lunch bags at random. It seems someone almost always gets the correct bag.

Now you are ready to look at another famous problem.

MATERIALS

Coin, Die, Slips of paper marked from 1 to 31

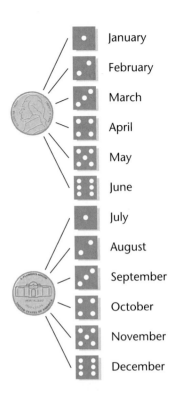

1. What is the probability that a person's birthday is August 28? What are the odds against it?
2. What is the probability that a person was born on any specific day?
3. Do you know anyone else with the same birthday as yours? Do you believe that it is rare for two people in a classroom to share the same birthday?
4. You can simulate birthdays using a coin, a die, and a bag of paper slips marked from 1 to 31.
   Flip the coin and roll the die for the month. Then draw a number from 1 to 31 from a bag. (If an impossible day comes up, like February 31, put the slip back, flip, roll, and draw again.)
5. Using this technique, list at least 30 birthdays. Do you find matching birthdays on your list?
6. Look at the pattern shown.

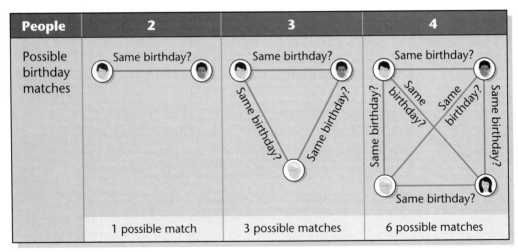

People	2	3	4
Possible birthday matches	1 possible match	3 possible matches	6 possible matches

What seems to be happening? Estimate the number of possible matches for 23 people.

7. The odds are 1 to 1 that you will get a match by the time you have 23 birthdays on your list. Why do you think this is true?

1. What is the purpose of a tree diagram?
2. What do you think makes a game fair? How does probability influence the fairness of a game?
3. How are odds and probability related?
4. Describe or make up a lottery game that uses an ordered arrangement. Describe a different game that uses a group of numbers. Which is easier to win?
5. Suppose a lottery ticket has 6 different numbers. What would happen to the probability of winning if numbers could be repeated?

Self-Assessment

1. Make a tree diagram to show all the outcomes when one coin is tossed three times.
   a. What is the probability of tossing three heads?
   b. What is the probability of tossing two tails followed by a head?
   c. What is the probability of tossing two tails and one head in any order?

2. In selecting a clown costume, Maricela can choose among 3 wigs, 4 suits, and 3 pairs of shoes. How many possible costume sets could she make?

3. A scout became separated from the rest of the troop on a hike, somewhere between Turtle Rock and Windy Hill.

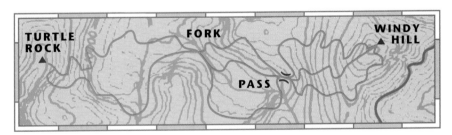

   a. How many different routes could the scout have taken?
   b. Guides say to stay on the northern-most trail. What is the probability that the lost scout would do this by choosing trails randomly?

4. In how many ways can 3 prizes be hidden in 100 packages
   a. if the prizes are all different?
   b. if the prizes are all the same? (Hint: Divide your answer to **4a** by the number of ways to order the 3 prizes.)

5. What is the difference between an arrangement and a grouping?

6. A license plate consists of two different letters followed by four digits. The address for the OK Ranch is 1230 Gulch Canyon. State the probability of receiving each plate.
   a. a plate with the letters OK
   b. a plate with the digits 1230 in that order
   c. the license plate OK 1230

7. In a student election, 5 people are running for president, and 5 different people are running for vice president.
   a. In how many ways can this election turn out?
   b. Suppose the vice president is chosen from the other candidates who were running for president. In how many ways can the election turn out?
   c. In how many ways could 2 council members be chosen from 5 candidates?

8. Prizes are to be awarded for first, second, and third place in a tournament of 36 golfers. Which calculation shows the number of ways this can happen?
   (a) $3 \times 2 \times 1$ (b) $36 \times 35 \times 34$
   (c) $1 \times 2 \times 3 \times \ldots \times 36$ (d) not here

9. Make a list of all the possible combinations of two vegetables selected from a restaurant menu offering carrots, broccoli, peas, and corn.

10. Draw a spinner for which the probability of getting 3 is $\frac{1}{4}$, and the probability of getting 4 is $\frac{1}{16}$.

11. Design a target that gives you a probability of $\frac{1}{6}$ of hitting the bulls-eye.

12. Solve each equation.[4-2]
   a. $10x - 8x = x + 20$ **b.** $-4x - 15 = 2x$

13. A bowling team has four players. In how many different orders can the team bowl?

14. At one time, men were selected for the military draft by drawing the birth month and day from a bin. What is the probability that a person's birthday was called on the first draw? on the second draw?

15. A sporting-goods store has four pairs of tennis shoes the same size but different styles. Sketch a diagram to show how many ways you can select a left shoe and a right shoe that do not match.

16. Walking at Work The amount of walking people do each day varies with their occupations.

Job	Miles per Day	Job	Miles per Day	Job	Miles per Day
Nurse	5.3	Waitress	3.3	Teacher	1.7
Security officer	4.2	Doctor	2.5	Homemaker	1.3
Retail salesperson	3.5	Secretary	2.2	Dentist	0.8

a. How many miles would a waitress walk in an average five-day week?

b. How many more miles than a homemaker would a teacher walk in an average five-day work week?

c. How many weeks would it take for a dentist to walk 100 miles?

17. In the game of jacks, ten jacks are picked up by ones, twos, threes, and so on up to ten. The leftovers are scooped at one time when the number of remaining jacks is less than the number for that round. Suppose you play a game straight through without a miss.

a. How many jacks will you pick up all together?

b. How many times will you pick up jacks in pairs?

c. How many times will you pick up jacks in threes?

18. Find the area of the shaded region. You will need to use a ruler to find the scale used and the missing lengths.

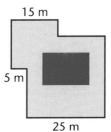

15 m

5 m

25 m

19. At a stadium, seven light bulbs make up each digit of the scoreboard. Suppose numbers are displayed for the same amount of time.

a. Which bulb has the highest probability of burning out first? Why?

b. Which bulb has the lowest probability of burning out first? Why?

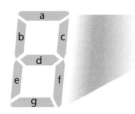

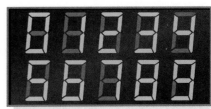

Chapter 7 Review

In Chapter 7, after thinking about how playing games involves skill and luck, you computed the probability of some everyday events directly. For other events, you ran trials and experiments first. Using spinners, dice, and random-number tables, you simulated events and compared experimental and theoretical probability. You learned to find the total number of possible outcomes.

KEY TERMS

arrangement [7-2]

Counting Principle [7-2]

even odds [7-2]

experimental probability [7-1]

grouping [7-2]

odds [7-2]

probability [7-1]

random-number table [7-1]

simulation [7-1]

theoretical probability [7-1]

tree diagram [7-2]

Write the letter of the word or phrase that best completes the sentence.

1. A method of finding all possible ways several things can be ordered is
   (a) a simulation
   (b) a tree diagram
   (c) random order
   (d) arrangement

2. If a spinner has 5 equal sections labeled 1 through 5, the probability of getting a 3 is $\frac{1}{5}$ by
   (a) theoretical probability
   (b) simulation
   (c) experimental probability
   (d) odds

3. If you roll a die and try to get a 2, then 5 to 1 is the
   (a) probability
   (b) odds in favor
   (c) odds against
   (d) claim

4. If a first thing can be done in 6 ways and a second thing can then be done in 2 ways, we can find the total number of ways to do both things by
   (a) random event
   (b) probability
   (c) random-number table
   (d) the counting principle

CONCEPTS AND APPLICATIONS

5. There are six ways to pick a pair of socks and two ways to pick a pair of shoes. How many different combinations are there? [7-2]

6. Consider the possible outcomes when using this spinner. [7-1]

   a. What is the probability of getting 2?
   b. of getting an odd number?
   c. of getting a number less than 10?
   d. of getting a number between 3 and 6?

7. Five celebrities, T, U, V, W, and X, have been invited to ride in the 4th of July parade. Only two can be in the first car. However, Ms. U and Mr. X refuse to ride in the same car. Make a list of the possible occupants of the first car. [7-2]

8. Decide whether each phrase describes an ordered arrangement or a grouping. [7-2]
   a. the number of ways to arrange 20 books on a shelf
   b. the number of ways to choose 2 books from a set of 20 on a shelf
   c. the number of 3-letter sets you can form from the letters in *random*
   d. the number of ways you can mix up the letters in the word *June*

9. There is a 60% chance of winning a game. The odds of winning are [7-2]
   (a) 6 to 10   (b) 3 to 5   (c) 40%   (d) 3 to 2   (e) not here

10. You are told that the odds against your winning a free vacation trip are 9 to 1. What is the probability that you will win the trip? [7-2]

11. Susan needs to go to the post office, the bank, and the bakery. [7-2]
   a. Use a tree diagram to show the orders in which she can do these errands.
   b. If she must go to the bank before going to the post office, in how many ways can she do these errands?

12. Two out of four students are going to be picked for the all-city spelling bee. Willa and William are among the four. [7-2]
   a. What is the probability that both will be chosen?
   b. What is the probability that neither will be chosen?
   c. What is the probability that one will be chosen, but not the other?

13. A spinner has 8 equal sections labeled 1 through 8. [7-1]
   a. What is the probability of spinning a 5?
   b. What is the probability of getting a total of 17 in two spins?

14. An office receptionist kept track of the calls received for a week. [7-1]
   a. What is the probability that the next call will be from a new customer?
   b. What is the probability that the next call received will be a personal call or a wrong number?

Calls from New Customers	84
Calls from Previous Customers	256
Personal Calls	42
Wrong Numbers	18

CONCEPTS AND CONNECTIONS

15. Statistics The Census Bureau keeps records on the number of children in American families. The table shows what percentage of the families counted in each census had children in age groups under 18. [7-1]

Percentage by Age Group					
	0	**1**	**2**	**3**	**4 or more**
1980	47.9%	20.9%	19.3%	7.8%	4.1%
1985	50.4%	20.9%	18.6%	7.2%	3.0%
1990	51.1%	20.5%	18.5%	7.0%	2.8%

Source: The Universal Almanac, *1993, p. 292.*

a. What trends do you observe in the chart?

b. In which year was the probability the greatest that a family selected at random had three children?

c. Your calculator is broken. What do you think is the total of the 1990 percentages? How does this relate to the sum of the probabilities?

SELF-EVALUATION

Write a summary about what you know about probability. Include examples of ways probability and simulations can add meaning to everyday situations. Mention areas that were troublesome and plans you have to review those areas.

Chapter 7 Assessment

TEST

1. The following ratios are probabilities of events. $\frac{3}{9}, \frac{2}{7}, \frac{1}{3}, \frac{2}{5}, \frac{4}{15}$

a. Which has the greatest probability?   **b.** Which has the least probability?

2. One hundred years of weather records for Dakkon City on July 4th show:

Rain, 11 years   Tornado, 1 year
Clear and hot, 80 years   Overcast and humid, 8 years

What is the probability that July 4th will be clear and hot this year?

3. For a safety poster, Andy can choose 1 of 5 themes, 1 of 10 different types of faces, and 1 of 3 sizes of poster board. In how many different ways can he plan his poster?

4. Sports fans entering this stadium split equally at each branch. What is the probability that a spectator enters the stadium through Gate B?

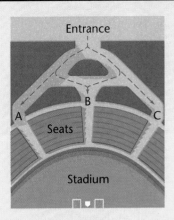

5. To win a game, a player must roll a number greater than 10 as the sum of two ordinary dice. What is the probability of winning on the next roll?

6. A basketball player has a record of hitting 6 free throws out of each 10 she tries. She picks this row of the random-number table to simulate what will happen in her next 30 tries. Digits from 1 to 6 stand for hits, and the others stand for misses.

78338 77881 90139 72375 50624 91385

How does this simulation match her record?

7. Three coins are tossed at the same time.
  a. What is the probability of getting 2 heads and 1 tail?
  b. What is the probability of getting 1 head and 2 tails?

8. A license plate is made up of three letters chosen from A, B, C, D, E, and F and three digits chosen from 1, 2, 3, 4, and 5.
  a. How many license plates can be made using this system?
  b. How many can be made if no letter or digit is used more than once?

9. Suppose your house number is 244. Make a list showing all the ways the digits can be mixed in the wrong order.

10. What is the probability of hitting the outer ring of this target?

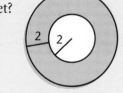

11. What number correctly completes the statement? [6-1]

$$\frac{100 \text{ runners}}{5 \text{ minutes}} \times \frac{60 \text{ minutes}}{1 \text{ hour}} = \frac{\boxed{} \text{ runners}}{1 \text{ hour}}$$

12. The probability of an event is 45%. What is the probability the event won't happen?

PERFORMANCE TASK

The school fair is coming. Your group will have a dart-throwing game. Design a dart board so that about one out of five players will win a small prize and one out of ten will win a large prize. Include reasons for your design, and list the assumptions you would be making.

Chapter 8 Functions

Project A
Shades of Gray
How do computers digitalize the continuous tones of photographs into black, white, and gray for high-contrast printing?

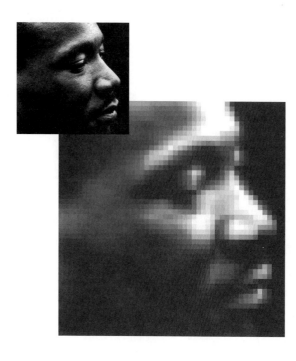

Project C
Off and On
What is the binary number system and how does it make computer technology possible?

ISBN 0-201-86700-1

Project B
Spring into Action
What is the relationship between a stretched spring and the weight it takes to stretch it?

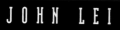

JOHN LEI

I was good at math in high school. I wanted to be an engineer.

I'm proud of working in educational photography. I don't have to sell a product or make people want to smoke. You have to know mathematical things to take good pictures—how to set and read a light meter, how to set the *f*-stops, how to get the correct light exposure, and how to proportion the subject to the background. Asking why a person should know math is like asking why you should know how to use a telephone or a calculator or a computer.

John Lei
Photographer
John C. Lei Studios, Inc.
New York, New York

Chapter 8

Overview   Functions

8-1 Dependent Relationships

Researchers for business or science frequently examine how changes in one quantity effect change in another. You will learn to identify dependent relationships, express the relationship between quantities as an equation, and represent the relationship as a graph.

8-2 Linear Functions

Reports for business or science sometimes need charts and graphs of relationships among quantities. Lines are useful in providing a visual representation of change among quantities. You will investigate linear functions as a specific type of dependent relationship. You will learn to determine the slope and y-intercepts of these functions.

8-3 Functions with Curved Graphs

Recording the altitude of a rocket over a period of time requires a curved graph. You will investigate several nonlinear functions. You will solidify your understanding of linear functions by seeing examples of nonlinear functions such as quadratic, square root, and exponential functions.

IT ALL DEPENDS...

Tenzing Norgay

Edmund Hillary

Mount Everest towers over the border between Nepal and Tibet in Asia's majestic Himalaya Mountains. At 29,028 feet, it is the world's tallest mountain. A series of attempts to climb it began in 1921. As successive expeditions made their way higher, the mountain revealed more of its secrets. But it was not until May 29, 1953, that the top of Mount Everest was finally reached. At 11:30 that morning, two members of a British expedition—former New Zealand beekeeper Edmund Hillary and his Sherpa guide from Nepal, Tenzing Norgay—reached the summit.

Hillary and Norgay quickly became internationally famous for their achievement. Both said modestly that their success depended on many factors for which they deserved no credit. Hillary said that they had climbed "on the shoulders" of all the mountaineers who had attempted Mount Everest before them. He and Norgay would have failed without a portable oxygen supply and other high-tech climbing gear and clothing. In addition, they had enjoyed good weather, good health, and the strong support of all the members of their expedition. Like most achievements for which individuals get credit, the ascent of Mount Everest was dependent on many factors over which the individuals themselves had no control.

?

1. What did Hillary mean when he said that he and Norgay climbed "on the shoulders" of other mountaineers?
2. Why did the two climbers need portable oxygen and other high-tech climbing gear?
3. Think of a great achievement by an individual whom you admire. Was it truly an individual achievement or did it depend to some degree on other people or factors?

← C O N N E C T → *The value of a variable expression changes as the value of the variable changes. The position of a figure changes if you slide, flip, or turn it. Change is central to mathematics. We will now look at how change in one quantity results in change in another quantity.*

Suppose you begin to climb a tall mountain. As you climb higher and higher, many changes slowly take place.

- The air temperature grows cooler.
- The air pressure decreases.
- Your distance from safety increases.
- The boiling point of water decreases.
- You see less plant life and more snow and ice.
- Each day you need more food energy than the day before to survive.

As you climb the mountain, each quantity listed above changes *because* the altitude changes. We say that each quantity *depends* on the altitude.

When one quantity depends on another quantity, drawing a graph can show how the quantities change in relation to one another.

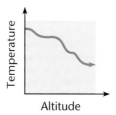

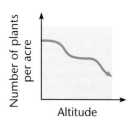

Notice that no numbers appear on the graphs. Even without numbers, however, each graph shows important information clearly. For example, the first graph shows temperature slowly falling as altitude increases. A person studying these graphs could learn a great deal about the changes that occur as a climber ascends a mountain.

CONSIDER

1. What can you learn from the second graph?
2. Compare and contrast the first two graphs.
3. The third graph has a step-like appearance. Why?
4. Suppose that you put on scuba-diving gear and descend into the ocean. What quantities might change? Would each quantity increase or decrease?

TRY IT

Sketch a graph showing how the quantity changes in relation to your altitude on a mountain.

a. air pressure
b. boiling point of water
c. amount of food energy needed daily
d. distance from the center of the earth
e. your height

EXPLORE: THE NATURE OF BALANCE

MATERIALS

Foot ruler, yard stick, or meter stick
Supply of pennies or other small, dense, identical objects

1. Place your ruler perpendicular to the edge of your desk or table. Slide the ruler over the edge until the ruler just begins to tip. Note the measurement at the balance point.
2. Place a penny at one end of the ruler. Find and note the new balance point.
3. Stack various numbers of pennies on top of the first penny. Note the balance point for each stack.
4. Explain how the position of the balance point depends on the number of pennies on the ruler.
5. What relationships can you find between the balance point and the number of pennies?
6. Sketch a graph showing the position of the balance point relative to the number of pennies.

Slide ruler until you find balance point.

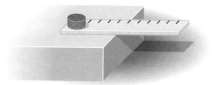

A graph that shows a relationship between quantities may tell a story.

EXAMPLE

Sarah bicycles to school each morning. The graph depicts one of her rides. The horizontal axis measures the length of time since she left her home. The vertical axis measures her distance from her home.

Tell the story of her ride.

Possible story:

During the first part of her ride, Sarah's distance from her home increased steadily. That means she must have traveled at a constant rate of speed.

During the middle part of her ride, her distance did not change as time went on. That means she must have stopped for awhile.

At the end of her ride, her distance increased at a faster rate than it did at the beginning, but also at a constant rate. She must have ridden faster at the end, perhaps to get to school on time.

TRY IT

f. The graph traces the weight of a puppy over several months. Tell a story that might be depicted by the graph.

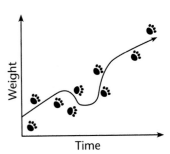

REFLECT

1. What does your grade in this class depend on? What does the score of a football game depend on? What does the area of a rectangle depend on?
2. Give examples of quantities that depend on the values of other quantities.
3. There is a relationship between the time that it takes to travel a distance and the rate at which you are traveling. As the time increases, does the distance increase or decrease? Explain.

Exercises

CORE

1. **Getting Started** The graph depicts the relationship between altitude and depth of snow on a mountain.
   a. As altitude increases, does snow depth increase, decrease, or stay the same?
   b. Where on a mountain would you expect the snow to be deepest?

2. Determine whether each statement is true or false.
   a. The length of time it takes a sky diver to reach the ground depends on the height from which the sky diver jumped.
   b. Your house or apartment number depends on your age.
   c. The sum of the measures of the angles of a triangle depends on the lengths of the triangle's sides.
   d. The square of a number depends on the number.

Tell a story depicted by the graph.

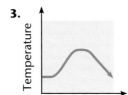

3.

4.

5.

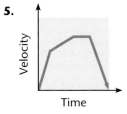

Name a quantity that each depends upon.

6. the mean of a set of data

7. the circumference of a circle

8. your age

9. the perimeter of a triangle

10. the value of the expression $a^2 - 3a + 5b$

11. the volume of a prism

Sketch a graph showing how the quantities change in relation to each other.

12. the height of a giraffe; the giraffe's age

13. the money you spend; the number of tapes you can buy

14. outside temperature; cost of heating your home

15. speed at which you walk; length of time it takes you to walk 5 miles

16. the price of an apple; the number of apples you can buy for $5

17. Astro Knots Suppose you traveled into space in a rocket.

    a. Name three quantities that would increase as your journey continued.

    b. Name three quantities that would decrease as your journey continued.

    c. Name three quantities that would neither increase nor decrease during your journey.

 # *LOOK BACK*

18. T.J.'s dresser drawer contains 2 red socks, 4 blue socks, and 6 white socks. If T.J. reaches in and chooses a sock at random, what is the probability that it will be white? [7-1]

19. A triangle with a base of 8 inches has a height of 2 inches. Find the area of the triangle. [5-2]

20. Which figure(s) have more than one line of symmetry? [3-1]

    (a) 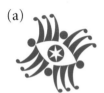   (b)   (c)   (d)

MORE PRACTICE

Tell a story depicted by the graph.

21.
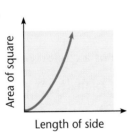

22.

23.
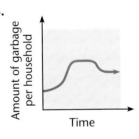

24.
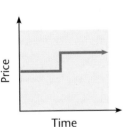

25.
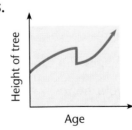

26.
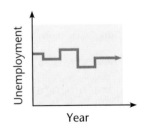

27. Choose the graph that best represents the height of someone on the Ferris wheel.

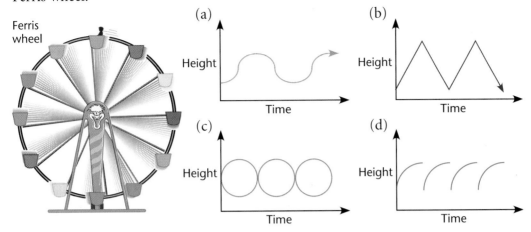

Ferris wheel

(a) Height / Time

(b) Height / Time

(c) Height / Time

(d) Height / Time

Name a quantity that each depends upon.

28. the size of a scale model of a boat

29. the surface area of a cone

30. your basketball foul-shooting percentage

31. the value of a baseball card

32. the value of a trigonometric ratio

33. the cost of a car

34. the amount a worker earns in a year

35. your bowling score

Sketch a graph showing how the quantities change in relation to each other.

36. the money you spend on gas; the distance you can travel on the gas

37. the radius of a circle; the area of the circle

38. the number of people cleaning out a garage; the length of time it takes to finish the job

39. a person's age; the person's height

40. the speed at which you type; the length of time it takes you to type 10 pages

41. the number of pennies on a ruler; the distance from the pennies to the balance point

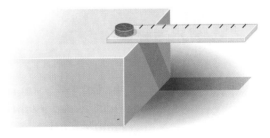

42. Pipe Up An organ pipe with a length of 20 to 25 times its diameter produces thin, sharp notes. Suppose you want to make the pipes longer. What must you do to be sure the sound stays the same?

MORE MATH REASONING

43. **Tell Me a Story** Describe a real-life situation that could match what is depicted by the graph. Tell what labels would go on the graph and what the graph indicates.

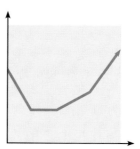

44. The graph depicts a race between Dana and Teri.
   a. Who won?
   b. Dana's line slants upward at a steeper angle than Teri's line. What does that tell you?

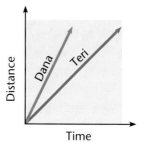

Explain how the numbers in the top and bottom rows are related.

45.

1	2	3	4
5	6	7	8

46.

−2	0	2	3
4	0	4	9

47.

1	2	6	9
6	12	36	54

48.

12	20	32	36
−3	−5	−8	−9

8-1
PART B Expressing Change

← CONNECT → *In the last part, you saw that change in one quantity can produce change in a related quantity. Now you will learn how to express these changes mathematically.*

Mathematical relationships sometimes appear in the most unexpected places. Now you will explore one such place—a pharmacy window.

Your job is to design window displays for retail stores. You have been asked to create an attractive display of toothpaste boxes for a local pharmacy. The illustration shows the kind of display you must build.

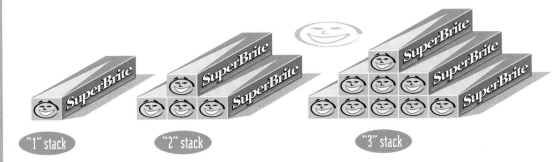

"1" stack   "2" stack   "3" stack

Each *stack* consists of rows of boxes. Each row in a stack contains two more boxes than the row above. The number in quotation marks tells the number of rows in a stack and is called the *type* of the stack.

1. Describe a "6" stack.
2. Copy and complete the table.

Type of Stack	"1"	"2"	"3"	"4"	"5"	"6"	"7"	"8"
Total Number of Boxes								

3. Describe the relationship between the type of stack and the number of boxes needed to build the stack.

> **Problem-Solving Tip**
>
> Look for a pattern.

4. How many boxes would you need to build a "32" stack? Explain your reasoning.
5. A stack of toothpaste boxes was built using 441 boxes. What type of stack was it? Explain your reasoning.
6. Write a formula for finding the number of boxes (b) in an "n" stack.

In the Explore, you looked at the relationship between the type of stack and the number of boxes in the stack. You saw that the number of boxes *depended on* the type of stack.

EXAMPLES

1. Make a table of six pairs of values for the equation $y = 3x - 5$. Choose small values of x that are easy to work with. Substitute each value in the equation and solve for y. One possible set of values is given below.

x	-2	-1	0	1	2	3
y	-11	-8	-5	-2	1	4

2. Jet pilots often use Mach numbers to express the speeds at which they fly. The formula $v = 740M$ relates the Mach number (M) of a plane and the plane's velocity (v) in miles per hour. Make a table of values showing a plane's velocity for Mach numbers 1 through 6.

For each value of M, substitute the value in the equation $v = 740M$.

Mach Number	1	2	3	4	5	6
Velocity (mi/hr)	740	1480	2220	2960	3700	4440

CONSIDER

1. In $y = 3x + 5$, is it easier to find the value of y if you know that $x = 10$ or to find the value of x if you know that $y = 10$? Explain.
2. Suppose you know a plane's speed. How could you find its Mach number?

a. Make a table of five pairs of values for the equation $y = 5x + 3$.

b. At Peak Experience, climbing rope sells for $0.68 per foot, plus a cutting fee of $0.20. The equation $c = 0.68f + 0.2$ can be used to find the cost (c) of a length of rope (f) in feet. Make a table of values showing costs for rope lengths of 100 feet, 110 feet, 120 feet, …, 150 feet.

You have seen many examples in which the value of one variable depends on the value of another variable.

> When the value of y depends on the value of x, y is called the **dependent variable** and x is called the **independent variable.**

Sometimes, by examining a table of values, you can discover an equation relating two variables.

CONSIDER

3. In Try It b, the relationship between the cost (c) of a rope and its lengh (f) is given by the equation $c = 0.68f + 0.2$. Which is the dependent variable and which is the independent variable? Explain.

EXAMPLE

3. Write an equation relating the variables in the table.

x	-2	0	1	2	4	7
y	-7	-5	-4	-3	-1	2

Each value of y can be obtained by subtracting 5 from the corresponding value of x. Therefore, an equation relating the variables is $y = x - 5$.

You can check any pair of values by substituting for x and y.

TRY IT

c. Write an equation relating the variables in the table.

x	-2	-1	0	1	2	3
y	6	3	0	-3	-6	-9

REFLECT

1. How does an equation or a formula show a relationship between quantities?

2. Describe what the word *dependent* means. Use numbers to describe a situation in your life where one quantity is dependent upon another.

3. Mrs. Chee works at an hourly rate. To analyze her pay, what quantities would you graph? What are the dependent and independent variables?

Exercises

CORE

1. Getting Started Copy and complete the table of values for the equation $y = 2x + 1$.

x	-1	0	1	2	3	4
y			3			

Complete each table of values.

2. $y = 7 - x$

x	-3	0	1	2	3	7
y						

3. $y = 4x + 5$

x	-2	-1	0	1	2	3
y						

4. $s = 40 - 16t$

t	s
-2	
-1	
0	
1	
2	

5. $k = \dfrac{4h - 2}{3}$

h	k
-4	
-1	
2	
5	
8	

6. $y = 3(x + 1)$

x	y
-1	
0	
1	
2	
10	

7. $n = m^2 - m$

m	n
-5	
-3	
0	
1	
7	

8. Independent Operator A trucker drove m miles in t hours at an average rate of 55 miles per hour. Complete the following sentence using the words *independent* or *dependent*.

The number of miles depends on t. We call t the _____ variable.

Look for a pattern to complete each table. Then give the equation that relates the variables.

9.

x	-3	-1	0	1		3	36
y	-15		0	5	10	15	

10.

x	-6	-2	0	1	3		36
y	0	4		7		11	

11. No Pain, No Gain A team of mountain climbers on Alaska's Mount McKinley used the equation $e = 450h$ to estimate their elevation gain (e), in feet, in h hours of climbing.
  a. Name the independent variable.
  b. Make a table of six pairs of values expressing the relationship between h and e.
  c. Modify the equation to show that the climbers start at an elevation of 17,825 feet.
  d. Use the equation from **11c** to find how long it would take to climb from an altitude of 17,825 feet to the 20,300-foot summit.

12. The illustration shows a "1-square," which has a perimeter of 4 units, and a "3-square," which has a perimeter of 8 units.
  a. Make a table of values expressing the relationship between the number of squares in a row (n) and the perimeter of the figure (p).
  b. Give an equation relating n and p.
  c. Use your equation to find the perimeter of a "500-square."

1-SQUARE   3-SQUARE

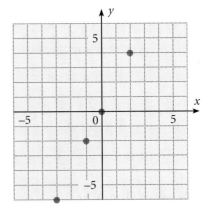
13. The points on the graph represent a relationship between x and y.
  a. Make a table of values for the relationship.
  b. Use the table to write the equation for the relationship.

MORE PRACTICE

Copy and complete each table of values.

14. $y = x^2 - 2$

x	y
-2	
-1	
0	
1	
2	

15. $c = 15 - 10m$

m	c
7	
5	
3	
1	
-1	

16. $f = \dfrac{g - 1}{2}$

g	f
-3	
-1	
1	
3	
5	

17. $s = 3t + 1$

t	s
1	
2	
3	
4	
5	

Look for a pattern to complete each table. Then give the equation that relates the variables.

18.

x	y
-5	-13
-3	-11
0	-8
1	
3	-5
6	-2
52	

19.

x	y
-6	3
	1
0	0
2	-1
4	
10	-5
52	

20.

x	y
	3
-8	2
0	0
4	-1
8	-2
20	
36	

21.

x	y
-2	4
-1	1
0	0
1	1
2	
3	9
36	

22. Mountains of Diapers Buying and washing cotton diapers costs an average of about $8.00 per week. Disposable diapers cost about $12.50 per week, and a diaper service costs about $9.25 per week.

a. Write equations giving the three weekly costs.

b. Use your equations to complete the table.

Number of Weeks	4	26	52	104
Buy-and-Wash Cost				
Disposable-Diaper Cost				
Diaper-Service Cost				

c. Why does the table use values like 26 and 104 for the number of weeks?

d. How much would you save over 2 years by buying and washing cotton diapers instead of buying disposable ones? instead of using a diaper service?

23. Former Surgeon General C. Everett Koop has cited estimates that every $15 bike helmet saves the country $450 in medical costs.

a. What do you think he meant by this statement?

b. Estimate the number of bike helmets that are worn in the United States, their total cost, and the medical-cost savings.

MORE MATH REASONING

24. This summer, Kaili has a job at $4.25 per hour. Next summer, she'll make $4.75 per hour. Each summer, her boss gives her a new uniform and takes $25 from her pay to cover its cost.

a. Write equations expressing the relationship between the number of hours Kaili works each summer and her total pay for the summer.

b. Copy and complete the table of values.

Number of Hours Worked	50	100	150	200	250
This Summer's Total Pay					
Next Summer's Total Pay					

25. The formula $F = 1.8C + 32$ can be used to convert Celsius temperatures (C) to Fahrenheit temperatures (F).

   a. Find the Fahrenheit temperature when the Celsius temperature is 55°.

   b. Describe a method you could use to convert Fahrenheit to Celsius temperatures.

   c. Use your method to convert 446°F to the Celsius scale.

   d. Would it be cold or hot if the temperature on each scale were about the same? Why?

Look for a pattern to complete each table.

26.

x	1	2	3	4	5	6	7	8	9	n
y	5	7	9	11	13	15				

27.

x	1	2	3	4	5	6	7	8	9	n
y	−4	−1	4	11	20	31				

8-1 PART C Graphing Change

← CONNECT →   *As you have seen, you can use an equation or a formula to express the relationship between two quantities. By drawing a graph, you can create a visual representation of the relationship that you may not be able to determine using numbers alone.*

A graph shows how two variables change in relation to each other.

When drawing a graph, it is customary to use the horizontal axis (*x*-axis) for the independent variable and the vertical axis (*y*-axis) for the dependent variable. You can use a table of values or a graphing utility to create the graph.

MATERIALS

Graph paper
Graphing utility

After a football running back was tackled, the ball was moved back 5 yards for a face-mask penalty.

Let x = the running back's gain on the play. Let y = the team's net gain on the play.

1. If the running back had lost 4 yards when he was tackled, the first entries in the table would be -4 and -9. Copy and complete the table, choosing your own values of x.

x	-4								
y	-9								

2. Find an equation in the form "$y = \ldots$" that expresses the relationship between x and y.

3. Look at each column in the table. Use the value of x and the value of y to write an ordered pair (x, y). (Hint: The first pair is $(-4, -9)$. What are the others?)

4. Draw a coordinate grid on graph paper. Plot the ordered pairs and describe your results.

5. Use a graphing utility to enter the equation you found in step 2:
Press $\boxed{Y=}$ and enter the expression from the right side of your equation.
Press $\boxed{\text{GRAPH}}$ to graph the equation in the calculator's standard graphing window.
Your screen should look like this.

6. Press $\boxed{\text{TRACE}}$ and the arrow keys to find the value of x closest to 0. What is the corresponding value of y? What meaning does this value have?

7. Compare and contrast the two methods of drawing a graph. What are the advantages and disadvantages of each method?

The Explore showed two methods you can use to graph an equation.

CONSIDER

1. The graph produced by the ordered pairs was a set of points. The graph produced by the calculator was a line. Which was correct? Explain.
2. How could you use each graph to find the value of y that corresponds to $x = -6$? to find the value of x that corresponds to $y = 7$?
3. The graph goes up from left to right. Why? What would it mean if the graph went down?

If the values of x and y are not limited to integers, you can connect the ordered pairs of a graph to produce a smooth line or curve.

WHAT DO **YOU** THINK?

Create a graph that shows the relationship between the length of a side of a square and the area of the square.

Rachel thinks ...

I'll let x represent the length of a side of a square, and I'll let y represent the area. Then I will use the equation $y = x^2$ to make a table of values.

x	0	1	2	3	4	5
y	0	1	4	9	16	25

I'll plot the ordered pairs and connect them with a smooth curve to draw the graph.

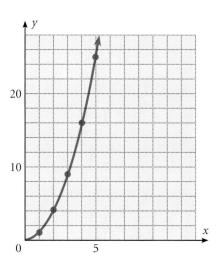

Ben thinks ...

I'll use my graphing utility. I'll use a window from 0 to 10 for x, and from 0 to 100 for y.

Then I'll graph the equation $y = x^2$.

Xmin=0
Xmax=10
Xscl=1
Ymin=0
Ymax=100
Yscl=10

Notice that Rachel's and Ben's graphs look different even though they represent the same equation. Ben used increments of 10 on the y-axis, and Rachel used increments of 2. Choosing which scales to use on the axes is an important step when using a graphing utility to create a graph.

CONSIDER

4. What do the graphs of the equation $y = x^2$ tell you about the relationship between the length of a side of a square and the area of the square?
5. Why did Rachel and Ben use the equation $y = x^2$? Why did they use only positive values of x?
6. How could you use Rachel or Ben's graph to approximate the value of 3.6^2? to solve the equation $12.8 = x^2$?

TRY IT

a. Graph the equation $y = -x - 3$.
b. Graph the equation $y = 0.5x^2 - 2x$.

REFLECT

1. How are a table and graph of an equation related?
2. When do you connect the points on a graph? Why?
3. How do you decide the highest and lowest values of x or of y to use when graphing?
4. Can two graphs of an equation have different shapes and yet both be accurate? Explain.

Exercises

CORE

1. **Getting Started** Use the equation $y = \frac{1}{2}x + 1$.

   a. Copy and complete the table of values.
   b. Were the choices of -2, 0, 2, and 4 as x-values good choices? Why or why not?
   c. List four ordered pairs given by your table.
   d. Draw a coordinate grid on graph paper and plot the ordered pairs.
   e. Graph $y = \frac{1}{2}x + 1$.

x	-2	0	2	4
y				

Determine whether each statement is true or false.

2. A rock falls from a cliff. The amount of time that passes before the rock hits the ground depends upon the distance that the rock falls.

3. The price of a paperback book depends upon the number of books that you buy.

4. The area of a circle depends upon the radius.

Graph each equation.

5. $y = 3x + 1$

6. $y = -2x + 5$

7. $y = x - 6$

8. $y = -x$

9. $y = x^2 - 1$

10. $y = 0.25x^2 - 12$

11. Use your graph from Exercise 7 to find the solution to each equation.
   a. $-2 = x - 6$
   b. $1.5 = x - 6$
   c. $4 = x - 6$

12. Use your graph from Exercise 9 to find the solution to each equation.
   a. $3 = x^2 - 1$
   b. $0 = x^2 - 1$
   c. $-1 = x^2 - 1$

13. **The Pressure's On** The formula $P = 14.7 + 0.45d$ gives the water pressure, in pounds, that a scuba diver at a depth of d feet feels on every square inch of skin.

   a. Make a table of five pairs of values. Use values of d ranging from 0 to 120.
   b. Plot the ordered pairs and draw a graph.
   c. The greatest pressure that the body can tolerate without special equipment is about 65 pounds per square inch. Use your graph to estimate how far an unprotected diver can descend.

   Problem-Solving Tip

   Think of P as y and d as x.

14. Pssst ... Wanna Buy a Mountain? The government of
Nepal charges a fee to mountaineering teams that attempt
to climb the nation's peaks. The climbing fee for one of
Nepal's peaks is $3000 plus $250 per team member.

  a. Does the climbing fee depend upon the number of
team members?

  b. Let y = climbing fee and let x = number of team
members. Write an equation $y =$ ___ expressing the
relationship between x and y.

  c. Graph the equation. Explain why you should not
connect the points on the graph.

  d. How many team members can go for $6000?

15. The Big Boom Next time you are in a lightning storm, count the number of
seconds between a flash of lightning and the resulting clap of thunder. This
number of seconds (s) depends on your distance (d), in miles, from the lightning. You will hear the thunder instantaneously, $s = 0$, if the lightning flashes
beside you. Otherwise, 5 seconds will go by for every mile the thunder travels
to reach you.

  a. Write an equation $s =$ ___ expressing the relationship between s and d.

  b. Graph the equation.

  c. Explain how you could use your graph during a lightning storm to estimate
the distance to a lightning bolt that you see.

LOOK BACK

16. What are the odds of getting a 4 rolling a number cube? [7-2]

17. Draw a net of a pyramid that has a pentagonal base. [6-3]

18. A room 20 feet long appears 6 inches long in a scale drawing. Find the scale. [6-2]

MORE PRACTICE

19. Complete a table of values for the equation $y = -2x + 1$. Use x-values of -2,
$-1, 0, 1$, and 2.

20. Sharon made a table of values for the
equation $y = 3x - 1$.

x	-2	-1	0	1	2
y	-7	-4	0	2	5

  a. Chang thought that the table contained a mistake. Was he right?

  b. Draw a graph of the equation $y = 3x - 1$.

Graph each equation.

21. $y = 4x - 2$ **22.** $y = -x + 3$ **23.** $y = x + 7$

24. $y = -\frac{1}{2}x$ **25.** $y = 2x^2 - 15$ **26.** $y = x^3$

27. Use your graph from Exercise 21 to find the solution to each equation.
     a. $-2 = 4x - 2$ **b.** $3 = 4x - 2$ **c.** $7 = 4x - 2$

28. Use your graph from Exercise 25 to find the solution to each equation.
     a. $11 = 2x^2 - 15$ **b.** $3 = 2x^2 - 15$ **c.** $-7 = 2x^2 - 15$

29. You have $1000 in a savings account in the bank. Your goal is to deposit $25 in your account each week. Let $A =$ the amount in your account and let $w =$ the number of weeks you have been saving.
     a. Which variable is the independent variable? Which is the dependent variable?
     b. Make a table of six pairs of values of w and A.
     c. Graph the ordered pairs given by your table.
     d. Write an equation $A = $ _____ expressing the relationship between w and A.

> **Problem-Solving Tip**
>
> Use different scales on your horizontal and vertical axes.

Write an equation that models each situation.

30. A community theater group pays $1250 to rent a theater for an evening and charges $4 per ticket. Let $E =$ the group's earnings for one night and let $n =$ the number of people who purchase tickets.

31. The library charges ten cents a day for each day that a book is overdue. Let $C =$ the charge for an overdue book and let $d =$ the number of days a book is overdue.

MORE MATH REASONING

32. The formula $F = 1.8C + 32$ can be used to convert Celsius temperatures (C) to Fahrenheit temperatures (F). The formula $C = \frac{5}{9}(F - 32)$ can be used to convert Fahrenheit to Celsius temperatures.
     a. Draw both graphs on the same set of axes.
     b. Use your graphs to find the temperature that is the same on both scales.

33. Write an equation for the surface area (S) of a cube with each side measuring s units.

Making Connections

← CONNECT →
You have looked at many different ways to express relationships between quantities. Now you will use them and some data you will collect to create an equation of practical importance.

Air temperature depends partly on *altitude*—elevation above the earth's surface. Therefore, as a mountain climber ascends a mountain, the temperature drops.

But air temperature also depends on other factors, especially *latitude*—position on the earth's surface relative to the equator and the poles. If two people are at the same altitude, the one at a higher latitude will probably be cooler.

Suppose you wished to investigate how the temperatures of two cities are affected by their altitudes. How could you eliminate the effect that latitude might have on your results? Easy—choose two cities with the same latitude!

Kakadu National Park, Northern Territory, Australia

Machu Picchu, Peru

EXPLORE: WHAT'S THE DIFFERENCE?

MATERIALS

Graph paper, Graphing utility, World almanac

1. Find the pages in your almanac with the following information about major U.S. cities.

    a. latitudes   **b.** altitudes   **c.** average monthly temperatures

2. Choose two cities that are at approximately the same latitude but have altitudes that differ by more than 3000 ft.

3. Find a mean annual temperature for each city. Because your almanac probably does not list this, you may have to calculate it using 12 average monthly temperatures or some other method.

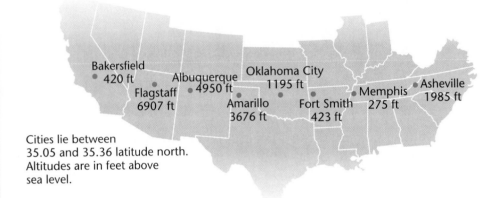

Bakersfield 420 ft
Albuquerque 4950 ft
Flagstaff 6907 ft
Oklahoma City 1195 ft
Amarillo 3676 ft
Fort Smith 423 ft
Memphis 275 ft
Asheville 1985 ft

Cities lie between 35.05 and 35.36 latitude north. Altitudes are in feet above sea level.

4. Calculate the temperature difference *per thousand feet* between the cities.

5. Let x = the altitude difference between two cities in thousands of feet.
Let y = the temperature difference between two cities.
Based on your results in this exploration, write an equation in the form $y = \underline{\hspace{1cm}}$ that expresses the relationship between x and y.

6. Graph your equation using graph paper or a graphing utility.

7. Explain how you could use your graph to predict the temperature difference between two cities at different altitudes at the latitude you used.

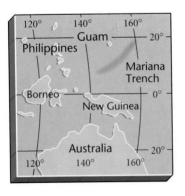

Our earth is a planet of great extremes. Altitudes range from 29,028 feet at the summit of Mount Everest to $-35,840$ feet at the bottom of the Mariana Trench in the Pacific Ocean.

Temperature extremes are equally dramatic. On September 13, 1922, the thermometer hit 136.4°F in Al 'Aziziyah, Libya. In 1963, Swedish cloud researchers measured a temperature of -225.4°F at an altitude of 50 to 60 miles above the earth's surface. By comparison, the coldest ground temperature ever recorded was a balmy -126.9°F at Vostok, Antarctica, on August 24, 1960.

REFLECT

1. How do you create a graph to show the relationship between two variables?
2. How does a graph show the change in the relationship between two variables?
3. Describe what is meant by a dependent variable.
4. What factors in addition to altitude and latitude might affect a city's temperature?

Self-Assessment

Determine whether each statement is true or false.

1. The volume of a cube depends on the length of a side of the cube.

2. Your height depends on your age.

3. The cost of gasoline depends on the number of gallons you buy.

4. The length of time a light bulb lasts depends on the price of the bulb.

5. **Lit Up** Light travels at a rate of about 186,000 mi/sec.

   Science

   Let d = the distance that a beam of light travels (mi).
   Let s = the length of time that the beam travels (sec).

   a. Write an equation in the form $d =$ ____ that expresses the relationship between d and s.
   b. Find the distance that light travels in 1 hour.

6. **Mean Wars** Professor Quincy Wright of the University of Chicago published a study in which he concluded that 278 wars took place between the years 1482 and 1940.

   History

   a. Find the mean number of wars per year.
   b. Let p = the length of a period of time (years). Let w = the number of wars during the period.
      Write an equation expressing the relationship between p and w. Assume Professor Quincy's figures are accurate for all periods of time.
   c. Identify the dependent variable and the independent variable in your equation.
   d. Draw a graph of the equation.

7. A triangle with an area of 96 cm² and a base length of 16 cm has a height of [5-1]
   (a) 6 cm   (b) 12 cm   (c) 18 cm   (d) not here

Choose the letter of the correct answer. [2-3]

8. Evaluate $7 + 5 \times 3 - 1$.
   (a) 24   (b) 35   (c) 21   (d) 17

9. Jan's 4-digit autoteller code has the numbers 1, 5, 8, and 3. How many possible orders are there for the code? [7-2]
   (a) 24   (b) 6   (c) 120   (d) 10   (e) not here

10. A right triangle has a hypotenuse of 17 cm and a leg of 8 cm. Find the length of the other leg. [6-3]
   (a) 18.8 cm   (b) 9 cm   (c) 225 cm   (d) 15 cm

11. Graph the equation $y = 4x + 3$.

12. Graph the equation $y = -\frac{1}{2}x - 2$.

13. Radar Readout Radar guns are not only used by police to ticket speeders, they are also used by baseball scouts. A radar gun can determine the speed of a ball coming directly toward it. But if the gun is at an angle to the path of the ball, it will not register the true speed. Use the proportion $\dfrac{\text{radar gun reading}}{\text{true speed}} = \dfrac{a}{c}$ to determine the true speed of the fast ball. [6-3]

14. Cresting A rainstorm caused a river to rise 52 in. above its normal level. Following the storm, the water level subsided at a rate of 2 in./hr.
  a. Define two variables that describe this situation.
  b. Make a table of six pairs of values expressing the relationship between your variables.
  c. Write an equation relating your variables.
  d. Graph the equation.
  e. Explain how to use your graph to find how long it took for the water to return to its normal level.

15. If You Would Like to Make a Call … The table of values shows the cost (c), in dollars, of making a long-distance call lasting m minutes.

m	1.00	2.00	3.00	4.00	5.00	6.00
c	1.40	2.20	3.00	3.80	4.60	5.40

  a. How much does each additional minute cost?
  b. Use the answer to **15a** to find the cost of a zero-minute call. This is the phone company's basic charge just to place the call, regardless of length.
  c. Write an equation $c = \underline{\quad}$ expressing the relationship between c and m.
  d. Graph the equation.

SLAM DUNKING

10'6"

"It begins with Michael swooping toward the basket. His tongue is out, the ball at the end of his long, muscular right arm. He takes one stride, and then he begins to rise. It is a magnificent thing, his rise, as articulate ... as the drawings of Leonardo or the joyous music of Louis Armstrong. His legs begin to churn in midair, mocking gravity, and he begins to climb even higher: he begins ... to fly. In his game, Jordan was the great African-American artist: improvisational, self-reflexive, bound only by the rules he made up as he went along." (*Newsweek*, Oct./Nov., 1993)

Michael Jordan is a hero to people across the United States. Different cultures have different heroes, but all heroes have one thing in common:

They inspire us to be better than we think we are. Heroes come from all walks of life—artists, scientists, entertainers, politicians, educators. Who is Michael Jordan's own hero? His Dad. He said, "If you're lucky, you grow up in a house where you learn what kind of person to be from your parents."

Be like Mike What are the physical [requirements] for dunking a basketball? The obvious requirement is ... that you have to be able to get the basketball over the edge of a 10-foot-high rim. This, in turn, calls for a combination of body height and jumping ability. ... As a minimum requirement, you have to get your wrist to rim level. This means that the sum of your *standing reach* and *vertical leap* must be at least 10 feet 6 inches.

10'3"

10'0"

1. Who is a hero to you? Why? Will this change over time?
2. Who are some heroes to specific ethnic groups—Native Americans, Latinos, Asian Americans, other groups?
3. What does *standing reach* mean? *vertical leap*? What happens to the *vertical leap* required to dunk as your *standing reach* changes over time?
4. Let *s* stand for *standing reach* and *v* stand for *vertical leap*. What does $s + v = 10.5$ show?

← CONNECT → *You have seen that graphs of equations come in many shapes and sizes. Now you will learn about an important class of equations that are graphed as straight lines.*

In mathematics, we use the word **function** to indicate that the value of one variable depends on the value of another variable. The value of y in $y = 3x + 2$ depends on the value of x. If we always choose 1 for x, we always get 5 for y. We say that y is a function of x.

CONSIDER

?

1. If substituting 1 for x in a formula could give you 5 one time, but 2 another time, what problems could result?

Physicist Peter Brancazio combines his love of sports with his profession. He has studied dozens of sporting activities including running, gymnastics, throwing and hitting a baseball, shooting a basketball, throwing a shot put, and delivering a karate chop. You can read about his findings in his book, *SportScience*. The following Explore is based on his research.

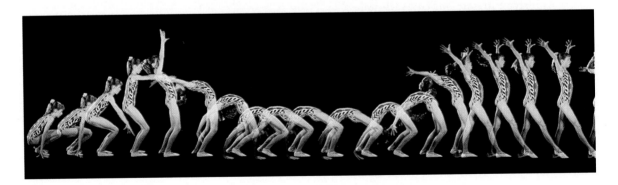

MATERIALS

Graphing utility or graph paper

How high would you have to jump to slam dunk a basketball? Peter Brancazio's answer is $v = 126 - \frac{5}{4}h$, where $v =$ your vertical leap, in inches, and $h =$ your height, in inches.

1. Estimate the vertical distance you must be able to jump to slam dunk.
2. Graph the relationship between vertical leap and height.
3. What conclusions can you reach by studying the graph?
4. Use the graph to estimate the following.
   a. the vertical leap needed by a 5-footer to slam dunk
   b. the height of a person who does not need to leap at all to slam dunk
5. Put chalk dust on your fingertips. Standing beside a wall, reach up and tap as high a point on the wall as you can. Then jump as high as you can and tap a second point directly above the first.
6. Measure the distance between chalk marks. This is your vertical leap. (Why?) Can you slam dunk on Peter Brancazio's team?

A function that is graphed as a straight line, like the one you have just drawn, is called a **linear function.** Linear functions involve proportions. Recall that in a proportion, equal changes in one quantity are matched by equal changes in another quantity.

Proportional Relationship

Equal changes in pairs of socks

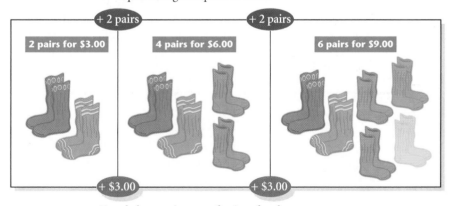

Equal changes in cost of pairs of socks

1. Ashley earns $5 an hour at her after-school job. Write and graph a function relating the number of hours she works to the amount she earns.

Let x = number of hours worked. Let y = amount earned ($). The table lists values of x and y for from 1 to 6 hours of work.

x	1	2	3	4	5	6
y	5	10	15	20	25	30

Notice that you can write a proportion involving any two ordered pairs.

$$\frac{2}{10} = \frac{5}{25} \qquad\qquad \frac{1}{5} = \frac{6}{30}$$

Because the value of y is always 5 times the value of x, the function is $y = 5x$.

Notice how the graph illustrates proportionality:

1 unit means ↑ 5 units

2 units means ↑ 10 units

and so on

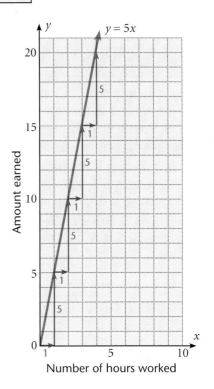

Because the equation is linear, the y-values always change by 5 units when the x-values change by 1 unit. Also, the y-values always change by 10 units when the x-values change by 2 units.

CONSIDER ?

2. Why was the function in the example only graphed for non-negative numbers?

3. How could you use the graph to find the amount Ashley would earn for a given number of hours? to find how long it would take Ashley to earn a certain amount?

4. How would the graph look if Ashley's rate increased?

a. David jogs at an average rate of 7 mi/hr. Write and graph a function relating the length of time he jogs to the distance he runs. Is the function linear?

EXAMPLE

2. A sky diver jumps from a plane. Is the relationship between time and the distance that the sky diver has been falling a linear function?

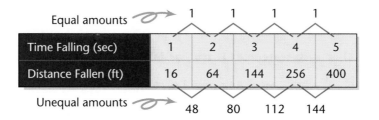

Equal amounts

Time Falling (sec)	1	2	3	4	5
Distance Fallen (ft)	16	64	144	256	400

Unequal amounts   48   80   112   144

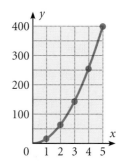

Notice that equal changes in amounts of time falling are not matched by equal changes in distances fallen. Therefore, the relationship is not linear.

You can verify this by looking at the graph, which is a curve rather than a line.

TRY IT

b. Is the relationship between a circle's radius and its area a linear function? Explain.

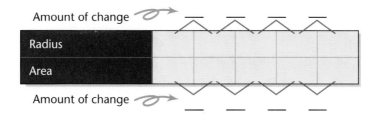

Amount of change

Radius				
Area				

Amount of change

REFLECT

1. How can you tell whether a function is linear from a table of values?
2. How can you tell whether a function is linear from its graph?
3. Can you write a true proportion involving any two ordered pairs of a *nonlinear* function?

Exercises

CORE

1. Getting Started Examine the function $y = \frac{1}{2}x$.

a. Copy and complete a table of ordered pairs for the function.

b. Do equal changes in x result in equal changes in y?

c. Is $y = \frac{1}{2}x$ a linear function?

x	1	2	3	4	5	6
y						

Determine whether each statement is true or false.

2. On the graph of any linear function, a horizontal change of 1 unit results in a vertical change of 1 unit.

3. Linear functions are graphed only in the first quadrant.

4. On the graph of a linear function, equal changes in x-values always result in equal changes in y-values.

Tell whether the function is linear. Explain how you know.

5.

Time Reading (hr)	1	2	3	4	5
Number of Pages Read	26	52	80	106	132

6.

Cost of Purchase ($)	1.00	2.00	3.00	6.00	7.60
Sales Tax ($)	0.05	0.10	0.15	0.30	0.38

7.

Height of Triangle with Base = 8 (in.)	1	2	3	4	6
Area of Triangle (in.^{2})	4	8	12	16	24

8.

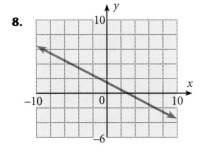

9.

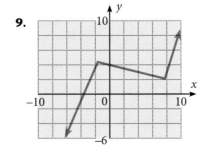

10. The moon is smaller than the earth, so its gravitational pull is less than the earth's. An object on the moon weighs only one-sixth what it weighs on the earth.

   a. On the earth a person weighs 150 pounds. Find the person's weight on the moon.

   b. On the moon a lunar rover weighs 215 pounds. How much does it weigh on the earth?

   c. Is the relationship between an object's weight on this planet and its weight on the moon proportional? Explain. (Hint: Use your answers from **10a** and **10b**.)

   d. Let $x =$ an object's weight on the earth. Let $y =$ an object's weight on the moon. Write y as a function of x.

   e. Make a table of values for the function.

   f. Graph the function.

   g. Is the function linear? Explain.

11. Fattening the Piggy Jeremiah deposits $20 in his piggy bank. Each month he saves another $5.

   a. Does the function $s = 20 + 5m$ correctly model the total amount (s) in the bank after m months? Explain.

   b. Graph s as a function of m. Should you connect the points on your graph?

   c. Is the function linear?

12. Recent data give disturbing information about a serious safety issue. They show that about 30% of Americans admit to sometimes driving while under the influence of alcohol.

   a. Write a function relating the number of people (p) and the number who admit to sometimes driving while under the influence of alcohol (d).

   b. Copy and complete the table of values.

p	50,000	100,000	250,000	500,000	1,000,000
d					

   c. Graph the function.

13. a. $y = \dfrac{1}{x}$ is not a linear function. Make a table of values for the function. Explain how the table illustrates that the function is not linear.

   b. Graph the function. Explain how the graph shows that the function is not linear.

Write a function relating the quantities. Then graph the function.

14. the diameter of a circle; the circumference of the circle

15. the length of time a snail crawls at a rate of 9 in./hr; the distance the snail crawls

 *LOOK AHEAD*

16. a. Make a table of ordered pairs for $y = 3x$, for $x = 1, 2, 3$, and so on.
   b. Do equal changes in x result in equal changes in y?
   c. Make a table of ordered pairs for $y = 3x + 5$, for $x = 1, 2, 3$, and so on.
   d. Do equal changes in x result in equal changes in y?
   e. How do the changes in y for $y = 3x + 5$ compare with the changes in y for $y = 3x$?

MORE PRACTICE

Tell whether each function is linear. Explain how you know.

17.

Time Working (hr)	1	2	3	4	5
Number of Trees Planted	3	6	9	12	15

18.

Number of Hours Leaking	1.0	2.0	3.0	4.0	5.0
Volume of Water Lost (gal)	4.6	9.2	13.8	18.6	23.2

19.

Side of Square (cm)	4	6	8	12	15
Perimeter of Square (cm)	16	24	32	48	60

20.

Age of Plant (wk)	5	10	15	20	30
Height of Plant (cm)	10	11	12	13	15

21.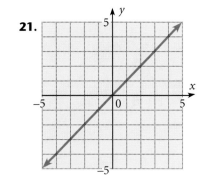

22.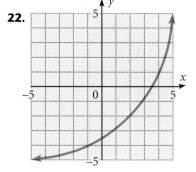

23.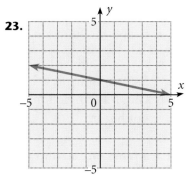

Write a function relating the quantities. Then graph the function.

24. number of days; number of hours in the given number of days

25. number of pairs of socks at $2 per pair; cost of pairs purchased

26. dimension of part of airplane; dimension of same part in model built to $\frac{1}{20}$th scale

27. It costs $40 per column-inch to place an ad in the *Town Weekly*. Write and graph a function relating the cost of an ad to the number of column-inches. Is the function linear?

MORE MATH REASONING

28. A baseball is thrown upward with a velocity given by $v = 40 - 32t$, where velocity (v) is in feet per second and time (t) is in seconds.

Science

a. Graph the velocity as a function of time.

b. Explain how you can use the graph to determine when the ball reaches its highest point, or *apex*.

c. What does it mean for a baseball to have negative velocity?

29. Decisions, Decisions Suppose Juanita has been offered two jobs. The first job will give her a starting annual salary of $26,000, plus annual increases of $1500. The second will give her a starting annual salary of $29,000, plus annual increases of $900.

Industry

a. For each offer, write the annual salary as a function of the number of years Juanita will work.

b. Graph the functions.

c. What do the graphs tell you about the annual amounts Juanita can expect to earn?

d. What points on the graph are meaningful for this situation?

Slope and Intercept

← **CONNECT** → *In the last part you looked at some of the characteristics of linear functions. Now you will learn to graph a linear function by finding its slope and **y**-intercept.*

The ramp *slopes* up to the door.

The *grade* of the highway is at most 7%.

The *pitch* of the roof allows the snow to slide off.

The mountain road is *steep*.

The picture was *tilted*.

CONSIDER

?

1. **What is the meaning of the italic words in the statements above?**

The equation of any linear function can be written as $y = ax + b$. These are all linear functions.

$$y = -3x + 4$$

a is -3 *b* is 4

$$y = \frac{1}{2}x + 0$$

a is $\frac{1}{2}$ *b* is 0

$$y = -x + -6$$

a is -1 *b* is -6
since $-x$ is $-1x$

Let's see if there is a relationship between the steepness or slope of a line and the equation of the line.

EXPLORE: GRAPHING, FROM A TO Y

MATERIALS

Graphing utility or graph paper

1. Graph the equation $y = ax$, using several different values of *a*. Be sure to include fractions and negative numbers among your values of *a*.
2. For each equation, note the steepness of the line. How does the value of *a* appear to affect the steepness?
3. Graph several equations of the form $y = x + b$, using different values of *b*.
4. For each equation in Step 3, note where the line intersects the *y*-axis. What relationship can you find between the value of *b* and the point of intersection?

CONSIDER

2. Two lines have the equations $y = 14x$ and $y = 20x$. Which line would you expect to be steeper?
3. A line has the equation $y = x + c$. Where would you expect the line to intersect the y-axis?

We use the word **slope** to describe the steepness of a line. A line that slants *upward* from left to right, like line ℓ, has a **positive slope.** A line that slants *downward* from left to right, like line n, has a **negative slope.**

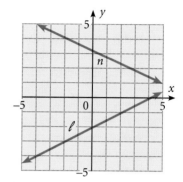

To find the slope of a line, choose two points on the line. Note how much the x-values and the y-values change as you move from one point to the other.

$$\text{Slope} = \frac{\text{Change in } y\text{-values}}{\text{Change in } x\text{-values}}$$

EXAMPLES

1. Find the slope of the line $y = \frac{2}{3}x - 4$.
   Choose two points on the line, for example $(3, -2)$ and $(6, 0)$.
   Change in y-values: $-2 - 0 = -2$
   Change in x-values: $3 - 6 = -3$
   Slope $= \frac{-2}{-3} = \frac{2}{3}$
   The line slants upward from left to right, so its slope is positive.

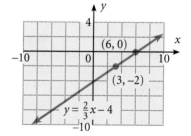

2. Find the slope of the line containing the points $(-1, 4)$ and $(3, 2)$.
   Change in y-values: $4 - 2 = 2$
   Change in x-values: $-1 - (3) = -4$
   Slope $= \frac{2}{-4} = -\frac{1}{2}$
   A sketch confirms that the line slants downward from left to right, so its slope is negative.

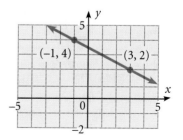

When you are finding the change in y-values and the change in x-values, be sure to start with the same ordered pair for both calculations.

EXAMPLE

3. Find the **slope** of the line containing the points $(-1, 8)$ and $(4, 3)$.

The change in y-values is $3 - 8 = -5$

The change in x-values is $4 - (-1) = 5$

The slope is $\frac{-5}{5}$, or -1.

TRY IT

a. Find the slope of the line $y = 2x - 1$.
b. Find the slope of the line containing the points $(5, 3)$ and $(1, -1)$.
c. Find the slope of the line containing the points $(-2, 4)$ and $(5, 4)$.
d. Can you find the slope of the line containing the points $(4, 1)$ and $(4, 6)$? What happens? Why?

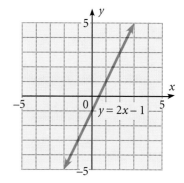

The *change in y-value* is sometimes called the *rise*.

The *change in x-value* is sometimes called the *run*.

So we can write the slope ratio, $\frac{\text{change in } y\text{-value}}{\text{change in } x\text{-value}}$, as $\frac{rise}{run}$.

 CONSIDER

4. How can you remember that *rise* means the "change in y-value" and that *run* means the "change in x-value"?
5. What would a negative rise value mean?

4. Find the slope of the line $y = \frac{3}{4}x + 2$.

Choose any two points on the line, such as $(0, 2)$ and $(4, 5)$.

To go from $(0, 2)$ to $(4, 5)$, you go to the right 4 and up 3.

So the run is 4, and the rise is 3.

$$\text{slope} = \frac{rise}{run} = \frac{3}{4}$$

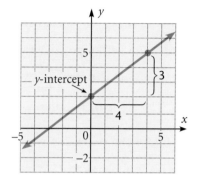

Notice that both the slope of the line and the y-intercept can be seen in the equation when it is in the form $y = ax + b$.

For the equation $y = \frac{3}{4}x + 2$

The slope is $\frac{3}{4}$.

The y-intercept is 2.

REFLECT

1. How can you find the slope of a line
   a. from the graph of the line?   **b.** from the equation of the line?
2. How can you find the y-intercept of a line
   a. from the graph of the line?   **b.** from the equation of the line?
3. How can you tell whether a line has a positive or negative slope
   a. from the graph of the line?   **b.** from the equation of the line?

Exercises

CORE

1. Getting Started
   a. Tell whether the slope of the line is positive or negative.
   b. What are the coordinates of A?
   c. What are the coordinates of B?
   d. Give the change in y from A to B.
   e. Give the change in x from A to B.
   f. Give the slope of the line.
   g. Give the y-intercept of the line.

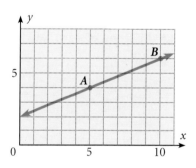

Tell whether the statement is true or false. If it is false, change the underlined word to make the statement true.

2. A line with a <u>positive</u> slope slants from lower left to upper right.

3. A line that slants <u>upward</u> from left to right has a negative slope.

4. The <u>slope</u> of the line $y = 3x + 2$ is 2.

Estimate the slope and *y*-intercept of each line.

5.
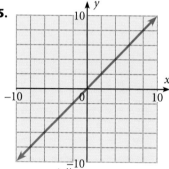

6.
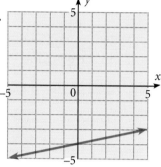

7.
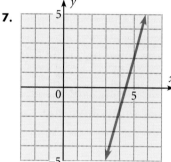

8.
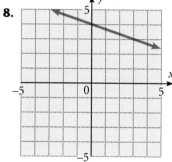

Tell whether each equation represents a linear function.

9. $5x - 4y = 3$

10. $y = 2x^2$

11. $-5y = 3$

> **Problem-Solving Tip**
>
> Make a table. Graph, if necessary.

Find the slope of each line.

12.
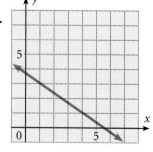

13.
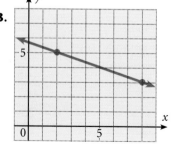

Find the slope of each line.

14. the line through $(2, 5)$ and $(6, 17)$

15. the line through $(-3, 4)$ and $(-1, -2)$

16. the line through $(1, 2)$ and $(6, 2)$

17. $y = -7$ (Hint: This is the same as $0x - 7$.)

18. the line that has a y-intercept of -3 and that passes through $(5, 0)$

Graph each line and find its slope.

19. $y = 5x + 3$

20. $y = -x - 3$

21. $y = -2x$

22. What's to Lose? A recent study showed that a person loses 2 hours of his or her life span for each pack of cigarettes smoked.

    a. Write an equation expressing the number of hours lost as a function of the number of packs of cigarettes smoked.

    b. Graph the function.

    c. Give the slope and y-intercept of the graph of the function.

    d. What does the graph tell you about the effects of smoking cigarettes?

Science

23. You've seen that the function $y = \frac{9}{5}x + 32$ expresses Fahrenheit temperature (y) as a function of Celsius temperature (x).

    a. Graph the function.

    b. Give the slope and y-intercept of the graph of the function.

    c. Use your graph to estimate the Fahrenheit temperature when the Celsius temperature is $-8°$.

Industry

24. Take That! A rental store charges a fee of $11 plus $4 an hour to rent a weed whacker. Draw a graph showing the rental cost of the weed whacker as a function of the rental time.

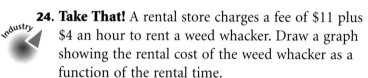 **LOOK BACK**

25. Sketch a graph showing how the quantities change in relation to each other: the number of school days you've had this year; the number of school days remaining in the year. [8-1]

26. How many ways can five books be lined up side by side on a shelf? [7-2]

27. What is the tangent of angle A? (Hint: Use the Pythagorean Theorem first.) [6-2, 6-3]

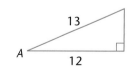

MORE PRACTICE

Tell whether the slope of each line is positive or negative.

28. line a

29. line b

30. line c

31. line d

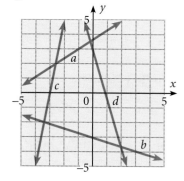

Give the slope of each line.

32. line a

33. line b

34. line c

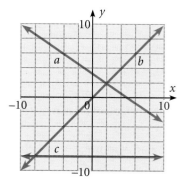

Estimate the slope of each line.

35. line m

36. line n

37. line k

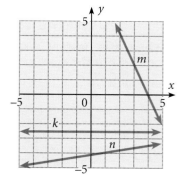

Find the slope of each line.

38. $y = -1.5x + 1$

39.

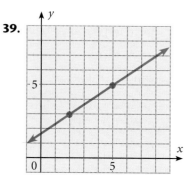

Find the slope of each line.

40. the line through (3, 4) and (2, 5)

41. the line through (−5, 1) and (7, −2)

42. the line through (5, 9) and (9, 5)

43. the line $y = 0$ (Hint: This is $0x + 0$.)

44. the line with a y-intercept of 4 that goes through (5, 0)

Tell whether each equation represents a linear function.

45. $y = \frac{2}{3}x + 6$

46. $y = \sqrt{x}$

47. $y = 2.5x + 3.7$

Graph each line and find its slope.

48. $y = -2x + 1$

49. $y = -x + 2$

50. $y = 5$ (Hint: This is the same as $0x + 5$.)

51. The function $y = 35x + 20$ approximates the Celsius temperature (y) of the earth as a function of depth in kilometers (x).
   a. Graph the function.
   b. Give the slope and y-intercept of the graph of the function.
   c. Use your graph to estimate the depth at which the temperature of the earth is 72°C.
   d. What is the ground-level temperature? Explain.

MORE MATH REASONING

52. The table gives the rates charged by two competing cab companies.
   a. Draw a graph for each company, showing total charge as a function of distance.

> **Problem-Solving Tip**
>
> Write equations in $ax + b$ form.

Company	Rate
Yellow Cab:	$1.75 + $0.30/quarter mile
Maroon Cab:	$2.05 + $0.25/quarter mile

   b. Use your graph to find the distance for which both companies charge the same rate.

53. Portions of Filbert Street and 22nd Street in San Francisco are the world's steepest streets, rising 1 foot for every 3.17 feet of horizontal distance. Find the slope of the two streets.

54. Colorado's 8940-foot-long Eisenhower Tunnel leads drivers from an elevation of 11,080 feet to an elevation of 11,160 feet. Find the slope of the tunnel.

Making Connections

← CONNECT → *Now you will use what you have learned about linear functions to explore a property of matter called elasticity.*

For a given throw, how high or far will a basketball bounce? For a given racket speed, how fast will a tennis ball rebound? The answers depend on *elasticity*. Elasticity tells us the amount of bounce or stretch of an object.

The law of elasticity was discovered by the English scientist Robert Hooke in 1678. Hooke found that the amount an object bends, bounces, or stretches is proportional to the size of the force acting on it.

EXPLORE: BIG STRETCH

1. Attach one end of a rubber band to a shelf or permanent fixture and attach the other end to a paper cup.
2. Measure and record the length of the rubber band.
3. Add marbles one-by-one to the cup, recording the length of the rubber band after each marble is added.
4. Graph the relationship between the weight in the cup and the length of the rubber band. Draw a line that comes as close as possible to connecting the data.
5. Find the slope and y-intercept of the line. Write an equation for the line by substituting in $y =$ (slope)$x + (y$-intercept).
6. What does the y-intercept of your graph represent?
7. Use the graph to determine how far the rubber band would stretch for a number of marbles that is different from any you tried.
8. Use the equation to determine how far the rubber band would stretch for 50 marbles. (Assume the rubber band would not break.)
9. What conclusions can you make?

MATERIALS

Paper cup, Rubber band, Supply of marbles or other objects equal in weight, Ruler, String

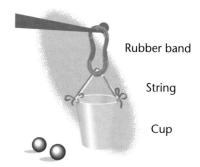

Rubber band

String

Cup

1. Suppose you repeated the Explore using heavier marbles. How would the graph compare with the one you drew?
2. If points of an exploration like the one on the opposite page do not fall perfectly on a straight line, can the function relating them be linear? Explain.
3. Describe what is meant by the slope of a line. What does the numerical value of the slope mean?

Self-Assessment

Tell whether each function is linear. If it is linear, write the equation.

1.

x	1	2	3	4	5	6
y	3	6	9	12	15	18

2.

x	4	8	12	16	20	24
y	−3	1	5	9	13	17

3.

x	1	2	3	4	5	6
y	1	4	9	16	25	36

4.

x	4	8	12	16	20	24
y	5	5	5	5	5	5

Write a function relating the quantities. Then graph the function.

5. number of weeks; number of days in the given number of weeks

6. number of pens at 29¢ per pen; cost of pens purchased

7. number of pages typed at 6 pages per hour; number of hours spent typing

8. Which is the correct slope of the line through $(-2, 3)$ and $(4, -5)$?

   (a) $-\frac{4}{3}$ (b) $-\frac{3}{4}$ (c) $\frac{4}{3}$ (d) $-\frac{1}{3}$ (e) -4

9. Graph the equation $y = \frac{3}{2}x + 3$.

10. A spring balance in the produce section of a grocery store stretches 3 cm when 0.6 kg of plums are placed on the scale.
    a. How far would you expect the spring to stretch under the weight of 2 kg of bananas? Explain.
    b. When Corey placed Brussels sprouts on the scale, the spring stretched 4.2 cm. Give the weight of the Brussels sprouts.

11. How many ways can the letters ABCD be arranged? [7-2]

12. An arrow is shot into the air. Its speed (*s*), in ft/sec, can be found using the function $s = 60 - 10t$, where *t* is the time, in sec, after the arrow is released.
  a. Graph the function.
  b. Use the graph to estimate the length of time the arrow will be in the air.
  c. Use the graph to estimate the speed at time $t = 3.2$ sec.

13. Sketch a graph showing how the quantities change in relation to each other: the number of 7-card packs of baseball cards purchased; the number of cards all together. [8-1]

14. For most people, effective exercise raises their pulse rates but keeps the pulse rates within a reasonable range of values.
  a. Why are there two lines? What does each line show?
  b. Why are the slopes negative?
  c. Why doesn't either line intersect the horizontal axis?

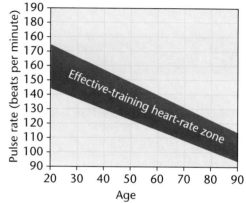

15. Radius Bone's Connected to the …
  Scientists can accurately predict a person's height given the length of the person's radius bone (*r*) in cm.
  a. Graph height as a function of radius length for both males and females. (Use the same coordinate grid or graphing-utility screen.)
  b. Explain how an anthropologist could make use of your graph.
  c. Find the height at which both males and females have the same length radius.

radius bone

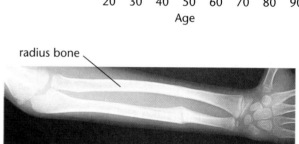

Height of Male (cm)	Height of Female (cm)
$3.6r + 81$	$4.2r + 62$

16. Damien has prepared a graph showing his month-by-month savings.
  a. What is happening when the slope is positive?
  b. What is happening when the slope is negative?
  c. What is happening when the slope is zero?
  d. What is the meaning of the *y*-intercept?

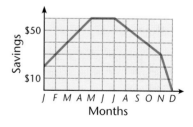

17. Find the length of $\overline{AB}$. Show how you found it. [6-3]

18. In a science-fiction story, a space creature grows as it moves *backward* in time. Sketch a graph comparing its size to time.

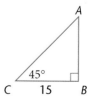

Coming Down to Earth

> "There is nothing more eloquent in Nature than a mountain stream."
>
> John Muir, *A Thousand Mile Walk to the Gulf*

Gravity can make your Fourth of July holiday great! When you visit a national park, the force of gravity provides you with the awesome experience of majestic waterfalls and the peaceful flow of mountain streams. At ocean beaches, you might play on sand kept wet by high tides. As you toss water balloons and volleyballs, you probably don't think of gravity at all.

The earth's pull shapes each jet of water spewing from the fountain at the local park. It ensures that every hit baseball—even home run balls—will come down. And at day's end, it determines the arc of each fireworks display.

Any object propelled into the air and then affected only by gravity—a drop of water, a baseball, or a rocket burst—traces a path called a **parabola**. The distance that the object travels depends on the initial angle of its flight. But the shape of its path is always that of a parabola.

1. At what angle should a batter hit a baseball in order to sock it a maximum distance?
2. What other things might have a parabolic flight path?
3. How does gravitational attraction affect tides?

Quadratic Functions

← **CONNECT** → *You have seen many linear functions, which are graphed as straight lines. Now you will investigate an important class of functions that are graphed as symmetric curves called parabolas.*

EXPLORE: LEARNING CURVES

MATERIALS

Graphing utility

1. Graph each of the following functions on your graphing utility. Copy each onto a piece of graph paper. On many calculators you use the $\boxed{\wedge}$ key to indicate that the next number is an exponent. Example: $y = -2x^2 + 1$.

   Enter $\boxed{y=}$ $\boxed{(-)}$ 2 $\boxed{x}$ $\boxed{\wedge}$ 2 $\boxed{+}$ 1

   The graph is shown at the right.

   a. $y = 2x^2$ **b.** $y = -3x + 4$

   c. $y = 7 - x^2 + x$ **d.** $y = \left(\frac{3}{14}\right)x + 5$

   e. $y = x^3 + 1$ **f.** $y = 2^x$

2. Which of these functions are linear functions, with straight lines for their graphs?

3. Which of these functions are **nonlinear functions,** with curved lines for their graphs?

4. Make a conjecture, or an educated guess, about how you can tell from looking at the equation whether it is a *linear function* or a *nonlinear function.*

5. Test your conjecture on the following functions. Decide whether you think the function is linear or nonlinear before you graph the function. Then graph each to see if you were correct.

   a. $y = 3x - 1$ **b.** $y = x^3$ **c.** $y = 1 - x + x^2$ **d.** $y = 1 - (2^2)x$

6. Graph each function. Make a conjecture about the effects of the coefficient of the x^2 term.

   a. $y = 4x^2$ **b.** $y = -4x^2$ **c.** $y = \left(\frac{1}{4}\right)x^2$ **d.** $y = -\left(\frac{1}{4}\right)x^2$

We will now take a closer look at a special type of nonlinear function, where a variable is squared.

$$y = -16x^2 \qquad y = \frac{2}{3}x^2 - 12 \qquad y = x^2 + 2.4x - 1$$

These functions are called **quadratic functions.** The graph of a quadratic function is called a **parabola.**

Many curves seen in everyday life have equations that are quadratic functions. You can use a graph to solve problems involving these curves.

EXAMPLE

1. On one of its bounces, a rubber ball follows a path given by $y = 8x - x^2$, where y is the ball's height (in.) and x is the ball's horizontal distance (in.) from the point where it last struck the ground. How far has the ball gone, horizontally, when it is 10 inches off the ground?

We want to find x when y is 10. Graph the function $y = 8x - x^2$ using a graphing utility.

Use the TRACE key to trace along the graph to see where y is 10. When $x \approx 1.5$, $y \approx 10$.

But y is also 10 at another point! When $x \approx 6.5$, $y \approx 10$. When the ball has gone 1.5 inches or 6.5 inches horizontally, it is 10 inches off the ground.

CONSIDER

?

1. Why are there two answers to Example 1?
2. How high does the ball in Example 1 bounce at its highest point? How did you decide?

You can find specific values for a function by evaluating the function for specific values of x.

EXAMPLE

2. For the ball in Example 1, which follows the path given by $y = 8x - x^2$, complete the table of values. Then plot the points on a grid and connect the points to sketch the graph.

x	0	2	4	6	8
y					

For each value of x, you can evaluate the expression $y = 8x - x^2$ to find y.

For $x = 0$,
$y = 8 \cdot \mathbf{0} - \mathbf{0}^2$
$= 0 - 0$
$= 0$

For $x = 2$,
$y = 8 \cdot \mathbf{2} - \mathbf{2}^2$
$= 16 - 4$
$= 12$

For $x = 4$,
$y = 8 \cdot \mathbf{4} - \mathbf{4}^2$
$= 32 - 16$
$= 16$

You can compute similarly to find y-values for $x = 6$ and 8, and complete the table.

x	0	2	4	6	8
y	0	12	16	12	0

Plotting the points, you get the graph shown.

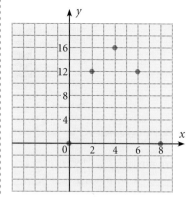

You can connect the points smoothly to sketch the graph of the function.

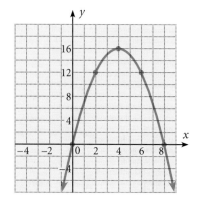

3. What is the meaning of $x = 4$ and $y = 16$ in the problem in Example 2?

TRY IT

a. A window washer drops a squeegee from a scaffold 400 feet off the ground. The relationship between the height of the squeegee (h), in feet, and the length of time it has been falling (t), in seconds, is given by $h = 400 - 16t^2$. Draw a graph and use it to estimate when the squeegee passes a window 100 feet off the ground.

b. Complete the table of values for $h = -16t^2 + 400$. Sketch the graph and explain what one ordered pair of values means.

t	0	1	2	3	4	5
h						

REFLECT

1. How can you tell by looking at the equation of a function whether it is a linear function or a nonlinear function?

2. How would you describe the shape of a quadratic function?

3. What is the difference between the graphs of the functions $y = 5x^2$ and $y = -5x^2$?

4. Describe how you can use your graphing utility to find the value of y for a function for a specific value of x.

Exercises

CORE

1. Getting Started Match each equation with the correct graph using what you know about linear and quadratic equations.

a. $y = x^3 - 5x^2 + 2x + 5$ **b.** $y = 2x^2$

c. $y = 3x - 1$ **d.** $y = -2x^2$

i.

ii.

iii.

iv.
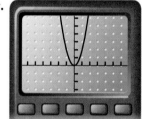

Write the word or phrase that correctly completes each statement.

2. The graph of a linear function is a ____.

3. The graph of a quadratic function is a ____.

Tell whether each is a linear function or a nonlinear function.

4. $y = 4x - 5x^2$ **5.** $y = 2x + 3$ **6.** $y = -2x^2 - 1$

7. $y = 1 - x^3$ **8.** $y = 4x^2 - 3x + 3$ **9.** $y = -\frac{1}{8}x$

10. $y = 4.5x^2 - 8.23$ **11.** $y = -x^4 + 8x^2 + 1$ **12.** $y = 1.25 - 18x$

13. Follow the Bouncing Ball On one of its bounces, a rubber ball follows a path given by $y = 6x - x^2$, where y is the ball's height (in.) and x is the ball's horizontal distance (in.) from the point where it last struck the ground. The graph of this function is shown at the right.

   a. Estimate the horizontal distance (x) when the ball hits the ground again.

   b. How high does the ball bounce at its highest point?

14. Complete the table of values for the function given in Exercise 13, $y = 6x - x^2$.

x	0	2	4	6	8	10	12
y							

Solve each equation for y. Then tell whether each is a linear function or a nonlinear function.

15. $2y = 6x^2$ **16.** $4.9 + y = 3.3x$ **17.** $6 = x^2 + 3y - 3$

18. Let $x =$ the length of a side of a square. Let $y =$ the area of the square.

   a. Write y as a function of x.

   b. Complete the table using the function.

x	1	2	3	4	5	6	7
y							

   c. Plot the points on a grid and connect the points to sketch a graph of the function.

   d. Use the graph to estimate the length of the side of a square with an area of 20 square units.

19. At the right is the graph of $y = 4x^2$. Sketch the graph of $y = -4x^2$.

20. The graph of a parabola is symmetric. What is the line of symmetry for the graph of $y = 4x^2$?

Evaluate the following expressions.

21. x^4 for $x = 3$

22. $3x$ for $x = 2$

23. $5x$ for $x = 2$

24. $\sqrt{x}$ for $x = 9$

25. $\sqrt{x}$ for $x = 100$

26. $\sqrt{x}$ for $x = 36$

27. Let $y = 2^x$. Evaluate this expression for $x = 2$, for $x = 3$, for $x = 4$, and for $x = 5$. What appears to be happening?

MORE PRACTICE

Determine whether each is a linear function or a nonlinear function.

28. $y = 13.2x - 18$

29. $y = 1 - 3x^2$

30. $y = x^2$

31. $y = \sqrt{3x}$

32. $y = 3 - 14x$

33. $y = 14 - 5x - 2x^2$

34. Match each equation with the correct graph using what you know about linear and quadratic equations.

a. $y = -3x^2 + 1$

b. $y = 5x - 3$

c. $y = \sqrt{x}$

d. $y = 3x^2 - 1$

i.

ii.

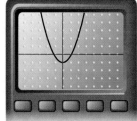

iii.

iv.

35. Use the function $y = x^2 - 4x + 1$.

  a. Complete the table of values for the function.

x	-2	-1	0	1	2	3	4	5	6
y									

  b. Plot the pairs of points and sketch a graph of the function.

An object is dropped. The distance it falls, y meters, is a function of time, x seconds. This function is $y = 4.9x^2$.

36. Use the graph to determine how long it will take the object to reach the ground from 10 meters up.

37. Use the graph to determine how long it will take the object to reach the ground from 20 meters up. (Hint: $y = 10$ is about halfway between the x-axis and the top of the screen.)

38. The area of a circle is given by $A = \pi r^2$, where r is the radius of the circle. Graph the function. Use the graph to estimate the radius of a circle with an area of 100 in.^{2}.

MORE MATH REASONING

39. Use a Graphing Utility On the Fourth of July, Liz took a picture that showed the parabolic paths made by the fireworks. A rocket's height above the water (h), in meters, is given by the equation $h = -6t^2 + 66t + 2$, where t is the time, in seconds, after the launch.

  a. Graph the rocket's height as a function of time.

  b. How long after the launch did the rocket hit the water?

40. Use a Graphing Utility You can use the formula $h = vt - 16t^2$ to find out about fireworks. In this formula, h is the height of a fireworks display, in feet; t is seconds after launch; and v is the launch velocity, in feet per second. A display is launched with an initial velocity of 100 feet per second.

  a. Express the information as a function. Then graph the function.

  b. Find the maximum height reached by the display.

  c. For safety, there should be no explosions within 120 feet of the ground. How soon after launch can safe explosions occur?

Square Root and Exponential Functions

← CONNECT → *Now you will investigate the properties of two important types of functions. The first is closely related to quadratic functions. The second has a variety of applications in science.*

How do objects fall through space? Does a heavy object fall faster than a light one? Does an object falling straight down fall faster than one launched at an angle?

During the late sixteenth century, the great Italian scientist Galileo discovered the answers to these questions. Legend has it that one of his experiments involved dropping an apple 175 feet from the top of the Leaning Tower of Pisa.

EXPLORE: APPLESAUCE

MATERIALS

Graphing utility or graph paper

You can use the function $y = 5\sqrt{x}$ to approximate the velocity (y) of a falling object, in miles per hour, where x is the distance, in feet, that the object has fallen. Because this function involves the square root of the independent variable, it is called a **square root function.**

1. An apple falls from the top of the Leaning Tower of Pisa to the ground. Draw a graph of the function $y = 5\sqrt{x}$ using your graphing utility. Enter 5 $\boxed{*}$ $\boxed{\sqrt{}}$ $\boxed{x}$. You may need to change the window settings to get a good look at the function.
2. Is this a linear function or a nonlinear function? How is it like a quadratic function? How is it different from a quadratic function?
3. Trace to find out what the velocity (y) is when the apple has traveled 1 ft, 2 ft, 4 ft, 5 ft, 7 ft, and 10 ft.
4. When does the velocity increase the most?
5. Galileo's discoveries about falling objects are true only for objects falling in vacuums. How would the velocity of an object falling through the air compare with that of one falling in a vacuum? Why?

You have drawn the graphs of many functions containing numerical exponents. Note that x is the same as x^1.

exponent = 1

↓

$y = 2x - 5$

Linear function

exponent = 2

↓

$y = x^2 - 1$

Quadratic function

Now we will look at a function called an **exponential function,** such as $y = 3^x$. Exponential functions have wide applications in science and social studies.

CONSIDER

1. The expressions $y = 2x - 5$, $y = x^2 - 1$, and $y = 3^x$ all have exponents. Why do you think that only $y = 3^x$ is called an *exponential function?*

EXAMPLE

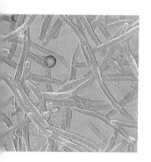

1. In a laboratory, the fast-growing bacteria known as *E. coli* can reproduce in 15 minutes. Suppose you start with one *E. coli* cell. Graph the number of cells you would have as a function of the amount of time since you began.

The number of cells doubles every 15 minutes. If you start with 1 cell, you will have 2 cells after 15 minutes, 4 cells after 30 minutes, 8 cells after 45 minutes, and so on.

Suppose we let x represent the number of 15-minute periods and let y represent the number of cells. We obtain the following table of values.

x	0	1	2	3	4	5	6
y	1	2	4	8	16	32	64

You can plot the points and sketch the graph. Because each y-value is a power of 2, we have the function $y = 2^x$. This is the graph of the number of cells as a function of the number of 15-minute periods.

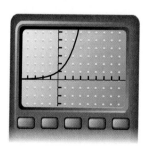

CONSIDER

2. Why do you think that an exponential function is sometimes called a power function?
3. How would the graph differ if we used minutes for x
   rather than 15-minute periods?

TRY IT

a. Graph the function $y = 3^x$ using a graphing utility. Use the [TRACE] key
to find what value of x is required to make $y \approx 8$ and to make $y \approx 20$.

When the **base** used with the exponent is less than 1, the shape of the
graph is different.

EXAMPLE

2. Graph the function $y = \left(\frac{1}{2}\right)^x$ and make
a table of values.

Graph [Y=] [(] 1 [÷] 2 [)] [^] [x]

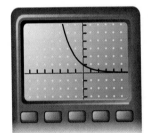

x	1	2	3	4	5	6
y	$\frac{1}{2}$	$\frac{1}{4}$	$\frac{1}{8}$	$\frac{1}{16}$	$\frac{1}{32}$	$\frac{1}{64}$

You have just seen an example of **exponential decay.** Example 1
illustrates **exponential growth.** Both of these types of exponential
functions are associated with many real-world situations.

REFLECT

1. What is an exponential function? How does it differ from a
   quadratic function?
2. Compare the function $y = \left(\frac{1}{2}\right)^x$ to the function $y = 2^x$.
3. How can you use the graph of the function $y = 2^x$ to prove
   that $2^0 = 1$?
4. Describe the graph of the function $y = 1^x$.

Exercises

CORE

1. Getting Started Use the function $y = 2\sqrt{x}$.

a. Complete the table of values.

x	0	1	4	9	16	25	36	49	64
y				6				14	

b. Why were the above values of x chosen for the table of values?

c. Why were no negative values of x chosen?

d. Graph the function using ordered pairs from the table.

e. How does the graph compare with the graph of the function $y = \sqrt{x}$?

Identify the function as linear, quadratic, square root, or exponential.

2. $y = x^2 + 2x + 1$ **3.** $y = \sqrt{x + 1}$ **4.** $-3x + 2y = 4$

5. $y = x - 7$ **6.** $y = 5^x$ **7.** $6^x = y$

8. The weight of an object above the earth's surface depends on its distance from the surface. The graph shows the percentage of weight on the earth as a function of distance. What kind of function would best model this curve? Why?

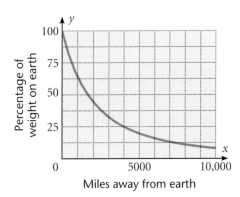

9. Look Out Below! The time (t), in seconds, that it takes a falling object to fall d feet is given by the equation $t = 0.25\sqrt{d}$.

a. How long does it take for an object to fall 100 feet?

b. Graph the equation. (Hint: Find t when d is 0, 1, 4, 9, 16, and 25.)

c. Use your graph to estimate the length of time it takes to fall 75 feet.

d. Use your graph to estimate the solution of the equation $1.4 = 0.25\sqrt{d}$.

e. According to the *Guinness Book of World Records,* in January 1942, Lieutenant I. M. Chisov of the Soviet Union survived a 21,980-foot fall from an airplane *without a parachute.* How long did it take Lt. Chisov to reach the ground?

10. **A Penny Saved …** Suppose you invest some money in a savings account that

pays 5% interest annually. You can find the amount of money you will have in
the account after n years by multiplying the amount of your investment by
$(1.05)^n$.
   a. Use a scientific calculator to make a table of values of the "multiplier"
      $m = (1.05)^n$ for values of n from 1 to 10.
   b. Use your table to graph the equation.
   c. What kind of function did you graph? Explain.
   d. If you invested $1000 in a savings account that paid 5% interest annually,
      how much money would you have after 10 years?

11. **Meltdown** Students have carved a huge ice statue for the Winter Math
Festival. The statue originally weighed 4000 pounds. Because of unseasonably
warm weather, however, it is losing half its weight every hour.
   a. Write an equation expressing the weight of the
      statue (w), in pounds, as a function of the number
      of hours since it weighed 4000 pounds (t).
   b. Graph w as a function of t.
   c. Use the graph to estimate when the statue weighed
      700 pounds.
   d. Use the graph to estimate the weight of the statue
      after $4\frac{1}{4}$ hours.

 LOOK BACK

12. Find the slope and y-intercept of the line $12x + 3y = 21$. [8-2]

13. An equilateral triangle measuring 6 in. on a side is divided into equilateral
triangles measuring 3 in. on a side. The small triangles are numbered consec-
utively, beginning with 1. If one of the small triangles is chosen at random,
what is the probability that triangle number 2 will be chosen? [7-1]

14. How far does the Leaning Tower of Pisa lean
over its base? [6-3]

15. The formula $E = \frac{9r}{I}$ gives the earned-run average
(E) of a baseball pitcher who has given up r
runs in I innings. Find the number of runs given
up by a pitcher with an earned-run average
of 3.50 over 126 innings of pitching. [4-1]

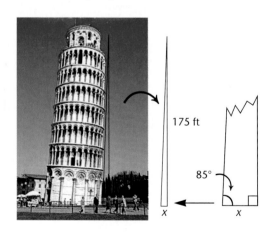

175 ft

85°

MORE PRACTICE

Identify the function as linear, quadratic, square root, or exponential.

16. $y = 0.3x$

17. $y = \sqrt{2}x$

18. $y = 9^x$

19. $y = x^2 - 7$

20. $y = 0.5^x$

21. $\sqrt{4x} = y$

Graph each function.

22. $y = 6\sqrt{x}$

23. $y = 2^{x+1}$

24. $y = \sqrt{x - 1}$

25. $y = (0.9)^x$

26. The radius (r) of a circle is related to the area (A) by the equation $r = \sqrt{\dfrac{A}{\pi}}$.
  a. Graph the radius as a function of the area.
  b. Use your graph to estimate the radius of a circle with an area of 36 square units.
  c. Use your graph to estimate the solution of the equation $2.5 = \sqrt{\dfrac{A}{\pi}}$.

27. Match the function with its graph.

  a. $y = 0.9^x$

  b. $y = \dfrac{1}{20}x^2 + 1$

  c. $1.1^x = y$

i.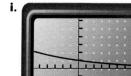

ii.

iii.

28. Decay Away Radioactive plutonium-246 has a **half-life** of 11 days. Every 11 days, a given amount of plutonium-246 will decay to half the mass with which it began the 11-day period. Suppose you start with 16 grams of plutonium-246. Graph the amount of material that remains as a function of the number of 11-day periods since it began to decay.

29. Since 1970, the number of physicians has increased 3.4% per year. $P = 349(1.034)^t$ gives the approximate number of physicians, in thousands, t years after 1970. Estimate the number of physicians for the year 1990 and the year 2000.

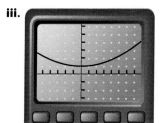

MORE MATH REASONING

30. On the same coordinate axes, draw the first quadrant of the graphs of the functions $y = x^2$ and $y = \sqrt{x}$. Describe your results.

31. Use a Graphing Utility Draw the graphs of the functions $y = x^{0.5}$ and $y = \sqrt{x}$. Describe your results.

32. A forest contained 100,000 cubic meters of lumber in 1985. Logging reduced the volume by 12% per year. Draw a graph showing volume as a function of time.

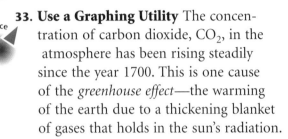

33. Use a Graphing Utility The concentration of carbon dioxide, CO_2, in the atmosphere has been rising steadily since the year 1700. This is one cause of the *greenhouse effect*—the warming of the earth due to a thickening blanket of gases that holds in the sun's radiation.

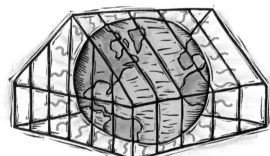

The function $C = 270 + 4.5(1.01)^t$ models CO_2 concentration, in parts per million, where t is the number of years since 1700. Graph and trace to find the year when the concentration of CO_2 will be double what it is today.

8-3
PART C Making Connections

← **C O N N E C T** → *You now have the skills to investigate the graphs of many of the equations that you encounter, even extremely complex ones. In this part you will graph two complex equations, both related to baseball.*

Through your work in this chapter, you have learned a practical three-step method for graphing a function.

1. Express y, the dependent variable, as a function of x, the independent variable.
2. Make a table of values.
3. On graph paper, plot ordered pairs, using values from the table.

If you have a graphing utility, you can bypass the table of values. Simply choose ranges for x and y, input the function, and draw the graph.

EXPLORE: DON'T GET BENT OUT OF SHAPE!

MATERIALS

*Graphing utility
or graph paper
Calculator*

What happens to a baseball when it collides with a bat?

In a split second, the shape of the ball compresses dramatically. Then it quickly snaps back to its normal spherical shape, giving the ball energy to fly off the bat.

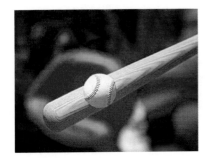

The amount of the ball's compression is a function of the combined speeds of the pitch and the swinging bat. The faster the pitch and the swing, the greater the compression. In this exploration you'll draw two cross-sections. The first will show a normal baseball. The second will show a baseball as it might appear when a mighty home run swing meets a 90-mile-per-hour fast ball.

1. Use the equation $y = \pm\sqrt{16 - x^2}$ to make a table of values. The $\pm$ sign tells you to use both the positive and the negative value each time you evaluate the square root. This will give you two values of y and two ordered pairs for each value of x that you choose.

2. Graph the equation. If you use a graphing utility, graph $y = +\sqrt{16 - x^2}$ and $y = -\sqrt{16 - x^2}$ on the same screen. If you use centimeter graph paper, your graph will be a cross-section of a baseball enlarged by about 5%.

3. Make a table of values using the equation $y = \pm\sqrt{50 - 8x^2}$. Then graph the equation as above. Your graph will be the cross-section of a baseball as it's about to take off on a trip over the center-field fence. The curve that you draw is called an **ellipse.**

4. Compare and contrast the cross-section of a normal baseball with that of a baseball under compression.

REFLECT

1. What are the types of functions you have learned about in this book? How do their graphs differ?

2. Are changes in y proportional to changes in x for functions you have studied in 8-3? Explain.

3. Is the area of a circle a quadratic function of some quantity? If so, what is the quantity?

Give the letter of the graph that most resembles the graph of the given function. Do not graph the function.

1. $y = \sqrt{2x}$

A.

2. $y = -x^2 + 5$

B.

3. $x^2 - x - 2 = y$

C.

4. $y = (1.4)^x$

D.

5. Which of the following pairs of transformations will leave a figure's position unchanged? [3-2]

    (a) two translations

    (b) two 180° rotations

    (c) two 90° clockwise rotations

    (d) a reflection across the x-axis followed by a reflection across the y-axis

6. Match each equation with the correct graph.

a. $y = \sqrt{x}$

b. $y = -1.5x$

c. $y = -2x^2$

d. $y = x^2 - 2$

i.

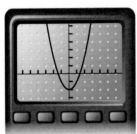

ii.

iii.

iv.

7. Solve for n: $\frac{9}{24} = \frac{12}{n}$. [6-1]

(a) 4.5

(b) 18

(c) 32

(d) 36

8. Write the letter of the second pair that best matches the first pair. Parabola: quadratic function as

(a) y-intercept: linear function

(b) slope: linear function

(c) line: linear function

(d) table: linear function

9. Same Slide According to the *Guinness Book of World Records*, the longest slide is in Peru, Vermont. It drops 820 feet as it covers a distance of 4600 feet How would you describe its slope? [8-2]

10. Two functions are graphed on the same axis shown on the right.

a. Which graph shows $y = x^2 + 2$?

b. Which graph shows $y = x^2 + 5$?

c. How would the graph of $y = x^2 + 3$ be similar to these?

d. How would $y = x^2 + 3$ be different from these?

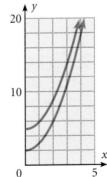

11. On the same coordinate axes, graph the first quadrant of $y = x^2 + 1$ and $y = \sqrt{x} - 1$. Describe your results.

12. How much do each of the identical spikes on the scale weigh? [4-2]

(a) $\frac{85}{3}$

(b) $\frac{75}{3}$

(c) $\frac{95}{3}$

(d) $\frac{105}{3}$

(e) not here

13. On the Rebound A ball dropped from a height of 36 inches rebounds to a height of 24 inches. Each bounce is proportional to the previous one.
  a. Make a table of values showing the maximum height of the first six bounces.
  b. Graph bounce height as a function of bounce number.
  c. What type of function have you graphed? Explain your reasoning.

14. Lukewarm The difference between the temperature of a cup of cocoa and room temperature is given by $T = 110(0.9)^t$, where t is the time since the cocoa was poured.
  a. What is T when t is 0? What does this mean?
  b. Graph the equation. What kind of curve is the graph?
  c. Explain what happens to the temperature of the cocoa.

15. Double Trouble A sheet of notebook paper is a rectangle. Fold it in half. If you open it up you will see two rectangles. Fold the folded sheet in half again. Count the rectangles. Continue this process through six folds.

$f = 0$
$r = 1$

$f = 1$
$r = 2$

$f = 2$
$r = 4$

  a. Make a table of ordered pairs (f, r), where f is the number of times you have folded the paper in half, and r is the number of rectangles.
  b. Graph your ordered pairs.
  c. Does it make sense to connect your points? Explain.
  d. Write a function to describe this situation.

Chapter 8 Review

In Chapter 8, you saw how change in one quantity can produce changes in related quantities, which led to the idea of a function. You learned to identify linear, quadratic, square root, and exponential functions. You used the graphs of these functions to understand how the ideas of slope, y-intercept, vertex, and maximum and minimum points apply to real-life situations.

KEY TERMS

dependent variable [8-1]   linear function [8-2]   slope [8-2]

exponential function [8-3]   parabola [8-3]   square root function [8-3]

independent variable [8-1]   quadratic function [8-3] y-intercept [8-2]

Determine whether each statement is true or false. If the statement is false, change the underlined word or phrase to make it true.

1. The <u>slope</u> of the graph of the equation $y = 3x + 4$ is 4.

2. The equation $y = 2^x$ is an <u>exponential</u> function.

3. The graph of the equation $y = -4x^2$ has its vertex at its <u>maximum point</u>.

Write the word or phrase that correctly completes the statement.

4. A line that slants downward from left to right has ____ slope.

5. A ____ function can be written in the form $y = ax^2 + bx + c$.

CONCEPTS AND APPLICATIONS

6. Name a quantity that each of the following depends upon. [8-1]
  a. area of a circle
  b. cost of a long distance phone call
  c. wages at $12 an hour

7. Look for a pattern to complete the table. Then give the equation that relates the variables. [8-1]

x	-2	-1	0	1	2	14	36
y	6		0			-42	

8. Tomato juice sells for $2.25 a can. [8-2]
   a. Make a table of five pairs of values expressing the relationship between the number of cans purchased (c) and the total cost (d).
   b. Give an equation relating the variables c and d.
   c. Identify which variable is dependent and which is independent.
   d. Is this a linear function? Explain.

9. Give the slope and y-intercept of line k. [8-2]

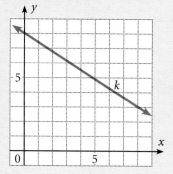

10. a. Graph the equation $y = 3x - 1$. [8-1]
   b. Explain how to use your graph to find the solution to the equation $11 = 3x - 1$.

11. Find the width of a rectangle with an area of 576 ft^2 and a length of 32 ft. [5-2]

Find the slope of each line containing the pair of points. [8-2]

12. (3, 7) and (4, 7)   **13.** (−1, 5) and (3, 2)   **14.** (3, −9) and (8, −5)

15. How long is a toy car that is made as a $\frac{1}{54}$ scale model of a 9-foot-long car? [6-2]

Give the slope and y-intercept of the graph of each equation. [8-2]

16. $y = -\frac{7}{2}x + 2$ **17.** $y = 3x + \frac{5}{3}$ **18.** $x - 2y = 6$

19. A typist charges a flat $10 rate to type papers, plus $1.50 per page. [8-2]
   a. Choose variables and write the total charge for typing a paper.
   b. Graph the equation using the slope and y-intercept.
   c. Use the graph to approximate how much he charges to type 15 pages.

Graph each equation and tell whether it is a linear, quadratic, square root, or exponential function. [8-2, 8-3]

20. $y = 2x$ **21.** $y = -2x^2$ **22.** $y = 2^x$

23. How many ways can you arrange three sports trophies on a shelf? [7-2]

24. A toy rocket is set off with a velocity of 96 feet per second. The rocket's height (h), in feet, after t seconds is given by $h = -16t^2 + 96t$. [8-3]
   a. Graph h as a function of t.
   b. Give the coordinates of the vertex.
   c. Give the maximum height reached by the rocket.
   d. Give the length of time the rocket is in the air.

CONCEPTS AND CONNECTIONS

25. Biology The number of bacteria in a culture triples each day.

    a. If you start with 100 bacteria, write a function that represents the number of bacteria in the culture as a function of the number of days since the culture began growing.

    b. Graph the equation. How many bacteria would be present on the fifth day?

SELF-EVALUATION

The function has been called the most important concept in mathematics. Write a paragraph explaining why you think functions are important. Give examples of equations, graphs, and applications of some of the functions you studied. Make a list of specific ideas you found difficult and plan time to get help with those areas.

Chapter 8 Assessment

TEST

Tell whether each function is linear, quadratic, square root, or exponential.

1. $y = \sqrt{x - 5}$ **2.** $3x + 6y = 8$ **3.** $y = 7^2 + 11x$

4. $-3x^2 - 2x = y + 2.3$ **5.** $6^x = y$ **6.** $y + x^2 = 1$

7.

x	1	2	3	4	5	6	7
y	1	4	9	16	25	36	49

8.

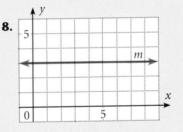

Determine whether each statement is true or false. If the statement is false, change the underlined word or phrase to make it true.

9. The length of your stride is a <u>function</u> of your leg length.

10. The graph of a quadratic equation is a <u>parabola</u>.

11. The slope of a line is the ratio of the <u>change in x-values to the change in y values</u>.

12. The <u>slope</u> of the line $2x - 2y = 3$ is 1.

13. Use the equation, $y = 3x + \frac{3}{2}$.

    a. Give the slope of the line and its y-intercept.

    b. Use the slope of the line and its y-intercept to graph the line.

14. How can you tell by looking at a line if its slope is positive or negative?

15. Find the slope of the line containing the points

    a. $(1, 7)$ and $(4, 7)$ **b.** $(-3, 5)$ and $(2, 1)$ **c.** $(5, -2)$ and $(8, -7)$

16. What are the odds of not getting a four when you roll a number cube labeled with the numbers one through six?

17. The temperature at 6 a.m. was 9°F. Between 6 a.m. and 3 p.m. the same day, the temperature rose two degrees per hour.

    Let $t =$ the temperature (°F).   Let $n =$ the number of hours since 6 a.m.

    a. Write t as a function of n for the hours between 6 a.m. and 3 p.m.

    b. Graph the function.

    c. Would this function make sense for values of n after 3 p.m.? Explain.

Graph each equation.

18. $y = 4^x$ **19.** $y = -3x^2 - 1$ **20.** $y = \sqrt{x + 5}$

21. Solve for m: $\frac{3}{17} = \frac{22.4}{m}$.

22. The kinetic energy (k), in joules, of an object with a mass of 1 kilogram is given by the function $k = \frac{1}{2}v^2$, where v is the velocity of the object in m/sec.

    a. Graph the function.

    b. Use your graph to estimate the velocity of a 1-kg object with a kinetic energy of 3 joules.

PERFORMANCE TASK

Use the trigonometric function, $y = \sin x$. Complete a table through 360° for x.

x	0°	30°	60°	90°	120°	150°	180°	210°	330°	360°
$\sin x$	0	0.5	0.87					-0.5	-0.5	0

Then use a graphing utility or coordinates from the table to graph $y = \sin x$. Compare your graph with the graphs you have worked with in this chapter. Identify some concepts in this chapter that you could apply to this trigonometric function and its graph and explain how they apply.

REFERENCE CENTER

SKILLS BANK

UNDERSTANDING MEASUREMENT

Numbers were first used to represent the measures of pieces of food and fuel. Today, the ability to measure is a skill used in every profession.

Joan and Marcy drove from New York City to Los Angeles. A friend asked them how far it was from New York to LA.

Joan said: "It was a long way. It seemed to take forever."

Marcy said: "When we got to Los Angeles, I checked the odometer. It read 3174 miles."

1. Who gave a more useful description of the distance? Why?

A **measurement** gives the size of something. A measurement consists of a **number** and a **unit**.

A football field is 100 yards long.

number   unit

The *unit* in a measurement is a fixed quantity with a size that is understood by most people. Most people in the United States know how long a yard is, so we often give measurements of length in terms of yards.

The *number* in a measurement tells how many units there are in the thing being measured. This allows us to compare the size of the thing being measured with the size of the unit.

Tell what is being measured. Give the number and unit of measurement.

2. A day is 24 hours long.   **3.** Joe drank 2 cups of water.
4. My cat weighs 8 pounds.

We often have a choice of the unit we will use in a measurement.

$$
\text{A football field is}
\begin{cases}
100 \text{ yards} \\
300 \text{ feet} \\
3600 \text{ inches} \\
91.44 \text{ meters}
\end{cases}
\text{long.}
$$

5. Which unit for measuring a football field is best? Explain your answer.
6. Does the actual length of a football field change if you use a different unit to measure the field? Explain.

Give the measure of each using at least two different units.

7. the length of September   **8.** the size of a milk carton

The **inch** (in.) is one of the basic units of length in the **customary** system of measurement.

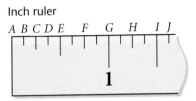
Inch ruler

TRY IT

1. Into how many smaller divisions is an inch divided on the ruler?
2. How long is each of the smallest divisions of an inch on the ruler?
3. What point represents a measurement of 0 inches? of 1 inch?
4. Give the measurement represented by each point.
   a. D   **b.** B   **c.** J   **d.** H
5. Give the point represented by each measurement.
   a. one-eighth inch   **b.** one-fourth inch   **c.** one and one-half inches
6. Suppose each of the smallest divisions were divided into two units. How long would each be?

The **centimeter** (cm) is one of the basic units of length in the **metric** system of measurement.

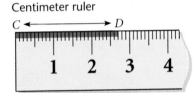
Centimeter ruler

TRY IT

7. Compare and contrast 1 centimeter with 1 inch.
8. Suppose you measured a length using both a centimeter ruler and an inch ruler. Which measurement would show the greater number?
9. Give the length of line segment $\overline{CD}$.
10. The measurement of a line segment is halfway between 1.7 cm and 1.8 cm. Give the measurement.

The **ounce** (oz) is one of the basic units of liquid measure in the customary system.

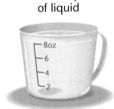
8-oz cup of liquid

TRY IT

11. Why aren't the distances between marks on the cup equal?
12. How would you locate a measurement of 5 oz on the cup scale?
13. What measurement on the cup would be triple a measurement of 2 oz?

REFERENCE CENTER: Skills Bank

667

UNDERSTANDING PLACE VALUE

The digits 0–9 are the basis of our numeration system.

The order of the digits 0–9 determines which of two numbers is the greater.

(Recall that "<" means "less than" and ">" means "greater than.")

• Which is greater, 685 or 691?

We can compare the numbers by comparing corresponding digits, moving left to right.

$$\left.\begin{array}{c} \boxed{6}85 \\ \boxed{6}91 \end{array}\right\}$$ The first pair of digits are equal, so we move to the next pair.

$$\left.\begin{array}{c} 6\boxed{8}5 \\ 6\boxed{9}1 \end{array}\right\}$$ 9 > 8, so 691 > 685.

• Which is greater, 136 or 9.87?

Write both numbers with the same number of digits to the left of the decimal point. Write zeroes if necessary.

$$\left.\begin{array}{c} \boxed{1}36.00 \\ \boxed{0}09.87 \end{array}\right\}$$ 1 > 0, so 136 > 9.87.

Write < or > for each ❑.

1. 81 ❑ 31   **2.** 3472 ❑ 3485   **3.** 62.17 ❑ 62.0185
4. 3 ❑ 1.76905   **5.** 156.44 ❑ 8.888   **6.** 40,000,000 ❑ 50,000

• Is 143 closer to 140 or to 150? Think of a number line to help decide.

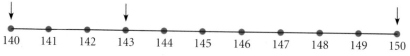

143 is closer to 140 than it is to 150.

Answer each question. You may wish to sketch a number line.

7. Is 7.84 closer to 7.8 or to 7.9?
8. Is 37,000 closer 30,000 or to 40,000?
9. Is 0.673 closer to 0.6 or to 0.7?
10. Is 0.49 closer to 0 or to 1?
11. Is 26.3811 closer to 26.3 or to 26.4?
12. Is 0.1059 closer to 0.1 or to 0.2?

Use a **place-value** chart to read numbers.

Billions			Millions			Thousands			Ones			Decimal Places					
Hundreds	Tens	Ones	Hundreds	Tens	Ones	Hundreds	Tens	Ones	Hundreds	Tens	Ones	Tenths	Hundredths	Thousandths	Ten-thousandths	Hundred-thousandths	Millionths
					8	5	0	6	2	9	1 .	7	3	4			

EXAMPLES

1. Give the standard form and the short word name of the number in the chart. Read the number.
Standard form: 8,506,291.734
Short word name: 8 million, 506 thousand, 291, and 734 thousandths
Read: Eight million, five hundred and six thousand, two hundred ninety-one, and seven hundred thirty-four thousandths

2. Give the value of the underlined digit: 345.6789.
Refer to the chart. The value of the underlined digit is 7 hundredths.

3. Round 34,863 to the nearest thousand.
Find the digit in the place to which you want to round.   34,863
Look at the digit one place to its right.   34, 8 63
If it is less than 5, round down.
If it is 5 or greater, round up. 34,863 → 35,000

TRY IT

Give the short word name of each number. Read the number.

1. 40,629   **2.** 0.0007   **3.** 23,000,000,020   **4.** 9300.45

Give the value of the underlined digit.

5. 427,630.57   **6.** 20,091.6   **7.** 2.035

Are they equal? If not why?

8. 2.5 billion   2,500,000   **9.** half a million   500,000

Round.

10. 47.3 to the nearest one   **11.** 36,772 to the nearest thousand
12. 56,999.8 to the nearest ten   **13.** 0.595 to the nearest hundredth

14. Is 84¢ closer to 8 dimes or to 9 dimes?

15. Is 3.72 cm closer to 3 cm or to 4 cm?

16. Is 3 closer to 2.74 or 3.27?   **17.** Is 0.1 closer to 0.1204 or 0.0891?

669

UNDERSTANDING FRACTIONS AND PERCENTS

A percent is a ratio that compares a number with 100. Percent means "per hundred."

One hundred percent of a quantity is *all* of the quantity.

100% = 1 whole quantity

If you remember the above fact, you can easily find the fraction and the percent represented by a portion of a quantity.

Think: One half of the circle is shaded. One half of 100% is 50%.

Think: One fourth of the square is shaded. One fourth of 100% is 25%.

Think: Two fifths of the rectangle is shaded. One fifth of 100% is 20%, so two fifths of 100% is 40%.

Give the shaded portion of each figure as a fraction and as a percent.

1.   **2.** 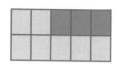   **3.**

Ray found that 7 of the 10 elm trees on his property were diseased. He reasoned: "Seven out of ten is the same as seventy out of one hundred. That means that 70% of the trees are diseased."

Use Ray's method to find each percent.

4. What percent of a dollar is 25¢?

5. What percent of 50 miles is 25 miles?

6. What percent of 10 pencils is 3 pencils?

7. What percent of 20 inches is 15 inches?

A portion of the whole can be represented as a percentage, as a fraction, or as a decimal. You can change from one representation to the others.

REFERENCE CENTER: Skills Bank

EXAMPLE

1. Write 36% as a fraction and as a decimal.

The percent symbol following 36 means "Compare 36 with 100."

Fraction $36\% = \frac{36}{100} = \frac{9}{25}$ Percent written as fraction in simplest form

Decimal $36\% = \frac{36}{100} = 0.36$ Percent written as decimal

The second example shows a simple way to write a percent as a decimal: Move the decimal point two places to the *left* and remove the percent symbol.

EXAMPLES

2. Write 0.65 as a percent and as a fraction.

Percent $0.65 = 65\%$ To write a decimal as a percent, move the decimal point two places to the *right* and write the percent symbol.

Fraction $0.65 = \frac{65}{100} = \frac{13}{20}$ Decimal written as fraction in simplest form

3. Write $\frac{27}{50}$ as a decimal and as a percent.

Decimal   Method 1: Calculator   Method 2: Equivalent fractions

$27 \boxed{\div} 50 \boxed{=} 0.54$ $\frac{27}{50} = \frac{27 \times 2}{50 \times 2} = \frac{54}{100} = 0.54$

Percent $\frac{27}{50} = 0.54 = 54\%$ Write the fraction as a decimal, then as a percent.

TRY IT

Write each percent as a decimal and as a fraction in simplest form.

1. 40%   **2.** 24%   **3.** 85%   **4.** 30%   **5.** 9%   **6.** 58%

Write each decimal as a percent and as a fraction in simplest form.

7. 0.13   **8.** 0.55   **9.** 0.32   **10.** 0.04   **11.** 0.375   **12.** 1.25

Write each fraction as a decimal and as a percent.

13. $\frac{7}{20}$ **14.** $\frac{1}{8}$ **15.** $\frac{19}{50}$ **16.** $\frac{87}{100}$ **17.** $\frac{9}{10}$ **18.** $\frac{23}{25}$

Estimate the percent represented by each fraction. Think: Is it more than half? Is it close to 0 or close to 1?

19. $\frac{1}{3}$ **20.** $\frac{1}{19}$ **21.** $\frac{35}{40}$ **22.** $\frac{3}{7}$

WORKING WITH PERCENT

Percentages are commonly used in commerce. For example, sale prices are often given as percent discounts, and mortgage and other interest rates are expressed as percents.

Val and Trevin go out to eat and spend $40 on their meal. They decide to leave a 15% tip for the waiter. How much should they leave?

WHAT DO YOU THINK?

Val thinks ...

15% = 10% + 5% = 10% + half of 10%

Therefore,

| 15% of the number | = | 10% of the number | + | half of 10% of the number |.

I can find 10% of $40.00 by moving the decimal point left one place.

10% of $40 = $4

15% of $40 = $4 + half of $4 = $4 + $2 = $6.

We should leave a $6 tip.

Trevin thinks ...

10% of $40 is $4. 20% of $40 is double that, or $8. Because 15% is half-way between 10% and 20%, we should leave halfway between $4 and $8.

We should leave a $6 tip.

Find 15% of each number mentally.

1. 60   **2.** $120   **3.** 80   **4.** 200   **5.** $160   **6.** 400

Describe a method that you could use to find each percent mentally.

7. 5%   **8.** 20%   **9.** 30%   **10.** 75%

11. Val thought: "I can find 10% of $60 by moving the decimal point one place to the left." Describe a similar method you could use to find 1% of a number.

12. Would doubling the sales tax on a restaurant bill where you live be a good way to calculate a tip? Why or why not

To find a percent of a number, write the percent as a decimal or as a fraction. Then multiply.

EXAMPLES

1. Find the cost of an $18 blouse including 6.5% sales tax.
   The percent does not have a simple fractional equivalent, so we rewrite it as a decimal: 6.5% = 0.065

   Paper and pencil

   $0.065 \times 18 = 1.17$ Multiply.
   $18.00 + 1.17 = 19.17$ Add.
   The cost of the blouse is $19.17.

   Calculator

   18 [+] 6.5 [%] [=] 19.17

   On some calculators it is not necessary to press [=].

2. Find the cost of a $750 sofa with a 20% discount.

   The percent has a simple fractional equivalent, so to find the cost using paper and pencil, we can rewrite the percent as a fraction $\left(20\% = \frac{1}{5}\right)$ or as a decimal (20% = 0.2).

   Paper and pencil

   $20\% \times 750 = \frac{1}{5} \times 750$ Rewrite.
   $= 150$ Multiply.
   $750 - 150 = 600$ Subtract.
   The cost of the sofa is $600.

   Calculator

   750 [−] 20 [%] [=] 600

3. Give 175% of 64.

   175% > 100%, so we expect the answer to be greater than 64.

   Percent as a decimal

   $64 \times 1.75 = 112$

   Percent as a fraction

   $64 \times 1\frac{3}{4} = 64 \times \frac{7}{4}$
   $= 112$

TRY IT

Find each number.

1. 25% of 80   2. 38% of 300   3. 16.3% of 45   4. 150% of 24
5. 77.9% of 135   6. 0.8% of 650   7. 225% of 12   8. 0.25% of 400

9. Find the cost of a $32.50 textbook including 5% sales tax.
10. Find the cost of a $2700 piano with a 15% discount.

Fractions are built from whole numbers. Operations on fractions depend on the properties of the whole numbers that compose them.

One number is a **factor** of another if it divides that number with no remainder. For example, 3 is a factor of 24 because $24 \div 3 = 8$ exactly. But 7 is not a factor of 24 because $24 \div 7 = 3$ R 3.

Think about the factors of the numbers in the two boxes below. How are the numbers in the first box different from those in the second box?

| 5, 13, 29, 41, 7 | | 10, 8, 15, 21, 27 |

The numbers in the first box cannot be divided by other numbers. If you had 29 house plants, for example, you could not divide them into smaller groups with the same number in each group. 29 is divisible by only 1 and 29. The numbers in the first box are **prime** numbers.

The numbers in the second box can be divided by other numbers. You could divide 21 house plants into groups of 3 or groups of 7. The second set of numbers are **composite** numbers.

Prime: 2, 3, 5, 7, 11, ...   Composite numbers: 4, 6, 8, 9, ...

To decide whether a number is prime or composite, look for factors of the number. You can use mental math or your calculator to find these.

| **48?** |
| I know that I can divide 48 by 2, by 6, by 8, and by other numbers, so 48 is composite. |

| **91?** |
| $91 \div 2$: no $91 \div 3$: no $91 \div 4$: no $91 \div 5$: no $91 \div 6$: no **$91 \div 7 = 13$** 91 is composite. |

When looking for factors, you do not need to divide by every number. Divide only by *prime numbers*. Also, remember these divisibility hints:

2 is a factor if: The number is even (ends in 0, 2, 4, 6, or 8).

3 is a factor if: The sum of the digits is divisible by 3 (567: $5 + 6 + 7 = 18$; 18 is divisible by 3).

5 is a factor if: The number ends in 0 or 5 (1435).

Decide whether the number is prime or composite.

1. 38   **2.** 45   **3.** 51

4. 71   **5.** 119   **6.** 247

A whole number can be expressed as a product of prime factors. The expression is called the **prime factorization** of the number. You can use a **factor tree** to find a prime factorization.

The **greatest common factor (GCF)** of two whole numbers is the greatest number that is a factor of the given numbers.

The **least common multiple (LCM)** of two whole numbers is the least number that is a multiple of the given numbers.

EXAMPLES

1. Find the prime factorization of 60.

Write 60 as a product of two factors.
Write each factor as a product of two factors.
Continue until only prime factors remain.
$60 = 2 \times 2 \times 3 \times 5 = 2^2 \times 3 \times 5$ Write the prime factorization.

```
        60
       /  \
      4  × 15
     / \    / \
    2 × 2  3 × 5
```

2. Find the GCF of 40 and 140.

Write the prime factorizations.
Circle each pair of common factors.
The GCF is the product of the common factors. The GCF is 20.

$40 = ②\times②\times 2 \times⑤$
$140 = ②\times②\times⑤\times 7$
$GCF = 2 \times 2 \times 5$

3. Find the LCM of 36 and 120.

Write the prime factorizations.
Find and circle the greatest number of times that each prime factor occurs in any one prime factorization.

$36 = 2 \times 2 \times \boxed{3 \times 3}$
$120 = \boxed{2 \times 2 \times 2} \times 3 \times ⑤$
$LCM = 2 \times 2 \times 2 \times 3 \times 3 \times 5 = 360$

The LCM is the product of the circled factors. The LCM is 360.

TRY IT

Find the prime factorization of the number using a factor tree.

1. 24   **2.** 100   **3.** 160   **4.** 186   **5.** 128   **6.** 315

Find the GCF of the pair of numbers.

7. 16, 24   **8.** 10, 17   **9.** 12, 28   **10.** 39, 52   **11.** 26, 32   **12.** 96, 120

Find the LCM of the pair of numbers.

13. 5, 6   **14.** 12, 16   **15.** 8, 10   **16.** 15, 25

ADDITION AND SUBTRACTION OF FRACTIONS

To add or subtract fractions with unlike denominators, we rewrite the fractions using the least common multiple of the denominators as our new denominator.

You can often perform calculations involving fractions by using your imagination.

Juli wanted to add $\frac{2}{4}$ and $\frac{1}{4}$. She thought: "I'm going to think of $\frac{2}{4}$ as two *quarters* and $\frac{1}{4}$ as one *quarter* and then add like money. If I had two quarters and then got another quarter, I'd have three quarters. So $\frac{2}{4} + \frac{1}{4} = \frac{3}{4}$."

She used the same kind of reasoning when she wanted to add $\frac{5}{9}$ and $\frac{2}{9}$. She thought: "I'm going to imagine that there's a coin called a *ninth*. If I had five ninths and then got two more ninths, I'd have seven ninths. So $\frac{5}{9} + \frac{2}{9} = \frac{7}{9}$."

Use Juli's method to find each sum or difference.

1. $\frac{2}{7} + \frac{4}{7}$ **2.** $\frac{3}{8} + \frac{4}{8}$ **3.** $\frac{9}{11} - \frac{5}{11}$ **4.** $\frac{14}{15} - \frac{8}{15}$

To add $\frac{3}{4} + \frac{5}{8}$, Juli thought: "Since fourths of an inch and eighths of an inch appear on a ruler, I can use a ruler to add these fractions."

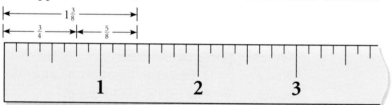

$\frac{3}{4} + \frac{5}{8} = 1\frac{3}{8}$

Use the ruler to find each sum or difference.

5. $\frac{3}{4} + \frac{1}{4}$ **6.** $2\frac{3}{8} + \frac{7}{8}$ **7.** $3 - 1\frac{3}{4}$ **8.** $2\frac{1}{2} - 1\frac{5}{8}$

To add $\frac{1}{3} + \frac{1}{4}$, Juli drew the figure shown here. She thought: "One third of 12 squares is 4 squares. One fourth of 12 squares is 3 squares. The sum is 7 out of 12 squares. So $\frac{1}{3} + \frac{1}{4} = \frac{7}{12}$."

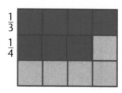

Draw a diagram to find each sum or difference.

9. $\frac{1}{2} + \frac{1}{5}$ **10.** $\frac{1}{2} + \frac{1}{3}$ **11.** $\frac{3}{4} - \frac{2}{3}$ **12.** $\frac{5}{6} - \frac{1}{4}$

To add (or subtract) two fractions with the same denominator, add (or subtract) the numerators.

EXAMPLE

1. Add $\frac{11}{15} + \frac{7}{15}$.

   $\frac{11}{15} + \frac{7}{15} = \frac{11 + 7}{15}$ Add the numerators.

   $= \frac{18}{15}$

   $= 1\frac{3}{15}$, or $1\frac{1}{5}$ Write the sum in simplest form.

To add or subtract two fractions with unlike denominators, rewrite the fractions using the LCM as the denominator.

EXAMPLES

2. Subtract $\frac{7}{8} - \frac{5}{12}$.

   $\frac{7}{8} - \frac{5}{12} = \frac{21}{24} - \frac{10}{24}$ Rewrite using 24, the LCM of 8 and 12, as the denominator.

   $= \frac{11}{24}$ Subtract.

3. Subtract $3\frac{3}{10} - 1\frac{3}{4}$.

   $3\frac{3}{10} - 1\frac{3}{4} = 3\frac{6}{20} - 1\frac{15}{20}$ Rewrite using the LCM as the denominator.

   $= 2\frac{26}{20} - 1\frac{15}{20}$ Rename $3\frac{6}{20}$ as $2\frac{26}{20}$ so that its numerator is greater than 15.

   $= 1\frac{11}{20}$ Subtract the whole numbers and subtract the fractions.

TRY IT

Add or subtract. Write the sum or difference in simplest form.

1. $\frac{5}{9} + \frac{1}{9}$

2. $\frac{10}{15} - \frac{4}{15}$

3. $\frac{8}{9} - \frac{2}{3}$

4. $\frac{7}{12} + \frac{5}{8}$

5. $\frac{1}{4} + \frac{9}{10}$

6. $\frac{13}{18} - \frac{5}{12}$

7. $\frac{7}{8} - \frac{5}{24}$

8. $1\frac{3}{5} + 2\frac{7}{10}$

9. $\frac{13}{15} + 1\frac{13}{20}$

10. $1\frac{5}{8} - \frac{11}{12}$

11. $3\frac{7}{15} - 2\frac{11}{12}$

12. $3\frac{2}{9} + 4\frac{5}{6}$

MULTIPLICATION AND DIVISION OF FRACTIONS

Each day we encounter fractions in a variety of contexts, from science to business to current events. Understanding fractions is essential to understanding our world.

When you multiply by a fraction, think of the multiplication sign as the word "of."

$\frac{1}{4} \times 20 = ?$ **Think:** What is one fourth *of* 20? Answer: 5.

$\frac{1}{4} \times 20 = 5$

Rewrite each equation as a sentence containing the word "of." Then give the product.

1. $\frac{1}{3} \times 21 =$ ____   **2.** $\frac{1}{6} \times 30 =$ ____   **3.** $\frac{3}{4} \times 16 =$ ____

Sometimes a diagram helps to clarify a product involving fractions.

$\frac{1}{2} \times \frac{1}{3} = ?$ **Think:** What is one half *of* one third?

In the diagram, *one third* of the squares are shaded. A circle is drawn around *one half* of the shaded squares. The circle encloses one of the six squares in the figure.

Therefore $\frac{1}{2} \times \frac{1}{3} = \frac{1}{6}$.

Draw a diagram illustrating each product.

4. $\frac{1}{2} \times \frac{1}{4}$ **5.** $\frac{1}{4} \times \frac{1}{3}$ **6.** $\frac{3}{4} \times \frac{1}{2}$ **7.** $\frac{1}{3} \times \frac{3}{4}$

You can use a diagram to clarify a quotient, too.

$1\frac{1}{2} \div \frac{1}{4} = ?$ **Think:** How many fourths are there in $1\frac{1}{2}$?

In the figure, $1\frac{1}{2}$ circles have been divided into quarter-circles. There are six quarter-circles. Therefore $1\frac{1}{2} \div \frac{1}{4} = 6$.

Draw a diagram illustrating each quotient.

8. $1 \div \frac{1}{3}$ **9.** $2\frac{2}{5} \div \frac{1}{5}$

10. $2 \div \frac{2}{3}$ **11.** $2\frac{1}{4} \div \frac{3}{4}$

To multiply two fractions, multiply the numerators and multiply the denominators. To divide by a fraction, multiply by the reciprocal of the fraction.

REFERENCE CENTER: Skills Bank

EXAMPLES

1. Multiply $\frac{2}{3} \times \frac{7}{9}$.

$\frac{2}{3} \times \frac{7}{9} = \frac{2 \times 7}{3 \times 9}$ Multiply the numerators and denominators.

$= \frac{14}{27}$ Write the product.

2. Multiply $1\frac{5}{7} \times 2\frac{5}{8}$.

$1\frac{5}{7} \times 2\frac{5}{8} = \frac{12}{7} \times \frac{21}{8}$ Rename mixed numbers as improper fractions.

$= \frac{12 \times 21}{7 \times 8}$ Multiply numerators and denominators.

$= \frac{\overset{3}{\cancel{12}} \times \overset{3}{\cancel{21}}}{\underset{1}{\cancel{7}} \times \underset{2}{\cancel{8}}}$ Simplify.

$= \frac{9}{2}$, or $4\frac{1}{2}$ Write the product.

3. Divide $\frac{3}{8} \div \frac{2}{5}$.

$\frac{3}{8} \div \frac{2}{5} = \frac{3}{8} \times \frac{5}{2}$ To divide by a fraction, multiply by the reciprocal.

$= \frac{15}{16}$ Write the quotient.

TRY IT

Multiply or divide. Write the product or quotient in simplest form.

1. $\frac{1}{2} \times \frac{2}{3}$ **2.** $\frac{2}{5} \times \frac{6}{7}$ **3.** $\frac{3}{4} \times \frac{2}{3}$

4. $2 \div \frac{1}{3}$ **5.** $\frac{4}{5} \div \frac{4}{3}$ **6.** $\frac{3}{8} \div \frac{9}{4}$

7. $20 \times \frac{3}{4}$ **8.** $0 \div \frac{5}{9}$ **9.** $1 \times \frac{3}{5}$

10. $1 \div \frac{5}{8}$ **11.** $\frac{8}{15} \times \frac{5}{12}$ **12.** $\frac{4}{5} \div 2\frac{2}{5}$

13. $1\frac{2}{5} \times \frac{15}{21}$ **14.** $1\frac{7}{9} \times 1\frac{7}{8}$ **15.** $1\frac{7}{18} \div \frac{20}{27}$

679

WORKING WITH DECIMAL NUMBERS

Understanding the decimal numeration system allows you to operate on the numbers you encounter every day.

Justin performed the following calculations.

$$573 \times 1000 = 573{,}000 \qquad 573 \div 10 = 57.3$$
$$573 \times 100 = 57{,}300 \qquad 573 \div 100 = 5.73$$
$$573 \times 10 = 5730 \qquad 573 \div 1000 = 0.573$$

He noticed that each product could be found simply by moving the decimal point of 573. He wrote the following rules:

To multiply by a power of 10: Count the number of zeroes in the power of 10 and move the decimal point of the other factor the same number of places to the right. $4.375 \times 100 = 437.5$.

To divide by a power of 10: Count the number of zeroes in the power of 10 and move the decimal point of the other factor the same number of places to the left. $85.31 \div 1000 = 0.08531$.

Find the product or quotient mentally.

1. 10×34 **2.** $687 \div 100$ **3.** 0.779×1000 **4.** $86{,}500 \div 10$

Justin saw that knowing how to multiply and divide by powers of 10 mentally enabled him to perform other mental calculations. For example, he bought five magazines priced at $2.90 apiece. To find the total cost mentally, he reasoned:

"Five equals ten divided by two. So to find the cost, I will multiply by ten and then divide by two."

$2.90 \times 10 = 29.00. \qquad 29.00 \div 2 = 14.50. \qquad$ The cost is $14.50.

Find the product mentally.

5. 3.4×5 **6.** 66×5 **7.** 8.2×50 **8.** 4600×0.5

Justin earned $180 in five days. To find his mean daily earnings mentally, he reasoned:

"I want to find one fifth of $180. One fifth equals two divided by ten. So to divide by five, I will divide by ten and multiply by two."

$180 \div 10 = 18. \qquad 18 \times 2 = 36. \qquad$ The mean is $36.

Find the quotient mentally.

9. $140 \div 5$ **10.** $600 \div 5$ **11.** $420 \div 50$ **12.** $1200 \div 25$

Operate with decimal numbers as you operate with whole numbers. The following examples will help you recall the rules for placing decimal points.

EXAMPLES

1. Add $36.05 + 2.7 + 0.0899 + 14$.

$$
\begin{array}{r}
36.05 \\
2.7 \\
0.0899 \\
+\ 14. \\
\hline
52.8399
\end{array}
$$

Align the decimal points.

Place the decimal point of the sum in line with the others.

2. Subtract $214.06 - 9.7$.

$$
\begin{array}{r}
214.06 \\
-\ \ \ 9.7 \\
\hline
204.36
\end{array}
$$

Align the decimal points.

Place the decimal point of the difference in line with the others.

3. Multiply 2.15×3.4.

$$
\begin{array}{r}
2.1\,5 \\
\times\ \ \ \ \ 3.4 \\
\hline
8\,6\,0 \\
6\,4\,5 \\
\hline
7.3\,1\,0
\end{array}
$$

It is not necessary to align decimal points when multiplying.

Use the same number of decimal places in the product as the sum of the decimal places in the factors.

4. Divide $11.4 \div 4.75$.

$$
4.75 \overline{)11.40}
$$

Multiply the divisor by a power of 10 to make it a whole number. Multiply the dividend by the same power of 10.

$$
475 \overline{)\,1140.0\,}^{\,2.4}
$$

Place the decimal point of the quotient above the decimal point of the dividend.

TRY IT

Find the sum, difference, product, or quotient.

1. $5.677 + 72 + 13.9 + 544.916$ **2.** $806 - 4.81$ **3.** $7 - 0.45$

4. $0.8845 + 18 + 0.6 + 409.83$ **5.** 3.14×9.5 **6.** 0.27×16.73

7. $1.4 + 38.79 + 5.077 + 0.98 + 234$ **8.** $16.24 \div 2.9$ **9.** $25.437 \div 8.34$

WHAT DOES IT MEAN?

Language is central to mathematics. For everyone to understand mathematical concepts equally, terms must be defined carefully and used with precision.

Many of the concepts you have studied in mathematics involve change.

- Adding 5 to a number changes 13 to 18.
- Taking 10% of a number changes 40 to 4.
- Calculating the square root of a number changes 81 to 9.

Describing change requires careful use of mathematical language. Five students each described a way in which 10 could be operated on to produce 20. What do you think of each description? Is it accurate? Can you improve on it?

Tomas: Change 10 into 20 by doubling 10.

Angela: Change 10 into 20 by maximizing 10 by an amount equal to 10.

Ming: Change 10 into 20 by multiplying 10 by 2.

Vanessa: Change 10 into 20 by adding 10 to 10.

Dennis: Change 10 into 20 by adding 100 percent of 10.

Jackie: Change 10 into 20 by increasing 10 by 10.

As precisely as possible, describe how the first quantity or figure can be operated on to produce the second. If you can think of more than one way to produce the change, describe each of them.

1. $5 \rightarrow 25$ **2.** $30 \rightarrow 10$ **3.** $\$50 \rightarrow \$60$

4. 18 snow tires $\rightarrow$ 9 snow tires

5. 75 bolts $\rightarrow$ 63 bolts

6. 20 baseballs $\rightarrow$ 60 baseballs

7.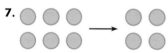

8.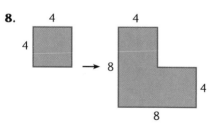

Certain terms are used to indicate a change in the size of a quantity.

EXAMPLES

Explain the meaning of the boldface term.

1. Jon's height **increased by** two inches during the summer.

To *increase* is to become greater. Jon grew two inches.

2. Greg's monthly income **decreased by** $98.

To *decrease* is to become less. Greg's monthly income shrank by $98. The term **minus** also means "decreased by:" Margo earned $5000 minus attorney's fees.

3. The price of GoldStar tapes was **twice** that of SilverStars.

Twice means "two times as much." GoldStar tapes cost two times as much as SilverStars.
The term **double** also means "two times:" Earnings of the Sophomore Class were double those of the Junior Class.
The term **triple** means "three times:" She was triple her son's age.

4. In the second trial, the rat's daily calorie intake was **cut in two.**

Cut in two means "reduced to half the original amount:" In the second race, the rat received only half the cheese it received in the first race.
The terms **halved** and **cut in half** also mean "cut in two." The term **cut in thirds** means "reduced to one third the original quantity."

5. The **minimum** age for driving is 18.

Minimum means "the least possible:" To drive, one must be 18 or older.
The term **maximum** means "the greatest possible:" The maximum speed is 65 miles per hour.

TRY IT

Explain the meaning of each sentence.

1. By taking the new job, Earl halved his commuting time.
2. The river's height decreased to 6 feet below flood stage.
3. Under the new president, the number of club members doubled.
4. Fire laws specify that the maximum number of diners allowed in the restaurant is 125.
5. Thanks to strict conservation measures, the number of whooping cranes has increased by 60.

GEOMETRIC FORMULAS

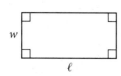

Rectangle

Area: $A = \ell w$

Perimeter: $p = 2\ell + 2w$

Square

Area: $A = s^2$

Perimeter: $p = 4s$

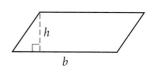

Parallelogram

Area: $A = bh$

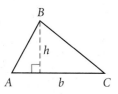

Triangle

Area: $A = \frac{1}{2}bh$

$m\angle A + m\angle B + m\angle C = 180°$

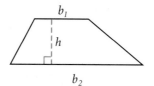

Trapezoid

Area: $A = \frac{1}{2}h(b_1 + b_2)$

Regular Polygon

Area: $A = \frac{1}{2}ap$

Circle

Area: $A = \pi r^2$

Circumference: $C = \pi d = 2\pi r$

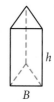

Prism

Volume: $V = Bh$

Surface Area: $SA = ph + 2B$

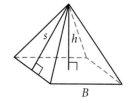

Regular Pyramid

Volume: $V = \frac{1}{3}Bh$

Surface Area: $SA = \frac{1}{2}ps + B$

Cylinder

Volume: $V = \pi r^2 h$

Surface Area: $SA = 2\pi rh + 2\pi r^2$

Cone

Volume: $V = \frac{1}{3}\pi r^2 h$

Surface Area: $SA = \pi rs + \pi r^2$

Sphere

Volume: $V = \frac{4}{3}\pi r^3$

Surface Area: $SA = 4\pi r^2$

MEASUREMENT CONVERSION FACTORS

Metric Measures Length
1000 meters (m) = 1 kilometer (km)
100 centimeter (cm) = 1 m
10 decimeter (dm) = 1 m
1000 millimeters (mm) = 1 m
10 cm = 1 decimeter (dm)
10 mm = 1 cm

Area
100 square millimeters = 1 square centimeter
(mm^2) (cm^2)
10,000 cm^2 = 1 square meter (m^2)
10,000 m^2 = 1 hectare (ha)

Volume
1000 cubic millimeters = 1 cubic centimeter
(mm^3) (cm^3)
1000 cm^3 = 1 cubic decimeter (dm^3)
1,000,000 cm^3 = 1 cubic meter (m^3)

Capacity
1000 milliliters (mL) = 1 liter (L)
1000 L = 1 kiloliter (kL)

Mass
1000 kilograms (kg) = 1 metric ton (t)
1000 grams (g) = 1 kg
1000 milligrams (mg) = 1 g

Temperature Degrees Celsius (°C)
0°C = freezing point of water
37°C = normal body temperature
100°C = boiling point of water

Time
60 seconds (sec) = 1 minute (min)
60 min = 1 hour (hr)
24 hr = 1 day

Customary Measures Length
12 inches (in.) = 1 foot (ft)
3 ft = 1 yard (yd)
36 in. = 1 yd
5280 ft = 1 mile (mi)
1760 yd = 1 mi
6076 feet = 1 nautical mile

Area
144 square inches = 1 square foot
$(in.^2)$ (ft^2)
9 ft^2 = 1 square yard (yd^2)
43,560 ft^2 = 1 acre (A)

Volume
1728 cubic inches = 1 cubic foot
(cu in.) (cu ft)
27 cu ft = 1 cubic yard (cu yard)

Capacity
8 fluid ounces (fl oz) = 1 cup (c)
2 c = 1 pint (pt)
2 pt = 1 quart (qt)
4 qt = 1 gallon (gal)

Weight
16 ounces (oz) = 1 pound (lb)
2000 lb = 1 ton (T)

Temperature Degrees Fahrenheit (°F)
32°F = freezing point of water
98.6°F = normal body temperature
212°F = boiling point of water

SYMBOLS

$+$	plus or positive	$\llcorner$	right angle
$-$	minus or negative	AB	length of $\overline{AB}$; distance between A and B
$\cdot$	times		
$\times$	times	$\triangle ABC$	triangle with vertices A, B, and C
$\div$	divided by	$\angle ABC$	angle with sides $\overrightarrow{BA}$ and $\overrightarrow{BC}$
$\pm$	positive or negative	$\angle B$	angle with vertex B
$=$	is equal to	$m\angle ABC$	measure of angle ABC
$\neq$	is not equal to	$'$	prime
$<$	is less than	a^n	the nth power of a
$>$	is greater than	$|x|$	absolute value of x
$\leq$	is less than or equal to	$\sqrt{x}$	principal square root of x
$\geq$	is greater than or equal to	$\bar{x}$	the mean of data values of x
$\approx$	is approximately equal to	π	pi (approximately 3.1416)
$\%$	percent	(a, b)	ordered pair with x-coordinate a and y-coordinate b
$a{:}b$	the ratio of a to b, or $\frac{a}{b}$		
$\cong$	is congruent to	$P(A)$	the probability of event A
$\sim$	is similar to	$\sin A$	sine of $\angle A$
$^\circ$	degree(s)	$\cos A$	cosine of $\angle A$
$\overleftrightarrow{AB}$	line containing points A and B	$\tan A$	tangent of $\angle A$
$\overline{AB}$	line segment with endpoints A and B	$n!$	n factorial
$\overrightarrow{AB}$	ray with endpoint A and containing B		

SQUARES AND SQUARE ROOTS

N	N²	√N
1	1	1
2	4	1.414
3	9	1.732
4	16	2
5	25	2.236
6	36	2.449
7	49	2.646
8	64	2.828
9	81	3
10	100	3.162
11	121	3.317
12	144	3.464
13	169	3.606
14	196	3.742
15	225	3.873
16	256	4
17	289	4.123
18	324	4.243
19	361	4.359
20	400	4.472
21	441	4.583
22	484	4.690
23	529	4.796
24	576	4.899
25	625	5
26	676	5.099
27	729	5.196
28	784	5.292
29	841	5.385
30	900	5.477
31	961	5.568
32	1,024	5.657
33	1,089	5.745
34	1,156	5.831
35	1,225	5.916
36	1,296	6
37	1,369	6.083
38	1,444	6.164
39	1,521	6.245
40	1,600	6.325
41	1,681	6.403
42	1,764	6.481
43	1,849	6.557
44	1,936	6.633
45	2,025	6.708
46	2,116	6.782
47	2,209	6.856
48	2,304	6.928
49	2,401	7
50	2,500	7.071

N	N²	√N
51	2,601	7.141
52	2,704	7.211
53	2,809	7.280
54	2,916	7.348
55	3,025	7.416
56	3,136	7.483
57	3,249	7.550
58	3,364	7.616
59	3,481	7.681
60	3,600	7.746
61	3,721	7.810
62	3,844	7.874
63	3,969	7.937
64	4,096	8
65	4,225	8.062
66	4,356	8.124
67	4,489	8.185
68	4,624	8.246
69	4,761	8.307
70	4,900	8.367
71	5,041	8.426
72	5,184	8.485
73	5,329	8.544
74	5,476	8.602
75	5,625	8.660
76	5,776	8.718
77	5,929	8.775
78	6,084	8.832
79	6,241	8.888
80	6,400	8.944
81	6,561	9
82	6,724	9.055
83	6,889	9.110
84	7,056	9.165
85	7,225	9.220
86	7,396	9.274
87	7,569	9.327
88	7,744	9.381
89	7,921	9.434
90	8,100	9.487
91	8,281	9.539
92	8,464	9.592
93	8,649	9.644
94	8,836	9.695
95	9,025	9.747
96	9,216	9.798
97	9,409	9.849
98	9,604	9.899
99	9,801	9.950
100	10,000	10

TRIGONOMETRIC RATIOS

REFERENCE CENTER: Trigonometric Ratios

Degrees	Sin	Cos	Tan
0°	0.0000	1.0000	0.0000
1°	0.0175	0.9998	0.0175
2°	0.0349	0.9994	0.0349
3°	0.0523	0.9986	0.0524
4°	0.0698	0.9976	0.0699
5°	0.0872	0.9962	0.0875
6°	0.1045	0.9945	0.1051
7°	0.1219	0.9925	0.1228
8°	0.1392	0.9903	0.1405
9°	0.1564	0.9877	0.1584
10°	0.1736	0.9848	0.1763
11°	0.1908	0.9816	0.1944
12°	0.2079	0.9781	0.2126
13°	0.2250	0.9744	0.2309
14°	0.2419	0.9703	0.2493
15°	0.2588	0.9659	0.2679
16°	0.2756	0.9613	0.2867
17°	0.2924	0.9563	0.3057
18°	0.3090	0.9511	0.3249
19°	0.3256	0.9455	0.3443
20°	0.3420	0.9397	0.3640
21°	0.3584	0.9336	0.3839
22°	0.3746	0.9272	0.4040
23°	0.3907	0.9205	0.4245
24°	0.4067	0.9135	0.4452
25°	0.4226	0.9063	0.4663
26°	0.4384	0.8988	0.4877
27°	0.4540	0.8910	0.5095
28°	0.4695	0.8829	0.5317
29°	0.4848	0.8746	0.5543
30°	0.5000	0.8660	0.5774
31°	0.5150	0.8572	0.6009
32°	0.5299	0.8480	0.6249
33°	0.5446	0.8387	0.6494
34°	0.5592	0.8290	0.6745
35°	0.5736	0.8192	0.7002
36°	0.5878	0.8090	0.7265
37°	0.6018	0.7986	0.7536
38°	0.6157	0.7880	0.7813
39°	0.6293	0.7771	0.8098
40°	0.6428	0.7660	0.8391
41°	0.6561	0.7547	0.8693
42°	0.6691	0.7431	0.9004
43°	0.6820	0.7314	0.9325
44°	0.6947	0.7193	0.9657
45°	0.7071	0.7071	1.0000

Degrees	Sin	Cos	Tan
46°	0.7193	0.6947	1.0355
47°	0.7314	0.6820	1.0724
48°	0.7431	0.6691	1.1106
49°	0.7547	0.6561	1.1504
50°	0.7660	0.6428	1.1918
51°	0.7771	0.6293	1.2349
52°	0.7880	0.6157	1.2799
53°	0.7986	0.6018	1.3270
54°	0.8090	0.5878	1.3764
55°	0.8192	0.5736	1.4281
56°	0.8290	0.5592	1.4826
57°	0.8387	0.5446	1.5399
58°	0.8480	0.5299	1.6003
59°	0.8572	0.5150	1.6643
60°	0.8660	0.5000	1.7321
61°	0.8746	0.4848	1.8040
62°	0.8829	0.4695	1.8807
63°	0.8910	0.4540	1.9626
64°	0.8988	0.4384	2.0503
65°	0.9063	0.4226	2.1445
66°	0.9135	0.4067	2.2460
67°	0.9205	0.3907	2.3559
68°	0.9272	0.3746	2.4751
69°	0.9336	0.3584	2.6051
70°	0.9397	0.3420	2.7475
71°	0.9455	0.3256	2.9042
72°	0.9511	0.3090	3.0777
73°	0.9563	0.2924	3.2709
74°	0.9613	0.2756	3.4874
75°	0.9659	0.2588	3.7321
76°	0.9703	0.2419	4.0108
77°	0.9744	0.2250	4.3315
78°	0.9781	0.2079	4.7046
79°	0.9816	0.1908	5.1446
80°	0.9848	0.1736	5.6713
81°	0.9877	0.1564	6.3138
82°	0.9903	0.1392	7.1154
83°	0.9925	0.1219	8.1443
84°	0.9945	0.1045	9.5144
85°	0.9962	0.0872	11.4301
86°	0.9976	0.0698	14.3007
87°	0.9986	0.0523	19.0811
88°	0.9994	0.0349	28.6363
89°	0.9998	0.0175	57.2900
90°	1.0000	0.0000	———

RANDOM NUMBERS

```
16247  67057  10251  98521  23049  90485  93472  54764  00881  21724
81610  35647  07547  50419  21362  85249  28479  33337  61331  58725
02190  78025  42193  97923  78377  86562  24007  91872  67410  46409
22649  91220  32179  21334  12788  40270  11138  82012  05998  10364
29001  56298  83778  69591  90123  04649  79227  25378  45715  52276

15234  02652  30047  49331  40652  73094  77908  06495  57351  84655
95577  61558  43018  33399  50975  19841  55339  80061  35990  70867
03283  51305  82814  21654  50927  38630  67102  80549  22337  07513
99335  43723  54336  85631  29536  09603  54311  96113  76841  44828
58948  06168  12821  68004  35025  10759  97747  32629  88242  00491

54133  08702  64190  41077  01227  97516  05049  56559  42675  47265
94799  15581  35844  12041  19406  87466  01987  47078  13721  48109
75132  50493  54738  45219  94101  96092  65224  75320  84902  26903
48977  35675  00748  76521  12774  65079  35629  65977  34438  77810
43718  63169  96092  60295  04520  84718  84185  83447  33832  56383

83235  42754  77728  24549  31299  33827  02580  08151  61013  64209
03943  82600  30461  68178  31421  45606  68730  67643  24547  02547
79539  24424  19473  67861  40210  93720  90758  15756  14016  87498
14345  28829  16266  16842  26986  54043  95243  46557  81167  23076
75046  17173  30543  53818  98718  05829  95943  80761  52074  82025

24104  86117  80507  08639  42463  75654  41821  60112  97561  19897
33613  79355  08460  86685  55409  23376  54838  88002  33788  44248
84566  42821  14117  23095  05460  41344  34675  45742  94992  30119
15381  02276  44307  16442  74366  89358  53839  02761  50312  57353
39197  98534  70506  15141  55602  88296  78648  94354  14021  26215

29438  19035  05663  43629  87598  31712  33425  70245  19872  89724
16896  25390  79264  91499  84895  51067  08280  19043  72150  06439
97488  01272  19365  29769  21290  70767  77075  42442  29501  61670
99594  66745  43395  35137  07272  09173  24535  38122  62297  15800
89511  11751  82672  60241  70856  59283  51723  78500  99274  18233

92577  01085  88766  40812  19507  62501  45282  58016  09959  03078
58842  29940  82262  62736  62662  06847  49078  00027  25074  65931
08077  87702  34975  62027  75216  87557  99511  32340  23759  61622
96879  60090  53736  39739  27926  05659  27462  07634  74308  06367
68789  36658  30747  11612  09789  21738  38828  45100  44629  03677

06529  83100  98943  94622  40181  01273  58858  32872  41946  23349
22907  81134  73706  19569  43287  97037  50344  37298  77070  99404
92424  89307  93253  27446  22804  09231  87923  13727  86029  97232
30633  25074  05013  29204  11182  05637  48176  51738  85491  23013
29653  93531  39615  76501  85789  26758  56465  84039  05240  94781

34341  99948  87936  50074  05483  28675  20234  44853  28390  03527
30246  01027  75868  30259  19520  56976  45638  10524  52088  93145
44507  05563  21277  86446  85367  31483  53302  35051  43977  07431
67968  15218  27442  45586  73238  26478  88436  39235  28046  06586
21478  63170  24055  11164  97908  70971  49306  11899  09692  70960

31761  44482  07138  82229  72904  53463  22562  43538  08418  43136
32242  50506  83191  80605  03160  65732  93419  42376  97444  86346
21740  36773  93368  95239  34207  30296  03575  70048  63427  44945
67507  71300  00713  45986  86034  86386  74371  60319  73904  95496
45447  53116  15622  62596  54807  46475  84234  61754  18274  57850
```

GLOSSARY

accuracy

The closeness of a given answer to the actual answer. [p. 105]

Addition Property of Equality

If you add or subtract the same number to both sides of a true equation, the equation will still be true. If $a = b$, then $a + c = b + c$. [p. 302]

adjacent

Next to or attached to. In a right triangle, the adjacent leg to angle A is the leg from A that is *not* the hypotenuse. [p. 493]

algebraic expression

A mathematical phrase involving constants, variables, and operation symbols. [p. 156]

algorithm

A mathematical process. [p. 134]

altitude

In a polygon, the perpendicular distance from a vertex to the opposite base. [p. 359]

angle

Two rays with a common endpoint.

angle of rotation

The measure, in degrees, of how far a figure is turned by a rotation. [p. 232]

area

The number of square units contained in a plane region. [p. 340]

arrangements

The ways to put a series of objects in order. [p. 564]

axes

The two perpendicular lines of a coordinate plane that intersect at the origin. [p. 15]

back-to-back stem-and-leaf diagram

A stem-and-leaf diagram that has numerical "leaf" bars from two sets of data: one to the left of the stem and one to the right. [p. 72]

bar graph

A graph of data with parallel bars. The length of each bar represents the value of a quantity. [p. 32]

base (number)

In 2^3, 2 is the base. In exponential notation a^n, a is the base. [pp. 97, 652]

base of a polygon

Any side of a polygon, or its length, that is used with the corresponding height in calculating the figure's area. [p. 359]

bases of a trapezoid

The parallel sides of the trapezoid. [p. 360]

bearing

The number of degrees clockwise from due north. [p. 6]

box-and-whisker plot

A display of sorted data showing the highest and lowest quarters of data as whiskers, the middle two quarters as a box, and the median. [p. 78]

cell

A location in a spreadsheet, at the intersection of a row and column, used to store a number, text, or a formula. [p. 19]

center of rotation

The fixed point about which a figure is rotated. [p. 232]

circle

All points in a plane that are the same distance from a point, the *center*.

circle graph

A graph representing parts of the data as sectors of a circle, where the relative sizes of the sectors represent the relative sizes of the data parts. [p. 32]

circumference

The distance around a circle. [p. 267]

clustering

Estimating a sum by estimating the mean and multiplying by the number of addends. $12 + 14 + 17 + 18 \approx 4(15)$ [p. 103]

coefficient

The numerical factor of a term. For $-2x$, the coefficient is -2. [p. 306]

column

A vertical series of cells in a spreadsheet. [p. 19]

combine like terms

Use the distributive property to express a sum or difference of like terms as a single term. [p. 181]

compatible numbers

Replacements for numbers in a calculation that make estimation or mental calculation easier. $3579 \div 119 \approx 3600 \div 120$. [p. 103]

concentric circles

Two or more circles with the same center. [p. 6]

cone

A solid with a vertex and a circular base. [p. 398]

congruent

Having the same shape and size. [p. 214]

congruent angles

Angles with the same measure. [p. 456]

consecutive whole numbers

Whole numbers whose difference is 1. [p. 109]

constant

A quantity with a value that does not change. [p. 156]

conversion factor

A ratio of two equal quantities used to convert from one unit of measure to another unit of measure. For example, to convert 90 minutes to hours, the conversion factor is $\frac{1\,\text{hr}}{60\,\text{min}}$. [p. 437]

coordinate

A number specifying the location of a point on a number line. [p. 7]

coordinate grid

Equally-spaced vertical and horizontal lines, centered on the origin and determined by the x-axis and the y-axis, used for noting position in two dimensions. [p. 15]

coordinates

The ordered pair of numbers specifying the location of a point on a coordinate plane. [p. 7]

corresponding

The matching vertices, angles, and sides of two similar geometric figures. [p. 462]

cosine (cos)

For an angle of a right triangle (not the right angle), the ratio of the length of its adjacent leg to the length of the hypotenuse. [p. 498]

counting principle

If a first thing can occur in m ways, and a second thing can occur independently in n ways, then these things can occur together in $m \times n$ ways. [p. 557]

cross multiplication

In the true proportion, $\frac{a}{b} = \frac{c}{d}$, multiplying this way results in $ad = bc$. [p. 444]

$$\frac{a}{b} \; > \!\!= \!\!< \; \frac{c}{d}$$

cross section

The figure formed by the intersection of a solid and a plane.

cube

A solid whose six faces are congruent squares. [p. 332]

cubic units

Units of volume, such as cubic feet, cubic meters, or cubic miles. [p. 349]

cylinder

A solid that has congruent parallel circular bases. [p. 398]

degree (°)

A unit used to measure the size of an angle. There are 360° in a full circle. [p. 454]

dependent variable

A variable whose value depends on the value of another variable. [p. 605]

diameter of a circle

A segment, or the length of a segment, that contains the center of the circle and has endpoints on the circle. [p. 267]

difference

The result of subtracting numbers or expressions.

distributive property

For any numbers a, b, and c, $a(b + c) = ab + ac$ and $a(b - c) = ab - ac$. [p. 175]

double line graph

A line graph showing two related sets of data for comparison. [p. 48]

edge

A segment between two faces of a solid connecting two vertices. [p. 332]

endpoints

Points A and B are the endpoints of line segment $\overline{AB}$. [p. 15]

A •———————• B

equally likely

Two events expected to occur with the same probability. If an event is equally likely as unlikely, it has a probability of 0.5. [p. 530]

equation

A mathematical sentence stating that two quantities are equal, written as two expressions separated by an equal sign. [p. 274]

equilateral triangle

A triangle with three sides of equal length. [pp. 200, 489]

equivalent

Having equal value. $\frac{7}{10}$ and 70% are equivalent.

equivalent ratios

Two ratios that show the same comparison and have the same value, such as $\frac{4}{10}$ and $\frac{2}{5}$. [p. 421]

evaluate an expression

Replace the variables in an algebraic expression with numbers to find the value of the expression. [p. 163]

event

Any possible result of an experiment or activity. [p. 527]

experimental probability

Probability found by collecting data or running an experiment. [p. 535]

exponent

Indicates repeated multiplication. In 2^3, 3 is the exponent. It tells how many times the base 2 is used as a multiplier. [p. 97]

exponential function

A function that can be represented by an equation of the form $y = ab^x$, where a and b are constants and $b > 0$. For example, $y = -2(3)^x$ [p. 651]

expression

See Algebraic expression.

face

Each of the flat surfaces of a solid. [p. 332]

factor

A multiplier. 2, 3, and x are factors of $6x$. [p. 97]

Fibonacci sequence

A pattern of numbers (1, 1, 2, 3, 5, 8, 13, 21, ...) named for the thirteenth-century mathematician Leonardo Fibonacci. Beginning with the third number, each number is the sum of the two numbers before it. [p. 241]

flip

A transformation that flips a figure over a line. The figure and the mirror image are symmetric over the line. A reflection. [p. 214]

formula

A mathematical statement showing how the value of one quantity can be found from the values of other quantities. [p. 266]

function

A relationship between two quantities where the value of one quantity is dependent upon the other quantity. [p. 622]

geometric probability

The probability of an event as determined by comparing the areas (or perimeters, angle measures, etc.) of parts to the total area of the figure. [p. 537]

glyph

A visual display of data that does not depend on words. [p. 55]

graph of a function

A graph of all the ordered pairs described by a function.

graph of an ordered pair

The point on a coordinate plane that corresponds to the ordered pair. [p. 14]

groupings

The ways to select a smaller group of objects from a larger group. [p. 570]

height

In a polygon, the length of the perpendicular distance from a vertex to the opposite base. [p. 359]

hexagon

A polygon with six sides. [p. 200]

hexagonal prism

A prism with hexagonal bases. [p. 391]

horizon line

In a one-point perspective drawing, the horizontal line containing the vanishing point. [p. 334]

hypotenuse

The longest side of a right triangle, opposite the right angle. [p. 479]

image

The figure resulting from a slide, flip, or turn. [pp. 215, 219]

independent variable

When the value of y depends on the value of x, x is called the independent variable. [p. 605]

indirect measurement

Calculation of a measure without direct measurement, such as by using trigonometric ratios. [p. 482]

integers

The whole numbers and their opposites: ... -3, -2, -1, 0, 1, 2, 3, ...

intersection

The points common to two or more lines, figures, regions, or sets.

interval

The scale distance between two consecutive tick marks on the axis of a graph. [p. 32]

inverse operations

Operations that undo each other: addition and subtraction or multiplication and division. [p. 301]

irrational number

A real number that cannot be expressed as the ratio of two integers, and so cannot be expressed as a repeating or terminating decimal. π and $\sqrt{2}$ are irrational numbers.

isolate the variable

Use properties of equality to solve an equation for a variable. [p. 300]

isometric projection

A drawing of a three-dimensional object as if the object is viewed from an angle without perspective. *Isometric* means "equal measure" or "same sized." [p. 332 F]

key

In a pictograph, it describes the quantity of data represented by one picture. [p. 54]

legend

The part of a map that describes the scale of the map. [p. 474]

legs of a right triangle

The two shorter sides of a right triangle. These sides meet at a right angle. [p. 479]

length of a segment

The distance between the endpoints of a line segment.

like terms

Terms in an expression with the same variables raised to the same powers. $3y$ and $-2y$ are like terms, x^2 and x are *not* like terms. [p. 181]

line of best fit

A mathematically derived trend line. [p. 81]

line graph

A graph of ordered pairs in which the points are connected, in order, by line segments. [p. 46]

line plot

A graph on a number line showing stacks of symbols as numbers of occurrences. [p. 64]

line segment

Points along a line consisting of two endpoints and all the points between these points. [p. 15]

line symmetry

Exists when two halves of a figure mirror each other over a line. Reflectional symmetry. [p. 200]

line of symmetry

A line that divides a figure into two mirror-image halves. [p. 200]

linear function

A function, whose graph is a straight line, that can be written in the form $y = ax + b$. Changes in one variable are proportional to changes in the other variable. [p. 623]

linear units

Units of length, such as feet, meters, or miles. [p. 340]

lower quartile

The middle value of data *below* the median. 25% of the data are below this value, 75% are above. [p. 78]

mean

The sum of a set of data divided by the number of data; the average. [p. 65]

measure of central tendency

A single, central value that summarizes a set of numerical data, such as mean, median, or mode. [p. 65]

median

When a list of data is arranged in numerical order, the middle value or the mean of the middle two values. [p. 65]

mirror image

The image of a figure after a reflection or flip. [p. 200]

mode

The most frequently occurring value in a set of data. [p. 65]

model

A representation of something in the real world, using geometry, algebra, or other mathematical tools. [p. 79]

Multiplication Property of Equality

If you multiply or divide by the same number on both sides of a true equation, the equation will still be true. If $a = b$, then $ac = bc$. [p. 302]

negative integers

The integers that are less than zero: -1, -2, -3, ...

negative slope

The slope of a line that slants downward from left to right. [p. 631]

net

A pattern that can be cut out and folded into a three-dimensional figure without gaps or overlap. [p. 384]

nonlinear function

A function that does not have a straight line for its graph. [p. 642]

number line

A line on which points representing numbers are labeled. [p. 7]

octagon

A polygon with eight sides. [p. 200]

odds

The ratio of the number of ways an event can happen to the number of ways it cannot happen. [p. 577]

odds against

The ratio of the number of ways an event cannot happen to the number of ways it can happen. [p. 578]

one-point perspective

Using a vanishing point to give perspective to a drawing. [p. 334]

opposites

A pair of numbers that are the same distance from 0 but on opposite sides of 0 on the number line, such as 5 and −5. [p. 125]

order of operations

Agreed upon rules for the order in which to do operations when evaluating an expression. The order of operations is (1) evaluate what is inside parentheses or above or below fractions bars, (2) evaluate powers, (3) multiply and divide in order from left to right, and (4) add and subtract in order from left to right. [p. 115]

ordered pair

A pair of numbers describing the location of a point on a coordinate plane. [p. 14]

origin

On a number line, the point with coordinate 0. On a coordinate plane, the point with coordinates $(0, 0)$, where the x- and y-axes intersect. [pp. 7, 15]

orthographic projection

A drawing showing the top, front, and side views of an object. [p. 368]

outcome

Any possible result of an experiment or activity. [p. 527]

parabola

The U-shaped graph of a quadratic function. [p. 643]

parallelogram

A quadrilateral with two pairs of parallel sides. Rectangles, rhombuses, and squares are parallelograms. [p. 206]

pattern

A predictable sequence of elements, such as figures or numbers. [p. 240]

pentagon

A polygon with five sides. [p. 200]

perfect square

A number that has an exact whole-number square root. 49 is a perfect square because $7^2 = 49$. [p. 110]

perimeter

The distance around the edge of a region. [p. 340]

perpendicular

Two lines that intersect, or meet, to form a right angle. [p. 225]

perspective

A shrinking effect given to parts of a two-dimensional drawing to add depth, making the drawing appear three dimensional. [p. 333]

pi (π)

The ratio of the circumference of a circle to its diameter. $\pi \approx 3.14$. [p. 267]

pictograph

A graph, similar to a bar graph, that uses a repeated picture or symbol, rather than a bar, to represent data. [p. 54]

pie chart

Common business or industry term for a circle graph. [p. 33]

polygon

A closed figure formed by line segments that intersect at their endpoints. [pp. 200, 358]

positive integers

The integers that are greater than zero: 1, 2, 3, ...

positive slope

The slope of a line that slants upward from left to right. [p. 631]

power

A number with a base and an exponent, such as 2^3. [p. 97]

prism

A solid with two parallel, congruent bases and rectangular sides. [pp. 332, 391]

probability

A number from 0 to 1 indicating the likelihood of an event. [p. 528]

product

The result of multiplying numbers or expressions. [pp. 97, 147]

properties of equality

Mathematical tools used to solve linear equations. [p. 302]

proportion

An equation stating that two ratios are equal. [p. 442]

protractor

A tool for measuring angles. [p. 454]

pure tessellation

A tessellation using only one figure. [p. 207]

pyramid

A solid with a polygonal base, with each vertex of the base connected by an edge to a point not on the base. [p. 398]

Pythagorean Theorem

In a right triangle, the square of the length of the hypotenuse is equal to the sum of the squares of the lengths of the legs. [p. 480]

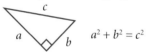

$a^2 + b^2 = c^2$

quadratic function

A function of the form $y = ax^2 + bx + c$, where $a \neq 0$. For example, $y = 2x^2 - x + 3$ or $y = -x^2$. [p. 643]

quadrilateral

A polygon with four sides. [p. 206]

quotient

The result of dividing numbers or expressions. [p. 148]

radius of a circle

A segment, or the length of a segment, from the center to any point on the circle. [p. 267]

random-number table

A list of digits without any pattern, where each digit has the same chance of occurring and is unrelated to the others. Note that 55555 and 28403 have the same chance of occurring in the table. [p. 542]

range (of data)

For a list of values, the difference between the highest and lowest value. [p. 65]

rate

A ratio that compares two quantities measured in different units. 12 miles in 2 hours is a rate of 6 miles per hour. [p. 435]

ratio

A comparison of two quantities by division. [p. 421]

rational number

A number that can be expressed as a ratio of two integers. 2 can be expressed as $\frac{2}{1}$, 1.5 as $\frac{3}{2}$, and 0.666 as $\frac{2}{3}$.

reciprocal

Two numbers are reciprocals if 1 is their product. 2 and $\frac{1}{2}$ are reciprocals, as are $\frac{5}{2}$ and $\frac{2}{5}$. For a number a (where $a \neq 0$), its reciprocal is $\frac{1}{a}$. [p. 306]

rectangle

A quadrilateral with four right angles. [p. 206]

rectangular prism

A prism with rectangular bases. [pp. 332, 391]

reflection

A transformation that flips a figure over a line. The figure and the mirror image are symmetric over the line. [p. 225]

reflectional symmetry

Exists when two halves of a figure mirror each other over a line. Line symmetry. [p. 227]

regular polygon

A polygon whose sides have equal length and angles have equal measure. A square is a regular polygon. [p. 200]

rhombus

A quadrilateral with four congruent sides. [p. 367]

right angle

An angle that measures 90°. In drawings, a right angle is marked by a square corner. [pp. 225, 455]

right prism

See Prism.

right triangle

A triangle with one right angle. [p. 455]

rotation

A transformation that turns a figure about a fixed point. [p. 232]

rotational symmetry

Exists when a figure can be rotated about a point onto itself with an angle of rotation of less than 360°. [p. 233]

row

A horizontal series of cells in a spreadsheet. [p. 19]

scale

The ratio of a distance on a map or model to the corresponding distance in the real world. [p. 471]

scale (of a graph)

The marked intervals on the axes of a coordinate plane. [p. 32]

scale factor

A ratio by which a figure is enlarged or reduced. [p. 471]

scatter plot

A graph showing a set of points based on two sets of data. [p. 79]

sector

A wedge-shaped part of a circle between one radius and another. In a circle graph or pie chart, it represents a portion of the data. [p. 32]

segment

See Line segment.

sequence

An ordered list of numbers. [p. 247]

signed numbers

Numbers written with their signs, such as +7 and −3. [p. 125]

similar

Having the same shape, but not necessarily the same size. [p. 461]

similar polygons

Polygons having the same shape, but not necessarily the same size, so that corresponding angles have the same measure and corresponding side lengths have the same ratio. [p. 463]

simplifying an expression

Finding a simpler form of an expression by distributing and/or combining like terms. [pp. 176, 181]

simulate

To use an experimental model to find probability, such as flipping a coin to determine the probability that a family with three children will have one girl. [p. 542]

sine (sin)

For an angle of a right triangle (not the right angle), the ratio of the length of the opposite leg to the length of the hypotenuse. [p. 498]

slant height of a cone

The length of any segment from the vertex of the cone to the circle bounding the base. [p. 401]

slide

A transformation that moves a figure a fixed distance in a given direction. A translation. [p. 214]

slope

A measure of the steepness of a line. It is the change in y-values divided by the change in x-values. For the line $y = ax + b$, the slope is a. [p. 631]

solid

A three-dimensional shape, such as a cube, a sphere, or a pyramid. [p. 332]

solution

A value of a variable in an equation that makes the equation true. [p. 275]

solve

To find the solution(s) of an equation. [p. 275]

spreadsheet

A table of rows and columns, usually used by computer programs, containing numbers, text, or formulas. [p. 19]

square (geometry)

A four-sided polygon with four right angles and four sides of equal length. [p. 200]

square (number)

A number multiplied by itself. The square of 9 is 9×9, or 81. [p. 98]

square root

A square root of 52 is any number whose square is 52. [p. 109]

square root function

A function involving the square root of the independent variable, such as $y = \sqrt{x}$. [p. 650]

square units

Units of area, such as square feet, square meters, or square miles. [p. 340]

stem-and-leaf diagram

A display that organizes data to show its shape and distribution. The digits of a number are used to create a numerical bar graph. [p. 71]

substitute

Replace a variable with a number in an algebraic expression.

sum

The result of adding numbers or expressions. [p. 133]

surface area of a prism

The total area of all of its faces, including the bases.

symmetric

A figure is symmetric if its image on one side of a line is a mirror image of the figure on the other side.

tangent (tan)

For an angle of a right triangle (not the right angle), the ratio of the length of the opposite leg to the length of the adjacent leg. [p. 493]

term (algebraic)

Numbers or parts of an expression that are added or subtracted. [pp. 133, 176]

term (sequence)

Each number of a sequence. For example, in the sequence 1, 3, 6, the second term is 3. [p. 247]

tessellation

A repeating pattern of figures that completely covers a plane region without gaps or overlaps. [p. 205]

tetrahedron

A pyramid with four triangular faces. [p. 389]

theoretical probability

When all equally likely outcomes are known, the number of outcomes of an event divided by the total number possible. [p. 535]

transformation

A movement of points that changes a figure by a slide, flip, and/or turn. [p. 216]

translation

A transformation that moves a figure a fixed distance in a given direction. A slide. [p. 219]

translational symmetry

Exists when the image of a figure after a translation is the same as the original figure. [p. 221]

trapezoid

A quadrilateral with exactly one pair of parallel sides. [p. 206]

trapezoidal prism

A prism with bases that are trapezoids.

tree diagram

A graphic representation, similar to the branches of a tree, of all possible outcomes of an event. [p. 554]

trend

The overall direction of increase or decrease shown by a graph. [p. 46]

trend line

The line that approximates the relationship between the two quantities of a scatter plot. [p. 79]

triangle

A polygon with three sides.

trigonometric ratios

The ratios of side lengths in right triangles. The sine, cosine, and tangent are the three basic ratios. [p. 493]

trigonometry

The study of right triangle measurements and ratios, useful for calculating indirect measurements. [p. 493]

turn

To move a figure around one point of the figure. A rotation. [pp. 214, 232]

unit rate

A rate in which the comparison is to one unit of a quantity. 55 mi/hr is a unit rate, since it means a ratio of 55 miles to one hour. [p. 435]

upper quartile

The middle value of the data *above* the median. 75% of the data are below this value, 25% are above. [p. 78]

value

The measurement, including a unit, of a measured quantity, or the number of a counted quantity.

vanishing point

A point used as a guide when giving one-point perspective to a drawing. [p. 334]

variable

A letter in an expression or equation that holds a place for or represents a quantity whose value may change or vary. [p. 156]

Venn diagram

A picture of a relationship between two or more sets of data shown as intersecting circles. [p. 59]

vertex

A corner point where two sides or edges intersect. [pp. 16, 332]

vertices of a triangle

The three corner points of the triangle. [p. 16]

volume

The number of cubic units contained in a solid. [p. 349]

whole numbers

The numbers 0, 1, 2, 3, ...

x-axis

The horizontal axis on a coordinate grid. [p. 15]

x-coordinate

The first number of an ordered pair. It describes the location of a point on a coordinate grid by its distance left or right from the vertical axis. [p. 15]

x-intercept

The x-coordinate of a point where a graph crosses the x-axis.

y-axis

The vertical axis on a coordinate plane. [p. 15]

y-coordinate

The second number of an ordered pair. It describes the location of a point on the coordinate plane by its distance above or below the horizontal axis. [p. 15]

y-intercept

The y-coordinate of a point where a graph crosses the y-axis. For the line $y = ax + b$, the y-intercept is b. [p. 633]

SELECTED ANSWERS

CHAPTER 1

1-1 Part A Try It

a–c.

−4.5, 4.5

b. Any coordinate x such that $-2 \leq x \leq 2$
c. $-1 \leq x \leq 7$

1-1 Part A Exercises

1. a. Coordinates
b. Miles from tower
c. Bearing (relative to North)
5. $(15, 135°)$ **9.** $(30, 135°)$
15.

17. To the right of 3; To the right of −3 **21.** Origin; 12 units **23.** 2.5 cm
25.

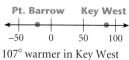

107° warmer in Key West

27. Above the origin
29. a. The plane is 5 miles due South from the airport.
b. The plane is 14 miles due North from the airport.
c. The plane on the west side of the airport.
d. The plane is on the north side of the airport.
35. $-3, 3$ **37.** $-6, 2$
39. To the left of −1
41. None exist **43.** $\frac{1}{2}$ in.
45. a.

City	% Change
New York	+3.55%
Detroit	−14.57%
Chicago	−7.37%
Seattle	+4.54%
Phoenix	+24.53%

b.

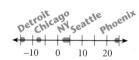

Detroit, Chicago, New York, Seattle, Phoenix

1-1 Part B Try It

a. $(3, 3)$ **b.** $(2, 1.5)$
c. $(3, -4)$ **d.** $(-3, -3)$
e. $(-4, 2)$ **f.** 2 left, 1 up
g. 3.5 right, 4 up **h.** 5 left, 2 down **i.** 2 right **j.** 4 left
k. 4.5 down **l.** No movement **m.** 3 left, 2 down

1-1 Part B Exercises

1. a. Two units right
b. Six units down
3. Down 2 **7.** Right 5, down 2 **9.** $(4.5, -1)$
11. $(0, -5)$

15.

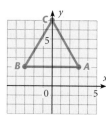

21. Hundreds **23.** 54, 126
25. 2.3456; $\frac{1}{100}$ of the previous number **27.** $(4, 3.5)$
29. $(-2, -1)$ **31.** Left 2, up 1 **33.** Right 3.5
35. Right 10, down 1
37. Left 2, down 2
39. Left 3, down 2
41. $(7, -2)$ **43.** $(0, 7)$
45. $(2, 1)$ **47.** $(0, 6)$

49.

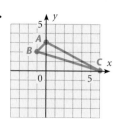

51. a.

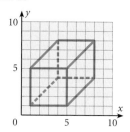

1-1 Part C Try It

a. Look in the rectangle where row 12 meets column K **b.** Tampa
c. 238 miles

1-1 Part C Exercises

1. In the cell where column D and row 15 meet **5.** B5
9. E5; Erie **11.** G7
13. H7 **17.** 246 miles
19. 399 miles **23.** $3.69
25. a. $\frac{3}{4}$ **b.** $\frac{6}{8}$ **c.** They are the same; Both shade $\frac{3}{4}$ of the picture to show that $\frac{6}{8} = \frac{3}{4}$. **27.** A2 **29.** 140 miles
31. City **33.** 4682
35. 58,622; Total number of homeless persons in these 5 cities **37.** Year; Number of cases argued, by year; Holds title for the study **39.** Number of cases appealed to the Supreme Court (not all of which will receive review); 1,158

1-1 Part D Self-Assessment

1. $(-3, 5)$

2. a, c, d.

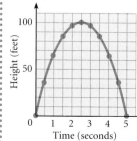

b. $(0, 0)$, $(0.5, 36)$, $(1, 64)$, $(1.5, 84)$, $(2, 96)$, $(2.5, 100)$, $(3, 96)$, $(3.5, 84)$, $(4, 64)$, $(4.5, 36)$, $(5, 0)$
e. The baseball is thrown up, gradually slows, stops (instantaneously), and falls at a faster and faster rate. The acceleration (deceleration) due to gravity varies with altitude.
3. Bear Haven; $(9, 45°)$ Running Creek; $(3, 75°)$ Cascades; $(8.25, 180°)$ Lookout Point; $(9, 240°)$ Pekoe Geyser; $(10.5, 315°)$
4. C6 **5.** C5, C6, C10
6. C3, C4, C12 **7.** Possible answer: Require all tankers to be double hulled.

8. a.

b. 1 p.m.; Moving +1 unit adds an hour
c. 2 p.m., 11 a.m., 3 p.m., 1 p.m.
d. 9 p.m. Monday; It is more than two hours earlier so it must be the previous day.

e.

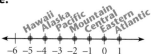

Both number lines show an interval of one hour between time zones.

9. (b) **10.** Axis; Coordinates are the numbers of the ordered pair used to describe the location of a point on a grid. A location on an axis is shown by one number or an ordered pair.
11. 40,352 **12.** $13.76
13. Possible answer: Maps, mileage charts (town to town), growth chart

1-2 Part A Try It
a. Number of home runs per season **b.** Year (season) **c.** 0; 60; 10 **d.** 1989 **e.** 1990 **f.** Approximately the same

1-2 Part A Exercises
1. a. Country **b.** 200 **c.** Japan **d.** 1600
7. a. Long distance running; Weights **b.** Long distance running plus Start Practice **c.** 100%; Because the total activities equal one workout.
11. 26.2 million **13.** 35.1 million; Possible answer: Almost everyone can walk, but not everyone has access to equipment (or a health club, for example) **17.** Pie charts **19.** 37.3% **21.** About 3,617,634; Possible answer: Mexico, Canada, Brazil, Colombia, Chile **27.** 12.5% **29.** 62.5% **31.** 25%; 15%; 10% **33.** 2.4 hrs; 8.4 hrs **35.** ≈ 215 kg **37. a.** ≈ 150 kg **b.** 330 lb **c.** 250% of his weight
39. The four schools had comparable scores; By graphing only the 100 points where they differ, it appears the schools' scores vary significantly with Tyler nearly twice the score of the other schools.

1-2 Part B Try It
1. a. Possible answer: 50

1-2 Part B Exercises
1. a. Sales region **b.** 0 to 50 thousand books **c.** 10 thousand books **3.** Possible answer: 5000 **5.** Possible answer: Number below the poverty level, 1960-1990 **9.** Possible answer: Life expectancy in six major industrialized nations

10. Possible answer: 80; 70; This will show the variability between nations **13.** Between −4 and 0 **15. a.** Minimum January temperature (°F) **b.** 10°F **c.** Yes, to include Minneapolis on the map.

21.

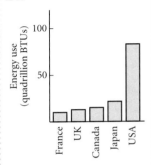

1-2 Part C Try It
a. Up **b.** Down **c.** Down

1-2 Part C Exercises
1. a. Decrease **b.** Increase **c.** Decreasing; The overall trend is downward with the March to April increase showing an anomaly in the data rather than a change in trend **2.** (c) **5.** Interval between tick marks is 10 seconds **7.** Each is less than previous olympiad's time; 4:35.0 **9.** 1976
11. ≈ $1900 million; ≈ $2950 million
12. ≈ $4030 million; ≈ $3800 million **17.** 6
19. $\frac{1}{2}$ **21.** 325 million **23.** 1983 **25.** 3465 million dollars **27. a.** 19% **b.** Cropland, Pasture, Forest, and either Developed or Federal **c.** 87%; Pasture, range and cropland

1-2 Part D Try It
a. The rail (train) ride takes 20 minutes to get to

Columbia and departs at 9:10. **b.** The trolley departs at 6:00 and takes 5 minutes to get to the aquarium. **c.** The bus leaves at 3:30 for the Dutch Mall and takes 45 minutes to get there.

1-2 Part D Exercises
1. 4.5 clocks per household

3.

5. Key

7.

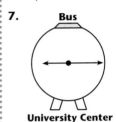

9. 80 million metric tons; 125 million metric tons
13. Right of −5 **15.** 2.5
17. 24

19.

21. 15 **23.** Soap Operas **25.** About twice as many chose baseball. **27.** 9; 5; 25 **29.** 48; 20; 36 **31.** 8

1-2 Part E Self-Assessment
1. Bar **2.** Circle **3.** Line **4.** Line **5.** Pictograph **6.** 13 cm; 10 cm² **7.** Possible answer: Height during growth years, weight, hours spent studying per day **8.** Possible answer: Personal income, number of days grounded over past 10 years **9.** Yes. The collection is one situation and can be represented

as percentages of its parts using types of music or artists.
10. A pictograph is a visual representation of data where symbols are used to represent specific quantities of the data.
11. (b) **13.** (1, 0)
14. a. Because the "days missed annually" is based on several situations.

b.

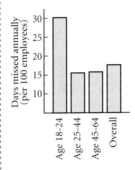

15. 82-88%; 35-55%
16. Japan **17.** Both are approaching U.S. productivity levels, but Japan is growing at a faster rate.

1-3 Part A Try It
a. $46.68 **b.** 12; Mode **c.** $101,350

1-3 Part A Exercises
1. a. 10.8, 11.0, 11.0, 11.3, 11.4, 11.4, 11.5, 11.6, 12.2; Range = 1.4 **b.** 11.4; 11.36; 11.0 and 11.4 (bimodal)
3. $552.50 **6. a.** Median because of large variability in data **b.** Median = 80 exams per 1,000 students
8. Mean = 1.06 kg; Median = 1 kg; Either measure would be appropriate.
11. Possible answer: 10 units per tick mark (and probably a jagged line to indicate a gap in the axis from 30 to 135)
13. Hundreds

15. Hundredths $\left(\frac{1}{100}\right)$
17. $6.75 **19.** 1108 (thousand) **21.** 32
23. Possible answer: 95; My school requires an average of 90 for an A

1-3 Part B Exercises

1. a. 17, 18, 22, 25, 27, 27, 30, 32, 33, 35, 35, 41, 41, 43, 45, 48, 50, 52, 56, 66
b. One

c–d.

Stem	Leaf
6	6
5	0 2 6
4	1 1 3 5 8
3	0 2 3 5 5
2	2 5 7 7
1	7 8

3. Possible answer: (c), (b), (a) by assuming more time was spent on TV than on the phone, and more on the phone than on chores, and selecting the diagram sequence which seems to show this pattern
5. There are left leaves that begin at the stem and increase outward to the left
7. City and state populations; City precipitation

11. a–b.

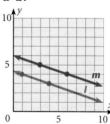

c. l and m are parallel

13.

Stem	Leaf
8	2 3
7	1 3 7 5
6	3 2
5	0 3 4 5 8 5
4	1 4 3 7 6 2
3	3 0 7 0

17. a. 43 **b.** 225 **c.** 67

702

---

19. a. 39.0, 59.0, 70.0, 77.2, 83.0, 83.1, 86.0, 86.0, 89.4, 91.2, 91.6, 93.5, 93.9, 94.4, 95.0, 97.1; Range = 58.1%
b. Median = 87.7; Lower quartile = 80.1; Upper quartile = 93.7
c.

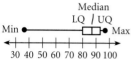

Median
LQ / UQ
Min ●——————□□□—● Max

30 40 50 60 70 80 90 100

d. Half of the countries solve 80-95% of their murder cases. One fourth solve a little over 95%, one fourth solve 39-80%.

1-3 Part C Exercises

1. a. 1980; 1984
b. No; Intercept edges of grid are at different locations.
c. $625; $650; Both appear to be reasonable figures.
3. Crime rate; Percentage of students in each state who graduate from high school
5. Approximately 600
7. As the graduation rate increases, the crime rate decreases; The trend line has a negative slope. **8. a.** 55%
b. 110 **c.** Not as dependable as predictions for data points located with the bulk of the data. The data are only moderately related which lessens the accuracy of the predictions. **11.** (a)
13. $\frac{13}{4}$ **15.** 4 **16.** $550
19. $715 **23.** A somewhat linear relationship should be found.

1-3 Part D Self-Assessment

1. Range = 2,895; Mean = 4064.4; Median = 3,486
2. a. Range = 34%; Mean = 40.06%; Median = 38.5%; Mode = 57%, 36%
b. Mean or median

c.

Stem	Leaf
5	1 7 7
4	2 6 7 8
3	1 5 6 6 8 9
2	3 7 8

---

d. The opinions are fairly evenly spread over the range 23% to 57% **3.** $\frac{18}{5}$ **4.** $\frac{7}{3}$
5. 4 **6.** $\frac{3}{2}$

7.

	Before	After
Range	28	24
Mean	82.08	115.9
Median	80	116
Mode	96	108, 120

Before: Median since asymmetric; After: Mean or median since symmetric

8.

Before	Stem	After
	12	0 0 2 5 9
	11	3 5 7
	10	5 8 8 9
6 6 6 2	9	
5 0 0	8	
6 6 2	7	
8 8	6	

Observe that the "before" data are asymmetric and the "after" data are symmetric.

9–10.

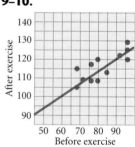

A modest positive linear trend

10. a. About 108 **b.** Moderately dependable. Pulse rate data clusters within 10 beats of the trend line. **11.** F
12. T **13.** (a)
14. a. Trend line $y = 3.14x$
b. Yes. A 0 diameter circle has 0 circumference.
c. 79 cm **d.** Yes; The relationship is exact.
e. $C = 2\pi r = \pi d$ so $\frac{C}{\pi} = d$; Here $d = \frac{126}{\pi} = 40.1$ m.

Chapter 1 Review

1. Coordinates
2. Spreadsheet **3.** Mean

---

4. Between and including -5 and $+5$

5. a. $A: (-3, 2)$, $B: (4, 1)$, $C: (-2, -3)$ **b.** $\overline{AB}, \overline{AC}, \overline{CB}$ are all line segments.
6. a. $(0, 0)$ **b.** Origin
7. (d) **8.** The cell located where the third or "C" column intersects the 17th row contains the cost of apple pie.
9. a. Range = $11,100; Mean = $3,800; Mode = $2,250; Median = $2250
b. Median, because the $12,000 data point has too much influence on the mean.
10. a. Tick mark to tick mark, 50,000 **b.** 350,000
c. Alaska–Its line starts below and finishes above that of Wyoming. **d.** Alaska has grown more and at a faster rate than Wyoming.
11. Possible answers: 30, 31, 32, ..., 39, 40; 1000, 1001, 1002, ..., 1009, 1010.
12. Whether there is a relationship between the variables; Kind of relationship; Strength of relationship; Whether the trend of the data is positive or negative
13. a. Mystery: 288; Romance: 216; Science Fiction: 144; Historical: 96; Other: 56

b.

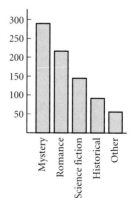

c. Pie chart

CHAPTER 2

2-1 Part A Try It
a. 9 **b.** 216 **c.** 2.25
d. $\frac{1}{8}$ **e.** 0.0016 **f.** 25

2-1 Part A Exercises
1. 3.2 **3.** 3.84 **5.** 4913
7. 52.5625 cm^2 **9.** 961
15. 3.375 **17.** 4
19. $2.29 **23.** Start at the origin. Move 4 units left then 3 units up and make a point with your pencil.
25. 132.02 **27.** 11.780972
29. -12 **31.** 23
33. 78.539816 **35.** 512
37. 20.25 **39.** 0.0025
41. $\frac{27}{64}$ **43.** $105.75
45. 96 tiles

2-1 Part B Try It
a. $2.30 **b.** 2.09 **c.** 18
d. 4300 **e.** 10 **f.** $3.20
g. 89.4 **h.** 64,000 **i.** $3

2-1 Part B Exercises
1. 2.24 **3.** 0.300 **5.** $9.60
9. 1260 **11.** 270
13. $18.59 **14.** (b) **17.** 5
19. 10 **21.** 432,400
23. $10.70 **25.** 927
27. 15,000 **29.** 20
31. 20 **33.** 35
35. 10 cakes

2-1 Part C Try It
a. 2 and 3; 2.8 **b.** 4 and 5; 4.6 **c.** 8 and 9; 8.7 **d.** 11

2-1 Part C Exercises
1. More **3.** 22.4 ft by 22.4 ft **5.** 4 and 5
7. 3 and 4 **9.** 9 **11.** 0.3
13. (b) **21.** $\frac{1}{5}$
23. $(0, -3)$ **25.** 3 and 4
27. 10 and 11 **29.** 4 and 5
31. 3 and 4 **33.** 0.0
35. 4.2 **37.** 3.5 **39.** 0.5
41. about 316 ft by 316 ft
43. 0.9
45. 5.4 **47.** 1,000 m

2-1 Part D Try It
a. 12 **b.** 10 **c.** 18 **d.** 20

2-1 Part D Exercises
1. $3 + 4$ **5.** 33 **7.** 19

11. 2.5 **13.** $\frac{3(10) + 6}{4} = $ 9 ounces **15.** First calculate $3 \times 2 = 6$, then $8 - 6 = 2$. The expression now equals $13 - 3^2 \div 2$. Next, calculate $3^2 = 9$, then $9 \div 2 = 4.5$. Finally calculate $13 - 4.5 = 8.5$ to get the final answer
17. $\times$ **21.** $2,379,400
23. 16; 16 **25.** 60; 60
27. 22.8 **29.** 35 **31.** 19
33. $2 \times 52 + 3 \times 13 = 143$ miles **35.** 90 **37.** 4
39. 66 **41.** $275; $625
43. $159.50

2-1 Part E Self-Assessment
1. 1 **2.** 14 **3.** 15
4. 144,000,000 **5.** 0.000036
6. 1440 **7. a.** 271,800 ft
b. 755 home runs $\times$ 4 bases per home run $\times$ 90 feet per base = 271,800 ft.
8. Possible answer:
$1 + 2 \cdot 3 \div 4$
$1 \div 2 + 3 + 4$
$1 + 2 + 3 + 4$ **9.** $\sqrt{72}$ is between 8 and 9; 8.49
10.

= 200 Cars

11. a.
$$\frac{5(80) + 3(90) + 2(92) - 1(3)}{10}$$
b. $\frac{5(85) + 3(80) + 2(85) - 1(0)}{10}$
c. Mia **12.** No; $8 \times 30 = 240$, so 273 is too high
13. 14.8 cm **14.** 96
15. 273 **16.** 92
17. Between 4 and 5
18. 4200 **19.** 85
20. $18.70 **21.** 55.1 ft
22. 62.4 Kilowatt-hours
23. Designer C

2-2 Part A Try It
a. -7 **b.** 5 **c.** -5.3
d. 12 **e.** -1 **f.** -4
g. -4 **h.** 2

2-2 Part A Exercises
1. 5 **3.** 10 **5.** -3
7. Possible answer: The national debt; $4.5 trillion;

the net worth of the U.S. government. **11. a.** She means there are 10 seconds until the rocket is launched.
b. "+5 and counting"
c. To indicate the number of seconds before and after the launch. **15.** -3
18.

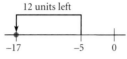

12 units left

21. 2 **23.** -1 **25.** 15
27. 2 **29.** 15 **31.** 2
33. $-$25 **35.** 6 **37.** 2
39. -14 **45.** $-427.7°$; $-247.7°$

2-2 Part B Try It
a. 3 **b.** -3 **c.** 25
d. -25 **e.** -66 **f.** -125
g. -5.3 **h.** -5.5

2-2 Part B Exercises
1. -3 **2.** Terms **7.** 3
9. -3 **11.** -10 **13.** -20.5
19. -24.6 **22. a.** $102 + (-16) + 25 + (-18.50)$
b. $92.50 **25.** $29.76
27. 642 **33.** -1 **35.** 8
37. 0 **39.** -23.7 **41.** 85.4
43. 5000 **45.** -1550
47. -912.2 **49.** $-$49.32
51. a. Dillon **b.** Louise got the jack; Dillon got the queen

2-2 Part C Try It
a. 1 **b.** 7 **c.** -12 **d.** -7
e. -16 **f.** 13 **g.** -80.6
h. 8 **i.** 20.4

2-2 Part C Exercises
3. $-14 + 12$ **5.** $-14 + 12 + 3$ **7.** -10 **11.** 10
13. 16.8 **15.** 15
18. a. Changes the 30 to -30
b. -35 **c.** $5 \boxed{-} 7 \boxed{+/-} \boxed{=}$; The answer is 12 **21.** 20; Yes
23. 50 **25.** 8.5 **27.** $-24 + 12$ **29.** $-1 + 14 + 32$
31. -19 **33.** 323
35. -101.6 **37.** 5.1
39. 45.6 **41.** -47.9
43. 2007 **45.** 170.8
47. a. $-1.5 + 0.8 + 0.3 - 1.9$ seconds

b. 3 minutes 58.7 seconds

2-2 Part D Try It
a. Negative; -160
b. Positive; 44 **c.** Negative; -250 **d.** Negative; -40
e. 15 **f.** 20 **g.** -21
h. -22 **i.** 7 **j.** 10 **k.** 4

2-2 Part D Exercises
1. 15 **3.** $+$ **5.** $+$ **7.** $+$
9. 30 **11.** -3 **13.** -12.5
16. (c) **19.** $-3,333$
21. 6.3 **23.** 16
27. A glyph is a visual display that conveys information without words.
29. $-$ **31.** $+$ **33.** $-$
35. -101 **37.** 72.6
39. 5.0 **41.** 2160
43. -300 **45.** 145.8
47. 28 **49.** $13\frac{1}{4}$
51. a. The population in 1990 = population in 1980 $- 3200 \times 10$ **b.** 638,900

2-2 Part E Self-Assessment
1. 6 **2.** 6 **3.** 46 **4.** $-3\frac{1}{3}$
5. -8.2 **6.** 1.7 **7.** 2950 years **8.** -27.5 **9.** 38.3
10. -8 **11.** 756
12. -12.5 **13.** Impossible; The product of any number multiplied by itself must be positive. **14.** Possible answer: $18 \div (-1)$
15. Possible answer: $-5 - (-10)$ **16.** 45.88
17. a. 82% **b.** 84,284,520 workers **18.** $-\frac{4.3 \text{ trillion}}{250 \text{ million}} = -$17,200$; Debt is negative. Population is positive. $\frac{\text{Debt}}{\text{population}}$ is negative.
19. a. 82 **b.** 5 **c.** 15
20. (d) **21.** Golfer B wins by 3 strokes **22.** 19,852 ft

2-3 Part A Try It
a. Constant **b.** Variable
c. Constant **d.** Variable
e. $2x + 5$

f. $2x - 1$

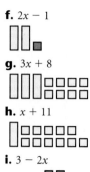

g. $3x + 8$

h. $x + 11$

i. $3 - 2x$

2-3 Part A Exercises
1. $2x - 4$

3. Constant   **5.** Constant

7.

9.

11. $20d$ **13.** $\frac{1}{3}j - 3.54$
15. $\frac{v-5}{7}$ **21.** $5.4x - 3(2)$
23. $8m - 2.3$ **25.** 5
27. -58.9 **29.** 43
31. Variable   **33.** Variable
35. Constant
37.

39.

41. $25q + 10$
43. $3 \cdot (h \cdot 4.35) - 5.50$
45. $0.15m - 48$
47. a. Your age; $0.54y +$
110   **b.** Increase
c. Possible answer: 115.4
d. 37

2-3 Part B Try It
a. -8.4 **b.** 42.7   **c.** 100π
d. 30   **e.** 7

2-3 Part B Exercises
1. 14   **3.** 5558   **7.** 123
9. -12 **11.** 84
13. a. y represents the number of years since you last cut your nails.   **b.** 15.5 in.; 30.5
in.   **c.** $24\frac{1}{3}$ years   **17.** 2
19. 67   **21.** 38   **23.** 0
25. 91   **27.** 10   **29.** 7
31. a. \$12   **b.** \$9   **c.** \$10
33. $0.31 + 22(x - 1)$; 8.6
minutes

2-3 Part C Try It
a. $3x^2 - x + 6$
b. $2x - x^2 - 2$ **c.** $3x - 2$
d.

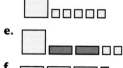

e.

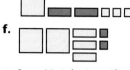

f.

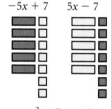

g. $3x - 11 + (-6x - 2) =$
$-3x - 13$ **h.** $3x^2 + 5x +$
$7 + (-2x^2 - 5x + 8) =$
$x^2 + 15$ **i.** $7x^2 + 4x -$
$10 + (-3x^2 + 3) = 4x^2 +$
$4x - 7$

2-3 Part C Exercises
1. $2x^2 - 2x - 2$
2. $x^2 + 2x - 3$

$-5x + 7$ $5x - 7$

$x^2 + 7x - 10$

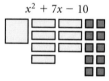

3. $2x + 3$ **5.** $3x^2 + 10x + 2$
9. $3x^2 + 2x - 10 +$
$(-3x^2 - 3) = 2x - 13$
11. 3   **15.** 25
17. $10x^2 + 12x - 1$
19. $7x - 39$
21. $6x^2 + 12x + 3$
23. $-2x^2 + 18x + 24$
25. $39x^2 - 15$ **27.** $32x$
29. $(5x - 10) + (-21x - 7) =$
$-16x - 17$ **31.** $(x^2 +$
$12x - 11) + (7x^2 - 3) =$
$8x^2 + 12x - 14$ **33.** -21
35. c.
$5 \cdot 1000 - 500 = \$4500$
$6 \cdot 900 - 500 = \$4900$
$7 \cdot 800 - 500 = \$5100$
$8 \cdot 700 - 500 = \$5100$
$9 \cdot 600 - 500 = \$4900$

2-3 Part D Try It
a. $12a - 6$ **b.** $-4x - 12$
c. $5x + 10y$
d. $-6y^2 - 12y + 3$

2-3 Part D Exercises
1. $-12x - 21$ **3.** $-5x +$
100   **5.** $10x^2 + 50x + 35$
7. $25d^2 + 100d$ **9. a.** $3a +$
15   **b.** $72b$ **c.** $2x$ **d.** $21b$
e. $30x$ **11.** -1 **13.** 12
15. 3   **17.** -7 **19.** 252
21. $21x + 77$ **23.** $5x^2 +$
40   **25.** $-2m + 70$
27. $21x + 14y + 77$
29. $-8x^2 + 20$ **31.** 90
33. 7   **35.** $1.98 +$
$0.07(1.98) = 1.98(1 + 0.07) =$
\$2.12

2-3 Part E Try It
a. $7y - 1$ **b.** $3x^2 + 10$
c. $7y^2 - 2y - 6$ **d.** $2x + 4$
e. $x^2 - 6$ **f.** $3y + 7$
g. $3y^2 - 2y$ **h.** $7x$

2-3 Part E Exercises
2. a. $(x^2 + 2x - 3) +$
$(-3x - 7)$ **b.** $x^2 - x - 10$
4. $25y - 10$ **5.** $9x^2 + 10$
9. $4x + 1$ **11.** $-10x^2 -$
$2x + 8$ **13.** $2y^2 + 8y$
15. $18y^2$ **17.** $4a + 1$;
$\overline{AB} = 1.6$; $\overline{BC} = 5.8$;
$\overline{AC} = 7.4$ **19.** -242
21. $\approx 194{,}253$ **23.** $4m +$
4   **25.** $103x + 64y - 22$
27. $-2y - 10$ **29.** $3k^2 +$
$4k + 3$ **31.** $11x^2 + 3y^2 +$
10   **33.** $5x^2 + 6x + 6$
35. $-6x - 12m$
37. 25   **39.** -7 **41.** -10;
Yes   **43.** $80 + 4y$

2-3 Part F Self-Assessment
1. $4\ell - 7$ **2.** $p + 1000$
3. -39 **4.** 447   **5.** \$334
6. $4x^2 - 4x + 21y$
7. $-24a^2 + 25a - 30b^2$
8. $x - 12y$ **9.** $-15b + 21$
10. $48x + 144y$
11. $-18c + 50d$

12. $(2(n + 7) - 4) \div 2 -$
$n = (2n + 14 - 4) \div 2 - n$
$= (2n + 10) \div 2 - n =$
$n + 5 - n = 5$
13. a. $30x + 35t - 20$,
not $30x + 7t - 4$ **b.** OK
c. $8x + 10$, not $8x + 14$
d. $43y - 40$, not $43y - 30$
14. a. A cube with sides of
length d.   **b.** $0.48d^3$
c. Basketball: about 408 in.^{3}
Baseball: about 12 in.^{3}
Volleyball: about 272 in.^{3}
Soccerball: about 322 in.^{3}
15. They added the population, the elevation and the
fine which are not like terms.

Chapter 2 Review
1. Multiply   **2.** T
3. Terms   **4.** Multiplication
5. Variable   **6.** 1.728   **7.** 1
8. 5   **9.** 11   **10.** -14
11. 0   **12.** 15   **13.** 58
14. 43   **15.** 8.125 yards
16. 7250   **17.** \$57.38
18. 45.2   **19.** Yes, but the
correct answer is 81
20. 10,251   **21.** 1401
22. 22   **23.** 11.2 ft
24. (c)   **25.** $7 \cdot 43 = 7 \cdot$
$(40 + 3) = 280 + 21 = 301$
26. The first coordinate, 2
27. 5   **28.** -10 **29.** 5
30. \$98.11   **31.** 0.7, 0.621,
0.6, 0.52, 0.5, 0.06

32–35.

-3.7 **(33.)** $\frac{1}{3}$ **(35.)**

-2.25 **(34.)** 3.7 **(32.)**

36. $102°F$ **37.** 165
38. $-3x^2 + 2x - 2$
39. $9x + 5$ **40.** $3k + 1$
41. $-10y + 15$ **42.** $-x^2 + 2$
43. $-12x + 28$ **44.** $5b - 1$
45. a. $6.29 + 0.17p$
b. \$10.37   **c.** \$10.03
46. $4x - 6$; 6; x cannot equal
2 because the side of a rectangle cannot have negative
length.   **47.** 18.1 square
centimeters

48. Sun; 28.7; Whatever was used as a reference was probably assigned a 0 magnitude. Brighter stars had to be assigned to either positive or negative numbers.

CHAPTER 3

3-1 Part A Try It
a. Yes; Either line is correct.

b. No
c. Yes; Either line is correct.

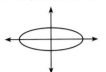

d. Yes

3-1 Part A Exercises
1. Yes; It divides the figure into two mirror images.
3. No; The line does not divide the figure into two mirror images.   **5.** (e)
9.

13. Yes, the right half of the door is a mirror image of the left half.   **15.** F; Hexagon
17. None
19.

23. $(-2, 3)$
25. No; The two sides are not reflections of each other.
27.

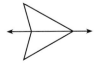

---

29.   **31.**

33.   **35.**

37. No lines of symmetry
39. a. Equilateral triangle = 3; Square = 4; Regular hexagon = 6; Regular octagon = 8
b. The number of lines of symmetry is the same as the number of sides; 5

3-1 Part B Try It
a. Equilateral triangles
b. Trapezoids   **c.** Hexagons

3-1 Part B Exercises
1. Tessellation   **3.** Triangle, square **7.** Possible answers: Equilateral triangle, square, regular hexagon   **11.** F
13. Yes; Hexagon   **15.** (e)
17. -5 **19.** Parallelogram

3-1 Part C Self-Assessment
1. Yes; It is a figure with three or more sides.
2. Possible answer: ▢
3. Possible answer:

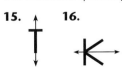

4. 158,120.5   **5.** -5
6. (d)   **7.** Yes   **8.** No
9. No   **10.** Rhombus; Snakeskin
11. Rectangle; Brick road
12. B   **13.** W
14. No lines of symmetry
15. ↑   **16.** K

---

17. Pentagon; Square; Hexagon; No; Pure tessellations use only one shape.

3-2 Part A Try It
a. Slide   **b.** Slide and turn

3-2 Part A Exercises
3. Slide and flip   **5.** Slide and turn   **7.** d and b
11. Possible answers: Congruent: football; Not congruent: sailboat racing, skiing, figure skating
13. Yes; They are the same shape and size.

15.

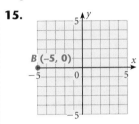

17. Slide and turn
19. Slide and turn
21. Slide   **23.** No; They are different lengths.   **25.** Yes; They are the same size and shape.   **27.** Slide and flip; Slide and turn

3-2 Part B Try It
a. Six units left and 4 units down   **b.** $A'(3, -5)$
c. $M'(-3, 3)$ **d.** $K'(2, -2)$
e. $O'(1, -1)$

3-2 Part B Exercises
1. $A'(3, 1)$

3.

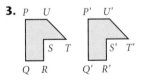

5. $B'(-4, -6)$
7. $F'(2, -3)$ **8.** $P'(0, 2)$, $Q'(4, -2)$, $R'(2, -6)$

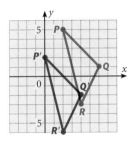

15. $3x^2 + 2x + 5$
17. Right 2 units and up 6 units   **19.** Right 2 units and down 6 units   **21.** Left 2 units   **23.** $B'(-2, -4)$
25. $S'(1, -2)$
27. $M'(3, 0.2)$
29. $F'(-1, -1)$
31. $K'(-3.3, -2.5)$
33. $<4, -2>$

3-2 Part C Try It
a. $A'(2, 3)$ **b.** $B'(-1, 2)$
c. $C'(-4, -2)$
d. $A'(-2, -3)$
e. $B'(1, -2)$ **f.** $C'(4, 2)$

3-2 Part C Exercises
1. a. D **b.** E **3.** $C'(1, 2)$
5. $L'(-4, 0)$ **7.** $C'(4, -3)$
9. $L'(0, 2)$ **13.** C **15.** B
17. $A'(3, 1)$ **19.** $X'(1, -2)$
21. $A'(3, 2)$ **23.** $X'(5, -3)$
25. $A'(-3, -2)$ **27.** $X'(-5, 3)$
29. $A'(-3, -1)$
31. $X'(-1, 2)$ **35.** $\triangle A''B''C''$ is a slide of $\triangle ABC$.

3-2 Part D Try It
a. 300° counterclockwise
b. 330° clockwise   **c.** 270° counterclockwise   **d.** 335° clockwise   **e.** 315° counterclockwise   **f.** 180° clockwise

3-2 Part D Exercises
1. 90° clockwise
3. Congruent; Rotation, translation, and reflection are all examples of transformations.
5. F **7.** F **9.** 340° counterclockwise   **12.** Yes; A stop sign is a regular octagon. Rotating it around its center will match itself 7 times before a full turn.

705

15. 360°; Same
17. $-6x + 12$
19. A **21.** F **23.** 325° counterclockwise **25.** 290° counterclockwise

3-2 Part E Self-Assessment

1. Rotational symmetry
2. Reflectional symmetry
3. 335° counterclockwise
4. 180° clockwise
5. 30° counterclockwise
6. Possible answer:

7. $4x^2 - 16x$ **8.** F **9.** T
10. (c) **11. a.** $A'(-1, 4)$, $B'(2, 4)$, $C'(2, 9)$ **b.** Left 3 units and up 2 units
c.

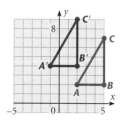

12.

13. $K'(5, 6)$, $L'(2, 6)$, $M'(4, 1)$

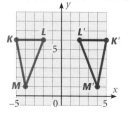

14. Translation, reflection

3-3 Part A Try It
a. 25, 36 **b.** MN, PQ
c.

d. 14, 17

3-3 Part A Exercises
1. a. 4; 5; 6 **b.** Add 1 to each successive number of sides.
c.

3. 81, −243, 729 **5.** $\frac{5}{6}, \frac{6}{7}, \frac{7}{8}$
7. UV, TU, ST **9.** 17, 21, 41
11. J, J, A **15.** $1.04
17. 1, 4, 7, 10, 13
19. 3, 9, 19, 33, 51
21. 95, 191, 383
23. IX, XI, XIII
25. 52, −62, 72 **27.** 4, 2, 1
29. 24, 35, 48 **31.** T, S, E
33. −21, −33 **35.** 16, 19, 28
37. a. 4; 5; 6 **b.** $x - 1$

3-3 Part B Try It
a. $2n$; 40 **b.** $2n + 1$; 41
c. n^2; 400 **d.** $3n - 1$; 59

3-3 Part B Exercises
1. −1, 1, 3, 5, 7 **3.** 6, 7, 8, 9, 10 **5.** 1, 3, 5, 7, 9
7. 0, 3, 8, 15, 24 **9.** $5n$; 45
11. $\frac{1}{n}, \frac{1}{25}$ **15.** (b) **17.** 20
19. 7, 9, 11, 13, 15 **21.** 6, 12, 20, 30, 42 **23.** 3^{n-1}; 2187 **25.** $n^2 - 1$; 99
27. $4n - 9$; 39

3-3 Part C Self-Assessment
1. 7, 4, 5 **2.** 15, 16, 19
3. XIV, XV, XVI
4. EV, UF, GT
5. Bird; Fibonacci sequence
6. Pattern **7.** Term **8.** 14
9. b. Add 7^n for each additional item. **c.** $1 + 1 + 7 + 7^2 + 7^3 + 7^4 = 2802$
d. Possible answer: I was the only one going to St. Ives. I only met the others. **10.** 49
11. Let t be the thickness of the paper. **a.** $2t$ **b.** $4t$
c. $8t$ **d.** $16t$ **e.** $(2^n)t$
f. $(2^{50})t = (1.126 \times 10^{15})t$; Yes **12.** −1, 4, 19, 364, 132, 499 **13.** 1, 5, 9, 13, 17
14. −1, 1, 0, 1, 1

Chapter 3 Review
1. T **2.** F; Right **3.** F; Possible answer: Parallelogram **4.** Pentagon
5. Ordered list of numbers.
6. 3 **7.** (b) **8.** Yes, they are identical. **9.** No, their shapes are different.
10. Yes, they are identical.
11. a. Slide and turn
b. Slide and flip **c.** Slide
12. Translation; Reflection; Rotation **13. a.** Left 5; Up 2
b. $A'(-4, 0)$, $B'(-3, 7)$, $C'(-1, 4)$

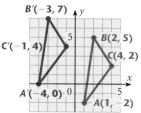

14. $M'(-3, 0)$
15. $T'(-7, -2)$
16. $P'(-4, 8)$
17.

18. (a) **19.** (c)
20. ≈ 53.3 **21.** $6x^2 - 2x - 4$ **22.** $-6x + 12$
23. 51, 66, 83 **24.** A, J, J
25. The pattern of squares is 1, 3, 5, ... while the pattern of circles is 1, 2, 3, ... □
26. $3n + 2$; 50 **27. a.** D
b. 225° counterclockwise
c. The center of the pendant
d. Yes; Yes

CHAPTER 4

4-1 Part A Try It
a. ≈ 87.92 in. **b.** 165 beats per minute

4-1 Part A Exercises
1. 24 ft² **3.** 24 m²
5. 26.325 ft² **7.** 165 miles
11. a. 240 **b.** 230 **c.** 80
d. Herta, Manny, Ricardo

13. 172,980,000,000 lb mi²/s² **15. a.** 30 units
b. −20 units **c.** −4 units
19.

A = area
r = radius

21. ≈ 199.49 cm
23. 42 ft² **25.** 468.6 cm³
27. a. $B = 96$ **b.** $R = 72$
c. $E = 24$ **d.** $A = 216$; Total surface area
29. a. C = the child's age; A = adult dose; M = child's dose **b.** 0.5 tablespoon
31. a. 26.25 ft **b.** 75 ft
c. No; The stopping distance depends on the square of the car's speed.

4-1 Part B Try It
a. $x = 4$
b. $\frac{1}{4}(400) - 1 = 99$
c. $t = 5$ **d.** $x = 1500$
e. $y = 100$ **f.** $x = 25$ ft

4-1 Part B Exercises
1. Yes **3.** (a)
5. Because $4 \times 100 = 400$, which is near 401; $x = 101$
7. A negative multiplied by a positive is negative; $x = -5$
9. $x = 13$ **10.** $y = 25$
13. $2y + 10 = 100$; $y = 45$
17. 20 lb per month
21. It tells us that the weight on each side is the same.
23. 300; $t = 100$ **25.** 10; $x = 11.4$ **27.** $6 \times 1 = 6$ is less than 10.2 while $6 \times 2 = 12$ is greater than 10.2; $x = 1.7$
29. $y = 1$ **31.** $s = -10$
33. $t = \frac{49}{4}$ **35.** $q = -0.2$
37. $5p = 107.50$ **39.** If it is true, then $A = B$. If the equation is false, $A \neq B$.

4-1 Part C Try It
a. $x = -3$ **b.** $-3x = 2 + x$

4-1 Part C Exercises
1. a. **b.**

c. None

3. $2x + 3 = -2x - 1, x = -1$
5. $2x = 0; x = 0$
7. $-6x + 3$ and $3(-2x + 1)$
11. $1 + x = 2x - 2; x = 3$

17.

19. $x + 3 = -3x - 1; x = -1$
21. $6x - 3$ and $3(2x - 1)$
23. $4x + 4$ and $4(x + 1)$

4-1 Part D
Self-Assessment
1. a. It gets more difficult to read. **b.** It gets easier to read. **c.** Possible answer:

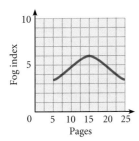

2. 16, 20 **3.** $3\frac{2}{3}, 4\frac{2}{3}, 5\frac{2}{3}$
4. $-2, -3, -4, -5$
5. $-1, -4, -9, -16, -25$
6. $5x + 13.5 = 100; x = 17.3$
7. $-3x + 20 = -22; x = 14$
8. a. The number of poles $= \frac{n}{10} + 1$ **b.** 13

9. a.

With Skate Rental	
k	P
10	41.67%
12	50%
14	58.33%
18	75%

b. $k = 24$
10. $3x - 3 = x + 7, x = 5$
11. a. $\frac{4}{3}\pi$ **b.** $1,679,616\pi$
c. 1,259,712 earths

12. a.

Without Skate Rental	
Hours	Cost
5	$9.50
6	$11.00
7	$12.50

b. $20 **c.** $2 **d.** $1.50 per hour **e.** Cost $= 2 + (h \times 1.5)$ where $h =$ number of hours.

f.

Without Skate Rental	
Hours	Cost
1	$1.50
2	$3.00
3	$4.50
4	$6.00

13. a. 2.2 years
b. Possible answer: It is relatively inexpensive but it is very dangerous.

14. a.

b.

c.

d.

e.

15. a. A is the surface area of the box (i.e., the amount of cardboard needed), and s stands for the length of a side of the box. **b.** 800 in.^{2}
c. $A = 6s^2$ **16.** (c)

4-2 Part A Try It
a. Yes; The objects on both sides have equal weights.
b. Yes **c.** No

4-2 Part A Exercises
1. a. Add 10 lb to the left.
b. Add 8 pears to the left.
c. Remove $\frac{2}{5}$ of the weight from the right. **d.** Remove 17.5 oz from the left.

3. $c + 2 = 28$ **5.** $4c - 5 = 41.8$ **6.** Remove two blocks from each side to get $c = 26$
8. Popping the balloon adds 5 to the scale's weight to give $4c = 46.8$. If we remove 3 cans that reduces the weight by $\frac{3}{4}$ leaving $c = 11.7$.
9. 0.6 lb **13.** Add $\frac{1}{3}$ of the total number of coins to the right side. **15.** Remove $\frac{2}{3}$ of the coins from the right side.
17. $3c + 3 = 102$
19. $2d - 7 = 53$
21. Remove five from both sides to get $4p = 120$. Remove 3 pencils from the right and $\frac{3}{4}$ of the weight from the left to get $p = 30$.
23. $x = 1000$ **25.** $y = 100$

4-2 Part B Try It
a. 1. Subtract 17.9; **2.** Subtract 6.34; **3.** Divide by 3.2
b. 1. $z = 137.5$; **2.** $x = 46$; **3.** $v = -50$ **c.** 190 ft

4-2 Part B Exercises
1. a. Add 73 to both sides
b. y is isolated **c.** Addition
3. (b) **5.** $x = 6.4$
7. $x = -11$ **9.** $h = 50$
11. $k = -1$ **13.** $y = 220\frac{1}{2}$
15. $t = 60$ **17.** $s = -11.3$
25. $t = 5.74; 5t + 49.3 = 78$
27. $x = 0.3$ **29.** $x = 7$
31. $t = 14$ **33.** $y = 2$
35. $y = 9$ **37.** $x = 1013$
39. $t = 100$ **41.** $k = 31$
43. $n = 100$ **45.** $x = 1800$
47. $x = 89.6$
49. $v = 180.3$ **51. a.** 1
b. 0 **c.** 0 **d.** 1
e. (b) and (c); (a) and (d)
53. Both pictures describe the equation $x - 237 = 48.6$.

4-2 Part C Try It
a. $\frac{1}{3}$ **b.** 1 **c.** 4 **d.** $\frac{7}{4}$
e. Multiply by $\frac{5}{2}$; $n = 2$
f. Multiply by $-\frac{5}{2}$; $n = -2$
g. Multiply by 9; $x = 2079$
h. Divide by 0.3; $n = 450$

4-2 Part C Exercises
1. a. Multiply by $\frac{1}{4}$.
b. Multiply by $\frac{5}{3}$.
c. Multiply by $-\frac{5}{3}$.
d. Multiply by 9.
e. Multiply or divide by 1.
3. $5; \frac{1}{5}; y = 86$ **5.** 1; 1; $w + 15 = 91$ **7.** $\frac{3}{8}; \frac{8}{3};$ $x = 40$ **9.** $\frac{1}{3}; 3; v = 300$
11. $x = 364$ **13.** $r = 65.6$
19. $\times \frac{1}{14}$ **21.** $\times \frac{1}{28}$
23. $\times 4$ **25.** $\times \frac{9}{5}$
27. $\frac{1}{3}; 3; x = 60$
29. $-\frac{1}{5}; -5; y = -35$
31. $200; \frac{1}{200}; t = 0.02$
33. $-\frac{1}{6}; -6; x = -6$
35. $3; \frac{1}{3}; y = \frac{2}{3}$
37. 1; 1; $w + 78.3 = 101$
39. $x = 18$ **41.** $t = 0$
43. $x = 20$ **45.** $x = -22$
47. 3572 cartons

4-2 Part D Try It
a. $m = 12$ **b.** $x = 60$
c. $t = 1$ **d.** $x = 6.5$
e. $k = \frac{35}{3}$ **f.** $a = 1.5333$
g. 13

4-2 Part D Exercises
1. Add 7.5 to both sides
3. $x = 25$ **5.** $h = 23$
7. $s = 16$ **9.** $x = -5$
11. $x = -102$ **13.** $5p + 22.5 = 88; p = 13.1$ lb
15. $7x + 2 = 44; x = 6$
17. $3m + 5 = 38; m = 11$
21. a. $x = 10$ **b.** $y = 15$
23. $-x$ **25.** $y - 2$
27. Octagon **29.** $t = 10$
31. $x = -7$ **33.** $x = 27$
35. $t = -5.2$
37. $4x - 7 = 13; x = 5$
39. $-6m + 17 = 5; m = 2$
41. $8y + 8 = 64; y = 7$
43. $2.5 + 2(d - 1) = 30.5;$ $d = 15$ days **45.** 6, 6, 7, 8, 9
47. $x = 11\frac{1}{3}$ ft

4-2 Part E
Self-Assessment
1. 2.76 **2.** 0 **3.** 3 **4.** $\frac{13}{3}$
5. a. Possible answer: In order to find a value for x so that $5x - 10 = 20$.

b. Add 10 to both sides.
c. $5x = 30$ **d.** Divide both sides by 5. **e.** $x = 6$
7. $x = 15$ **8.** $w = 75$
9. $t = 100$ **10.** $x = 23$
11. $r = -35$ **12.** $d = \frac{500}{3}$
13. $q = \frac{26}{3}$ **14.** No solution
15. a. $491 **b.** $4000 = s -$ 1865 **c.** $5865 = s$ **d.** No
16. a. $A = 52$
b. $21.15\% = P$ **c.** 29.26
d. It would go lower.
17. Possible answer: Kevin has $1.05 in quarters and nickels. He has only one quarter. How many nickels does he have? **18.** Possible answer: At the end of the day, Vanessa has $8. She put $\frac{1}{3}$ of her money in the bank and then spent $10. How much money did she start the day with? **19.** Both modeled the equation $4s = 6.8$.
20. Possible answer: A number multiplied by a sum of numbers equals the sum of the products of the first number times each of the other numbers. **21.** About $0.31
22. Put the 50-g weight on the left side and the 20-g weight on the right side. Add clay to the right side until the scale is balanced. If $x =$ the weight of the clay we added, then we must have $50 = x + 20$ because the scale is balanced; $30 = x$ is obtained by subtracting 20 from both sides. Now, using the scale without the weight we divide the clay of 30-g weight into clumps of equal 15-g weight, putting the clay on each side of the scale until the scale balances.

Chapter 4 Review
1. (a) **2.** (e) **3.** 44
4. 65.94 **5.** Because $4 \times 25 = 100$ **6.** Because $\frac{1}{3}(30) = 10$ is less than 10.5
7. $t = 50$ **8.** $d = 0.35$
9. $y = 11$ **10.** (d)

11.

12. $2x = 4$; $x = 2$
13. $-7x = 3x + 10$; $x = -1$
14. $-2x + 4 = 3x - 1$; $x = 1$ **15.** $3x - 6 = -x + 2$; $x = 2$ **16.** If $e =$ weight of one egg, then $5e = 1$, $e = \frac{1}{5}$, (divide both sides by 5). One egg weighs $\frac{1}{5}$lb. **17.** If $p =$ weight of one pencil, then $12p + 12p = 50 + 50 + 50$, $24p = 150$ (simplify), $p = 6.25$ g (divide both sides by 24). One pencil weighs 6.25 grams. **18.** If $m =$ weight of one muffin, then $8m = 1 + 1$, $8m = 2$ (simplify), $m = \frac{1}{4}$ (divide both sides by 8). One muffin weighs $\frac{1}{4}$lb.

19. Possible answer:
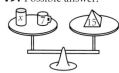

20. $\frac{1}{6}$ **21.** $\frac{7}{4}$ **22.** $-\frac{1}{3}$
23. -4 **24.** $s = \frac{100}{3}$
25. $d = 140$ **26.** $d = 82$
27. a. x **b.** -3
28. $x = 2$ **29.** $s = -18$
30. $t = -25$
31. Possible answer: Devan is 2 years more than 3 times as old as Gail. If Devan is 17, how old is Gail?
32. a. $s + 5 + s + s + 4 = p$ **b.** $s + 5 + s + s + 4 = 45$ **c.** $s = 12$ **d.** The new perimeter would be 81.
e. The new perimeter would be 27. **33.** If $x =$ cost of a six-pack, then $2x = 2.04$, so $x = 1.02$ by dividing both sides by 2. **34.** $0.36
35. Use the cost of one six-pack. Divide by 6 to get the cost of one can, and subtract the 3-cent refund.
36. $12y = 2.04 - 0.36$

CHAPTER 5

5-1 Part A Try It
a.
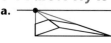

5-1 Part A Exercises
1. 6 **3.** Isometric projection **5. a.** iv, E **b.** vi, B **c.** i, C **d.** iii, D **e.** ii, A

7.
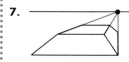

9. 4 vertices, 6 edges, 4 faces
13. 21 **15.** 18 **17.** -10
21. 6 vertices, 9 edges, 5 faces **22.** 8 vertices, 12 edges, 6 faces **23.** 6 vertices, 12 edges, 8 faces

5-1 Part B Try It
a. 28 units; 26 square units
b. 28 units; 34 square units
c. 20 cm^2 **d.** ≈ 70 cm^2

5-1 Part B Exercises
1. a. Two of the sides are 2 units long. The other two sides are 10 units long.
b. 24 units **c.** 20 **d.** 20 square units **2.** Perimeter: 38 units; Area: 25 square units **5.** Perimeter: 10 m; Area: 6 m^2

7. Possible answer:
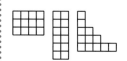

9. 9 **11.** Perimeter: 42 ft; Area: 62 ft^2 **14. a.** Possible answer: Georgia: ≈ 1000 mi; Ohio: ≈ 850 mi **b.** Possible answer: Georgia: $\approx 59,000$ mi^2; Ohio: $\approx 41,000$ mi^2 **c.** Georgia is larger than Ohio. **15.** 32 m^2
17. $259 **19.** 9
21. $-3, -28, -53$ **23.** 3
25. 50 units; 55 square units
27. 48 units; 34 square units
28. Circumference
29. 16 in.; 16 in.^{2}

---

31. 11 km; 6 km^2
33. 36 m^2 **35. a.** ≈ 29 cm
b. ≈ 37 cm^2
37. 36.6 yd; 45.9 yd^2
39. $\approx \frac{1}{16}$ mi^2
41. 40 units
43. About 1.15 in.

5-1 Part C Try It
a. Area; Square units
b. Length; Linear units
c. Volume; Cubic units
d. Area; Square units
e. 30 ft^3

5-1 Part C Exercises
1. Volume **3.** 6 cubic units
5. 24 cubic units **7. a.** 24 cubic units **b.** 27 cubic units **c.** 12 cubic units
d. 36 cubic units
9. Volume; Cubic units
11. Volume; Cubic units
13. Volume; Cubic units
14. 64 cubic units **21.** 33 square units **23.** 128 cubic units **25.** Cubic
27. Square **29.** Square
31. 27 cubic units **33.** 40 cubic units **35.** 36 cubic units **37. b.** No **39.** 12 cubic units

5-1 Part D Self-Assessment
1. (c) **2.** One-point perspective **3.** 26, 37, 50
4. (c) **5.** 18 square units; 18 units **6. a.** 7.6 cm **b.** 3 in.

7.

8. 63 mi/hr **9.** 4 in.; 1 in.^{2}
10. 34 units; 18 square units
11. 60 ft; 216 ft^2

12. a.
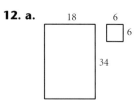

b. 18
c. $x \times 6 \times 6 = 18 \times 34$
d. 17

e. Yes; 17 sprinklers would cover the necessary square footage, but not in the shape of Monica's yard.

13. Possible answer: 56 yd^2

14. Possible answer: 60 m^2

15. a. 15 **b.** 15 **c.** 15 **d.** 15

16.

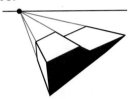

17. a. Linear **b.** Cubic **c.** Square **18.** 2 cubic units

19. 24 cubic units

20. 30 cubic units

5-2 Part A Try It

a.

b.

c.

d. 2 in.^{2} **e.** 24 in.^{2} **f.** 21 in.^{2}

5-2 Part A Exercises

1. Match: $A = \frac{1}{2}(b_1 + b_2)h$, trapezoid; $A = bh$, parallelogram; $A = \frac{1}{2}bh$, triangle.

2. 2 in.^{2} **3.** 50 in.^{2} **4.** 28 in.^{2} **5.** 12 cm; 6 cm^2

7. 6.45 cm^2 **11.** 7.8 cm^2

13. a. 8.75 ft^2 **b.** 12 ft; To help decide the amount of framing material needed

c. 12 ft^2 **17.** 28 in.; 40 in.^{2}

19. $\frac{10}{3}$ **21.** (2, 5)

23. Trapezoid **25.** Triangle

27. 180 cm^2 **29.** 9.62 cm^2

31. 6.84 cm^2 **33.** 6.3 cm^2

---

35. 400 ft^2 **37.** 5.8 cm^2

39. 29,700 mi^2 **41.** 1.72 in.^{2}

5-2 Part B Try It

a. Front Top Right

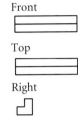

b. Front

Top

Right

c. 15.7 cm

d. about 30.6 cm^2

e. 72 in.^{2}

5-2 Part B Exercises

1. a. 12

b.

c.

d.

e.

3. Front Top Right

5. 7.85 cm.; 4.91 cm^2

7.

9. 7960 miles **10.** (b)

11.

13. a. 324 ft^2 **b.** 295.7 ft^2

19. 2.35 ft^2 **21.** 6 cubic inches

23. Front Top Right

25.

Front Top Right

---

27. 28.27 mi^2 **29.** 94.2 m

31. 7,050,000,000 square miles

5-2 Part C Self-Assessment

1. 250 in.^{2} **2.** 72 in.^{2}

3. 175 in.^{2} **4. a.** (b)

b. (c) **5.** (b) **6.** (c)

7. (c)

8. a. Possible answer:

b. $x^2 + 2x = A$ **c.** $4x + 4 = P$

9. 36 in.; 60 in.^{2} **10.** 48 m; 96 m^2 **11.** 56.5 cm; 254 cm^2 **12.** 64 in.; 222 in.^{2}

13. 6 **14.** -17 **15.** 15

16. $\frac{3}{4}$ **17.** $\frac{22}{5}$ **18.** $-\frac{4}{5}$

19. The 9-in. square pan comes closest, so that pan is most likely to give results similar to the round pan.

20. Front Top Right

21. a. 2918.4 ft^2

b. $315 **22. a.** 24 ft

b. 19 ft **c.** 456 ft^2

d. 156 ft^2 **e.** 86 ft

23. a. 14.215 ft^2

b. Possible answer: $4\frac{1}{2}$ ft^2

24. The station's claim is a bit of an exaggeration.

25. a. Yes; By measuring the distance across the rounded figure in different places.

b. They are the same size. This is found by measuring both circles.

5-3 Part A Try It

a. Possible answer:

376 cm^2

5-3 Part A Exercises

1. a. There are four rectangles and two squares.

Possible answers:

b. 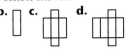 **c.** **d.**

3. (a)

5. Possible answer:

190 in.^{2}

7. Possible answer:

2036 cm^2

9. 118 cm^2

11. Possible answer:

13. 255 in.^{2} **15.** 3

17. Cylinder

19. One answer:

32.6 m^2

21. Possible answer:

880 in.^{2}

23.

25. No net can be drawn for a sphere using pieces that are all the same size and shape.

5-3 Part B Try It

a. 2160 in.^{3} **b.** 2400 cm^3

5-3 Part B Exercises

1. a.

b. 160 in.^{3} **3.** 4.5 in.^{3}
5. 0.7 in.^{3} **7.** $12\frac{1}{2}$ in.^{3}
10. 27 ft^2 **11. a.** 1080 in.^{3}
b. 4.68 gallons **17.** $d = 55t$
19. 3960 cm^3 **21.** 4340 in.^{3}
23. 1671.2 cm^2
25. 1761.25 in.^{2}
27. $\approx$ 27 liters
29. a. 24,000 ft^3
b. 179,532 gallons

5-3 Part C Try It
a. $\approx$ 31.8 in.^{3}

5-3 Part C Exercises
1. Cone: $\frac{1}{3}Bh$/Volume, $\pi r\ell + \pi r^2$/Surface Area; Prism: Bh/Volume; Pyramid: $\frac{1}{3}Bh$/Volume
3. 160.8 ft^2; 120 ft^3
5. 256 in.^{2}; 240 in.^{3}
8. 1.6 ft^3 **9. a.** 22.9 in.^{3}
b. Less **11.** 2,311,875 m^3
13. 6900 m^3 **15. a.** Cylinder
b. $8\pi \approx$ 25.12 in.^{2}; $3\pi \approx$ 9.42 in.^{3} **17.** 10 cm^2
19. 41.69 **21.** 24 cm^3
23. 8 cm^3 **25.** $300\pi \approx$ 942 in.^{3} **27.** $4.32\pi \approx$ 13.6 in.^{3} **29.** $54\pi \approx$ 169.6 in.^{2}; $54\pi \approx$ 169.6 in.^{3}
30. $600\pi \approx$ 1885 in.^{2}
31. 69.35 in.^{3}
33. The volumes are the same: $\frac{1}{3}(20)(3) = 20$ cm^3
35. The short cone is larger in capacity than the tall cone.
37. Possible answer:

39. 215.69 cm^3

5-3 Part D Self-Assessment
1. Possible answer:

2. a. 30 cm^3 **b.** 62 cm^2
3. (d) **4.** $1088\pi \approx$ 3418 cm^2; $4608\pi \approx$ 14,476.5 cm^3
5. $360\pi \approx$ 1131 in.^{2}; $800\pi \approx$ 2513 in.^{3} **6.** 40.7 gallons

7. St. Paul's Cathedral is 190,000 m^3 ÷ 105 m^3 = 1810 times as large as the living room. **8. a.** Cubic meters
b. Square meters **c.** Meters
9. a. Possible answer:

b. Enough to cover 56 ft^2. You wouldn't paint the bottom. **10. a.** The volume is doubled **b.** The surface area is increased, but not doubled. **11. a.** 141.4 ft by 141.4 ft **b.** It will increase by 100,000 ft^3 **c.** $123.75 more **12.** 21.5%
13. 2396 m^2 **14. a.** Possible answer: First add 5.1 to both sides of the equation. Then multiply both sides of the equation by $\left(\frac{1}{3.2}\right)$.
b. $x = 4.8125$ **15.** Possible answer: (3, 0), (−3, 0), (0, 3), (0, −3) **16. a.** 4800 ft^2
b. 2040 ft^2 **c.** No **17.** (d)
18. 29.48, 8447.79, 0.25, 4.67, 100.00
19. Possible answer:
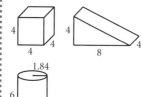
20. 340.8 yd x 340.8 yd; 1022.5 ft x 1022.5 ft

Chapter 5 Review
1. Height **2.** One-point perspective **3.** Edge
4. Linear **5. a.** 42 in.
b. 108 in.^{2}
6.
7.
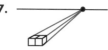
8. Front Top Right

9. 6.075 in.^{2} **10.** 1.8 in.
11. 89.5° **12.** 48.6 cm; 138.78 cm^2 **13. a.** 7 in.
b. 43.96 in. **14. a.** $a^2 + a - 3$ **b.** $3a^2 + 9a - 6$
15. 115.73 mm^2 **16. a.** Possible answer:

b. 94 in.^{2} **c.** 60 in.^{3}
17. a. 5 **b.** 9 **c.** 6
d. Possible answer:
18. −39, 43, −47
19. 81, 64, 49 **20.** 40 in.^{3}
21. a. 48.7 cm^2 **b.** 9.5 cm^3
22. a. 24 mm^2 **b.** Small-grained soils, since for a given volume small-grained soils will have more surface area.

CHAPTER 6

6-1 Part A Try It
a. 40%

6-1 Part A Exercises
1. $\frac{1}{10} = 10\%$ **3.** $\frac{6.5}{250} = 2.6\%$
5.

4	8	12	20
30	60	90	150

7. a. $\frac{2}{3}$ **b.** $\frac{1}{3}$ **c.** $\frac{1}{2}$ **d.** $\frac{2}{1}$
13. 0.40 **15.** 80%
17. 33.3% **19.** $\frac{1}{5}$; One out of five visitors to the White House has been there before.
23. 7 **25.** −17 **27.** 3
29. 54 units^2

31.

8	12	16	20	24	80
10	15	20	25	30	100

33. $\frac{1}{5}$ **35.** $\frac{1}{2}$ **37.** $\frac{1}{1}$
39. $\frac{3}{8}, \frac{3}{5}$ **41.** $\frac{1}{4}, \frac{1}{3}$
43. 0.20 **45.** 0.60
47. 5% **49.** 20% **51.** $\frac{10}{25} = 0.4 = 40\%$ **53.** $\frac{8}{24} = 0.333... \approx 33.3\%$ **55.** Yes, it is; $\frac{3.5}{10} = 0.35 = 35\%$

6-1 Part B Try It
a. $\frac{20}{60} > \frac{15}{50}$;
$\frac{20}{60} = \frac{1}{3} = 0.33... \approx 33\%$;
$\frac{15}{50} = \frac{3}{10} = 0.3 = 30\%$;
$33\% > 30\%$ **b.** $\frac{25}{30} > \frac{20}{25}$;
$\frac{25}{30} = \frac{5}{6} = 0.8333... \approx 83\%$;
$\frac{20}{25} = \frac{4}{5} = 0.8 = 80\%$;
$83\% > 80\%$ **c.** about $\frac{1}{20}$
d. $\frac{6.5}{151}, \frac{151}{6.5}$; The Statue of Liberty is over 23 times as tall as Cindy.

6-1 Part B Exercises
1. (c) **3.** 9 **5.** $\frac{300}{4} > \frac{1000}{15}$;
$\frac{300}{4} = 75$; $\frac{1000}{15} = 66.666...$;
$75 > 66.666...$ **7.** $\frac{5}{55} > \frac{2}{24}$;
$\frac{5}{55} = \frac{1}{11}; \frac{2}{24} = \frac{1}{12}; \frac{1}{11} > \frac{1}{12}$
9. a. $\frac{2}{8}$ **b.** $\frac{8}{2}$ **c.** $\frac{6}{16}$
d. $\frac{2}{16}$ **11.** $\frac{2}{3}; \frac{3}{2}$
13. a. 25π m^2 **b.** 100π m^2 **c.** $\frac{4}{1}$ **15.** Bar graph; A circle graph would imply that the monuments were parts of a whole. **17.** 365 **19.** 36
21. 9 **23.** 10 **25.** 137.5
27. $\frac{67}{183} > \frac{17}{57}$, since 0.366 > 0.298 **29.** $\frac{1.69}{25.95} > \frac{4.03}{64.50}$, since 0.065 > 0.062
31. a. $\frac{1}{21}$ **b.** $\frac{21}{1}$
33. Beetles/day: yellow, 47.2; white 15.7; green, 31.5; blue, 14.8 **35.** $\frac{170,756}{101,572}, \frac{101,572}{170,756}$
37. $\frac{1040}{1} = \frac{\text{circumference}}{24}$, circumference = 24,960 mi

6-1 Part C Try It
a. About 4 cents
b. 0.067 cm per minute

6-1 Part C Exercises
1. a. $\frac{20 \text{ miles}}{5 \text{ hours}}$ **b.** $\frac{4 \text{ miles}}{1 \text{ hour}}$
c. 4 miles per hour
3. 1.5 quarts per tablespoon
5. 1.67 calculators per student
7. 1 **9.** 10 **11.** 128.6
13. $\frac{4 \text{ quarts}}{1 \text{ gallon}} \cdot \frac{2 \text{ pints}}{1 \text{ quart}} \cdot \frac{2 \text{ cups}}{1 \text{ pint}} = \frac{16 \text{ cups}}{1 \text{ gallon}}$ **15. a.** $\frac{5 \text{ toes}}{1 \text{ foot}}$
$\frac{10 \text{ toes}}{1 \text{ person}}, \frac{0.5 \text{ person}}{1 \text{ foot}}, \frac{0.1 \text{ person}}{1 \text{ toe}}$
b. 170; 850 **17.** $\frac{51.627 \text{ miles}}{1 \text{ gallon}}$

19. a. 0.04 sec/ft
b. 25 ft/sec **23.** 83.92 in.²
25. The nth term is $3n$; 60
27. Not equal **29.** 500
31. $\frac{1 \text{ hour}}{60 \text{ minutes}}$; 0.05 gallon
33. 504 **35. a.** 1,037,446
b. Not very useful
37. a. 5,601.4 dollars per
person **b.** 3,816,769,863
dollars per day

6-1 Part D Try It
a. $\frac{16}{10} = \frac{6}{1}$; F **b.** $\frac{40}{25} = \frac{8}{5}$; T
c. 16 **d.** 12 **e.** 35
f. 550 ft

6-1 Part D Exercises
1. $\frac{4}{10} = \frac{40}{100}$; T **3.** $\frac{60}{60} = \frac{15}{15}$;
T **5.** 1.5 **7.** 200 **9.** 6
11. 6 **13. a.** 20 quarts
b. 5 quarts **c.** 2.5 quarts
d. 15 quarts **21.** $\frac{1}{5}$
23. $\frac{1}{2}$ **25.** 16 in.²
27. a. T **b.** F **c.** F
29. $\frac{3}{4}$ **31.** 200 **33.** 6
37. a. 4.5 in. **b.** 16 months
39. a. 8 times as strong
b. 1.728 times as strong
41. b. $\frac{1}{47}$ square mile per
person.

6-1 Part E Self-Assessment
1. $\frac{6 \text{ min T.V.}}{1 \text{ min homework}}$
2. $\frac{0.43 \text{ computer}}{1 \text{ student}}$
3. $\frac{\$700,000}{1 \text{ mile}}$ **4.** $\frac{78 \text{ gallons}}{1 \text{ day}}$
5. 16 **6. a.** $\frac{\$0.06}{1 \text{ mile}}$, $\frac{\$0.09}{1 \text{ mile}}$,
$\frac{\$0.10}{1 \text{ mile}}$, $\frac{\$0.14}{1 \text{ mile}}$
b. Possible answer: Travelers;
To compare the cost of
traveling by air with other
ways to travel. **c.** In 1993, it
cost 8 cents per mile more to
travel to Los Angeles than to
Phoenix. **7.** Possible
answer: Find out how many
raisins are in one ounce. Use
this information to convert
$\frac{12 \text{ ounces}}{5 \text{ doz cookies}}$ into $\frac{\text{raisins}}{\text{cookie}}$.
8. 4.67 speeches per day
9. 0.094 love note per day;
Yes; It describes the rate at
which they wrote love notes

to each other. **10.** 50.8
miles per hour **11.** $x = 7.5$
12. No; Only the number of
women surveyed can be
found from this information.
There is not enough information to find the number of
men surveyed.
13. 14 and 16; She should
have compared the number
who selected dogs to the total
(30), not the number who
selected dogs to the number
who selected cats.
14. a. $\$100 \times \frac{1 \text{ pound}}{\$1.48} =$
67.57 pounds **b.** 100
pounds $\times \frac{\$1.48}{1 \text{ pound}} = \$148$

15. a.

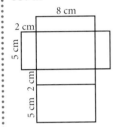

b. 40 cm² **c.** 80 cm³
d. $\frac{1 \text{ cm}^2}{2 \text{ cm}^3}$ **16. a.** 16,800 lb
b. 0.53 **c.** 2.4 **d.** 12%
e. 116,200 lb

6-2 Part A Try It
a. 43° **b.** 135° **c.** 90°
d. 65°

6-2 Part A Exercises
1. a. 55° **b.** 20° **3.** 32°
5. (a) **7.** 30° **9.** 45°
12. 65° **13.** 75°; 75°
15. 140° **17.** 155°
19. 115° **21.** 102°
23. 17° **25.** 80°
27. 85 liked; 80 disliked;
15 no opinion
29. $m\angle d = 50°$; $m\angle b = 50°$;
$m\angle c = 130°$; Vertical angles
are congruent.

6-2 Part B Try It
a. $m\angle A = m\angle D$; $m\angle B =$
$m\angle E$; $m\angle C = m\angle F$;
$\frac{AB}{DE} = \frac{BC}{EF} = \frac{AC}{DF}$; Therefore,
$\triangle ABC \sim \triangle DEF$ **b.** 26

6-2 Part B Exercises
1. a. Y **b.** $\overline{YZ}$
3. Protractor **4.** Similar
5. Measure **6.** Angles
7. The same or equal
9. Not similar **11.** 14
15. The larger triangle has
four times the area of the
smaller. **19.** 0.5 **21.** 20
23. 150 mi **25. a.** E
b. $\overline{CD}$ **27.** The corresponding angles are congru-
ent and corresponding sides
have the same ratio of $\frac{5}{12}$.
31. a. $\angle LJK$ and $\angle MNK$ are
right angles **c.** All corresponding angles in $\triangle LJK$ and
$\triangle MNK$ are congruent and
have the same ratio of $\frac{3}{1}$.
d. 16 ft 6 in. **33.** Similar
35. $x = 14$; $y = 12.5$
37. No. **39. b.** Possible
answer: Making clothing patterns; The different sizes of a
clothing design are similar to
one another.

6-2 Part C Try It
a. $\frac{4}{5}$ **b.** $\frac{2}{5}$

6-2 Part C Exercises
1. a. $\frac{24}{16}$ **b.** $\frac{18}{12}$ **c.** $\frac{36}{x}$
d. $\frac{3}{2}$ **e.** 24 **2.** $\frac{3}{4}$ **5.** 1 ft
7. 4 cm **11.** The second
volume is eight times the
first.
13. $\frac{1}{3}$, $\frac{1}{2}$, $\frac{3}{4}$, $\frac{7}{6}$, $\frac{5}{2}$, 4
15. Possible answer:
$\frac{1 \text{ inch}}{2000 \text{ feet}} = 1{:}24{,}000$;
This would enable you to
make your drawing on a
regular sized piece of paper.
17. Possible answer: 20:1.
This scale factor would allow
the drawing to fit on an 8.5 in.
by 11 in. piece of drawing
paper. **21.** is less than
23. is greater than
25. is equal to
27. Possible answer:

29. 6 **31.** 7 **33.** 7:2
35. 30 cm **37.** 24 ft
39. a. 1:12 **b.** 12:1

41. a. 1:25.86 **b.** 18.63 ft

6-2 Part D Try It
a. 15 **b.** 12 in.

6-2 Part D Exercises
1. (b) **3.** Not a right triangle
5. ≈ 6.4 **7.** 24
9. 150 ft **11.** $x = 24$;
$y = 30$ **13.** 16 ft
15. a. 0.375 km per min
b. 94 words per min
c. 5.5 miles per hour
17. 72π in.² **19.** Is a right
triangle **21.** Is a right triangle **23.** 5.83 **25.** 21.19
27. 3.5 **29.** (b) **31. a.** 2
b. 1.73 **33. a.** all 90°
b. all 10 **35.** 30 m

6-2 Part E Self-Assessment
1. 170° **2.** 27° **3.** 85°
4. Draw each line of the original drawing twice as long but
keep all the angles the same.
5. It is $\frac{1}{3}$ the size of the
original. **6.** (b) **7.** 60 ft
8. 10 **9.** 8 **10.** Not a
right triangle, since $6^2 +$
$10^2 = 136 \neq 144 = 12^2$
11. a. $(-4, 2.5)$
b. $(-2.5, 4)$ **c.** $(2.5, 4)$
d. $(4, -2.5)$ **12. a.** 3:2
b. 2:3 **13.** 46 m; 80 m²
14. a. 60° **b.** 23.38 in.
c. 81 in.; 315.67 in.²
15. Mexican nutmeg = 21 oz;
Portuguese nutmeg = 14 oz
16. a. Possible answer: 1 in.
= 20 ft; This is an easy scale
and makes the house a reasonable size. **b.** 60 by 32.5.
18. 20 ft **19.** All the corresponding angles are congru-
ent and all the corresponding
sides have the same ratio.
20. Split the octagon up into
triangles by drawing lines
from one vertex to the other
vertices. Count the number
of triangles and multiply by
180°. The result is the sum of
the angles of the octagon; If
the octagon is regular, divide
the sum of the angles by 8 to
find the measure of each
angle of the octagon; A stop
sign

21. The billboard is 8 ft by 18 ft; 24:1

6-3 Part A Try It
a. 0.7314 **b.** 5.1446
c. 0.1736 **d.** 0.7; 0.7002

6-3 Part A Exercises
1. a. 0.6018 **b.** 0.7986
c. 0.7536 **d.** 0.9962
e. 0.0872 **f.** 11.4301
3. $\frac{24}{7} \approx 3.4286$ **5.** (c)
9. 757.9 mi **11.** 68.7 ft
13. 1.06 mi **15.** A rectangle; The length of the label is the can's circumference.
17. 26.70 cm **19.** (a)
21. $\frac{9}{40}$ **23. a.** $\frac{40}{9}$ **b.** $\frac{9}{40}$
25. a. 7.07 **b.** $\frac{1}{1}; \frac{1}{1}$ **c.** 1
27. Possible answer: The tangents of their corresponding angles are the same.
29. 0.3057, 17; It finds the angle measure from the tangent ratio.

6-3 Part B Try It
a. 6.4279 **b.** 43.0337

6-3 Part B Exercises
1. a. $\frac{4}{5}$ **b.** $\frac{3}{5}$ **c.** $\frac{4}{3}$ **d.** $\frac{3}{5}$
e. $\frac{4}{5}$ **f.** $\frac{3}{4}$ **3.** 3
5. 0.4686 **7.** 449.02
9. 27.3512 **11.** 138.5641
13. 70.6 ft **16.** (b)
17. 1.4 **19.** 10 **21.** −32
23. 18 **25. a.** $\frac{5}{12}$ **b.** $\frac{12}{13}$
c. $\frac{5}{13}$ **27.** 6 **29.** $\frac{192}{5}$
31. 33.1785 **33.** 24.2574
35. 136.4 **37.** 3.2361
39. $x = 50$ ft, $y = 70.71$ ft

6-3 Part C Self-Assessment
1. 261.08 **2.** 2.6496
3. 65.15 **4.** Adjacent leg; Hypotenuse **5.** 384.74 ft
6. 39.6 in.; Possible answer: No; The slope is too steep and could be hard to push a wheelchair up. **7.** 31,509 ft
8. Possible answer: Use the tan function and her horizontal distance from the totem pole to find the distance from

her eye level to the top. Then add her height to obtain the total height of the totem pole.
9. Weight per clip = (weight of dish with paper clips − weight of dish) ÷ 50
10. 80 ft **11. a.** 24.6 ft
b. The angle, the height of the observer's eyes above the ground. **12.** Possible answer: Use tan $m°$ and solve for the side opposite $\angle B$.
13. 4.71 ft per sec
14. 8148 miles **15.** Possible answer: 14.3 inches
16. a. 12 ft **b.** 15 yards
17. 47.3 ft; 86.6 ft^2
18. Attempt to keep the pool heated to about 80.5°. The largest number of people will be satisfied, and it will balance the number of people who say it is too hot or cold.

Chapter 6 Review
1. Proportion **2.** 90
3. Opposite **4.** Angles
5. Hypotenuse
6. $\frac{3}{4} = 0.75 = 75\%$
7. $\frac{5}{20} = 0.25 = 25\%$
8. 2.24 **9.** −7 **10.** 92
11. 8.75 cm^2 **12.** (a)
13. 20.17 **14.** 2.5 in.
15. Possible answer:

For a right triangle, the length of the hypotenuse squared equals the sum of the squares of the lengths of the two legs. In the figure, $c^2 = a^2 + b^2$. In this case $a = 5$ and $b = 12$. Thus, $c^2 = 5^2 + 12^2$, $25 + 144 = 169$, $c = \sqrt{169}$ or 13
16. a. Yes; By inspection, we can see which vertices correspond. $\triangle CAB \sim \triangle TRS$. Then $m\angle T = m\angle C = 27°$, $m\angle B = m\angle S = 70°$, and $m\angle A = m\angle R = 83°$.
b. Yes; Since all sides have the same ratio, namely $\frac{3}{6} = \frac{1}{2}$, $TR = \frac{1}{2} \times 10 = 5$ in.

c. We could find the lengths of all three sides. **17.** 19
18. $\sin B = \frac{x}{y}$; $\cos B = \frac{w}{y}$; $\tan B = \frac{x}{w}$
19. $\sin S = \frac{3.5}{8.7} \approx 0.40$, $\cos S = \frac{8}{8.7} \approx 0.92$
$\tan S = \frac{3.5}{8}$ **20.** For example: $\frac{3 \text{ miles}}{10 \text{ minutes}} \cdot \frac{60 \text{ minutes}}{1 \text{ hour}} = \frac{180 \text{ miles}}{10 \text{ hours}} = \frac{18 \text{ miles}}{1 \text{ hour}} = 18\text{mi/hr}$.
21. a. $\frac{4}{6}; \frac{3}{6}$ **b.** $\frac{4}{6}$; Since both ratios have the same denominator the one with the larger numerator will be greater. **c.** 72 ft^3; 108 ft^2
22. 300 words **23.** Possible answer: Converting all data to minutes per mile, we find that Darwin, Nicole, Mike and Miranda run 6-, 8-, 5- and 12-minute miles, respectively. The rates are all reasonable, although Miranda may be able to run a bit faster than she thinks, and Mike should be on the track team. **24.** Use the tangent function; The length of a line segment TP along one road and the measure of $\angle m$ between $\overline{TP}$ and $\overline{TS}$ where point S is on the other road and $\overline{SP}$ is perpendicular to $\overline{TP}$; Stand with a transit at point P and locate point S on the opposite road. Mark off the distance $\overline{TP}$ past the transit at point T and measure $\angle m$.

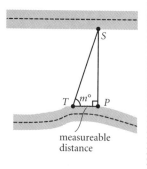

measureable distance

CHAPTER 7

7-1 Part A Try It
a. Would be 14 points, but the player wins immediately

7-1 Part A Exercises
1. Jump over the lamb and end up at the bottom.
3. Move the tiger to the bottom. **5.** $\frac{5 \text{ pieces}}{11 \text{ positions}}$
9. 23 **11.** 15 **13.** One of each face **19.** 20
21. 3600 **23.** Area of $\triangle CBD = 145.6$; Area of $\triangle ABD = 78$; Area of trapezoid $ABCD = 223.6$; $145.6 + 78 = 223.6$ **25.** 15
27. 11 **29.** 2 dogs and 2 vulcans; a prince, 2 vulcans, and a dog **31.** 9; 116
33. (b) **35. a.** $\frac{1 \text{ fox}}{13 \text{ geese}}$; $\frac{14 \text{ pieces}}{33 \text{ positions}}$
b. 4; 7 **39. a.** All games will end in a draw.

7-1 Part B Try It
a. No **b.** 50% **c.** 0%; No cat has lived past 40.
d. 100%; Almost all English words contain a vowel.

7-1 Part B Exercises
1. a. iii **b.** ii **c.** i
3. 65% **4.** Close to 0; Holidays are usually vacation days. **5.** Close to 0; Louisiana is very warm in July. **6.** Either 0 or 1
7. Close to 50% if applicable; Some grades will be good while others will not.
9. a. 61 **b.** $\frac{3}{61}$ **13.** $\frac{1}{3}$
15. 0.65 **17. a.** 62.5%; 0.625 **b.** 44%; 0.44
c. 44.4%; $0.\overline{4}$ **d.** 36.2%; 0.362 **19.** 1 **21.** 0.5
23. 0.5 **25.** Close to 1; School usually dismisses students before 4:00 p.m.
27. Close to 1; Tuesday always follows Monday.
29. a. 0.72; 0.28 **b.** Age 56–65 **c.** It decreases through age 65. **31.** The chance that it will rain is more than that it will not rain. **33. a.** 0.68 **b.** 0.83

7-1 Part C Try It
a. $\frac{1}{2}$ **b.** $\frac{3}{4}$ **c.** 6 **d.** $\frac{1}{6}$
e. $\frac{5}{6}$ **f.** $\frac{200}{750} \approx 0.267$
g. $\frac{600}{750} = 0.8$

7-1 Part C Exercises

1. a. $\frac{1}{6}$ **b.** 2, 4, 6 **c.** $\frac{1}{2}$
3. a. $\frac{1}{5}$ **b.** $\frac{3}{5}$ **c.** $\frac{2}{5}$ **d.** $\frac{3}{5}$
e. 4 **f.** 5; $\frac{1}{5}(25) = 5$
7. a. 1st band = 1, 2nd band = 3, 3rd band = 5, 4th band = 7 **b.** 1st band = $\frac{1}{16}$, 2nd band = $\frac{3}{16}$, 3rd band = $\frac{5}{16}$, 4th band = $\frac{7}{16}$
c. They should add to 1. This helps confirm the answers.
9. a. $\frac{1}{2}$ **b.** $\frac{1}{4}$ **c.** $\frac{1}{8}$ **d.** 1
11. $\frac{1}{4}$; $\frac{3}{16}$ **13.** Dark
15. 1, 2, 3, 4, 5, 6 **17. a.** $\frac{1}{4}$
b. $\frac{1}{4}$ **c.** 1 **d.** $\frac{5}{8}$ **e.** $\frac{7}{8}$
f. 0 **19.** $\frac{5}{7}$ **21. a.** 2, 3, 4, 5, 6, 7, 8, 9, 10, 11, 12; 11
b. No **c.** green 1 + red 1; green 6 + red 6
d. green 1 + red 6; green 6 + red 1; green 3 + red 4; green 4 + red 3; green 2 + red 5; green 5 + red 2
23. a. No, the theoretical probabilities are 3 heads: $\frac{1}{8}$, 2 heads: $\frac{3}{8}$, 1 head: $\frac{3}{8}$, 0 heads: $\frac{1}{8}$.

7-1 Part D Try It

a. Check students' numbers. It is possible that students will be overlooked. It is unlikely that a student would get as much as $500.

7-1 Part D Exercises

1. 5 should occur $\frac{1}{10}$ of the time when picking from numbers from 0 to 9; Students will have answers close to $\frac{1}{10}$. **2.** Consonant
3. a. B **b.** Both occupy $\frac{1}{4}$ of the spinner. **4. a.** 0.3
b. About 0.27 **c.** Answers should be close to 0.06.
5. a. $\frac{1}{32}$ **b.** The probability should be about 31%.
11. $\frac{1}{3}$ **13. a.** 6 **b.** 12
c. 20 **15. a.** Answers should be close to 25.
b. Answers should be close to $\frac{1}{2}$. **17. a.** $\frac{3}{10}$ **b.** $\frac{7}{10}$
19. $\frac{1}{9}$

21.

7-1 Part E Self-Assessment

1. a. $\frac{1}{6}$ **b.** $\frac{5}{6}$ **2.** Possible answer: It would be more difficult to collect all six cards because the probability of getting a 4, 5, or 6 would be reduced. There would be more duplicate cards for 1, 2, and 3. **3. a.** $\frac{1}{8}$ **b.** 1 **c.** 0
d. Possible answer:

4. 0.2 **5. a.** $\frac{1}{4}$, $\frac{1}{8}$ **b.** $\frac{5}{8}$
c. 3; 12 **d.** $5.53; The average of all the prices, using $6.75 twice. **6. a.** $\frac{1}{2}$ **b.** $\frac{1}{4}$; $\frac{1}{2}$ **c.** 10 **d.** 14 **e.** Luck; There is no strategy to the game.
7. Possible answer:

8. a. About 8 meals
9. a.

b. $\frac{7}{16}$; $\frac{9}{16}$ **c.** White; The probability of hitting within the white area is greater.
10. Yes; 8 times out of ten would yield a higher score.
11. (b) **12.** (c) **13.** (b)
14. 0.66; 1 **15.** $\frac{13}{28}$
16. Both glasses hold the same amount; Their volumes are both $\approx$ 75.4 in.³

7-2 Part A Try It

a. Cows run; Cows hide; Cows call out; Cows stop; Pigs run; Pigs hide; Pigs call out; Pigs stop; Chickens run; Chickens hide; Chickens call out; Chickens stop

b. $\frac{1}{12}$ **c.** $\frac{1}{3}$ **d.** $\frac{2}{3}$

7-2 Part A Exercises

1. b. 12 **c.** 4 **3. a.** 16
b. $\frac{1}{2}$; $\frac{1}{4}$; $\frac{1}{16}$ **5.** 36 **7.** 702
9. 6,760,000 **13.** 120
15. 1320 **19.** 24 **21.** $\frac{1}{16}$
23. 72 **25. a.** 48 **b.** $\frac{1}{36}$
26. b. No **c.** $\frac{1}{32}$ **d.** $\frac{7}{32}$
e. $\frac{1}{32}$ **27. a.** $\frac{1}{6}$; $\frac{1}{6}$ **b.** $\frac{1}{3}$
c. $\frac{1}{3}$

7-2 Part B Try It

a. $\frac{1}{720}$ **b.** 60

7-2 Part B Exercises

1. a. 4 **b.** 3 **c.** 2 **d.** 1
e. 24; The number of possible arrangements of the four objects **2.** 6; Possible answer: 3 people, Soo, Gary, and Lehri can be seated at a concert in the following ways: Soo, Gary, Lehri; Soo, Lehri, Gary; Gary, Soo, Lehri; Gary, Lehri, Soo; Lehri, Gary, Soo; Lehri, Soo, Gary **3.** 120
4. a. 362,880 **b.** $\frac{1}{362,880}$
5. $\frac{1}{120}$ **7. a.** 720 **b.** 6477 seconds ($\approx$ 1 hr 48 min)
11. 24 **13.** $x = -2$
15. $x = 11$ **17.** $\frac{2}{3}$
19. 5040; The number of arrangements of 7 objects.
21. 24 **23. a.** 720
b. $\frac{1}{720}$ **25. a.** 60 **b.** $\frac{1}{60}$
27. a. 5040 **b.** $\frac{1}{5040}$
29. The five-letter word jumble has only 120 arrangements, while the six-letter word jumble has 720 possibilities. **31. a.** 5 **b.** 3
c. No matter how the digits are arranged the number is 222.

7-2 Part C Try It

a. ABC, ABD, ABE, ACD, ACE, ADE, BCD, BCE, BDE, CDE

7-2 Part C Exercises

1. a. Arrangement
b. Group **c.** Group **2.** 4
3. Ann and Bob, Ann and Carly, Ann and Damien, Bob and Carly, Bob and Damien, Carly and Damien

5. 5; ABCD, ABCE, ABDE, ACDE, BCDE
7. a. Arrangement
b. Group **c.** Group
d. Arrangement **11.** 11; 14; 17 **13.** 16; 25 **15.** 5
19. ABCDE, ABCDF, ABCDG, ABCDH, ABCEF, ABCEG, ABCEH, ABCFG, ABCFH, ABCGH, ABDEF, ABDEG, ABDEH, ABDFG, ABDFH, ABDGH, ABEFG, ABEFH, ABEGH, ABFGH, ACDEF, ACDEG, ACDEH, ACDFG, ACDFH, ACDGH, ACEFG, ACEFH, ACEGH, ACFGH, ADEFG, ADEFH, ADEGH, ADFGH, AEFGH
21. Yes **23. a.** 1234, 1235, 1236, 1245, 1246, 1256, 1345, 1346, 1356, 1456, 2345, 2346, 2356, 2456, 3456 **b.** $\frac{2}{3}$
c. $\frac{1}{15}$ **25. a.** Let A = Ana, B = Barry, C = Cecilia, D = Damon, E = Elizabeth, F = Felix, G = Gary, and H = Hannah

ACE BD	ACE DF
ACH BD	ACH DF
AEH BD	AEH DF
CEH BD	CEH DF
ACE BF	ACE DG
ACH BF	ACH DG
AEH BF	AEH DG
CEH BF	CEH DG
ACE BG	ACE FG
ACH BG	ACH FG
AEH BG	AEH FG
CEH BG	CEH FG

b. $\frac{3}{4}$ **c.** $\frac{1}{2}$ **d.** $\frac{3}{8}$ **e.** Female

7-2 Part D Try It

a. 2:3

7-2 Part D Exercises

1. a. $\frac{3}{4}$ **b.** 25% **c.** 3:1
2. 9:7; 7:9 **3.** 3:1 **4.** $\frac{4}{5}$
5. a. 20 **b.** Possible answer: For $1, only if the prize is worth $5; For $5, only if it is worth $25.
9. $x = 8.25$; $y = 9$
11. $12.98 **13. a.** 3:9
b. $\frac{1}{4}$ **15.** 9:1 **19.** 1:3

7-2 Part E
Self-Assessment

1. a. $\frac{1}{8}$ **b.** $\frac{1}{8}$ **c.** $\frac{3}{8}$ **2.** 36
3. a. 18 **b.** $\frac{1}{18}$
4. a. 970,200 **b.** 161,700
5. Possible answer: Order is not important in grouping.
6. a. $\frac{1}{650}$ **b.** $\frac{1}{10,000}$
c. $\frac{1}{6,500,000}$ **7. a.** 25
b. 20 **c.** 10 **8.** (b)
9. Let C = Carrots, B = Broccoli, P = Peas, and R = Corn; CB, CP, CR, BP, BR, PR

10. Possible answer:

11. Possible answer:

12. a. $x = 20$ **b.** $x = -\frac{5}{2}$
13. 24 **14.** $\frac{1}{365}; \frac{1}{364}$

15. Possible answer:

16. a. 16.5 **b.** 2 **c.** 25
17. a. 100 **b.** 7 **c.** 4
18. 150 m² **19. a.** f; It is used the most; i.e., 9 times when lighting digits 0 through 9. **b.** e; It is used the least, i.e., 4 times when lighting digits 0 through 9.

Chapter 7 Review
1. (b) **2.** (a) **3.** (c)
4. (d) **5.** 12 **6. a.** $\frac{1}{2}$
b. $\frac{1}{2}$ **c.** 1 **d.** $\frac{1}{4}$ **7.** TU, TV, TW, TX, UV, UW, VW, VX, WX **8. a.** Arrangement **b.** Group **c.** Group **d.** Arrangement **9.** (d)

10. $\frac{1}{10}$ **11.** Let P = Post Office, B = Bank, and K = Bakery

a.

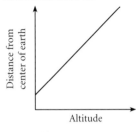

b. 3 **12. a.** $\frac{1}{6}$ **b.** $\frac{1}{6}$
c. $\frac{2}{3}$ **13. a.** $\frac{1}{8}$ **b.** 0
14. a. $\frac{21}{100}$ **b.** $\frac{3}{20}$
15. a. Possible answer: There are fewer children per family as time progresses.
b. 1980 **c.** Possible answer: 100%

CHAPTER 8

8-1 Part A Try It
a. Possible answer:

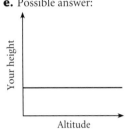

b. Possible answer:

c. Possible answer:

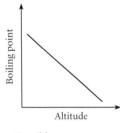

d. Possible answer:

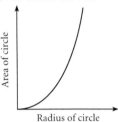

e. Possible answer:

f. The puppy's steady weight gain was interrupted by a brief illness.

8-1 Part A Exercises
1. a. Increases **b.** At the summit **7.** Possible answer: The radius **9.** Possible answer: The lengths of the sides **13.** Possible answer:

15. Possible answer:

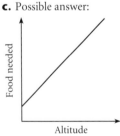

19. 8 in.² **21.** Possible answer: A square swimming pool's area increases with the length of its side.
23. Possible answer: Households put out more garbage in the summer than in the spring or fall.

25. Possible answer: A tree grows with renewed vigor after drastic pruning.
27. (a) **29.** Possible answer: The slant height
31. Possible answer: Number of cards in circulation **33.** Possible answer: Number of options selected
35. Possible answer: Number of hours of practice
37. Possible answer:

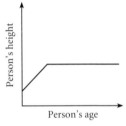

39. Possible answer:

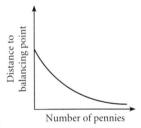

41. Possible answer:

43. Possible answer: A driver brakes while approaching a turn, coasts through the turn, then accelerates while shifting. Time on the horizontal axis, speed on the vertical.
45. They differ by 4
47. The bottom row is 6 times the top row

8-1 Part B Try It
a. Possible answer: (0, 3), (1, 8), (2, 13), (3, 18), (4, 23)

b. (100, 68.2), (110, 75.0), (120, 81.8), (130, 88.6), (140, 95.4), (150, 102.2)
c. $y = -3x$

8-1 Part B Exercises
1. $(-1, -1)$, $(0, 1)$, $(1, 3)$, $(2, 5)$, $(3, 7)$, $(4, 9)$ **3.** $-3; 1; 5; 9; 13; 17$
5. $-6; -2; 2; 6; 10$
7. $(-5, 30)$, $(-3, 12)$, $(0, 0)$, $(1, 0)$, $(7, 42)$ **9.** $y = 5x$; $(-3, -15)$, $(-1, -5)$, $(0, 0)$, $(1, 5)$, $(2, 10)$, $(3, 15)$, $(36, 180)$
13. a. $(-3, -6)$, $(-1, -2)$, $(0, 0)$, $(2, 4)$ **b.** $y = 2x$
15. $-55; -35; -15; 5; 25$
17. $4; 7; 10; 13; 16$
19. $y = \frac{x}{-2}$ $(-6, 3)$, $(-2, 1)$, $(0, 0)$, $(2, -1)$, $(4, -2)$, $(10, -5)$, $(52, -26)$
21. $y = x^2$ $(-2, 4)$, $(-1, 1)$, $(0, 0)$, $(1, 1)$, $(2, 4)$, $(3, 9)$, $(36, 1296)$ **25. a.** $131°$
b. Solve $F = 1.8C + 32$ for C as follows: $1.8C = F - 32$; $C = \frac{F - 32}{1.8}$ **c.** $230°C$
d. Cold; The temperatures are the same at $-40°$ on either scale. **27.** $44; 59; 76$; $n^2 - 5$

8-1 Part C Try It
a.
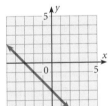
b.
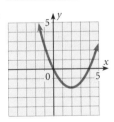

8-1 Part C Exercises
1. a. $0; 1; 2; 3$ **b.** Possible answer: Yes; They produced y-values which are whole numbers. This simplifies the graphing process.

c. $(-2, 0)$, $(0, 1)$, $(2, 2)$, $(4, 3)$
d.
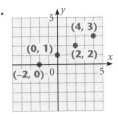
e.
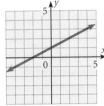
7.
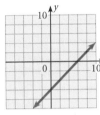
11. a. $x = 4$ **b.** $x = 7.5$
c. $x = 10$ **13. a.** Possible answer: $(0, 14.7)$, $(30, 28.2)$, $(60, 41.7)$, $(90, 55.2)$, $(120, 68.7)$
b.
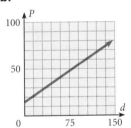
c. About 112 ft
17. Possible answer:

19. $5; 3; 1; -1; -3$
21.
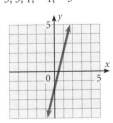

23.
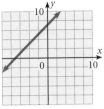
25.
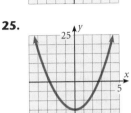
27. a. $x = 0$ **b.** $x = 1.25$
c. $x = 2.25$ **29. a.** w is independent; A is dependent.
b. Possible answer: $(1, 1025)$, $(5, 1125)$, $(10, 1250)$, $(20, 1500)$, $(30, 1750)$, $(50, 2250)$
c.
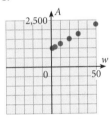
d. $A = 1000 + 25w$
31. $C = 0.10d$ **33.** $S = 6s^2$

8-1 Part D Self-Assessment
1. T **2.** T **3.** T **4.** F
5. a. $d = 186{,}000s$
b. 669,600,000 mi
6. a. 0.6 war per year
b. $w = 0.6p$ **c.** w is the dependent variable; p is the independent variable.
d.
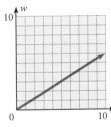
7. (b) **8.** (c) **9.** (a)
10. (d)

11.
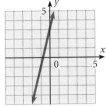
12.
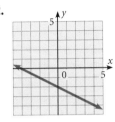
13. 91.4
14. a. Possible answer: $h = $ hours, $w = $ water level above normal, in inches
b. Possible answer: $(0, 52)$, $(1, 50)$, $(2, 48)$, $(3, 46)$, $(4, 44)$, $(5, 42)$
c. $w = 52 - 2h$
d.
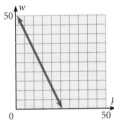
e. Locate the point whose w-coordinate is 0. Whatever the corresponding h-coordinate is at that point will represent how long it took.
15. a. \$0.80 **b.** \$0.60
c. $c = 0.60 + 0.80m$
d.
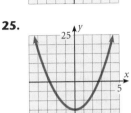

715

8-2 Part A Try It

a.

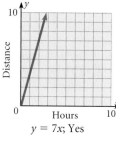

$y = 7x$; Yes

b. No. Possible answer: The area is linearly related to the square of the radius.

8-2 Part A Exercises

1. a. $\frac{1}{2}$; 1; $\frac{3}{2}$; 2; $\frac{5}{2}$; 3   **b.** Yes
c. Yes   **5.** Not linear, because as x changes from 1 to 2, y changes by 26, but as x changes from 2 to 3, y changes by 28.   **7.** Linear, because each change of 1 unit in x results in a change of 4 in y.
9. Not linear, because the graph is not a straight line.
11. a. Yes; For each successive month, the original savings of $20 increases by increments of $5.
b. No

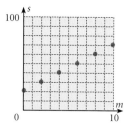

c. Yes
17. Linear; Each change of 1 in x results in a change of 3 in y.
19. Linear; Each change of 2 in x results in a change of 8 in y.   **21.** Yes; Graph is a straight line.   **23.** Yes; Graph is a straight line.
25. $c = 2p$

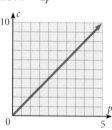

27. $C = 40x$; Yes
29. a. 1st job: $s = 26,000 + 1500y$; 2nd job: $s = 29,000 + 900y$

b.

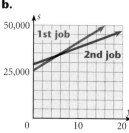

c. The graphs show that the second job pays more in the short term, but the first pays more in the long term.

8-2 Part B Try It

a. 2   **b.** 1   **c.** 0   **d.** No; The calculation results in a division by zero, which is undefined.

8-2 Part B Exercises

1. a. Positive   **b.** (5, 4)
c. (10, 6)   **d.** 2   **e.** 5   **f.** $\frac{2}{5}$
g. 2   **5.** 1; 0   **7.** 3; −10
9. Linear   **11.** Linear
13. $-\frac{1}{3}$ **15.** −3   **17.** 0
23. a.

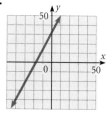

b. $\frac{9}{5}$; 32
c. About 18°   **27.** $\frac{5}{12}$ **29.** Negative
31. Negative   **33.** 1
35. −2   **37.** 0   **39.** $\frac{2}{3}$
41. $-\frac{1}{4}$ **43.** 0   **45.** Linear   **47.** Linear
49.

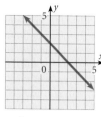

slope = −1

51. a.

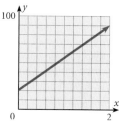

b. 35; 20   **c.** ≈ 1.5 km
d. 20°C, which is the y-intercept   **53.** 0.315

8-2 Part C Self-Assessment

1. Linear; $y = 3x$
2. Linear; $y = x - 7$
3. Not linear   **4.** Linear; $y = 5$

5. $d = 7w$

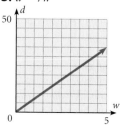

6. $c = 0.29p$

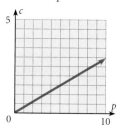

7. $p = 6h$
8. (a)
9.

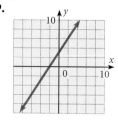

10. a. 10 cm, since $2 \times \frac{3}{0.6} = 10$
b. 0.84 kg   **11.** 24

12. a.

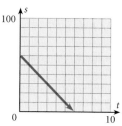

b. 6 sec   **c.** 28 ft/sec

13.

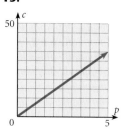

15. a.

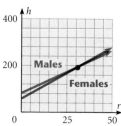

b. Possible answer: To identify the skeletons as male or female.   **c.** ≈ 32 cm
16. a. The account balance is increasing.   **b.** The account balance is decreasing.
c. The account balance is holding steady.   **d.** That is the initial account balance.
17. This is a 45°-45°-90° right triangle. In this type of triangle the two legs $\overline{AB}$ and $\overline{CB}$ are the same length. Therefore $\overline{AB} = 15$.

18.

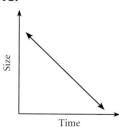

8-3 Part A Try It
a. 4.3 sec

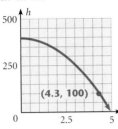

b. (0, 400), (1, 384), (2, 336), (3, 256), (4, 144), (5, 0)

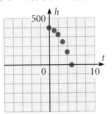

(0, 400) represents the height of the squeegee at the moment it was dropped. Each other *h*-value represents the height of the squeegee at the corresponding time (*t* seconds) after it was dropped.

8-3 Part A Exercises
1. a. iii **b.** iv **c.** i **d.** ii
5. Linear **7.** Nonlinear
9. Linear **11.** Nonlinear
15. $y = 3x^2$; Nonlinear
18. a. $y = x^2$ **b.** 1; 4; 9; 16; 25; 36; 49

c.

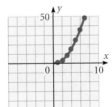

d. ≈ 4.5 units **21.** 81
23. 10 **25.** 10 **27.** 4; 8; 16; 32; Each *y*-value is the previous one multiplied by 2.
29. Nonlinear
31. Nonlinear
33. Nonlinear
35. a. 13; 6; 1; −2; −3; −2; 1; 6; 13

b.

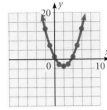

37. ≈ 2.0 sec.
39. a.

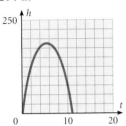

b. ≈ 11 sec

8-3 Part B Try It
a.

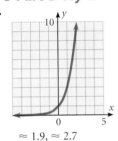

≈ 1.9, ≈ 2.7

8-3 Part B Exercises
1. a. 0; 2; 4; 8; 10; 12; 16
b. Each value chosen is a perfect square. **c.** The square root of a negative number is not defined.

d.

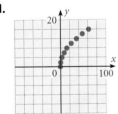

e. It rises more steeply than the graph of $y = \sqrt{x}$.
3. Square root **5.** Linear
7. Exponential
9. a. About 2.5 seconds

b.

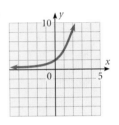

c. 2.2 seconds **d.** 31.4 feet
e. 37 seconds **13.** $\frac{1}{4}$
15. 49 **17.** Linear
19. Quadratic **21.** Square root

23.

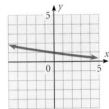

25.

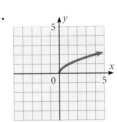

27. a. i **b.** iii **c.** ii
29. 681 thousand; 952 thousand

31.

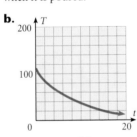

They are the same.

33. 2160

8-3 Part C Self-Assessment
1. C **2.** D **3.** B **4.** A
5. (b) **6. a.** iii **b.** ii
c. iv **d.** i **7.** (c) **8.** (c)
9. $-\frac{820}{4600} \approx -0.18$; Not very steep **10. a.** The lower graph **b.** The higher graph **c.** It would have the same shape.

d. The first point would be at 3 instead of 2 or 4.

11.

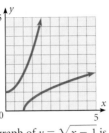

The graph of $y = \sqrt{x - 1}$ is the mirror image of $y = x^2 + 1$.
12. (d) **13. a.** (1, 24), (2, 16), (3, 10.67), (4, 7.11), (5, 4.74), (6, 3.16)

b.

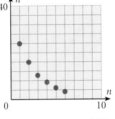

c. Exponential; $h = 36\left(\frac{2}{3}\right)^n$
14. a. 110; The cocoa is 110° more than room temperature when it is poured.

b.

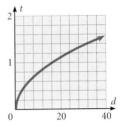

Exponential

c. It drops until it approaches room temperature.
15. a. (0, 1), (1, 2), (2, 4), (3, 8), (4, 16), (5, 32), (6, 64)

b.

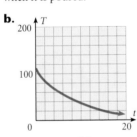

c. No; It doesn't make sense to make a fraction of a fold.
d. $r = 2^f$

Chapter 8 Review

1. F; *y*-intercept **2.** T
3. T **4.** Negative
5. Quadratic **6. a.** Possible
answer: Radius **b.** Possible
answer: Number of minutes
on the phone **c.** Possible
answer: Number of hours
worked **7.** $y = -3x$ $(-2, 6)$,
$(-1, 3), (0, 0), (1, -3), (2, -6)$,
$(14, -42), (36, -108)$
8. a. $(1, 2.25), (2, 4.50)$,
$(3, 6.75), (4, 9.00), (5, 11.25)$
b. $d = 2.25c$
c. *c* is independent;
d is dependent **d.** Yes; It is
of the form $y = mx + b$, with
$m = 2.25$ and $b = 0$.
9. $-\frac{5}{8}$; 8
10. a.

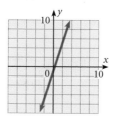

b. Find the *x*-value where the
line intersects $y = 11$.
11. 18 ft **12.** 0 **13.** $-\frac{3}{4}$
14. $\frac{4}{5}$ **15.** 2 in. **16.** $-\frac{7}{2}$;
2 **17.** 3; $\frac{5}{3}$ **18.** $\frac{1}{2}$; -3
19. a. Let $p =$ the number
of pages and $c =$ total cost;
$c = 10 + 1.50p$
b.

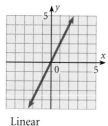

c. $\approx$ \$32
20.

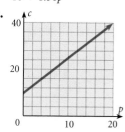

Linear

21.

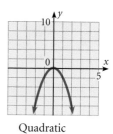

Quadratic

22.

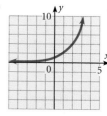

Exponential

23. 6

24. a.

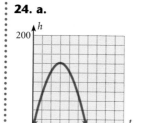

b. (3, 144) **c.** 144 ft
d. 6 sec **25. a.** $y = 100(3^x)$
b.

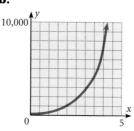

c. 24,300

▼ CREDITS

PHOTOGRAPHS

Front Cover **Left** Thomas Kitchin/Tom Stack & Associates **Right** Giraudon/Art Resource, NY

Spine **Left** Thomas Kitchin/Tom Stack & Associates **Right** Giraudon/Art Resource, NY

Back Cover **TCL** Giraudon/Art Resource, NY **TCR** Jerry Jacka Photography **TL** Thomas Kitchin/Tom Stack & Associates **TR** Jon Feingersh/Tom Stack & Associates **BCL** Art Resource **BCR** Cheryl Fenton* **BL** Jerry Jacka Photography: Museum of Northern Arizona, Flagstaff **BR** Antonio M. Rosario/The Image Bank

Front Matter **FM4–5** Roger Ressmeyer/Starlight **FM5** Ken Karp* **FM6–7** Scott Camazine/Photo Researchers **FM6BL** Lance Nelson/The Stock Market **FM6C** America Hurrah Antiques, New York, NY **FM6T** Michael Holford **FM7** ©1994 M.C. Escher/Cordon Art/Baarn, Holland. All Rights Reserved **FM8–9** GHP Studio* **FM8C** John Marmaras/Woodfin Camp & Associates **FM8T** Pete Turner/The Image Bank **FM9BC** Globus Studios Inc./The Stock Market **FM9BR** D. & J. Heaton/Stock, Boston **FM9TR** Ken Lax* **FM10** Spencer Swanger/Tom Stack & Associates

Getting Started **i** Ken Karp* **ii** David Madison **vii** Ken Karp*

Chapter 1 **2B** Brownie Harris/The Stock Market **2C** David Madison **2T** Bob Daemmrich/Stock, Boston **3** (background) Jack Gardner/Stock South **5C** Joe Towers/The Stock Market **5L** Doug Milner/DRK Photo **5R** Bill Sumner/The Stock Market **6** Charles Feil/Stock, Boston **9** Cheryl Fenton* **12C** Photoworld/FPG International **12L** Beechcraft Air Corporation **12LC** Cessna Aircraft Company **12R** United Air Lines Photo **12RC** Photoworld/FPG International **13** Jim Anderson/Woodfin Camp & Associates **17** Roger Ressmeyer/Starlight **20** Dave Bartruff/Stock, Boston **22** Dan McCoy/Rainbow **25** J. Wengle/DRK Photo **26** Norbert Wu/Peter Arnold, Inc. **29** Natalie Fobes/AllStock **31CL** Tony Duffy/Allsport **31CR** Duomo **31L** William R. Sallaz/Duomo **31R** Focus on Sports **34** The Topps Company, Inc. Photo by GHP Studio* **38** David Madison/Duomo **45** ©1993 Time Inc. Reprinted by permission. Photo by Cheryl Fenton* **47** Tim Davis* **58** Don & Pat Valenti/DRK Photo **61** Momatiuk-Eastcott/Woodfin Camp & Associates **66** Otto Greule/Allsport **67** David Madison/Duomo **68** Ken Karp* **69T** Tim Davis* **71** Tim Davis* **72** Tim Davis* **73** Tim Davis* **74** Shelby Thorner/David Madison Photography **80** Scala/Art Resource **83** Pete Saloutos/The Stock Market **84** Grant Heilman Photography **85** Hank Morgan/Rainbow **86** George E. Joseph **87** Tim Davis*

Chapter 2 **92** Cheryl Fenton* **93** (background) Will & Deni McIntyre/AllStock **95** (background) John Gerlach/DRK Photo **95** (frame) Tim Davis* **96** Ken Karp* **100** Cheryl Fenton* **101** Cheryl Fenton* **102** The Bettmann Archive **103** Ken Karp* **104** GHP Studio* **106** Cheryl Fenton* **107** Cheryl Fenton* **108** Shattil-Rozinski/Tom Stack & Associates **112B** Bob Daemmrich/The Image Works **112T** GHP Studio* **116** Ken Karp* **117** Tim Davis* **121** Kevin Morris/AllStock **122** Phyllis Picardi/Stock South **123** (inset) Brian Parker/Tom Stack & Associates **123T** Wes Thompson Photography/The Stock Market **124** Ken Karp* **125** Ken Karp* **128** Ken Karp* **130** Photograph by Ansel Adams. Copyright ©1994 by the Trustees of the Ansel Adams Publishing Rights Trust. All Rights Reserved **131** Jerry Cooke/Photo Researchers **134** Ken Karp* **137** Ralf-Finn Hestoft/Third Coast Stock Source **138** FPG International **140** The Bettmann Archive **141** Stephen J. Krasemann/Peter Arnold, Inc. **144** Courtesy of the Illinois State Historical Library **146** Steven E. Sutton/Duomo **149** Ken Karp* **150** Ric Ergenbright/AllStock **153L** Michael Holford **153R** Art Resource **154** David Madison **155L** Ken Karp* **155R** Shell Gorget, A.D. 1400, #9025.451. From the collection of Gilcrease Museum, Tulsa, Oklahoma **159** Cheryl Fenton* **160** Steve Martin/Tom Stack & Associates **162** Cheryl Fenton* **163** David Madison **164** H. P. Merten/The Stock Market **165** GHP Studio* **167** Bob Daemmrich/The Image Works **171** Ken Karp* **178** Springer/Bettmann Film Archive **183** David Madison **187** J. Lotter/Tom Stack & Associates **188** Ken Karp*

Chapter 3 **194BR** Cheryl Fenton* **194CR** Cheryl Fenton* **194L** Dallas & John Heaton/Westlight **194TR** Cheryl Fenton* **195** (background) Cheryl Fenton* **197BL** Cheryl Fenton* **197BR** Cheryl Fenton* **197C** AP/Wide World Photos **198L** Lance Nelson/The Stock Market **198R`** The Kobal Collection **200BL** Darwin R. Wiggett/Westlight **200BR** C. Bruce Forster/AllStock **200TL** A. & F. Michler/Peter Arnold, Inc. **200TR** Jeff Greenberg/Photo Researchers **201** Magnum Photos Inc. **202** Courtesy: Museum of Northern Arizona. Jerry Jacka Photography **203B** Jerry Jacka Photography **203T** Werner Otto/AllStock **205** ©1994 M.C. Escher/Cordon Art/Baarn, Holland. All Rights Reserved **207** America Hurrah Antiques, New York, NY **208B** Scott Camazine/Photo Researchers **208C** Ken Karp* **208T** M. Thonig/H. Armstrong Roberts/AllStock **211** Kevin Morris/AllStock **212B** Steve Proehl/The Image Bank **212T** David G. Barker/Tom Stack & Associates **213C** Maxwell Museum **213L** (border) Courtesy: Heard Museum, Harvey Fine Arts Collection. Jerry Jacka Photography **213L** (inset) Jim Olive/Peter Arnold, Inc. **213R** (background) Courtesy: Margaret Kilgore Gallery, Scottsdale, Arizona. Jerry Jacka Photography **221B** Cheryl Fenton* **221C** Cheryl Fenton* **221T** GHP Studio* **223** Jon Feingersh/The Stock Market **223T** ©1994 M.C. Escher/Cordon Art/Baarn, Holland. All Rights Reserved **227** Scott Blackman/Tom Stack & Associates **229** R. Y. Kaufman/Yogi/AllStock **230L** GHP Studio* **230R** Courtesy: Gallery 10, Scottsdale, AZ. Jerry Jacka Photography **233** Tim Davis* **234** The DOBAG Project, Western Turkey. Photo courtesy of Return to Tradition, San Francisco **235R** Marty Loken/AllStock **236** Courtesy: The Heard Museum, Phoenix, AZ. Jerry Jacka Photography **238** Cooper-Hewitt Museum **239B** Bob Daemmrich/Stock, Boston **239T** Ann Hawthorne/Black Star **241** John Cancalosi/Peter Arnold, Inc. **246** Robert Brons/Biological Photo Service **253B** Ken Karp* **253T** Cheryl Fenton* **255** Giraudon/Art Resource **259** GHP Studio*

Chapter 4 **262B** Michael Holford **262C** Cheryl Fenton* **262T** Cheryl Fenton* **263** (background) Cheryl Fenton* **265** AP/Wide World **267** Ken Karp* **269** Ken Karp* **271B** Stephen J. Krasemann/DRK Photo **271T** Elena Dorfman* **272** Global Hobby Distributors **273** Frank Whitney/The Image Bank **275** Ken Karp* **276CR** Ken Karp* **276L** Cheryl Fenton* **277** Art Wolfe **279** Elliott Smith* **280** Ken Karp* **281** Ken Karp* **288** Larry Ulrich/DRK Photo **291** Robert Frerck/Woodfin Camp & Associates **293L** The Bettmann Archive **293R** The Bettmann Archive **294** Cheryl Fenton* **298** Cheryl Fenton* **300** Ken Karp* **304** UPI/Bettmann

35a, 40a, 42a, 46a, 52b, 54a, 62c, 70a, 84c, 118a, 318c, 326a, 428a, 533a, 543a, 581a, 609a

TEXT AND ART

Chapter 1   Opener 1-3: p. 63, text from Charles Corbin and Ruth Lindsey, *Fitness for Life,* 2nd Edition (Scott Foresman, 1983).

Chapter 2   2-2 Part B: p.132: text from Merriam-Webster's Collegiate® Dictionary, Tenth Edition. © 1994 by Merriam-Webster, Inc. Reprinted by permission.

Chapter 3   Opener 3-2: p. 213, upper left text from *Multiculturalism in Mathematics, Science, and Technology,* p. 127 (Menlo Park, CA: Addison-Wesley, 1993). Copyright ©1993 Addison-Wesley Publishing Company.

Chapter 4   Opener 4-1: p. 265, upper left text from Lister Sinclair, *Centennial Centre of Science and Technology,* 1969. Copyright ©1969 Centennial Centre of Science and Technology. 4-1 Part D: p. 288, Fog Index adapted from Robert Gunning and Richard A Kallan, *How to Take the Fog Out of Business Writing,* published by Dartnell, 1994. The FOG INDEX℠ scale is a service mark licensed exclusively to RK Communication Consultants by D. and M. Mueller. Opener 4-2: p. 293, text from Isaac Asimov, *X Stands for the Unknown* (Garden City, NY: Doubleday and Company, 1984). Copyright ©1984 by Isaac Asimov. 4-2 Part E: p. 322, Exercise 22: Problem adapted from *Performance Assessment— An International Experiment,* Center for the Assessment of Educational Progress, Princeton, NJ.

Chapter 5   Opener 5-1: p. 331, text from Clovis Heimsath, *Pioneer Texas Buildings, A Geometry Lesson* (Austin, TX: University of Texas Press, 1968). Copyright ©1968 by Clovis Heimsath. Opener 5-2: p. 357, upper left text from Robert Hughes, "Signs of Anxiety," *Time,* March 1, 1993, p. 60. Copyright ©1993 Time Magazine. 5-3 Part D: p. 411, Exercise 20: caption text from Stanley J. Herd, *Crop Art and Other Earthworks,* p. 25 (New York: Harry N. Abrams, 1994). Copyright ©1994 Stanley J. Herd.

Chapter 6   Opener 6-1: p. 419, lyric excerpts of "Do-Re-Mi" by Richard Rodgers and Oscar Hammerstein II. Copyright ©1959 by Richard Rodgers and Oscar Hammerstein II. Copyright Renewed. International Copyright Secured. Used by Permission. All Rights Reserved. Opener 6-2: p. 453, text from Kathleen Caccavale, "Sand Visions," *Vista USA,* Summer 1989, pp. 11–15. Opener 6-3: p. 491, text condensed from William Schaff, "An Adventure in Postage Stamps," *Mathematics and Science,* p. 22 (Reston, VA: NCTM, 1978). Copyright ©1978 National Council of Teachers of Mathematics.

Chapter 7   Opener 7-2: p. 553, text from Marilyn vos Savant, "Ask Marilyn," *Parade Magazine,* 1991.

Chapter 8   Opener 8-2: p. 621, text from John Leland, "and thanks …," *Newsweek,* Special Issue, October/November 1993. Copyright ©1993 Newsweek, Inc. All rights reserved. Reprinted by permission. 8-2 Part A: p. 623, Explore activity developed with the cooperation of Peter Brancazio.